THE ODDFELLOWS, 1810–2010

FRONTISPIECE

In the spring of 2000 members took a break
from the AMC in Scarborough to spell out
the word 'Oddfellows' on the beach. In doing
so they made the point that it has been the
members who have been central to the
Oddfellows. For 200 years amid the ebb and
flow of political and social changes the Society
has relied on members' commitment to
friendship, love and truth.

The Oddfellows, 1810–2010

Two hundred years of making friends and helping people

DANIEL WEINBREN

CARNEGIE

The Oddfellows, 1810–2010

Copyright © The Oddfellows, 2010

First published in 2010 by
Carnegie Publishing *in association with* The Oddfellows
www.oddfellows.co.uk

Carnegie Publishing Ltd
Chatsworth Road,
Lancaster LA1 4SL
www.carnegiepublishing.com

British Library Cataloguing-in-Publication data
A catalogue record for this book is available from the British Library

ISBN 978-1-85936-207-5   *hardback*

Designed, typeset and originated by Carnegie Publishing
Printed and bound in the UK in association with Jellyfish Solutions Ltd

Contents

Foreword

by the Oddfellows' Board of Directors

As the Society reaches its 200-year anniversary, this book looks back over our distinguished history. It is a chance for both members and non-members to discover our origins; our part in British (indeed world) history and how we became the much loved Society we are today. Many things have changed over the past 200 years both outside of the Society and within but our motto of 'Friendship, Love and Truth' still remains as relevant as ever.

Our bicentennial year also provides us with an opportunity to look towards the future and plan the next 200 years. We will continue to build on our theme of 'Making Friends, Helping People' providing opportunities for socialising in all our Branches as well as delivering a first class care and advice service to help those members when they need it most.

The arm of friendship has been extended even further with the introduction of International Membership online, meaning that anyone anywhere in the world can become part of our family of Oddfellows.

We would like to take this opportunity to thank all our members and friends who have helped to tell our story. With the on-going commitment and enthusiasm of our members we look forward to being as relevant in people's lives in the next millennium.

Finally we hope you enjoy reading about our history and discovering more about our fascinating Society.

Board of Directors:

Dorothy Deacon	Alan Cole	Nicola O'Riordan Finley
Philip Howcroft	Jane Nelson	Roger Burley
Sue Doulton Smith	Andrew Porter	Charles Vaughan
Karen Stuart	George Lickess	Bill Connolly
Martin Jackson		

February 2010

Dedicated to
all Oddfellows,
past, present and future

Acknowledgements

I AM INDEBTED to the Independent Order of Oddfellows Manchester Unity Friendly Society for its support in the writing of this book. I was provided with access to materials and with help contacting members. All the Oddfellows staff in Manchester who I met went out of their way to be helpful. Much of my contact with the Oddfellows was through Philip Howcroft, Dawn Walters, Ian Wallace and Hannah Clark, and I am grateful to them. Paul Eyre and Karen Stuart shared ideas and commented on a draft. Ian Jones helped me by finding photographs. Catherine Pont made me a loan of materials from Australia. I carried out some of the interviews but most were conducted by Mary French who also provided good humour and astute remarks. I transcribed some recordings but much of this work was done by Brenda Barnett with some help from Sarah Batt. They tackled the work with enthusiasm and diligence. There are no footnotes for the quotations from the recordings and the biographical notes about those interviewed for this book aim to provide only an indication of the level of their involvement and periods when they were active. However, applications to access the recordings can be made through the Oddfellows. Mark Dennis, Christine Payne, Michael Greatorex and Tony Marsh were particularly obliging in regard to photographs. I am grateful for the assistance provided by Anna Goddard, Judith Franks, Alistair Hodge and Chris Quinn of Carnegie Publishing. I have built on the work of many scholars, some of them members of the Oddfellows. It has been a pleasure to read their work, and I aimed to represent the views of others in a fair way. Their contribution is acknowledged in the notes section. I have found the mutual aid of many within the Friendly Societies Research Group to be of considerable value. Particular thanks are due to Simon Cordery, Andy Durr and Bob James. The patience, forbearance and delightful distraction of Miriam, Bethany and Jacob were important in the creation of this text. I am indebted to Rebecca for her support and for so readily living with the book. My greatest thanks go to her.

Daniel Weinbren, Milton Keynes, 2010

Introduction

FOR 200 YEARS the Independent Order of Oddfellows Manchester Unity Friendly Society has appealed to the best in people, treated them as capable of exercising responsibility, and empowered them to face the challenges of leadership and self-organisation.[1] The Society has been able to spread prosperity, trust and co-operation because members created structures for loyalty and reciprocity and developed distinctive ideas about space, temporality and sociability. Building on, and being integral to, many of the changes within society in the nineteenth century its popular associational culture embodied understandings of mutuality upon which numerous working-class communities were reliant. The Oddfellows offered reciprocity as an alternative, sometimes complementary, sometimes transgressive and resistant, ordering of society to that of the market economy. Adapting ideas associated with magic, the theatre, trade unions, Freemasonry, guilds and insurance companies, it focused on the construction of social relationships and the institutionalisation of benevolence. This enabled members to be empowered as they came to terms with, and sometimes challenged, economic and social conventions. The 'great object of Oddfellowship', pronounced one of the Society's Directors, James Burn, was 'to teach the members to rely upon themselves for mutual support'.[2] Through foregrounding these developments by the Society, particularly within the context of the UK, this book illuminates the development of the wider society and the shaping of national policies.

Reciprocity was not unique to the Society. The centrality of a related notion, collective self help, was emphasised by a leading member of the Ancient Order of Foresters Friendly Society, the journalist T. Ballam Stead:

> When the historian will arise who will picture the marvellous patience, the indomitable perseverance and the unswerving determination of the people in their efforts of self-help, then will their history in its truest sense have been written and the rise of the great Affiliated friendly societies be eulogised as the distinguishing glory of the century.[3]

Reciprocity was not always practised within the Society. As the Unity's frequent reminders of the importance of its principles might indicate, many members have found it difficult to live up to the ideas of Oddfellowship. Some focused on peripheral concerns or perceived the Society in instrumental terms, as one survival strategy among many, not as a central element of their lives. Others misused or stole the funds, creating vicious rather than virtuous circles.[4] Nevertheless, at the heart of the Society remains a form of uneven and contested reciprocity derived from the values of the neighbourhoods in which the Society was nurtured. Burn made the point that while there were ungenerous, 'plodding and designing' members, the Society still managed to promote mutual aid:

> I am not aware of a single individual who truly and faithfully served the interests of the Society who has not either been repaid by some substantial token of their esteem or by some public expression of their grateful sense of the obligation conferred.

The Society did not simply rely on people being helpful. It was structured to encouraged mutual aid. It recognised, as others have subsequently, that huge differences in behaviour flow from differences in circumstances, that people are more inclined to behave in a virtuous fashion if encouraged so to do.[5] Burn stressed the structured nature of that reciprocity:

> I am not aware of any society of men who possess a better conservative principle for protecting and watching over the interests of both the Society and its members individually.[6]

Insurance was long central to the Society's structured reciprocity. It offered the security of sharing risks, of knowing that money paid in during good times could be the source of support during leaner ones. Pooled money was used to protect members against the consequences of not being able to work at their normal trade due to a variety of problems including injury or old age. It supported bereaved spouses and offspring in the event of the death of a member. Although it built upon the concept of insurance it had other ideals. It was the Society's system of structured exchange which enabled abstract notions of, to quote its motto, friendship, love and truth, to be further embedded in the communities the Unity served.

As it was run by elected members, offered opportunities for sociability (through social drinking and feasting) for public demonstrations of fraternity (on parades and at funerals) and for private affirmations of solidarity (through visiting the sick) the Unity has been categorised with trade unions.[7] Thompson presented friendly societies as

> the sub-culture out of which the less stable trade unions grew … they facilitated regional and national trade union federation … the friendly society helped to pick up and carry into the trade union movement the love of ceremony and the high sense of status of the craftsman's guild.[8]

However, in 1842 the Society declared, when making the case for legal status, that

> another feature of the constitution of the Order is that it does not countenance trade unions and that no officer or brother is allowed a travelling certificate or the travelling

relief who may have left his employ through a strike or turn-out for wages under any circumstances.[9]

In 1920 Sidney and Beatrice Webb saw the industrialisation of the nineteenth century as a break from the past and asserted 'with confidence, that in no case did any Trade Union in the United Kingdom arise either directly or indirectly from descent from a Craft Guild'.[10] Although this is a reference to unions, the Webbs also noted the close connections of the unions to the Oddfellows:

> If the reader were to seek out, in some tavern of an industrial centre, the local meeting place of the Foresters or the Carpenters, the Oddfellows or the Boilermakers, he might easily fail, on a first visit, to detect any important difference between the Trade Union branch and the court or lodge of the friendly society. [They] all seem to be clubs managing their own affairs. Every night sees the same interminable procession of men, women and children bringing the contribution money.[11]

While the Society shared much with the trade unions and the guilds, it remained different to them. It was more than a stepping stone between social and economic formations.

Friendly societies have also been classified with welfare organisations.[12] Gorsky has shown how in eighteenth-century Britain many charities were 'coloured by mutualist sentiment', and Prochaska argued that in the nineteenth century 'the boundaries between religion, philanthropy and mutual aid were less marked than in the past'.[13] The Society's banners, sashes and aprons and the claims to mythic origins indicate the importance attached to collective heritage. Rituals aided the maintenance and transmission of sophisticated, multi-faceted, historiographies which linked a notion of trustworthy, vigilant fictive fraternity to mutuality, loyalty, trades, locality, Empire and Christianity. In part because of its rituals the Oddfellows has also been compared to Freemasonry.[14] Burn's account of the Society opened with a comparison of the two fraternities.[15] Another account argued that 'as Freemasons had a beginning, so must Oddfellows', and then presented a suggestion that the Society's roots lay within Roman society.[16] It is insufficient to present the Society as the offspring of only one ancestor. The Oddfellows' distinctive blend of collective self-help, mutuality and charitable, social and financial activity based on networks of trust can be understood as part of a matrix which connected commercial companies, religious bodies, unions and other organisations.

In the twentieth century the Society had to adjust to changes in the role of the state, the broadening of the franchise, the increase in medical possibilities and in longevity, the rise in recreational and political opportunities and the growth in social mobility. It has also had to survive total war and the reduction of the faith and self-confidence which had been associated with British prosperity and imperial grandeur. At the 1900 AMC, Annual Moveable Conference, a gathering of Oddfellow delegates – called Deputies – from all over the country, the Grand Master make a comparison, 'that Oddfellowship, like the empire, was becoming

as the sea'.[17] Certainly the rapid loss of membership which occurred when new
.re was provided mirrored the withdrawal from empire.

.society has been kept alive because members recruited and involved others. Many
.nised that their personal goals and the wider goals of Oddfellowship could only be
.ieved with the help of others. The memories of some members were recorded during 2008
for this book. They joined at a variety of ages and in a number of years. As the focus of this
book is on the UK, most were from that country. Their willingness to talk about their lives
and, in a number of cases, to share their photographs and memorabilia, has been very helpful.
Some had close family ties, some 'went through the chairs', and rose through the ranks, all
offered thoughtful insights. In an address to his fellow Society members in 1934 Stanley
Baldwin, who within a few months would once again be Prime Minister, said: 'Your story has
been a very human one – trial, error, victory, success. It is not the story of a superman. That
is what I like about it so much.'[18] Perhaps he was wrong about these not being super people,
but he was right about the humanity of the Society.

The interviewees were not selected in order to support any thesis or to represent the views
of anybody but themselves. Listening to those who have built, maintained, developed this
organisation over a long period of time provided a better understanding as to why it has
succeeded and a clearer sense of the engagement of those who keep it going than can be gained
from written sources alone. These individual contributions are only a selection of the voices
of Oddfellowship. Oddfellowship need not be seen as an inadequate or marginal version of a
trade union or an insurance company but in its own right, as a coherent, flexible set of ideas
which can be understood through the reflections of those who have been involved and shared
their memories. The personal accounts of members born in every decade of the twentieth
century between the centenary and the 1970s and who have held every post in the Society
can be used to explain the shifts in policies. They also serve to remind us that members of
the Society are not the ciphers of history, but its active agents and that to understand the
Oddfellows requires the zoom and the wide-angle lens, the individual and the international,
the particular and the general.

The principles and practices of Oddfellowship have developed over a long period of time
and it was clear from these accounts that current Oddfellowship is a living tradition informed
by the past in many ways. In recognition of this, the book has been structured in both a
chronological and thematic fashion. Although some themes cross temporal boundaries and
some illustrative ideas presented by interviewees illuminate elements of the nineteenth-century
story, in general, Chapters 1, 2, 3 and 4 are about the first century and in Chapters 5, 6, 7 and
8 the focus is on the second century.

Note on old-style money

Before the decimalisation of sterling in the early 1970s, there were 12 pence (12d.) in 1 shilling (1s.),
and 20 shillings (20s.) in £1. Throughout this book old-style money is given in the form £1 16s. 8d.

CHAPTER ONE

Early years

T H E *Oddfellows' Magazine* of 1847 has it that, on 10 October 1810, the Independent Order of Oddfellows, Manchester Unity, was formed 'by 27 individuals, working men in Manchester'.[1] This date was accepted in 1910, when the centenary was marked and again in 1985 when the 175th anniversary was celebrated.[2] Nevertheless, other dates have been proposed and these are considered in the first section. The claims that the origins lay in Biblical or Roman times, the views that the Society first developed in the seventeenth or eighteenth century and the proposal of dates in the first half of the nineteenth century will be assessed. The Society's growth in the early nineteenth century initially derived from the lodges of the north-west of England. The effect on the Society of the conurbation based on Manchester is addressed in the second section. The Society swiftly became one of the most popular of the bodies that offered formal, structured, lodges where men could share information, give vent to their feelings, find fellowship and nurture common values. In the third section the early development within and beyond the north of England is outlined.

I Long gestation, multiple births

In 1810 tales of the origins of the Society reflected popular ideas of the period. This was a time of social unrest in the north of England and the Oddfellows' interest in establishing an ancient, honourable, linage was a means by which it could elevate its own status as a secure association. The Society's solidity and longevity could be enhanced by the claim that Oddfellowship was derived from ancient roots, that the events in Manchester in the early nineteenth century were only the latest stage in a journey which commenced with the exile of the Israelites in Babylon 587 years before Jesus was born, or even earlier. During and immediately after the French Wars, 1793–1815, there was an increase in support for the monarchy.[3] In 1819 Walter Scott popularised Saxon chivalry when he made Robin Hood an important figure in *Ivanhoe*. There was a contemporary interest in what might be seen as creation myths.[4] Thompson noted it became more acceptable for working men to express ideals in the late eighteenth century. Indeed, 'one of the strangest consequences of the language of "social man" of the philosophical Enlightenment is its reproduction in the rules of obscure clubs meeting in the taverns'.[5] Burn noted that 'Some Oddfellows very modestly claim old Father Adam' as a founder.[6]

Paradoxically, members of the Oddfellows who asserted its antiquity in the early nineteenth century were also indicating its modernity as part of a contribution to the creation of the new national identity. Linda Colley argued that an over-arching British identity was developed in the eighteenth century. Independent Protestant loyalty to the Crown and Parliament was presented as an attractive alternative to Catholic France. This was not simply imposed by an élite but was also constructed at other levels of society. She noted the 'innumerable Masonic and quasi-masonic societies catering to the male delight in secret rituals and dressing up'.[7] When James Anderson compiled a rule book for Freemasons in 1717, *The book of constitutions*, he explicitly linked the creation of the Freemasons to the Hanoverian succession. For him, Freemasonry helped to cement the British nation. That Freemasonry was also alleged to be a cover for Jacobite subversion and was the form adopted by Irish rebels indicates the importance of the part played within the notion of a nation by fraternal societies such as the Oddfellows.[8] Colley was influenced by Benedict Anderson's work. He suggested that the Enlightenment and the French Revolution undermined the legitimacy of the divinely ordained, hierarchical dynastic realm. Nations became 'imagined communities' in which members did not need to know every other fellow-member but could imagine their affinity to one another because

> regardless of the actual inequality and exploitation that may prevail in each, the nation is always conceived as a deep, horizontal comradeship. Ultimately it is this fraternity that makes it possible, over the past two centuries, for so many millions of people, not so much to kill, as willingly to die for such limited imaginings.[9]

At a time when a new sense of national identity was being forged with fraternity at its core, the Oddfellows' myth of origins was a contribution to that process.

The stress on the longevity of the Society enabled it to emphasise both the novelty and the continuity of membership. Through its own accounts of the past the Society incited speculation about the authenticity of market exchange, challenged elements of legal orthodoxy and promoted the intellectual shift from an Enlightenment ideal of universal truth. Its dramas encouraged both ethical reflection and recruitment. Moreover, because they were open to a variety of interpretations regarding the roles of respect, aspirations and independence and justice, these spectacles served to mute internal divisions. Members could move back in time to ancient Egypt or be reborn before entrance to a symbolically hierarchical, violent lodge through which they could progress, measured by 'Degrees' and 'jewels', into positions of authority. Burn referred to 22 men who were 'initiated into the craft and secrets of Oddfellowship' as 'new-born brothers'.[10] They might also look forward, for, as a Victorian member proudly marched, in his spotless white gloves, beneath banners covering in multi-vocal symbols to hear sometimes defiant graveside orations, he could envisage his own well-attended funeral and beyond it to when his grieving widow would benefit from the support of his respectful brothers. There might be 'upwards of 100 brethren' at his funeral all wearing black silk scarves and white gloves, as there was at the funeral of Lionel Kipling of Darlington in 1839, there might be 'about four hundred brethren' as there was at the funeral of Henry Hurst of Hull or he might even be the subject of an eight-verse poem as 'democratic', philanthropic, Mancunian boilermaker John Roach was, in 1880.[11] In common with the idealised nation, the Society existed long before the individual and had the capacity to memorise that person.

Stories of ancient origins were one way of countering the potentially disruptive claims regarding more recent origins. The early years of the Society were ones when the Order was

a name without a reality – composed of the discordant elements of pride and poverty, fraud and benevolence, strife and goodwill to mankind – attractive in the exterior, rotten in its internal government – without the pale of the law – the victim of knaves and charlatans.[12]

Amid the uncertainty the Romans appeared solid and dependable. Tales of the distant past were developed and in 1842 the Board of Directors asserted that the name of Oddfellows was granted by Titus Caesar in 79 CE. This was the story told in 1909 by a PPGM, George Brindley. There was some justification for the claim, in that, although the Roman labour system was more coercive than that of the medieval or subsequent periods of British history, the Roman *collegia*, trade groupings, provided burials for members and existed in Britain and indeed across the Roman Empire. Fraternities have existed since classical times and could well have drawn on ideas from all over the Roman Empire including Babylon and Roman Palestine. For example, the Roman God Mithras was the central figure of a fraternal cult which was popular among Roman soldiers in Britain and elsewhere from the first to the fourth centuries of the Common Era. Mithraism was an initiatory order, passed from initiate to initiate, and there were seven degrees of membership, following the initiation ceremony. Many fraternities were suppressed following the adoption of Christianity in the fourth century CE, but others adapted and became the basis for guilds, a type of organisation that flourished in Britain under the Normans. While a direct connection between Babylon and Manchester is unproven, the Romans left valuation techniques, the law of contract and the notion that it was the right of the state in intervene in economic matters for the Oddfellows. They also had a goddess of justice, Iustitia, who had scales, for weighing out justice, and a sword for enforcing it. Sometimes she also has a torch, the light of truth, and a bundle of rods, the fasces, which cannot be broken when united. From Roman sources the Oddfellows could have taken a number of its enduring images.

Traditions of longevity were maintained within the Society. In 1867 Corresponding Secretary James Spry suggested that 'Our Creator … kindly implanted in our natures various gifts [from which] we may trace the establishment of Odd-Fellowship'.[13] In 1909 a Provincial Grand Master placed the origins in the Garden of Eden and also made a case for early women membership: 'that Adam was an Oddfellow no one can doubt and that Eve was another is a matter of fact; and that they constituted in the Garden of Eden the first Oddfellows' Friendly Society is a matter of History.'[14] Members of the Oddfellows have also claimed roots in the Old Testament Jews of ancient Babylon.[15] The Unity was possibly drawing on a tradition of

Jews as symbols of loyalty and power. The convention was retained by the Archdeacon of Ely who told the Oddfellows' annual conference, AMC, in 1914 that

> St Paul in his day was a member of what it is not an exaggeration to call a great friendly society. The people of Israel as a friendly society … was bound up in faith in the God of Israel like modern friendly societies in many of its characteristics.[16]

In 1945 a Trustee of the Society claimed:

> There is no power on earth capable of destroying Oddfellowship founded on Friendship Truth and Love. It has existed from time immemorial. Moses was an Odd Fellow when he went to the assistance of his brethren in the brickyards of Egypt. David and Jonathan knew a good brand of Odd Fellowship. The Independent Order of Odd Fellows had a good brand of it long before 1812, with branches spread over the whole inhabitable globe … Odd Fellowship is getting acquainted, getting better acquainted, being so interested in the welfare of each other that you are willing to help one another in Friendship, Love and Truth.[17]

This appeal to longevity made when the upheaval of the Second World War was still fresh and there was considerable change to the role of the Society, suggests that the Society sought to present itself in terms of permanence during a difficult period.

Histories of the Society which stressed the origins within the early modern and modern period are indicative of a shift in perceptions as to how history should be written. The writing of history at the end of the eighteenth century involved little systematic use of primary sources, and there was often a limited sense of the idea of change through time. It was not a discipline in the way that it was by the nineteenth century, when the idea that historians should write narratives based on primary sources became popularised. Moffrey, writing in 1910, invited readers to 'smile' at the 'romantic genealogy' of the story of the Roman origins and gave greater credence to the 'documentary evidence' of Spry's work of 1867.[18] There was a greater interest in secular origins. The suggestion was made in the *Complete Manual of Oddfellowship*, 1879, that the Ancient Order of Oddfellows met in the Bull Inn, where members took a solemn oath of mutual support and promised to act with justice to all men. A variation of this was printed 35 years later, when it was argued that an Order of Odd Fellows was established in 1452 by various knights who were said to have met at the Boulogne-sur-Mere (Bull and Mouth) London and formed a fraternity.[19] Collections were made at meetings for a common fund out of which payments would be made to any members in need. It merged with another group to form the Grand United Order of Oddfellows. Members of that body possibly sang a song written in 1788 by James Montgomery, the first line of which 'When Friendship, Love and Truth abound, among a band of brothers'. The lyrics were echoed in verses in later IOOFMU songbooks and indeed the song is reproduced in some.[20] One Edwardian Oddfellow history argued that in 1710 there was a Loyal Lintot of Oddfellows in London.[21] Lintot was a place in Normandy from which Huguenots had fled to London. Between 1683 and 1710 they formed many friendly societies such as the Société des Enfants de Nîmes, the Society of Dauphiné, the Society of Parisians and the Society of Lintot.

Greer claimed that Oddfellowship dates from 'sometime before 1650'.[22] Another source mentions the Aristarchus Lodge No. 9 of the Order of Odd Fellows which met at a Globe Tavern, London, in 1748. Neave called this 'the first authentic reference to an Oddfellows' society', although his source was Spry's *The history of Odd-Fellowship: its origin, tradition and objects with a general review of the results arising from its adoption by the branch known as the Manchester Unity*.[23] This lodge was numbered nine, so presumably there were, or had been, at least eight associated Odd Fellows lodges at that time. In 1964 the Grand Master, J. A. McBryde, suggested that the Order was 'conceived in the early days of the eighteenth century', and in 1997 the Grand Master, Roger Burley, when addressing the AMC, referred to 'the eighteenth-century lodges of Oddfellows'.[24] In this respect he was following an American 'Grand Secretary of the Sovereign Grand Lodge', T. A. Ross, who claimed that the Order of Odd Fellows 'originated in England in the eighteenth century'. He also suggested the officers' titles derived from the 'Order of Gregorians' which met in 1736, and that the Society was mentioned by Daniel Defoe and the *Gentleman's Magazine* of 1745.[25] In 1940 the Oddfellows in Australia, while admitting that 'mystery of long-past ages enshrouds the origin of Oddfellowship', then added that 'the first definite memorandum of an Oddfellows lodge indicates that there was one in existence in London during the year 1736'.[26]

More recently, Hutton said that the Society 'developed out of a drinking club which had existed since the early eighteenth century'.[27] There was a lodge of the Union Order of Oddfellows in London in 1750 and one in Derby in 1775. In 1838 the *Oddfellows' Magazine* suggested that, following a dispute, some members declared themselves 'Independent' from the 'Union Order of Odd Fellows'.[28] In 1769 John Wilkes, the radical MP and journalist, was said to be a member of the Union Grand Lodge but it is not clear that this was an Oddfellows lodge.[29] Possibly the Unity grew out of (was 'Independent' of) the Union or London order whose headquarters were at the Bohemia Tavern in Wych Street. Possibly the Union Order itself was formed in about 1779 by the partial amalgamation of two earlier Orders the 'Ancient' and the 'Patriotic'. Although no primary evidence of these Orders is available it has been argued that they were convivial, political and charitable and on their merger the benevolence aspect became the principal aim of the brethren. The *Oddfellows' Magazine* 1888 included a picture of a medal presented to the secretary of a lodge of the Grand Independent Order of Oddfellows, in 1796–1797 and reported that in 1798 the *Gentleman's Magazine* suggested that the 'Original United Order of Oddfellows' consisted of 50 lodges, 39 of them in London and its environs. According to a history of the Grand United Order of Oddfellows written in 1914 by a member, John Thornley of Burton-on-Trent, 1798 is also the date on the oldest document in the possession of the Grand United Order of Oddfellows.

The eighteenth-century understanding of the value of such associations was so ubiquitous that heaven was visualised as one large friendly society.[30] By 1800 there were thousands of friendly societies in England and Wales with perhaps 650,000 members.[31] In 1804 there was one benefit club to every 710 people in the north-west of England and each club had an average of 87 members.[32] This must have rendered familiar the term 'friendly society'. The words Independent, Order and Unity were ones in use by a number of societies. In naming their enterprise Oddfellows the founders were connecting not only to previous lodges of which they may have been members but also to a widely popular brand. By the end of the eighteenth century there were many Odd Fellow organisations in England including the Imperial Odd Fellows of Nottingham; the Ancient Noble Odd Fellows, Bolton and the Grand United Odd Fellows, Sheffield, the Economical Odd Fellows, Leeds and the National Odd Fellows, Salford. In 1891 Wilkinson argued that the Grand United existed 'before 1798', the Nottingham Ancient Imperial Order of Odd Fellows by 1810 and that the IOOFMU started in 1812.[33] The founders may well have known that many friendly societies had short lives often ending in financial disaster and wanted their name to indicate reliability.[34] The name was used all over England. There is mention of a humorous print of a meeting night of a club of Oddfellows in 1789, references in the press to a 'Grand Original Lodge of Odd Fellows' in 1790, the union of the Imperial and United Lodges of Odd Fellows in 1793, accounts, in 1796, of a Society of Oddfellows with a Vice Grand, a Most Noble Grand and a Secretary. There was a Society of Oddfellows in Gravesend in 1797 and 1798, according to *True Briton*, and in 1798 both a meeting of the Loyal and Constitutional Third Lodge of Odd Fellows in Birmingham and a reference, in the *Whitehall Evening Post*, to the Town Lodges of the United Order of Odd Fellows.[35] When James Hadfield or Hatfield attempted to kill King George III in 1800, his trial was widely reported. At it the prisoner told the court that he had been made an Oddfellow and was a member of the Society.[36]

It has been argued that in 1803 one of the grouping of lodges known as the London Union (or United) Odd Fellows Society declared itself to be the 'Grand Lodge of England' and assumed authority.[37] Although Gosden suggested that such Oddfellows clubs in London 'were convivial clubs only', a member who is a Londoner, Douglas Potter, claimed that 'London has just claims to regard itself as the birthplace of Oddfellowship. We consider that Oddfellowship started in the London area.'[38] An Ancient Independent Order of Oddfellows, Kent Unity, was formed in 1805.[39] An account from 1806 of the death of a Manchester man, J. J. Seger, reported that he was an Oddfellow.[40] There were lodges of Oddfellows in Halifax from at least 1804. According to reports of the fifth and second annual meetings of Lodge No. 6 of the Odd Fellows of Halifax, in 1804 and 1807 the members 'repaired in procession to a Methodist chapel with their 'flags, trappings, insignia and entire regalia' and 'excellent band of music'.[41] There is a contemporary account of Lord Cochrane being invited to join an 'Odd Fellows' club at 'The Feathers', Pimlico, in 1807 and a reference to a meeting of the Bon Accord Lodge of Ancient Oddfellows a few months later.[42] The 1888 *Oddfellows' Magazine* refers to a 'Free and Independent Order of Oddfellows', in Dover in 1807. A journal, *The Odd Fellows Miscellany* was published in London in 1808. In 1809 Richard Barnes of Harwich recorded in his diary that he witnessed a procession in Colchester: 'I saw an Odd Fellows funeral. He was carried to All Saints Church, where there were prayers.'[43] According to Ross it was in 1809 that the lodges united into the Manchester Unity.[44] In 1810 three lodges which had been part of the London Grand Lodge of the United Order of Oddfellows formed, it has been argued by Neave, a Sheffield Grand Lodge which eventually became the Grand United Order of Oddfellows.[45] The term was sufficiently popular that by 1811 a dictionary satire was able to provide a definition of Odd Fellows as 'a convivial society: the introduction of the noble grands, arrayed in royal robes is well worth seeing at the price of becoming a member.'[46] A song book published in that year recommended the contents on the grounds that they were sung in Oddfellows' lodges.

The Society has claimed 1809 as the foundation date but a year later proposed 'about the year 1821'.[47] The *Complete Manual of Oddfellowship*, 1879 claimed that the 'first authentic date of (an odd fellows) dispensation' was that of Trafalgar Lodge, Halifax, Yorkshire, 13 August 1810. Members of the Oddfellows in the Manchester District became dissatisfied with the way the United Order was being run from Sheffield and broke away to form an independent Order with the title 'Manchester Unity'. These dissidents then encouraged other lodges to leave the United Order and become part of the Manchester Unity.[48] Certainly a membership card for the 'Grand Lodge of Odd Fellows, Sheffield', dated 1812 refers to 'Lodge No 34', which suggests that there were Oddfellows in Sheffield.[49] There is also a report of a Festival of the Original and Fraternal Lodges of Odd Fellows at the Bull and Mouth and Pleasant Inns, Sheffield in 1811. There was a procession to a church and reports of visiting brothers from Leeds, Halifax and elsewhere. Mention was made of 26 lodges and of wardens, supporters, secretaries, Fathers of the Lodges. It was also referred to as the United Order of Oddfellows and, to judge from the account of the sashes, jewels and wands, it was well-equipped with regalia.[50] A booklet produced to mark the Unity's 175th anniversary noted that there were Oddfellow lodges in South Wales and six English towns, including Sheffield.[51] Burn suggested that 'it is very probable that the first Odd-fellows made their appearance in North Wales'.[52] The Grand United Order of Oddfellows' claim to be the branch friendly society from which the IOOFMU broke away is based on a Bond of Union, held in its Head Office, which was issued to establish a lodge in 1798.[53] Although no evidence is available to substantiate the claim that a 'Grand Lodge of the Ancient Order of O'Fellows' was established in Sheffield under a dispensation from London, there are a number of references to a 'Society of Oddfellows' in the *Leeds Mercury* from the 1790s, and in 1804 a charter to open a further lodge of Oddfellows was granted to William Leay of London.[54] Neave's account, drawn from Oddfellow sources and records in Sheffield, indicated that this was also the year that the Grand Lodge of the United Order of Oddfellows was dissolved.[55] Those who selected the name Oddfellows for the body which became the IOOFMU were developing a well-established idea.

Possibly a marble mason called Bolton received a dispensation to form a lodge, the Victory. He then moved to Manchester and in 1809 declared its independence of the Grand Lodge of England.[56] By 1800 up to 17 trades may have been organised in national or regional club networks, the idea of seeking to extend such contacts may well have been familiar to Bolton.[57] Either this lodge or the Prince Regent Lodge of Odd Fellows joined with a social club started in 1808 which was associated with Robert Naylor. Harris, writing in 1946 followed Stillson, 1897 and put the emphasis on Naylor (who became Grand Master in 1832) rather than Bolton.[58]

Moffrey cautiously offered that Bolton is 'credited by some with having opened a lodge' in 1809 which 'may afterwards have joined' the IOOFMU.[59] In 1948 William Beveridge concluded that while 'the honour of founding the Manchester Unity of Oddfellows is sometimes disputed, the leader seems clearly to have been Robert Naylor, landlord of the Ropemakers' Arms in Salford who gathered there a group of men to follow him into secession'. However, he also noted that mutual aid movements have often been the 'creation of a group of men … this is true above all of the friendly societies'.[60] The disputes about the roles of individuals and locations in the creation of the Unity may be related to personal disputes and rival claims to the 'mother' lodge and these persisted during the nineteenth century. At the centenary Moffrey concluded that 'one or other of these men, for accounts differ as to the real founder, took hold of the traditions and laid the foundations of a united society'.[61] Whoever was the more significant figure, the lodge met at the Ropemakers Arms, Chapel St, Salford, or (as Naylor may have been the landlord there) at the Robin Hood Hotel, Church Street. Whichever the pub, a new united organisation declared itself to be the Lord Abercrombie Lodge from which, it is said, 'the greatest of all the orders sprang'.[62] Other lodges declared their allegiance to the new lodge which in 1811 proclaimed itself as the 'Lord Abercrombie Grand Lodge of Independent Odd Fellows'.[63] In 1812 the organisation of these lodges was revised and a management committee elected.

There have also been claims for 1812 as a foundation year. Burn cited a Memorial petitioning for legal status dated 1842 which opens with the words: 'The Society was formed about the year 1812'.[64] In 1892 the claim was made by Edgar Webbe that:

> The Manchester Unity was established in 1812. It is presumed that it originated by secession from the Union Order of Oddfellows at the instigation of Mr Naylor, who became Grand Master.

The *Leeds Mercury* of 1900 and Brindley, writing in 1909, agreed that the foundation was in 1812.[65] Spry quotes a petition to the Commons from the Unity which is dated 1850. This claimed that the Society 'has been in existence since 1812', though he also stated that it was formed 'about the year 1812'. Cordery also proposed 1812.[66] In 1879 *The Complete Manual of Oddfellowship* suggested that the Oddfellows was formed following secession in 1813 from the Patriotic Order. In December 1963 the Lancashire Provincial Corresponding Secretary Brother Aspinall, referred to the 'invisible bridge which spanned the history of Odd Fellowship', and 'recalled the foundation of the Unity 150 years ago [i.e. 1813] when 27 men gathered together'.[67] Although not an official history, when first published Gosden's work was available at a discounted rate to Society members and the Secretary of the Order noted that 'it is felt that a copy of the book should be available in every District'. Gosden opted for a foundation date of 1812, though he also argued that it was in 1813 that a convention was called of the lodges in and around Manchester in sympathy with the new movement, an organisation of the lodges was effected, and the title "The Manchester Unity of the Independent Order of Odd Fellows" adopted.[68] Ross argued that although there had been lodges 'the first Lodge was chartered July 21st 1813 … the Unity as a body was organised in 1813.'[69] This was when a Grand Committee or district grand lodge was provided, a form of government adopted, and a Grand Master and a Deputy Grand Master appointed. In January 1814 a Grand Master was elected. Solt Dennis put forward 1813 as a foundation date.[70] Other recent historians have opted for 1814 and 1816.[71] However, in the 1990s two historians echoed an account of 1845, and plumped for 1823.[72]

Claiming the status of original 'mother lodge' enabled members to charge other groups for charters and take a percentage of subscriptions. This might have been an incentive to conceal or destroy information about the origins of a lodge. There were other reasons to be economical with the truth. There are a number of examples of societies suffering from organisational problems about record-keeping, abuses of the funds or actuarial deficiencies. It was not a statutory requirement to be financially sound although legislation in 1819 attempted to introduce this. Witnesses to the Parliamentary Committee of Friendly Societies, 1825 claimed that there were few solvent societies. In such circumstances there could be many men who favoured concealment of data. Furthermore, members might have been concerned about spies. Working men's associations were subject to governmental regulation from the 1790s. To keep records of meetings may not have been popular with those who attended. The Corresponding Societies Act, 1797 made communication between lodges illegal while the Seditious Meetings Act, allowed meetings of more than 50 people to be banned. Subversive organisations had been outlawed under the Unlawful Societies Act, 1799, and friendly societies' secret words and signs aroused the concern of government.[73] Some supporters of Tom Paine argued that it was their business to 'worm themselves' into friendly societies. Although Thompson argued that there 'little evidence' of this, there were possible connections.[74] There are reports in 1819 of a procession of 35,000 people on Cronkeyshaw Common, Rochdale, with banners. The slogans displayed included 'The memory of Paine, Brandreth etc.' and 'Success to Female Societies'. Furthermore, a representative of the Stockport Union Female Society addressed a reform gathering in Macclesfield. However, these claims were disputed.[75] The Treasonable and Seditious Practices Act, 1795 and the Combinations Acts 1799 and 1800 indicated the concern to prevent men uniting to raise wages or follow the example of the French who in 1789 overthrew their Monarchy and government. Worrall claimed that 'Britain 1790–1820 was a spy culture'.[76] Those early nineteenth-century members of the Society who were suspicious of authority may have sought to evade surveillance by destroying or falsifying records. For them to focus on the longer roots of their associations may have been a necessary fiction.

There were disadvantages to the promotion of ancient linage. It might have made governments and courts suspicious of the oaths being sworn within lodges and it might have given comfort to those who did not want to adopt the new actuarial regulations which came into force in the 1840s. To marginalise the distant antecedents helped to situate the Society as a provider of rational modern mutual insurance. In 1845 a Past Provincial Grand Master, James Burn dismissed the Edenic story of 'the first Odd-fellow fresh from Creation's mould', and 'supposed' that 'the first foundation-stone of our present magnificent superstructure was laid' at the opening of the 'Loyal Abercrombie' in Salford in October 1810.[77] He also belittled the 'puritanical cant and phraseology of the ancient order' that persisted in the USA. He argued that the British had, 'very properly discarded the mummery of the old school'.[78] In the same year, when Benjamin Disraeli addressed 1,000 members of the Society at a festival in South London, he tactfully suggested that 'it had originated silently'.[79] Those who have presented the foundation in the period since the early nineteenth century have often sought to emphasise modernity. Spry argued that it was only in 1864 that the structure of financial reform was completed, though he noted that 'the foundation stone of this pillar of was laid in Glasgow in 1845, the shaft was erected at Preston in 1853'.[80] Moffrey agreed that it was only in 1845 that the Unity took the 'first step to security'. This was echoed, about a century later, by the American populariser of the notion of 'social capital', Robert Putnam, who claimed that friendly societies in Britain were 'invented by mid-Victorian social reformers to restore community bonds', while Martin Daunton proposed that the political economy of Victorian Britain was 'an act of construction of new forms of organisation – co-operatives, friendly societies, trade unions'.[81]

Rather than inventing traditions upon which many could agree, another way to try to settle disputes was to emphasis the modernity and familial nature of Oddfellowship. Burn argued that there was a decisive break from the 'old order' which he dated from 1745. Its 'forms and ceremonies were composed of the most stupid and ridiculous nonsense'. He described the 'downright buffoonery and unmeaning frivolity', of the initiation, the blindfolds, the soaking, the sword. Once he had dismissed 'the nonsensical ordeal', he sought to 'change the scene'. He stressed that while the Society had been 'cradled in vice', it grew into be able to unite 'the greater part of the human family in the bonds on good fellowship'.[82] In 1845, when Burn was writing, an important element of the Chartist critique of the Poor Law of 1834 was that it undermined the family. It meant that husbands and wives were separated in workhouses and that the whole burden of supporting an illegitimate child fell onto the mother. There was also opposition to the view, often associated with Thomas Malthus, that poorer people should marry when older than they might have wished, so as to be sure that they could support their offspring.[83] In mentioning how Oddfellowship supported family life Burn may have sought to reassure readers about the solidity of the Society. He was not alone as the metaphor of the family was widely employed within the Society. When he addressed the AMC in 1842 J. L. Ridgely of Baltimore called the Oddfellows across the world 'members of one great family … children of one great parent', and suggested that American Oddfellows offered prayers 'for the welfare of the Mother', before he asked 'What had they received from Mother?'[84] The notion of maternal beneficence was reinforced by the Society's emblem. It featured Britannia attended by Europe, Asia and Africa, bestowing the Grand Charter upon the USA through a native American while the Past Officers' Certificates included the Arms of Australia, New Zealand, Cape Colony and the USA, these being 'the homes of many of our foremost members, whose connections with the mother country and with our Order is thus symbolised'.[85] The image of the family involved not merely rhetoric about international brotherhood but also metaphorical parental control from the organisation which Ridgely called 'The Mother of the Order'. In 1867 Spry mentioned that the growth of the Unity had been 'for the benefit of the Brotherhood of the human family'.[86] While emphasising modernity those who employed terms such as brethren and mother staked a claim to a linage back to the early church (in which monks were brothers and the Pope the Holy Father) and to the notion of kinship between those not related by blood or marriage.

It took many years for a statistical approach to mortality hazards to be adopted. Partly this was because of popular views about, for example, the recklessness of youth compared to the sobriety of older men appeared to make more sense than tables of data. Moreover, although their advertising stressed the mathematical certainty of their calculations, different insurance companies adopted different rates and emphasised the importance of local knowledge and many of them failed due to poor management or fraud.[87] The Oddfellows presented itself as at the forefront of scientific reform in the works of Hardy in 1888, Watson in 1900 and Moffrey in 1910.[88] *The Oddfellows' Companion and Guide to Derby*, produced for the 1892 AMC, which was held in the town, argued that if 'seeking for definite truth and enlightenment' an enquirer needs to 'research many centuries'. Readers could learn about 'labour unions' in relation to the Temple in Jerusalem and Greek and Roman life but they were firmly told that to assert that Oddfellows 'have any claim to such remote antiquity as Masonry, is only to create a wrong impression'.[89] Writing in 1897, a period when the Oddfellows was keen to promote actuarial science, Henry Stillson described the formation of the first Oddfellows lodge as 'spontaneous organisation, by self-institution'. He also referred to Naylor's initiation rites as 'an absurd and ridiculous ceremony for the admission of applicants', which were only modified when it joined the Prince Regent.[90] He marginalised the roots which stretched back far beyond an early nineteenth-century Mancunian pub, and stressed instead that the new body had a 'somewhat improved initiatory ceremony', and introduced 'appropriate paraphernalia … to restrain the ancient usages of the lodge'.[91] Stillson mentioned the importance of the guilds, but avoided any more recent comparisons, and concluded that 'the present age has borrowed but little from the models of ancient times … whatever its early formation, the institution as we know it today was not moulded in the dim centuries of the past but in the present, which is the golden age of the world.'[92] Ross agreed that 'intelligent Odd Fellows in Europe and America place no reliance upon the old and mythical story', which he then repeated.[93]

It has been argued that, 'The main purpose of a friendly society is to provide life assurance and to assist members during sickness and unemployment'.[94] Carnes made a similar case in 1989 when he claimed that 'Odd Fellowship originated in the late 18th century in Britain. Its working-class founders sought to mitigate the effects of the Industrial Revolution and the English Poor Laws.'[95] Such accounts can narrow Oddfellowship to a product of sudden industrial change and marginalise the impact of early eighteenth-century societies which emerged from the guilds. They are in danger of reducing members' engagement with funeral rites and group solidarity in the event of the death of a member to fears of a pauper's grave. The emphasis on a periodisation of modernity as a unified, coherent, historical epoch which occurred after a dichotomous break may tell us more about the Webbs than about how far the Oddfellows was an outcome of an epochal shift towards rational economic market needs. Moreover, accounts which stressed modernity can less easily address Frederick Eden's question. In his *Observations on friendly societies for the maintenance of the industrious classes during sickness, infirmity and old age* (1801) he asked why a bachelor who wanted to protect himself against illness should pay to bury his neighbour's wife. If one assumes that the bachelor was driven by a desire to maximise his own material possessions, then efficient impersonal exchanges may have been his best strategy. However, if expenditure was linked to obligation and community, if the money spent on burying a neighbour's wife, beer and ritual were part of a cycle of giving and accepting which connected individuals to coherent collective entity it was not a waste of money, it was a means of connecting to long-held social traditions.

Contextualisation of all the accounts of the origins may not tell us the truth in the conventional sense, but an assessment of that which the narrators sought to highlight, and that which they sought to conceal, can reveal much about the culture which produced the tales. Disputes over the precise pub and exact year of foundation reveal tensions between the competing demands for civility, commerce, community and charity which have been central to much of the development of Oddfellowship and which constitute important elements within its structured reciprocity. A focus on the Romans may have distracted from contemporary tensions. The history of the Society, like its symbols and rituals, could be perceived and revealed in many ways. Members from Yorkshire could take pride in the Oddfellows from their county, those from London could also have a sense of parochial satisfaction. While this could lead to discord it was also the basis for growth because different facets of Oddfellowship, some scientific, some mystical, could be presented to potential members. Moffrey recognised that ambiguity about the origins could be helpful. He noted that as records were not available, 'the frail ties which bound the branches to the "Grand Lodges" were severed, and all traces of the existence of the lodges as branches of their Orders were lost.' For him 1810 was only 'a convenient date to start' for

> it must not be assumed that the opening of the Abercrombie Lodge marked the dawn of Oddfellowship. Oddfellows' Lodges had been in existence for a long period anterior to 1810 … sufficient has been written to show the antiquity of the elementary principle of mutual help in which Oddfellowship is based and to prove that the principle had been carried out by societies bearing the name of Oddfellows for upwards of half a century.[96]

Either for the financial gain associated with being the parent of other lodges or through suspicion of the authorities, some may have deliberately concealed information about the foundation of the Oddfellows. Others may have written down ill-recalled stories or conflated information about a variety of organisations, some of which had the word Oddfellows in their titles. Some have sought to present the Society in a particular light, as part of a fraternal tradition reaching back to the guilds, as connected to trade unionism and Freemasonry. Different accounts focused on its independence and its modern approach to finance. Whatever its origins it has been made and remade within each generation. The expression of its values, through its mottos and Ritual, has been adapted and the balance within its structured reciprocity has altered.

II Growing up in 'Shock City' [97]

Initially Oddfellowship was particularly popular in Lancashire (as Table 1 indicates) where the early friendly society was 'an insurance company, savings bank, associational status grouping and trade union all in one'.[98] Manchester was associated with rapid industrial and urban development, a relatively unhealthy population, social protest, new insurance and financial services and distinctive managerial and gender roles. The character of the town informed the nature of early Oddfellowship particularly because men based in Manchester sought to dominate the early years of the Society. An account written a century later by a Past Provincial Grand Master of West London indicated that a few 'men in the Manchester district were determined to keep the government entirely in their own hands. Manchester members only were to rule the Manchester Unity.' Their arrangements 'exhibited a peculiar lack of vision, a selfish short-sighted policy ... The Directors, although elected by the whole of the Manchester Unity, still had to be chosen from the districts in and around Manchester.' [99] Three tiers emerged, the lodge, the district committee and the AMC where the directors were appointed. This structure, which proved durable and effective over many years, was developed in Manchester.

The mechanisation of the long-established wool and linen textile industry in the late eighteenth century helped Manchester and its surrounding towns to expand. The soft water,

Industrialisation in north-west England

The rapidity of the changes can be seen in two descriptions. The first is of Lancashire in about 1780:

Their dwellings and small gardens clean and neat – all the family well clad the men with each a watch in his pocket, and the women dressed to their own fancy – the church crowded to excess every Sunday – every house well furnished with a clock in elegant mahogany or fancy case – handsome tea services in Staffordshire ware ... The workshop of the weaver was a rural cottage, from which, when he was tired of sedentary labour, he could sally forth into his little garden, and with the spade or the hoe tend its culinary productions. The cotton wool which was to form his weft was picked clean by the fingers of his younger children and was carded and spun by the older girls assisted by his wife, and the yarn was woven by himself assisted by his sons.[100]

The below is a description from about 1814:

There are hundreds of factories in Manchester which are five or six stories high. At the side of each factory there is a great chimney which belches forth black smoke and indicates the presence of the powerful steam engines. The smoke from the chimneys forms a great cloud which can be seen for miles around the town. The houses have become black on account of the smoke. The river upon which Manchester stands is so tainted with colouring matter that the water resembles the contents of a dye vat ... To save wages, mule jennies have actually been built so that no less than 600 spindles can be operated by one adult and two children ... In the large spinning mills machines of different kinds stand in rows like regiments in an army.[101]

humid climate, local coal, labour supply, economic infrastructure, canals, and later railways, enabled Manchester, the 'Shock City' of the period as historian Asa Briggs called it, to become the location where it was technologically, politically, economically and socially possible to produce textiles in factories and mills. Between 1781 and 1791 imports of cotton into Britain quadrupled, reaching 100 million pounds in 1815. In 1751 Britain exported £46,000 worth of cotton cloth. By 1800 this figure was £5.4 million and in 1811 there were more than 5,000,000 spindles at work in the Britain. Central to this change was the Manchester area.

While historians have noted the long roots of many changes, to many of those living in Manchester urbanisation would have appeared rapid and frightening.[102] In 1835 commentator Alexander de Tocqueville noted the great economic wealth, extraordinary vitality and

The new industrial Manchester had the capacity to fascinate, amaze and shock contemporaries: the spread of industry, the huge physical expansion of the town, the squalor of much working-class housing, and the enormous wealth being accumulated by merchants, mill-owners and traders. This is Baines's map of Manchester, which dates from 1824. Inset (*bottom right*) is his depiction of the town as it had appeared in 1650, before industrialisation had transformed the town.

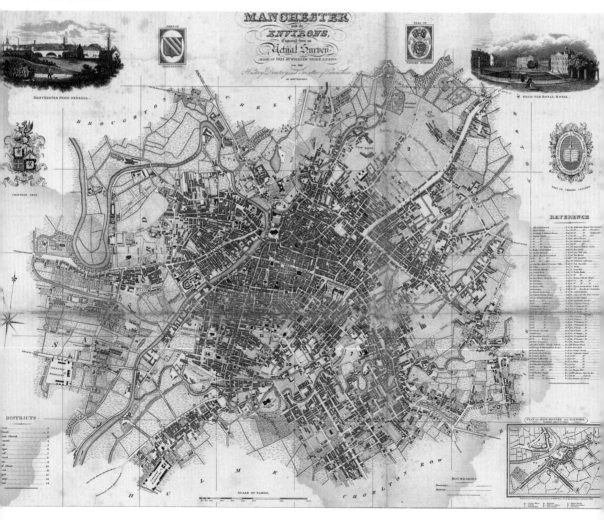

There are accounts of numerous fish in the River Irk at Manchester in the early part of the nineteenth century. However, it soon became polluted. The old Manchester can be seen in the form of Chetham's College on the riverbank. New Manchester can be seen in the background, with mill chimneys and industrial premises crowding the skyline.
CARNEGIE COLLECTION

considerable social and environmental problems of the town and characterised Manchester as 'a foul drain from which the greatest stream of industry flows to fertilise the whole world. From this filthy sewer pure gold flows.' Being the pioneer of many industrial activities came at a social price. Many people lacked financial security, solidarity and social networks. In 1810 there were about 2,000 power looms. By 1834 the number of power looms in the country had risen to 110,000, many of them in the north of England. The number of handloom weavers remained at about 250,000, and it was only by the 1840s that handloom weavers went into decline. In Oldham in the 1820s 50 per cent of the workforce were handloom weavers, and only 7 per cent worked in the new mills, while by the 1840s the number in the mills had risen to 60 per cent. By 1835, 90 per cent of the British cotton industry was concentrated in and around Manchester, and goods manufactured out of cotton amounted to 51 per cent of all British exports. In 1853, the British cotton industry supplied 45 per cent of the total world consumption of cotton cloth. In Manchester alone the population rose from 77 000 people in 1801 to over 316 000 in 1851.

Table 1   *Lancashire Oddfellow Lodge foundations, 1828–1841*

District	Number of Lodges founded		Total in 1875	Earliest foundation
	1828–34	1835–41		
Liverpool	4	21	27	1818
Manchester	3	2	11	1814
Preston	3	17	20	1815
Blackburn	3	17	24	1819
Bury	4	10	19	1814
Wigan	3	5	13	1819

In Lancashire the Poor Law Amendment Act was applied to the whole of the county by 1842, with the exception of Ashton-under-Lyne, Oldham and Rochdale. It was also the county with the largest number of newly founded Oddfellow lodges between 1834 and 1841. This Table indicates the number of lodges founded in Lancashire during both the seven years before and the seven years after the passage of the Poor Law Amendment Act. The number founded in Manchester was relatively low as a high proportion of the earliest lodges were in that area and also because the Oddfellows Manchester district did not cover the entire conurbation of Manchester.

Source: Gosden, *The friendly societies*, p. 208.

As the number of new general workers grew, the population of Manchester tripled between about 1775 and 1830; men were increasingly at risk of falling sick among strangers. Organisations which offered practical social insurance, beyond philanthropy and state poor relief, developed. The Oddfellows offered solutions to working people in uncertain times, to those in danger of social isolation or who had limited financial means and could not rely on savings, higher salaries or the support of blood kin. Many of the early members of the Oddfellows would have lived in overcrowded, damp, poorly lit and inadequately ventilated accommodation with little sanitation. Typhus spread among cotton-mill employees in 1796 and cholera in 1831–32. Infant mortality in Manchester in 1798 may have been as high as 300 per 1,000 live births. Respiratory diseases were common among adults, exacerbated by the dusty and damp conditions in the mills. Many died of smallpox and after vaccination reduced deaths from that disease, the principal causes of death were from whooping cough and diarrhoea.

In many towns doctors promoted charities associated with hospitals and provided their services free to some patients. This aided their prestige and may have gained their additional business. Whereas in the past men might have been wary of those who sold exotic potions and dubious pills, the status of doctors had improved by the time that the Oddfellows was founded. This may have made membership, and the associated medical aid, more attractive. 'Old poison peddlers were becoming new civic worthies,' as Corfield put it.[103] Moreover, doctors also had their mutual aid such as the Benevolent Medical Society, founded in 1787. This provided assistance to the widows and orphans of surgeons, apothecaries and physicians in Kent. In 1815, the London-based men-only guild, the Society of Apothecaries, was licensed by statue to provide a system of education, assessment and registration. The Oddfellows had

Industrialisation changed everything. Tens of thousands flocked to find new opportunities and work in the factories that were concentrated in northern towns such as Manchester. There they found a raw, new society which had not yet had time to develop adequate facilities for welfare, housing, education or even sanitation. Here mule spinners toil ceaselessly to keep their machinery working. Cotton thread is being drawn and twisted as the whole bank of machinery moves backwards and forwards on the rails. A child risks serious injury to sweep up the cotton waste from underneath the mechanism.
CARNEGIE COLLECTION

a clear model of men who had gained respectability and status through charitable activity and mutual aid.[104]

In such circumstances men might find the need to join a friendly society more pressing, particularly if they were not defined as 'settled' under the Poor Law, and thus could not rely on the parish for poor relief. Prior to 1834 poor people received relief from the parish where they were settled. Often this was conditional upon a check on other possible sources of income, such as kin, and there was a need to engage in casual labour. In Lancashire, during the period of late eighteenth-century industrialisation, it was rare for the local authorities to give relief, that is payment in cash or kind, to able-bodied men as a matter of routine.

There were many friendly societies in the north-west of England. By 1794 452 had registered under the 1793 legislation. One estimate concluded that 17 per cent of the population were friendly society members while another suggested that 50 per cent of the adult men of Oldham were members. A meeting of delegates from 128 local friendly societies representing 14,000 people was held in Manchester in 1793 and by 1815 it was said that there were over 147,000 friendly society members in Lancashire.[105] It was organisations such as these which provided a model for the Oddfellows. They helped to validate its status, legitimate its activities and train its first officers. In 1800 in Manchester a union of friendly societies collected donations, purchased in bulk, distributed food cheaply to the poor and was reputed to have saved its members £5,000.[106]

More generally, clubs and societies were an important element of eighteenth-century sociability and networking in Manchester. Many were social, such as the Billiard Club, 1792 and the Scramble Club, 1801, others overtly Tory Anglican such as the Church and King Club, 1791 and the Pitt Club 1812. In John Shaw's, established in 1738, of the 57 members in 1825, 38 were involved in the cotton trade. Others were involved in local government and the Church of England. Over 60 per cent were involved in other clubs as well. To create the Oddfellows was to follow well-established local precedent.[107]

Life insurance was localised, the character and development of financial services in Manchester being different to London. In Manchester insurance was an important part of the social cement. It developed rapidly during the period when the Oddfellows was being founded. Between 1770 and 1830 Manchester cotton merchants moved into fire insurance as part of a strategy of collective diversification to consolidate their economic and political power. Over the course of a few years fire insurance expanded from a dozen offices insuring £110 million worth of property to nearly 60 offices insuring £487 million, or 49 per cent of the insurable assets.[108] More generally, fraternity was perceived as integral to the development of business. In promoting reform to the law relating to limited liability the *Westminster Review*, claimed that limited liability could enable investment in large communication schemes such as road building which would help men

> to associate with one another ... feelings of good will, sympathy and friendship would inevitably spring from laws which placed men in relations of mutual dependence and reciprocal benefit; and the happiness which such institutions would bring to individuals, and the strength they would give to the social fabric, are beyond estimation.

In a similar vein the *Quarterly Review* argued that limited liability was like charity but without the paternalism in that 'it combines all the requisites and avoids nearly all the prohibitions which mark out the legitimate path of philanthropic aid'. Moreover, through investment and saving the working man would become 'a tranquil and conservative citizen'.[109]

Private banking in England is generally thought to date from when the medieval scriveners guild (sometimes called brokers or notaries) and the goldsmiths issued receipts for goods deposited with them. The goldsmiths also lent deposits to borrowers and allowed clients to draw drafts on demand. Guilds, the ancestors of private banks, were also the ancestors of many friendly societies. The two descendents shared a number of features. For example, local English country banks adopted the trunk-and-branch system during the period when the Oddfellows developed its system of affiliation. Both sought to reassure potential customers or members as to their solidity and trustworthiness. Following the passage of the 1797 Bank Restriction Act the number of private banks rapidly increased from about 80 in 1793 to 700 in 1810 and 900 by 1815. However, so too did the number which collapsed. Between 1790 and 1826 334 banks failed.[110] Information about such failures was reported in greater detail than previously as 'by the end of the century a column entitled "remarks on trade" was a staple of nearly every British newspaper [and] the reading public was accustomed to reading about financial and commercial topics in local papers'. City columns appeared soon afterwards.[111] In the circumstances, opting to become an Oddfellow appeared to be a relatively secure means of gaining financial security. The Oddfellows was developed during a period of rapid growth of the insurance and banking sector, when investment was perceived as a means of aiding the development of communities of citizens.[112] The circumstances which benefited the Unity, the interest in security, thrift and prudence, also supported insurance companies. These were parallel solutions to similarly conceptualised problems.

In May 1811 there was considerable economic and social distress in Manchester. Unemployment was high and poverty endemic. A petition of protest signed by 40,000 people in the area was sent to the Commons. Another petition of a similar nature, signed by 7,000 weavers, spinners and labourers in Bolton was also sent.[113] People who had known modest prosperity appeared to be condemned to a life of filth, food lacking in quality and quantity, poor accommodation and the likelihood of illness. They had no vote and no representatives as Manchester, Leeds, Sheffield and Birmingham had not a single MP between them and although almost a million people lived in Manchester, Salford, Bolton, Blackburn, Rochdale, Ashton-under-Lyne, Oldham and Stockport there were only two MPs for Lancashire. Stockport was part of Cheshire, and that county also had two MPs.

The new machines were perceived as one of the causes of misery. In 1811 in Nottinghamshire threats to damage machinery were issued and some new stocking frames were destroyed by men calling themselves Luddites. There had been disturbances before, for example riots in Rochdale in 1795 and 1808 when the gaol was burnt down and the militia called in, and there was still considerable tension. '1812 opens with a gloom altogether so frigid and cheerless,' said the *Manchester Gazette* 'that hope itself is almost lost and frozen in the prospect.' In February 1812 it became a capital offence to destroy stocking frames but people attacked them and commandeered market stalls to hand out foodstuffs. There were food riots in Manchester, Oldham, Ashton, Rochdale, Stockport and Macclesfield. A group gathered on a field near Stockport and held a 'Luddite Congress', and in March 1812 some power looms in Stockport were attacked. A letter of March 1812, signed by 'the General of the Army of Redressers, Ned Ludd, Clerk' called upon Parliament to pass legislation 'to put down all Machinery hurtful to Comonality [sic] and repeal that to hang Frame Breakers'. It was felt that 'Comonality', the older system of manufacture, which involved considerable mutual dependency upon manual skills and masculine solidarity, was being replaced by competitive, alienating labour. In order to oppose this shift, to defend what were perceived as more desirable modes of work and employment and customary bonds of household, community and marketplace, men were requesting Parliamentary intervention. Some were also organising in secret, pledging oaths, inventing passwords and making ritual use of clothing (there were instances of men cross-dressing as General Ludd's wives in Stockport).[114] In April several thousand men attacked

Burton's Mill at Middleton near Manchester. The Prince Regent offered a reward of £50 to those 'giving information on any person or persons wickedly breaking the frames', and there was a demonstration at the Manchester Exchange, coordinated in secret by weavers' committees, against a plan to send him a loyal address. Luddism and the reaction to it, was another element of the social order within which the Oddfellows developed. Luddism was effectively countered in the summer of 1812. In June 1812 at the end of a meeting of 38 weavers in a public house in Manchester, the Deputy Constable of Manchester arrived. The weavers were accused of attending a seditious meeting and put on trial for swearing illegal oaths. Between 12,000 and 14,400 troops were moved into the area to protect mills and factories. Eight men in Lancashire were sentenced to death. Thirteen people were transported to Australia for attacks on cotton mills. Fifteen were executed at York and four at Chester.

The underlying concerns remained. In 1803 many weavers would have been able to afford to join the Oddfellows because they were being paid around 15 shillings a week. Following the conclusion of the French Wars in 1815, wages fell to about a third of that figure. Moreover, bread prices rose because of the Corn Laws, which were an attempt to protect British grain prices. In 1817 25,000 people assembled in Manchester to launch a march to London petitioning for constitutional reform. In 1819 about 60,000 to 80,000 people gathered at a rally in Manchester organised by those who sought political change. The crowd was dispersed violently in what became known as the Peterloo Massacre. Poor men in Manchester may have seen the pollution, the poverty, the lack of support from their families and their parishes and the violent reaction of the authorities to expressions of concern. They may also have seen the ways in which wealthier men arranged insurance, and seen part of the solution to their problems as lying in Oddfellowship.

Oddfellowship may also have appealed in Manchester because industrialisation and mechanisation resulted in a reduction in the number of women employed in agriculture as they moved to sex segregated work in the new mills. During the seventeenth and eighteenth centuries the number of single women who were more independent for longer periods of time (i.e. worked as servants for about a decade, while saving for marriages) grew. Compared to their mothers they had more choice in their selection of husbands and they were more likely to behave as economic partners within the marriages. Many had babies at an older age, which led to greater age gaps between generations and less reliance on extended kin networks and legal traditions that emphasised both spouses as producers of wealth and allowed widows extensive rights over household property. The convergence of women's and men's lives and the prospect of greater economic partnerships between men and women may have created a heightened preoccupation with gender difference and female inferiority among men. Tosh has argued that 'the requirements of an urbanised, market-led and increasingly industrialised society' aided the growth of specific ideas of masculinity and that the new 'dual commitment to work and home' was to be found in the lives of the middle class and had a 'hold over the labour aristocracy: working men proud of their hard-earned skill, their "independence", their domestic habits and their self-improvement'.[115] Barker noted the possibility of regional variation in regard to notions of politeness. He concluded that, 'Northern manners then might have been more sober than those of the polished national elite and closer to the respectability or self-governance which historians have identified marking social relations for a later period.'[116] The Oddfellows' offer of single sex solidarity, a space where men could develop rituals of civility and masculine reciprocity may have been particularly warmly welcomed in Manchester.

The new mills of the north were of managerial as well as technical significance. They have been associated with wage negotiations which were an 'escape from the market' into co-operation and which could have provided an additional model for the Oddfellows.[117] In Lancashire the language of labour was characterised by moral concepts of both employers and employees having responsibilities to one another.[118] Millowner John Robinson was an Oddfellow who ran his workplace as a 'paternal regime' with close personal supervision and 'the fiction of a shared purpose imagined in the myth of the father and his family'.[119] When the *Oddfellows' Magazine* provided a tour through a Manchester warehouse it noted that 'each animated atom has its particular place and use, tending to the unity as a whole'. It went on to suggest that 'Good masters make good men: and the best proof that the principals in our Manchester warehouses are what they should be is the perfect concord which exists between them and their subordinates'.[120] The fraternity and co-operation proposed by the Oddfellows did not imply subservience to the mill owners but a viable means of resolving deadlocks and gaining respect. The promotion of a vision of brotherhood which transcended antagonistic class relations was an aspiration to a better world and acceptance of this one. It was acquiescence to a fixed social order and a claim for greater justice.

By the mid-century there had been a shift among employers away from 'Christian kindness to "rational" and "scientific" considerations'.[121] Men who worked within mills had relatively little control over their hours and speed of work, and over the implementation of technical innovations, compared to the weavers who had worked in dispersed cottages. As social relations in the craft workshops changed and the fraternal bonds between masters and men disappeared, the ideals of fraternity became more difficult to realise in the workplace. Friendly societies' social fraternity outside the workplace, their creation of togetherness through ritual, offered both a critique of capitalist development and accommodation to it. An idealised moral community, which if it had ever been there, had vanished from the workplace, could be reconstructed in the Oddfellows lodge. The activities of the Oddfellows echoed and bolstered social relations in their workplaces. John Watts an Owenite lecturer who became a propagandist for the millowners, linked King Cotton to the friendly societies in his *The Facts of the Cotton Famine*, 1866:

> The discipline of the cotton mill has spread its influences beyond the workshop, and regularity and punctuality have become essential parts of Lancashire life … the effects of manufacturing discipline have not been less upon the workpeople than upon their employers. The habit of working together has taught them to associate for other purposes, and the necessity of submission to strict rules within the mills has led them to make rules for their own guidance in matters which seem to concern themselves more immediately.[122]

Many members of the Society were adversely affected by the Cotton Famine of the 1860s. In 1862 60,000 of the approximately 350,000 members lived in the cottons districts in and near Lancashire. However, the Society raised considerable sums for the distressed areas.[123] The Oddfellows informed, and were informed by, life in the mills. The men of Salford and Manchester would have been familiar with the values of self-reliance, thrift, solidarity, sociability and the benefits of federation. They may also have had personal experience of managing a club. The Unity's success helps account for why two thirds of the adult male population of Lancashire, 258,000 men, were friendly society members by 1847, compared to 30,000 in Kent.[124] As the Industrial Remuneration Conference Report, 1885 noted:

> The working men of Lancashire were tied into a whole system of unions, co-operatives building and benefit societies. Cooperatives, trade unions with large reserve funds and their accident, sickness and out of work benefits, insurance and benefit societies … They are staffed with working-class members.

Men have found in the Oddfellows an organisation which reflected the familiar rhythms of life in the Manchester mills and which also offered a vision of brotherhood which took them out of those same mills. The experience of being a part of the growth of Manchester provided the Society with significant generic, transferable skills which informed much subsequent development. During the late eighteenth and nineteenth centuries a number of fraternal associations presented themselves as the embodiment of the modern civic virtues of obedience and equality before the law. They sought to demonstrate that they could aid discipline in the new towns by modelling systems of control and categorisation and by promoting formal rules, surveillance and punishment. They developed their own forms of protection and information exchange which echoed and bolstered many developments within the legal code and policing systems. When personal morality became more clearly defined as being of interest to government, the Oddfellows with its millions of members and strict, popular hierarchies, emerged as a central agent of governance, sanctioning legislative and societal norms and supporting the diffusion of civic codes. Its regulation of communal behaviour through members, in particular Sick Visitors, acting as active citizens, comparable to the patrolling constable, aided the maintenance of a fluid social order. The years in Manchester and its environs helped the Oddfellows to become familiar with the requirements of an urban industrial society.

III 'Rearing the infant Society'[125]

Between 1810 and 1814 new lodges were authorised by and affiliated to the Abercrombie Lodge and existing lodges were encouraged to accept the leadership of the 'Mother' Lodge. From 1814 it had a Grand Master. In 1816 the first Corresponding Secretary (CS) was appointed.[125] At one time the CS was the only paid officer and men often held the post for a number of years. Burn explained that 'there are two qualifications requisite in the person who fills that office;

he must be a man of the most regular business habits and of strict integrity'.[126] The question of adopting degrees into the order was also discussed, the degrees of White, Royal Blue, and Scarlet were established and the Patriarchal, the Covenant, and Remembrance degrees were added later.[127] In 1819 the question of a site for the central government of the Order was settled by the establishment of a movable committee. This held annual sessions in locations agreed upon at a preceding session. The Society had regulations about funerals, regalia, contributions and it weathered several disputes and expulsions. It had a system of relief for travellers.[128] In 1822 the first movable committee convened; it was composed of past and present officers of districts and lodges, and had the power to adopt or reject laws proposed by districts. There were concerns at the powers of the Grand Committee. These may reflect that some members had memories of having declared independence from the Grand United Order in Sheffield and had no wish to be subject to further governance in that style. In 1826 the Abercrombie Lodge was ordered to surrender its powers. It refused and was suspended from the Unity. It was decided that the term Grand Lodge would no longer be used. From 1827 the AMC elected a Board of Directors to replace the Grand Committee and the term was not used again until the Directors reintroduced it in 1919.[129] It was also from 1827 that the Society had Directors, paid staff, an office for them (No 45, Smithy Door) and central funds. A system of checks on the activities of the Directors was made from 1828 when the AMC appointed seven members to examine and report on the books of the Directors. The Society ran the *Oddfellows' Magazine* from 1824. It included news of the Society and improving features on, for example, Italian history and William Cowper which rendered the Unity more seemly by association. By 1831 the Unity was holding AMCs which lasted for five days and in 1833 there were 225 Deputies in attendance. Further growth in the UK and abroad occurred. By the time that the Society was 25 years old it was so well established that the AMC could be held in an Oddfellows Hall (in Kendal) with over 40,000 members.[130]

Given the importance of trust to ensuring the smooth running of the Society it was of significance that power remained with the lodges. Although the Oddfellows had lodges all over the world, it was important that men who joined their local lodge would not be concerned that decisions about their fate would be taken without their consent in Manchester. The importance of this was remarked upon by a Past Provincial Grand Master in 1909:

> This great and powerful organisation is only what the districts make it. The districts are only what the lodges make them and the lodges are what the members make them. You see therefore, how important it is for each individual to exert himself in promoting and encouraging others to join us in spreading our glorious and philanthropic principles. Just as the greatest rivers are made up of the smallest streams so is the Manchester Unity made up of the smallest units.[131]

The structure also valued experience. The Oddfellows was run by the Grand Master and Board of Directors which aided continuity. One commentator who prepared detailed reports on friendly societies noted:

The moveable and variable character of the Foresters' executive council makes it impossible for the Order to trust them with the powers that might well be given to such a body as the Board of Directors of the Manchester Unity.[132]

Spreading risks and costs led to some powers of the lodges being conceded to district level. A Manchester district central funeral fund was established and this pattern spread. Lodges started to run both their own sick funds and a district fund as well. In 1815 a general rule established that 'each lodge shall relieve its own sick', and rates were set nine years later as James Roe, a Provincial Grand Master in North London told a Select Committee:

Up to 1824 there was no regular rate of payment in sickness, nor in contribution. About that time, when sickness occurred, the members used to contribute among themselves. It was found more convenient and more certain to have a rate of contribution.[133]

In the early 1830s the AMC decided that separate funds needed to be established 'for all expenses other than sickness and funeral benefits'. This shifted the balance of payments to orphans and widows from lodge funds or charitable fund-raising events to individual members. Although it was lodge members who administered widows' pensions, and there remained scope for fraternal leniency, it was no longer a collective brotherly responsibility. Members had to make provision which would then be controlled by the lodge. Even with cross-subsidy (not always popular with healthier members) the structure encouraged members to recruit young men, partly because the sickness benefit rates, set in each lodge, were often set higher than the lodge income permitted.

From its base in the north-west of England, the Oddfellows rapidly grew. Within a decade of 1810 there were Oddfellow lodges across Manchester and the Unity reached Liverpool in 1816, the USA in 1819 and London, Yorkshire and Wales in 1820.[134] From these locations it spread, initially to areas of rapid industrial development. Williams connected industrial growth and the foundation of friendly societies, arguing that 'there is a distinct correlation between friendly society formation and the fortunes of industry'.[135] In 1825 there were 19 lodges in Yorkshire and there were 50 lodges in Wales by 1830, this rapid progress partly being attributed to 'the failure of the Trades' Union Clubs that had been formed among the workmen.'[136] By 1832 there were 31,000 members in 561 lodges in the UK and by 1838 there were 90,000 members within 1,200 lodges. Lodges opened in Sunderland in 1832, in Darlington in 1833 and in the new town of Middlesbrough in 1835.[137] The first lodge was opened in Scotland in 1837. It was Aberdeen and a year later there was a lodge in Greenock and one in Glasgow by 1839.[138] In Coventry three lodges were opened between 1838 and 1840. The first Worcester lodge was opened in 1840 and there were five by 1842.[139] By 1842 friendly societies had become a prominent feature of the Godiva processions and by 1845 there were 17 lodges with 686 members.[140] Across the country there were 3,500 lodges with 220,000 members.[141] Glasgow had 12,000 members by 1845 and there were lodges in 'almost every town in Scotland … In England there is scarcely a city, town or village where Oddfellow lodges do not exist.'[142] Burn declared in 1845 that 'if the soil of any part of Great Britain was congenial to growth of Odd-fellowship, London ought to stand first'.[143] In that year there were lodges in every English county and also in Ireland, Germany, New Zealand, Australia and other parts of the empire. Out of a total population of men over the age of 20 in Britain of about 5.5 million, about 1.5 million were friendly society members and around 40,000 were Oddfellows.[144] It was perhaps because there was considerable interest in encouraging the development of the Society that AMCs were held all over the country, including Glasgow in 1845, Dublin in 1851 and Swansea in 1858.[145] There was further considerable growth in the UK in the latter half of the nineteenth century. Unemployment grew and profits fell but the price of food went down and real wages rose and the number of members of the Oddfellows almost doubled. Working men had more money available to insure against sickness and by 1910 there were probably over one million members making it the most popular friendly society in the country.[146]

There is some dispute about who opened the first lodge in the USA and whether it was a lodge of the Unity or another Order of Oddfellows but the Unity was established there by the

Oddfellowship thrived in New Zealand, where members developed the idea of travelling brothers when they arranged for the Oddfellows Hall to be moved across Christchurch in 1903. The local newspaper, *The weekly press*, 25 Nov. 1903, p. 45 reported that 'This was one of the largest undertakings of this class which have been known in the district. The distance the building was taken was about three-quarters of a mile and it was decided to use greased skids instead of the usual trolleys, doubtless on account of the danger of breaking the telegraph wires under which the building had to pass.' Members of the Ashley District, Christchurch, which had been formed in 1880, gathered in 1898 for the photograph above.

391

ODDFELLOWSHIP IN THE COLONIES.

Oddfellowship in the Colonies.

A COLONIAL ROLL OF HONOUR.

J. C. CORDLE, P.P.G.M., P.P.C.S.

THE portrait of Bro. John Christopher Cordle, P.P.G.M., P.P.C.S., of Barbados District, West Indies, shows that the Manchester Unity recognises no distinctions of creed or colour. We appraise the man by his worth and his work. The choice of Bro. Cordle by the Barbados District, with the approval of the Grand Master and Board of Directors, for the second Colonial portrait is a fitting recognition of the sterling qualities of an Oddfellow who has done real service to the cause in the West Indies.

Bro. Cordle was born at Bridgeton, Barbados, on the 18th December, 1827, and received his education at the elementary school of St. Giles, under Mr. E. W. Archer, himself an Oddfellow. After serving as assistant in the school in which he received his education, Bro. Cordle subsequently held several appointments as schoolmaster, until his retirement upon a pension. As a result of the zeal and interest evinced in Oddfellowship by his schoolmaster, Mr. E. W. Archer, who was then Prov. C.S. of the Barbados District, Bro. Cordle joined the St. Michael Lodge, on the 26th of May, 1853, and on the following lodge night was appointed assistant secretary. After passing through the lodge offices, Bro. Cordle continued his active interest in the work and served two terms as Grand Master of the district, in 1859 and 1860. From that time up to the present his record has been one of continuous hard work in the interest of the Order. For thirty years he served the office of C.S. of the district, and now, in the evening of his days, he continues to do whatever his hand findeth to do for the progress of Oddfellowship in the West Indies. It would be a pleasurable task to write more fully of Bro. Cordle's work as an earnest, active Odd[fellow] ... of new lodges in Jamaica, at Trinidad, and elsewher[e] ... orphan fund, but sufficie[nt] ... honour conferred by th[e] ... portrait—a selection ap[proved by the] Directors of the Unity.

MEETING OF TH[E]

The half-yearly meet[ing] ... held at the Board Roo[m] ... Melbourne, on Wednesd[ay] ... Grand Master J. Reid p[resided] ... J. Sternberg, C.S. J. Ta[ylor] ... C.S. of Port Phillip Di[strict] ... Rose of Brunswick Lodg[e] ... certificates describing t[he] ... old age. The officers o[f] ... answer given to a simi[lar] ... for July, 1897, to the ... caused by old age. In ... A.M.C., the officers of ...

The Society has long made a point of promoting international brotherhood and of crediting brethren who have made significant contributions, as these images from 1901 (*left*) and the 1910 AMC (*below*) indicate.

1820s. Burn claimed that a lodge of the Society was opened in New York in 1818 by Thomas Wilde, or Wildey, and this story has been repeated many times since.[147] The Oddfellows had reached New Zealand, by 1842 and by 1908 there were 39,000 Oddfellows in the country.[148] In 1846 ten lodges opened in Toronto, Canada.[149] In 1852 new lodges were opened in Calcutta, the East Indies and the Cape of Good Hope District opened one in Natal.[150] By the 1860s lodges had opened in South Africa, South America and Constantinople (Istanbul) and representatives from abroad attended AMCs. The first 50 members of the 'Star of the East Lodge' in Constantinople were largely artisans employed on public works, and within four years there were three lodges and 150 members. Rule and lectures were translated with a view to 'implanting principles of self-reliance in place of sluggish fatalism'.[151] By 1865 there were nine districts in Australia, 120 lodges (10 per cent opened in the last year) and over 10,000 members, over 1,000 of whom had joined in that year. Over 60 per cent of the members lived in the South Australia District. In that year also lodges opened in Mauritius and Port Louis.[152]

A number of accounts suggest that in 1843 the Grand United Order of Oddfellows was founded in America and that the Oddfellows in America formally broke away from those in the UK. It is likely that the story is more complex, with many divisions and regroupings over much of the course of the first half of the nineteenth century. One claim is that the Americans sought to restrict membership to 'free white males' (according to an account of the 1845 AMC) and another is that there were disputes about ritual procedures.[153] It has also been suggested that the US-based Grand United Order of Oddfellows, which permitted black men to join, was offered support from the UK when it received a charter from the Oddfellows in 1842.

Keeping track of lodges was difficult because, as Burn pointed out, communication was often slow. It was because dispensations to open new lodges could take up to nine months to reach Canada that from the 1840s the Board sent out blank charters to the districts in Canada and parts of Australia.[154] In addition to the secession by many lodges in the USA there were other set backs for the Society. The funds of a lodge in Barbados were exhausted when cholera affected the members and it had to be subsidised in 1854.[155] However, despite the divisions, there was communication between the UK and North America. In 1879 the UK Grand Master was well received on a tour of the USA.[156] During the 1880s there were 'further efforts to open up communication with the American Order of Oddfellows'.[157] In 1906, following the devastating San Francisco earthquake in which around 3,000 were killed and around quarter a million left homeless, a halfpenny levy was raised throughout the Unity for the relief of those affected. The sum of £1,000 was raised, but some of the money was reported to have been 'ungraciously returned,' and, following this dispute, the Unity Directors withheld most of the money. Yet the return of the money does not necessarily indicate that the Americans had taken offence. Rather, it was normal practice of lodges with the USA to return unspent funds once the immediate distress had been alleviated. Moreover, the action 'drew attention to the universality of the Manchester Unity'. It might also be noted that the sum of £500 was sent to Jamaican lodges after a similar disaster there and this was disbursed without disagreement.[158]

IV   Conclusion

While it might be undiplomatic to mark the bicentennial of the Society by questioning its age, the categorisation of the different claims regarding its antiquity indicates the importance attached at different times, to personal and lodge rivalries, secrecy, longevity and modernity. This in turn clarifies the role of the Society as a source for the renewal of reciprocity and helps to reframe wider understandings of social developments over a two hundred year period. Burn predicted that 'the day will come when everything connected with the early history of the Order will be eagerly sought for, both by the chronicler, the antiquarian and the historian'.[159] However, he may not have been among those eager seekers, just in case an unfortunate truth was revealed. Through ambiguity about its origins the Unity could gain legitimacy for the new social bonds it was forming when it borrowed from the individualistic contractual society around it and also drew on living traditions of mutuality and continuity.

To those arriving in the new cotton mills bewildered and alone the Oddfellows offered the familiarity of mutual aid and rituals within an easily recognised framework. There was the possibility of being both a donor and recipient of charity and the guarantee of financial support from a body with a trustworthy name. Within the lodge there was a version of family life in which men were in control and opportunities to ascend through the ranks of a hierarchy which might have helped to compensate men for their lack of control at the workplace. It also offered an important lesson. In the mid-1840s a leading Oddfellow, James Burn, described how membership offered a means of dealing with some of the difficulties of town life. He mentioned the 'pleasure which was "dressed in a thousand fantastic shapes"', how 'sly and insinuating vice in the garb of virtue besets the paths of the innocent', and that the density of people in London helped to destroy 'the healthy influence men exercise over each other's feelings and actions in smaller communities'. He also stressed that 'the loneliness of a large city exceeds any other solitude I know of'. Oddfellowship, he argued, offered to restrain members, to ameliorate the 'moral and physical position' of working men and to teach 'them the dignity of their own honest independence'.[160] By imitating ecclesiastical mysteries within its own myths, the Oddfellows could elevate its own moral and social status and carve out a space for its model of the best way to live and organise regulated, egalitarian, but hierarchical, communities. It grew because members were able to build on an understanding of clubs, insurance, gender relations and masculinity, migration patterns, dramatic economic change and the dynamics of mill life and politics in order to create and to recreate, a vibrant Society.

Why is the Society called the Oddfellows?

Andrew Porter, the Grand Master in 2004, said, 'We have torn ourselves to pieces over the name. Our official title is The Independent Order of Oddfellows Manchester Unity Friendly Society. Always too much of a mouthful, always too difficult.' So why does the Society have that name? In 1997 the Grand Master Roger Burley reported to the AMC:

> Throughout the twentieth century there have been spasmodic arguments over the name ... at present we have an uneasy compromise, but I have a feeling that the only acceptable solution is a new name. One that can be explained and does not cause embarrassment, unlike Odd Fellows. One that is individual and not easily confused, unlike Manchester Unity which is usually called Manchester United.

Derek Winbush added that that we 'get called all sorts of things and we have got a massive name [I have a] cheque for a gilt interest at home that came to us for the Manchester United Friendly Society. I have banked it but of course he hasn't got my sympathy because I am a Villa supporter.' Perhaps the name has encouraged members to try harder. The preface to the Laws of the Society used to state that members should 'living examples to others' so that 'the odium hitherto attempted to be thrown at us, merely on account of our name will quickly be obliterated'.[161] While there has been derision and mirth for well over 200 years there has also been the curiosity which has provided members with an opportunity to inform people about what Oddfellowship means to them.

Some have suggested that the original Oddfellows were men who were engaged in various or odd trades at a time when there were organisations for some of the larger trades. They were not eligible to join the master craftsmen's guilds and therefore banded together as lodges of 'odd fellows'. The *Oddfellows' Magazine* September 1888 explained:

> Those who have made it their study to dive into the hazy past incline to the belief that the Oddfellows are revivals of the old trade guilds, which flourished in the sixteenth century ... the Masonic Order maintained intact a collection from all the others, which were not strong enough in themselves to carry on a distinctive club. Thus they were not mercers, nor dyers, nor smiths, nor girdlers, not drapers but an *omnium gatherum*, and hence Oddfellows.[162]

This idea was reflected in the *Freemasons' Monthly Magazine* which referred to the Oddfellows as 'the illegitimate offspring of Masonry', and as 'the *omnium gatherum* of mock masonry', and also as one of the 'illegitimate institutions'.[163] Burn suggested of the first Oddfellows that 'in all likelihood some of the party were Free Masons, which will sufficiently account for the various Masonic symbols formerly made use of in the Society.'[164] Although the first part of *omnium gatherum* is Latin (it is the genitive plural of omnis meaning all) the second word is pseudo-Latin in that a Latin ending (um) has been added to the English gather. This may add to the joke of the name. Not only was the Society a miscellaneous mélange but even its name was a jumble and a play on gather 'em all.

The notion of banding together was taken up by a leading officer in north Wales. In 1883 a procession through Bangor, which involved members from 14 lodges, concluded with a large-scale meeting at which Mr H. Barber, in addressing the crowd, provided a definition. He said that he

> had made inquiries as to the origin of the word 'Oddfellow'. It seemed to suggest something grotesque or eccentric, but there was nothing grotesque about it at all, it merely meant a large assembly bound together for the common good of all.[165]

The idea that the name had changed its meaning was echoed in more recent times. In Worcester, where the Oddfellows remained 'mostly unknown to the wider public', John Bradley, the Provincial Corresponding Secretary, was often asked about the Society's activities: '… The name has come to have other connotations in modern times and not everyone wants to have the Oddfellow label.'[166]

Possibly the Society was originally composed of members who were not Masons but labourers who served the Masons, hence 'hod' fellows. The name contrasts the members of the Society and the allegedly more exclusive brethren: while Freemasonry was relatively familiar, these fellows were odd, or uncommon. The Masonic Aristarchus Lodge, it is said, refers to 'Our Great Odd-Master, invisible, incomprehensible and eternal'. James Spry claimed to have been shown the portion of the laws of an Aristarcus Lodge of Oddfellows dated 1748.[167] The Deity is so far removed from the ordinary as to be alone. Odd Fellows are God's Fellows. In 1934 Dr Foxley Norris, the Dean of Westminster Abbey, echoed this idea:

> I suppose nobody really knows what is the meaning of the term 'Oddfellows' and yet there was a time when the word odd had a very different meaning from that it now commonly has. There was a time when, with the utmost reverence, God, the almighty ruler of the universe, was described as 'odd' because he was wholly unique from any other being. Odd in that regard has the most honourable meaning and 'Oddfellows' are those who have been separated from the common run of men to make something different.[168]

It has been argued that the ceremonies practised in the lodges were strange, that is odd. This was because it was unusual for labouring men to form a fraternity for fellowship and mutual help. It has sometimes been suggested that orders and sects that rendered aid to members in times of sickness and distress were exceedingly rare. Another possibility is that the word odd is a corruption of the word oath.

Perhaps the title was bestowed by Titus Caesar on members of his loyal Israelite legion who, having proved their fidelity to the Emperor became in 79 CE, Fellow Citizens and Odd-Fellows.[169] Burn added that the name was given 'very likely for being stopped on their march when going to the siege of the Holy City by a huge Boa constrictor'.[170] According to the *Complete Manual of Oddfellowship*, 1879, many of these largely autonomous lodges of Oddfellows formed a Patriotic or Union Order in the late eighteenth century. This had five degrees, one of which, the Royal Arch of Titus (or Fidelity) refers to this story. There were passwords, grips, oaths of secrecy, rituals with props, lighting and sound effects.

A further possibility is that the name was intended to be comical, that it is a joke dating from when the Unity was one of many convivial Georgian societies. In the eighteenth century there were a number of tradesmen societies with comical names, such as the Codheads, the Friendly Bachelors and the Knights of the Brush. Burn argued that

> as to the origins of this strange and unmeaning name there can be little doubt that it was christened at the font of Bacchus [by] a set of jovial souls who caught the inspiration while worshipping at his shrine. Thus the name might be conjured up in the dream of their hilarity without any other motive than that of sending the sand the hour gaily and fleetly through the glass of time.[171]

Perhaps the conviviality within the lodge was of such significance that members needed distinguish themselves from ordinary men. They were the odd ones out. The connection between a jocular nomenclature and conviviality has been maintained. Derek Winbush told the AMC in 1997 'If Foresters talk to us privately or we go for a drink with them, hopefully with them paying, we are the "Oddies"'. It would seem that, as Moffrey suggested, 'like the actual commencement of Oddfellowship, the reason for the adoption of the name must remain buried in obscurity.[172]

CHAPTER TWO

The setting

T HE ODDFELLOWS offered the security of a form of insurance which could not be gained through personal savings. Legal, rational and magical concepts of safety and reassurance framed the development of the Society in relation to insurance. It is this which is the subject of the first section. The second section is an assessment of the different fraternal bodies from which ideas of Oddfellowship may have been drawn both prior to its inception and soon afterwards. By 1810 there were many member-run organisations which facilitated risk sharing and the transfer of money between members. Some also offered opportunities for social drinking, feasting and, through parades and funeral processions, public demonstrations of fraternity. Many also supported private affirmations of solidarity, through visiting the sick and were strengthened because of their notions of rites and rights.

In addition to being built on the traditions of fraternities and on the popularity of recent insurance schemes, Oddfellowship also emphasised charity. The description of the Oddfellows' White Degree (which was part of an internal system of accreditation) began: 'The first point upon which our Order ordains to admonish you is no less than that of the first friendly duty to mankind – Charity.'[1] The third section considers the relationship of Oddfellowship to charities. Many charitable bodies were constructed on Christian principles and the Oddfellows, itself a charitable organisation, also drew heavily on Christian images and discourses. The relationship with Christianity is the subject of the fourth section. To the traditions of socialising in pubs, reciprocity and mutual aid, the Oddfellows brought an understanding of the needs of migrants to a rapidly growing urban area dominated by sex-segregated work in mills. In order to create Oddfellowship the Society adapted ideas from many sources and built upon the security offered by the well-established parish relief system. The support offered to the men who travelled seeking employment is considered in the fifth section.

I The development of insurance and saving

In order to be created and then to prosper the Oddfellows required the security of a legal framework, and in particular the national system of identity registration, initiated in 1538, and the network of magistrates and the legislation for the relief of the poor passed in 1598, 1601 and subsequently. This legislation made clear the responsibilities of parishes, reduced free riding and encouraged labour mobility. Knowing that there was provision for the subsistence of all subjects, even in the face of local crises, provided a basis which encouraged people to consider the broad issues of welfare, health and responsibility for the strangers in their midst. This bolstered the development of philanthropic, mutualist, kin and neighbourly support. The Oddfellows was one of a number of locally devolved and funded pooled insurance risk schemes which required such stability and which benefited from the 1793 legislation and that which had been passed prior to the Friendly Societies Act.

Throughout the eighteenth century the state had 'employed money to regulate the movements of its labouring population'.[2] At around the time that the Oddfellows was being founded new attitudes towards money were emerging. Hierarchies defined by money, rather than earlier notions based upon religious, social, or political standards, began to be of greater significance. There had been considerable efforts to measure and value lives such that 'the commodification of people appears natural and unquestionable'. The result, argued Valenze, was a 'triumph of the monetary self', as 'people situated their sense of selfhood within the hierarchies and reversals revealed through money, incorporating the medium into experiences of personal achievement and autonomy'.

It was against this background that the Oddfellows was able to put a value on fraternity while appearing not to be putting a price on members. Legislation abolished some of the British slave trade in 1809 and the laws regulating child labour were amended in 1819, both attempts to separate people from commodities during this period. Such legislation was the other side of the coin which recognised that money need not only be a source of fear and suspicion, that it could provide charity and be used to reveal members as ethically superior. The period was one notable for that which Valenze called the 'detoxification of money', and as some lodges had their own currency, paying rent for the hire of the lodge room in tokens, the Oddfellows played its part in helping to bring about the 'reconciliation with money'.[3] Medallions and coins could carry a pocketful of messages including helping to promote the idea that risks could be quantified in monetary terms, bridging the gap between the literate and illiterate and providing a visual reminder of the Unity. During the period 1800 and 1810 there little enthusiasm for bank notes in Lancashire, the purchasing power of paper notes fell dramatically and it became clear that paper money was only as good as the bank which issued it (as when a bank failed, its money became worthless).[4] The circulation of a rumour, particularly prevalent in Lancashire, that government intended to pay for the national debt by seizing the funds of friendly societies had to be quashed by the Chancellor of the Exchequer in the Commons.[5] During a period of strikes and unrest in the north-west of England in 1842 when the troops were sent in, notices were posted around Manchester calling for a general strike. *The Times* reporter saw other posters which proclaimed:

Run for gold! Labour is suspended! Public credit is shaken! Labour is worthless! Run for gold! Every sovereign is now worth 30s. Paper cannot be cashed. Run middle class men, trades, Odd fellows, sick clubs and money clubs to the savings-banks and all banks for gold! Gold! Gold![6]

During a period of change when people may have feared for their savings, the Society offered reassurance. As magic moved from being associated with fear and the supernatural and became a form of entertainment and as the idea of a fixed, pre-ordained future became less popular and belief in magical prediction declined, so the Oddfellows' atemporal rituals may have reassured people who felt threatened by modernity. The Society offered the rational predictions associated with commercial insurance companies but also the 'confusion between actor, rite and object' which Mauss said was 'a fundamental feature of magic'.[7] Mauss argued that 'all ritual is a kind of language; it therefore translates ideas.' He went on to note the connections upon which the Oddfellows may have drawn: 'in the Middle Ages magic was always seen as the work of fraternities … We find that magicians usually follow a set of rules, which is a corporate discipline. These rules sometimes consist of a search for moral virtues.'[8] He noted that magicians would 'draw a magical circle or square', and concluded, 'we shall find magical origins in those early forms of collective representations'.[9] That there was a mutual aid society for astrologers in the 1820s and 1830s suggests both the ubiquity of the notion of friendly societies and that those who worked within the world of prediction did not see fraternity as a contradictory position to adopt.[10]

Although the ideas of regulated mutual aid had been accepted for years, in the period shortly before the foundation of the Oddfellows there were changes in people's views about how to cope with the uncertainties of everyday life. Whereas before the eighteenth century people often referred to luck or to Divine Providence, that is the idea that there was a pre-designed purpose, the events of the late eighteenth century, notably industrialisation, the French revolution and the challenges to absolutism and Catholicism, were connected to understandings that people developed which countered the notion that there was a form of Providential order to the world and that there were laws that connected time, space and matter. There was wider acceptance of the Newtonian model of the universe as a machine bound by fixed relations of cause and effect. The emergence of the Oddfellows occurred in a world where the future was deemed unknowable in ways that had not been as evident before to as many people. They were living during a period when the possibility of change by rational action appeared to have been reduced. Oddfellowship offered to take a lone individual, to socialise him in a group of his own kind and then, by taking a set of known factors in the present, predict a pattern for the future. This did not make the future more certain, but it made it easier to weigh up the possibilities. From the seventeenth century the notion that misfortune was a sign of God's particular disfavour declined and the notion that risk could be calculated and rationally managed spread. Many aspects of life appeared more reliable. Bubonic plague had receded; building materials were less susceptible to fire, and fire-fighting became more effective. Risk management became more predictable due to innovations in public finances, notably the Bank of England, the creation of a national Debt and the formation of structures which aided the flow of information, for example the organisation of a stock exchange. Being able to generalise about likely events in order to minimise loss and maximise gain provided individuals with a guide for rational action and gave them a sense of control over uncertainty. They did not know what the future held but they could know that they were acting in line with the current principles of risk management.

The earliest recorded life insurance contract is of the life of William Gibbons in 1588, but it was not until the end of the next century that the market grew. John Gaunt is credited with creating a table of mortality in 1662 and others followed which suggested that it was possible to calculate the length of time a person would live. Halley's tables of mortality for Breslau were produced in 1693; the Church of Scotland's 1779 scheme for widows' pensions was based on the lives of past Church of Scotland ministers. The Equitable rates, which most life offices copied until 1820, were based on Richard Price's investigation of the mortality records of a Northampton parish between 1735 and 1780. In 1815 the Sun's actuary, Joshua Milne, produced better tables based on birth and death records from Carlisle between 1779 and 1787.

In the early seventeenth century life insurance was mainly associated with overseas merchants and large-scale moneylenders, by the early eighteenth century the market had expanded considerably. Mutual insurance schemes existed for cover against fire including insurance by the Corporation of London from 1681 and The Friendly Society from 1683. In 1696 the Amicable Contributors for Insuring Houses From Loss by Fire, later the Hand-in-Hand, was established in London and Union Fire (1714) and Westminster Fire Office (1717) soon followed. They insured goods and merchandise but the Sun Fire Office (1710) had a wider range as did the Bristol Crown (1718) and the Friendly Society of Edinburgh (1720).[11] By 1721 between 3,000 and 12,000 lives were insured.[12] Some friendly societies employed the term assurance, such as the British Assurance Society, formed 1773, while some insurance companies used the term friendly society. Some friendly societies became industrial life insurance companies, including the Refuge, founded 1858, the Pearl, 1864, the Wesleyan and General and the Royal London.[13] The Friendly Society was a joint stock company and Richard Carter's Friendly Society of Widows formed in 1696 was designed to make a profit, although the mode of organisation mimicked the friendly societies and box clubs.[14] Carter's society very probably swiftly folded but in 1699 a very similar firm, the Society of Assurance for Widows and Orphans, was launched. Risk management became more predictable. Even though the Institute of Actuaries made it clear that the notion of a fixed rate of mortality was untenable, the periodical press was 'full of laws and tables of all kinds while the publicity surrounding insurance institutions admitted to no uncertainty regarding the law of mortality'.[15] There was also the growth of insurance for ships and their cargoes. The first ship owners' mutual club was established in 1778 and the number of such clubs grew rapidly. In 1809 the London Union Society, a mutual insurance club, paid premiums of 5 per cent.[16]

There were other precedents for the notion of mutual insurance. In 1555 the Incorporation of Carters in Leith enrolled journeymen in a convivial mutual insurance scheme. Sea box societies were mutual aid clubs funded by a head levy on sailings from the port, invested in land and made loans to fund the distribution of benefits to their members. Both the Sea Box or Prime Gilt Societies of Fife and the Crail Sea Box Society (founded by 1630) performed functions later associated with the Oddfellows, notably ensuring that members were buried in an appropriate fashion.[17] The Sea Box Society Bo'ness, founded in Borrowstounness on the

Firth of Forth in 1634 received 10 per cent of the profits from successful voyages and made payments to the needy.[18] There is evidence of similar societies dating from the 1670s.[19] During the 1680s many of the Huguenot who left France to avoid persecution came to London and formed mutual aid organisations in the early 1700s.[20] In around 1700 a treatise called *A scheme for erecting a friendly society for insuring lives* was published and it was followed in 1728 by *A method for the regular management of those societies called box clubs*.[21] The Goldsmiths' Friendly Society, founded in 1712 was still functioning in 1945 with 74 members.[22] The Coal Miners of Neath, near Swansea, had formed a trade-based body in 1768 and the textile spinners of Oldham had their own society by 1796.

In 1796 the Equitable Life Assurance Company had about 5,000 current policies. This was said to be the first life insurance company to make use of sound actuarial methods in that it charged level annual premiums related to the age of the insured.[23] Previously companies had been 'dependent more on rough and ready guesses than life-tables'.[24] Founded in 1762, its products remained distinctive for most of the rest of the century. Horton and Macve concluded that its main innovations were:

> It was a self-capitalising mutual fund which offered level premiums that enable people to continue insurance into their high-risk years without penalty and payments were made in cash.[25]

A typical policy at the Equitable was more expensive than was required to meet the claim. In 1809, a £1,000 Equitable policy taken out in 1770 had increased almost fourfold in value to £3,900. For the policyholder this might be seen as evidence of wartime inflation following forty years of overcharging. However, the bonuses attracted new members and did not stop long-term investment, in municipal bonds for example. This was an opportunity which was open to few companies. Several life offices opened which linked insurance and fund management in this way. The mutual constitution was a popular model employed, for example, by the Norwich Union, established in 1808.

Although these organisations were aimed at the well-heeled there was interest in provision for the poorer. In 1798 Sir Frederick Eden proposed the establishment of a multi-functional financial institution to provide cover for fire, life and endowment insurance, grant annuities, death benefits of widows and children to manage the savings of friendly societies and to act as a working-class deposit account. These ideas were further elaborated in his 1801 *Observations on friendly societies*.[26] The existence of annuities can be traced back to Roman times when those who sold marine insurance arranged contracts for payments for a fixed term or for life. A table of annuity rates was calculated in about 230 CE and annuities were used by UK governments to raise money until the 1690s when their use diminished as they were insufficiently liquid. Annuities were then increasingly issued by private companies, such as the Equitable Life Assurance Society. In 1808 government life annuities began to be priced according to the age of the nominee and to be based on the data the Equitable used which had been collated by Richard Price. However, the government, unlike the Equitable, priced actuarially with no mark-up, and the discrepancy between the assumed and actual mortality led to the government losing millions of pounds. Despite the losses, it was realised that deferred annuities could assist the elderly poor, and from 1819 legislation encouraged sales by allowing them to be sold through friendly societies. Government interest in both saving money and providing for the poor framed the formative years of the Unity.

In 1816 the Equitable restricted its bonus to the 5,000 people who had been with the society the longest. The number wishing to join rapidly declined while the Norwich Union announced its first bonus of 20 per cent on all premiums paid and nearly tripled its new premium income.[27] The advertisements of the Norwich Union Life Insurance Society stressed both that its premiums were 10 per cent lower than the Equitable and that it paid high bonuses due to the mutual system. In 1815 its income was such that it paid 20 per cent on all premiums.[28] The Equitable paid out what appeared to be attractive bonuses in 1776, 1781 and during the inflationary French Wars, 1793–1815. The Westminster was founded in 1792, the Pelican in 1797 and eight new London companies were founded between 1803 and 1808. Altogether during the French Wars 15 offices were created and another 29 before 1830. The repeal of the Bubble Act in 1825 led to many insurance companies being formed. They were often small, speculative and failed. It has been observed that mutual organisations are often a response to market failures and state crises.[29] In the case of the Oddfellows there were threats to the stability of the state during the French Wars, both at home and abroad, and insurance companies, while popular, were also not always successful.

Another 56 insurance companies were created between 1830 and 1844. In that latter year the Joint Stock Companies Act was passed. This enabled people to learn more about companies and sought to reduce insolvency. There was some resistance to the government gathering information not only by Oddfellows but also by insurance companies. The actuary of the Royal Exchange took the view that 'if you allow the company furnishing the account to append a valuation, the Government will become a publisher of puffs [advertisements]'.[30] Around 80 more insurance firms were formed between 1845 and 1852 but many failed. In 1853 the Select Committee on Assurance Associations was told by the Secretary to the Treasury that many new companies were 'of a mushroom description', deserved the name 'swindling establishments' and that 'hundreds of associations were springing into existence one day and falling like the autumn leaf the next'.[31] In the first half of the nineteenth century there was at least a tenfold increase in insurance per head of population.[32] However prone to collapse insurance companies were, they were part of the landscape in which the Oddfellows was formed.

Another aspect of these schemes which may have inspired the Oddfellows was the way in which finance-based networks were used to strengthen credit relationships. A number of moneylenders insured their clients as collateral on loans. People related by service, kinship or residence bought sold and traded in policies on each others' lives as a way to collateralise loans. Life insurance was employed as a medium in social transactions, creating and maintaining relationships and aiding family security. People insured their servants, boarders and neighbours who in turn insured others in the household or locality. Such strategies helped to create webs of multiple relationships. The crest of the Amicable Society for a Perpetual

Assurance Office, founded in 1706, included a handclasp encircled by a serpent and the words *Esto Perpetua*, the hope being that this friendly union will endure forever. Similar ideas can be found within the Oddfellows crest. By the 1860s the Oddfellows were claiming that it was the source of such ideas. Charles Hardwick argued that insurance companies 'generally employ an artist to design for them an allegorical emblem, which they may display as conspicuously as the Oddfellows do theirs'.[33] The Oddfellows lodge system and emphasis on communities, echoed these ties across social groups of the eighteenth century.[34] Structures which mixed charity and insurance would also have been familiar to the founding Oddfellows because life insurance companies had an interest in charity. Although some invested in the stock market, one society planned to run a hospital for its destitute members. The promotional literature of these co-operative life insurance companies indicated how by helping widows and orphans they combined benevolence, the public good and enlightened self-interest and that these companies acted 'as a means to cement or extend familial, household or commercial ties, often accompanying credit relationships'. The Amicable Society for a Perpetual Assurance Office claimed that it aided charity schools, poor debtors and poor clerics and 'the propagation of Christianity in foreign parts'. Through participation in a co-operative charity members could prevent their own decline into the ranks of those requiring charity and reduce the burden of the rates. The Amicable Corporation for the Benefit of Seamen Taken or Lost at Sea and For the Relief of their Widows and Familys (1711) aimed 'to keep many families from being a charge on their parish'.[35] This was an important aspect of the rationale for friendly societies. The 1793 Friendly Societies Act 'for the encouragement and relief of friendly societies' indicated that societies were expected to support members 'in Sickness old Age and Infirmity ... by promoting the Happiness of Individuals and at the same Time diminishing the Publick Burdens'.

The system used for much life insurance was that each member paid equally into a common fund, part of which was redistributed to claimants or beneficiaries proposed by the deceased. Under one popular scheme up to 2,000 people paid in each time a member died. In a mortuary tontine (such as that run by the Amicable Society for a Perpetual Assurance Office founded in 1706) there were fixed rates for members, the total being annually divided among the nominees of members who had died that year. These voluntary mutual-insuring ventures checked on claimants in ways which would have been familiar to members of fraternities used to the 'sick visitor'. Daniel Defoe, writing in 1697, termed the co-operative redistributive schemes which affluent tradesmen and professionals found attractive, 'assurances in the way of a friendly society'.[36] Societies began to provide banking facilities to members for, as Geoffrey Clark noted: 'a fund of credit accessible through a life insurance policy could capitalise on co-operative association to provide a timely reserve of cash'.[37] The Oddfellows was also a form of credit networks designed to reduce economic risks. Furthermore, the Oddfellows' rules which regulated democratic discourse may have also have built on the practices of insurance companies. In the seventeenth century, when life insurance was restricted to professional, genteel urban families, it was this social stratum which was most deeply influenced by the promoters of polite manners.

> Life insurance fostered politeness by [encouraging] thousands of individuals of different political persuasions and religious affiliations … voluntarily to embark on a common enterprise of mutual benefaction and support. This social solidarity was reinforced by annual meetings to elect boards.[38]

Life insurance was promoted as evidence of moral improvement, devotion to family and a means to kindle Christian fellowship among members. It was seen as related to friendly societies. For example, when tables for government annuities and insurances were being investigated by the 1827 Parliamentary Select Committee on Friendly Societies it was Charles Babbage, an actuary with the Protector Life Assurance Society, to whom it looked for evidence.[39] Familiarity with such ideas may have aided the development of tables within the Oddfellows.

For ideas about mutual insurance the Oddfellows could also have drawn on building societies and savings banks. Building societies, which developed from the late eighteenth century, fined miscreants, met in pubs (where the landlord often held the strong box) held feasts and in some cases had regalia.[40] Peter Greenall, 1796–1845, made the connection. A brewer who owned 14 pubs in St Helens, he instigated the foundation of the first terminating building society in the town (many of the houses were built on his land), piped water from his brewery ponds to those who could afford it, and dominated the local Oddfellow lodge from when it was opened in 1825. He swiftly became a Provincial Grand Master. H. H. Brimblecombe, a Provincial Grand Master in Devon was a director of the first Exeter Starr Bowkett Building Society, secretary of the Exeter and Devon Mutual Benefit Building Society as well as being in the Artillery Volunteers and a member of the Royal Arch chapter of Freemasons.[41] Savings banks, too, can be seen as evidence of the encouragement of self-help by patrons and, like friendly societies, they were subject to recognition and regulation through legislation proposed by George Rose. His Saving Bank Act of 1817 encouraged friendly societies to deposit within them. These banks were seen as another element of self-help for poorer people and were concentrated in developing industrial towns. They were managed by trustees, often local philanthropic dignitaries and viewed as an aid to social stability because they helped to give people a stake in society. Preston in Lancashire had one from 1816. One of the trustees was a magistrate, another an alderman and mayor, and both were partners in Horrockses' Mill, a leading employer.[42] The depositors tended to be single or childless men, much as many early Oddfellows probably were.

Building societies and banks may have helped to promote the idea of saving or even acted as a spur to mutual aid. It was the failure of the Rochdale Savings Bank which may have given the impetus to the formation of the co-operative movement in that town.[43] The Oddfellows Foresters, Free Gardeners and other benefit societies had their funds invested in the bank as did various sick clubs in the town.[44] The closeness of the co-operative movement to the Oddfellows can be demonstrated by the tactics of one lodge which was expelled in 1827 following a dispute over the price of initiation and the use of the local Savings Bank for lodge funds. Members of the Co-operative Lodge, Brighton went on to form the Brighton Co-operative Benevolent Fund Association.[45] Both building societies and savings banks came to rival friendly societies as a location for the funds of working men. They were the beneficiaries of legislation designed to foster working men's providence. However, at the time that the Oddfellows was being formed they can be seen as supportive in that they drew on elements of the benefit club format and, by being part of the intellectual, cultural economic and social climate of the period, helped to provide a vision that Oddfellowship could be realised.

II   Fraternal antecedents and connections

In addition to the elements derived from the state and the insurance sector the framework within which the Society developed was also derived from other fraternal bodies. Since the eighth century there have been benevolent organisations which enabled members to assist one another materially and socially and which had religious and ceremonial roles. Under the Normans these bodies, many of them called guilds, developed further and there is evidence that, for example, by the eleventh century members of the Thanes' Guild agreed to attend the funerals of fellow members and help one another in times of trouble.[46] The guilds were very popular. A survey of 1388 revealed that 160 were listed in Norfolk alone.[47] Half the men in King's Lynn, Norfolk were members of religious and merchants' guilds.[48] Many wage-earning employees, fellows, sometimes formed their own guilds for those associated with a variety of trades, that is odd fellows. In the Prologue to Chaucer's *Canterbury Tales*, 1400, there is a description of members of one guild who came from different trades. The similarity of rules among the weavers of London, Oxford, Marlborough and Beverley and the existence of merchant and craft guilds in different towns with reciprocal agreements with one another indicates that complex networks existed. The guilds emphasised the 'fundamental common bond of fellowship ... the ostentatious observance of members' funerals [and] the quest for respectability.'[49] In fifteenth-century London there were 160 cofraternities. In these oath-bound, lay-controlled voluntary organisations 'the spiritual agenda always took precedence over any monetary benefits', and hooded members marched in funeral processions to pray for their brethren. Furthermore, 'in theory and to a great extent in reality, cofraternities were democratic and egalitarian.'[50] Guilds supported poor, sick and aged members and provided funerals. Some made payments for apprenticeships, dowries for members' daughters and in Stamford 'beyond the reach of memory' the guild provided the beast for the annual bull-running. There was also a sophisticated tramping system similar to the clearances and cards of the Oddfellows.[51]

Although during the Reformation of the 1540s religious guilds were dissolved, their property confiscated and the Statute of Apprentices, 1563, removed their regulation of apprenticeships, craft guilds were maintained. They adapted to new economic conditions and were of considerable relevance to the regulation of trade during the eighteenth century.[52] Some guild functions were developed by others. In Lynn the Corporation fulfilled similar functions providing opportunities for collective self-help, processions, rituals and feasts and the channelling funds to the poor.[53] In the sixteenth century 66 per cent of Lynn merchants left money to the poor by entrusting funds to the Corporation.[54] The marblers and quarrymen of Purbeck, Dorset, called themselves the 'Freemen of the Ancient Guild' and in Salisbury the Rainbow Society, part of the Friendly Society of Cordwainers from 1784, paraded with the guilds in the city's processions. There was strong guild interest in ritual and several examples in the Manchester area on which the Oddfellows might have drawn. Moreover, in the textile industries (which played a significant role within the Mancunian economy) a direct lineage can be traced between a guild and a trade combination. The Worsted Small-Ware Weavers of Manchester looked to the guilds as an exemplar which legitimised their own activity. Formed in 1747 it had rules of conduct for the club room and favoured 'unity concord and brotherly love'. It compared itself to Chartered worshipful companies but it can also be compared to the roles that the Oddfellows played. Its rules indicate a 'meticulous attention to procedure and to institutional etiquette', including rules about where members might sit, how they must behave and the ways in which the 'box' would be kept secure.[55] As its chair pointed out in 1756, 'a great many worshipful Companies now held by charter in this Nation, had once no better a Beginning and acted as much contrary to the Law'. Margaret Jacob argued that guilds evolved into what she calls a 'quasi-religious form of corporatism, complete with oaths, rituals, regalia and 'secret truths'. This was eighteenth-century Freemasonry which was closely identified with the promotion of laws and regulations.[56] Malcolm Chase concluded that 'the place of ritual within guild life may well have been stronger in the early eighteenth century than at any time since the Reformation ... Elaborate ritual, hierarchy and the language of brotherhood was one means by which the frontier of skill was defended.' When the ironmoulders of Bolton, a new mill town on the outskirts of Manchester, formed a society in 1809 they explicitly drew upon 'an ancient and most laudable custom' of men forming societies 'for the sole purpose of assisting each other in cases of sickness, old age, and other infirmities and for the burial of the dead'. At the time that the Oddfellows was being formed, to draw on the guild traditions was an attempt to strengthen the friendly societies. While the law was hostile to workers' combinations, the guild regulations of 1563 could, until repealed in 1813 and 1814, be enforced by a Justice of the Peace. Guilds fined members for swearing, missing meetings and aggression. Members' visited homes to ensure rules were being kept. They were fined if they behaved indecorously, including the incorrect wearing of regalia, did not attend meetings or did not take on duties when elected to the hierarchy. Many guilds had a box with keys held by separate officials. It was from this that payments were made to the bereaved and ill. Some ran their own almshouses and convalescence homes.[57] It was through their provision of sick relief, pensions and burials that the guilds provided 'the germ of modern Odd Fellowship', and were 'certainly the forerunners of the groups of friendly societies which have finally culminated in the powerful Manchester Unity'.[58]

The term 'mutual improvement' was used throughout most of the eighteenth century, for example by a plebeian poet in 1731 and within the Easy Club, founded in 1712 in Edinburgh. This mutual improvement society was 'a friendly society devoted to education', and were part of a wider working-class tradition.[59] There were 51 working-class libraries in Scotland by 1822 including the Leadhills Reading Society founded 1741, the Wanlockhead Miners' Library (founded 1756) and the Westerkirk Library (founded 1792). There were 35 reading societies recorded in Scotland by 1797. Many were associated with miners and weavers, trades which developed within industrial Lancashire. Rose noted that 'in the eighteenth century autodidact culture flourished … particularly among weavers', and that it was 'an overwhelmingly male territory'. Such societies became linked to radicalism and also to temperance and the widely recognised 'reformation of manners' that occurred between about 1780 and 1851.[60] They were part of the milieu within which the Oddfellows developed. In Rochdale, for example, there was an Oddfellows' Literary Institute which was 'established for the enlightenment of the Oddfellows and the education of their children by means of a Day-School'.[61]

In 1793 some of these associations were given legal standing under the Act for the Relief and Encouragement of Friendly Societies while others were made illegal under the Combination Acts of 1799 and 1800. The intention was to distinguish organisations 'of good fellowship [and] mutual relief and maintenance' from trade unions. However, there was a continuum between the two. From 1793 friendly societies were exempt from some taxation and could sue for stolen funds (a common problem) if they provided a set of their rules for the local JPs. Registration was voluntary and many societies chose not to register. In 1817 registered societies were permitted to deposit their funds in savings banks at favourable interest rates. The government sought to support those organisations of which it approved and to outlaw the rest but that distinction was difficult to maintain. In the early nineteenth century miners in the north east formed the Brotherly Friendly Society, which was also known as the Union of Pitmen.[62] The Manchester weavers' strike of 1808 was sustained by friendly societies. In Wiltshire and Somerset, where there was a federation of shearmen's box clubs, the Home Secretary Spencer Percival noted when Wiltshire shearmen destroyed some gig-mills in 1802: 'it is most probable that they are too cunning to keep any papers but such as would be referable to little more than a friendly society.'[63] Thompson suggested both a distinction and deliberate blurring of the boundaries when he argued that some friendly societies were 'covers for trade union activity' or Jacobin organisation; 'it was a continual complaint of the authorities that friendly societies allowed members to withdraw funds when on strike,' and in 1812 Macclesfield was said to be 'full of sick and burial societies which are the germ of revolution'.[64] As Malcolm Chase concluded: 'in trying to explain both the rise of trade unions and the great political mobilisations of the early nineteenth century, it is to the bedrock provided by the early friendly societies as much as any other single factor that we should look.'[65] The Oddfellows, although not a trade union or guild, enjoyed a symbiotic relationship with such bodies.

An important way to demonstrate the respectability required of an organisation which offered to structure reciprocity was to be seen to be orderly. The Oddfellows did this by adapting some of the ideas of other fraternal bodies. The guilds had introduced three separate degrees, apprentices, fellows and masters, members were headed by Grand Masters, wore regalia and engaged in elaborate Rituals and feasting. They became recognised associations of master craftsmen, that is employers (some of whom may also work for wages) with some control over training and apprenticeships. Trade guilds had further ceremonies when a Fellow was raised to the status of Master craftsmen and when an officer was installed. Each ceremony included the reading of a lecture, or "charge", outlining the duties, ethical standards and responsibilities expected of the candidate. Late medieval York for example, had a plethora of crafts, fraternities and guilds which provided mutual support and promoted religious rituals and processions.[66] In the eighteenth century the weavers of Taunton had an association with a seal tipstaff and colours, the woolcombers in Alton, Hampshire elected their supervisors, and had a bookkeeper, a common seal and entry qualifications.

In common with the guilds, the Oddfellows also punished rule breakers (see Tables 2 and 3). The Good Samaritan Lodge, Hedon opened with 32 members and met at a pub until 1841 when the publican, an Oddfellow, was expelled for divulging the secrets of the Order. On other occasions notions of fraternity were encouraged through a system of fines. The Reverend W. T. Lawson was a Deputy from the Joseph Warburton Lodge, Middlesbrough to at least one AMC. He wrote an account of the first century of the lodge and recorded that 'fines were frequently inflicted'.[67] It was part of a wider movement to create frameworks for benevolence, social relationships and loyalty to transcend economic transfers. Sometimes these regulations were misdirected, as George Fretton, writing towards the end of the nineteenth century, suggested. He argued that members had focused on rules rather than the wider financial circumstances, that the Oddfellows was

> bound by a narrow, almost extinct red-tapism. We notice in our earlier resolutions an almost intolerable coercion in matters of minor importance while in regard to subjects of vital consequence there is either too much laxity exhibited or entire indifference. For

Table 2   *Extracts from Wellesbourne Lodge Fine Book, 1842*

Name	Infringement	Fine
Mr Gardner	Late	6*d.*
Fred Cobb	Not giving countersign	3*d.*
VG Wm Langford	Late	1*s.* apology
George Maric	Absent	6*d.* apology
Richard Charles	Not knowing charge	6*d.*
Richard Lea	Arrears	1*s.* reminder
James Kibler	Not accepting chair*	3*d.* pd 3rd October
Sec Carles	Not accepting chair	3*d.* pd 3rd October
John Freeman	Offering to bet wage	1*s.*
J Bettridge	Not visiting sick	1*s.*
John Freeman	Quarrelling and Striking	5*s.* March

* Posts were held on a six months rota. Kibler was later fined for saying the word 'Dam'.

Source: C. M. Cluley, 'Mutuality, discipline and respectability, with special reference to nineteenth-century friendly societies in mid-Warwickshire', Warwick, MA 1997. Christine Cluley acknowledged the help of Derek Winbush with this thesis and he told the 1997 AMC 'I've got a researcher from the University of Warwick doing a big research project on my own District records in 1840'.

Table 3   *Reasons given for fines imposed by the Henry Jenkins Lodge, Scorton, 1839–55*

Non-attendance at meetings/funerals:	70 per cent
Late for meetings	13
Improper conduct at meetings. This included 'falling asleep', 'lighting his pipe' and 'opening the lodge door' during a meeting and 'leaving the room without giving the correct sign'.	12
Refusing to take office	6
Improper conduct outside meetings (all for the same offence: 'being intoxicated on a Sunday')	3
Violating sick pay rules	2
Other	3

Source: Turner 'Friendly societies', p. 324; Lodge Fines Book, 1839–1855 ZDR 2 1 NYCRO.

instance, I find that no delegate at a District meeting was to absent himself for 15 minutes without leave of the presiding officer under a fine of 2s. 6d. which was the same penalty as if he had stayed away altogether, while on the other hand there is a complete absence of any investigation into the financial condition and prospects of the District for some years after its opening.[68]

In 1884 the Philanthropic Lodge, Coventry, expelled William Burbidge after he was convicted of felony. It made a Provisional Grand Master apologise for drunken behaviour at a ball in 1886 and in 1871.[69] The need to be seen to impose orderly respectability was an important part of the Oddfellows fraternal tradition. It was an echo of earlier associations of working men as well as being evidence of modernity in that was the division of labour applied to administration.

James Inglis, writing about Newcastle, New South Wales, Australia in 1880 noted that there was little malingering because members watched each other. The records of the Loyal Prince of Wales Lodge, Wallsend, New South Wales indicate the consequences for those found to be claiming while capable of work. In 1870 Brother Madison said that he saw Bro Isaac Parker:

On New years night at a quarter past ten o clock i was in the Township And i saw Isac Parker comming out of the train i asked him if he was on the Lodge he said yes then said i would stop his money he made no answer [signed]

Brother Curry acted as witness:

I was on Shepards Hill playing the Concertina and Bro.Parker was Dancing [signed]

I plead guilty to the Charge of Dancing but not to being out after hours i had Business in Newcastle to se the Doctor and i lost the train [signed]

Brother Parker's sick pay was withheld, he was fined and suspended for three months. *Source*: Green and Cromwell, *Mutual aid*, pp. 56–7.

The Society's rituals indicate that some of its roots lay in other fraternal bodies, particularly the Freemasons. Part of the attraction of Ritual is the sense of longevity, as Karen Stuart explained:

I just like the fact that we are a society that is almost two hundred years old. The Ritual has evolved a little bit, but primarily it's not a lot different from the 1834 Ritual and it's certainly no different from the Ritual at the turn of the last century. To that extent it's something that we are, it makes us very different and I am very, very keen to keep that difference.

Some of the Society's rituals have drawn on ideas far older than two centuries. The initiation rites of the Leeds wool-combers, the London tailors, the West country weavers and the Operative Stone Masons all involved a blindfold initiate calling for admittance to the Lodge room, the chanting of Psalms and passages from the Old Testament and oaths of secrecy administered by an officer in a robe. Through such ceremonies the illiterate might have been helped to understand and remember the teaching being presented. In outlining some aspects of current Oddfellow Ritual Mike Trenchard noted some of the ways in which Oddfellowship mimics Freemasonry:

The structure of lodges is a square. If you come into a lodge room you will find the four main offices on the sides of that square. In the normal adult lodge the Noble Grand, a chairman is the furthest away from the door. Opposite he or she would be the Vice Grand. To the right hand of the Noble Grand would be the Secretary and to the left hand the immediate Past Noble Grand ... The sign for someone coming in after a lodge is open is given to the Noble Grand and the Vice Grand before the person who has arrived sits down. It's a way of saluting the Noble Grand and Vice Grand, to say 'Good Evening'.

The Initiation Ritual, used for much of the late twentieth century, promotes similar ideas to those of the Freemasons:

There are three great moral duties which you, as an Oddfellow, ought always to inculcate – namely to God, your neighbour and yourself. To God, in never mentioning his Holy Name, but with that humble reverence which is due from you to your creator ... To your Neighbour, by acting upon the Golden Rule laid down in the unerring standard of Divine Truth. Doing unto others that which you wish others to do unto you. To yourself, by avoiding all intemperance and excess, whereby you might be rendered incapable of following your daily occupation, or to be led into behaviour unbecoming our laudable profession.[70]

This idea has been frequently echoed by members. In 2000 John Sharp, then a Director summarised his own involvement when he stated, 'being an Oddfellow means doing unto others as you would be done by'.[71]

Freemasonry was formally organised in England from 1717 through the United Grand Lodge. There as a web of Masonic lodges by the 1720s and by the 1730s Freemasonry was 'the most pervasive and influential form of secular voluntary organisation in most English towns'.[72] There was a schism within Freemasonry with one faction called Ancients and the other Moderns. Reunification was only achieved in 1813. By the 1740s the greatest proportion of English Modern lodges were found in the north of England and this remained an important centre for Modern Freemasonry until the end of the century by which time there were about 500 Modern lodges, many of those in the north being artisan-based. In 1807 the highest proportion of Ancient Lodges was in industrial towns, 19 per cent, which has been attributed to the support of artisans.[73] Some lodges had clearly designated benefits. The Lodge of Relief, which was founded in Bury, Lancashire in 1733, paid, in 1771, four shillings a week to any sick member of three years' standing instead of leaving the amount to be fixed by the majority of the brethren. In the event of a death a shroud, sheet and oak coffin were provided.[74] Just as the Freemasons borrowed from the box clubs, the Oddfellows could develop ideas associated with the Freemasons. The Society also adopted the widespread traditions of orderly, colourful ritual and parades which helped to bind together members of fraternal organisations. Freemasons engaged in social drinking, feasts and processions. For example in 1796 in the North West the Bolton, Chorley and Wigan Freemasons united to parade to church in their regalia. In 1813 the Duke of Sussex, who played an important role in unifying the Freemasons of England into one system of lodges, employed Godfrey Higgins to find out the links between Freemasonry and the pre-Christian worship of the sun. The Duke's view that his modern Grade Lodge required ancient antecedents parallels views held within the Unity.[75] In early nineteenth-century Bradford artisans used their meetings in the Freemason's lodge to retain a sense of community in the face of industrialisation.[76] Freemasons supported their elderly members and promoted self-help. There is evidence of a system of Masonic tramping. In the late 1840s one of the leading Magazines of the Freemasons, *The Freemason's Quarterly Review*, was renamed the *Freemason's Quarterly Review and General Assurance Advocate*.

Since the eighteenth century fully initiated Master Masons (i.e. members) have attended monthly lodge meetings and been obliged to help fellow Freemasons if this does not conflict with their own interests. Oddfellowship is similar to Freemasonry in that there is a duty and tradition of members helping one another and their widows. The Masons' Ritual involved death and resurrection and the Oddfellows also focused on mortality. Both encouraged fellowship, conviviality (often they met in pubs) and also respectability (they fined for swearing and drunkenness and forbid discussion of religion and politics). Members wore regalia and exchanged grips and signs and processed in public with banners. Both elected the men who headed the hierarchies and had degree systems. Officers had titles (for example both Oddfellows and Freemasons refer to the doorkeeper as the Tyler and both have branches called Lodges which have both names and numbers). The Masonic Third Degree involved the acting out of the murder by three men of Hiram Abiff, the man who is said to have used his secret knowledge to build Solomon's Temple in Jerusalem. Hiram (played by the candidate) perambulates around the lodge room, falls into his grave and is then pulled from his grave, at the third attempt, by brothers using the appropriate grip, and the candidate rises to a new status within the lodge. He is given new information but the revived Mason does not have the secrets lost as a result of Hiram's death. He must search for them. It is his duty to strive, with his brothers, to figuratively rebuild the temple. Although Moffrey did not provide evidence when he argued that the Oddfellows was 'founded in imitation of Freemasonry', it was a view often found within the Society, reiterated in the *Oddfellows' Magazine*.[77] The organisations appear to have common roots and similar appeals. Perkin, for example, noted that friendly societies flourished due to the attraction of 'goodfellowship, conviviality and a sense of belonging to a secret and powerful masonry'.[78] One entrepreneur spotted the connection and established *The Era*, 'the only journal devoted to licensed victuallers, Freemasons, Foresters and Odd Fellows'.[79]

John Money has suggested that the Freemasons conceived of charity in terms of mutual aid, that they saw

> charity primarily in terms of their own self-realisation. To 'make' a mason, archetypically formed and regularly tested to the 'working' of his lodge was itself the best form of charity because it conferred those attributes of 'character' without which charity was wasted on the recipient.[80]

This notion parallels Oddfellowship and the organisations had similar aims. Freemasonry described itself as 'a system of morality, veiled in allegory and illustrated by symbols'. It sought to improve the membership through allegorical guidance based on the tools and craft skills of stonemasons.[81] The Freemasons claimed to trace their roots back to Jerusalem, had passwords, initiation and other rituals, ceremonial impedimenta, notably chairs, aprons and jewels, and were clearly influenced by the guilds. They had rules against religious and political debate and were committed to mutual aid and charity. Their elected head was called a Noble Grand Master. For the early Oddfellow the first sight in the lodge was the emblem of death and motto 'Remember thy end'. The initiate was asked 'What do you make of the emblem,' and replied 'As a guard upon my lips – like unto it be as silent as the grave: recollecting that the day will come when the secrets of all the hearts will be laid open.'[82] This Ritual is similar to that of the Freemasons, indeed the historian Peter Clark characterised the Oddfellows of the period as 'masonic style' but as Masonic ritual was amended in 1815–16 there may have been some cross-fertilisation between the two organisations.[83] Although it appears that Freemasonry could well have set the organisational pattern for the Oddfellows, a connection was denied by the US Odd Fellows Grand Sire in the 1880s. John H. White asserted, 'It is sometimes said that Odd Fellowship is the offspring of Masonry but this is in no sense true.'[84] He pointed out the Freemasons assisted the needy as a charity, whereas the Oddfellows made payments as a right. However, the Oddfellows were charitable and the Masonic Benevolent Society operated 1799–1830, like a friendly society while the Temple Lodge Benefit Society, in Bristol, was also a Masonic Lodge.[85] The Freemasons linked trade networks to charity and ritual through a concept of 'fraternal charity' which Andy Durr called 'an ideology of interdependence, its practical manifestation being giving and receiving'.[86] Durr distinguished the Oddfellows and the other affiliated orders from village societies arguing that to the former 'self-help was secondary and the primary purpose was to spread among their members ideas of benevolence, love and charity. The Oddfellows had more in common with the masons than with the county or village friendly society.'[87]

By the time that the Oddfellows was formed the Freemasons enjoyed considerable status. For example the Masons were able to negotiate a degree of exemption from the legislation outlawing secret societies, the 1797 Unlawful Oaths Act. From an early period there appear to have been close ties between the Oddfellows and the Freemasons in that in March 1815 the Oddfellows Grand Committee resolved 'that in consequence of information received from the Masonic Grand Lodge, John Wood never be admitted into our Order'. In November 1815 when a new lodge was opened in Ashton-under-Lyne there was a toast to 'The Hon. Society of Freemasons', before the toast to the 'The Hon. Independent Society of Oddfellows'. In September the following year another man was rejected for membership on the advice of the Freemasons.[88] The Oddfellows continued to make links to the Freemasons. In 1829 the *Oddfellows' Magazine* stated:

> The Order of Oddfellows was originally initiated on Masonic principles, the object of which is to cement more firmly the bonds of social feeling and sympathetic intercourse between man and man.[89]

There is other evidence of an overlapping of membership between these fraternal orders. In Australia the charitable Ballarat Benevolent and Visiting Society was established in 1857 and it soon established an asylum which received funding from the local Unity and the local Freemasons. The President was a prominent Oddfellow in the town, William Scott, a bootmaker from a Catholic Irish background.[90] In 1880 the Oddfellows held its AMC in Lynn. Some 400 Deputies represented the society in a procession and at a banquet with a reception in the town's Guildhall. The influential Oddfellows Estimates Committee was chaired by a Freemason who was also a civil servant and later a Grand Master, Robert Moffrey. The conference was supported by a number of prominent local men including the MP for West Norfolk. He was a Freemason, a local landowner, patron of at least three local churches and a former Sheriff of Norfolk. The Prince of Wales, who was another Freemason, invited conference Deputies to Sandringham.[91] Moffrey found this to be a significant event:

The incident furnished proof of the change which had come over public opinion of those in high places in respect to the position and the operations of the society. The Manchester Unity was no longer an institution to be sneered at, or to be suspected of nefarious designs. Its usefulness was recognised by the highest in the land.[92]

Hamon L'Estrange the Freemasons' Provincial Grand Treasurer 1876–86, Grand Deacon and Grand Master, initiated an Oddfellows Lodge in the town where he lived, Hunstanton, 17 miles from his Masonic Lodge in Lynn. John Rust, who in 1892 was the Worshipful Master of the Lynn lodge of Freemasons, the Philanthropic, was another Unity Grand Master. As the *Oddfellows' Magazine* noted on his death in 1900, 'His interest in Oddfellowship continued undiminished until the end.'[93] Philanthropic Lodge member James Lister Stead was also a prominent Oddfellow. In 1866 Charles Theophilus Ives became Provincial Grand Master of the Lynn District of the Oddfellows and in 1867, seven years after he joined, he became Worshipful Master of the Philanthropic Lodge of Freemasons.[94] Charles Edward Ward, a solicitor's clerk in Lynn, was a Master and Provincial Grand Senior Warden in the Freemasons, a patron of the Oddfellows and, in 1906, the Forester's High Chief Ranger (a rank equivalent to Grand Master).[95]

Many Oddfellows were proud of their connections to Freemasonry. In 1900 Edgar Horne, a Freemason and member of the Oddfellows, was elected mayor of Derby.[96] In 1901 the Unity's Grand Master Richard Rushton was entertained at a banquet held by the mayor of Accrington, the town where Rushton had first joined the Oddfellows aged 18 in 1866. Rushton, 'an active Mason' (he became both a Provincial Grand Treasurer of the district and was also a member of a supra-local lodge grouping of Freemasons, Royal Arch) told the mayor, councillors and others assembled that 'he was not unmindful of many friends with whom he worked in another society which did a great deal of good – the Order of Freemasons'.[97] In nominating the Grand Master who was elected in 2001 a colleague from Reading mentioned that David Phillips had led his team to victory in Ritual competitions and was 'a keen Ritualist which may stem from his strong Masonic connections … He has made certain improvements to the Ritual which we in Reading agree are much neater.'[98] Terry Moore, a Freemason as well as an Oddfellow called the former 'a gathering of like-minded people who support each other help each other and encourage each other when they need encouragement. The Oddfellows come into the same bracket but they are much more down to earth, and meaningful in a day-to-day way.' Others have found themselves being a little more circumspect. Mike Trenchard explained some aspects of the continuing relationship between Freemasonry and Oddfellowship:

My children were joined at the same kind of age as I was joined and my daughter is still a member, my son is not. He is very religious and he equated some of the Ritual with Freemasonry. I have tried to explain that the Oddfellows is a friendly and paternal society.

A lot of Oddfellows are also Masons but I am not and my Dad [Ron Trenchard] never has been either. The Ritual that Oddfellows use is just a means of explaining to the membership what its fundamental principles are and wrapping that round with some aspects of Freemasonry ritual like knocks and signs and passwords. It's very simple, it's nothing as complicated as Freemasonry ritual and in fact, the current Ritual of the society is very much a watered down version that was used in the 19th century.

Freemasonry is not the original fraternity from which all the friendly societies copied. Rather the Oddfellows, the Freemasons and the trade unions have common roots. They have exchanged ideas about supporting fraternity and shared ideals of fellowship and produced some common notions. Oddfellowship has informed and been informed by, the rituals and principles of a variety of fraternal bodies. Its success is in part due to its ability to adapt ideas and to rebalance the elements of reciprocity which are central to it.

III   Charity

If reliable help was to be offered to members of the Oddfellows the organisation had to be well structured. For ideas on organisation the founders may have turned not only to insurance companies and fraternities but also to charities. The founders of the late eighteenth-century charity the Strangers Friend Society made visiting a regular part of its work with a system of checks similar to those developed by many friendly societies. Members subscribed money and placed suggestions as to suitable recipients in a box. A committee assessed the proposals and dispatched visitors to check on the recommended individuals. If appropriate, a second visitor would check again and then make a donation.[99] Subscriber democracy, as this was known, spread to other charities. Funding was collected from the members who elected a committee of higher status members and constructed an elaborate hierarchy of grades of membership. 'Voting charities' drew up a list of candidates eligible for relief and provided subscribers with a number of votes proportionate to their subscriptions. The Society of Friends had a national, organised, charitable system to support travelling Friends, apprentices and paupers with medical and funeral costs, while the organisers of the Anglican-run charitable mothers' meetings ensured that recipients were deserving by sifting through their membership to reduce the number of 'travellers' who abused the system.[100] The Oddfellows sense of mutual obligation and insistence that relief met institutional as well as individual needs echoed many charities. Harris has suggested that there was a porous boundary in the nineteenth century and argued that because it was viewed with ambivalence by recipients, some charitable activity was presented in terms of mutual aid.[101] Networks of obligation, self help, independence, loyalty and a sense of community were important for both the Oddfellows and charities.[102] Both forms of organisation were capable of generating varying degrees of solidarity and had roots in the guilds. Both had a continuing common interest in institutionalising benevolence through creating social relationships and mutual ties based on loyalty. Both had an interest in transcending economic transfers between recipients and donors, or members, by extending connections in order to involve emotional and social relationships.

Charity and mutual aid drew on the guild traditions of helping the poor through binding together recipients and donors and they continued to overlap. As Gorsky noted, in eighteenth-century Bristol the annual meetings of charities typically included a Christian service, a procession and a feast in one of the old guild halls. Some charities had costumes and ceremonies, such as the Warwick Bread Dole or the buttons decorated with shears on the clothing provided by a tailor's charity in Atherstone, Warwickshire.[103] To aid institutional survival some charities developed a sense of obligation and commitment to the public good.

One of the points of convergence was the Sunday School. Attendance was common to working-class children.[104] A number of friendly societies developed from within Sunday Schools. In Lancashire many Sunday Schools had their own benefit societies.[105] Gosden suggested that there were 'numerous' Sunday School-type friendly societies, though few registered ones outside Lancashire, Yorkshire and Cheshire.[106] The Harborough Congregational Sunday School in Leicestershire dated from before 1794 and had an associated sick fund and the Brotherly Society of Birmingham grew out of the Sunday Schools movement.[107] In 1789 one writer coupled advice for establishing Sunday schools to that for instituting friendly societies.[108] In the 1820s the Farningham Sunday School, Kent, received annual payments from the Oddfellows, and both organisations were closely associated with the vicar.[109] Like the friendly societies some of the schools relied on rich patrons while others were dependent on contributions from trade unions or the scholars themselves.[110] Almost all children in the first half of the nineteenth century would have known a sibling or neighbour to die. In 1850 overall life expectancy for English males was 40 but only 24 in Manchester.[111] Many Sunday School teachers both visited sick pupils and ensured that other pupils also visited. Sometimes school bands would visit and in Stockport teachers were urged to report death scenes and the superintendent kept records because 'last moments were thought of as a public rather than a private occasion'.[112] Like the Oddfellows, Sunday Schools held processions with banners. Biographies of societies' leaders often mentioned the significant role that Sunday School played in their lives. For example, the Oddfellows recounted how an active member, the Reverend Thomas Price, started out as a Sunday School teacher.[113] For the Oddfellows it was a matter of pride that among the best Sunday school teachers were 'some whose minds were first cultivated by a benefit society'.[114] By the late nineteenth century 'it was customary for the Sunday School to follow the friendly society procession'.[115] The Oddfellows derived a sense of security through drawing on the experiences, ideas and models provided by charitable organisations. Through charitable activity the Society became a route through which men could gain and cultivate the civic identities associated with citizenship.[116]

A further connection between Oddfellowship and charity was that the state authorities often categorised charities and friendly societies as means by which the rates, local taxation, might be reduced. In 1757 an Act of Parliament encouraged coal-heavers on the Thames to 'make provision for such of themselves as shall be sick, lame or past their labours'. This could encompass charitable activity. The 1793 Friendly Societies Act referred to happiness as well as reducing the rates.

That the protection and encouragement of Friendly Societies in this Kingdom for securing by voluntary subscriptions of the members thereof separate Funds for the mutual relief and maintenance of the members in sickness, old age, and infirmity, is likely to be attended with very beneficial effects by promoting the happiness of individuals and at the same time diminishing the public burdens.

This legislation envisaged friendly societies as reliant on either the subscriptions of the members or on voluntary contributions. The Act was amended in 1795 to include benevolent and charitable institutions. However, later the language of legislation focused more on the cost to the public purse. From 1809 JPs were empowered to enforce the observance of the Rules and to compel payment of arrears due to a society. This echoed the 1807 proposal of Samuel Whitbread for a Government Savings Bank. While his 'Fund and Assurance office for investing the Savings of the Poor' was not adopted his interest is indicative of the widespread concern that working men save money and that this saving be controlled.[117] In 1819 legislation referred to the need for friendly societies to be based on 'principle of mutual insurance for the maintenance or assistance of contributors thereto' There was also firmer cajoling:

the habitual reliance of poor persons upon parochial relief rather than upon their own industry tends to the moral deterioration of the people and to the accumulation of heavy burdens upon parishes, and it is desirable, with a view as well to the reduction of the assessment made for the relief of the poor as to the improvement of the habits of the people, that encouragement should be afforded to persons desirous of making provision for themselves or their families out of the fruits of their own industry.

Throughout the nineteenth century charities and friendly societies were part of a broad concern, expressed in part through the considerable growth in the collation of government data, with occupational ill-health, morbidity and morality which were conceptualised as the main causes of working-class poverty.[118] Indeed, 'if there is a single thread running through early English population statistics it is insurance'.[119] Although Burn argued that he was 'not thus pleading for charitable assistance', he concluded his study of the Society by seeking

to prove to the middle and higher orders that it is both their duty and interest to patronise it; their duty because it is admirably fitted to better the condition of the labouring community, and therefore make them independent of either charitable or parochial aid. Secondly, because both the duties and responsibilities of the higher orders will be made lighter. And thirdly, that the working classes may have a greater respect for their character.[120]

One commentator argued in 1867 that charitable hospitals were, as a means of reducing reliance on relief, 'an important agent against pauperism'.[121] There was an attempt to use a charity to support ratepayers in another way in the early twentieth century. In 1900 William Sutton left his fortune to provide housing for the poor. By 1913 the Local Government Board and several councils had become dominant trustees of the charity. They sought to use it to maintain the income of ratepaying local landlords.[122] The widespread importance attached to 'self-help' and the discourse of the 'deserving poor', a discourse which was articulated through legislation, framed much charitable and friendly society activity.

The Oddfellows made it clear that a commitment to solid finances did not undermine the need for fraternal charity. Charitable activity burnished the image of the Oddfellows. A poem composed by Thomas Crossley, of Queen Victoria Lodge, for the occasion of the opening of the Oddfellows hall in Halifax opened with the lines:

> Brothers! We've met on this auspicious day,
> Not for vain pomp, nor yet for vain display,
> But here, this towering Structure – nobly great!
> To deeds of charity to consecrate![123]

Stories such as the one that in 1841 in Australia the Felix Lodge, Melbourne, helped a brother who had been shipwrecked and the wife of another brother who wished to join her husband in the bush, revealed Oddfellows as caring brothers.[124] There are accounts from England which also indicate the charitable role that the Society took. In 1846 nearly £900 was sent to those who were suffering through the failure of the potato crop in Ireland.[125] In 1861 the Grand Master permitted a petition on behalf of the distressed ribbon weavers of Coventry to be circulated. Within nine months over £200 had been raised and distributed. In 1864 the Distressed Brethren in the Cotton Districts, received over £2,140.[126] In 1862 nearly £10,000 was raised for the relief of members in those areas, such as Preston, where the lack of cotton due to the American Civil War had led to lay-offs and deprivation.[127] In 1869 in Coventry a Tea Party and Ball attended by 600 Oddfellows raised money for Ragged Schools and two local philanthropic societies, 'thus showing' the 1870 Annual Report noted,

> that while Friendship Love and Truth are the prevailing characteristics of our vast Brotherhood, we are not unmindful of the urgent requirements of our less fortunate and distressed fellow creatures.

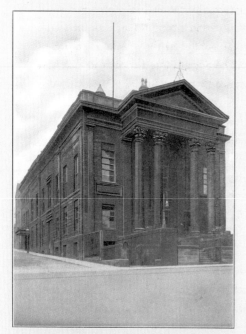

FRIENDLY & TRADES CLUB, HALIFAX.

Headquarters of the Halifax District Independent Order of Oddfellows, (Manchester Unity).

Halifax Oddfellows Hall was opened in 1840, hosting public meetings and theatrical performances. It later became a cinema, and was demolished in 1963 to make way for a new bus station.
BY COURTESY OF THE AUTHOR

Godiva Oddfellows Hall, Coventry. Processions and celebrations relating to Lady Godiva have long been part of the traditions of Coventry. Naming a hall after this local heroine emphasised how rooted within the city the Society was.
ODDFELLOWS COLLECTION

Three years later there was a call for a hardship fund for the Coventry District. This was to be

> on a similar basis to that of the existing Philanthropic Institution for the relief of special cases of distress occurring among the brethren of the district and their families, through poverty, accident, long continued sickness or any other misfortune and to met such special circumstances for which the ordinary rules of our sick and funeral fund do not provide.[128]

A number of lifeboats carried the name of the donors. Since 1863, when the AMC resolved to ask lodges to raise money, there has been support for the Royal National Lifeboat Institute.[129] There was a Cleethorpes-based *Manchester Unity* from 1868 and when, in 1884 four men were rescued by the *Manchester Unity* lifeboat, the story was publicised through the *Oddfellows' Magazine*.[130] It also featured in the centenary book.[131] The Society frequently expressed how its particular form of fraternity was of greater significance than its actuarial tables, as in this example from the *Oddfellows' Magazine* 1886:

> It is very often said that although our great aim and object is the promulgation of these principles of forethought and thrift amongst our fellow men which ultimately lead to their protection in times of sickness and death, raising them in their own estimation and in the estimation of others, yet our primary object is to promote that spirit of brotherly love in our fellow creatures which is necessary for the well-being and success of any institution, no matter what its object.[132]

Many Oddfellows raised funds for the 1889 London Dock strikers and the Melbourne *Oddfellow* commented, 'We glory in the manner in which the matter has been taken up in the lodges, as it is one of the fundamental principles of true Oddfellowship to assist their fellowmen in times of distress and tribulation.'[133] In 1910 an explosion of firedamp in a mine killed 139 men and boys, including 11 Oddfellows at Whitehaven, Cumberland. There was considerable publicity given to the 50 guineas sent by the Oddfellows to the relief fund.[134]

There are also documented instances of charity within the Society which may have strengthened the ties between brethren. After a clergyman who controlled a local charity refused help to silkweaver Joseph Gutteridge, an atheist, his neighbours saved his wife and five children from the workhouse or starvation, and the Oddfellows helped him to bury his fourth child, who died from smallpox. In the autobiography he published when he was aged 77 he described how on one occasion his father was taken ill:

> During a violent fit of coughing he ruptured a blood vessel. As soon as he possibly could he insisted on going back to work again, being in a manner compelled to take this step by the fact that the Benefit Society to which he belonged had for some time suspended payment for sickness.

Gutteridge himself received 10s. a week from the Oddfellows during illness in 1851 and was the beneficiary of Oddfellow charity. In 1845 he reported that

> We had been without work for many weeks, but I had made up my mind that come what might I would not appeal to the parish for relief. Help at last came from an unexpected quarter. On New Year's Day 1845 while acting as a door keeper at a ball given by the Philanthropic Lodge of the Manchester Unity of Odd Fellows at St Mary's Hall, my despondency attracted the attention of two senior officers of the lodge, Thomas Barnes and James Rushton. I had cause to be down hearted; my boy lay at home dead and I had not the means to bury him. The two gentlemen enquired the cause of my grief and on learning my story they expressed their sympathy and when the ball broke up at about two o'clock in the morning they bade me stay awhile and presented me with a sum of money obtained from friends which enabled me to bury my child decently.[135]

In 1837 a quarter of the deaths in Glasgow were due to typhus, a disease closely associated with poverty. When James Burn's family caught typhus he was the recipient of considerable Oddfellow generosity:

> As soon as my calamity became known to the Odd Fellows' Lodges several of them sent me various sums of money. The 'Banks of Clyde' in Greenock, of which I was a member cleared me of their books and sent me three pounds and ten shillings. I may remark that I had long been out of benefit in consequence of not being able to pay my contribution. One of the lodges in Edinburgh sent two pounds. One of the country lodges also sent the same sum; and two of the town lodges sent five pounds between them ... The man who dries the tears of sorrow and relieves the wants of suffering humanity with acts of charity is the greatest among sons of men.[136]

An emphasis on its charitable roles may have reduced the number of members who claimed benefits while not ill. The tradition of charity enabled lodges to interpret regulations with more flexibility than other insurance bodies would have done. In the King William IV Lodge, Lancaster, in 1861 William Huddlestone was fined 5s. for drunkenness whilst claiming 'on the box'. However, because he had a wife and several young children he was allowed to keep his sick pay of 9s. When James Richardson was arrested for drunkenness his wife rushed to the shop of the appropriate Oddfellow official, Edward Gardner, so that he could be declared well and thus avoid a fine and the stopping of sick pay. The fine was remitted but the family lost the sick pay. In 1866 the Preston District allowed a £5 benefit to a widow with seven children who was not entitled as her husband had been suspended from membership at the time of his death.[137] Similar accounts can be found in the Coventry records. The Philanthropic Lodge, Coventry, expelled Henry Hollis after he was convicted of robbery. However, Hollis appealed and 81 members attended a meeting to hear his case. If he was expelled he would be unable to access any money that he had contributed and may have been ineligible to join another society on grounds of age. He stated that he had not stolen the society's beer, but only helped to drink it and that he had been punished.

> I have been in the lodge for many years and am now getting old. I hope and trust you will do what is right by me and take me again into the lodge as I suffered imprisonment for the whole of the workmen who drank the beer.

The lodge agreed to reinstate him but this was overturned by the District. In 1875 Henry Aires of the same lodge was spotted by the Noble Grand working whilst in receipt of sick pay. When reminded of the rules Aires broke another rule by using insulting and abusive language. He was expelled but on appeal to the District and then to Grand Master his sentence was reduced to suspension for a year.[138] The Oddfellows was a rule-based organisation but it did not forget its charitable roots and indeed promoted these. There was room for appeals for leniency and charity, both of which could aid member retention and loyalty.

IV   Christianity

Edward Thompson argued that organisation such as the Oddfellows owed much to Methodists:

> by the 1790s Dissent was enjoying its own evangelistic revival … Methodism provided not only the forms of the class meeting, the methodical collection of penny subscriptions and the 'ticket', so frequently borrowed by radical and trade union organisations, but also an experience of efficient centralised organisation at district as well as national level.

He went on to argue that in the complexity of competing sects and seceding chapels we have a forcing-bed for the variants of nineteenth-century working-class culture'.[139] Nevertheless,

INDEPENDENT ORDER OF ODD FELLOWS.

Manchester Unity Friendly Society. Mersey District.

LOYAL LORD STANLEY LODGE, No. 2084.

Order of Service

AT

ST. CLEOPAS CHURCH,
BERESFORD ROAD, LIVERPOOL, 8,

On SUNDAY, APRIL 28th, 1935,
at 3 p.m.

Attended in State by THE LORD MAYOR OF LIVERPOOL,
(Bro. Alderman F. T. RICHARDSON, J.P.)

MEMBERS OF THE CITY COUNCIL
and
THE DISTRICT OFFICERS.

Preacher :

Rev. E. J. M. ELDRIDGE, O.B.E., C.F.(T.A.)
(Vicar of St. Cleopas).

INDEPENDENT ORDER OF
ODDFELLOWS (Manchester Unity)
— HALIFAX DISTRICT —

1833   1933

CENTENARY THANKSGIVING · · SERVICE · ·

SUNDAY, July 2nd, 1933,
at 3·15 p.m., in the
HALIFAX PARISH CHURCH

Conducted by

The Right Reverend Bishop Frodsham, D.D.

Lodge histories and church services could help to reinforce messages about the respectability and longevity of the Society. The celebration of the first anniversary of the Loyal Barnard Lodge, South Cave, in 1838, for instance, was marked by a church service, a dinner for 60 provided by a local benefactor and a collection for the Sunday School. One of the toasts ran:

> May our activities as Oddfellows be faithfully guarded by the rules of our Order and by the unerring Book of Truth so that when we leave this our earthly lodge we may be furnished with the countersign of the heavenly lodge above and be forever shut in with our Supreme Grand Master.
>
> (FROM *THE HULL PACKET*, 18 MAY 1838)

These illustrations come from a variety of lodges, including the Mersey District and Halifax.

SOUVENIR COVER COURTESY OF JAMES BEARD; SERVICE COURTESY OF BETTY MOSTYN

INDEPENDENT ORDER
OF
ODD FELLOWS
MANCHESTER
UNITY
FRIENDLY SOCIETY

REGISTERED UNDER THE FRIENDLY
SOCIETIES ACT AND APPROVED UNDER THE
NATIONAL HEALTH INSURANCE ACTS

LOYAL
"FOX" LODGE
No. 668.

Centenary Souvenir
1832—1932.

there was some unease with some aspects of Oddfellowship among Christians, notably the idea that to gamble on lives questioned the wisdom of God to decide on when people should die. Commercial insurance firms sought to reassure that their products aided piety. Regulations sought to distinguish between gambling and investment in life insurance and the firms tried to present themselves as part of familial obligation 'to put chance in the form of risk in the service of morality: family life, foresight, prudence and parsimony'.[140] The Oddfellows also tried to associate itself with religious propriety. Although the Society has enjoyed close connections with Christianity and has a Golden Rule derived from the words of Jesus, Oddfellows Ritual has been presented as anti-Christian. In Yorkshire one Anglican cleric condemned the Oddfellows' funeral service as 'ancient heathenism' which maintained 'the ignorance and barbarism of Pagan Britain'. Another minister declared:

> I care not for your badges – they are the emblems of wickedness – and you are worse than devils or infidels; and if you do not forsake your badges you will not only go down to the grave as this man has done, but you will sink to eternal hell.

A Methodist minister writing in the *Magazine* referred to the Oddfellows 'horrid oaths' and said God condemned the society. According to a report in the *Magazine* a Leeds vicar refused to officiate at an Oddfellow event (a lower church minister took his place).[141] However, in 1842 a Leeds vicar lent the Society his church, was given the collection which was taken at the Service (70s.) and joined the Society the next day.[142] Hutton argued that the ritual set the Society apart, 'Something very apparent about both Freemasonry and the affiliated orders is that the religious language that they used, and the tradition which it implied was not a Christian one. It implied no necessary hostility towards Christianity.'[143] In Woodhouse the Reverend Bywater told the Oddfellows, 'I intend to give you a short lecture and then turn my back on you forever. I care not for you … You are a disgrace to society.' In 1838 a vicar refused to let an Oddfellow read a Society speech over the grave at the funeral of an Oddfellow in Silkstone.[144] In Wakefield a year later a vicar also refused to let members read at the graveside. The local newspaper speculated that, 'it is said that the clergymen of the Church have received orders from a high quarter not to allow the reading of any of these orations at the graveside'.[145] The Archdeacon of Durham argued that the Oddfellows' graveside oration was 'a novelty savouring in its character more of Deism than of Christian faith, for we find no mention of the Saviour'.[146] The Bishop of Oxford pointed out that as some of the Oddfellow lecturers were written by George Holyoake the lectures must be atheistic.[147] It was the independence of the Oddfellows, with their own distinctive activities, which may have alarmed the advocate of public health, reformer Edwin Chadwick. He proposed that gatherings in graveyards be suppressed, churchyards closed and mourning be individualised.[148] In 1859 in Maitland New South Wales, Australia a Roman Catholic Dean refused to perform the last rites over the grave of a deceased Oddfellow. This, the local newspaper reported, was because his church did not recognise 'secret societies' and indeed all societies 'over which she does not exercise a guiding and controlling influence'.[149] In 1848 the Oddfellows had to answer questions about the religious view taken by the Order from a Parliamentary Committee. William Benjamin Smith argued that the Order did not challenge churches:

> *Q.*   What is the object of having a funeral service connected with your Society?
>
> *A.*   I am not sure I can hardly tell what was the object of it.
>
> *Q.*   Is not the effect of it in a certain degree to set yourselves up as a separate religious Sect?
>
> *A.*   No, I think not; because political opinions or religious tenets, and every thing of that kind, are not allowed to be entertained or discussed or thought of or talked about.

He also explained that members had to be 'of good moral character … sober, honest, steady, and so on'.[150] In 1850 a vicar in Preston told members of the Society that 'the principles and practices of your Order are such that a Minister of the Gospel may entirely approve'.[151] In 1901 the *Oddfellows' Magazine* published a poem which referred to Heaven as 'the Eternal Grand Master's abode', and in 1910 Moffrey felt the need to reprint some favourable comments by clerics.[152] In 1914 the Bishop of Winchester said he valued being initiated as a member of the Society because he felt that he found 'right at the heart of a great movement the real secret of its life and strength'. He went on to trust that it would remain 'a society of sisters and brothers and not a society of participators in some scheme of financial and industrial benefits. I plead for your initiation ceremony … as a symbol of something greater.'[153]

Lodges were often treated in a similar way to that which people treated spaces designated for Christian worship. In the lodge brethren looked inwards into a space in the centre, reminiscent of Friends' Meeting Houses, perhaps to remind members of the belief in seeking inwardly and in the communion of every brother directly with the Supreme Grand Master. However, there were also spatial distinctions within the lodge as members were also encouraged to focus on the places where officers sat. This perhaps drew on the location of the alter in Anglican churches. It echoed the difference between the nave (where congregation sat) and the chancel (often reserved for the choir). The symbolic movement between locations (for example during initiation in Oddfellows' lodges) may have derived from the processing that occurred during communion. To control the space where Ritual occurred reinforced the idea of members as free, moral agents, part of an elect (to employ a Calvinist term) who were developing a new order of society. There is a similarity between some activities in church, in terms of formal, repeated symbolic actions and some of those of the lodge. The Eucharistic drama of Anglican Communion involves a re-enactment of the transformation of Jesus' body and blood in which those who eat the bread and wine can be reminded of the idea of resurrection.[154] Burn made the connection to Christian ritual when he described the City of Glasgow Lodge where 'the elective officers dressed in full pontificals with white cotton gloves on their hands'.[155]

A few snapshots over the years can be used to indicate the close links between the Oddfellows and many clerics. In Warwickshire an advertisement placed in the local press by the Oddfellows in 1845 described how

The members will proceed to the Episcopal Chapel, Upper Parade, Leamington, where William Grice, MA incumbent of Wroxall (a member of the order) will preach a sermon. Collection in aid of the parish church.[156]

In east Yorkshire they 'openly courted the Anglican church'.[157] William Duke was secretary of the Cranswick Oddfellows, 1889–1901, and also a preacher in the local Primitive Methodist chapel.[158] Arthur Jackson recalled the role of Oddfellows in building links between the Church of England and the chapel in inter-war Kettleshulme, Cheshire:

> There were two occasions in the year when 'them and us' was forgotten. The Remembrance Sunday service when the Rector of Taxal joined forces with the Whaley Bridge Wesleyan Minister in conducting the service, and the Oddfellows annual procession held in September. Here again the two would take part in the united service, held alternatively in church and chapel.[159]

Another member, now in her thirties, mentioned a more recent connection:

> We have got strong links with the local Methodist Church … We have a Carol Service every year there which we sponsor. We do all the hymn sheets, the order of the service. We will bring the members in and we do a reading as well. We will make sure all the other parishioners have teas, coffees and mince pies afterwards. The minister … he will be coming to the AMC this year.

Both Pauline Pettigrove and Arthur Jackson compared the activities within a lodge to those which occur in a church. 'You no longer call it a Ritual you should call it ceremony because it's ceremony like the Sunday service or a marriage service,' she said, while he said: 'you had to say "I will" like when you get married. All verbal, nothing written down.'

The Society was not an attempt to counter Christianity with diabolic secrets. Many members of the Oddfellows were Christians and the Oddfellows drew upon Christian images and rituals in the design of its rules and banners and sought to present itself as an open, Christian, organisation. It was deeply imbued with many of the values of Christian faith as the following part of the Ritual performed when a new lodge is opened makes clear:

> In the name of the Grand Master of the Universe unto whom all hearts belong, whose All-Seeing Eye watches our every action, who has given us the Golden Rule for our guidance we Dedicate this Lodge Room to the dissemination of Friendship Love and Truth to the cultivation of Faith, Hope and Charity, to the protection of the fatherless, to the relief of all distressed Odd Fellows and to the promotion of Universal Brotherhood.

While being open to a variety of readings has left the Oddfellows open to criticism by clerics who felt threatened by its popularity the ambiguity meant that Ritual was not banal and one

The All-Seeing Eye

The Oddfellows often made use of the image of an All-Seeing Eye of the protective Great Architect (or Grand Master) of the Universe. This may indicate the influence of the Freemasons, but it has iconographic echoes reaching back to ancient times.[160] Moreover, it was a familiar nineteenth-century metaphor.[161] The All-Seeing Eye may also represent the members themselves, read as evidence that the friendly societies were open to inspection, that members watched over one another and that the central executive was ever vigilant.[162] The All-Seeing Eye reminded people that, from the time they joined, when a doctor examined applicants on behalf of the members, the Oddfellows' rendered members' lives visible and knowable. In order to calculate the number of deaths of a population at various ages, the Society required surveillance. It needed to monitor members in order to relate financial risk to morbidity and mortality. On Oddfellow banners the All-Seeing Eye could remind those who saw it not simply that surveillance was pervasive but that good members internalised that gaze and watched over their own activities. There was a further prompt to memory below the banner on the parade. It was part of the job of the club doctor to be seen there, as the Commons Select Committee on Medical Poor Relief, 1844, made clear. The friendly societies 'expect him to walk in their processions and they thank him for his services at annual feasts'.[163] The connection was made by Jeremy Bentham who wrote favouring friendly societies and also designed a prison, the Panoptican ('all-seeing') in which the incarcerated could be constantly watched. That which was hidden came to be seen as a source of fear. In 1838 a Select Committee reported its concerns about those parts of London where there was 'a dense population of the lowest classes of persons ... entirely secluded from the observation and influence of better education neighbours'.[164] During the nineteenth century there were shifts in how people came to understand the notion of masculinity. Manhood was 'defined above all as an honest, straight-forward conduct' as distinct from 'subtlety and obliquity of any kind.'[165] Those in receipt of sickness benefit were not supposed to work and one lodge

> agreed that some members go to Stockton to see whether a Brother member is attending to any business. Also to make enquiries secretly with the Eston lodge concerning the behaviour of another member.

In 1905 the sick visitor of the Erimus Lodge, Middlesbrough, heard from a women whose sister had recently been deserted by an Oddfellow. The women claimed that her brother-in-law 'was not ill' and was 'not keeping club hours' (i.e. that he was out of-doors when he was supposed to be resting at home). After an inquiry the man was expelled.[166] Members also watched over the morality of members' activities to ensure compliance with rules regarding numerous matters including sexual conduct and drinking. The All-Seeing Eye could serve to indicate that it was the members who kept watch, that they were self-regulating citizens, contributors to civic virtue, creators of social capital, family providers who watched over one another to ensure their collective financial and bodily health.

A lodge of Oddfellows was established in Burton-upon-Trent in 1830, but it was not until 1983 that the Society Branch purchased the former hall and renamed it Unity Hall. A new lodge, based on the original one and several others, met here.
ODDFELLOWS COLLECTION

dimensional but multi-layered and understandable at different levels. It had to represent different conceptualisations of secure, reliable structured reciprocity. It also needed to be immediate and recognizable, offering the comfort of repetition and a sense of universal truth.

V   Travellers and networks

Being part of a network of lodges was of importance because it offered greater security. Between 1795 and 1832 19,787 societies deposited their rules with the Clerks of the Peace and yet in 1836 only 5,409 of them were in existence. The Registrar of Friendly Societies estimated that between 1793 and 1867 36 per cent of societies collapsed.[167] Many failed because limited number of members led to insolvency in the face of a poor harvest, an epidemic or local unemployment. The Oddfellows enabled risks to be spread. Friendly societies which were for one particular trade or locality tended to suffer if there was a localised depression. In New Malton two societies which started in 1817 and 1818 became involved in disputes over enrolment. The seceding members formed two lodges of Oddfellows. When the Yarm Union Club closed in 1834 members joined the Oddfellows lodge which opened soon afterwards.[168] In 1895 746 people joined the Society when their societies joined the Oddfellows.[169] Other affiliated orders also spread their risks. When, in 1847 most of the Foresters 75 courts (the Foresters' equivalent term to lodges) in Liverpool had to close due to a cholera epidemic the organisation made a loan to the district (which was not repaid) in order to aid recovery.[170] In 1894, when ten members of the Society's Hallow Lodge in Worcestershire joined a local Foresters' court, they had to first demonstrate their solvency.[171] Being part of a network had other benefits. According to a press report in 1844, fishermen from Aberystwyth, driven by poor weather conditions, were forced to land at Pwllheli, 52 miles away. The two Oddfellows in the crew appealed for help and the whole crew was supported for a week at the expense of the lodge and then given towards the cost of getting home.[172] In 1852 a flood in Holmfirth killed 65 people. Officers from the Oddfellows and other friendly societies,

> with feelings highly creditable to them, busied themselves where relatives did not come forward to own the bodies, in searching them out from distant towns, and paying them the sums for which the societies were liable in cases of death, either of the members or of the children of members, for funeral money.[173]

For the idea of a network the Oddfellows could have drawn on a number of federation organisations in which local lodges retained considerable autonomy. The Free and Easy Johns, the Independents, the Lumber Troop, the Bucks, the Albions and Antigallicans were 'lodges and societies were designed to provide mutual assistance for their members in order to help them become socially, economically and politically independent.'[174] During the 1760s coal heavers created a society of Bucks and another called the Brothers.[175] In their 1993 account, *The Three Link Fraternity – Oddfellowship in California*, Smith and Roberts claimed that in the eighteenth century the Ancient Order of Bucks met in pubs, had a leader known as Most Noble Grand and had emblems including three bucks with their antlers intertwined and a bundle of sticks which symbolised strength in union. The Select Society of Free and Easy Johns in Chester-le-Street was established as a convivial club in 1813 but started to make payments for funerals and illness in return for contributions and a Free and Easy in Stockton registered as a friendly society in 1838.[176] The Free and Easy Johns Lodge No 3, formed in Newcastle-upon-Tyne in 1795 'for the reciprocal relief of each other' may, like the Bucks, have predated the Oddfellows.[177] There is a reference to the 'Odd Fellows, Free and Easy and the Jolly Friars' in 1799 where a musician could receive a diploma and which met at the Goose and Gridiron.[178] However, it appears not to have survived into the nineteenth century. Burn suggested that 'many friendly societies have sprung from the same bacchanalian free-and-easy source'.[179] Although the Society was not the first one with a network of lodges it was, as Gosden notes 'the first of the affiliated societies to grow'. By 1832 it had 561 lodges and 31,000 members.[180]

Its connected lodges, similar to Freemasons' network, enabled the Oddfellows to develop the tradition of hospitality to the tramping stranger. Manchester was a town of migrants. In 1851, as only 45 per cent of the 401, 000 inhabitants of Manchester–Salford had been born locally, it is appropriate that accounts of the foundation of the Oddfellows indicate the importance of Brother Bolton the newcomer to Manchester who, it is said, helped to found the Order. The Oddfellow's offer, to support, preserve and protect members by providing a network in place of the blood ties many had left behind, may have sounded more plausible when made by a man such as Bolton. There was also a tradition in London, of which Bolton may have been aware, of 'county feasts' at which migrants from the specified counties would raise money to help those from that county apprentice themselves in the capital. There is evidence of similar societies in other towns.[181] Martin Gorsky has demonstrated that, 'if there was such a person as an average friendly society member, he was probably a migrant who had been absorbed

Table 4   *Oddfellows' occupations, 1846–1848*

Occupations	percentage of the Order	approximate number	percentage of occupied males in 1851
Labourer (rural). Defined as labourers in lodges located in towns of fewer than 5,000 people.	8.70	21,800	24.5 (agricultural labourers and related)
Labourer (town)	6.80	17,160	classification not compatible
Carpenter and joiner	6.00	15,000	2.68
Miner	4.93	12,325	3.03
Shoemaker	3.90	9,750	3.63
Blacksmith	3.80	9,500	1.6
Tailor	3.40	8,500	1.90
Weaver	3.00	7,500	classification not compatible
Stonemason	2.96	7,400	1.32
Domestic servant	2.61	5,175	classification not compatible
Mill operative	2.17	5,435	
Plumber	1.89	4,725	0.81
Spinner	1.82	4,550	classification not compatible
Bricklayer	1.80	4,500	1.15
Clerk	1.40	3,500	classification not compatible
Butcher	1.20	3,000	1.03
Baker	0.98	2,450	classification not compatible
Printer and compositor	0.78	1,950	0.40
Wheelwright	0.74	1,850	classification not compatible
Woolcomber	0.68	1,700	
Sawyer	0.66	1,650	
Hatter	0.58	1,450	
Dyer	0.54	1,350	
Potter	0.41	1,025	
Millwright	0.39	975	
Cooper	0.35	875	
Total	62.45	155,095	
Sundry occupations or no data	37.55		

Sources: H. Ratcliffe, *Observations on the rate of mortality and sickness existing amongst friendly societies*, 1850, pp. 39–60 and 1851 Census cited in Gosden, *The friendly societies*, pp. 75–6.

successfully into an urban labour market but had to purchase insurance as a substitute for the customary prerequisites and poor relief which had supplemented the rural wage.'[182]

There were long traditions of organisations which would find accommodation or work for members who arrived 'on the tramp' and the Oddfellows swiftly adopted and developed these. These were both informal and organised. Hospitality had long been offered to migrants on the basis of letters of introduction and word of mouth contact. A witness at court in seventeenth-century Southampton said that he was provided with food and clothes when he delivered the 'commendations' of his neighbours elsewhere and there was similar accounts from London.[183] A 'tramp' could expect his society brothers to provide food, drink and accommodation for the night. The traveller had to have a card from his lodge indicating that he was 'in benefit'.[184] In the morning he would receive either an introduction to an appropriate employer or, if there was no work, a small sum to tide him over until he had tramped to the next society lodge. A drinking pot made for a friendly society is illustrated with a picture of a traveller asking the foreman, 'Brother craft, can you give me a job?' the reply being: 'If we cannot we will relieve you.'[185] Eric Hobsbawm described the tramping artisan:

> The man who wished to leave town to look for work elsewhere received a 'blank' or 'clearance' or 'document' showing him to be a member in good standing of the society. This he presented to the local secretary of relieving officer in the 'lodge house' or 'club house' of 'house of call' of the strange town – generally a pub – receiving in return supper, perhaps beer and a tramp allowance. If there was work he took it; the call book (if there was one) was of course kept at the house of call, an unofficial labour exchange.[186]

To the early members of the Oddfellows, 'travelling relief' was 'probably the most useful benefit, indeed the principal one', and while by 1839 there was a recommended rate (1s. 6d. a day) there were variations.[187] In Stockton, in 1842, 94 'distressed brothers' received 5d. each and in Middlesbrough that year it was 3d. and the following year one brother received 2s.[188] This was an area where the population was growing. In County Durham between 1866 and 1914 between one and 19 travelling cards were issued to members each year and the highest number of 'clearances' issued was 30. However, between 54 and 397 members of the Oddfellows arrived each year looking for work.[189] Through this system the Oddfellows helped to support the unemployed, regulate the supply of skilled labour and enabled men to travel. While it may have been efficient to pay men to stay at home the 'artisans' Grand Tour' as Hobsbawm put it, was encouraged in some trades.[190] It enabled information to be passed around and potential blacklegs to be dispersed in times of industrial dispute. The Loyal Constitution Lodge, Great Easton, Lincolnshire, paid 1s. 6d. a day to members travelling for work, for one night only providing that the traveller's home lodge had granted him a card valid for six months. It had an additional proviso, 'that no member shall be allowed a card who has lost his employ through a strike or turn-out for wages – trades' unions not being countenanced by the Order'.[191]

Table 5   *Oddfellows' occupations, 1846–1870*

	Approximate number
Agricultural labourer	107,760
Labourer (town)	85,774
Miner	77,161
Carpenters and Joiners	74,760
Cordwainers	49,076

Source: Hopkins, *Working-class self-help*, p. 34 from the 1874 Fourth Report of the Royal Commission. A further 21 occupations were listed. There is a very large 'sundries' group.

There were more labourers who were Oddfellows than any other single trade, for them, even in the new urban areas, employment was often seasonal and casual.[192] There were also a large number of carpenters, miners, shoemakers, blacksmiths and tailors as Tables 2 and 3 indicate. All of these trades practised tramping and may have been attracted to the Oddfellows because, as one Bolton Oddfellow and printer claimed in 1844, 'the travelling system is the one grand principle contemplated by the constitution and laws of Oddfellowship'. An Oddfellow songbook of 1823, reprinted in 1866, contained the lyrics to the 'Song of the Wanderer' by 'Jewel'. This began:

> I've wandered far on foreign strands,
> Where fate had bade me roam;
> And oft tho' strange in stranger lands,
> I've found a welcome home.
> A friendly Brotherhood I've met,
> Co-mingling age and youth;
> And never can I e'er forget,
> Their Friendship Love and Truth.[193]

Table 6   *Oddfellow Clearances, 1870–1875*

Year	Number
1870	964
1871	694
1872	863
1873	896
1874	554
1875	540

Source: F. G. P. Neison 'Some statistics of the Affiliated Orders', *Journal of the Statistical Society*, 40, 1877, cited in Gosden, *The friendly societies*, p. 222.

As Malcolm Chase has shown, 'the great age of the tramping artisan was the first two-thirds of the nineteenth century'.[194] Parliamentary concern about vagrancy was reflected in the frequency of enquiries. Select committees reported in 1841, 1848 and 1851. By 1848 the iron moulders had concluded that tramping was injurious to the health of tramps. It ruled against loans and payments to those 'on the tramp'. In 1871 the Local Government Board, which replaced the Poor Law Commission as the central government body responsible for poor relief and public health identified only types of vagrants: 'working men seeking employment' and the 'habitual tramp'.[195] Nevertheless, at local level a more discerning analysis could be made. Neave argued that the travelling system was less in evidence in rural areas. However, Logan felt this view required 'modification'.[196] In Howden, Yorkshire, it was recognised that vagrants were 'generally men engaged in different trades passing from the chief towns of the West Riding to those of the East, and vice versa and are generally well conducted'.[197]

The Oddfellows continued to offer support. If a member permanently moved to a different area then, if he was paid up-to-date he could receive a 'clearance certificate' from his lodge which could be presented to another lodge. The Oddfellows paid out £5,200 to tramping members in 1842. In 1850 a reciprocal arrangement was made with the Universal Independent Order of Odd-Fellows, an American body, for the exchange of the 'travelling pass-word'. In 1853 the form of the Travelling Cards was changed and also similar reciprocal arrangements were made with the Canadian Order of Odd Fellows in that year, which strengthened ties between the three bodies.[198] Between 1863 and 1873, 94,476 Oddfellows in the UK received relief to help them to travel to seek employment. In 1862 when there was a depression in the cotton trade, the Oddfellows issued 1378 travelling cards.[199] There were 943 issued in 1863 and then further changes to Travellers' Cards were made in 1864 and the number of cards granted almost halved to 557 and then fell again to 378 in 1865. The average paid to each person fell by over 68 per cent.[200] Tables 6 and 7 indicate the continuing popularity of tramping. In 1884 the dilemma in a story in the *Magazine* is resolved by the helpful intervention of a travelling carver known as the Bear (the Oddfellows' PGM at the time was R. C. Bear).[201]

Table 7   *Oddfellow Travellers, 1848–1872*

Period	Number of cards issued	Sums paid to travellers (in £)	Number of payments made
1848–52	4,721	4,468	
1853–57	2,500	1,619	
1858–62	3,797	3,590	
1863–67	2,864	2,406	44,278
1868–72	2,204	1,750	50,218
Total	16,086	13,833	

Source: F. G. P. Neison 'Some statistics of the Affiliated Orders', *Journal of the Statistical Society*, 40, 1877, cited in Gosden, *The friendly societies*, p. 76 and Hopkins, *Working-class self-help*, p. 29.

Table 8   *Membership of some friendly societies 1845–2007, in thousands*

Affiliated order	Oddfellows	Ancient Order of Foresters	Independent Order of Rechabites	Ashton Unity Shepherds
1845	248	77	26	14
1846	259	77	18	14
1848	249	84	12	16
1850	225	80	9	15
1852	225	90	7	14
1854	232	100	6	17
1856	251	114	6	18
1858	276	135	6	19
1860	305	166	6	23
1865	373	301	–	31
1870	434	377	15	33
1875	496	491	–	56
1880	532	555	35	61
1885	551	595	68	67
1886	597	572	60	72
1890	595	640	95	89
1895	665	654	103	107
1900	736	666	137	118
1905	754	652	176	126
1910	749	606	213	122
1912	753	656	227	146
2007	95	170	17	25

Sources: various records of the Oddfellows and others, cited in Neave, *Mutual aid*, pp. 23, 106; AFS, *Key statistics*, 2007, pp. 6–7. There are some contradictions in the sources. The Oddfellows appear to have gained 10,000 members between 1845 and 1846, and then to lose 10,000 members the following year.

In 1886 Brother E. Brown, walked from Hull to Bristol in search of work. When he called on the Lord Hill Lodge in Kidderminster he was given accommodation, food and £2 to help him on his way.[202] Some chose to retain membership of their mother lodge. They empowered their new local lodge to act as an agent and report when the member was entitled to draw on funds. This could operate across thousands of miles. In Norfolk in 1891 the Loyal Trafalgar Lodge of Oddfellows granted 'clearance' to Brother Henry Hollis when he went to America and in 1908 made a sick payment to Brother Ward, who, although 'residing in Australia' had

The Oddfellows Hall at South Creake, Fakenham, Norfolk, a modest brick building in a predominantly rural district. From its early beginnings in northern industrial towns, Oddfellowship did eventually spread southwards and into less industrialised areas.

maintained his membership.[203] In 1876 a Royal Commission in Victoria, Australia found that in the previous decade the Oddfellows in the state had accepted 2,724 clearances while 2,517 had left by clearance.[204] Robert Moffrey, reflecting at the centenary of the Order in 1910, was particularly proud of the success of the Unity there, noting that 'so firm has a root has the Manchester Unity taken in Australia that there are now four subsidiary Orders each with its own Grand Master and directors, all working in harmony with each other and the Order in the Motherland.'[205] The connecting of travel, fraternal, Christian, charity and insurance was proving popular across the Empire.

VI   Conclusion

The Society could offer sociability and support because it built on the fraternal networks and structures of the friendly societies, the guilds, the trade unions and the Freemasons. The Oddfellows was developed within a milieu in which it was familiar for men to meet together in order to help themselves and others. The organisational ideas of insurance companies and charities also played a part. During a period when British people had to become accustomed to urban industrial society the Oddfellows offered both a critique of, and a means of working within, the notion of the classical political economy and the new exchange relations. Its formalised fraternity, offered relief to the sick and the possibility of a reduced poor rate and showed that it had rules against embezzlement and drunkenness. It also offered opportunities for working men to meet and assess common concerns. Taken together these factors offer part of the explanation for the success of Oddfellowship. However, it also required considerable effort by members. If they had not assiduously promoted the Society and turned the narratives of ancient linage into a lived culture the Unity would swiftly have followed so many other fraternal bodies and fallen apart.

CHAPTER THREE

Respect and reciprocity

W H E N the Oddfellows challenged individual members to behave better it did this within popular understandings as to what constituted better behaviour. It combined notions of neighbourliness and respectability in a distinctive fashion without straying too far from the familiar. The first section indicates that the notion of a cycle of exchange whereby people give, receive and reciprocate within a gift economy and which Marcel Mauss claimed lay at 'the heart of normal social life' was well established within British Victorian society.[1] In a gift economy exchange is mediated through a vast number of person-to-person transactions. This can exist alongside relatively impersonal social institutions which organise specialised occupations and which are dependent on the payment of fixed sums for specific activities. Ceremonies provide 'an ideal vehicle for conveying messages that concern authority, legitimacy and power', and the other four sections are about how the Oddfellows aided reciprocity through a system of payments, public displays, notions of secrecy, demonstrable respectability and social activities.[2]

I The gift

According to Samuel Johnson's 1755 definition a gift was both a 'bequest, endowment, or alms to the poor' and also 'an obligation, offering, bribe'.[3] The Scottish word for mutual help, giff-gaff, and the English term 'give and take' also suggest the unity of the two actions of donating and receiving. Under the aegis of charity, donors could create an obligation and aid the preservation of the status quo. Gifting has been seen as of significance to the development of the market. Ilana Krausman Ben-Amos suggested that informal support was pervasive and was often stimulated by the market.[4] However, it has also often been seen as dying out. The notion that long-established formal and ritualised structures for the exchange of credit and charity collapsed as people ceased to be members of *Gemeinschaft* communities and became part of contractually organised *Gesellschaft* societies has been proposed by a number of scholars.[5] In the early twentieth century Max Weber argued in *The Protestant ethic and the spirit of capitalism* that as society became more modern so people became more selfish. They tended to think in terms of calculation rather than obligation. A few years later Mauss concluded that gift exchanges, by which people were connected by the fact that if they received they were obliged to give, were an aspect of the pre-modern marketplace where exchanges were dependent on credit and typically were solidified only after hours of negotiation in a local tavern, over drinks and in front of witnesses. He suggested that by the nineteenth century there had been a 'victory of rationalism and mercantilism'.[6] This shift has been associated with the Reformation, the rise of markets, urbanisation and the Poor Laws. Others too have stressed the importance of gifts and gifting in the early modern period. Craig Muldrew argued that 'as the market became all pervasive reciprocity and forgiveness, tempered by thrift and discretion, became more pervasive in notions of charity'. He pointed to the interconnection of charity and credit noting that the value of unpaid debts to the poor was 20 times as large as donations to charity and the value of poor relief combined.[7] Taylor has suggested it is related to the development of the modern state.[8] Karl Polyani argued that a system of reciprocity was being replaced by the self-regulating market by the end of the eighteenth century. Deborah Valenze thought that the seventeenth and eighteenth centuries 'constituted a transitional period during which a traditional notion of the individual as embedded in social relationships of obligation came into conflict with a new definition of the individual as severed from ties of dependency'. John Gillis suggested that 'by the end of the nineteenth century the old gift economy had virtually disappeared'.[9] Gareth Stedman Jones took the view that in the late Victorian period, 'in a large urban area where the rich and poor had been separated, the social powers supposedly inherent in the gift had disappeared'.[10] Howard Newby made a similar point about East Anglia from the 1880s arguing that the weakening of the economic position of agricultural landowners and the divisions between landlords and tenants meant that it became obvious to 'even to the loyal agricultural worker that the "organic community" was beginning to fall apart'.[11]

If it was dying out, gifting took a long time to go. However, the metaphor of death suggests a sudden change, a clear distinction. Such a notion of dualism might be ascribed to Romans 4:4 and 6:23 where favours and gifts were presented as moral while wages were deemed to be material. The Authorised Version renders these verses as: '4.4 Now to him that worketh is the reward not reckoned of grace, but of debt' and '6:23 For the wages of sin is death; but the gift of God is eternal life through Jesus Christ our Lord'. Rather than posit a clear-cut distinction between archaic and modern societies in terms of antithesis between the gift and commodity exchange, it aids understanding to recognise these as parallel options.[12] The middle class, for example, continued to extend credit only to those of good character and notions of personal credit and a moral economy persisted well into Victorian times.[13] In Ireland farmers did not pay off their debts to suppliers in order to maintain a state of mutual indebtedness.[14] Writing about transport, water, gas and electricity in Victorian Britain Daunton concluded that 'the market was permeated by notions of fairness and morality'.[15]

Evidence of reciprocity being the basis of relationships can be found in many working-class areas of the United Kingdom. In early nineteenth-century Wales, community not conjugality was highlighted at weddings when the entire neighbourhood was invited to give presents. Each practical gift would be noted and an appropriate gift returned, if not to the individuals then to their descendants.[16] There is also evidence of reciprocity in urban and industrial areas. Reports of the 1832 pay negotiations between the Durham and Northumberland-based Coal Miners' Friendly Society and the employers indicate that 'the language of fairness and reciprocity was central to this culture of bargaining and negotiation'.[17] On other coalfields friendly societies promoted co-operation between employers and workers.[18] County court judges refused to enforce credit contracts which had not been mediated by personal contact between traders and poor consumers. They articulated 'their own distinctive conception of a moral economy insulated from the full force of market mechanisms'.[19] In rural England one of the most popular forms of supported self-help were allotments. Familiar from the 1840s and provided for one in three male agricultural labourers by 1873 these were a means by which clerics and landowners provided assistance in order to improve morality, reduce the rates, local taxes, and increase social stability.[20] Provided for the deserving and taken from rule-breakers, allotments were 'about moral issues and moral improvements', and often linked to other landlord-inspired improvements such as medical and clothing clubs.[21]

Archie Cameron described the 'mutual aid' between the poor of the island of Rhum, which, between 1843 and 1957, was a privately owned estate.[22] In rural Perthshire *lovedargs* were both a system of neighbourly reciprocity and used by the wealthy to embed their social superiority.[23] Fixed price retailing only became a convention in the 1790s.[24] By the mid-nineteenth century high volume, low-mark-up, multiple shops were selling at single publicly posted fixed prices for cash. However, small shops continued to offer items 'on tick' in return for loyalty. Customers only settled their accounts and purchased goods elsewhere if the cycle of reciprocity broke down. In 1844 Manchester factory owner Frederick Engels was one of many observers who commented upon the extent of working-class mutual help.[25] In the early 1870s a report on Poor Law administration commented on the practice of collections to help widows:

> what amounts to interchange of charitable assistance among the poor in London is not uncommon … they assist each other to an extent which is little understood … It is scarcely possible to conceive a form of charity which combines so completely its highest reciprocal benefits with the absence of mischief so frequently incident to almsgiving.

According to the satirical magazine *Porcupine* in 1880 the poor 'have a system of mutual assistance, a habit of helping each other, which prevents many of them ever becoming rich in anything but nobleness of character'.[26] In London vicar Arthur Jephson wrote of the Waterloo area in the south that in the 1880s 'as long as one person has anything to share, they are willing to share it … The starving can always secure help from neighbours in distress, for the poorest never know when their turn to starve may not come.'[27] More recently, historians have described mutual aid in the UK capital. 'Irish neighbours contributed money for funeral expenses, if the dead person's kin could not raise enough. Neighbours loaned money.'[28] In east London 'the bulk of women's day-to-day sharing was exchange: in theory at least reciprocity was the rule.'[29] In Islington, north London, there were 'pudding bowl collections for bereavements' … neighbourhood-based 'diddlum' clubs for savings and credit and … the Vernon Help-One-Another Society', formed in 1899.[30] In Preston it was 'well-nigh essential to make every effort to keep in contact with, or enter into reciprocal assistance with, kinsmen, if life chances were not to be seriously imperilled', and in the Potteries there is evidence of

Crockery advertised the Society, reminding users of the orderliness of the Order and the tenets of Oddfellowship. It may have been used to spark conversations about the benefits of membership. The 1860 Song Book celebrates 'the cup of joy', which may refer to the two-handled cup. Some of the lines also appear on the jug from Taddington:

When 'Friendship, Love and Truth' abound,
Among a band of Brothers,
The Cup of joy goes gaily round,
Each shares the bliss of others.
Sweet roses grace the thorny way
Among this vale of sorrow;
The flowers that shed their leaves today
Shall bloom again tomorrow.

Chorus:
How grand in age, how fair in youth
Are holy 'Friendship, Love and Truth'.

SONGBOOK TAKEN FROM GOSDEN, THE FRIENDLY SOCIETIES, PAGE 135

TOP: PHOTOGRAPH BY COURTESY OF CHRISTINE PAYNE
CENTRE: PHOTOGRAPHS OF JUGS FROM DAVE BATHE COLLECTION, UNIVERSITY OF SHEFFIELD
RIGHT: BY COURTESY OF THE LIBRARY AND MUSEUM OF FREEMASONRY

'reciprocity negotiated between family members.'[31] There is considerable evidence of informal mutual support networks within working-class communities, particularly of reciprocal domestic labour arrangements between women.[32]

Material such as this can be employed to support Simon Cordery's view, that the Oddfellows developed 'during the shift from paternal reciprocity to the creation of a free market in labour', and that rituals 'smoothed the transition from the old order to the new world of commercialism'.[33] In the nineteenth century reciprocity and trust within economic relations were familiar and stabilising notions. Employing the language of reciprocity made sense to many people.[34] The point was often made that malingering or moral hazard were reduced if friendly society members or charitable donors or recipients felt that they would be adversely affected if they lost the regard of others. In order for the Oddfellows to build on the notions that gifts were not isolated but implicated in social conventions it had to be respectable. Respectability was closely connected to networks of credit and information exchange, particularly for those who had to deal with people far removed about whom they knew little, who were, for example, from another lodge.[35] The law offered only limited protection against defaulters.[36] In 1836 when the Order was well established in Merthyr, there was a dispute involving a man who had joined two friendly societies and the magistrates ruled that the Oddfellows were a 'voluntary association not regulated by law'.[37] In the 1840s Burn described the difficulties associated with the illegal status.[38] Gifting was a means of addressing the problem of moral hazard whilst also working within notions of honour and civility between members during a period when masculine affability, courtesy and reliability oiled the wheels of commerce.[39]

For the Oddfellows cycle of giving, receiving and returning of gifts helped to create and maintain relationships. Most of these examples of mutual aid relied on personal trust, of dealing with known individuals. Oddfellowship united those with common interests, even when they were physically separated, and through rule-based lodges, enabled trust to be spread. The Society's benefits offered were a gift in this sense, as the case of the Grand Master of the

The Oddfellows Hall, Brighouse, near Huddersfield, was built on Bradford Road in 1850, and acted as the town's first concert hall. The building was demolished in 1972 to make way for a new road.

ODDFELLOWS COLLECTION

Rose of England lodge, Middlesbrough indicates. He was censored in 1848 'for going out to gather mushrooms while receiving the gifts of the lodge'.[40] Moffrey pointed out that money paid to the ill was often described as a 'sick gift' and that 'the description of sick ailment as a "gift" and as funeral money as a "donation" lingered long after the system was changed to a definite benefit in the heading to the tables in the General Rules'.[41] The first returns of sickness experience in the Society, published in 1850, refered to the 'Sick Gift', while the second one, issued in 1862 treated the terms 'gifts' and 'sick allowance' as synonymous.[42] Spry used the term 'Sick Gift' in 1867.[43] This use of the term gift maintained a social convention of the eighteenth and nineteenth century employed by other friendly societies. For example, the 1772 rule book of the Yarm Tradesman's Society indicated that fines could be imposed on a member 'who reflects upon his fellow for having received the gift of this society'.[44] By accepting a 'gift' the recipient also accepted the obligation to reciprocate. Gifts were a mixture of altruism and selfishness based on the principle of *do ut des* (I give so that you may return). As Mauss pointed out, 'generosity and self-interest are linked in giving'. Seeing benefits as gifts was a way of reminding members that they were obliged to the 'donor', other Oddfellows. An inequitable relationship had been created and, because reciprocation cannot be immediate, the relationship would need to be maintained.

The act of giving can turn into an act of revenge and respect into rivalry, it could be a means of asserting status. Thus when a member of the Rose of England Lodge Middlesbrough was given a vote of thanks 'for the manly manner he has acted in not laying himself on the lodge fund while sick', and he rejected this gift he was establishing his position in regard to the cycle of exchange.[45] The commonplace advice to be wary of Greeks bearing gifts and to inspect the mouths of gift horses indicates that gifts are not free, they structure and maintain relations between people, they are the medium of social relations, bound up with pride and prestige, never free of obligation and debt. They are a means of survival they connect rituals and institutions of exchange which specify what, when and how, it is appropriate to give, to accept and to receive. Whereas some wealthy people may have seen their relationship with poorer people in terms of patronage which they could bestow as they saw fit, for the Oddfellows one way of maintaining a sense of obligation was by returning fines to the member. This restored his status as a grateful member and gave him a motive for remaining within the Society. In 1844 a lodge official who had been keeping fines imposed on other members was himself fined but, after five months the fine money was returned to him.[46] John Carter joined the R. H. Bulman Lodge, Middlesbrough, in 1874 became a Noble Grand in 1875 and was then fined for drinking while in receipt of sick pay and in 1884 was imprisoned for receiving stolen goods. Nevertheless he was reinstated into the lodge.[47]

This desire to evade what some could have perceived as a vicious circle rather than a virtuous cycle, was not an isolated incident. Writing in 1933, a period when the role of the Oddfellows was dramatically different in that it was far more involved in the administration of state aid, one observer claimed that 'an appreciable proportion of members of the old friendly societies … never had the slightest intention of drawing benefit and this type of member has now largely ceased to exist'.[48] More recently Joan Henry recalled, 'In those days you didn't very often take it because the lodge couldn't afford it. It was more a question of what you could put in rather than what you get out,' and Lesley Bull also felt that there was a need to see the Oddfellows in terms of mutuality not simply a business relationship: 'I don't feel I should take out if I don't put in. I pay contributions but I feel I should do more instead of just expect them to pay to help me out with my dentist treatment.' In noting that 'My Dad used to swear by the Oddfellows for a bit of help and a bit of company' Ken Harding connected social activities to the business ones and suggested a sense of reciprocity. He also attributed this notion to himself in that he noted that once he had received a mortgage from the Oddfellows he felt a sense of obligation and for eight or nine years during the 1960s he and his wife ran 'sausage sizzles' in their garden for younger Oddfellows.

> When we got married it was like opening up a new life to us with all the help we got and we tried to do our best to repay it. I didn't want to be one of the officers and we couldn't do anything monetarily but we decided, with a bit of persuasion that we could run the youth club. We paid for all this because we felt we were quite indebted to the Oddfellows. I was really pleased to think we could thumb our nose at the people who had refused us a loan.

Andrew Porter said that the ethos of Oddfellows was 'If somebody comes along says "Help," we'll say, "How much and when?" What Oddfellowship is, it's paying it forward. It's making sure that whatever you get, you pay back to somebody else, or somewhere else, double. We are looking to put out more than we take.' Douglas Potter made a similar point:

> My wife and I we look after our next door neighbours who are unfortunately are widows and they need a man about the house at times. We can give them help and that is what Oddfellowship taught me. If you help others you can hope that in time they will help you … the ethos, what we did, I respected, I thought it was worthwhile. You were helping your fellow men all the time and that as been my purpose in life.

Oddfellow gifting has aided the 'detoxification of money' (to use Valenze's phrase). It has supported the maintenance of a culture apparently dominated by possessive individualism by clearing the pathway towards it. Its formalised fraternity has also provided a haven within that culture where members might seek respite and fellowship.

II 'Matters appertaining to the Order which its Rules or customs declare shall be kept secret'[49]

From its inception the Society in common with other financial bodies, needed to balance secrecy and openness. On the one hand secrecy was associated with hiding the financial truth. The collapse of the South Sea Bubble in 1720 was said to be due to secrecy according to many sources, including a Commons Committee of Secrecy. On the other hand secrecy was

VISIT OF THE MANCHESTER UNITY OF ODDFELLOWS TO THE GROUNDS OF OSBORNE HOUSE.

Photo by Mr. F. G. O. Stuart, Southampton

The respectability of the Society was demonstrated in 1893 by an invitation to attend a function at one of Queen Victoria's residences, Osborne House. Approximately half a century earlier the Deputies who took a trip there were 'shadowed by detectives, lest they might have nefarious designs against the person or property of Her majesty'.

INFORMATION FROM MOFFREY, A CENTURY OF ODDFELLOWSHIP, PAGE 119. ILLUSTRATION FROM ILLUSTRATED LONDON NEWS, 3 JUNE 1893

perceived as a necessary facet of competitive trade. Guild and company secrets were guarded by practitioners as were those of trade unions. Through secrecy a competitive advantage might be gained.

In 1834 six men in Tolpuddle, Dorset, formed a trade union or friendly society – there was little distinction at that time – and, as part of this process, they swore an oath. They were convicted under the 1797 Unlawful Oaths Act and transported to Australia. Four years later, at the trial of five cotton spinners for conspiracy and murder, trade unions were represented as dangerous secret societies. Much was made of these events, indeed as Edward Thompson argued, in the early nineteenth century 'the government needed conspirators to justify the continuation of repressive legislation which prevented nationwide popular organisation'.[50] The Oddfellows, a society with secrets, wished to distance itself from accusations that it was a secret society. One MP made the connection between allegations of insurrection and the Oddfellows. He admitted that he had been ignorant of the 1797 legislation and added:

During the nineteenth century British society became less parochial as improved communications and new opportunities for travel fostered contacts and exchange with like-minded people from much further afield. This change was aided by the Oddfellows. The Society's structure ensured that members got to know and trust one another within a local lodge, and that they were also offered opportunities to make regional, national and international connections. These examples, from Barrow-in-Furness (*right*) and Portsmouth (*below*), reflect these different dimensions of the Society. Lodge members may have felt that their reputation for dependability, respectability and Christian connections would be enhanced by being linked to images of the ruined abbey or the town hall. On many banners there was a general message, or the arms of the Society, on one side and evidence of civic or local pride in a specific area on the other side.

UPPER IMAGE: BY COURTESY OF THE DOCK MUSEUM, BARROW-IN-FURNESS; LOWER IMAGE: REPRODUCED WITH THE KIND PERMISSION OF PORTSMOUTH MUSEUMS AND RECORDS SERVICE

Indeed, if secret oaths were illegal and punishable by this Statute he was himself indictable as he belonged to the Society of Oddfellows and had taken a secret oath in that Society, over which presided at the time an eminent lawyer, now high in the administration of the law, who actually administered the oath to him.[51]

The Oddfellows made public its commitment to reliability, a useful attribute in a Society which offered to enhance families' security, by amending its Ritual and publicly marginalising its significance. In 1826 Gold, Purple, Covenant and Remembrance Degrees had been added. In July 1834 John Tester, writing from Devon, reported the existence of a National Association for the Protection of the Price of Labour with hundreds of members in Bradford, Leeds, Dewsbury and Huddersfield. He claimed that this organisation's oath was the same of that of the Kidderminster carpet weavers and 'the initiation mode was the same as was practised by the flannel weavers of Rochdale'. He went on:

> A great part of the ceremony of the Trade Union society, particularly the death scene was taken from the ceremonial of one division of the Odd Fellows. The Society, as a combination for regulating the price of labour, originated with a party of Odd Fellows who were flannel weavers at Rochdale, in Lancashire; and all that could be well turned from the rules and lectures of one society into the regulation of the other was so turned, with some trifling verbal alterations. It soon spread extensively among the flannel-weavers of the place just mentioned, producing great excitement and at one time considerable confusion. One of the lodge rooms was broken into by the civil authorities and a lawsuit was the consequence.[52]

It has been said that deputies rushed from the AMC that year to destroy their record books and membership records.[53] In 1834 AMC modified the Ritual. It dropped the use of prayers, cassocks and Bibles and the Covenant and Remembrance Degrees. Burn mentioned of the AMC in 1834 that 'One very essential reformation was effected at the Bury AMC, in the abolishing the obligation of oaths'.[54] Spry stressed that since 1834 no oaths have been required during initiation or at any other time.[55] As Moffrey put it, 'The Hull AMC of 1834 was remarkable for the abolition of the oath at initiation and the adoption of a form more in accordance with the newer spirit of the Unity'.[56]

Expressions of loyalty became more common and the Making (initiation) and other degree lectures simplified. The Oddfellows instituted a promise on initiation rather than an oath. In 1837 the Oddfellows declared that

> If any member sing or give a toast or sentiment on religious or political subjects he shall pay a fine for the breach of the law ... the order discountenances Trades Unions and does not allow assistance to be given to those who leave their employment in strikes or turnouts – by this means promoting good will to all men.[57]

In 1841 the Oddfellows added a rule promising 'to assist every brother who may apply through sickness, distress or otherwise, if he be well attached to the Queen and Government, and faithful to the Order'. In 1848 the Grand Master, William Benjamin Smith, claimed that ritual and secrecy were 'secondary matters' to conviviality and that insurance was the priority for members, that the Unity was not a religious sect and that in due course those who focused on regalia 'would be looked upon as being so ridiculous that they will abandon [it] of their own accord'. Joseph Barrow, an Oddfellow leader from Rochdale said that signs and passwords were 'an honorary distinction more than of any real use'. Nevertheless, Deputies who took a trip from the Southampton AMC to the Isle of Wight, where the Queen had a residence, were 'shadowed by detectives, lest they might have nefarious designs against the person or property of Her Majesty'.[58] In 1849 James Roe, the secretary of the north London district reassured a select committee of the Commons that 'As a member of the association I am taught, even at my initiation, and by the general rules, that my first duty is to be faithful to the Queen and Government.' An official of the Order in Liverpool, Thomas Luff, told the same committee that Oddfellows were unlikely to be seditious as members were 'in the middle class of life, and who have property at stake and who would not risk anything of the kind'. He added that the 1848 change in rules requiring the consent of the minister prior to the delivery of a graveside oration was evidence of the loyalty of the Order to the Church.[59]

The Society continued to defend its privacy. The Noble Grand opened the Lodge with the words 'Guardian, Tyle the Door!' This meant that outsiders were excluded while the Warden examined the credentials of all those present and, if necessary, checked passwords. This was to establish that only members (i.e. those entitled to benefits) were present. Nevertheless, it appeared to promote secrecy. The 1855 Laws for the government of the Oddfellows regarding the lecture books made the continued importance of concealment clear.

- That the lecture book and supplement shall be kept in a box with two locks in the desk of some safe place; the Noble Grand shall keep one key and any Past Grand appointed by the lodge shall keep the other.

- That no officer or other member shall be allowed to take the lecture books or supplement out of the lodge under the penalty of two pounds two shillings which shall be paid into the district fund.

- That lodges occupying lodge rooms in outbuildings shall remove the box containing the lecture book and supplement into some safe apartment in the house where the lodge is held.

This description makes clear that while the Ritual was modified, the justifications of secrecy remained valid in the eyes of the Society.

For some it was the unknown and secret aspects of Oddfellowship which were the attraction. Secret societies were perceived as a route to power. Roberts argued that during the first century of the Oddfellows 'a large number of intelligent Europeans believed that much of what was happening in the world around them only happened because secret societies planned it'.[60] Secrecy was associated with gaining access to a higher truth. In 1847 Thomas De Quincey argued that secret societies were repositories of sublime truths. Secrecy was legitimate because it derived from a privileged access to a higher truth. Being a fraternity with secrets helped to ensure that the Freemasons were valued and that their activities endorsement by the social elite.

Other élite bodies also had secrets. Doctors, lawyers and MPs sought to maintain their distinctiveness through the symbolic swearing of oaths. To visit the Royal Society a man had to be introduced by a member who would introduce him to the secretary. He would then have to observe various ceremonies including the ritual transfer of the silver mace. In *The English Constitution* 1867, Walter Bagehot suggested that while it might be reasonable to extend the franchise (most adults in the UK were not allowed to vote until the twentieth century) the nation should be ruled by the Cabinet, 'the most powerful body in the state' the meetings of which were 'not only secret in theory, but secret in reality'.[61] Georg Simmel, the eminent nineteenth-century sociologist, writing about 'the role of the secret in social life', concluded that the secret offered, 'the possibility of a second world alongside the manifest world; and the latter is deeply influenced by the former'. He also noted that secrecy can be associated with power and jealousy of hidden information and that 'British parliamentary discussions were secret for a long time; and as late as under George III, press communications about them were persecuted as criminal offences, explicitly as violations of parliamentary privilege'. He saw secrecy as a social form, a strategy comparable to that of an 'adorning possession', perhaps like the jewels or regalia that some members wore. These indicated status, that the wearer was a person of mystery and power as some secrets were only for the ears of the higher ranks of the Order. The content of the symbols was not the most important factor. Status derived from the ways in which they were exchanged, the mechanisms of power through which they were conferred. That which was presented as true at the lower levels was revealed as shallow by further revelations. Joseph Burrows reviewed one of the secrets; 'we confine or ought to confine our family disputes within the walls of our own temples; and in this consists the true mystery of the order … Our order is an extended beneficial association. To this end all our forms, all our ceremonies tend.'[62] However, there were always further layers of secrecy, deeper, or possibly higher, levels of truth.

The Oddfellows sought to secure its acceptability as part of the mainstream by offering access to sacred truths, controlled recruitment and elaborate symbols and allegories. Simmel argued that there was a 'peculiar attraction of formally secretive behaviour … that what is denied to many must have special value'.[63] In that it can be possessed information can be seen as a form of property which can be given, acquired, sold or exchanged. The lodge can be seen as being like a market place where deals could be struck and information exchanged. Even if this information was seen as dangerous, illegal or threatening it was still desirable. Secrecy fuelled talk between people who do not know and those who do. Derek Elmer reiterated these aspects of the attraction of secrecy. He used to go to the pub with a friend

The gift to the corporation of Sunderland of a fountain which commemorated a Past Provincial Grand Master both emphasised that the Society supported the community and indicated members' respect for the memory of William Hall.

whose father was an Oddfellow. The Lodge met in the room above the pub. The two youths were initiated together in 1965. They joined, said Derek, because 'we wanted to see what the guys did upstairs'. In the latter part of the nineteenth century the Unity began to emphasis its modernity. In 1869 the Society replaced two of the degrees Scarlet – Knowledge and Gold – Science with Benevolence and Purity while White – Charity and Blue – Truth remained. The lectures, instead of being those of a campaigner for secularism who was often presented as an atheist, Holyoake, were written by Oddfellow actuary Charles Hardwick. This may

The Loyal Triumphant Hope Lodge, No. 1543 Winster opened in 1838. One of the earliest members was Joseph Greatorex, and many members of the family subsequently joined, including Arnold, Kenneth and Michael, pictured here. Michael Greatorex recalled:

I have a treasured photograph of the banner about to be put on parade at the bottom of Leacroft Road. It was taken on Wakes Sunday, 1955 when I was 10. The banner was carried by Henry Gregory and my father with the support of my late brother, Kenneth and me. Armistice Sunday was another time when the Oddfellows paraded behind the banner, wearing their sashes with pride.

MICHAEL GREATOREX, 'WINSTER ODDFELLOWS', WINSTER LOCAL HISTORY GROUP NEWSLETTER, NO. 30, NOVEMBER 2004. PHOTOGRAPH BY COURTESY OF MICHAEL GREATOREX

have been a signal that the Oddfellows craved the image of being dependable. However, the *Complete Manual of Oddfellowship* noted that many lodges continued to 'adhere to the older ceremonies and practise them in conjunction with the Lectures officially promulgated'.[64] In 1889 Baernreither suggested that rituals

have now only a subordinate importance, although certain formulas and passwords are retained which, together with the often most eccentric names of functionaries devices, symbols and emblems of the orders present a strange contrast to the thoroughly practical and sober objects of insurance against sickness and accident.[65]

By the 1920s there was less need for passwords and secrecy was perceived as a cause of the First World War and contrasted to the 'open diplomacy' promoted within Woodrow Wilson's Fourteen Points. It was also associated with spies and subversion. In its first century the Society was able, through recourse to notions of respectability and reciprocity to resolve the tensions between the need for compulsion and the benefits of voluntary engagement, the interest in open orderliness and the enthusiasm for secrecy. It found this balancing act more difficult to perform in the twentieth century.

III Reputable parades and excursions

A further means by which respectability was demonstrated was through parades and orderly, educational trips. Although it has been claimed that it was in 1841 that Thomas Cook pioneered the excursion, friendly societies had been organising such events, often with brass bands and feasting, before that date. For example in 1840 both the Oddfellows and the Foresters organised trips from Leeds to the north-east coast and Scarborough.[66] The tradition was maintained. Almost half the excursions leaving Birmingham in 1846 were organised by friendly societies, prominent among them being the Oddfellows. An Oddfellows' trip to London included a guide and was viewed as a potentially uplifting educational visit.[67] By the 1850s there were annual excursions, for example, the Metropolitan Oddfellows visited the Crystal Palace in 1856.[68] In 1877 more than 700 of the Foresters and Oddfellows of Coventry took a trip to Matlock and Chatsworth on Fair Tuesday, which was intended to be the first of a series of excursions.[69]

There are many accounts of the Society associating itself with loyalty, royalty and civic pomp. The Oddfellows of Partington parade in 1838 included many typical elements:

> On Monday last [27 August 1838] at Partington, the officers and brothers of the Loyal Thomas Hildyard Lodge of Oddfellows, of the MU held their first annual meeting. At an early hour Patrington was a scene of unusual animation; crowds were seen arriving from the several villages anxious to witness the proceedings of the day. At half past ten o'clock the officers, brothers and their friends assembled at the lodge and proceeded in procession to the church, headed by the band of the Hull Kingston Odd Fellows, who played several airs &c in their usual masterly style and were followed by almost every respectable inhabitant in the neighbourhood.[70]

The parade to mark the opening of the Derby Arboretum in 1840 was led by the town councillors who were followed by the Rechabites and the Oddfellows and then a number of smaller friendly societies. All the societies had at least one banner and the larger societies boasted several.[71] An Oddfellows banner was carried on the 1856 Salisbury peace parade at the end of the Crimean War.[72] In Lewes Oddfellows banners prominent during a Royal visit during which the crowds were policed by Oddfellow officers.[73] On another parade to honour the King a newspaper reported:

> The Independent Order of Oddfellows appeared the greatest in numbers, most respectable in appearance and most orderly in conduct of any of the numerous societies that attended on this occasion.[74]

On this Heart of Norfolk District banner fraternity is represented by a cross-class alliance of a man in a tailcoat and a man in a flat cap. There are a number of symbols of loyalty, Christianity and parochial pride. On the other side of the banner females feature as victims and virtues.

Parades and public demonstrations appear to have aided recruitment. John Tidd Pratt, the first Registrar of Friendly Societies, noted how the Oddfellows 'comes into the Parish or Village and takes all the young men away; they are led away by the music or paraphernalia which they have in their processions'. A report in *The Odd Fellow*, 1840, noted:

> On the whole the inhabitants of Newport have never witnessed such a procession, nor was any procession ever honoured with so many thousands of followers and spectators who were to be seen from every window fronting the streets as they passed.[75]

Some 30 years later Sir George Young made a similar point about the Foresters. Sometimes after a feast a Foresters court was founded 'because the people in the neighbourhood had observed the banners and decorations which were very pretty'.[76] When the AMC met in Worcester in 1865 there was a procession through the decorated streets with five bands, a gala with balloon ascents, entertainers and fireworks. There was also a banquet. The local newspaper editorial concluded:

> We heartily congratulate the Oddfellows upon their great meeting at Worcester. It is many years since a gathering of such social import took place in this city. As an institution almost wholly governed by working men, Oddfellowship is a monument of industry, perseverance, providence and administrative talent.[77]

The point was also made in Crewe in 1909 when there was 'plenty of room for improvement as far as Crewe lodges are concerned', and it was suggested that musical evenings might attract younger people to otherwise 'dull meetings'.[78] Parades might also have raised money. After marching behind the Volunteeer Band to the church, attending a service the Oddfellows of Aynho, Northamptonshire, 'paraded with the band through the village of Clifton to call upon the principal residents for subscriptions for defraying the expenses of the day'. These included a meal for 70, sports and dancing into the evening.[79] Similarly a procession in Bangor of members mainly of the 'artisan classes', called at a solicitor's, a bank, a coal merchant's, a coach maker, the house of Colonel the Honourable Sackville West and other places. At the meeting which followed the honorary members were thanked for their support.[80]

This interest in parades and regalia was a cause of concern to the Reverend Samuel Green, who presumably wore a dog collar and cassock and took part in church ceremonies and processions. In 1850 he argued that

> the Odd-fellows associations … and the like are but suspicious affairs. If their intention is to economise your resources and provide real help why do they spend so much of their funds in foolish feasting and nonsensical parades?

He advised readers, without suggesting an alternative venue, that they should 'have nothing to do with any club that meets at a public house or beershop'.[81] Reflecting on such views

A day out in Monmouth

The below account from 1828 of a feast day outing to Monmouth indicates that whatever occurred on the trip, the record was of an event which was seemly and joyous. This is conveyed by the elevated language ('The tinkling strings of the harp now summoned the votaries of Terpsichore to the pleasures of the mazy dance') and the reminders of the image of Oddfellowship as respectable. Within the space of the first sentence the Oddfellows both declares itself independent and also refers to the patronage of a Duke. The support of the church is implied by the reference to the merry bells and later the author makes clear that although the Headquarters for the day was a pub, the first thing that the members did on arrival was to be 'unanimous' in their admiration of the castle. It is probable that the 'foreign weed' was the respectable drug of the period: tobacco.

The Waterloo lodge of the Independent Odd Fellows made their annual summer excursion on Monday the 4th [of August] within the celebrated ruins of Ragland Castle, eight miles distant therefrom, the use thereof being kindly granted to them by A. Wyatt Esq. agent of the Duke of Beaufort. The preparations for the occasion were conducted with the same spirit-stirring zeal which has ever marked the proceedings of the Waterloo lodge. At six o'clock the merry bells of St Mary's tower proclaimed, in clamour loud, the commencement of this Odd Fellows' holiday. A little before nine, the full band marched up to the lodge house, in the street leading from which to the river the conveyances took their ground. The signal for starting off being given, the procession moved off, headed by the band with two cars and led by the Grand Master of the district in an open chariot-and-four followed by six other chariots, whilst the rear was made up of gigs, cars etc. making an aggregate of twenty-five conveyances on its entry into Ragland, besides numerous horsemen, pedestrians etc. At the village of Mitchel Troy the inhabitants had erected an arch of flowers and their example was followed at the turn-pike gate near Thloft-y-thloi and a third rose in its arial bow at the top of the hill leading into Ragland. The brethren and their friends dismounted at the Beaufort Arms Inn (the headquarters for the day) and immediately repaired to the Castle, in the Yellow Tower of which floated the Union Jack. Unanimous was the feeling of admiration on the survey of these far-famed remains of castellated splendour. After a cursory glance and slight refreshment being partaken of, a procession was formed on the terrace in front of the entrance gateway and eighty-four brethren walked in full costume with the insignia of the Order through the village returning to the castle in the same order amid the assembled crowds that lined the road. At two o'clock dinner was announced to which nearly 200 sat down under a large tent in the Fountain Court. The cloth being removed the usual routine of toasts were given and the pleasures of the evening were enlivened by some excellent singing and recitations composed for the occasion. The tinkling strings of the harp now summoned the votaries of Terpsichore to the pleasures of the mazy dance and two parties were soon formed on the bowling green to enjoy this, their favourite amusement. The Castle, at this time presented the most animated appearance the dancers on the green, tea parties in the tent, the porter's lodge crowded with an attentive audience to the vocal exertions of Mr and Mrs Allford who were professionally engaged, the summits of the South-West and other towers filled with lovers of the foreign weed and cheerful glass, the broad shadows of the mossy walls relieved by the scattered smiling groups employed in exploring the widely extended ruins adding to the general picturesque effect of the scene whilst the music of the band stationed in the Fountain Court reverberated through the 'proud baronial pile' devoted to ruin by the iron hand of Cromwell these were amid the sources of enjoyment to the numerous visitors on whom the shades of evening stole with but too rapid strides to interrupt the pleasures of the day.[82]

from a distance of many years John Clapham addressed the matter of public ritual through a rhetorical question:

> If too much of the savings went into banners, aprons, initiation ceremonies and liquor, there was some precedent in the history of gild pageantry, and a good defence in the failure hitherto of the new industrial society to furnish the colour, the ritual, and the cheer which men need and 'hands' had not been given. There were still crowns and garters and college feasts and city dinners. How could Manchester or Leeds, without 'public walks', art galleries, new buildings worth looking at or any civic splendour, expect these adult 'sons of toil' never to flout sound actuarial principles, or play with 'the follies and baubles of youth', when, by their own saving, they got the chance?[83]

Despite the Reverend Green, support for parades continued. Indeed

> the outdoor public meeting as a social phenomenon achieved a sort of apogee in late Victorian England … It is no coincidence that the word demonstration in the sense of a meeting entered the English vocabulary in the eighteen-sixties.

The Oddfellows of Fringford, Oxfordshire, leave the village church during the Edwardian period.
BY COURTESY OF MARTIN GREENWOOD

Images such as the bundle of sticks that cannot be broken – which appears here on the Fringford, Oxfordshire, banner – would have been familiar, and a reminder of the values of the Society.

On 9 August 1872 *The Times* commented that organising demonstrations was 'becoming a recognised branch of industry in this country', and by the 1880s it had, become a 'national mania', reinforced by official processions such as those for the Jubilees.[84] Cannadine has demonstrated that there was a rise in civic ritual and pageantry between the 1880s and 1914 and suggested that 'spectacles were not just the expression of this sense of community: perhaps they were the community'.[85] For the Society such events provided opportunities to inform people of the centrality of trust and order to Oddfellowship.

Parades frequently involved flags and banners. A banner was like military standards borne aloft in battles. It could remind people of the importance of collective male endeavor (because some banners were so large and prestigious that it was felt that only a group of men would have carried them) and could communicate a message which could be read above the noise at rallies where there were often several platforms with competing speakers and bands playing music. Later in the century they could be seen in the half-tone photographs which appeared in the popular press in reports on large-scale events.[86] Some Oddfellows' banners indicated the extent of their wealth on their banners. For example the 1894 banner of the Loyal Lodge, Provincial and Humane, No. 1448, Portsmouth District includes information about its longevity ('Estd 1844') and its security ('Members: 2000, Capital: £27,000'). This is framed in terms of respectability. It has the All-Seeing Eye above the Portsmouth Town Crest, a moon, a six-pointed star and a handclasp and mentions its name ('the Loyal Lodge') and the monarchy ('Jubilee Festival 1894').[87]

In 1890 when Cabinet Minister Henry Matthews, MP for East Birmingham, made the case against a ban on street demonstrations he gave the example of friendly societies. He wrote that 'these men are the pick of the working classes, perfectly orderly with an excellent object in view. It would be disastrous to get the police in collision with them.'[88] In 1894 in Warwick an annual feast and procession was announced in the local press in terms which stressed decorum:

> The members will proceed to the Episcopal Chapel, Upper Parade, Leamington where William Grice, MA incumbent of Wroxall (a member of the Order) will preach a sermon. Collection in aid of the parish church. The use of Newbold Wood walk having been granted members will dine together in Pleasure Grounds and will dance in the evening. Surplus funds will be devolved to the Widows and Orphans Fund.[89]

In 1906 there was a dinner in Leicestershire:

> The annual dinner of the Loyal Beaumont Lodge of Oddfellows, Manchester Unity took place on Tuesday. The members walked through the village [Coleorton, Leicestershire which had been dominated by the Beaumont family since 1426] to church headed by the Ibstock Excelsior Band. The sermon was preached by the Rev A.G. Meakin, vicar of Breedon on the Hill who took the subject of 'Benefit Societies on Earth and Benefit Societies in heaven'. On returning to the 'Beaumont Arms' the headquarters of the lodge,

The steps of the Taddington dance were said to resemble those of Maypole dancers in the village. Wearing Oddfellow regalia rather than Morris dancers' clothes the Taddington Lodge danced on their procession. The Taddington banner had guide ropes so that it could be borne by several men. It was illustrated with an image of the arms of the Society on one side (*opposite above*) and a picture representing the Good Samaritan on the other (*opposite below*).

the members sat down to dinner ... The band played selections during dinner and also in the afternoon.[90]

These are two of many examples of the Society demonstrating Christian orderliness. The 1910 AMC planned a public procession to church 'to offer thanks to Almighty God for the guidance vouchsafed and for the gigantic results which had sprung from the modest beginnings of 1810', and a banquet which the heir to the throne, the Prince of Wales had promised to attend.[91]

Irene Osborne, born 1910, and the daughter of an Oddfellow recalled the Society's parades in Taddington Derbyshire in the 1920s: 'They used to parade up to Church and have a service in Church and then they used to go back and have a good dinner ... then they'd start out after tea and do the morris dancing up the village.' Every year the Oddfellows would meet at the club room, parade to church at 10 a.m., accompanied by the band, 'there was the banner, two big flagpoles and two chaps used to walk under the banner with crossed swords,' said one of the dancers, Bill Needham. The banner was two-sided, showing the arms of the Unity on one side and an image of the Good Samaritan on the other. Bernard Brocklehurst, born 1906, remembered the 'high officials of the Order in their brilliant sashes ... and they'd all be walking smartly.' Bert Boam of Winster, which is just over 12 miles from Taddington, recalled the Loyal Triumphant Hope Lodge parades in his village, 'up the street with a band in front of them. And it was a big occasion!'[92] Elsewhere in Derbyshire Arthur Jackson recalled Oddfellows processions during the inter-war period:

> We had an annual procession round the village and collected for the local hospitals, because there was no health service then. [There was also an] annual concert in the village hall for the hospital fund ... All the Juveniles had rosettes, we hung them round our necks and me Dad had a huge sash. The NG had a purple sash. They were all very smart, bowler hats, like the men of Ulster.

In the 1920s in Tideswell, Derbyshire, the secretary of the Oddfellows, Norman Hill, told Cecil Sharp that in the June 'Wakes Week', the Oddfellows walked in procession to the church at noon and then held a dinner with the vicar present and toasts. This was followed by a procession around the village attended by members in regalia with a banner and a band. This ended at the club house where the band played the National Anthem. Norman Hill went on:

> At 6.30 Morris dance takes place. Some form of procession, but each dancer takes off his coat and carries 2 handks. They stop at chief inns and dance processional dance in stationary position. They make arrangements with public houses by which they pay a lump sum in return for which the landlord supplies them all with free drinks. They usually go to Dr. Parkes and dance some country dances on his lawn. On the Thursday, School Feast day, processional dance again performed by school-children and adults of both sexes. On Saturday the younger members of the Club dance in the same way as their elders on the previous Monday.'[93]

In nearby Taddington until the early 1930s the church service and parade were followed by a form of traditional, respectable dancing. Joe Gregory, c.1900–82, a member of the Society, recalled events there:

> They'd parade up and down the village, following the band and then the men used to be dancing with their white handkerchiefs. Me father and me eldest brother used to. Oh it was a great time. Relations used to come.

This Oddfellows Hall, at Haydon Bridge near Hexham, was built in 1869. Like many other such buildings it has found a new use. It became an Indian takeaway in 2000.

SILVER TABLEAU, 54 PIECES.
1ST PRIZE, FRIENDLY & TRADE SOCTYS DEMONSTRATION.
AUG. 7TH 1905.

Members in Newcastle won first prize when they demonstrated their regalia and ideas on a float in 1905.
BY COURTESY OF THE AUTHOR

Members joined hands, crossing over the road and waving white handkerchiefs to a tune, 'Pudding in a Lantern'. One observer, Gladys Copper, born 1911, said that it was similar to the maypole dance and her brother, Fred Percival, born 1908, referred to how sometimes the dancers would 'stop and do this circular dance'. The Oddfellows paraded through the village to the vicarage and then to the furthest pub and back, via all the other pubs (of which there between three and at least seven) with performances of the dance. Bill Needham, one of the dancers, recalled:

> When we got into the village from the Vicarage we started doing the Morris dancing. We used to do that all the way down the village as we were going along. We didn't do it up, [the George was at the lower end of the village] we used to do it coming back and where we stopped we'd give them a real good session … then we'd come back down to the George.

Like other public displays the event was a pleasant activity for both participants and spectators. Moreover, it aided unity and social intercourse. Fred Percival said that the event united those who had left the village.

They used to come from far and wide – you'd see them coming from Millers Dale station, whole families. They'd all come to the club feast, they'd never miss that. I can reel off dozens as were Taddington born as used to come.[94]

Ceremonies, both public and private, helped to remind members and potential members of the importance of ordered, organised mutuality. The joy of Oddfellowship was communicated to members and potential members alike. Church parades, feasts and processions were opportunities to demonstrate the orderly nature of the Order, to advertise to potential recruits that insurance could be convivial, that charity need not be cold and to potential patrons that members were respectable. Although he was not always an enthusiast of it, Grand Master Charles Hardwick argued that regalia was a form of advertisement.[95] Parades and sickness benefits were different sides of the same coin of Oddfellowship, there was a symbiotic relationship. Joan Henry remembered processions at the AMCs she attended. They were, she said, 'part and parcel of Oddfellows'. Dulcie Pauley remembered that in 1994:

When I became the Provincial Grandmaster of Plymouth Truro, the conference was held in Plymouth. On the Sunday we had a big service at the Pavilions and we assembled on Plymouth Hoe and marched down through the main street, the Royal Parade of Plymouth with all our emblems. We have a number of silver emblems and we had our service which was very uplifting and everybody enjoyed it.

Commercial firms also held parades. There were so many demonstrations designed to hold up the traffic in London that these were outlawed in 1853.[96] However, whereas insurance companies and other financial institutions employed bill posters, advertised in the press and featured in a number of novels, the Oddfellows relied on its own magazine and its own members.

The incentive for members to recommend to other men that they join was that their personal security and status within the Unity could be enhanced by ensuring growth. A member who joined in Durham in 1835 said it was 'a time when Oddfellowship was despised by many in this city, tolerated by a few and loved only by isolated individuals', while a Hartlepool rulebook of 1838 referred to the need to overcome 'obstructions' and the need to prove 'that Oddfellowship is more than a name'. Although there were pieces in the local newspapers about the benefits of thrift and the extent to which Oddfellowship was 'practical Christianity', and the Society had its own newsletter, largely the Oddfellows advertised by word of mouth.[97] In 1839 *The Odd Fellow* complained that 'it has often been a matter of surprise to us that of all the vast number of publications which in this age of bookmaking are constantly issuing from the press not one of them should notice Odd Fellowship, even by name'.[98] A poem recited at an Oddfellows Ball in 1842 and reproduced in a local newspaper might have been read as an advertisement for the Society as the below extract indicates:

To you, ye brethren of a sacred band,
Whose deeds bear witness for you o'er the land,

Oddfellows within village life

Robert Hird (1768–1841) a shoemaker who lived and worked in Emgate, Bedale, was not an Oddfellow. His description of the establishment and activities of the Philanthropic Lodge of the Unity where he lived is of interest because it presents the Society as an outsider saw it. Between 1832 and 1838 he wrote three sequences of a thousand verses each. The below rhymed quatrains date from 1835. He mentions the customs of attending funerals in white gloves and linking fingers, of ceremonial swords and a feast day and indicates the importance to the Oddfellows of conviviality, adornment and being a part of the village celebrations. This lodge had 220 members within five years and 390 at the time of the Royal Commission of 1874, with funds totalling £2,543.[99]

The Green Dragon's known for a good Inn
Jan Sadler she dwells there
And in her house vast company's seen
She don't let attention spare.

Her accommodation is well known
Her liquor mostly good
And in her house is many a room
Which is well understood.

Twas here the scheme it did commence
Young men they hither drew
Theirs not all a drinking sense
They'd try what they could do.

For one another's general good
Whilst on earth did stay
And pittance spare in youth which would
Assist them in decay.

In form and earnest they commenc'd
And entered their name
Within a book and their door fenc'd
With swords till an explain.

For a password each man receives
When that members go
Which is quite good and it relieves
And quite intruders too.

Thus their beginning it spread round
In numbers it did grow
And soon by death its good was found
For help the man did draw.

What was agreed if wife did die
For her interest then
Was seven pound then all did cry
The scheme was good for them.

And brethren like they did condole
And funeral attend
And o'er the corpse they had the paul
And all went, as one friend.

The process it was very grand
The brethren all in black
Silk scarfe, white gloves, but no hatband
But this it was no lack.

To church they moved, two by two
In union did go,
With finger link'd each couple through
Quite brotherly the shew.

And this, when it made men keen
And wives could not say nay
Another day was in the scheme
The grand processions day.

The talk'd of day it soon came on,
And members they did come,
With horse and gig, they came anon,
They flock'd into the town.

> Ye who go forth the widow's home to bless,
> Ye who are fathers to the fatherless,
> Ye who march onward in benign crusade,
> And the pale realms of woe and want invade,
> Waging with poverty untiring war,
> Benevolence your ever-guiding star,
> Whilst a proud banner floats your ranks above,
> Bearing your watchwords, 'Friendship Truth and Love'.[100]

For a brief period the Society was able to take advantage of the taxation and postal privileges of the Isle of Man. There was a tax on newspaper from 1830 but papers published on the Isle were entitled to free postage throughout mainland Britain after 1840. In addition, advertisement tax, stamp duty and paper duty were not due. William Shirrefs, a Chartist, printer and publisher was a member of the Mona Lodge, the first Oddfellows lodge on the Isle of Man, which opened in 1839. He launched the monthly *Odd-Fellows Chronicle* in 1844 which was sold for a penny halfpenny. This 'Journal of Literature, the Arts and Compendium of News' acquired official approval at the next AMC (Burn mentioned 'the chaste and useful character of its articles') and soon had a circulation of 10,000.[101] Profits went to the Isle of Man Widows and Orphans Fund.[102] The need for appropriate representation in the press was recognised at the time of the 1845 secession. The *London Journal and Pioneer* was established to present the case of the Society and this joined the *Odd-Fellows Chronicle*.[103] Despite these efforts adverse publicity may have influenced those contemplating membership of the Oddfellows. In these circumstances the Society needed its processions and banners to help members make members.

IV   Fraternity beyond the grave

Another form of parade which demonstrated the values of Oddfellowship was the funeral. When people moved to the new towns the Oddfellows provided structures, derived from familiar and living traditions of reciprocity, which helped families to survive. To those whose families might be far away it offered brotherhood and the reassurance that even after death, the brethren would show their appreciation of a worthy sibling. The evidence of the popularity of a brother, as demonstrated by an elaborate funeral, may have aided recruitment. The first resolution preserved in the Minutes of the Grand Committee stated 'that every brother provide himself with an apron at his own expense'. The second was 'that each member subscribe one shilling towards purchasing funeral regalia'. In 1815 it was decided 'that the death supporters carry drawn swords and be attired in caps and gowns', and 'that none but death supporters and tylers walk in caps and gowns during the procession'. It was further resolved

> That every brother appear in a white napkin and white stockings; also a white apron with
> the following binding:- Past and Present grands: scarlet sash with mazarine blue rosette

on the shoulder and tied with a mazarine blue; mazarine sashes to be tied with the sky sashes to be tied to the mazarine.[104]

A funeral fund was created at the annual session of 1816. Members were instructed to attend funerals and in some villages after the service the brethren would attend the home of the widow and hand over the sum due thanks to the membership of the Society of her late spouse. In 1817 Charles Tiplady, 1808–73, had his first encounter with the Society. It was in Blackburn when, aged nine, he saw

> a procession representing the funeral of the Princess Charlotte. There was a very long procession of Oddfellows, dressed in all the paraphernalia of that time, and many of them looked most lugubrious. Four men, dressed in white surplices, carried a coffin, in which was a representation of the Princess. Taste has improved in the town since that ghastly-grotesque feature of a street procession was conceived.[105]

The event did not deter Tiplady who became Oddfellows' Treasurer for the local Widow and Orphans' Fund for a decade. For the Society funeral processions, like other processions, were an opportunity to promote Oddfellowship.

Interest in the provision of a publicly acceptable funeral was boosted by legislation in the 1830s. The Anatomy Act, 1832, gave doctors and medical students access to corpses, often those of paupers that were unclaimed after death. It was not until 1844 that it became illegal for workhouse masters to sell corpses to medical schools. The 1832 legislation was very unpopular. Sheffield School of Anatomy was sacked by an angry crowd in 1835.[106] As the Act was passed to deal with the activities of resurrectionists and justified by the methods of delivery employed by Burke and Hare in Edinburgh, dissection was associated with criminality. Furthermore, there were widely held beliefs regarding the integrity of the corpse on Judgement Day.[107] *The Lancet* noted that throughout England

> the dread of dissection is there carried to such an extent that nothing is more common than for strangers to club together to bury a friend or neighbour, rather than allow the body to be taken to the dissecting-room.[108]

Radicals in Ashton argued that the legislation gave people a stark choice 'to be buried by a penny sick club or else send your bodies to the anatomical theatre'.[109] The legislation was both an opportunity and a challenge to the Unity for while many may have joined the Oddfellows following the passage of the Act, others were attracted to the newly developed joint-stock cemetery companies. These maintained their own fleets of coaches and hearses and assured potential clients of their modernity, tastefulness and low prices.[110]

The 1834 Poor Law (Amendment) Act was probably of greater significance to the growth of the Society. This legislation led to a fall in government expenditure on poor relief by 50 per cent to 1 per cent of the national income. The responsibility for the poor shifted from

Burial in Woking

In Woking Cemetery there was an 'Oddfellows' Acre' of land for the burial plots of Society members with an inscribed pedestal of white marble.[111] A broken column marked the place where Oddfellows gathered for funerals. The *Oddfellows' Magazine* described its opening ceremony in 1861:

The broken column marks the special gathering place of Odd-Fellowship at Woking Cemetery. An inscription on the pedestal tells us that this is 'The Burial Ground of the Metropolitan Districts of the Independent Order of Odd-Fellows, Manchester Unity Friendly Society. Inaugurated October 14th, 1861.' The emblems of the Society, beautifully cut in a block of white marble, shine out in fair relief from the rest of the monument, which is modestly and durably composed of Portland stone. On this autumn morning, the date of which is thus recorded – a breezy morning, with thin clouds scudding before the upper currents, and veiling the sun at times, hut never breaking into showers – a morning rich in all the variable beauty of light and shade, and fresh with sudden swirls and eddies of wild odour from the furze patches on the surrounding moorland – between four and five hundred of the brethren took solemn possession, on the part of themselves and their Order, of the four acres of ground assigned to them for a burial place in perpetuity.

The ceremony began with a religious service, after which a procession was formed, and the members traced the boundaries of the ground, which is very prettily laid out. Subsequently the Secretary of the Necropolis Company read aloud the deed of gift, consigning this portion of the land to the Society, and an appropriate address on the part of one of the members followed.

being that of individual parishes to being placed in the hands of newly created local Boards of Guardians which had jurisdiction over areas known as Poor Law Unions. The poor could, under certain circumstances, be offered places in sex-segregated workhouses rather than be assisted while living at home. Inmates received free food and accommodation but life in the workhouse was often bleak so as to deter any but the truly destitute from applying to live there. The prospect of the workhouse and dissection may have led many to join a friendly society. In the case of the Oddfellows, of the 30,074 lodges active in the 1870s nearly half (14,700) were established in the decade after 1835. Another effect of the legislation was greater official encouragement of friendly societies. In 1837 the Secretary of the Poor Law Commissioners Edwin Chadwick, issued an 'Instructional letter addressed to various Boards of Guardians on their formation'. This stated that

The Commission trust that you will, each in his own neighbourhood, do all in your power to promote the formation of habits of forethought, of frugality, and self-dependence as will keep them [the able-bodied poor] from falling back into pauperism, by aiding the establishment of sick-clubs, savings banks and annuity societies.

Although the law was supposed to apply across the entire country there were difficulties with implementation in some areas and it was never uniformly applied. Thomson argued that in the north and west of England there were lower levels of entitlement than elsewhere.[112] In such circumstances alternative arrangements became of considerable importance. There was considerable speculation about the regime within workhouses and agitation against them. Workhouses and their staff were attacked in a number of places. The resultant publicity might have made the benefits of membership more apparent to many men.

The following description, written in 1839, is of the first Oddfellow to be buried on the Isle of Man. It indicates the care and ceremony with which the Oddfellows ensured that a brother was laid to rest. Both those who attended and those who read the newspaper account would have been reminded of the respectful attitude of the Society towards their dead brethren.

On Sunday Afternoon, one of the members of the lodge of the above Order in this town, was interred in Kirk Braddan church yard. This being the first funeral of an Odd Fellow in the Island, the novelty of the occasion attracted a large concourse of spectators, amounting to many hundreds, who accompanied the procession of the brethren to the parish church, and we feel pleasure in stating that the whole proceedings were conducted in a manner which reflects credit upon the order at large, and more especially those of the brethren who accompanied their deceased brother to his last home.

In the following year a large crowd attended the funeral of Thomas Dinwoody an Oddfellow who was interred on the Isle of Man 'agreeably to the prescribed form adopted by the Order' according to the report in the local press.

The corpse was accompanied to the grave by upwards of one hundred of his brethren wearing black sashes and white gloves and an immense concourse of spectators who were attracted by the novelty of the scene. The oration was read in an impressive manner by Mr J. Stephenson Pro G.M. of the Isle of Man District which concluded the ceremony.[113]

In the same year, 1840, *The Hull Advertiser* reported:

On Sunday last the remains of David Hebden of North Frodingham, a young man aged 23, were interred at Skipsea. The deceased, being a member of the Briton's Pride lodge of Oddfellows at Frodingham a large number of members of the different lodges at Bridlington, Driffield and several of the adjoining villages attended the funeral to the place of sepulchre. The body was borne on a bier surmounted by a neat pall from the Driffield lodge provided for all similar occasions. The members followed in procession dressed in their funeral costumes of white aprons and white gloves and black sashes. As the long procession moved from North Frondingham to Skipsea … it formed a novel and imposing spectacle and attracted many villagers who seemed to be deeply interested in the proceedings. Upwards of 600 persons followed in the funeral train. After the burial service had been conducted the usual funeral oration of the order was read by Noble Grand Nicholson of the Briton's Pride lodge.[114]

Thyme is of the essence

In presenting Oddfellowship as a form of fraternity which could extend beyond the grave the Society was building on well-established conventions of how gifts could sustain communities and loyalty, be used as expressions of friendship and could help to ensure moral exchanges and continuous relationships.[115] For its ceremonies it also built on the familiar. At a funeral in Birmingham in the 1830s the members and officers of a wood sawyers society turned out as did representatives from other societies. Each man carried a bunch of thyme and, after the coffin had been lowered and the doxology sung, 'the trades came two by two to the grave, dividing at the foot, one on each side, shook hands and dropped the thyme on the coffin and returned to the deceased's house'.[116] The use of thyme became associated with the Oddfellows.[117] In 1839 thyme was dropped on a coffin in Chesterfield according to an account in a local newspaper headlined 'Funeral of an Oddfellow':

> On Sunday last the remains of Joseph Booth, of the Scaresdale Lodge, Chesterfield, were interred in the parish church yard when upwards of 130 members of the Order attended his funeral, in procession, wearing white gloves and black sashes. At the conclusion of the funeral service, an address (usually read on such occasions) was delivered by Henry Ford, a member of the Order, after which each of the members walked up to the grave and dropped into it a sprig of thyme.[118]

The tradition was maintained into the twentieth century. When William Spencer a PPGM and Lodge Secretary and when PPGM W. H. Plumb CS were buried in 1901 mourning brethren dropped sprigs of thyme on their coffins.[119] Fred Cooper, c.1910–82 recalled that in Taddington, Derbyshire, 'when there was a burial of an Oddfellow member there were Oddfellows' rites read over the grave thyme, a herb, that was thrown on the coffin during the ceremony.'[120] Echoes of such rites can be found in Oddfellow Arthur Jackson's memories of Kettleshulme, Cheshire, between the wars:

> If anybody died, a member, shortly after they were buried we went up to the church and everybody had white gloves on and we linked fingers and walked over the grave from top to bottom. The NG read a short service and that was that. Very tastefully done. All the people would go in black suits and bowler hats. After the church service we had the service by the grave.

In the 1990s a leaflet outlining procedures for an Oddfellow funeral opened with the words:

> Lodges shall have power to make such arrangements as they think proper for the attendance of members at the funeral of a deceased member or the wife of a member. Sprigs of thyme (or similar) to be provided to members.

There was a funeral address and then

> Members are to respond 'Amen' and immediately after, to file past the grave or coffin and throw the sprigs of thyme (or similar) in token of esteem.

While not obligatory the Noble Grand can refer at the Lodge of Remembrance, to the member who has 'passed to the Grand Lodge above'. There is a silent toast, using signs without words and the singing 'The Day Thou Gavest'. This ritual helped to unite both those present at a funeral with one another and to connect them to long gone Oddfellows and, perhaps to future ones. It reminded people that Oddfellows cared for their brethren.

The details as to the requirements of a funeral changed but interest in one being arranged did not. In 1867 the Coventry District Annual Report noted that which was supplied for a funeral:

A Mourning Coach and Hearse, also Pall, Hatbands and Scarves are now supplied at the expense of the District at the funeral of any member or his wife whose internment takes place within a radius of eight miles of Coventry.[121]

In an account of the life of gardener and handyman Frederick Grover (called Bettesworth in the book) who died in 1905 aged about 68, George Bourne recounted how a couple of months before his death Bettesworth, who had recently been both seen by the Oddfellows' doctor and spent time in the workhouse, was concerned that payments be maintained. Although he was illiterate 'he produced two membership cards in support of his statements'. When his wife died he was able to make a claim to cover some funeral expenses and ensure that she was buried in an elm coffin.[122] Anybody who saw members of the Society parading, whether to a church service or a graveyard, would have seen the message that this was an organisation which could be trusted. The idea that paying final respects might also be instructional was echoed in Australia in 2005. A report of a 'Lodge of Sorrow' held for Sister Dot Maher, a Past District Grand Master noted:

This was the best way for members to pay their respects in true Manchester Unity style – it was a full Lodge Meeting and our Social Members found out at first hand how we revere the memory of members when they pass to the Grand Lodge above.[123]

It has always been useful for the Society to be able to adapt to local conditions. In Watford, the Oddfellows Hall used by the Grand Union Lodge of the Great Berkhampstead District is located in The Avenue. The address and appearance of the building will be familiar to those who live in the area.
ODDFELLOWS COLLECTION

By contrast, in the nineteenth century, non-members might leave their families destitute, might be neglected in times of illness and might be buried in a pauper's grave following dissection by medical students. Ownership of the corpse and many commemorative rites were denied to paupers' next of kin. Some Poor Law Guardians replaced coffin nameplates with chalked numbers and forbade mourners from throwing soil on the coffin, entering the cemetery chapel or providing headstones. Stretford Burial Board stipulated that ownership of private graves reverted to the municipality if owners failed to install a headstone within six months of the first interment.[124] Many Oddfellows also maintained connections with the deceased through gravestones noted their membership such as the one which informed readers that Thomas Fletcher provided '50 years of continued usefulness to the Order'.[125] A gravestone in St Peter's Church, Wakefield has the inscription:

> Joshua Stringer who died Jun. 23 1866 aged 71. He honestly discharged the duties of corresponding secretary for the Wakefield District of the Independent Order of Oddfellows Manchester Unity during the period of 17 years. His los [sic] they lament and whose memory they revere. This stone was erected by members of the above district. Ann Stringer wife of the above died 16 Dec. 1860 aged 49.

The period was one when burials and memorials were considered of great importance. The Oddfellows had its own plot in Pimlico which had a seven-foot high sculpture of figures representing Faith, Hope and Charity 'together with the symbol of the order "Friendship, Love and Truth"'.[126] The Society was not unique in providing inscribed stones, it was reflecting and buttressing the experience of respectable men.

The Oddfellows presented a form of fraternity that was law-abiding and rested on long-standing traditions of respect of duty towards the earthly remains of a departed brother. It has been suggested that there was clear social division between the roughs, who were reckless, cowardly and dishonest, and the respectable who outwardly conformed to what were deemed to be appropriate levels of moral rectitude, economic continence and self-sufficiency.[127] Bailey has argued that, 'to the Victorian bourgeois there was no confusion as the elect and non-elect in working-class life.[128] While this may have been an overly neat compartmentalisation, the Oddfellows made some attempt to adhere to elements of the external form of those Bailey called 'the elect'. Through its processions, including the funerals it provided, it demonstrated that it was not a trade union, a charity, an insurance company, a Freemasons' lodge or a Sunday School, though it might have had affinities with such bodies, and that it did not threaten the values and beliefs of the Established Church.

V   Respectable leaders

While it oversimplifies to argue that that membership of a friendly society 'was the badge of the skilled worker', as Gilbert claimed, it was often the conventionally respectable skilled workers who played significant roles in running the Oddfellows.[129] Even though, as Neave indicated, 64 per cent of Oddfellows in the East Riding were involved in heavy outdoors labour on farms, the formal printed sources presented to Royal Commissions stressed that the Society was dominated by craftsmen.[130] This aided the presentation of the Oddfellows as respectable. As labourers rarely had the flexible time or organisational skills to run a lodge many village societies called upon the better-off to take on such tasks. Peter Gosden found that business-owners constituted a majority of over 100 principal leaders of the Oddfellow and the Ancient Order of Foresters in the nineteenth century.[131] David Neave found that the Oddfellows' leadership included such men as George Kendall. A land surveyor and insurance agent, assistant overseer, assessor of taxes, clerk to the School Board, Churchwarden, Kendall was a sometime schoolmaster and also a leading figure in the Oddfellows' Aeneas Lodge.[132] Other studies have found a preponderance of skilled men running the Order. Between 1835 and 1863 the *Oddfellows' Magazine* presented brief biographies of leading Oddfellows. The occupations of 69 of them can be traced. There is a clerk to a Poor Law Union, a saddler (employee) and two full-time Secretaries of the Order (William and Henry Ratcliffe). None of the others is an employee.[133] Among those who appeared to be able to afford to take time off work to attend meetings without remuneration were several proprietors, doctors and farmers, a Baptist Minister, the Principal of a school and the owner and editor of the *Southampton Examiner*. It may have been that initially members, who were recruited by other members, sought out those with similar outlooks and resources to those men whose trades encouraged them to go on the tramp.

All over the country the Order often attracted respectable men to positions of public prominence. The Earl of Warwick Lodge, Stratford was established by a trunkmaker and a tailor, eight years later in 1839 a doctor became a member and in 1842 an upholsterer became an honorary member.[134] In Stockport in 1840 there were only a few unskilled men among the 1,533 Oddfellows in the District while between 1859 and 1873 the admissions register of the Oddfellows 'reveals the strong presence of craft, skilled and lower-middle-class occupations'. The 'appeal was to the broad mass of regularly employed and relatively well-paid operatives'.[135] Many of the officers of the Loyal Vale of Clun Oddfellows Lodge, based near Lydbury North were 'the more substantial members of rural society'.[136] A study of friendly societies of Cambridge, where there were a number of Oddfellows' lodges, concluded that 'although the majority of ordinary friendly society members were from the working class, the leadership of the movement was dominated by members from the lower middle class'.[137] The leadership of the King William IV Lodge, Lancaster, was dominated by men with higher incomes than many in the town, including many employers involved in the building trades and independent artisans.[138] The Rev Dr Hook of Leeds joined 'upwards of 40 MPs and numerous clergymen and dissenting ministers of every persuasion' when he was initiated as an Oddfellow in 1842.[139]

Those members of the Pleasant Retreat Lodge, Preston whose names appear in the 1851 and 1861 censuses include master artisans, a journalist, the owner of the *Preston Chronicle*, a local councillor, a magistrate and a manufacturer. It also attracted Joseph Nicholson, a spinning master whose son Tom (see *Biographical notes*) followed his father into the lodge.

Fetes and dances have long been popular within the Society. The advertisement from 1852 (*above*) indicates the support of a duke, a marquess, an earl and a dozen MPs. This emphasis on respectable supporters might have been a reaction to the publicity resulting from an Old Bailey court case of 1848. At a trial it was claimed that on one Oddfellows Thames steamer excursion members' riotous behaviour had culminated in their threat to throw the captain overboard.

BY COURTESY OF CHRISTINE PAYNE

The 1960s saw an attempt to attract younger people through the creation of Intermediate lodges. These offered a variety of social activities, including (*top right*) dances.

BY COURTESY OF FRANCES WILKINSON

Impresario and showman on the London variety stage Sam Torr gave John Merrick – the Elephant Man – his first stage work in 1884. He also recognised the market for an Oddfellows song sheet (*right*): 'I'll sing about Oddfellowship, the Order I adore ...'

BY COURTESY OF THE LIBRARY AND MUSEUM OF FREEMASONRY

Those joining the Joseph Warburton and Rose of England lodges in Middlesbrough between 1841 and 1845 included traders, a grocer and a merchant who was later a leading Teesside ironmaster and MP, skilled men (including a tailor, a brewer and a mason) and a professional, a doctor.[140] In Durham the occupations of the 557 men who joined one lodge between 1868 and 1914 have been examined and compared to the census figures for 1871. It appears that joiners, grocers and police constables were over-represented in the Star of the North while miners and masons were under-represented. In the lodge 33 per cent of the men were skilled. 16 per cent were shopkeepers, hotelkeepers and publicans and 13 per cent white collar workers. Although Johnson argued that clerks, who may not have earned more money than many blue collar workers, tended to avoid friendly society fellowship, perceiving it as incompatible with their aspirations, there were some white-collar members of the Society.[141] Almost all the Corresponding Secretaries of the District of South Durham and North Yorkshire 1837–73 were skilled men. Publicans dominated, followed by shoemakers, joiners and tailors and there was also a solicitor. There was a similar social profile among the occupations of the district's examining and relieving officers, while Provincial Grand Masters tended to be initially skilled manual workers but latterly white collar workers. The exception was an unskilled foundry worker who became a PGM.[142]

The occupations of half of those who held the posts of Provincial Grand Master, the Deputy Provincial Grand Master, the Corresponding Secretary or Trustee of the Lynn District Oddfellows 1867–1915 have been identified and only one was an agricultural labourer. Others were traders, merchants, landowners, a solicitor and a ship owner.[143] By contrast, in 1849 there were 24 Foresters' Courts (the equivalent of lodges) in the King's Lynn and West Norfolk District. Most of the members were labourers while within the 17 Oddfellows' lodges which charged a higher entry fee, there were farmers, shopkeepers and artisans. The fee differed depending on the age of the person seeking to join. In 1854 at the upper age bracket it was 12s. 6d. for a man aged 35–40 to join the Foresters and a £1 (20 shillings) for him to become an Oddfellow.

In some areas poorer men joined, but they may well still have been among the wealthier in their locality. In Middlesbrough, over a quarter of the 61 men who joined the Victoria Lodge, 1898–1910 were labourers with 25 occupations mentioned overall while of the 53 who joined either the R. H. Bulman or the Erismus lodges between 1892 and 1912 only ten per cent were labourers with clerks and skilled men joining in significant numbers.[144] When the Oddfellows opened a lodge in Banbury it attracted labourers but in general poorer men favoured village or county societies (which often had the support of wealthy patrons) or the Foresters.[145] One account of life in an Oxfordshire village at the end of the nineteenth century suggested that to join the Oddfellows was significantly more expensive than to become a member of the Compton Pilgrims Friendly Society.[146] Although the evidence suggests that most of those who joined the lodge in Chipping Norton, Oxfordshire were agricultural labourers there were also many who were artisans and clerks, shop assistants and deliverers.[147]

In 1880 the Oddfellows valuation revealed a deficit of greater proportions than had been expected because the actuaries included, for the first time, the additional liability caused by members following hazardous occupations.[148] Scales of payments were developed which took account of age, health and occupation. The need to retain financial stability and respectability took on a different aspect. Although the Oddfellows attracted miners, they constituted 4.93 per cent of all Oddfellows in 1848, there was some ambivalence about their membership. In 1862 Henry Ratcliffe, the Corresponding Secretary argued that lodges with more than the average number of miners and colliers as members, by then almost 6 per cent, should pay greater contributions as the nature of their work made it difficult to allow them to remain members while still enforcing actuarially sound scales of contributions and benefits. That year a ruling was made which allowed districts to raise the initiation fees, or reduce the pay-outs in the event of their deaths, of those engaged in such work. In some parts of Derbyshire lodges refused to admit miners, though in other parts miners dominated the lodges. In 1874 the Corresponding Secretary of the Plymouth District, James Spry, reported on effect on the tin miners of the area when the Oddfellows sought to charge them more:

> They are a strange race. When they take a thing into their heads, they will follow each other all over the district and nothing can stop them. Thus formerly there was a West Cornwall District, with centre at Hayle, several lodges and some hundreds members. When the first step was taken towards a graduated scale, great discontent ensued; and a great battle in which Mr Ratcliffe, the Secretary was ousted for deflacations caused the collapse of all credit in the society. [A survey of 1874 suggested that only about 10 per cent of lodges were solvent, although this does not take not account of the many secessions]. The lodges began breaking up and seceding and of all the district only the Truro lodge was left … The miners have taken to the Philanthropic [i.e. the Loyal Philanthropic Association, a local miners' order] and we do not in all lodges admit them.[149]

Similarly in 1905, following what was probably a dispute over the level of contributions, two lodges of mainly iron-stone miners seceded in Guisborough, Yorkshire, and re-registered as Pease Oddfellows Friendly Society and the Chaloner Oddfellows Friendly Society.[150] In order to ensure that payments received could be balanced with payments to members the Oddfellows tried to be actuarially sound. This caused resentment and confusion and was sometimes unpopular. However, sound membership, respectable figureheads and firm leadership were increasingly perceived as being of importance to the survival of the Society. In 1930 it was decided to relieve members following hazardous occupations and who were initiated before 1921 of an additional payment of 25 per cent on their contributions when their lodges required Unity relief.[151]

VI Conclusion

In *Hamlet* Shakespeare had a unpleasant character advise his son against one version of reciprocity: 'Neither a borrower nor a lender be, For loan oft loses both itself and friend, And borrowing dulls the edge of husbandry.'[152] Countering Polonius' view that loans can cause resentment and supplant thrift ('husbandry') the Oddfellows took another well-understood and successful economic and social idea, that of the gift. It offered a solution: a structure rooted in conventional wisdom which could promote friendship and money in hard times without undermining frugality. The Society strengthened this by adapting gifting to the burgeoning market economy, creating a system of formal fraternity. It still had to rely on trust and brotherly behaviour and, to encourage these, the Order promoted order. To attract and keep members the Oddfellows had to demonstrate that it structured reciprocity, that a person who joined could expect, over the course of time, to both give and receive and that the gifts would be proportionate, measured and agreed. The Oddfellows relied not on advertisements in the press but appearances by its members. It was the members who made members. It was they who were the public face of Oddfellowship, who could belie the view that it was an organisation committed, through secret oaths, to the Devil or the revolution. Travelling the country, as tramps or on trips, or in orderly processions, members demonstrated the values of Oddfellowship. Its parades and funerals were opportunities to indicate its discipline and loyalty to both brethren and the wider social order. Beneath their banners, wearing their sashes, they sought to show that the Society was respectable, trustworthy and that potential recruits should have no fear that their money would be stolen or ill-spent or that the Society would collapse under the weight of its debt. Its internal structure ensured that there was both continuity and the possibility of change. Its hierarchy favoured the men with the skills to run the Unity in a sound manner. Although there were dishonest members, divisions, disputes and local difficulties, the system of quasi-autonomous lodges, in which men could rely on those they knew, and if necessary call upon thousands across the globe, was robust. It was the well-established procedures for the redistribution of wealth to those brethren in need, as well as to others requiring charity, which enabled the Oddfellows to become respectable and to create an international network of trust and reciprocity.

CHAPTER FOUR

Citizenship and security

T HROUGHOUT the nineteenth century mortality tables were developed and the Oddfellows had, despite considerable internal divisions, considerable recourse to such data. By the end of the century it was producing its own data which was considered so sophisticated and accurate that it became the basis for government action on National Insurance. It was by drawing on such data that the Oddfellows could see the changing age and health profile of the membership and could make an informed decision to try and reduce its commitments by campaigning for the introduction of state pensions. 'What was wanted,' the Grand Master explained in 1907, 'was a properly devised old-age pension scheme to suit all classes of friendly society members as well as the community at large.'[1] The increasing importance of what the Bishop of Winchester elevated in his address at the centenary AMC Service to 'your *principles* of financial stability and actuarial statistics' will be considered in the first section.[2] In common with many friendly societies the Unity 'employed respectability as a resource throughout the nineteenth century ... to forge an arena of autonomy for working-class mutualism'.[3] Members' campaigns for political rights were an important element of the Society's construction of respectability. It is this aspect of how it sought to secure sociability that is addressed in the second section. The connections between struggling for political status and economic security are addressed in the third section. This examines one of the most widespread images in the Society, which appeared on banners, badges and in the names of lodges: the Good Samaritan. The parable can be employed to illuminate the important aspects of Oddfellowship. Its popularity demonstrates the importance to the Oddfellows of well-structured reciprocity, tempered by masculine, Christian, charity towards strangers.

I   Financial safety

Although the fraternal elements of Oddfellowship were of considerable importance, there were other organisations which offered fraternity. During the period when the Oddfellows was experiencing rapid growth, other affiliated orders were being developed in the north-west of England and elsewhere, including the United Order of Free Gardeners, formed in 1820, the Loyal Order of Ancient Shepherds, Ashton Unity, formed in Lancashire in 1826, the Ancient Order of Foresters, formed in 1834 (from an earlier organisation which had branches from 1813) and the Independent Order of Rechabites which opened its first 'tent' (equivalent to a lodge) in Salford in 1835. In order to grow the Oddfellows needed to distinguish itself from such organisations. Many friendly societies were caught, as Simon Cordery noted:

> between their economic function as insurance bodies and their cultural role as suppliers of leisure activities and fellowship. Maintaining financial solvency was a balancing act which involved satisfying convivial demands to remain in business and retaining sufficient funds to meet sickness and death benefits.[4]

To ensure its own survival in this competitive market the Oddfellows had to reformulate the contemporary notion of the gift in a distinctive fashion. Perhaps because it also noticed the success of insurance companies during the first 40 years of the Society it presented itself not only as a charitable, civil, community with a culture of reciprocity but also as a commercially viable operation.

The English life insurance scene has been characterised as enjoying 'a rash of company flotations' in the 1840s with 56 viable life offices floated between 1830 and 1844 and a further 80 between 1845 and 1852. In January 1837 there were 74 life companies in operation and 152 by the end of 1851. In 1840 the Yorkshire Fire & Life Insurance Company had a prospectus which could have been aimed at potential Oddfellows. It claimed:

> He who will not insure will be looked upon as a not less detestable wretch than he who will not work for his children's bread and his memory after death will not be held in less contempt.[5]

Life insurance developed swiftly with the formation of a mutual life insurer in 1843. By 1847 there were seven mutuals owned by their policy owners and 19 by 1849. Most of the investor-owned companies had stopped selling life insurance by 1853. Treble concluded that growth was due to three inter-related factors:

> First most life offices accepted over time the bonus principle, linked to 'with profits' policies, as the most dynamic strategy for building up new business. Second, effective use was made of the evolving skills of the actuary to produce more reliable tables of mortality experience and to lower premiums on certain types of risk. Third, advertising techniques and an evolving network of insurance agents were employed to sell the virtues of life insurance to a burgeoning middle class.[6]

The Oddfellows may not have had the same range of policies or paid agents but it could make effective use of mortality data in order to advance. The Oddfellows was able to move from simple redistribution to more complex forms of redistribution as actuarial data became more sophisticated. In 1816 John Curwen MP 'the father of National Insurance' and owner of several collieries, and his wife, both of whom ran friendly societies, made data available and publicised the disbenefits of faulty actuarial information.[7] In 1824 the Highland Society of Scotland published actuarial data which was of considerable accuracy. In 1835 an actuarial textbook provided a set of tables based on the experience of friendly societies in England was produced. However, levies, whip rounds and charity and payments made to the landlord for room hire 'wet rent' were ignored which made the figures of limited value as a reflection of Oddfellow practice.

There were also attempts by the government to gather data and promote actuarial soundness. The first legislation specifically to mention friendly societies, the 1793 Act for the Encouragement and Relief of Friendly Societies aimed at 'diminishing the Publick Burdens'. A desire to reduce the rates drove much of the subsequent regulation and quantification of friendly societies. The poor, and particularly the ill poor, were perceived as a burden on the rates, and in the nineteenth century the emphasis was on selective, coordinated, effective, efficient and educative relief. Societies registered under the 1793 Act had to have their rules approved by Justices. The Oddfellows did not register for many years. In 1818 a Bill was introduced to appoint public valuers to examine tables and rules but the Bill was not passed. In 1819, influenced by parliamentary committee discussions on the Poor Law, legislation was passed that all rules and tables should be checked by actuaries and approved by Justices.[8] There were insufficient actuaries to do this and the data was inadequate. JPs were authorised to publish general friendly society rules but many accepted as 'persons skilled in calculation', local schoolmasters and others who had no real knowledge of the technical difficulties of the subject. At that time ratepayers could receive rates-funded assistance with pensions or funeral expenses and friendly society arrears could be paid from the rates in order to stop people becoming more of a burden on the rates.[9] The legislation simplified the system of society registration and encouraged regular returns of sickness and mortality experience from societies. Registered societies had to make quinquennial returns and have their rules confirmed by a barrister, John Tidd Pratt who became first Registrar of Friendly Societies.[10] He was one of those who drafted the 1834 Poor Law (Amendment) Act. It was in part based on the 1829 Friendly Societies Act which has been perceived as a significant stimulus to the growth of friendly societies.[11] The 1834 legislation was in turn a model for the 1875 Friendly Societies Act.[12] Both friendly societies and poor law administrators were regulated in regions by district auditors and both sought to measure lives in similar ways.[13] The connection was made in the press. The *Northern Star* reported in 1839 that during the last six months the Oddfellows of Leeds had paid over £517 for funerals and about £200 a week to sick members and that this 'must be a great relief to the parochial funds'.[14] The regulation of those in receipt of friendly society pensions and those in receipt of state pensions, former military, postal and naval personnel, reflected the similarities in the ways that these bodies rewarded those who were loyal and moral.[15]

In encouraging the Society to move towards actuarial security governments were pushing at an open door as far as many within the Society were concerned. Information derived from the quinquennial returns to the Registrar for the period 1836–1840 was published in 1845. The data and the fact that many lodges were starting to falter, led some within the Society to look towards a change in the benefits strategy as a means of survival. In 1842 there were some 3,500

Oddfellow lodges but in 1843 alone 225 closed through lack of funds. Lodges were setting contribution levels which were too low and much of the AMC's time was spent considering individual cases in need of relief. The solution to such problems was a matter of dispute. In 1843 the *Magazine* argued that 'experience is one of the best teachers, and we generally find that there are amongst our members men possessed of sufficient judgment and forethought to enable them to take proper measures of precaution.' On the other hand, five months later, in 1844, one writer proclaimed that, 'if anything can be done to extend or perpetuate the benevolent objects of the Order, to a greater degree than has hitherto been done, no man living would be more eager to entertain and accomplish it then myself.' Another opined that fraternity attracted new members arguing that 'Hundreds have joined our order, knowing as has been eloquently observed, that the Oddfellows has higher and holier ends than mere pecuniary recompense.'[16] If the majority of Oddfellows were to maintain their allegiance to the Order then changes would need to be made with the agreement of those members. The tensions between government regulation, leaders who recognised that they had to comply and membership resistance arose many times over the course of the first two centuries of Oddfellowship.

The solution agreed at the 1844 AMC was that lodges should provide information about membership figures and funds on an annual basis in order for tables of benefits to be created. A table of contributions devised by the actuary of the Guardian Assurance Company was circulated. There was, reported Moffrey, a 'stormy discussion' and it was decided that lodges which failed to make returns were to be suspended. Despite the warnings that to retain the *status quo* would be to break the virtuous circle of structured reciprocity, change was not universally popular. Opponents of the plans produced 'a flood of scurrilous songs and pamphlets', and lodges representing almost 16,000 members refused to comply.[17] Many of them left to join the breakaway National Independent Order of Oddfellows.[18] A high proportion of the secessionists lived in Lancashire and Yorkshire and would have been members of the older lodges, which had controlled their own funds for many years. These lodges would have been included older men, who were more likely to want to call on sickness benefits.[19] In addition, the 1844 AMC restructured the districts in a way which reduced the influence of the older lodges of the Manchester area. Directors could come from any district, not just in and around Manchester. This may have been another reason why 'the Manchester and Salford lodges threw down the gage of war [as] the cradle of the Order became a hotbed of sedition,' as Moffrey put it.[20] Gosden suggested there were two reasons for the breakaway, noting that the 'struggle for reform and solvency dominated the story of the Oddfellows in the middle years of the century'.[21] One of those involved in the dispute, James Burn, recognised that the argument was being waged within different intellectual frameworks:

The opponents of the proposed change were not attempting to disprove or impugn the accuracy of Mr Smith's statements and calculations but contending that it was an insidious attempt to divert the Order from its original benevolent purposes and designs and to assimilate it in principles to an assurance company.[22]

The Mr Smith to whom Burn referred was W. B. Smith of Birmingham, a Director and Grand Master in 1847. He drew on the Highland Society's experience and explained the probability of financial collapse if changes were not made. Spry also put the matter in broader terms when he called the actuarial sophistication of the Society 'a blessing to the country and the whole Anglo Saxon race, wherever they may be found, who seek shelter under its branches'.[23]

In 1845 there was what one witness called 'a strong discussion' over a motion to promote financial stability. It was realised that a large number of lodges had in financial terms, 'deplorable practices'. The AMC required increased contributions and ordered lodges to keep separate sickness and funeral benefits and separate district management funds. Management funds were separated from benefit funds and lodges were instructed that although they could fix their own rates they had to be such that each halfpenny a week contribution provided 1s. a week sickness benefit and a £1 at death. These rates limited branch autonomy and were still inadequate in that they were not graduated by age. Francis Neison, having examined the figures for the entire Unity noted that while there was a deficit of £200,000 and the Order had £700,000 in its reserves, it should have ten times that figure. The Order had recently recruited a lot of young men and that 'the majority of lodges have not yet found the weight of their liabilities and will not do so until young men have grown old'. He concluded that the 'inevitable dissolution of the Order of Odd Fellowship ... is certain'.

The decision to move towards a sound basis for rating was a significant signal that the Oddfellows wished to lead the way among the affiliated orders.[24] It also promoted greater legal security. Following the theft of funds by a Corresponding Secretary the Society petitioned for protective legislation and gave evidence to the Lords Select Committee. In 1848 a Bill was drafted and although, following disagreements it was withdrawn, the 1850 Friendly Societies Act increased protection for registered lodges. The growth areas for the Society were in the south, where similar problems relating to income and expenditure occurred a few years later. Between 1846 and 1849 membership fell from 249,261 to 234,490 and by 1875 a further 1,215 Unity lodges had been dissolved or expelled or had withdrawn.[25]

Potential members of the Society might have read of rogue insurance schemes in popular novels. 'Literary writers repeatedly – and after 1845 increasingly – appropriated economic and financial themes and real-life situations for fictional treatment.'[26] Thackeray's *Great Hoggarty Diamond* satirised the scandal of the Independent and West Middlesex Assurance Company (which claimed to have a million pounds when it opened in 1837 and whose directors fled the country with £250,000 in 1840) while Dickens described the fraudulent Anglo-Bengalee Disinterested Loan and Life Assurance Company in *Martin Chuzzlewick*. There were also cases of embezzlement in his *Hard Times*, securities fraud in Margaret Oliphant's *Hester*, and a lying banker who misinvests in Eliot's *Middlemarch*. Moreover, although Poovey argued that during most of the nineteenth century 'economic and literary writers both continued to stress the generic differences between them', many working-class readers may not have made that distinction. Rose concluded that they 'read all these texts in the same way: as ripping yarns but also as gospel truth'.[27] In the circumstances the case being made for the actuarial tables which the Society promoted may have been bolstered.

The Oddfellows sought legal protection under the provisions of the 1846 Friendly Society Act, a piece of legislation which, by shifting the supervision of friendly societies from local JPs to central government, concluded a process begun in 1829. The Society wished to register partly because it would allow it to prosecute in cases of fraud and refusal by Trustees to surrender money in their trust. In 1847 the Irish Oddfellows appealed for help to enable them to cope with the effects of the failure of the potato crop. It was agreed that all subscriptions would be channelled through the Corresponding Secretary, William Ratcliffe. However, he then placed the funds into his own account claiming that the money would be safe there. He was suspended and his brother Henry took over as CS. William removed the books and the capital and was expelled and prosecuted. The issue of legal protection took on a new urgency. Lodges petitioned the Commons for change but the Directors were also instructed not to accept alterations which undermined the autonomy of the lodges. During a period when the Order was, in some areas at least, closely associated with radical politics it did not want government interference in its federal structure. In addressing a question as to whether the Society would change its rules as a condition of receiving legislative concessions William Benjamin Smith's evidence to Parliament in 1847 made clear the importance of legal protection. Speaking only a few years after the secession of the Americans in 1843 and the 'civil war' of 1844–45 he claimed that many Oddfellows were prepared to change.

> I have no doubt there would be strong opposition on the part of many of the members of the Society to any extensive organic change; and on the other hand I know that a great many would sacrifice anything and everything belonging to the Society for the purpose of obtaining legal protection or a legal title.[28]

Having weathered the storms of disputation, the Society sought the reward of legal protection which was required if it was to achieve actuarial soundness. In 1850 the Oddfellows became recognised as a legal entity but the effects of the crises still continued. The number of members fell from 249,300 to 234,500 in 1849 and to 224,900 in 1850. If 'a period which might be termed the dawn of actuarial science in the Manchester Unity' began, then that dawn came after the darkest hour that the Society had known.[29]

During the next twenty years numbers rose to 434,100 in 1870, an increase of 74 per cent on 1848.[30] However, the number of lodges in Lancashire fell from 737 to 507 between 1845 and 1875 and in the West Riding from 600 to 444.[31] Part of the reason for the decline in the number of lodges is that the numbers in each lodge grew, a measure which improved actuarial soundness. The average number of members in a lodge rose from 70 in 1845 to 132 in 1875 and 142 by 1886.[32] While having more members in each lodge was actuarially sound it could be socially divisive. Only one of the 17 lodges in Coventry had more than 47 members in 1845 and seven had fewer than 22 members. George Fretton described how 'a spasmodic effort was made to popularise and spread the Order by opening seven new lodges. This ended after a struggle for existence for a few years, disastrously for most of them.' There were only eight lodges by 1851 and six by 1860 with only 583 members. It was only slowly that the sound principles embodied in the tables were consistently used within the Society. However, the Oddfellows prioritised centralisation long before other affiliated orders. The emphasis on financial viability reduced the importance of individual members and the autonomy of individual lodges. It was in 1847 that, as Gosden put it, the leadership 'succeeded for the first time in limiting the financial autonomy of the lodges'.[33] Although there were secessions, this focus on standardisation did not deter people from joining and the Society recruited very well in comparison to the Foresters which proceeded towards actuarial soundness at a slower rate. The Oddfellows administered death benefits at district level whereas Foresters' Courts varied in regard to the sums paid and the system of payment.[34] It was only in 1855 that a Forester drew up a table based on mortality and sickness records.[35]

Ensuring the financial security of all the lodges of such a vast organisation was difficult. This was partly because of embezzlement. One Oddfellows' leader carefully commented on 'unenrolled' societies rather than his own Society. Nevertheless, his comments may have drawn on his experience of the Unity:

> I have often heard it argued that if the members would always be careful, and choose 'honest men' for their treasurers and officers, legal protection would be superfluous! Perhaps if all mankind were all practical Christians, and gifted with the privilege of peeping into futurity, we might contrive to get on without any social compact whatever. But, unfortunately, I have never yet heard of a defaulting treasurer or trustee who was not, at the time of his appointment, regarded by those who had selected him as a most exemplary individual! It is generally some exceedingly 'good character', some 'very nice person' or some 'highly respectable gentleman' whom nobody distrusts that contrives to decamp with the funds of unenrolled Friendly Societies or impudently demands 'something handsome' before he will transfer his trust to a properly appointed successor.[36]

Another factor which made financial stability difficult was that the Highland Society tables were, as Moffrey recognised, 'crude'. The Society began to collect its own data.[37] Corresponding Secretary Henry Ratcliffe collected the sickness and mortality experience of the Order over the period 1846 to 1848. He produced the first of the Oddfellows' life tables in 1850. In recognition of the evidence that older people tended to claim more time off for sickness, graduated contributions were agreed by the AMC. In 1853 the AMC introduced graduated premiums for new members, scales of contribution instead of flat rate contributions irrespective of age.[38] Over time these scales were amended to take account of hazardous occupations. Both the data and the regulation grew and in 1872 Provincial Grand Master Samuel Daynes argued that all lodges should be required by law to file quinquennial valuations with the Society's headquarters.[39] Although the proposal was not enacted it indicates that the balance had shifted further towards finance and away from unstructured fraternity.

In 1849 one Staffordshire Oddfellow told a Commons committee that 'we find a great advantage in self-government in having the means within our hands immediately to correct anything that we find wrong, while if we were under the authority of the registrar we should not be able to act until we got his certification.' Affiliated orders, such as the Unity, were not registered, as a fee had to be paid by each lodge. According to Grand Master Charles Hardwick, the Registrar of Friendly Societies, Tidd Pratt, treated the affiliated orders much 'as the master of a union workhouse, a militia drill-sergeant and the governor of a convict prison' treated their charges, and insisted that each lodge register as a separate society.[40] In 1855 Tidd Pratt shifted his position in regard to the affiliated orders and abolished the registration fee which he had introduced in 1850. It was not until 1851 that the Society gained the benefits of registration. This gave it the right to place money with the National Debt Commissioners which paid a guaranteed rate of 4.5 per cent per annum. Many patronised societies took advantage of this regulation. These bodies could avoid the disbenefits associated with small local autonomous lodges. Looking back some decades later 1871 District Auditor George Fretton noted that the notion of actuarial soundness was not widely understood and described this development as

prejudicial, for it is better to have a few strong lodges than many weak ones for several reasons. In a lodge of small numbers the distribution of sickness liability is insufficient to secure safety while the expenses of management are proportionately heavy … The early pioneers of Odd Fellowship never troubled their heads about financial matters, 'sufficient for the day is the evil thereof' and 'takes no thought for the morrow' were their mottoes. The possession of a fund of some sort was sufficient for them if that fund increased year by year so much the better, Whether it did so in such a ratio to met their future liabilities never entered into the calculations and so a rigid economy was never insisted upon.[41]

Recognition of the Society's commitment to sound finance was such that by 1874 the Assistant Commissioner of Friendly Societies, Sir George Young, could argue that the Foresters was 'in most respects half a generation behind the Oddfellows, Manchester Unity' and the Royal Commission to whom he was giving evidence could concur. In 1882 the Chief Registrar of Friendly Societies reported that he had made over 6,500 valuations, that just under a quarter showed a surplus and most of these were Oddfellows' lodges. The Society's strategy of ensuring reliable finances was not enthusiastically adapted by other friendly societies not only because actuarial soundness relied upon the creation and correct use of robust tables indicating life expectancy, charges and benefits based on statistical evidence, but also because it required implementation within largely autonomous lodges. A French medical statistician, Dr Jacques Bertillon, carried out a survey of mutual aid in 1892. He did not refer to the Oddfellows specifically when he concluded that when the British friendly societies

grant compensation they attach less importance to their regulations than to the state of their till. A rich society gives its help more liberally than a poor one; and this is absolutely the sole cause of the large English societies, which are often very old and generally rich, granting more daily indemnities than the French.[42]

The Oddfellows' efforts to base its payments on the best available data were poorly understood. Possibly this became more socially acceptable. Poovey suggested that by the mid-nineteenth century

> imaginative writers' tendency to mine contemporary financial events for characters and plots paradoxically cultivated in readers a tolerance of ignorance about the very financial mechanisms that political economists thought to explain.[43]

Gilbert argued that 'to a poorly educated working man for whom statistics were a mystery, friendly society finance was an enigma'.[44] In addition data was frequently presented in terms of a dichotomous dilemma, either fraternity or finance. In *Little Dorrit* Dickens' financier, Merdle, was based on a MP who embezzled but central to the novel is the redemptive capacity of love. As Poovey points out reform is 'not by an explanation that might enable readers to discriminate between a sound investment and irrational speculation but simply through the moral transformation that Amy inspires'.[45] Gilbert also noted how, during the late nineteenth century, friendly societies, beset by actuarial danger and the loss of the fraternal spirit, began to decline. He asserted that

> the old type of friendly society man – the backbone of the movement, for whom the lodge was the centre of life … was becoming rare. And with his disappearance the friendly society movement, whatever the membership figures showed, began to decay.[46]

Sound finances required a sound structure and that was difficult to ensure even when the pressure for change mounted. The Friendly Societies Act 1875, in continuation of the 1829 Act, required every registered society to make quinquennial returns of the sickness and mortality experienced by its members and valuations of assets and liabilities.[47] By the year 1880 ten periods of five years had been completed. The experience of nearly four and a half million years of life were tabulated in 1896, and indicated an increased liability to sickness. This inference was echoed by Oddfellows' actuary, Alfred W. Watson. His work was based on an investigation of the sickness and mortality experience of the Oddfellows between 1893 and 1897. It drew on the experiences of 800,000 individuals, more than 3,000,000 years of life and 7,000,000 weeks of sickness. When improved living standards were enabling more men to seek individual forms of self-help and turn away from friendly societies, the Oddfellows needed, at very least, to recruit far more young men and raise the level of its funds.

The actuarial tables that were used were based on mortality between 1836 and 1854 and indicated that a 16-year-old male could expect to live to 58.4 years and at 20 to live to 59.5 years. During the period 1890–1900 the average age of death of males reaching maturity had increased by about two and a half years while during the same half century the proportion of the English and Welsh male population over 65 grew from 4.4 per cent to 4.7 per cent. Friendly society members tended to live even longer, by maybe three or four years.[48] Largely due to the reduction in infant mortality life expectancy rose from just over 40 years of age in the 1860s to more than 50 by 1912. In addition, Oddfellows began to accept that they might retire rather than working until they died. Between 1881 and 1911 the percentage of men aged over 65 who were still in work fell from 74 per cent to 57 per cent. Those Oddfellows who lived longer were more likely to suffer from illness than their younger brethren who bore the cost of that sickness. Members over the age of 70 were twice as likely to be sick as those under that age and between 1846–48 and 1893–97 the percentage of those in the Oddfellows over 65 increased 23-fold.[49]

In the 1870s and 1880s not only did men began to live longer but the age of the average Oddfellow rose from 35.62 years to 36.91 between 1868 and 1893.[50] Moreover, the Friendly Societies Act 1896 (which consolidated and replaced the 1875 Act) barred those under 16 (from 1875 and 21 from 1887) from full membership and in 1895 those under the age of one could not join. Attracting young men became an important activity, and one in which other societies were engaged. In 1905 for example in Deddington, Oxfordshire, a friendly society had to close when all the younger men left and formed an Oddfellows Lodge but in Scorton, Yorkshire, it was the Oddfellows who the younger men deserted. The older members of the lodge were suddenly considerably worse off and were saved only when the AMC approved a payment of £265 from the Unity Sick and Funeral Fund to the 'loyal remnant'.[51] In such circumstances solvency became more difficult to achieve or maintain. Raising membership charges was unpopular and so was a Superannuation Fund which the Society established in 1882.

Until the late 1860s many records of illness noted the frequency of sickness, not the duration. When they were of sufficient rigor to establish a base for comparing short-term and long-term sickness it became clear that many members claimed sick benefit because they were unable to work at their usual trade, in the last years of their lives. This might have been because of shrinking labour market opportunities or it might have been that people were earning more and thus able to survive on reduced pay for longer periods of time, that is higher living standards permitted 'affordable convalescence', or there may have been a reduction in the stigma attached to claiming.[52] This put up the cost of sickness claims. In Nantwich membership of the Poor Man's Friend Lodge rose by 15.3 per cent between 1890 and 1894 which resulted in a rise in contributions of 20.7 per cent. However, sickness benefit pay-outs also rose. In 1890 the lodge received £198 and paid out £287. In 1894 that deficit had risen from £89 to £115 because while contributions amounted to £239, £354 was spent.[53] While some lodges appeared happy to provide what were in effect pensions for older brothers, in one Bristol lodge the younger members voted to charge 'over-age money', a levy of an additional 6d. on all older members on the grounds that 'the old men had had too much out by way of benefit'.[54] In the 1890s lodges at which the valuation indicated a solvency of less than 85 per cent (anything under 100 per cent indicated a deficiency) had to both reduce benefits and increase contributions. Assistance was provided by the Order as a whole taking over all or part of the liability of older members and financing that liability though a charge on those lodges which were in surplus. The AMC took a number of similar decisions to support financially unsound lodges.

The cost of providing pensions out of the sickness funds became even clearer when in 1903 actuary Alfred W. Watson examined four surveys of sickness among Oddfellows for the years 1846–1848; 1856–1860; 1866–1870 and 1893–1897.[55] Watson also surveyed information available from other registered friendly societies from the period 1876 to 1880. He discovered that there was four more weeks of sickness per member in the 65–69 age group and over five more weeks per member in the 70–74 age group in the 1890s than there had been during the 1840s. In 1893–97 the percentage of Oddfellows aged over 65 was 23 times as large as it had been in 1846–48.[56] He concluded that 'The broad results of these comparisons, viewing them chronologically from 1846–48 and 1893–97 are that sickness rates are constantly rising, whilst mortality rates, except at the later ages, are declining.' The frequency of sickness among members was more than twice the actuarial calculations at all age levels and the duration of a sickness claim averaged 4.26 weeks for those under 40, 8.42 weeks for those aged 40–60 and 23.7 weeks for those aged over 60. The AMC intervened in a number of cases. In 1909 the Chester-le-Street district was fined for inefficiency and in 1910 it was refused help because the management was still considered inept.[57] However, the AMC decided to take responsibility for the funeral liabilities of 24 members of the Loyal Tar Lodge in Scarborough and 301 members in the Durham district.[58]

It also became clearer that some lodges were failing to ensure that they had sufficient funds to meet costs. For some this was due to lack of managerial expertise, for others because of the hazardous nature of the work that members undertook. In 1871 in Coventry only 28 per cent of the lodges were solvent or in surplus. District Auditor George Fretton criticised the Loyal Dunsmore Lodge, Coventry, for the structure of its accounts explaining that

> a separate account of members paying extra annual contributions should also be kept, it is quite impossible to detect any omission when they are entered with the ordinary accounts. Separate accounts should also be posted on account of money for defraying the expenses of the anniversary.

Membership of these lodges grew and by 1877 the district was in surplus as were five of the eight lodges, even though members of the older lodges who joined before 1853, still paid the older, flat rates. In 1880 40 per cent of all the lodges in the country were in surplus and the rest close to it.[59] There were accusations, for example in 1875 made by the Grand Master of the Order of Druids, that the Oddfellows did not pay the claims made on the funds 'again and again' and that the Oddfellows had 'nothing to boast about when the poor were left to take care of themselves while the rich [lodges] kept all they could get for their own exclusive use'.[60] Others too expressed concern about the future security of funds and benefits as George Young reported in 1874

> Many elderly working men have said to me, with reference to the uncertainly which hangs over the future of the Odd Fellows and all other sick clubs 'If I had to begin again I would not spend a farthing on a sick club but invest all my savings on insurance of my life, at least you get something for your money.'[61]

While there are examples of fraternity, for example in May 1884 Brother Evans of the Philanthropic Lodge, Coventry paid the 4s. contributions of Brother Smith, thus clearing him of the books, more generally, survival was partly at the expense of those members who found it hard to maintain payments. In the 1890s one in eight Oddfellows lapsed within a five-year period. Another estimate indicated that half of all members lapsed.[62] This was not a sound basis for the longevity of the Society. If it was to be able to continue to offer fraternal bonds to the young and the old and promises of support in the event of death it had to look in new directions. As the members became older, sicker and more likely to wish to retire, the attractions of pension schemes increased and the Oddfellows launched a voluntary superannuation fund in 1882.[63] Another option was also considered, that of state annuities for the aged poor. This idea, like the idea that friendly societies could be subsidised or encouraged to provide or administer pensions, had been raised in the eighteenth century. It became more prominent in the late nineteenth century as men lived longer. Prior to that many Oddfellows do not appear to have believed that they would live long enough to collect a pension and indeed actuarial tables also made that assumption. There was general working-class scepticism about the benefits of state intervention. There was specific concern about compulsory contributions to a state-administered pension fund. It was felt that state pensions could undermine the incentive to become an Oddfellow, reduce thrift and be expensive.[64] As Grand Master Sidney Campkin put it:

> the friendly societies did not want grandmotherly legislation. They were capable of managing their own affairs without State intervention … Friendly societies were jealous of any interference by the State; they had built themselves up without its assistance and felt they could certainly continue without it'.[65]

In a story published in the *Magazine* in 1885 a blacksmith is offered three wishes by the fairies.[66] The blacksmith rejects the proposal that he wish for a pension. Many within the Society took the view that wages should be improved to enable people to save for themselves, rather than be dependent on state provision and indeed the blacksmith is criticised for undercharging and thus remaining in poverty. In the same year the *Magazine* published a poem by Thor Coles which indicated hostility towards Canon Blackley's proposal for a state pensions scheme:

> *An Elegy (National Insurance is as Dead as Queen Anne)*
> The Canon's scheme is dead and gone
> No patriot could approve it
> And if in case it came full blown
> T'would take a power to move it.[67]

After a Royal Commission recommended in 1895 that pensions remain the responsibility of individuals within the friendly societies the Oddfellows was pleased that it was to be 'left alone' untouched by 'the poison of state interference'.[68] In addition, although the Oddfellows did not wish to be unfraternal, by forcing older members into the workhouse, it also did not wish to place additional burdens on younger men (during a period of intense competition for younger members) by ensuring that they subscribe to a pension fund. Instead the Oddfellows stuck to its general principle that if men behaved in a thrifty and moral fashion then poverty would be reduced.

In 1896 the Oddfellows' AMC narrowly resolved that it would support state pensions providing that the scheme did 'not create any power of government interference in the general management of the Manchester Unity'. In 1898 a government departmental committee (members of which included the Chief Registrar of Friendly Societies Sir Edward Brabrook, representatives of the friendly societies and Sir Alfred Watson, Chief Actuary of the Oddfellows) gathered evidence from the largest friendly societies about pensions.[69] Those who gave evidence included Tom Hughes, who was on the Oddfellows Board of Directors. Its report, produced in 1898, indicated that all but five of the 179 friendly societies approached, supported their aged members at a median average of 3s. a week and all but two supported the idea of a state pension. Although the Oddfellows AMC of that year voted against state pensions, the Unity's evidence, taken before the AMC, indicated the contrary view.[70] The Oddfellows may have also been influenced when other countries, initially New Zealand in 1898, introduced state pensions. In addition, the TUC started to campaign for them, as did some friendly societies (for example the Hearts of Oak). Some Oddfellows members highlighted the benefits: 'There are a lot of old men whose lodges cannot provide benefit.' 'Most men over 40 cannot afford to pay for the Oddfellows Old Age Pension. Why shouldn't the State help?'[71]

In March 1902 the National Conference of Friendly Societies called for state pensions, added the rider that 'the cost of the same shall be raised without any interference with the funds of thrift societies'.[72] In 1908 the views of friendly societies about pensions were requested. There were 151, about half, favouring state pensions. The announcement of the outline of legislation was greeted with calls to reduce the age limit from 70 to 65 from the TUC and *The Times*. William Beveridge, whose views on friendly societies were to be very influential, called for a contributory scheme as this would enable working people to retain a sense of obligation towards both self-help and others.[73] He saw this as 'the first instalment of a wider ranging programme of remedies for the major causes of need'.[74]

The Oddfellows was also faced with another problem at this time: the death of members in the Boer War, 1899–1902. The news that British troops had taken Pretoria broke while deputies were in attendance at the 1899 AMC. There was an outbreak of patriotic fervour and it was decided that those who were incapacitated by wounds or disease while at the front should be entitled to sick pay. The 1900 Portsmouth AMC approved a proposal of the Board to meet the contributions of Reservists and military members by a special levy so as to spread the liability equitably over the entire membership. It was carried by an almost unanimous vote. A further proposal to assist the lodges in South Africa in re-organising and restarting their operations on a proper basis also commanded the approval of the meeting.[75] The Grand Master told those attending the AMC that the events of the year had afforded a practical example of the value of their colonial lodge, for information had reached them of Canadian and Australian Oddfellows being among the first in the colonies to volunteer for active service. In South Africa they fought shoulder to shoulder with members of their British lodges in the common cause of the empire.[76]

The *Magazine* issued a warning:

> The prolongation of the campaign imposes further sacrifices on us as citizens and as members of the Manchester Unity – sacrifices which we feel assured will be cheerfully borne. The lodges continue to bear the heavy liability of sickness and wounds which must always accompany war. We do not disguise from ourselves that the latter will be much the more grievous liability. Men are returning home from South Africa enfeebled in health by the ravages of enteric and of dysentery – more insidious foes than Boer bullets. It is to be feared that many of these victims of the war young in years but broken in health, will remain almost permanent burdens on the sick funds of their lodges. It is well that this should be realised and where surpluses exist the money ought not to be lightly dispersed.[77]

The Unity decided to make sick payments to serving members injured or ill due to the Boer War and that their contributions of all those serving 'under the African sun' should be paid by management or distress funds. A special distress fund was established and assistance provided for those lodges which were closed due to the war.[78] This action echoed that of half a century earlier when £20 was voted for the relief of widows and orphans of soldiers killed in the Crimea at the 1854 AMC and subsequently £2,582 was subscribed for this cause.[79] It may also have led to the campaign for the formation of military lodges. These were soon approved by the War Office and the Woolwich Garrison Military Lodge was opened. It was from the Woolwich District that the Order spread to Malta and Gibraltar. At the 1910 AMC it was approved that 'further facilities are to be afforded to men in the naval and military forces to become members'.[80]

The standard of living of English workers increased sharply during the second half of the nineteenth century. Real wages for manual workers doubled and even the pay of agricultural workers rose by 73 per cent. Although probably more than half of working-class men were members of societies which paid sickness benefit, many workers found it difficult to save for their old age. Somewhere between 33 and 40 per cent of adult males were eligible for a friendly society or trade union pension, which often amounted to no more than 3 shillings a week. Few older people could live on savings or benefits and many turned to charity or the Poor Law. In the 1860s more than half of the working class who were aged over 65 were receipt of poor relief. A report in 1895 by Beatrice and Sydney Webb indicated that provision from friendly societies and from local government was not satisfactory.[81]

In 1908 the Old Age Pensions Act was passed and the duties and responsibilities of the

Oddfellows were reduced. The new law provided people over seventy whose annual income was not above £21, with between 1s. and 5s. a week. Only 5 per cent of people lived beyond 70 and most were women. Those who had recently been in receipt of poor relief or who had been convicted under the Inebriates Act were disqualified as were those who had failed to work. However, that could be countered if they had contributed to a friendly society before the age of 60. As initially the legislation benefited the elderly respectable poor it had little impact on many members of the Oddfellow. The Society was acquiescent, but not enthusiastic.[82] The suspicion towards the scheme may account for why it was 'implemented in ways calculated to reassure the beneficiaries, that it promoted the independence of the elderly … and that it helped to modify popular attitudes towards the state'.[83] Moreover the legislation was inexpensive, straightforward to administer and designed 'to be of maximum benefit to the friendly societies'.[84] The year that the legislation came into force, 1909, the Oddfellows AMC ordered a study to ascertain the effects of ending sickness benefit at 70. The report revealed that those lodges in deficiency would become solvent and those which were solvent but paying reduced sickness benefits to pay full benefits.[85] While members may have welcomed the prospect of a state pension, there was less incentive to join the Oddfellows, less need for thrift or the training in actuarial and civil activities that the Oddfellows offered and less incentive to stay a member.

Although data improved in accuracy, insurance companies grew in strength and rival affiliated orders grew in number actuarially sound tables were not always adopted by members of the Oddfellows. This was despite the pressure from government to improve solvency and from the experience of witnessing the closure of lodges and the resultant poverty of men who had invested their money over a long number of years. Actuarial soundness was perceived as a tool by which some within the Unity would gain advantage, by which the government would gain information and by which fraternity would be undermined. The struggles over these issues were lengthy and even after the AMC has reached a decision, agreement within the Society was only reached after a period of years. When it became clear that members were living longer, making greater claims for sickness benefit and that the Boer War was likely to have a detrimental effect on funds, there was a change in opinion. The idea of state intervention in regard to pensions grew in popularity.

II   Joining the political nation

In the mid-1840s there was a large secession from the Oddfellows. This became the National Independent Order of Oddfellows. Many of those who joined it came from areas where there was widespread support for Chartism. This was the campaign for the extension of the franchise and related social and political reforms. Its peak of popularity was in the 1840s in the north of England. Some Chartists gathered names for vast petitions, Charters, which were delivered to Parliament.[86] The 48 lodges suspended in 1845 were all in the north. There were 2,770 members suspended in the Rochdale area, 1,894 from Salford and 1,139 from Stockport (all of which are near Manchester), 184 from Manchester itself and 1,666 members from the

Huddersfield District.[87] Although Burn characterised the division as being about 'selfish men', it is possible that divisions over Chartism fuelled the acrimony within the Oddfellows.[88] Some may have been Chartists suspicious that the information they divulged would be sent to the government. It was widely reported when, in 1844, a Commons Committee report made it public knowledge that the government intercepted and opened mail.[89] Koditschek noted the connections in Bradford.

> What kept the Oddfellows together was that its working-class leaders, unlike the bourgeois officers of the Temperance Society, seem to have shared a common affinity with their members for the Chartist creed ... They rented their hall to Chartists when the latter found other meetings closed off ... In May 1839, with very little legal justification, the magistrates summarily threatened to revoke the Oddfellows' license if they rented to the Chartists again.[90]

The *Northern Star* reported that Bradford Oddfellows Hall was used for radical meetings.[91] The growth in Oddfellowship in this period may have been in part because membership of the Oddfellows disguised or supported other connections members had. Writing in the 1840s Burn declared Oddfellowship to be 'the first attempt' at British working-class self-government and also called it 'the best attempt which has been made by the working classes at self-government'.[92] Addressing the Oddfellows in the USA in 1834 a leader, Joseph Burrows stressed the loyalty and legality of the members, noting that 'We owe a duty to our God, our country and our families, paramount to any by which we are bound to the order'. By contrast, while Burn also stressed that in the UK, 'The Society is based upon the principle of loyalty to the Sovereign and obedience to the laws', he noted that this did not involve 'blind obedience to the Government'. Moreover, when he pointed to the 'nobility' of 'the plodding artizan' and described the period when 'the labouring community sought a more equal representation and a share of the legislative power', this indicated where his sympathies lay. He also noted that 'the labouring community of Great Britain have much reason to be proud of their class.'[93]

There are many examples of those who were involved in both Chartism and the Oddfellows. Hobsbawm indicated one connection when he saw self-organisation in the

> concentration of workers' mutual and friendly societies in the new industrial areas, especially in Lancashire, but above all in the serried thousands of men, women and children who streamed with torches onto the moors for Chartist demonstrations.[94]

The first issue of *The Odd Fellow* in 1839 had an editorial which supported the 'intrepid advocates of the just and meritorious "People's Charter"'.[95] The concerns of many Chartists echoed those of Oddfellowship.[96] In Merthyr on Christmas Day 1838 400 Oddfellows turned out in full regalia to 'distract attention from a Chartist meeting impending on Heolgerrig Hill'.[97] In 1839 there was a large-scale armed rebellion. About 5,000 men, many armed, marched on Newport, Monmouthshire where they fought the army. At a trial which followed the disturbances in Newport in 1839 an engineer, Lloyd Lewis, gave evidence that a mason called John Gwillam had explained that there was to be a rising among the Chartists.

> He also told me to be sure to go to the presiding officers of our society – that is, the Oddfellows Lodge, and tell them to go and draw our money out of the saving bank, so I did so and the money was drawn out.[98]

Although Lewis also explained 'I am not aware that he belongs to any other society than the Oddfellows' and Gwillam was discharged, the Oddfellows raised money for the 1839 Newport Rising in which, it is said, their ceremonial swords were used in the fighting.[99]

In 1840 on Teesside two Oddfellow lodges agreed to invest £120 from lodge funds in shares in the Chartist Co-operative Society together with £75 of members' own money. Four months later this co-operative venture was registered under Friendly Society legislation.[100] A radical newspaper which made the connection between the Unity and political activity, *Tracts for Oddfellows and Social Reformers* was published in Sheffield. In Dundee there was an Oddfellows Democratic Society which appointed men to deliver Chartist lectures across Fife.[101] James Dawson Burn, the illegitimate son of itinerant beggars, became active in campaigns for the extension of the franchise and rose to prominence within the hatters' trade union before being joining the Oddfellows in about 1838.[102] In December 1840, when Henry Vincent initiated a campaign to persuade Chartists that they should become teetotallers, he did so via the Chartist newspapers, the *Northern Star*, and the *English Chartist Circular* and also in *The Odd Fellow*. Abel Swann, a master tailor in Ashton-under-Lyne was an active Oddfellow and chaired a Chartist lecture in Ashton-under-Lyne, October 1840.[103] On his release from Lancaster Castle Chartist leader Bronterre O'Brien immediately went to Kendal to address a crowd gathered in the Oddfellows Hall.[104] In 1841 the Chartist *Northern Star* cried 'hurrah! for the tailors and hurrah! for the Oddfellows' when an Oddfellow secretary and tailor agreed to stand for Parliament on a Chartist ticket.[105] When in 1844 Richard Close, a Todmorden weaver and subscriber to the National Land Company, sent a donation to the Chartist funds he gave his address as the Oddfellows Hall.[106] In 1846, an estimated 66,000 British workers were present in France and branches of the Land Company existed in Rouen, Boulogne and elsewhere. Thomas Sidaway, an innkeeper and Chartist activist in Rouen advertised his Oddfellow connections in *The Norman Times*, a short-lived paper produced for British workers in the city.[107]

Six members of the Joseph Warburton lodge, Middlesbrough, established in 1835, were Chartist activists. James Hollinshead was Treasurer of the Middlesbrough Charter Association, which met in his home and Noble Grand in 1842. John Ward was Lodge Secretary and a shareholder in the Chartist Land Company as was David Jackson, a founder member of the lodge who was also elected to the Middlesbrough Improvement Commission with Chartist support. John Anderson was a Corresponding Secretary of the District and secretary of the Middlesbrough Chartist Association. The District Grand Master, William Gendle, was a Chartist. John Jordison was a mortgagor of the Oddfellows Hall and a member of the Chartist Land Plan. The Chartist Land Company was registered as a friendly society. *The*

Stokesley News and Cleveland Reporter was printed and owned by a prominent local Oddfellow and Chartist, George Tweddle. He also produced the *Oddfellows Reciter* for use at lodge anniversaries and other special events.[108] Other Grand Masters in Middlesbrough included William Blakiston who attempted to establish a Political Reform Association at a meeting in the Oddfellows Hall in 1859 and W. G. Appleyard who was a President of the North East Coast Alliance of the Federation of Master Printers.[109] When one of the shareholders of the Chartist *Northern Star* was tried for seditious speeches Newcastle Oddfellows contributed to his defence fund.[110] In Barnsley and in Bradford public meetings were held to support him in the Oddfellows Halls.[111]

Edward Thompson has argued that in Yorkshire too 'in the simple cellular structure of the friendly society, with its workaday ethos of mutual aid, we can see many features which were reproduced in more sophisticated and complex forms in trade unions, co-operatives, Hampden Clubs, Political Unions and Chartist lodges'.[112] Dorothy Thompson added that 'Most of the male Chartists of Halifax were Oddfellows', and that Oddfellow lodges made loans to both a radical community in Hampshire and striking miners in Yorkshire.[113] In Barnsley the Oddfellow Hall was used for Chartist meetings, including one addressed by Fergus O'Connor.[114] This was one of the largest building in the town as 2,000 people could gather there with women in the gallery.[115] The *Northern Star* reported a meeting of 2,000 women Chartists at Oddfellows' Hall, Halifax on 9 August 1847. Radical poet Eliza Cook, 1818–89, wrote in support of the 1848 Chartist petition ('A Song: to '"The People" of England') another piece to raise funds for an Asylum for the Poor and Aged Masons ('Address to the Freemasons, 1848') and a third promoting Oddfellowship ('Odd Lines for "Odd Fellows"').[116] The lyrics of this last song, which indicates that 'proud Independence' is greater than 'sweet Charity', were reproduced in the history of the Society produced for the centenary.[117] Oddfellow funds supported radical printer Joshua Hobson, who produced both the Chartist *Northern Star* (between 1838 and 1844) and the radical *New Moral World* (between 1839 and 1841).[118] William Aitken, a cotton spinner who later ran his own school and was imprisoned for sedition due to his Chartist activities, was a Chartist organizer in Ashton and Stalybridge and an active Oddfellow.[119] He was central to the successful campaign to open an Oddfellows' Hall in Ashton in 1856 and a portrait, that is a biographical account, appeared in the *Oddfellows' Magazine* July 1857. William Marcroft, 1822–94, was a Chartist, an Oddfellow and active in the co-operative movement in Oldham. He demonstrated considerable business acumen when he helped to create and run the successful co-operative Sun Mill Company. William James Linton and Henry Hetherington, who were leading Chartists, edited *The Odd Fellow* during the period 1841–42.[120] Hetherington, 1792–1849, had previously published *The Poor Man's Guardian* 1831–35 and been fined and imprisoned on a number of occasions. He was the first Treasurer of the London Working Man's Association and helped to draw up the first Charter. Abram Fielden of Todmorden was an active Chartist and Oddfellow according to the autobiography of his son, Samuel.[121]

Such overt political activity might appear to sit uneasily with the emphasis on respectability that the Oddfellows presented for much of the nineteenth century. In addition, Chartists may have wanted access to the Oddfellows' funds. Oddfellow Charles Tiplady claimed that

Chartist and Oddfellow

Following the death of Chartist Ben Rushton in 1853, a hand-loom weaver in Ovenden in the West Riding, 140 Oddfellows escorted his coffin and between 6,000 and 10,000 people are estimated to have attended his funeral. This description was provided by a witness in an autobiography:

> At the entrance of the village the Odd-fellows were waiting at their lodge to the number of 140, and walked in advance. On approaching the house of the deceased patriot they opened out in double line. The sight was magnificent … The coffin was carried by six veteran Chartists, and the splendid pall by six Odd-fellows … The wish of the departed patriot was that no paid priest should officiate at his funeral. Mr. Gammage spoke at the grave side, and after him a member of the Odd-fellows said a few words.[122]

Chartists who dominated a local burial society transferred its funds to the Chartist land scheme.[123] It is probable that some Oddfellows did not wish the Society to be seen to be taking sides in a political dispute. Others opposed the Chartists.[124] At an Oddfellows dinner in London in 1843 the Chair, Sir G. De Lacy Evans, KCB pointed out that the Society members included MPs and clerics. He added that

> all members amongst the lower orders who are guilty of joining disorderly or insurrectionary movements are uniformly expelled from the society which, although repudiating all party politics and sectarian exclusiveness is desirous of inculcating and maintaining sound loyal, conservative and constitutional principles.[125]

In 1843 Magistrate William Chambers suggested that the Board of the Oddfellows should issue an order to all the lodges in the counties of Carmarthen, Pembroke, Cardigan and Glamorgan, expressing their disapproval at the recent unlawful acts committed in these areas. These included murder and the destruction of property. Possibly Chambers thought Oddfellows were more likely to be law-abiding, or possibly he thought that the Society could help to discipline its more unruly elements.[126] The Society did not permit party political conversations within the lodge. Rules published in 1841 make it clear that could be imposed for 'singing an indecent or political song, or giving an indecent or political toast or sentiment', and Rule 254 forbade the publication of 'advertisements of a political or religious nature' in the Order's quarterly magazine.[127] However, an important element of Oddfellowship was the promotion of the support for the family, and many Chartists advocated a sober, domesticated manhood in which men supported their families.[128] A further aspect of Oddfellowship was that it sought to make more Oddfellows. Many of the men who were attracted to Chartist meetings could well have made stalwart Oddfellows and attending the places where civic-minded artisans were gathered could have aided recruitment to the Unity with its notions of fair exchange.

Many Oddfellows were engaged in political activities. There are numerous examples reported in the *Oddfellows' Magazine* of Oddfellows who attained civic and political office and of politicians who felt that the support of the Oddfellows would aid their cause. William Duke was a Liberal on the Cranswick School Board the first chair of the parish council and an Oddfellow.[129] In 1841 one candidate 'got himself made an Oddfellow' as 'an electioning manoeuvre', according to the *Manchester Guardian* editorial.[130] When in 1873, Sir George Bowyer stood for Parliament in Abingdon, Oxfordshire, he led a procession under a banner he had donated to the Loyal Bowyer Union Lodge of Odd Fellows. The local newspaper reported that 'electioneering tactics had something to do with it'. He was returned to the House and subsequently met at the station on his homecoming to Abingdon by a crowd with the same banner.[131] It may have also been that the Oddfellows hoped to gain members through connections with local politicians. In 1875 the Naval Commander-in-Chief and Colonel Sir Frederick Fitzwygram, Bart., became honorary members in Portsmouth, at an event 'crowded to excess by members of the Royal Naval Lodge'.[132] In Derby in 1891 when a local alderman was initiated he was welcomed by a number of fellow councillors and the local MP who stressed that the Society was 'non-political'.[133] In 1892 the local newspaper reported that 'another batch of local gentlemen were initiated honorary members'. These were to include the local Conservative candidate but he was unexpectedly unable to attend.[134] In 1910 the Strangers Home Lodge, Crewe enrolled the mayor as an honorary member.[135] Two editions of the *Oddfellows' Magazine* furnished many examples members who achieved civic office. In January and February 1913 it was reported that the Mayor of Newport had 'filled the chief offices of the Earl Yarborough Lodge [Isle of Wight] with great distinction', that Wallace Dashwood became the youngest town councillor in Portsmouth, that a brother from Tything Lodge Worcester district became an alderman and that a senior Trustee of the Order, Sidney Campkin, was a former mayor of Cambridge. It was an Oddfellow who represented the marine engineers at the Titanic disaster inquiry, and a PPGM of the Preston district who became general secretary of the Lancashire Federation of Rural Friendly Societies.[136]

The skills developed in the lodge, of civil discourse, of strict procedures and hierarchies and of wealth collection and redistribution were ones which were also required in the Commons and the council chamber. Indeed, one of the arguments for the extension of the franchise in 1867 was that working men had demonstrated their acceptability through their associational activities.[137] The Foresters recommended that members be sober and industrious in order to 'purchase your own electoral rights'.[138] Evan M. Richards told his fellow MPs in 1869 that

These societies are teaching men the duties of citizenship. I believe that the future of this country will be a great deal better than its past, and that, in great measure, from the education which its working men are receiving in its Oddfellows and other kindred societies. As an honorary member of one of them, I may say that from what I have seen in the Lodges, in order and decorum, they are equal to the House. Every member on entering the room is required to make the same acknowledgement of the authority of the Chair as is customary here. No undue drinking, no swearing, no political or religious discussion is allowed to be introduced. I believe that a system of education is practised in these societies which tends very much indeed to improve men as citizens, and to improve them in every way that conduces to the welfare of the community.[139]

Chartism was a means by which the Society might hope to advance members' interest in civic engagement and support for respectable domesticity. In common with the Oddfellows 'there was a constant tension in Chartist politics between class antagonism and a longing for class conciliation'.[140] Mauss noted that the Hebrew and Arabic words *sadaka*, and *ʒedaqa* initially meant 'justice' and only later 'alms' and suggested that alms are the 'gift morality raised to the position of a principle of justice'.[141] The connection was made in Charles Kingsley's *The Water Babies*, 1863, the two female figures representing mercy and justice, Mrs Doasyouwouldbedoneby and Mrs Bedonebyasyoudid turn out to be one person. She embodies the Golden Rule. The Oddfellows, by linking justice and alms through its notion of the gift was able to present itself as involved in the promotion of both and therefore to make a connection to campaigning for the extension of political rights. Membership of the Oddfellows, because it entailed thrift, regulated cordiality, prudence and engagement in civil society epitomised the model of working men's respectability to many observers. It was an aid to skilled men's economic and social stability, because it enabled them to form and maintain the exclusive cycles of exchange which helped their survival. However, the link which so many made to Chartism suggests that the values of respectability, as handed down the social scale, were reformulated to fit with the values associated not only with individualistic striving but also the traditions of reciprocity. It was a negotiated response to the coercive structures which valued sober, hard working, law abiding, pious artisans. In their support for the extension of political rights members of the Society helped to 'provide an education in the duties of citizenship through the practice of self-government', while making it clear that its practices were not created simply in accordance with pre-existing middle-class tutelage.[142]

III   The Good Samaritan

The parable known as the Good Samaritan is part of Jesus' response to being asked how eternal life might be attained and has long been popular within the Oddfellows.[143] In 1840 'an exhortation to strangers, to be said or sung at an opening or anniversary dinner', included the lines

> We love to help our friends in need
> Relieve their wants, the hungry feed
> We are Samaritans indeed.[144]

In 1874 the Coventry District ordered a banner 'full size, made of the best silk' costing over £27 with a painting of the Good Samaritan on it. In the 1890s, Director Henry Whaite put the Good Samaritan into his design of the Widow and Orphans' Emblem No 2. A few years later, at an Oddfellows' celebratory Church service in Aynho, the vicar remarked at such events

'I helped to buy the banner. "Go thou and do likewise": £20. I done all degrees. NG. My father was secretary,' recalled Whitty Whitlock. The arms of the Society appeared on the Loyal Travellers Home Lodge, Blisworth, Northamptonshire banner. Between the fruit and flowers and above the Latin is an image of the Good Samaritan. William John 'Whitty' Whitlock, 1873–1966, was a carpenter, coffin maker and sexton. His father John was a carpenter and undertaker.

INTERVIEW WITH GEORGE FREESTON, C.1966 AVAILABLE AT HTTP://WWW.BLISWORTH.ORG.UK/IMAGES/AUDIO/AUDIO.HTM ACCESSED 22 FEB. 2009. PHOTOGRAPH BY COURTESY OF WALTER ALEXANDER, BLISWORTH

'many had chosen for their subject the parable of the good Samaritan'.[145] In December 1963 the Grand Master, J. W. Morgan summarised Oddfellowship as 'the modern expression of the parable of the good Samaritan', and in 2008 Terry Moore, an Oddfellow Anglican lay preacher, suggested that, 'the Oddfellows' Golden Rule, that we should treat others as we would wish them to treat us, is connected to the parable of the Good Samaritan.'[146] Many elements of importance to the Oddfellows can be illuminated through an assessment of the parable.

The story, told to Jews by Jesus, concerned a relatively well-resourced, but despised, adherent of a minority branch of Judaism, a Samaritan. Jesus was asked how to gain immortality and also who was a neighbour. He replied by relating the parable. The Samaritan helped a robbed and injured man who was by the roadside and who had been ignored by the representatives of established aid agencies. The injured man in the parable relied on a wealthy one, just as the Oddfellows' had patrons. The Samaritan built a relationship across social boundaries with the injured man. At some risk to himself the outsider, the Samaritan, gave the ill man alcohol and (indicative that he had sufficient funds) made a payment towards his healthcare. For Oddfellows both benefits and sociability in the pub were important. The symbol of the Good Samaritan could be seen as a defiant reminder to those who complained about the use of pubs as meeting places by friendly societies.[147]

The Samaritan then promoted a cycle of exchange when he asked another man, an innkeeper, to provide for the injured man and be repaid later. This may well have brought to mind hospitals' admission policies. These were determined not by doctors, but by hospital patrons. For much of the nineteenth century for a poor person to be treated in many hospitals required them to present a letter from a subscriber or governor.[148] Prospective patients needed a subscriber who was prepared to recommend them, just as the Good Samaritan vouched for the injured traveller to the innkeeper who was to care for him. When the Oddfellows took their banner to the 1831 opening ceremony of Huddersfield Infirmary they were pointing out both that the Society was a donor to the hospital and that members might expect to receive medical treatment. The Oddfellows donated to hospitals in, for example, Northampton, Wakefield and Huddersfield and secured places for their members.[149] There was surveillance of the sick when the Samaritan acted like a Sick Visitor and promised to return and check on the results of the care. Within the Oddfellows, from the time they joined, when a doctor examined applicants on behalf of the members, the Oddfellows rendered members' lives visible and knowable. Members watched other members to ensure compliance with rules regarding numerous matters including sexual conduct. Furthermore, lodge meetings often involved analysis of the merits of claims. 'The most common medical item discussed in the minutes of local meetings,' was suspicions about the merits of claims.[150] Society officers then facilitated a cycle of exchange in which they transferred money from the society to the ill members and reported back to the Lodge on the claimant's health. The connection was made within the Oddfellows. In March 1966 one Past Provincial Grand Master wrote to *The Odd Fellow* and suggested that the title of Sick Visitor should be amended to Samaritan. He also wanted this person to collect arrears and recruit new members. His focus was also on fellowship:

> What better propaganda can we have than to hear an Odd Fellow say, 'It was a big blow to me and my family moving to a strange area but thanks to the Odd Fellows of which I am a member, we found real friends in our new home who have really made us feel at home with them.' That is our target.[151]

The Samaritan's help was reciprocated through the granting of eternal life. He ascended the hierarchy of society, from outsider to immortal. A member of the Oddfellows could rise through the ranks and gain, if not power over life and death then at least power and status. Furthermore, there was provision for the name of a departed brother if not immortalised, at least commemorated. As indicated in Chapter 3 the Society followed a long tradition of indirect, posthumous reciprocity. In return for a bequest a donor's reputations could be confirmed. In 1688 Caleb Trenchfield pointed out that it was better for the poor to follow your coffin than to have the town talk of 'thousands behind you in your coffers', and there were many examples of the names of donors being perpetuated in almshouses or their portraits in guild halls. Funeral sermons and tombstones were testimony to visible generosity.[152]

Just as there are stories of the birth of the Oddfellows there are stories of death. In 1901 the *Oddfellows' Magazine* reported that in Paisley the Alexander Wilson Lodge lost is oldest member PPGM William Allen in November 1900, aged 72. Instead of attending church as usual he 'sat down at the fireside to read his Bible and almost instantly fell forward and expired'. He had retired only six months earlier. A lodge member for almost 50 years he had twice won first prize for the person who introduces the most members into the lodge.[153] The *Magazine* reminded members that even after death their Oddfellowship would not be forgotten. On the one hand the parable of the Samaritan enabled those who saw within Oddfellowship a critique of capitalist relations, the market economy in which transactions led only to material gain and who yearned for pre-capitalist, non-contractual form of association and mutual aid, to gain some comfort. On the other hand it could be seen as an example of how in a society which lauded individual advancement social solidarity could be complementary not antagonistic and there could be assistance for those who fell by the wayside. The Golden Rule at the initiation refers to members' moral duties to God, neighbours and themselves. This parable reiterates that view. The importance attached to kindness to strangers, could have been seen as of significance by Oddfellows as they tramped the country in search of work as could the evidence of reciprocity. Indeed one of the Society's toasts was 'The Stranger'.[154]

All the people mentioned in the parable are male, a reminder that Jesus had made it clear that neighbourliness and charity were obligations for men, not merely the prerogative of wealthy women. Those Oddfellows, who were members during the 83 years when the Society did not have women as full members, may have found that image of single-sex solidarity to be one which spoke to them. The Widow and Orphans' Emblem No. 1, instituted in 1851, shows Charity, a woman, supported a widow and her children. She is 'flying from grim Want and is seeking refuge within the ranks of our society'.[155] Urbanisation made many families more dependent on the father's wage and societies promoted the idea that it was the husband and father, not the wider community, who was obliged to make provision for widows and orphans. Domestic money, increasingly derived from wages, legally belonged to a husband and if he chose to place it in a friendly society, where it would usually be controlled by men, it would only benefit a wife and children on his sickness or death. The image of the Samaritan could have reminded those thinking of joining, and reassured members, that membership aided male control over the domestic income. One Preston Oddfellows lodge forbade 'members sending their money … by women and children', reminding members of their status.[156] Burn mentioned the lodge in Glasgow where 'a gigantic black fellow with a drawn sword in his hand … acted as the Cerberus to guard the Lodge-room door against the ladies and children'.[157] When women were mentioned it was clear where control should lie. In making a presentation in 1837 a District Grand Master said that the members 'meet as brethren of one great family

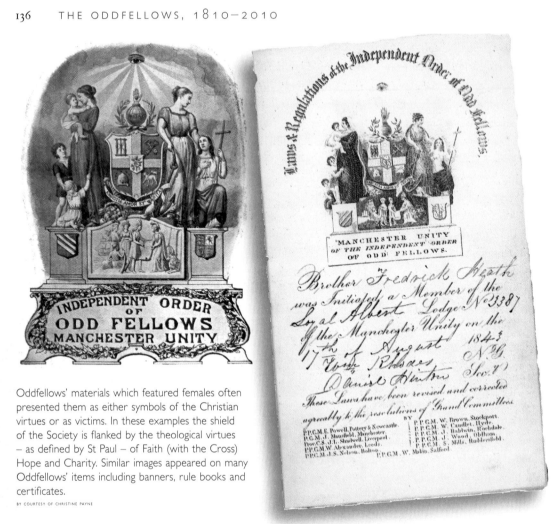

Oddfellows' materials which featured females often presented them as either symbols of the Christian virtues or as victims. In these examples the shield of the Society is flanked by the theological virtues – as defined by St Paul – of Faith (with the Cross) Hope and Charity. Similar images appeared on many Oddfellows' items including banners, rule books and certificates.

BY COURTESY OF CHRISTINE PAYNE

– a family united in the most sacred tries of brotherly love and charity'. He went on to mention the welfare of a member's wife and children. What, he asked, 'is more calculated to soften the pains of a dying hour than the assurance that those dear objects of our affection shall still find comfort and consolation from our brethren'. He went on to hope that after they died the members would meet 'in that grand lodge above'.[158] In the same year in Burton-upon-Trent, the Marquess of Anglesey Lodge admitted women, but only the 'wives, relations and sweethearts' who attended for 'tea-drinking' and a ball.[159]

For some members the ideas associated with the image of the Samaritan might have been reinforced by the image of the Hand and Heart described by Spry as

an emblem of friendship: because it is supposed to exhibit that confidence which Odd Fellows (especially those who have properly learned what our Lectures seek to inculcate) should repose in each other, after taking upon themselves the solemn obligations at their Initiation.[160]

Central to this image is Mercy in a feminine form. She is comforting a respectable widow and her well-shod and smartly dressed children, aiming perhaps to shield them from a male figure representing death or destitution who stalks them menacingly from the right. Even though attendance at Society functions took men away from their wives and children, the Society presented itself as protecting the family. The other human element on the image is the heart on an open hand. This may have reinforced the message that the society offered more than a hand-out: it also offered love.

BY COURTESY OF CHRISTINE PAYNE

The 1910 AMC was an excellent location to remind Deputies and visitors about the tenets of the Society. Here they are being greeted and reminded of the longevity of the Society. Banners on the other walls read 'Harmony Peace and Concord' and 'Prosperity to our branches'. These emphasised the difficulties which could arise if disputes were not settled amicably, and the need to focus on financial issues. Although local autonomy had been eroded over the years, the leadership chose to stress the importance of the lodges.

The Oddfellows recognised that it operated within a world where the distinctions between charity and mutual aid were blurred. The Oddfellows developed in a town where friendly societies and charities had been hand-in-hand. In 1800 in Manchester a Union of Friendly Societies collected donations and distributed food cheaply to the poor and there was a close association between social status and a reputation for altruism and care. Members could present themselves as a version of the 'Manchester men'.[161] Like many friendly societies membership of the Unity was organised 'around notions of friendship, brotherly love charity whilst any self-understanding in terms of risk or insurance was largely absent from their cultural world'.[162] The Unity stress on its charitable ideals was prominent. In 1849 Oddfellow James Larkin, a mechanic in the Woolwich Dockyard noted that, 'the great aim of the members of the Order is to do good to each other, and to improve the character of the human race, by inculcating the doctrine of self-reliance'.[163] In 1855 the Unity made an overt link between conviviality and a higher purpose:

> The lodge is always considered as sacred ground: and no sooner do those who in any other place might come together as enemies, enter into its precincts, then their bad feelings seem to vanish ... the sectarian feeling which is apt to prevail amongst religious

enthusiasts and heart burnings of violent political partisans are for a time obliterated and forgotten by those who meet in the temples of Oddfellowship. There must then be some great and good moral principle amongst us by the aid of which we accomplish all this: there must be some powerful and virtuous influence connected with the Order.[164]

In his sermon to a Centenary service in 1910 the Bishop of Winchester suggested that an organisation which had been an outsider had now become so elevated that its financial stability was comparable to the Proverbs. He pointed out that the Oddfellows was

no longer a small band emerging into a precarious existence, amid ridicule and prognostications of failure but the greatest of all friendly societies, whose numbers are more than a million, whose organisation spreads over the globe, whose membership has been thrown open to women and to juveniles and whose actuarial security has become proverbial.

He went on to argue that the Society had 'upheld a strict and searching standard of financial probity', had deepened 'the brotherhood amongst men' and spread 'a knowledge of the power of self-control and of the happiness that springs from a share in giving to relieve the common misfortunes of human life.'[165] The linking of 'actuarial statistics' 'self-control' and 'giving to relieve' also echo the motifs of the Samaritan parable. It was a concept which could be employed to express more than one set of meanings and to fuse together apparently irreconcilable elements. It enabled the commitment to the improvement of financial modelling and risk analysis to be connected to fraternity.

The Oddfellows' interest in the Biblical story can be seen as a reflection of the parable's wider acceptability. When members of the Society in Coventry selected that image for a banner they may well have recognised that it was important for the Unity not to stray beyond the limits of acceptability. As Gwyn Williams pointed out, 'banner art is no counter-culture. Its duty was to communicate with the generality, it employed the media of the commons … No banner can move far from the common discourse.'[166] The image appeared on many Oddfellows' banners.[167] Even if only glimpsed on a fluttering banner above a crowd, the Good Samaritan would have been a familiar, enduring icon which could remind people of the role of Christianity within the Unity's origins and practices and suggest that the while the Unity produced mortality tables it did not seek to commodify sickness and death.[168] The parable would have been a familiar to potential recruits and friendly society members as The Good Samaritan appeared on many Sunday School's banners and one banner-making company 'would use the same set of standard designs for them all … the Good Samaritan was especially serviceable'.[169] Quite apart from their Biblical knowledge many would have been familiar with the use of the Samaritan within other narratives. In *Hard Times* Dickens has a dislikable character, Mr Gradgrind, trying to prove 'that the Good Samaritan was a Bad Economist', while in *Oliver Twist* the same author used the parable to highlight the unpleasantness of the eponymous hero's persecutor.[170] It might reasonably be expected that onlookers, on seeing at the bearers of the Coventry banner would perceive them strong, caring, disciplined Christian men, united for mutual support, eager for citizenship, in favour of social relationships created through rituals and actions, respectful of hierarchy and yet defiant of middle-class strictures regarding expenditure by friendly societies on banners.

IV   Conclusion

During its first century the Oddfellows enjoyed growth and prosperity. By 1910 it had 1,033,000 members and capital valued at £14,600,000. It was, as the Bishop said in 1910, 'no longer a small band emerging into a precarious existence, amid ridicule and prognostications of failure but the greatest of all friendly societies'.[171] Maintaining the balance between commercial, charitable, civil and community considerations was difficult. Prioritisation of one thread within the tapestry had led to contestation, lodges seceding and members being expelled. Many tensions remained. When the Oddfellows enabled men to travel for work through the tramping system, it found itself relatively unpopular among those whose skills tied them to specific locations. When it offered secure provision in times of need, it excluded those who could not afford to be members and alienated those who placed charity and fellowship as superior to, and distinct from, actuarial soundness. When it enabled men to control their own finances and administer their own healthcare, it found those responsibilities were sometimes subject to abuse and ineptitude. When it provided fraternal activities and rituals, it found some preferred that their money be spent on insurance and savings rather than regalia and feasting. The Oddfellows succeeded because it supported a highly mobile population (in the mid-1800s more than one out of every three rural residents of Great Britain left for an urban area), during a period when there were few institutional barriers to geographic mobility (some aspects of the Poor Laws apart) and considerable incentive to move for economic gain especially since there was little occupational mobility. It also grew because it adapted to changes in the legal framework and was at home in urban areas where new ways of working and gender and familial divisions occurred. It was not simply the object of external forces, it was also active in the creation of Manchester and of the social and legal regulatory frameworks and able to employ familiar ideas and activities in distinctive ways. The provision offered by the Oddfellows was welcomed because it was built on a recognition that people's needs were social and relational, that individuals required the mutuality of friendship and the experience of self-realisation in a common endeavour. During a period when mutual aid was in its zenith, a period, 1790 to 1890, which has been described by Yeo as one when there was a 'making of a culture of co-operation and mutuality among English working people' the Society's way of connecting insurance to the promotion of ethical and moral teaching designed to inspire both charity and mutual aid, of supporting families through male fellowship and of enabling men to engage in political activity by providing a stable civic environment and single-sex structured social networks, proved to be of enormous popularity.[172]

CHAPTER FIVE

Administering National Health Insurance, 1912–1948

AT its centenary in 1910 the Oddfellows appeared to be enormously successful. The Society had built upon the experiences of a variety of existing bodies which promoted collective self-help. It had presented itself as a body of convivial men (and recently women) capable of engagement in civil functions, sound investment and involvement in a regulated cycle of exchange. It had successfully appealed to those with regular incomes who wished to be associated with a charitable, rule-based organisation which, through the sound management of funds, was able to support families against some of the problems which arose due to the illness or death of a breadwinner. In 1826 in Manchester 95 elected Deputies, representing fewer lodges, attended the AMC. In 1834 there were 70,000 members. In 1910, following 'a century of silent, unobtrusive growth', there were 678 deputies who attended the AMC. They represented over a million members in 4,000 lodges in 400 districts.[1] However, even as Moffrey claimed that 'the hundredth anniversary will be but the starting point of renewed youth and fresh triumphs', negotiations were in progress which resulted in the National Health Insurance Act, 1911 which came into force in January 1912.[2] That celebrations at the centenary AMC in May 1910 were cancelled, due to the death the King ten days earlier, was perhaps prescient because a traditional feast would, if the effect of the forthcoming legislation had been known, probably have come to be seen as a Barmecidal banquet.

In November 1912 the Grand Master spoke of how the 'State has exploited our experience', and argued that Lloyd George, the Chancellor of the Exchequer, had promised not to harm the friendly societies and yet had engaged in negotiations with industrial insurance companies adding: 'he must have known when he did this that, with their house-to-house organisation, their methods of canvassing and their autocratic government he was striking a deadly blow at the friendly societies'.[3] In 1913, a year after it came into operation, Past Grand Master A. H. Warren concluded that 'if we were true to our ideals no cold-blooded State organisation would ever wipe out the Society in which we were all so proud to be workers'.[4] The Secretary of the Charity Organisation Society and an Honorary member of the Oddfellows, Charles Loch, wrote that the National Health Insurance Act was 'the death warrant of the friendly societies'.[5] In 1949, a year after the demise of the Act, Douglas Cole concluded that 'the friendly societies, including the Orders, despite their large membership, have ceased to count as a social force to anything like the extent to which they used to count in the Victorian era'.[6] Another 50 years later David Green came to a similar conclusion, that 'when national insurance was introduced it attended only to the material dimension and in separating the cash benefits from the moral and educational role of the societies destroyed their essence.'[7] Although the Oddfellows survived its passage the legislation speeded the 'gradual abandonment of those aspects of mutuality and fellowship that had been the hallmark of friendly societies in Victorian Britain'.[8] The first section indicates the ways in which the legislation contributed to the unpopularity of the Society with doctors (with whom there were already tensions) with the civil servants who implemented the Act, with the Labour Party, which supported the replacement of the Act, and with many of its own members, who were dissatisfied with the implementation of the Act.

The second section indicates that matters fail to improve for the Oddfellows once its approved status was removed, following the establishment of a Ministry of National Insurance in 1944 and the National Insurance Act, 1946. This was for a number of reasons. Although the focus in many studies has been on the impact of the legislation, a monocausal explanation marginalises longer-term concerns. In 1911 the Society was already finding it difficult to adjust to a world where expectations about health care and insurance were changing and the average age of the members was increasing. The adoption of new techniques and medications pushed up the cost of medical care. The main cost of the sickness of the breadwinner for a family changed from the loss of his income to the payment of medical bills. This entailed a demand for larger and more varying sums, a pattern which fitted better the less personal, and more business-like methods of commercial insurers. By agreeing to administer the 1911 Act for the government the Oddfellows proceeded in a new direction. It would have been marginalised if it had not taken on such a role but its engagement with the new legislation may have rendered it less able to adapt to the considerable social changes of the first half of the twentieth century.

I '9d. for 4d.': Implementing the National Health Insurance Act[9]

As the legislation to introduce state pensions appeared to have helped rather than hindered the Unity there was some hope that the legislation to introduce state national insurance would also be useful. The intention was to provide a system of compulsory health insurance for lower-paid employed people and for these workers to select a friendly society through which this scheme would be administered. Initially the Bill appeared to be supportive of collective self-help, but there were significant changes made during the latter stages of debate. The Society was divided about the forthcoming legislation. In 1909 a piece in the *Oddfellows' Magazine* claimed 'friendly societies are apolitical', but went on to express a 'confirmed belief in the voluntary principle as opposed to state compulsion'. This contradiction was partially explained by a further item in the same issue of the *Magazine* that equated politics with parties and argued that the Oddfellows 'kept outside altogether of politics, working only for the good of the Society and its members'. The Society, although many members were in members of political parties, insisted in presenting itself as above party politics.[10]

Although some MPs were members, for example Captain A. H. Lee MP was initiated into the Loyal Volunteers Pride Lodge, Cosham immediately prior to the annual dinner in 1900, the industrial insurance companies, such as the Prudential, were also adept at lobbying.[11] Founded as the Mutual Assurance and Loan Association in 1848, by the end of 1886 the Prudential had over seven million industrial assurance policies in force. It had 10 million policies by 1891 and by 1901 it claimed that a third of the population was covered by the Prudential. In 1912, for the first time the number of commercial insurance policies was larger than the number of friendly society members. Pledges of support for the commercial interests were provided by 590 of the 670 MPs returned in the December 1910 General Election. These companies, and some trade unions, were allowed to form societies which could be approved by the government to administer the national insurance scheme. Approved societies were not required to provide medical benefits (which had never offered by the commercial interests). One of the people who drafted the Bill referred to a 'betrayal', and claimed that the friendly society representatives who were discussing the proposed legislation were duped following 'a very good lunch (with wine)'.[12] At the 1909 AMC it was resolved that the Unity was opposed to any scheme of compulsory State insurance against sickness for persons eligible for membership in voluntary thrift societies.[13] However, following legislation, the Oddfellows decided, by 501 votes to 59, to apply for approved status.[14]

Although the rationale for government administration and expenditure on welfare, through the Poor Law system, was widely accepted, the cost of the Poor Law and the complexity of local government finance helped to make the case for intervention at national, not local, level. Using a narrow, regressive property tax, the rates, as a means of funding welfare was perceived as expensive. Local expenditure amounted to about a fifth of total

THE DAWN OF HOPE.

Mr. LLOYD GEORGE'S National Health Insurance Bill provides for the insurance of the Worker in case of Sickness.

Support the Liberal Government
in their policy of
SOCIAL REFORM.

This Liberal Party poster has used an image familiar to many members of the Society. Lloyd George is portrayed as a Sick Visitor and the member, instead of gazing upon his membership certificate on the wall is looking at the illusion conjured up by the Chancellor.

GETTY IMAGES

Jewel marking attendance at one of the most significant AMCs in the history of the Society, which was held in the wake of the National Health Insurance Act, 1911. The letters M and U can be seen in the art nouveau styling.
THE LIBRARY AND MUSEUM OF FREEMASONRY

government expenditure in 1840 and about half in 1910.[15] The Liberal Party was threatened by the possibility of working-class voters choosing Labour, which sought to develop redistributive tax-funded welfare, and middle-class voters voting for the Conservative Party, which promoted protective duties (in opposition to free trade) as a means of resolving the problems associated with poverty. Contributory social insurance imposed an obligation upon employers and involved only a modest state subsidy. In addition, the government could build upon not only the payment traditions and structures of the friendly societies but also some of the trade unions. Daunton has argued that the state had long 'delegated' powers to voluntary associations such as the Oddfellows.[16] Unemployment pay was already offered by those unions for relatively well-paid men who were susceptible to cyclical unemployment, such as ship builders and engineers. In order to provide elementary schooling there had been state subventions to Anglican and Nonconformist educational societies since 1833 and it was occasionally suggested that grants be given to hospitals.[17] The Liberal government built upon the general fiscal flexibility and capacity of national government, the well-developed, if sometimes parsimoniously administered, Poor Law and the actuarial knowledge, administrative experience and normative assumptions of the Oddfellows and other friendly societies when it created its social insurance scheme. While the Unity was critical of the outcome, presenting it as centralised and bureaucratic, it also shaped it.

The principles of Oddfellowship were already under threat through the decline in interest in migration, processions and regalia. Although the Oddfellows' Fete at Shipston in July 1886 involved a 'comic singing contest', within a few years one member noted that the traditions of Oddfellowship were endangered by recorded music.[18]

Why go to a sing song to hear Bob Turner the blacksmith sing some song fifty years old when they can go to the tuppenny gaff next door and hear the latest music hall artist or hear Harry Lauder repeated on the gramophone – he can get into a tram and go and see his friend at the other end of town and every year see fresh openings for social intercourse which did not exist fifty years ago.[19]

In the twentieth century, there were reports that the Oddfellows failed to make use of the interest in popular music among the young to attract them to the Society. In 1913 a Past Grand, I. C. King of North London contrasted current lodge nights which were 'in some cases a bore' with 'the happy period when the NG was wont, little caring for musical accompaniment, to lead off with a catchy chorus song. Taking their cue from their chief brother threw themselves heart and soul into the fun and happiness ruled supreme.' He reported that one lodge with a membership of over 200 had to count a visitor to make the quorum of five. He proposed singing, card games, debates and concerts. 'It is unreasonable to expect men – particularly young men to attend a stagnant lodge'.[20] At the same time the lodges of South London planned a ramblers club, 'a bowling club for our middle-aged brethren' and a fund-raising oratorio choir 'augmented by an orchestra'. All this was in order

> to develop the higher intellect and mould our social character so as to leave no doubt in one's mind that Oddfellowship has a deeper and broader interpretation than may be placed thereon by 'the man in the street' even those who constitute the rank and file of our numerical strength.[21]

Other forms of entertainment appealed to a wider audience. Robert Roberts wrote about growing up in Salford after the First World War:

> My mother recalled the complaint of our burial club collector. 'Some of 'em are reading mad!' he grumbled. 'They buy paper after paper, but won't pay the weekly penny these days, to bury their dead!'[22]

Cinemas, dancehalls and later television were all perceived as threats to the popularity of the Society. Furthermore, Daunton noted another role that the Society played became of less significance:

> charity was increasingly marginalised ... voluntary hospitals became less important ... Neither did charities any longer provide a means of negotiating class relations [and] could even be counter-productive as symbols of deference and dependence. The significance of philanthropic welfare provision declined as a central element in the stabilisation of urban society.[23]

The legislation provided between 11 and 12.4 million people with health insurance in 1912 and this figure rose in subsequent years as the population grew and the threshold for eligibility changed.[24] By 1942 some 21 million workers were covered. All employed persons aged between 16 (or, after 1937 younger but employed) and 70 (65 after 1928) if they earned less than £160 (£250 after 1920) per annum or were manual labourers in the same age group regardless of earnings, had to join a society which had been approved by the government. In 1911 only 2.25 million of the roughly ten million employed workers were declared eligible for unemployment Insurance. Most were in occupations labelled 'precarious' which included engineering, shipbuilding, construction, and machine- and tool-making. By 1919 the number had risen to four million.[25] If they lost their jobs they did not contribute to the scheme but were still allowed to claim.[26] Approximately 10 per cent joined a friendly society, a few joined approved trade union societies and most joined societies established by industrial life insurance companies. Employers paid three pence, male workers 4d. (women 3d.) and the government 2d. a week. The benefits included 10s. a week sick pay (7s. 6d. for women) for the first 26 weeks, payable from the fourth day of sickness, disability benefit of 5s. a week payable for periods beyond 26 weeks (these last two payable up to age 70), sanatorium treatment for TB sufferers and maternity benefit of 30s. in cash or in kind towards the expenses of confinement. Women whose husbands were also insured qualified for double benefit.[27] Jim Tolley recalled paying half-a-crown (2s. 6d.) each month and receiving 10s. a week when unable to work through illness. He went on to become a Trustee of the Worcester District.[28] These were not sums which acted as an inducement to fain illness as Ralph Dawes, 1920–2008, a member of the Royal Musgrove Lodge in Shillington noted. He saw the Unity as a safety net, but pointed out that 'if you were completely incapacitated you only drew 7s. 6d. a week or something like that and as a last resort there was parish relief'.[29]

One of the difficulties that the Oddfellows faced was that the Act undermined the lodge system. When the Act was passed there were over 15,000 separate approved society units (that is lodges, courts or branches). A departmental committee noted that 'where so many lodges are insignificant in size [this leads] to the perpetuation of inefficient methods and lax systems of administration'. Many of those friendly societies which were deemed to be too small to be approved were reformed as part of an approved society of which there were 2,208 in 1912. For example, a society based in Radcliffe-on-Trent was formed in 1821, joined the Nottingham Ancient Imperial Order of Oddfellows in 1844, left in the 1870s and joined the IOOFMU in 1912.[30] The Eliot Arms Friendly Society in Tregadillet, Cornwall, decided to join the Oddfellows and then changed its mind and became one of the 133 new Foresters courts which arose following the legislation.[31] Such gains were not made in a structured, strategic fashion, they meant that the growth of the lodge network remained uneven and related to areas of economic growth.[32] In 1915 the Oddfellows' Directors asked lodges with fewer than 100 members to merge with nearly lodges. The number of lodges fell dramatically over the years within the Oddfellows and in the other affiliated orders. Between 1918 and 1932, 2,700 branches of the larger societies had ceased to operate and total membership had fallen below three million. By 1938 only 5,700 of the 15,000 lodges which had been open remained. For many members the pleasures of convivial company were reduced because membership involved more travel and social activity in unfamiliar lodges. The larger lodges survived because they had the resources to run the new scheme efficiently. Tony Crouch recalled the period:

> The Grays Thurrock lodge was a very big lodge and a very wealthy lodge because, before National Health came into being [in 1948], the lodge administered all that the

state does today. You had two full time secretaries at the Grays Thurrock lodge. They had a nice office and one used to look after what you called the state side and the other one looked after what you called the voluntary side. I used to pay one and eleven pence halfpenny a fortnight and if I was sick I used to get a pound a week and that was the voluntary side.

Lodges were also put under pressure because of the work expected by local secretaries. Contributions were paid through a complex system. Employers purchased stamps at the post office and fixed them to the workers' contribution cards and deducted the workers' portion directly from wages. These cards were returned to the member's approved society, which returned them to the Ministry as proof of contributory income. Although the day-to-day administrative decisions were supposedly left to the approved societies in practice transactions between centre and society were monitored through the process of audit. Collectively, the Controller, the official auditors and Government Actuary determined the ways in which the scheme developed. The process of audit forced the Oddfellows to ensure that its lodges conformed. This was expensive and reduced local autonomy. One Oddfellows official in evidence to Departmental Committee in 1914 noted: 'Our secretaries are simply being converted into State officials ... it is said that the funds have been administered by self-governing societies but then we know as a matter of fact that they are not self-governing.' Every lodge had to keep track of nine different account books, 21 different categories of insured people and 22 different items of information about each member. The secretaries sent the books to the Ministry as proof of income which was then credited to the Society twice yearly in arrears. This was after the Ministry had checked on claims and certification and if appropriate withheld payment for 'improper' expenditure. The Ministry then credited the Oddfellows with their share of contributions and the state's subvention and audited the accounts. It decided every five years how much each approved society could offer in additional benefits. This was calculated following consideration of the 'panel' doctors' per capita fee and data about the reserve values, contingency funds and investment.[33]

The Oddfellows soon became concerned about the complexity of the system:

The year will be remembered by secretaries as a particularly trying one. Their work has been made more heavy by uncertainty from day to day as to what is required of them. The simple methods of a voluntary society, giving satisfactory results to the members have been superseded by a complex system designed to create unnecessary work and for Insurance Commissioners to bind in red tape the officials of the approved societies as helpless parts of the departmental machine. What has been the result? The resignation and retirement of many efficient and honest officers who declined to undertake the duties of the new regime ... The whole system of administration has been changed. If the friendly society is to hold its place among the approved societies many of our secretaries will have to devote their whole time to the work and the numerical development of their lodges.[34]

At the 1913 AMC the Grand Master, Walter Wright, said that the Unity had 'to a great extent transformed' by the decision to become an approved society and pointed to some of the dangers of 'the most revolutionary measure which has ever been adopted by the Legislature of this country'. His concerns included forgetting the need 'to build up character as well as to build up health' and to educate 'men and women in the virtues of self-denial and self-help'. He felt that the Unity was veering towards being 'a mere commercial undertaking', that 'social and educational gatherings are becoming a rarity' there was less Ritual and there was a danger of 'creating a nation of spoon fed puppets instead of a nation of free and independent men and women'. He also said that the old system of sick visiting was no longer working and that the detection of malingering was more difficult and that it was proving difficult. It was also difficult to accommodate women members as some lodges had not found meeting places outside licensed premises and in mixed lodges there were no women sick visitors.[35] He claimed that some trade union-run approved societies were interpreting 'incapacity of work' to justify paying unemployment benefit while others were very strict and that the rule which stated that industrial societies had to be subject to the control of their members was 'a dead letter'. He complained about the 'control and interference' of the government and noted that membership, excluding state membership, had fallen. The problems catalogued in 1913 were to continue to plague the Society for much of the period when it was approved.

The Oddfellows expressed further concerns about the demanding and intrusive nature of the legislation. 'We thought that National Insurance could be run in the same way as voluntary insurance,' a representative told the Departmental Committee on Sickness Benefits in March 1914 and went on:

> We never dreamed ... we would be so governed by regulations. We had no idea that the Treasury grant would be bound up in so much red tape. We were very unsophisticated, innocent people, knowing nothing whatever about state departments. We had an idea that all these people would come in through us, that we should receive the stamped cards and convert them into money, that the societies would be self governed, that the members would conserve their funds and look after them, just as they do on the voluntary side and that we should pay out benefits according to our own rules. I believe that if the friendly societies had really known what it meant and entailed ... they would in fact have asked the state to take the thing and administer it themselves.[36]

The regulations which framed the activities of the Oddfellows were not only time consuming and confusing but also often changed. There were numerous tweaks made to the scheme in almost every year between 1913 and 1945.

The Oddfellows felt obliged to pay for some secretarial work. In Exeter district as a result of the Act four female lodges with 2,500 members were opened. The Provincial Corresponding Secretary resigned and was replaced by a full-time Prov CS on a salary of £150 a year.[37] However, there were still concerns expressed in the *Oddfellows' Magazine*:

Lament of the Prov CS

The 'Lament of the Prov CS' appeared in the *Magazine* in June 1914. It first verse and chorus are as follows:

> The Government Auditor stands at my left,
> The Directors are close to my right –
> And behind and before Secretaries galore –
> I can't sleep by day or by night.
>
> Yes! I'm a gay CS
> And my life is naught but play:
> I get in my office at ten in the morn
> And at three go home for the day
> (I don't think).[38]

The approved societies are being asked to do work which will according to the secretaries be three or four times as heavy as in the past for 3*s*. 8*d*. per member per annum while extravagant salaries are paid to Commissioners and officials to supervise their work.[39]

The work of Harry Bagshaw, the Secretary of the Loyal Adventurers of the Peak Lodge Taddington, Derbyshire in the 1920s was recalled by his daughter, Mary Williams:

The Oddfellows work was a full time job. He issued the Insurance Cards – I used to help him to write the Insurance Cards out, about twice a year. They had what they called Club Nights, where they went to the pub – they all had a card and paid a subscription. He had about 700 or 800 members. It was called Baslow and Buxton District – he was the Secretary and there were so many lodges under him; about 13 or 14.[40]

Winifred Felgate recalled the administrative workload imposed on her father by the scheme. He was a lodge secretary in Dereham, Norfolk in the 1930s and he

got a small remuneration not enough to give up his work. He did that as well as his job. It involved doing all the books and paying the money out and collecting the money, running the lodge meetings. He had piles and piles of books to fill in and he had every member entered. Before 1948, when the National Health Service came in, he did the State sickness benefits. I can remember him having a special pad with all withdrawals in of all the members who were state registered with him. They had to have cards stamped, a stamp every week from their employer and Dad was responsible for that as well. Dad had a big wooden office built in our back garden and he had all his Oddfellows books there. We didn't have room in the house for all the books and insurance cards that had to be stamped. He used to collect the money for the contributions at the lodge meeting or people brought them round to our house. There were three doctors in the town and he used to go round to each of their surgeries and pay them for any of our members who had visited.

Moreover, these efforts were not always appreciated in Whitehall. In 1914 the Local Government Board concluded that 'the tragedy of voluntary effort is that it finds it difficult to maintain a high standard of efficiency'.[41]

The effect on the Oddfellows was, as one Oddfellow pointed out, that members became 'actuarial friendly society men rather than actual friendly society men [whose] souls were in pawn to the devil of arithmetic, who blew our ideals sky-high'.[42] The Oddfellows recognised that that its powers had diminished:

On the State side we are mere hewers of wood and drawers of water for the State. To talk of us retaining any shred of independent control or initiative is to delude ourselves as vainly as the fly which imagines itself to be driving the wheel on which it has alighted. The amount of the contribution, the amount of the benefit, the handling and investment of all the funds, the administration of the medical benefit have all been taken from us; these are all arranged now by the Insurance Commissioners, or by Insurance Committees, they are no longer in the control of the working men who will have to find the money either directly or indirectly. The right of our own members to administer all these things for themselves was the glory of our voluntary institutions. In all these things the Insurance Act carries us backward to the servile Middle Ages, instead of forward to a fuller and more enlightened freedom.[43]

The effect of this seemingly retrograde step was that the number of members of the Oddfellows fell. In a 15 year period in the late nineteenth century 250,000 adults joined but after the Act membership declined and through the 1914–1918 war the downwards trend continued. When the war broke out in 1914 the Society's Grand Master Tom Hughes argued that the mission of the Unity was a peaceful one: 'We are a peace-living people and as Oddfellows, crusaders in a cause that seeks to diminish human suffering, not to inflict it; to brighten homes not to desolate them.' Nevertheless, it was the duty of members to serve 'manfully and courageously', and the *Magazine* reported that the 10 per cent of the Loyal Earl of Pomfret Lodge, Towcester, had already joined up, and that the percentage was higher in other lodges.[44] In 1916 the *Oddfellows' Magazine* reported that secessions, of which there were 25,712, were 14,000 fewer than the 'abnormally high figures of a year ago', but that juvenile membership had fallen and

only 19,225 new members have been initiated into adult lodges as voluntary members. The loss is theirs and not the Manchester Unity. It is a big financial risk to accept any male member of military age; the liability which he brings to the lodge from the possibility of military service is enormous.[45]

There were still over one million 'independent' members and almost as many state members. During the Boer War some lodges had paid the contributions of those serving in South Africa and there had been concern that the sick funds of the Society would be severely depleted by those 'young in years but broken in health' and a levy was raised but the war did not prove to be economically disastrous for the Society.[46] In 1914 the Oddfellows promised to meet the contributions of those who served in the Forces. This was the cause of much pride as a poem in the *Magazine* which had the lines below indicates:

> So through our Order rang the words,
> Of which we're proud today –
> Brothers on active service will
> No contributions pay![47]

It was also proposed that the contributions of the wives and children of serving members be paid as this would be 'a splendid advertisement and should help us a lot in obtaining new members'.[48] However, the promise was severely amended in 1915.[49] Many of those to whom the Oddfellows expected to make payments did not live to receive the benefits due to the war, a period when the number of claims made fell. The decline between 1921 and 1922 was, it was 'confidently stated' by the Grand Master at the AMC 'due to the industrial depression during the past 12 months'. He noted that the overseas lodges had increased their membership by 8,156 and juvenile membership had increased by 2,862 while there has been an overall decrease in adult membership of 2,604. There had also been a decrease in state membership of 24,905 taking it to 922, 998 as former soldiers and women war workers left the scheme. As a result of the legislation the Oddfellows became part of a system which 'extended social protection at the price of undermining social autonomy – a process reinforced by recession', argued Whiteside who went on to suggest that 'central regulation throttled the possibility of popular participation.'[50] It was also in this period that a distinction that the Oddfellows had over other financial service providers was whittled away. The 1921 Finance Act introduced an exemption from income tax for trust-based pension schemes. This brought them into line with the treatment of friendly societies but without the restrictions on the size of benefits.

As well as the quasi-autonomous lodge system being ill-suited to the National Health Insurance scheme, there was an increase in savings by about 24 per cent among working people in the period 1916–21. Many purchased War Savings Certificates or National Savings Certificates. Industrial insurance and collecting societies increased their share of the market.[51] They issued more policies than they might otherwise have done. The number of policies issued by collecting societies rose by more than 350 per cent between 1915 and 1945.[52] The Hearts of Oak Friendly Society, which provided no social activities, had fewer than 33,000 members in 1872 and over 239,000 by the end of the century. Between 1910 and 1926 the Oddfellows lost one percent of its members while, insurance-only societies, such as the National Deposit, grew by over 200 per cent.

Although the Act specified that an approved society had to be subject to the 'absolute control of its members including provision for the election and removal of the committee of management', this requirement was satisfied when a dozen clerks who worked for the Prudential held a meeting in its London office.[53] When questioned about this matter by an MP the Prudential representative, J. A. Jefferson, said:

> all the present members of the committee are those who have been agents or superintendents and have worked up to their present positions by sheer ability, therefore they are persons who thoroughly know and understand the British public ... and know absolutely all their interests and everything of that sort.[54]

The Prudential officers and committee were appointed by the Prudential Assurance Company and could not be removed until at least four years hence and that there was no reasonable provision for local autonomy. If a member had a grievance there the route to satisfaction was complicated as Deputy Grand Master Walter Wright pointed out in 1913:

> He has no voice or vote in any matter connected with the administration of his society unless he pays his own expenses to London to attend the annual meeting. If he desires to ventilate a grievance he must get 1,000 of his fellow-members to sign a requisition for the holding of a district meeting and must guarantee the expenses of such a meeting. When the meeting is called he finds that no resolution can be submitted to a district meeting until it has first been submitted to a special meeting of the society and if he so desires to have a special meeting of the society he has to get another 1,000 signatures and guarantee the still heavier expenses of a large meeting in London. No member of the society who is in arrears to an amount greater than 13 weekly contributions a year on average is entitled to vote at any meeting and thus the unfortunate member who has had a long spell of unemployment is deprived of his elementary rights of membership.[55]

The depressed economy also led to further squeezes on the Oddfellows. The influence of the Actuary and the auditors increased in the 1920s. The government reduced its contribution to the cost of the scheme and, as the number of unemployed rose, their contributions fell. The government had found a revenue-raising measure which fitted the political culture of the country and was popular because contributions to national insurance through friendly societies were not seen as a tax.[56] Furthermore, it could evade criticism of the low level of benefit payments, the different levels of benefit payments and the fact that many people were not covered at all by blaming the approved societies. Frank Field has called this

> the political battering ram which was used to break down the defensive gates of mutuality. The charge that the system had failed immediately to provide cover for everyone in the land carried with it the capital sentence. Yet, ironically, a major responsibility for this very state of affairs rested with governments which, by raiding the reserves, crippled efforts to move towards a greater universalisation of provision.[57]

The Oddfellows was pushed into making good deficits from their own resources and to implementing new regulations governing questions of access, levels of benefit and the policing of claimants and doctors. While the recession reduced contributions and raised the incidence of claims, the cost to taxpayers was very little because the Exchequer contribution was only paid on reimbursement of expenditure. Large sums were held within Whitehall as contingency funds and the interest used to offset the Exchequer contribution. Furthermore, any money that the Oddfellows made was held by the government. The conservatism of the actuarial science practised by the Exchequer was such that by 1938 over £220 million was held, ostensibly as society investments, in centralised reserve funds – outstripping the assets of the Unemployment Fund (£130 million) and the Pensions Fund (£50 million) combined. The interest accruing from this sum (c.£7 million p.a.) was used to offset the annual Exchequer contribution of £9 million to the scheme. Funds which might previously have swelled the Oddfellows coffers ended up as savings for the Treasury. Furthermore, it was easy for the government to unilaterally tighten regulations. In 1922, following the Geddes Report and twice in 1925, following the introduction of contribution pensions and the Economy Act, the Society's income from the Exchequer was reduced. In 1932 women's benefit rights were cut and cover was removed from some unemployed. As the regulations became more complicated, so the autonomy of the Oddfellows was reduced. The Oddfellows received a flat rate, per capita subsidy. It had to pay for its own running expenses and overheads. The Treasury paid one sixth of the total administrative costs. The Oddfellows found it had high administrative costs compared to the cost of the benefits delivered. Its request that it be allowed to pool the surpluses of lodges (an idea that the 1926 report of the Royal Commission on National Health Insurance recommended) was not allowed. The Directors, the 1932 AMC was told, had done 'all that was humanly possible' to lobby.[58]

The scheme was expensive and complicated for the societies which administered it and not designed for a friendly society which valued lodge democracy. It also had the effect of maintaining and exacerbating tensions between the Oddfellows and many doctors. Before 1912 lodges had appointed their own doctors. Since the 1840s medical attendance was provided by many lodges but it was not in the national regulations of the Society and of course many people could not afford to join the Oddfellows.[59] Lodge appointments might be based on perceptions of qualifications, performance, bedside manner or ability. There were disputes. For example in 1844 the Oddfellows employed 27 surgeons to attend lodge members in Glasgow at the price of 3s. 6d. a head. Those who did not receive contracts felt this sum was unprofessional and brought medical attendance into disrepute. However, the Select Committee on Medical Poor Relief received evidence in the same year that the usual rate was between 2s. and 3s. There was no significant rise in the rate for the next 30 years and even as late as 1900, according to the *British Medical Journal*, doctors were accepting between 3s. and 4s.

By the mid-Victorian period the Oddfellows had developed a well-organised system of attendance and certification. Each lodge had a nominated medical officer who provided certificates and who was paid according to the number of lodge members. This meant that members could make what might otherwise have been deemed clinical decisions. When, in 1856 a sick member was away from home at unauthorised times and 'in a public house drunk and disorderly', Good Samaritan Lodge, Cambridge ordered him to pay a fine of 5s., to return the one week's sick benefit that he had received and to be suspended from the lodge for six weeks. In 1860 one member of the same lodge allowed one member to draw half sick pay while following his employment and when Brother Attwood was diagnosed as ill Merton Hall Lodge sought a second opinion. Unanimity Lodge, Cambridge argued that the certificate signed by the doctor did not specify a disease and refused to pay a member.[60] The same doctor would both certify that a member was ill and treat that member. His loyalty was to the employer, the Society, not to individual patients and Oddfellows members could not move to another doctor.[61]

The Oddfellows was allowed to decide who joined as Bert Bowker, the son of a coach-driver, later caretaker, recalled. In early twentieth-century Preston his family were members of the Oddfellows but he was not:

> I was the only one who never passed for the Oddfellows. My sister took me by the hand to the doctor and we had to pass a doctor in those days to go to a friendly society who then for a penny a week provided you with a free doctor ... The doctor said 'Well, what do you want?' The doctors were very severe in those days. 'My mother has sent us to see if you'll put Bert into the Oddfellows.' He said, 'You can take him back and tell your mother she should have drowned him when he was young and I'm not going to do it.'[62]

Although the comprehensive national system offered by the Oddfellows was superior to those offered by village societies or patronised societies, concerns remained. Most lodges only paid medical officers on a part-time contract basis and often the medical officers had to travel long distances to visit members. Some areas tackled these problems through the formation local medical associations, such as the Bradford Oddfellows Medical Aid Association. This body employed a surgeon full-time with a house and medical supplies, providing that he took on no other work. Lodges paid three shillings for each member or individual members could join for 3s. 6d. a year or 10s. 6d. for the whole family. There were also some tensions as an advertisement in a medical journal of the 1890s made clear:

> BATTLE OF THE CLUBS: Before replying to advertisements for Medical Officers to any society in the Wigan District medical men are requested to communicate with the Hon Sec Wigan and District Medical Guild, Wigan.[63]

After 1912 those covered by the scheme could call on the services of a 'panel' doctor. Money accrued under the scheme went to the Ministry of Health while the Oddfellows administered the benefits and paid the panel doctors and dispensaries through local insurance committees. Before the Act was passed many Oddfellows' club doctors had reduced visits in favour of a getting more patients through the surgery and the panel doctors often maintained this system. Doctors were paid per approved society patient on their panel and this encouraged GPs to recruit the maximum number of panel patients and to spend the minimum time treating them. Payment was not for treatment and doctors who made use of a laboratory for tests paid for it themselves. It was calculated that a doctor gave on average three-and-a-quarter minutes to each insurance patient in the surgery, and four minutes when on a visit to the patient's home. This resulted in tensions between doctors and Oddfellow patients because the emphasis was on the quantity not quality of care delivered. It was linked to a low standard of patient care, to over prescription and to a reluctance to treat difficult cases (for no remuneration) rather than to refer them to hospital outpatient clinics or elsewhere.[64] There was little incentive to invest in modern equipment and premises.[65] The quality of services provided varied widely, as it did in the hospital sector.

The distribution of General Practitioners did not necessarily correspond to the areas where their services were most needed. General Practitioners were independent contractors, not salaried employees of a state-provided medical service (a status they preserved under the NHS). Panel patients frequently queued at a back door to enter cramped, barely furnished surgery, there to wait their turn for the doctor during fixed surgery hours. In contrast, their middle-class counterparts chose personally convenient times for appointments, were greeted by a maid at the front door, and waited in a comfortable room in the doctor's house for more extended medical interviews. Appliances which were sanctioned by the NHI authorities in each locality were listed varied. In Burnley panel patients were given grey bandages, private patients were provided with white ones. There was neither incentive nor coercion for the doctor to improve accommodation.[66] Although panel patients had the right to choose their insurance practitioners, only between 3 and 5 per cent were estimated to have initiated a change in their doctor by giving notice at the end of a quarter. This may be due to ignorance, low expectations or satisfaction. Among the most common complaints were those from patients about rude or late doctors and charges made for procedures not covered by the insurance. This may have been because standards of practice varied between individual doctors and between insurance committees in different areas. Moreover, there were problems with inadequate certification in cases involving society members as insured patients with many complaints, usually upheld, by the Oddfellows against panel doctors. A BMA survey of 1926 indicated that doctors tended to visit panel patients less frequently than private ones. Some also admitted providing certificates indicating a person was unfit for work to prevent that patient joining another practice. Indeed a Ministry of Health report in 1937 concluded that the panel doctor 'tends to become little more than an agent for signing certificates'.[67]

The Society was running a scheme over which it had little control and which produced mediocre results for its members. Whereas in the past collecting contributions, processing claims and policing against fraud had been balanced by the pleasures of voluntary thrift, proud parades and democratic self-government, the Act shifted the focus of the Oddfellows. The change in the role of the lodge membership was noted by in the *Oddfellows' Magazine*. In one account the 'warm-hearted, sympathetic sick visitor' was contrasted to the 'cold officialism that will only perform so much service for so much monetary consideration'.[68] In another the 'sympathetic visitor' brought 'into the house of the afflicted brother … not only the benefit which the sick member has contributed for, but also a word of cheer and comfort from his brothers in the Order'. Following the legislation the visitor 'rushes round on Friday night or Saturday, hands the money in … takes a receipt for the benefit and goes.' [69]

Iris Capel was a juvenile Oddfellow in the 1930s and described how the system operated for her father:

When I was child I had rheumatism very badly for about 10 weeks. The doctor used to come and my Dad used to have to get him to sign a form to say he visited. In those days you had to pay the doctor and the lodge used to give you benefit towards the payment.

The 1922 'Special Rules' of the Loyal Adventurers of the Peak Lodge, Taddington, Derbyshire

These rules emphasised the financial and medical benefits and indicated the priorities of the Society:

(1) The objects of the Lodge shall be to provide contributions, fines, donations, levies, and interest on capital for:

(a) Insuring a sum of money to be paid on the death of a member, or for the funeral expenses of a member's first wife or the widow of a deceased member.

(b) The relief of maintenance of members during sickness or other infirmity.

(c) Payment of annuities to members in old age, if contributing for such Benefits.

(d) Proper medicine and surgical attendance for members.

(e) Assisting members in distressed circumstances.

(f) Contributing such sums to the Unity and District funds as may from time to time be determined by the Annual Movable Conference or a District Meeting.

(2) Grants may be made to any hospital, infirmary, charitable or provident institutions, under and subject to Sect. 37 of the Friendly Societies Act.[70]

In addition to the weekly provision of a Doctor's Certificate, members were bound by the following instructions in the 'Special Rules':

11: Sickness Benefits.

(l) A member in receipt of Sickness Benefit shall abstain from work of any description – the ordinary work of a household included.

Any member found undertaking such duties whilst in receipt of Sickness Benefit shall be liable to a fine, or suspension of Benefits, as set out in general Rule 167.

(2) A member in receipt of Sickness or Disablement Benefits shall not be absent from home between the hours of 6 pm and 8 pm between the first day of October and the first day of March and between 8 pm and 8 am between the first day of March and the first day of October, and shall not be absent at any time without leaving word where he may be found.

Many others recall the strict rules that were imposed. The conditions for receiving sickness benefit were stringent, and a Sick Visitor was appointed by the Lodge to make weekly visits to sick members within a specified radius of the Lodge to ensure compliance with the rules. Albert Fox acted as Sick Visitor in the Loyal Adventurers of the Peak Lodge in Taddington, Derbyshire:

> Now in those days you had to visit everybody on sick within a four mile radius once per week and report at the next Lodge meeting. There was one before I took over, he was pruning his roses and the Sick Visitor of the day saw him doing it and reported him and he had his sick pay stopped for that. There was another old man, he lived up Stanedge here, and his wife was ill and he was an old man, and he'd been down to Nelsons on Buxton Road for ½lb of sausages for their dinner, and he saw it and got stopped just the same – he was carrying ½lb of sausages. Oh they were strict, yes. It was terrible really. If they were out after 9 o'clock in summer, 7 o'clock in winter … I know when I was a Visitor, there was one man, he did like his beer, and it were about five minutes past nine. And I were on me round, sick visiting, and he said, 'I'm going straight 'ome, I'm going straight 'ome.'

Frank Bagshaw, a member of the same lodge, also recalled the rules for receiving benefit when interviewed by Dave Bathe:

> It was very keen, though. If you were off work they used to have a Sick Visitor, and he'd just drop in on you, any time. If he saw you – exaggerating I suppose – cleaning your boots, you were in trouble. You really couldn't do anything if you were sick you were sick and you had to stay in the house until you were signed off.

In nearby Disley the rules were also enforced according to Margaret Graham. She remembered that the Sick Visitor

> had a list of people who would claim the benefits. We used to go round to their houses regularly to make sure that they were still as incapacitated as they said they were and pay out their few shillings … If you were on the club you couldn't go out after 7 o'clock at night otherwise you lost your club money.

The Order had to deal with more illness than prior to the Act. This may have been because the policing of who was allowed to join the Oddfellows had been relaxed. It may have been because people who were more likely to claim sickness benefits joined and possibly it was because more people felt that malingering was acceptable and would go unpunished, As one report noted: 'We never saw toothache, earache and headache [on a doctor's certificate] until the National Insurance Act commenced operations.' Dr Alfred Cox, Secretary of the BMA, argued that the effect of the Act was that 'persons who formerly did not go to the doctor until they were really ill now go for more trifling ailments'.[71] At the 1914 AMC there was concern that there had been a rise in claims. One lodge of 600 members paid out £345 in one year and £640 the next while another the bill rose from £7 10s. to £26. Brother Jolly of South London said that this was not malingering but that 'the responsibility was with the medical men'.[72] The number of claims between the wars soon outstripped the rates established in the period 1912–14 and even rose above the averages that the Oddfellows had described during the mid-1890s. The decision to claim may have been guided by other factors than deciding that one felt ill. For example, by 1934–35 one third of the chronic disability cases were caused by nervous disorders, a trend partly explained by the recent respectability and prominence of psychiatric medicine and diagnoses. In addition, the criteria for payments under the National Insurance scheme were different to those made under the unemployment scheme. This may have encouraged people to claim the former, particularly as access to the latter was reduced and made more complicated.[73]

By contrast to the Oddfellows' high level of regulation and investigation by fellow members the Prudential hired full-time Sick Visitors who were not members but licensed nurses, if women, and former sales managers, if men. Prudential clerks were issued with medical dictionaries and guidelines on how much time off work could be claimed for any illness. The company wrote to doctors as a matter of routine to indicate the company view of a patient's ailment. The Oddfellows felt alienated and resentful that there was less reliance on brothers checking on one another. It had lost some if its status and it felt that the doctors had lobbied

Within a few years of being permitted to join the Society women were attending AMCs, as this picture of Deputies at the 1914 Aberystwyth AMC indicates.
ODDFELLOWS MAGAZINE

with considerable success in order to improve their pay at the expense of the Order. Doctors' pay increased by about 50 per cent for about 4s. to about 9s. per patient and in real terms GPs 'were almost 50 per cent better off at the end of the inter-war period than at the beginning'.[74] The Grand Master in 1912 argued that 'the doctors last year declared war on the societies'.[75] The *Magazine* claimed that

> They have beaten the Chancellor of the Exchequer all along the line … it is the members of the approved societies who will have to suffer by way of the payment of an extortionate contribution for medical service … the majority of our lodges secured efficient medical service and medicine for their members for an average of 4s. per annum.[76]

This may also account for the report in the *Oddfellows' Magazine* that in Newport, Isle of Wight the Oddfellows had helpfully permitted some doctors to rent its hall for a meeting. The members debated this action until one reminded his brethren that it was permissible to take an ox out of a pit on the Sabbath; 'so surely it is not wrong to help 50 asses to get themselves out of a hole'.[77]

The difficulties related to the new roles that it was expected to play were compounded by the Unity's continued adherence to a relatively inflexible version of Oddfellowship. This focused on lodge meetings in pubs which excluded women and ensured men maintained control over expenditure. The Oddfellows had long assumed a separation of men and women. It had been unexceptional for men to socialise away from women, indeed Victorian working-class masculine self-respect demanded the exclusion of women.[78] In the nineteenth century part of the attraction of Oddfellowship might have been the enthusiasm men had for meeting in all-male environments. Data gathered by Alfred Watson of the Oddfellows suggested that women tended to be paid less than men and make more claims. It was argued that for many their wages were so low that membership was unaffordable.[79] Although from the 1893 women were permitted to join, in 1900 there were only 1,227 women in the Society in 44 female lodges, of which 14 had been opened that year.[80] By contrast, the AMC was attended by 645 Deputies, almost all of them men. However, there was interest in encouraging women to join. Market Drayton district proposed that mixed lodges be formed, an indication that change was being considered.[81] In 1901 PGM Sydney Campkin called for greater efforts to recruit women by offering maternity benefits and pension schemes. He said that although women were liable to many ailments, 'there was as much honour among the women of the land as among the men', and that 'just as the Society had established an ideal of manhood, it should set up an ideal of womanhood'.[82] In 1902 there were only 70,000 women in friendly societies.[83]

It was also in 1902 that a trade unionist active among the London bus workers, A. G. Markham, told a select committee about how expenditure on friendly societies was the prerogative of men:

> The ordinary domestic economy of a workman's household is this: You might put it roughly that the average earnings of a wage earner [are] about 30s. a week; he would give

the wife 20s. to 25s. out of that 30s.; the other 5s. he would use as his private spending money and for his Oddfellows or other friendly society's subscription.[84]

A year later the *Reading Co-operative Record* reported that the Oddfellows was focused on men noting: 'The Oddfellows are undoubtedly doing good work in propagating the principles of good fellowship and it behoves every young fellow to join one of the lodges without delay.'[85] The *Oddfellows' Magazine* of January 1907 concluded that almost two thirds of the lodges in Wales met in pubs.[86] The issue of gender roles was addressed by others within the Society. During the discussions prior to the National Health Insurance Act the Grand Master argued that the Order offered 'invaluable training in acquiring business habits and the management of affairs', while the *Oddfellows' Magazine* June 1909 suggested that friendly societies 'have formed character, they have made men, strong, self-reliant men who have had the courage to work out their own destinies'. State insurance, on the other hand, 'must make for the degeneration of the race, for the sapping of the manhood of the nation'. In 1913, writing in the *National Insurance Gazette* A. H. Warren said that Oddfellows should use the Act as a means to 'building up ... manly self-reliant characters' among the state insured members.[87]

By 1909 there had been women members for many years and an interest in a different form of masculinity was expressed:

> We don't know any sects, clans, classes or creeds, either theologically, politically or nationally; we stand on strict neutral ground and recognise only the broad principles of the Brotherhood of Man and the Fatherhood of God ... There was in Florence some years ago a beautiful statue of a woman carved in marble. The face was declared to be one of such singularly benignant expression that it fixed the eyes of the beholder. Her right arm was extended, and from her open palm there flowed a stream of pure, sparkling water. Is it not suggestive? Take a lesson home with you by it conveyed. Strive to be pure and flawless in your nature. Be generous and open-handed; it's better to give than to receive. Be womanly in your tenderness. Let your brethren have the pure and simple truths of God at your hands, that they may live for that nobler and better life.[88]

The 1911 legislation reflected the idea that women depended on men for survival. The scheme was open to workers but not their spouses or children. Men were expected to be the breadwinners. David Levine characterised the period between about 1875 and 1939 as 'the breadwinner economy' when work and identity were closely associated with gender.[89] Susan Pedersen made the case for 'the centrality of male breadwinner ideals to the mid-Victorian settlement'.[90] There was considerable sex segregation at work between 1860 and 1914. Many women worked within domestic service, few within industry or transport. Working men's associations, notably trade unions, came to see their independence and citizenship in terms of the ability of men to support their wives and children. Keith McClelland suggested that there was a 'belief that those who were independent and in possession of their 'manhood' were those able to maintain dependants'.[91] In the UK there was political competition for the votes of newly enfranchised men, and there was strong support for the organised men's claim for male breadwinner wages, a notion reflected in the Liberal government 1911 scheme. In 1911 Liberal intellectual Leonard Hobhouse argued that the state should not 'feed house or clothe' its citizens but rather it should 'take care that the economic conditions are such that the normal man who is not defective in mind or body or will can by useful labour feed, house and clothe himself and his family'.[92] Assessing the scheme, and Hobhouse's view, historian Susan Pedersen said that it 'set in motion a process whereby a man's role as family breadwinner – and hence the practice of providing for children through the male wage – would be guaranteed ... by targeting working men and strengthening their capacity to maintain [it] can be seen as representing one approach to the problems of family dependence.' The status of the family as what Pedersen called 'a haven of non-market mutuality in a world wracked by economic competition' was increasingly difficult to sustain.[93] In 1913 the National Insurance Act was amended to break the link between the Oddfellows and their male membership in order to enable wives of insured men to be paid maternity benefit directly. This Society was in danger of losing its appeal to women through being embroiled in a debate which arose because of the position in which the legislation had placed it.

Although the Society's association with what appeared to be old-fashioned forms of masculinity made it difficult to recruit and retain women, when women joined the National Insurance Scheme in large numbers, as domestic servants and war workers, the Society needed to respond. During 1912 the Oddfellows opened almost 900 new lodges, the vast majority of them for women.[94] During the First World War a lot of women did jobs previously done by men. After the war in the new industries, light electrical and chemicals, many women found it easier to get work than men. A lot of it was unskilled, casual, low paid manual labour in the sweated trades, cleaning offices, hotels and restaurants, working in laundries and domestic service. There was male resentment of the new economic and political significance of women. Those aged over 30 got the vote in 1918 and another 1.5 million women joined the electorate in 1928. Doris Bailey's father was put on short-time as a french polisher and she got a job in an underclothing factory in Holborn: 'Plenty of work around,' her father said bitterly, 'Take a penny bus-ride and walk through Shoreditch. Lots of vacancies for girls. No need for you to be out of work. It's only men who are not wanted.' Women were patronised. Welsh Labour MP Aneurin Bevan asked in the *Western Mail* 1935: 'Are unemployed men to live lives of celibacy and their young girls to leave their homes to become the playthings of wealthy people in other parts of the country?'

Women were marginalised in social surveys. The Pilgrim Trust report of 1938 argued that work was about femininity and seduction:

The girl of 14 tends to drift into the most remunerative employment immediately available, keeping the alternative of marriage always in view ... she is readily enticed into any kind of factory.[95]

The expectation was that this was work until marriage and the TUC was also interested in women as wives not workers. There was a marriage bar in many trades, local authorities and the civil service and relatively few women joined trade unions. The secretary of the Tailors and Garment Workers argued that often women were not dismissed but retained on a part-time basis, particularly in factories without union organisation.[96] Domestic service still employed huge numbers of women but even within that sector there were changes. Vera Brittain dismissed her maid in 1918 'because she was clearly an amateur prostitute who painted her face ten years before lipstick began to acquire its present fashionable respectability'. Virginia Woolf was concerned that cooks were picking up the left-wing *Daily Herald* and entering the drawing room for a chat and that this was a sign of changing human character. Women were presented as frivolous by hostile, contemptuous, serious men. Socialist novelist John Sommerfield in *May Day* wrote off both women and their aspirations when he referred to these 'silly girls in their synthetic Hollywood dreams, their pathetic silk stockings and lipsticks, their foolish strivings'. Edith Hall worked a 50-hour week in an electric cable factory in Hayes after she left school in 1922 aged 14:

> I was often told, 'As a girl, keep your place,' but I was never quite sure where my place was. And on my way home from the factory I was shouted at by passers-by, 'Girls taking men's jobs'. It was all so confusing.

The image of unemployed cloth capped men in the north being threatened by lipsticked working girls in the south was difficult for the Oddfellows to counter. Compared to commercial bodies little support was offered to the Society's new female members. Rather, the Society sought to defend what appeared to be traditional fraternal values. In explaining that it sought to retain the loyalty of the men the Oddfellows suggested that they were married to their brethren, not their spouses and once again contrasted the warmth of fraternity with the coldness of the state:

> the man who has become an Oddfellow has been wedded to its principles and refused to be divorced from it by the action of the State. The future of the Manchester Unity depends upon the extent to which it is possible to foster the same love of our fraternal principles among those who are compulsorily insured. It may be a more difficult task to achieve but it ought not to be an impossible one. The Manchester Unity stands for brotherhood and kindly human sympathy in the hour of sickness and of suffering; these principles will continue to appeal to men in a way which the cold officialism of the State system can never hope to appeal. In the one case things will be managed for men; in the other they will manage things for themselves.[97]

By 1937 women constituted almost 37 per cent of the workforce of Greater London. The workforce was changing and the Oddfellows was finding it had to adapt.

Maintaining an enthusiasm for fraternity and management by men may have alienated some of the potential women members. In addition some men felt distanced from the Unity. The 1926

Report of the Royal Commission observed 'the apathy of insured persons in these matters', while Grand Master Walter Wright noted that these state members were 'practically taking no interest whatever' in management.[98] Paul Johnson has claimed that few members ever had an interest in the community of Oddfellowship, their focus was private and instrumental.[99] In 1934 there was an international conference of Oddfellows with representatives Australia, Canada, South Africa, New Zealand, Gibraltar, Bermuda and other parts of the Empire. Four people attended from the USA. It was comparatively easy to secure agreement about the status of overseas lodges, co-operation, clearances of members and how to deal with the exchange rates. However, it was reported that 'the subject upon which sharp differences of opinion have been raised is in relation to the ritual of the Order'. In 1936 it was disclosed that thousands of members had not been initiated.[100] The Directors proposed that the membership of a person who failed to be initiated within six months of joining would be cancelled and any payments made would be forfeit. This was rejected.[101] The 1937 AMC heard that of the 72,000 who had joined within a three-year period, 5,700 had been accepted without formal initiation. At this time there were 880,855 state members.[102] However, there is evidence of a lack of interest well before the inter-war period. The records of the Henry Jenkins Lodge, Scorton, indicate that 75 per cent of the fines imposed 1839–55 were for late attendance, non-attendance or missing the funeral of a brother.[103] In 1888 Frome Wilkinson, an Oddfellow, told the Druids that

> 90 percent of our members do not put in an appearance, save at the specially summoned meeting or on a quarter night [club life had ossified into] mere routine of receiving contributions, going through the modicum of business, taking a glass it may be and hearing the old songs.[104]

By contrast, commercial agencies were popular and expanded fast; they helped foster private saving against social adversity while simultaneously absorbing unorganised, poor risk, industrial workers (notably women) into the state insurance scheme.

In order to enable women to attend meetings approved societies were forbidden to meet in pubs. This 'dictatorial, autocratic, imperialist action' offended at least one Oddfellow, while another complained that school rooms 'were the most uncomfortable places it was possible to find [whereas] a village inn, if properly conducted, was as good as any other place'. Bill Needham, 1904–83, joined the Oddfellows in 1919. His recollections suggest the importance of the pub:

> We had a monthly meeting and it was always held in a pub – there was quite a few pubs in the village then – and we had it once a month on a Saturday night … It was run properly then, with a full committee, secretary, the lot … I used to enjoy going to them meetings, because it was a night out, and there was no television and you had to make your own amusement and although we were a bit young for having a drink we did used to sneak a drink … We used to have anything from about 20 to 30 chaps used to come once a month on a Saturday.

Another member of the same lodge, Frank Bagshaw, born 1916 pointed out such meetings might benefit women, but that control remained with men:

> If you were off ill you got two or three shillings a week of this thing. It was actually a very necessary benevolent society in the days before the social security came in, you know. Oh it was, my word, because you'd get nothing, there was no money from work or anything, was there, in those days. If you had a family you just couldn't risk not being in something like that at all.[105]

The solution proposed to the loss of enthusiastic members was not to try to embrace the new sisters but to look backwards. In 1922 the Grand Master proposed a reversion to 'our former principles' of the 'social and fraternal'.[106]

When the Oddfellows established separate female lodges, some of which had to have large catchment areas which meant travelling to lodge meetings was difficult, it rarely made any specific appeal to young women. In Manchester two women organised a whist drive in a 'prettily decorated room' for the Loyal De Trafford Female Lodge of lady clerks.[107] Many lodges met in locations such as draughty schoolrooms and initially, were run by men. Some of

Bill Needham pointed out that in the 1930s, 'there was no television and you had to make your own amusement'. The item often seen as persuading members not to attend meetings was in the 1970s being presented by Winfred Felgate (*fifth from right*) as a sign of appreciation for long service. There were many such presentations.

Bill Needham (1904–83) was a quarry worker who joined the Loyal Adventurers Lodge, Taddington, Derbyshire, in 1919. He was Noble Grand three times.

DAVE BATHE COLLECTION, UNIVERSITY OF SHEFFIELD

the older men may have had little in common with young working women. For example, Brother Tom Gutteridge PPGM, aged 83, was elected Treasurer of Kensington Female lodge in November 1912. At that time he was a Sick Visitor, had been an Oddfellow for 54 years and 'has never been out of office during his whole career as an Oddfellow. He has been through the chairs of his lodge 15 times and has also acted as NG in many other lodges in the district.'[108] By contrast, other organisations offered opportunities for involvement to women. Before the First World War the Labour Party had involved women 'as canvassers and fund-raisers' far more than the Conservatives, partly because it had fewer financial resources.[109] Between the wars, women became the majority of individual party members.[110] The party ran a newspaper and conferences for women and every June there was a Women's Week with processions, such as that of 1925, which attracted 3,000 women across Greater London.[111] Mr F. A. Broad from Edmonton Labour Party told the 1929 Labour Party conference that 'locally, we raise and spend in the work of the Movement perhaps ten times the amount that is handled through the central organisations and the bulk of that money is raised by women'. He added that 'nine-tenths of my canvassing is done by women'.[112] The party also publicised the fact that the first woman on Harlington council, the capital's first woman mayor and London's first woman JP were all Labour. Although Beatrice Webb characterised Poplar Labour Party as 'essentially a working-class benefit society', the Party was not a friendly society.[113] However, it was a competitor in that it offered social activities, marches, opportunities for social and political advance and the possibility of greater individual and collective financial security.[114]

Gilbert pointed out how the commercial companies promoted control of the household economy by women:

The lower-class housewife who carefully saved pennies in a sugar bowl over the mantelpiece for the weekly call of the funeral benefit collector could not bring herself to carry those pennies a few blocks to the post office savings bank. Still less could she enjoin her husband to become a member of a friendly society.

Gilbert described the collector-salesman as a 'sharp, unabashed young man from the slums', Lloyd George described these men in 1910 noting 'they are indefatigable, they are often very intelligent'.[115] Their visits may have had more appeal to than a trip to the Oddfellows Hall. The Prudential did not have to concern itself with traditions or how to deal with members who forgot passwords or whether women members should be allowed a vote or not (the franchise for General Elections was extended to women aged over 30 in 1918) or disputes about meetings in pubs. It was not interested in participation, did not have any ideals about the promotion of thrift within its membership and could focus on selling policies and checking claims. The industrial insurance companies did not expect members to attend meetings to collect and deliver their cards or participate in the running of the society. They did not offer dances, dinners and outings but instead provided opportunities to buy life insurance. This meant that the Prudential could be sufficiently flexible to create a women-only Domestic Servants Approved Section which attracted 18 per cent of the potential market of 2.1 million state-insured female servants.

The Prudential was also adept at attracting women to the purchase of its policies. The Oddfellows argued that it was different to the door-to-door sales reps of the Prudential because of its distinctive traditions:

The friendly societies will have to compete with great organisations who look to State Insurance acting as a feeder to the profit-making industrial insurance. The competition is at present unequal. The death-hunting canvasser takes the State's business as a side line. Sickness Insurance has been the main line in the work of a friendly society and if we are to equalise the conditions it will be essential to widen the range of our activities.[116]

In December 1915 a Provincial C. S. from Brighton argued that people were 'fast becoming sick and tired of "the man on the knocker", for whom they now have a positive loathing', and in September 1916 Brother Whitelegg of Warrington told his brethren that

When all is said and done we are not a collecting society. The Manchester Unity has been made what it is today by sentiment; not by men saying, 'How much can I get out of it?' … to cultivate this spirit of commercialism was going to be a bad day for the Unity'.[117]

Eric Ogden's characterisation of commercial insurance agents as focused on sales rather than fraternity accords with the view presented at the time by many Oddfellows. He said:

If you were an insurance agent in those days, knocking on the door on Friday night to collect the premiums for the policies that your clientele had, there was a famous expression, 'come along madam you're only a eleven pence halfpenny off the shilling'. It was your job to sell them more and more insurance, these penny policies and all the rest of it and so you became an insurance agent and you knocked on the door on Friday night and one the basis of your book, your insurers book, that was the basis upon which you were paid. You were paid a commission on the premiums that you collected and if you were a very good insurance agent, you'd be promoted to a desk job at head office in the town centre.

The industrial insurance companies sold more endowment policies and fewer burial policies. People were living longer and more began to plan for old age rather than the death of an infant. Despite the recognition of the need to widen the range of products the Oddfellows returned surpluses to the members in the form of additional benefits while the industrial insurance companies' agents made the same number of visits to policyholders (now nominally members of separate approved societies) and were in an excellent position to make further sales or prevent lapses. The Oddfellows membership declined by 2 per cent between 1929 and 1935, during the depression but if only one in five of the lapses had been prevented there would have been an increase in membership.[118] By contrast, the Pru's sale force of thousands were able to recruit on the doorsteps of Britain. The portrayal of the man from the Pru as a death-hunter missed the similarities between the approved societies. The recollections of one salesman who started work with the Prudential in 1935 and spent over 30 years with the firm are similar to those of some Oddfellows. Clients trusted the salesman as a financial advisor and friend, Hyman Kaye was invited to clients' weddings and this may well have increased sales.

At one time you would walk into a room where a person had just given birth to a child and pay them the maternity benefits, you insured the baby for a penny a week and you got used to seeing and helping people to advise them. And when they grew up, they would go to work and they would say, you know, 'Mr Kaye, we want to save money, what do you suggest what we do?'[119]

Through their weekly visits to working-class households, the commercial insurance sales teams offered a personal service to clients, combining public administration with private business. They tailored their delivery and collection. 'Often weekly visits were timed to take place just after the "breadwinner" arrived home on pay-day.'[120] When lobbying prior to the passage of the 1911 Act MPs were reminded that an insurance agent would enter many houses in their constituencies and there he was considered 'a philosopher, guide and friend [and] looked upon as a member of the family, consulted on many matters quite apart from his business'.[121] One more recent customer made the same point:

when I was little I went to my grandma [born 1880] and she used to hold the insurance man in great esteem. It was like he was on a pedestal and he used to collect on Friday. I used to think this man was something special.

A sales manager said,

> If grandma has had a policy, if a mother's had a policy, daughter has had a policy [then] when she has a child they … want a policy. You'd be surprised how many people, when we take maturities to them, want to maintain that contact.

A manager at another company took a similar view, noting that a typical customer

> will have had their policy passed down from family to family, generation to generation to generation. The collector, if they've been working in that area for a number of years, they're treated like a family friend … At the time of death that's really where a collector comes into their own, because they have befriended the family for so long.[122]

Although the Oddfellows sought to distinguish itself from the agents of proprietary concerns, 'who are getting "a bob a nob" and who enticed the unfortunate', it was, as an approved society, categorised with them.[123] Despite the Oddfellows' scorn, people trusted the commercial companies' agents.

The Labour Party was unenthusiastic about all non-state organisations being involved in health care, particularly commercial insurance companies. In 1913 Beatrice Webb told the Labour Party conference that no approved societies should be allowed to make a profit. In 1925 R. J. Davies argued at conference that the scheme should be democratised so that the people should have something to say in the election of those who controlled and administered their approved societies. In 1926 Labour was associated with the minority Report of the Royal Commission on National Health Insurance. This recommended that the approved societies be replaced by local authorities as this would enable the electorate some control over proceedings. In 1931 the Secretary of the Prudential, Sir George May, was commissioned to write a report on the changes required to counter the economic crisis. The May Report was widely held to have led to the fall of the Labour government, a fall so large that Labour did not win power again in the Commons until 1945. In 1934 the Party conference decided in favour of a state medical service built upon the existing local authority services and proposed not a universalist system but that the approved societies remain, although with the income limit for participation raised to £500 per annum. Labour made no further pronouncements on public health until the war, when it produced a policy which did not give the approved societies a role but, despite views expressed earlier, left the private insurance system alone.[124]

It has also been claimed that the approved societies 'had excellent links with the Conservative Party', and that 'for some Labour leaders in the 1920s and 1930s the approved societies came almost to be the embodiment of blood-sucking capitalism'.[125] Stanley Baldwin, 1st Earl Baldwin of Bewdley, was not a typical Oddfellow in that he was educated at Harrow and Trinity College, Cambridge, and inherited one of the Britain's largest iron and steel firms, Baldwins Ltd, from his father, a Conservative MP. He was an enthusiast for the area in which he lived. He lived at home until he married where his father had built a church, a school, and a vicarage. Playing fields were also provided where the Baldwin Works' cricket team played, and most employees lived in company houses. Baldwin became a parish and county councillor, a magistrate, and a member of the Oddfellows' and the Foresters' friendly societies. While in Wilden his interest in the welfare of his employees may have been appreciated. Others may have taken another view. Apart from any general dislike of Conservative leaders, some within Labour's ranks will have recalled that Baldwin was PM during the 1926 General Strike (he was PM for over seven years between 1923 and 1937) he was associated with appeasement and he was perceived as the de facto Prime Minister in a coalition government headed by Ramsay MacDonald, the Labour Prime Minister who was expelled from the Labour Party. That Baldwin was a member of the Society may not have enhanced its reputation on the left.

There was a comparable cold-shouldering of another part of the mutual enterprises sector. In 1936 Harold Laski, called the co-op as 'an oasis in a capitalist world' which represented a 'philosophy of life'. However, in 1942 Labour's *The Old World and the New Society*, had only one reference to the co-op and the 1945 manifesto, *Let us face the future* had none. Lancaster and Maguire concluded that, after the Second World War, the co-op 'found itself in increasing conflict with a government that did not replicate with co-operators the close association that prevailed with trade union leaders', while Mercer said that Labour ministers treated the co-op with 'studied indifference', and noted that the party in general had a 'nonchalant attitude' towards the co-op.[126] Like the co-op the Oddfellows perceived itself as means of changing society though a form of consumer-orientated voluntarism. Labour saw these bodies less as organised, loyal and engaged citizens and more as trading concerns which increasingly failed to offer the prosperous working class what they wanted.

Between the wars the Labour Party was relatively unsuccessful in the Commons and was far more popular at local level. The 1911 scheme was so restrictive that many women and children turned to other sources of help, such as Labour-run out-patient clinics and maternity and infant welfare clinics. The 1926 Royal Commission argued for the separation of the medical service from the insurance system and for it to be supported from general funds. In the end it was decided that local authorities would be permitted to expand and improve the health care services offered to the unemployed and the poor, and that the insurance system, which provided medical care only for the insured individual and not for his or her dependants, would be retained. The Labour-run London County Council developed sophisticated, integrated health facilities which became a model for the National Health Service.[127] In 1915 an analysis by an American economist found the UK health insurance system to be inefficient. He saw the solution as lying within the scope of local bodies and proposed a coherent localised (that is state rather than federal) scheme for the USA.[128] The government prevented the Oddfellows from extending or making their services more attractive as it did not want to increase its contribution. It used the Society as a buffer against pressure for the expansion of welfare.[129] At the same time the Oddfellows failed to make connections with Labour local authorities. By 1938, Ministry of Health officials were convinced that the future of public health policy did not lie with the approved societies:

It was generally agreed that any provision of specialist and institutional services must be made part of the public health services and not an additional insurance benefit, since not only was this the only way in which the necessary institutional accommodation could be provided, but also it would help to co-ordinate the whole of the health services in a consistent and comprehensive plan.[130]

In 1945 a Fabian Society publication made Labour's position clear:

No amount of patching and improving can give the present system the necessary change of aim. The scheme which was remarkably progressive thirty years ago has not moved forward with the times and is now obsolete. Health insurance has served its turn.[131]

Until the passage of the 1911 Act the primary interest of the Oddfellows had not been to provide health insurance and it struggled within this new role. By 1942 the Oddfellows was still trying to implement a scheme which 30 years old, not designed for either total war or mass unemployment and which failed to engage many members beyond the level of instrumentality.

Contemporary observers noticed a reduction in the sense of shame, particularly among younger adults, about claiming state allowances. This in turn reduced the importance of the independence from the state that the Oddfellows offered to members. Those who had participated in World War I either in the armed forces or in war work, joined a national trade union or become an active within the Labour or Communist Parties were among those most likely to have accepted that state intervention could be beneficial. In 1929 George Lansbury, then a Labour Councillor, later the party's leader, argued that there had been 'a complete revolution in man's and woman's attitude towards the social services, and things which the old Charity Organisation Society would consider as anathema, were now taken for granted'.[132] There was less of a stigma associated with resorting to the Poor Law authorities in the area of east London where he lived, Poplar. He claimed that there 'the people who were victims of poverty or unemployment … would not be treated as other than ordinary decent citizens'. This view was supported by the wide-ranging report which examined change since the Charles Booth's survey of London at the turn of the nineteenth century. In the 1930s *The New Survey of London Life and Labour* found that the

public attitude to poverty today is greatly changed. In the first place the numbers of recipients of relief are so much greater both absolutely and as a proportion of the population that they cannot be regarded as a separate class, or as abnormal cases … It would seem that recourse is now had to Poor Law relief just as to other forms of social assistance so that a person no longer feels that in applying to a relieving officer he is crossing a Rubicon.

It went on to argue that as a result of mass unemployment, payments, subject to a means test, which were made to those who were not entitled to payments under the system of selective national insurance were perceived as a right, not as a gift. The Poor Law was seen as one

The Society presented itself as supportive of families and encouraged children to be paraded through the streets. On the left we see an image of a Juvenile Float. In the image from Staffordshire on the cover of Odd Fellow in 1966 (*right*) the three links can be seen in the flowers.

The three links also appeared on the float paying tribute to Sir Gordon Richard, who was knighted and won the Derby in 1953.

BY COURTESY OF LESLEY BULL

service among many, 'no less honourable than the various health, education and insurance services [and] something to which they feel themselves equally entitled'.[133] A recent assessment of the evidence concluded that

> by 1939, East End residents of all ethnicities were making much greater use of state welfare services in the areas of unemployment, health, maternity and child care, and even of public assistance, than they had done in 1919. The most obvious reason for this transition was that the voluntary and mutual aid societies that they had relied on since the second half of the nineteenth century in order to avoid resorting to the dreaded Poor Law, were no longer viable alternatives by the 1930s.[134]

Moreover, the case for reform was strengthened by the increased intervention by central government during the 1939–1945 war. There was state support for those who had lost their homes through enemy action and those whose pensions had been eroded through inflation. Furthermore, in the period since 1911 the Labour Party had run innovative health services at local level, had categorised all the approved societies as inappropriate bodies to run national insurances and had decided that it favoured a comprehensive health plan run at national level by state officials.

The Society in Australia

In Australia the development of the Oddfellows followed a similar path to their brethren in the UK.[135] A comparison with Australia brings to the fore some of the key issues for the UK Oddfellows. The Unity was probably not the first friendly society to reach Australia.[136] It possibly arrived in 1840. The tale of the founding of the Stranger's Refuge in Sydney by eight members from England and a ninth man has been repeated in a number of texts. The centenary publication of the IOOFMU in Australia quoted a notice from *The Australian* newspaper 14 March 1840, to substantiate the claim.[137] Sydney had 25,000 people and the first popular elections in the colony in 1842. By then there was a lodge in Victoria another in South Australia and four in New South Wales. The Society reached Tasmania in 1843, Queensland in 1848 and West Australia in 1851. The Society spread rapidly as enthusiastic members recruited from vessels arrived on the shores, formed bands and cricket teams, which kept the Oddfellows in the public eye and reminded those who the Society sought to recruit and retain of its convivial activities. It established a school in 1844, a library in 1845, an AMC in 1857 and halls, ten in Queensland alone by 1871. One of the first buildings in Mount Morgan, the centre of a gold rush in 1889, was the Oddfellows Hall. It was built when the church was still under construction.[138] In 1889 a Past Grand's Lodge was established, the first juvenile lodge was created in 1893 and the first lodge for women in 1920.[139]

An important element of the success of the Oddfellows was its association with health care. The Unity in Australia was developed in the mid-nineteenth century by working men who, within a few years, employed medical staff. As in the UK, lodges employed doctors to examine those seeking to join the lodge, to examine the sick and certificate them if they were unable to carry on their usual work and to prescribe medicines and carry out minor operations. They received an annual fee which was open to negotiation, depending on such matters as the services offered by the doctor or the number of doctors who applied for the posts. Initially, most doctors worked part-time for the Lodge and had private practices as well. In 1847, the Oddfellows opened what has been claimed as the world's first medical institute in Sydney. Full-time, salaried doctors worked at the Oddfellows' Medical Institute and Dispensary, which was managed by a committee of delegates from affiliated lodges. This provided low-cost medical care with unadulterated medicines. It proved very popular. By the mid-1890s it served 11,700 members and their families in seven affiliated lodges. There were four doctors and members paid 7/6d a year for attendance only. Graduated tables of payments were introduced in 1894 and sick and funeral funds consolidated in 1908. Benefits were made uniform and payments of them guaranteed. By the late nineteenth and early twentieth centuries there were similar tensions in the UK and Australia between friendly societies and doctors and competition with commercial bodies. Each country introduced a system of national insurance that was administered by friendly societies, but Australia only did this in 1938 and the system was soon discontinued. In both countries there was state intervention after the Second World War which led the Oddfellows in both Australia and the UK to reduce their roles in health care provision and funeral benefits and to focus on investment in property and leisure.

During a period when the doctors in the UK were gaining professional status there were parallel developments in Australia where doctors were also concerned that their status was undermined because of their employment by friendly societies. Between the 1890s (when a third of doctors in Australia were serving the lodges) and the 1920s there was a long-running dispute between the doctors and the friendly societies. This resulted in a reduction of the Oddfellows' control over health provision. In Melbourne the Oddfellows planned to provide a clinic staffed by specialists. They would be paid an annual fee which would make the scheme accessible to poorer members. It was blocked by the doctors' association and had to be abandoned. The 1920s and 1930s were also ones when commercial companies sought to restrict the activities of the Oddfellows. In the UK the main competitor was industrial insurance companies, in Australia drug manufacturers restricted supplies to friendly society dispensaries. The Oddfellows initiated a scheme for friendly societies to make their own drugs. In the UK it was the National Health Service and changes to the administration of National Insurance which undermined the roles which the Oddfellows had played. In Australia after the Commonwealth's introduction, in 1945, of sickness benefits and funeral benefits, the rationale for Oddfellow membership declined and the National Health Act in 1951 forced the Oddfellows out of what had been one of its main fields of service. The parallels with Australia suggest that Oddfellowship was of value in times of individual crisis but was weaker when in a competitive marketplace regulated by an unsympathetic government during a period of widespread economic downturn and high unemployment. This broader contextualisation indicates that to focus on the UK 1911 legislation is to marginalise other reasons for the decline in the status of the mutual aid offered by the Oddfellows.

II 'The needs that remain in a social service state' [140]

By 1942 there were 1,000 more members than the two million that there had been just after the First World War and again in 1932. Its aggregate capital was over £31 million and it had a net surplus of almost £2 million. [141] The Society was active in its engagement in the war effort. In 1940 the Unity Propaganda Fund presented mobile canteens to the Church Army, the Salvation Army and the YMCA. In 1942 £500 was given forwards a YMCA Forces Hostel. [142] Further grants were made in 1943. In June 1945 the canteen was still busy and there was a hostel in Derby which the Oddfellows had made 'more homely'. Later that year it was reported that the Church Army Mobile Canteen that the Oddfellows provided and the hostel it supported continued to be valued by the Transport Command of the RAF and that the Women's Services Hostel at Bridge Street, Derby was still as popular as ever. 'During the four months ended October 27th 510 beds have been occupied and there have been 18, 293 users of the Club.'[143] The Society also raised money from members overseas. In 1942 it was reported that £3,500 had been received from Canada and the United States and that £11,000 had been donated by members in the UK.[144]

Although the legislation of 1911 adversely affected the promotion and development of Oddfellowship, the Society was deeply enmeshed in it. It was concerned by plans for change. The government established a committee on the reform of social insurance and allied services, chaired by Sir William Beveridge, the civil servant who was responsible for much of the 1911 Act. His report, 'Social Insurance and Allied Services', published in 1942, met with popular acclaim. The Directors told the 1943 AMC that they were 'in full agreement' with the National Conference of Friendly Societies. The AMC, it was announced, 'welcomes the acceptance by his Majesty's Government of the main principles contained in the Beveridge report for the purpose of making provision for post-war social security'. However, it also felt the need to stress that the legislation should 'leave room and encouragement for voluntary insurance by friendly societies'.[145] The government accepted many of Beveridge's proposals and in February 1943 it was announced that the status of approved societies would to be abolished and their work transferred to a Ministry of National Insurance. The Oddfellows lobbied against this change. Beveridge himself had suggested in paragraph 379, that as a large number of people were members of friendly societies it was 'unnecessary for the State to take any action in regard to voluntary insurance against sickness, except to leave scope and encouragement for the friendly societies'. In 1944 the Society's secretary, H. A. Andrews, argued that 'the friendly societies were the forerunners of social insurance', that the statistical experience of the Unity had been the basis for calculating the rates for of insurance in 1911 and that Beveridge's plan was 'a further evolution of the schemes and ideals of these societies'. He went on to conclude that

> the right national policy at present is not to make changes which tend nearer and nearer to a totalitarian state but rather in achieving 'social security' to do everything possible to preserve existing voluntary organisations so essentially British.[146]

In January 1945 lodge secretaries were commended to follow the example of Beacon Lodge, Penrith and produce a leaflet which encouraged members to lobby in the face of the 'government's intention to abolish friendly societies'.

> The present method of co-operation with the State is to be discontinued and friendly societies with 120 years practical experience of the work on the Independent side and over thirty years in Health Insurance administration are not to be retained under the new system. Now is the time to make your effort to induce the government to utilise the existing machinery which has worked so effortlessly in the past.[147]

Watford's Wonderful Women.
Presentation of Mobile Kitchen Car.
A Torrent of Tributes.

WATFORD has a group of wonderful women doing splendid work as war workers. At the outset they had no equipment. Now, thanks to the Order, they have a mobile kitchen car which enables them to go where their services are needed, and the Corporation of Watford has provided a motor vehicle which can draw it to the desired place. The women workers are all members of the Pride of Watford Women's Lodge, and at their head is Sister Minnie Swain, who has received from all sides tributes to the quality and value of her services and the services of those under her direction.

On Wednesday, February 26th, the presentation of the working classes to realise that they could not only do things for themselves, but did do things for themselves. He praised the work of the W.V.S., which had answered the very first call to provide for the evacuees, to care for the homeless, and to feed the sick and wounded soldiers from Dunkirk, where thousands of meals had had to be improvised at a moment's notice. He was grateful that so many of their organisation had taken part in those activities. When he and his fellow-directors had seen such good work hampered through poor equipment and inability to find funds for emergencies, they had decided that the provision of a canteen would be the best way they could

MAYOR UNLOCKS DOOR.

kitchen car was made by the Grand Master of the Order, who visited Watford for the purpose of making the presentation to the members of the W.V.S. who by happy circumstances are members of the Order, too. In addition to the Grand Master and Sister Meadmore, among those present were the Mayor of Watford (Councillor F. J. Baxter), the Mayoress, Lady Herbert, the Town Clerk (Mr. A. Norman Schofield), the Matron of the Peace Memorial Hospital (Miss L. A. Brooks), the Commandants of the Watford W.V.S. and V.A.D.'s and representatives of the Casualty Services. Bouquets were handed to the Mayoress and Mrs. Meadmore by Sister M. Barnes and Sister Joan Jays.

GRAND MASTER MAKES PRESENTATION

In making the presentation on behalf of the Directors, the Grand Master spoke of the part voluntary organisations had played in moulding the character and determination of our people, and one had only to look at the many Co-operative Societies and Friendly Societies formed by the help. A trailer canteen would contain much more apparatus than a motor canteen, and the W.V.S. already had a car for it. He hoped that the mobile kitchen would also be of assistance should troops be billeted in neighbouring villages. He praised the work of the 400 women in the Pride of Watford Lodge, who were doing such amazing work as a purely voluntary organisation. He was proud of them, and of Sister Swain, their leader. He then handed the key of the canteen to Sister Swain.

SISTER SWAIN'S STORY

Sister Swain was warmly received on rising to acknowledge the gift. She said she could hardly say how much the vehicle would mean to the Unit in its work. In the early days of intensive raiding they had to make journeys between the station and Odd Fellows' Hall in order to provide the evacuees with hot food. In the vehicle now presented to the Unit they had ample equipment for keeping food hot, and meals could be provided for 200 people at once. She believed that her squad, a self-contained group in the

Oddfellow Halls could be used, as this one was, to help the war effort and to remind passers-by of the solidity of friendship, love and truth. Members supported the war effort in many ways, one of which was to allow the Oddfellows Hall in Watford to be used to help evacuees.

The Oddfellows called on members to write to their MPs to remind them of the services that the Society had rendered over many years.[148]

If any members wrote making the case that the existing machinery worked as 'effortlessly' the Society they had little impact. One account of 1945 General Election campaign mentioned that when Herbert Morrison (the Deputy Prime Minister and Leader of the House of Commons after the election) was asked 'Are you aware that eight or nine million votes depend on Labour's attitude to friendly societies?' he gave 'no impression of being worried on this point'.[149] Similarly, the claim by Henry Goodrich, a Labour MP who was Parliamentary Agent to the National Conference of Friendly Societies, that he told the Minister of National Insurance to expect demonstrations, appears not to have worried James Griffiths[150] In January 1946 H. A. Andrews pointed out that the Society's staff equipment and offices were used for both voluntary and state members and that the Society stood to lose an income of £240,000 a year. He also said that it was relatively inexpensive to run the state and voluntary sectors together.[151] Although the Labour Party had pledged to abolish approved society status but retain the friendly societies as administrators and although Beveridge was angered by the differences between his report and the White Paper in regard to the role of friendly societies, the 1946 the National Insurance Act was passed. People in work, except married women, paid a flat-rate national insurance contribution (for the average worker, amounting to nearly 5 per cent of their income) of 4s. 11d. a week in National Insurance contributions. This entitled them, and their wives, if married men, to sickness, maternity and pension benefits funded by employers, employees and the government. This was followed in 1948 by the National Assistance Act, which gave financial help to those without other sources of income and the National Health Service Act which instituted a state health service providing free diagnosis and treatment of illnesses at home or in hospital, including dental and ophthalmic treatment. Within this centrally administered, comprehensive system of national insurance which covered most of the population there was no room for the Oddfellows. Grand Master, G. H. Barrow was sombre on the subject of the outlook:

> It is inevitable that Levies for Unity and District purposes will rise and in the Lodges almost every item will cost more. These blows, heavy as they are, are not 'knock-outs' however, and recovery from them is possible if we will, as a Society, give up all thought and talk of 'throwing in the towel'.

The newly expanded civil service required the skills of those who had worked within the approved societies who would otherwise be unemployed. Many Unity staff joined the new Ministry of National Insurance including Barrow. He had joined the Order in 1916 and, like his grandfather before him, become Provincial Corresponding Secretary. He had been a Director for 12 years and his departure was a loss to the Unity. The transition between the Unity and the civil service should have been a smooth one. To outsiders to leave one gendered, elaborately hierarchical, organisation staffed by bureaucrats who followed established procedures, collated actuarial data and were directed to focus on mathematical objectivity, for another such organisation might appear straightforward. However, Eric Ogden, who joined the Ministry of National Insurance in 1952, aged 17 suggested that there were difficulties at local level:

A lot of people went off to work for the Ministry of National Insurance and retained their job as lodge secretaries. It produced problems. We did have a lodge secretary who, in fact, worked for an insurance company and he was permitted to be the lodge secretary. They circumvented painful necessity by appointing his wife as the lodge secretary. The insurance employee couldn't be a lodge secretary so his wife was formerly appointed lodge secretary. She drew the salary in effect and he did the work and that was how it was overcome.

Eric Ogden also pointed out that one of the problems caused when people who had previously worked for the approved societies, such as the Oddfellows, became state employees was that they were appointed to a grade which was commensurate with the salary they had previously been paid. For some insurance sales representatives door-to-door collection was more remunerative than supervision of collectors.

The civil service took no notice of this, took these people on board and you ended up where the fellow that had been sitting behind the desk on a salary was appointed to be a clerical officer. The fellow who is out on the street, under his direction collecting the premiums and getting more money became an executive officer. Overnight the people

Lodge President Ellen Hayes salutes members of a meeting of the under-16s section of the Pride of Clapham Lodge, 1939.

who had been supervising on the fourth of July became the supervised on the fifth of July.

While this may have caused difficulties within Whitehall and tensions within the office where Eric Ogden worked, the Oddfellows had other problems as a result of the legislation.

In 1938 over 6.6 million people, one in seven of the UK's population, was a member of a friendly society. In 1945 8.7 million people were members of friendly societies and 10 per cent (871, 233) were adult members of the Oddfellows. If widows, members of female societies, honorary members (of whom there were 1,913) and other members are included there were over a million members. There were also over a million National Health Insurance 'state members'.[152] In that year, there was a decrease in Oddfellow membership of 6,800 members. The Secretary of the Order presented a positive face arguing that the nation had become more insurance-minded and that there remained a role for friendly societies while the Grand Master, M. V. Sweeney, stressed that although welfare was of importance, 'we are part of the great traditional social life of the country'.[153] Nevertheless, a further 9,500 left in 1946, almost twice as many in 1947 (18,600). The total number of friendly society members had also fallen to 6.3 million. The decrease doubled again to 35,500 in 1948. This was largely due to lapses rather than deaths. Men returned from the Services and did not resume payment. In 1939 the Society agreed that these members who were called up under the Military Training Act should be excused payment of contributions to the sick and funeral, management and distress funds for the period of service. This included those called up under the Act who satisfied the appropriate tribunal that they had a conscientious objection. The cost of this was borne by the Society.[154] It was difficult to trace many of them and when subscriptions also rose, membership fell. In 1948 only 6,170 joined the Oddfellows and that included 2,400 Juveniles. This was the lowest figure for over 50 years and no Gold Merit Awards (awarded for introducing at least 40 new adults) were presented that year. In 1950 the AMC heard how the 1938 adult membership of 725,000 had fallen to 570,000 by 1949.[155] The Unity published a list of Lodges closed under the National Insurance Act which came into force in July 1948. It ran to 205 lodges including the Mechanics of Belford and Pedrog in Caernarvon, three female lodges in Leominster and two Jewish ones in Stepney.

In 1945 the need for women to help with the changes which occurred after the war was recognised:

Ritual of a lodge makes a personal appeal to the women of the Order far deeper than the case of the men. We have in this a facet of the many-sided problem of what we call our religious life. Such congregations as are now seen in Churches are composed of an overwhelming majority of women. The eye of a woman sees so much more than the eye of a mere man and the result is that many of us men talk of the spirit of Odd Fellowship but women are stirred by the something we call spirituality ... It is necessary to be prepared to recast methods and styles and upon the changes that may be made I would rather have the judgment of ten women then ten times ten men.[156]

Although the Oddfellows is not a religious body, the language employed above was not an isolated case. In February 1945 'Uncle Tom', writing for 'Young Odd Fellows' informed readers that in Australia Oddfellows saw their membership as 'a part of their religion. This is what we should like to see here.'[157] Certainly in that year the *Queensland Oddfellows' Magazine* employed religious imagery when it argued against state intervention to help the destitute because this did not counter the cause of poverty, underemployment but rather it undermined the friendly societies: 'while the state can effect this total insurance it cannot make free independent and self-reliant citizens by that means. It may build up the machinery but it cannot give it a soul.'[158] Charles Willard was an Oddfellow from the age of six. Reflecting, in the 1970s, on 'the sole interest in my life apart from the occupation of printer that was the means of supplying my financial resources', he said that felt that 'here in this lodge one could rise above the ordinary material life and pass into those spiritual levels where all were friends and each worked for each others' welfare'.[159] This echoed the sentiment expressed in July 1914 by the UK Grand Master who said:

> A mere Government machine was a cold, calculating sort of being, with no soul. But the friendly societies had a soul – a great soul animated by the great principles of friendship, love and truth.[160]

In the UK a Special Conference on how to reconstruct the Unity was held in 1945 in which the emphasis was put on women within the family: 'every lodge should be built like the nation, upon the basis of the family and be encouraged to have men women and juvenile members'.[161] This appeal was not heard with enthusiasm by all. Prejudice against women taking positions of authority outside Ladies Lodges was mentioned by Pat Morgan:

> If you had any problems you sometimes got it with the 'Old Codgers' lodges. They were never very happy when women came in or in fact, to see a woman with a chain [of office] on. Dolly [Merrell] was the first one after the war to get the rough end of that. They didn't like to see the ladies with chains on, you know ladies should be in the kitchen doing the sandwiches and tea. All the men came home from the war, Dolly should have gone through district office earlier than she did. They got pushed back so that the men could go through.

Dolly Merrell worked for the Oddfellows for over 50 years, became a branch secretary and then the first woman to join the Board before she became the first female Grand Master in 1978. Pat recalled an officers' visit to a lodge at Chelmsford:

> You weren't allowed in the lodge room until they had finished doing their business because you weren't even allowed to know what business they were discussing. You were invited in after they had finished doing everything they had to do correspondence and accounts. *Then* you were invited in which isn't the idea. An officer's visit really is to see

how the lodge is running but they would not, they were very much down on women. There were two or three lodges like that.

The Ritual made it clear than a member needed to promote the Society by example: 'Let a strict attention to your domestic duties procure you the esteem of your friends and family.' The restriction on roles for women may have deterred some people and rendered the commitment to families difficult to enact.

In 1949 the Grand Master recognised that some members thought that the Oddfellows was 'of no further use to the community and should fade away', but he saw the future in youth, 'who should be given every encouragement to further their interests in the Society' and in 'the Social side of the Order'.[162] However, a survey in 1947 of 150 friendly society members revealed only three who said that they attended meetings regularly, and only 25 who had occasionally attended. The others never went. An Oddfellows secretary in Tottenham was interviewed about his lodge which had 150 adult members and 14 junior members. He said that about 30 attended the annual meetings and 'ten to twelve', including the committee members, attended the fortnightly ones.[163] The same branch secretary added:

> In 1912 when the National Insurance Act came in, they said it was the death knell of the friendly societies and a lot of them did go out of existence. The same thing is applying today. What applies then applies now. When people get used to paying the contributions from their wages with money they never handled they suddenly found out they could continue with the other and reap the benefit in times of sickness. The same thing will apply these days.[164]

The report noted negative attitudes towards friendly societies, even among the members, and that such attitudes were more pronounced among younger people. The conclusion was that

> membership today is predominantly passive one concentrating almost entirely upon payment of subscriptions and receipt of benefit. To some extent, as with other organisations, this may well be symptomatic of post-war apathy. It seems possible, however, that it may also be related to the present centralising and impersonalising of friendly society organisation, useful enough in the interests of efficiency but perhaps not calculated to arouse much interest and enthusiasm among members.[165]

Beveridge came to similar conclusion. He said that following the passage of the National Health Insurance Act 1911 that the focus of the friendly societies had shifted. They had 'became more official and less personal. More of insurance agencies and less of social agencies.' He added, 'only a very few people appear to have joined a friendly society with the idea of participating in the social functions which it might provide … to a large extent the assumption was that the main object of the friendly society was to administer national health insurance.'[166] Syd Bolton explained the impact on him of this lack of interest among the young:

After the 1948 National Health Service came in there wasn't the necessity. Up to that time people had to be in some kind of union or friendly society to draw benefits. Most of the people I met in those days who were older than myself, I was the youngest when I was a district trustee at 35 with a 70-year old and with a 72-year old.

Writing in 1949 one observer noted that there was little control by members and little interest in control:

On every hand there is a growth of centralisation and a lack of interest both in the member and by the member. With the lack of interest has come minority control and a façade of self-government. Meetings not attended, members and representatives are not known to one another and have very little opportunity of knowing one another and the choice of who represents whom is very largely in the hands of local officials.[167]

Eric Odgen found that the new situation enabled him to swiftly rise through the ranks:

I fairly quickly graduated through the chairs because of course, they were still suffering from the repercussions of 1948. My experience in the Ministry of National Insurance stood me in good in standing about where the friendly societies were coming from and I quickly went through the chairs of the lodge and became a delegate to the district meetings. In fact, I attended my first conference of the society in 1958 [aged 23] at Blackpool on an auto cycle. All 34 miles of it from Southport.

Younger people would have grown up during a period when the Oddfellows was often associated with the administration of benefits more than conviviality, community engagement or the extension of personal responsibility for social protection. If those around them had not attended lodge nights they would still have received the sick pay. They would have witnessed the effects of increased political opportunities for working men who were being elected to town councils and to the bodies which supervised local education and, until abolition in 1929, the administration of the Poor Law. Attendance at lodge meetings was not required as a vehicle for training in civic life, it was not required to gain health insurance and it was not the only form of recreational activity available. In 1949 Douglas Cole noted that the decline in the influence of the Oddfellows was because people had more 'opportunities for social and political activity than they used to be in the heyday of the Oddfellows'.[168] These were all rival attractions to the fellowship of the lodge. Friendly society membership became only one of a number of survival strategies which included campaigning for improved wages and conditions through political parties or trade unions.

The services provided by the Society failed to change in new circumstances. The Oddfellows continued to provide health care and to meet its commitments to members but the sums paid out were relatively small and the impositions on members relatively onerous, as these witnesses recalled. Denis Rose's father, Henry was a sub-postmaster. When his eyesight failed his wife took over but the shop still closed in 1927. The Oddfellows paid Henry until his death in 1964. These activities were time-consuming as Jean Facer mentioned:

> In the 50s the social side was more like a periphery. Business was the main object of the meetings, looking after their sick members and anybody who was in distress or needed help.

Bertie Miles remembered how when he contracted jaundice shortly after the war and was unable to work for six weeks. 'My father applied for some money and every week in the post he used to send me a ten shilling note which he got from the Oddfellows.' Mary Wheeler said that in the 1950s:

> My Dad used to go off sick in November when the smogs came because of his chest. He had chronic bronchitis and never worked a full twelve months. As there was no sick pay scheme he relied on hand-outs from the union and the Oddfellows. The Sick Visitor used to come and pay him a 10 shilling note. You had to sign a declaration and they had to see your sick note.

Betty Mostyn echoed memories of the inter-war years when she pointed out that 'each lodge used to have a Sick Visitor. If you were on the sick you were not supposed to go out after nine o'clock.' A system which had been designed for a different era was no longer vital to many members and alienated many of them. One newspaper account of 1958 suggested that the Societies had a relatively small part to play in people's lives.

> As a system the 'friendly' does fill in the gaps in social security left by the Welfare State and through its lodges its approach retains a human touch responding to need rather than merit or rule-book categories. For this reason it is useful in helping in the marginal cases which fall outside State regulations.[169]

Whereas previously the Society had offered security and hope, by this period its schemes included one for marriage endowment advertised as 'the price of a cigarette a day can bring you £100 on your wedding day'.[170] The lack of a role within the new system was demonstrated in 1966 when, to aid recruitment, the Poole, Bridport and Yeovil District parked a carnival float and had members distribute leaflets around it on the theme of 'Bridge that Gap' (the name of a film released in 1965). While connecting modern individuals on the one side to the NHS on the other side of a broken bridge was a useful task the image lacked the clarity and immediacy of the appeals of earlier periods with their references to grieving widows or injured workers.

III   Conclusion

The diminution of many aspects of Oddfellowship was noted by David Green who saw the problem in terms of the defeat of reciprocity:

> The friendly societies were not just benefit societies. They treated people as if they had a moral dimension to their character as well as a material one. They appealed to the best in people and enabled them to face the challenges of leadership and self-organisation … The welfare state that replaced mutual aid was built on a complex of ideas standing in opposition to older doctrines of reciprocal obligation evolved by the friendly societies … This tradition of reciprocal obligation treated people as capable of exercising responsibility. It sought to increase their human capital and, by fostering civil society, to increase their social capital so that no one stood alone.[171]

Simon Cordery was more succinct when he placed the 1911 Act onto a wider stage saying that it 'represented another act in the drama of squeezing sociability'.[172] Martin Daunton noted the 'collapse of the approved societies', and although he felt that 'friendly societies were by no means defunct', he agreed with Paul Johnson that they were less popular for reasons beside that of the new legislation:

> The political contingencies of 1911 were important but there were signs that the friendly societies and active participation would not have survived in any event. Serving on committees of friendly societies, taking part in rituals with regalia and a culture of fraternity were means of achieving status and respectability within the working-class community. Such activities were losing their appeal before the First World War and the growth of membership was increasingly in centralised 'collecting' societies such as Hearts of Oak … as income levels rose and working-class families were able to save rather than merely combine against hardship friendly societies would become less significant.[173]

At the beginning of the nineteenth century to join the Oddfellows required a man to have the appropriate opinions, imagination and expectations. Ritual helped people to negotiate the changes within economic structures. By the early twentieth century there was greater familiarity with mathematical approaches to the economy and different ways of coping with the present and the future. The Oddfellows' structured version of gifting was developed within a legislative framework. When that framework was altered the ground on which members had planted their reciprocity was cut from under their feet.

Roger Spear provided a framework which encourages a longer perspective when he produced a list of the 'key features of the co-operative advantage'. While he recognised that 'legislation for UK mutuals was very constraining', he also argued that the 'public perception that the co-operative idea is one that belongs to a past generation', that mutuals could be 'effective in responding to market failures and state crises', that they were 'regarded as more trustworthy', that they were 'suited to build on the spirit of self-help' and 'solidarity within the community', that they 'empower people', and that they generate 'positive externalities', that is wider benefits.[174] It was not only the Liberal government's changes which had an impact because the 'advantages' the Society enjoyed were broadly based. Spear also argued that 'associative factors and social movement forces' were of importance, while Ware noted that friendly societies' success was closely related to their social and fraternal purposes and Lyons pointed to the importance of the social as well as the economic to the non-profit sector.[175] George Yarrow went further and argued that if the 1911 Act had not made national insurance compulsory, 'friendly societies would have grown significantly larger in the inter-war years'.[176]

While the legislation of 1911 had a decisive effect, the Oddfellows needed to change during the first half of the twentieth century because everything around the Society changed. Others noticed the need to adapt to new circumstances. In 1907 the Foresters' High Chief Ranger (National Chair) declared:

> Brotherhood is forgotten and members are impressed with one fact only, that is that they have joined a huge sick and burial society. That is exactly what our forefathers did not teach, preach or practise in the infancy of our organisation.[177]

Although the Society contributed to a scheme which relied on the life tables of the Unity, removed the stigma of the Poor Law from publicly funded health services and gave people a sense that health care was a right, at least for those capable of work, it got little credit for these changes. Indeed Stanley Baldwin claimed that the tables on which the legislation of 1911 were based cost the Society £20,000 for which 'no official word of thanks or gratitude was ever received by the Order'.[178] Rather, it was associated with a system in which seven different government departments were involved, with three different and mutually exclusive benefits for unemployment, three different types of pension and different schemes for the blind, the disabled, those with industrial injuries and the sick who earned less than £250 a year. The Oddfellows having shifted its perspective in 1911 was then relieved of its role and had to struggle to find a new one.

CHAPTER SIX

Inside the lodge

WHILE for many members of the Oddfellows it was the business of the lodge which was of primary importance notably the health provision, the mortgages or the social activities, Ritual enveloped all of these. It could take members out of the everyday world into a mystical place derived from mummery, Masons and ideals associated with the Abrahamic faiths. Ritual was practised in order to comply with the rules, to demonstrate respect and affiliation, to satisfy emotional requirements and nourish relationships, to strengthen social bonds and for pleasure. It had practical applications, being useful for checking on members' status, informing them of the ideals of Oddfellowship, structuring change and networks within the Unity and uniting members across time and space in common activities. By sharing Rituals members have been linked by a sense of exclusivity.[1] The first section is about some of the reasons why Ritual has been of importance to the Oddfellows. As it can encompass many different meanings Ritual enables Oddfellows to disagree without arguing inside the lodge, to express, indirectly, conflicts within society, to symbolically both oppose and welcome urbanisation and industrialisation, cultural changes and the overt imposition of new structures and roles.[2] Interviews with members of the Labour Party indicate that 'activists agree that the debates, rituals and rhetoric of the Labour Party gave them heart while boosting recruitment and funds'.[3] Similar conclusions can be reached about the fraternity of the Order. The second section considers how far the structures of the Oddfellows supported learning and loyalty. The combination of the unreal and the realistic has worried governments, Oddfellows and potential members. For some people aprons, Guardians and the singing of 'Enter Boldly' were seen as evidence of security through longevity and familiarity, for others they have been unsettling, archaic distractions from the core business of the Society.[4] The third and fourth sections are about the impact of Ritual on people's lives and the debates within the Order about ceremonies. Ritual was a means by which members could explore and support the Society's notion of the gift. As that idea was undermined so Ritual came to be seen to be of less relevance.

I Communicating identities and ideas

One of the strengths of Oddfellowship is that it is built on foundations reaching back to 1810 and beyond. In order to understand the roots of Ritual within the Oddfellows it is helpful to place people's ideas about and memories of secrecy, passwords, lectures and degrees within a longer-term perspective. While Ritual is flexible and ideas have developed, there is considerable continuity. Instructions issued in 1875 indicated that, at funerals, members were to wear 'black sashes, white gloves and aprons'.[5] When Arthur Jackson spoke about white gloves at funerals he was evoking conventions which stretched back at least 200 years and were recorded all over the country.[6] For example, John Winkley recalled the funeral of his father in 1953:

> I can see all the members as you came out of church they were lined up on either side which was quite impressive. They probably would be all in dark and probably white gloves as well. They put regalia on for these sorts of occasions. He had been a Provincial Grand Master; he had been a trustee of the Trafalgar Lodge as well and Noble Grand a number of times.

When Brenda Francis recalled her first impressions of the 'colourful sashes, aprons and collarettes', her words are a reminder that Oddfellowship has connections with mummery and the guilds.[7] When Syd Bolton said 'A lot of work is done at the bar, things were arranged and fixed by people, ideas got transferred and people would persuade', he was drawing on drink-related networking traditions going back to the Anglo-Saxon guilds.[8]

> We would go out and have a drink and then we would go for a meeting for an hour and then we would have two or three drinks and a game of snooker, then go home. Two or three nights a week we were out. Same as when I ran the Conciliator [Lodge]. The meeting would take from eight 'til nine and at a minute past nine we were in the pub on the other side of the road having a drink.

For two hundred years rituals both within the lodge and in more public places, have provided comfort and respectability for Oddfellows. The rituals are open to many readings and yet at the same time they bind people together and act as an anchor in a changing world. This may have been an important aspect of early Oddfellowship. The Ritual may have been developed to support those who faced the dislocations caused by capitalist development and a market economy in which transactions led to material gain rather than fellowship. In such cases Ritual may have been a reassuring link to the past.

Eric Hobsbawm has argued that 'the nineteenth-century liberal ideology of social change systematically failed to provide for the social and authority ties taken for granted in earlier societies, and created voids which might have to be filled by invented practices.'[9] The ceremonies of the Society continued to provide a focus for meetings and help ensure that members understand the account of the past that the Society wished to promote. The Ritual has been heartening, for as Derek Winbush said, 'Wherever you go and see a ceremonial lodge you should immediately feel at home because it should always be the same'. In the 1970s Joan Henry attended, with her husband, Reg, an international conference in Australia about Ritual because, as she pointed out, 'the whole thing about Ritual it's not much good if everybody is doing their own thing. With Ritual everybody has to do the same thing.' They both echo an Oddfellows lecture of 1840 which made clear one of the benefits of Ritual: 'If I should wander to the farthest part of England or take flight across the wide Atlantic I should still feel at home.'[10] Even when Ritual was different there was communication and connections. Derek Elmer recalled meeting the American Order, which had sex-segregated lodges, in Holland. 'In the 70s we got invited to go to Rotterdam and we took enough to demonstrate an English lodge. We took all the regalia and chains.' Members indicated that Ritual helped to fulfil spiritual needs by indicating an ethical behaviour. When Joan Henry said, 'There is precept in the Order of friendship, love and truth and possibly Ritual helps people with those precepts', her views echoed the Oddfellow Rules of 1855, which referred to the lodges as 'sacred ground' and 'temples of Oddfellowship' where they could promote moral principles'.[11]

When, in the early years of Oddfellowship, a person claiming to be travelling brother arrived at lodge expecting hospitality, his authenticity needed to be verified. Ensuring that he had a grasp of Ritual was one means of checking his identity. This tradition has been maintained. Mike Trenchard explained, 'If someone enters the lodge after it's opened then they will be asked for certain password at the door to get in. The passwords were to stop imposters.' This idea drew on the medieval guilds. Within the craftworkers' guilds 'mysteries' could mean both trade secrets and an ethical code of conduct. The 'craft' of Oddfellowship was not tactile skills required of tradesmen but the more generic skills and virtues necessary for living in harmony with God and the brethren. These have been secret in the sense that they are not self-evident. They need to be learned and practised. The description of Ritual procedures in his village lodge in the 1920s provided by Bill Needham, 1904–83, indicates the difficulties an imposter would have with pretending to be a member of the Oddfellows:

> We always had a club room in them days. It was upstairs in the George Hotel. There used to be a member on the door and he were called the Tyler and nobody strange would get into that meeting because you had a secret sort of code. You would have to knock on the door with your first two knuckles, twice. The Tyler would be behind the door, fastened on the inside. He would open the door and say 'Brother Needham wishes to be admitted'. There was a Committee consisting of a Right and Left Supporter for the Vice Grand. The man in the chair used to wear a collaret round his neck and he had the initials on what he was. The first man was a VG, the Vice Grand and the next one, above again, sat in a chair, just at the back but slightly higher up was the NG, Noble Grand. Then there was another chair at the back again, raised up and he was the GM, the Grand Master. I was the Grand Master three times because nobody was very keen on accepting it because the Grand Master hadn't a lot of talking but the Noble Grand, he chaired the meeting. The secretary was sat on my side. When the member knocked on the door with those two knocks he'd turn straight to the NG, Noble Grand, and it was up to him whether he was admitted or not. If it was me who was Noble Grand I'd say 'Admit him', 'cause I knew who he was. Then he'd come in and sit down and take his place with the others.[12]

A report in 1930 indicated how this form of identification was employed at a conference:

> five of the delegates failed to justify their presence by an ability to repeat a necessary password with which they had been made acquainted twenty years ago on reaching what is known as 'the Purple Degree' in the hierarchy of the Order … However, no harm was done at yesterday's gathering, the backsliders proved their identity in other ways.[13]

In addition to ensuring that an individual was a member Ritual has been used to ensure that members gained experience before they took on key tasks. Karen Stuart made this point.

> You wouldn't expect somebody to say 'I've decided I want to be a teacher,' and then walk into a classroom and teach. You would expect them to have qualified in the appropriate way. In the same way I don't expect somebody to join the Society and walk straight in at a senior level. This is a means of proving that they've served their time.

She also pointed to the continuing value of the regalia which is associated with the Ritual. Members of the Society, she noted, were able to read regalia and make judgments about other members.

> It shows that you have achieved a level of service. Wherever you go in the Society

Aprons were worn for protection in the seventeenth and eighteenth centuries, with different shapes for different trades. Some trade bodies permitted only senior workers to wear certain aprons, and by the time that the Oddfellows was founded the idea of the apron as a badge of membership and a symbol of authority was well established. Commercially printed silk squares were used for aprons throughout the nineteenth century. Members could then add decorative elements. The use of collars, such as that on the left, derives from the collars worn by guild officers or within orders of chivalry. Some members wore collarettes as a badge of office. Cuffs, originally part of gauntlet gloves, were sometimes worn and were often elaborately decorated.

COLLAR BY COURTESY OF CHRISTINE PAYNE; APRON: BY COURTESY OF THE LIBRARY AND MUSEUM OF FREEMASONRY

Membership certificates and Degree certificates were often ornate; they were displayed with pride by owners.

BELOW

The membership certificate of Brother Charles William Simpson of Newark, 1904.

BY COURTESY OF CHRISTINE PAYNE

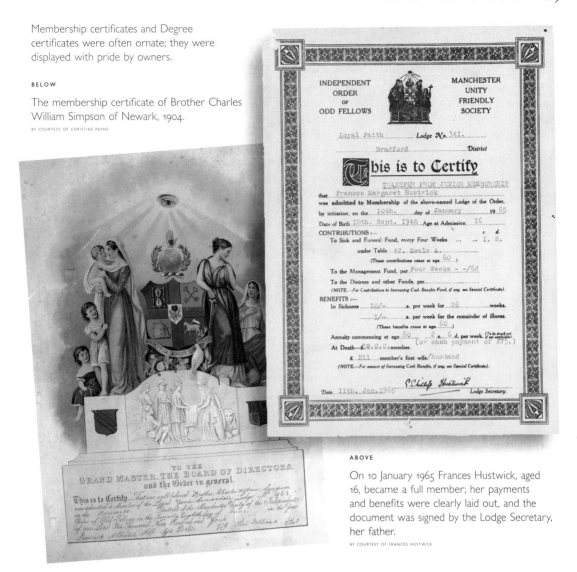

ABOVE

On 10 January 1965 Frances Hustwick, aged 16, became a full member; her payments and benefits were clearly laid out, and the document was signed by the Lodge Secretary, her father.

BY COURTESY OF FRANCES HUSTWICK

you can take the Purple Degree with you because there are collarettes, there are jewels that go with these things. When you are, for example, a Past Provincial Grand Master, you've a collarette of one style, it's purple with the gold tramlines on the outside. When you are a Past Noble Grand of a lodge there are two different jewels. There is one for a Past Noble Grand who has not done the Purple Degree, that's orange and gold, and then there is one that for somebody who has, which is scarlet and purple. So that it's very easy to look at the jewels that somebody wears for the collaret and know whereabouts they are in the progression. The Benevolence Committee, the Investigation Committee, the Special Arbitrators are central committees so their collarettes are purple with a single gold medium stripe down the middle that goes round. They are Unity Committee

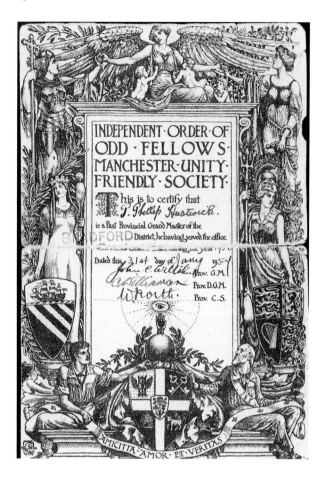

INDEPENDENT·ORDER·OF
ODD·FELLOWS·
MANCHESTER·UNITY·
FRIENDLY·SOCIETY·

This is to certify that
J. Phillip Hustwick
is a Past Provincial Grand Master of the
BRADFORD District, he having served the office

Dated this 31st day of Jany 195...
John C. Wildish Prov. G.M.
Williamson Prov. D.G.M.
W. Routh Prov. C.S.

AMICITIA·AMOR·ET·VERITAS·

A certificate from the 1950s confirming Phillip Hustwick's service as Past Provincial Grand Master of the Bradford District. Women support the royal coats of arms (*right*) and the Manchester coat of arms (*left*), while men support the arms of the Society.
BY COURTESY OF FRANCES HUSTWICK

collars and when you reach the Board of Directors then the collarettes there are just pure purple.

John Winkley took a matter-of-fact approach:

I took a purple degree. The degree themselves, apart from the signs, were common sense and the matter of the correct way to do things and the kind of attitude that one should have towards the various aspects of life or the society … My main interest in the first place of course was the financial side of it, coming from that point of view, I am afraid in my early days of activity I was more concentrating on that than the thinking behind the thing, that you are trying to help people which is the essence behind it.

Initiation was a way of passing on information, of introducing the mysteries of Oddfellowship, of acting out its ideals. Daphne Stephenson was told in advance that 'I would be making promises to the lodge', while Mike Trenchard suggested:

Initiation was to introduce a new member to each of the officers and to tell the new member some of the principles on which the society was founded and about the signs, knocks and passwords that the society uses in a normal lodge.

George Kilford called it 'a series of introductions and lectures about what Oddfellowship was all about, giving me the password and the method of entering the lodge, if the lodge was already opened'. Karen Stuart explained, 'You have to make certain promises that you will be a good person and that you will always endeavour to ensure that you don't treat the Oddfellows badly, I think that's the easiest way to put it. The initiation was something that excited me.' She added that the four degrees 'epitomise what Oddfellowship is. Each one deals with an element of who we are, who we were and what we were and I think that's important. I think of all the degrees probably the Purple Degree is the one that epitomises it and is the most special for me.' George Kilford pointed out that:

> People were introduced to the Society and were given the opportunity to read small parts in their lodge room. Increasing their understanding of things and also the acceptance of responsibility in the various offices would all help to build their confidence and give them the opportunity to express themselves. It's benefited me tremendously and I had a reasonable education. For others who had a lesser start that has been a great boon to them.

Dorothy Deacon provided other reasons as to why she favoured Ritual:

> if it's done properly there is nothing better; it is a way to run a meeting. To go into a lodge meeting with members wearing their full regalia and have it done properly is as good as going to see a good film or theatre.

In the twenty-first century there were other ways on which to check a person's identity, but the need to check on the status and qualifications of an individual remain. Passwords are required to take money from the bank, certificates can be demanded to prove the right to drive a car and it is an offence to wear some uniforms without authorisation. Ritual was a means by which poor, possibly illiterate, members of the Society could identify one another. It is also a way to structure networking and reciprocity, provide a path to higher ranks within the Society and pass on information.

II Structured for learning

The structure of the Oddfellows enabled members to gradually acquire the skills necessary to run the lodge. People could practise civil and social skills, learn how to run meetings, organise finances and co-operate in fellowship. Members would start with smaller tasks and once in positions of authority have the advice of the Immediate Past officer on which to call. The rules of confidentiality, instilled through the Ritual, could reassure a member who made an error while learning that knowledge of mistakes would not be known outside the lodge. In 1880 the Traveller's Rest lodge in Norwich initiated the local MP and member of an important local family, J. J. Colman. At his initiation Colman said that the Society aided the development of business talent, adding, 'Many a man owes his rise in social position to the practical lessons learned whilst filling honorary office in his society … [The Oddfellows] taught their members a respect for constituted authority, thus making them better citizens, while the capital under their control gives them a stake in the country.'[14] Olive Hare provided the example of her father, a farm labourer born in the late nineteenth century who learned new skills through running

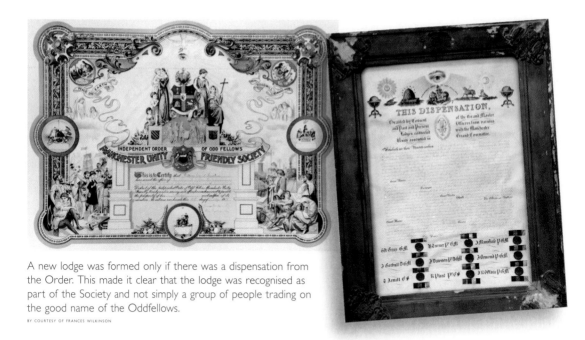

A new lodge was formed only if there was a dispensation from the Order. This made it clear that the lodge was recognised as part of the Society and not simply a group of people trading on the good name of the Oddfellows.

the local lodge in Shillington, Bedfordshire.[15] Keith Adamson pointed to other possibilities, arguing that 'the Oddfellows is the only place that I know that an ordinary man off the street can join the society today and become chairman of the board of a £300 million society.' The Oddfellows sought to help members on many levels, not only the financial.

Several Oddfellows mentioned that through the lodge they gained self-assurance and understanding. Tony Crouch felt that being a member of the Society: 'gave me a lot of confidence, it gave me a lot of knowledge that I probably wouldn't have got anywhere else; how to deal with people, how to talk to people, how to approach people and how to be my own man … It gave you a sense of learning something and being of use to people.' Jean Facer said, 'I am glad I joined Oddfellows I had an awful lot of fun, I was taught a lot and I found out a lot. It helped me to grow and appreciate other people. It helped me with my own development.' Jeff Barlett gained the auditing qualification available through the Society, the CAMU, and said, 'I'll always be grateful to the Oddfellows in regard to the knowledge I picked up of investments.'

Syd Bolton also gained auditing and book examination skills through his involvement in the Oddfellows. He gained the CAMU certificate and became an auditor of the Manchester Unity. His recollections of the examination indicate the mixture of formality and flexibility which characterised much of the Society's activities. During the examination the invigilator H. A. Andrews (after whom a Memorial Fund was named in 1971) allowed the candidates to have a break:

Halfway through the exam he said, 'I helped write the rules for this examination so I think if I want to I can break them. Providing you don't talk to one another about the

---

CAMU

An advertisement in 1984 claimed that the CAMU correspondence course will

Make you more effective in your lodge and district.

Help you to think more clearly.

Give you a useful basis from which you conduct your business and private affairs.

Keep your mind actively employed.[16]

---

examination, I am going to knock for twenty minutes and give you all a cup of tea.' We had a cup of tea and talked about Manchester United Football Club and then we started again and went on with the exam.

Syd went on to note that if the sums involved were relatively small it was not a requirement that a chartered accountant do the auditing.

I did a lot of those for about twenty years. It was a little part-time job, you had a fiver for doing it and it took you about an hour. It gave you some inside knowledge working there.

Mike Trenchard was another who recognised the personal benefits. He spoke of how through the Oddfellows he had gained 'experience of organising things, speaking publicly, finance responsibility'. This was a point made by Oddfellows in the past. In 1901 the mayor of Rotherham, a PPGM, said that if it had not been for his training within the Society he would not have been able to become mayor.[17] Frances Wilkinson said that being a member boosted her confidence and skills:

There is a lot of things we wouldn't have done if we hadn't had been in Oddfellowship. Being in your middle to late teens when you are able to organise a dance and get your tickets printed and get the food and make supper and prepare food and get your times right. We had great fun organising these things and you were very much left on your own to do it, there was help there if you needed it and you could ask for it and people would, the brothers and sisters would come and support your evening.

She went on

It probably gives you a maturity and that enables you to do things and have the confidence to do it. I didn't think I had confidence to enter this intermediate lodge competition but I found myself there and I was mortified that I was the first interviewed but I came through it OK. I wouldn't have volunteered to do it, I was pushed into it and I think you get pushed into it like going through the chairs. You're young and managing a meeting with a lot of experienced brothers and sisters sat around so people are hanging on your word at times. I think you really do get confidence in your own abilities really, I think if you did get things wrong people weren't too harsh on you, they just tell you the way it should have been done.

Tony Crouch explained about the civility that the lodge encouraged:

People learnt the rules and they debated things. They debated a problem and they learnt how to argue it out. It wasn't quite like the Houses of Parliament where everybody shouts at once and it's like a dog sale. They all respected each other and they didn't shout at each other. They all debated and you came to what I call a sensible conclusion about what you were talking about. Also you learnt how to conduct a meeting. When you're the Noble Grand it is important that you can control a meeting. Only one person in the lodge room, as in Parliament, stands at any one time when they are speaking. Even the speaker of Parliament sits down when somebody else is speaking in the Chamber and that's the basis of the Oddfellows. If you were the Noble Grand you sat down while somebody was speaking but if you got fed up with him you banged your gavel and stood up and he had to sit down. That's based on Parliament, if you watch the speaker of the Houses of Parliament that's exactly what he does.

Terence Pauley presented the rules in a slightly different light when he recalled being initiated in 1950, aged 16. He was familiar with the Society because:

All the family had to become members and those that were married into the family. Granddad used to collect the contributions and then pay it to the Lodge secretary each quarter.

Nevertheless, it was ordered:

We used to use a section of the Masonic Hall, one of the smaller rooms, we were called in and given a lecture on what the society stood for what we were to do what we were not to do. It was a very disciplined area in those days.

The importance of the rules can be measured by the fact that the lodge of Oddfellows in Parwich, North Staffordshire, fined one member, G. H. Brownson, 6d. for 'not being upstanding when speak [sic]'.[18] The same lodge had a strictly regulated annual parade. In 1876 the Anniversary Committee stipulated when members needed to attend, that they had to 'proceed to Church in an orderly manner at 11 o'clock, or be fined 1 shilling', and 'that any member leaving the church during the service with the exception of the two waiters shall be fined one shilling'. It was made clear that the band was only allowed '1 gallon of ale at each house' and there were fines for smoking during the procession, leaving the feast table without permission and not wearing white gloves. The tradition that new members had to carry a golden axe and bring up the rear of the procession was maintained until at least the 1970s.

Pat Morgan also recalled how her father was very firm in ensuring that rules were kept at the AMC:

> My Mum had never been to the mic[rophone] but when we were at Morecambe and my Dad was Grand Master she went up to the mic[rophone]. What you are supposed to do when you go to the mic, is to give your name and district because it is recorded. She goes to the mic and she goes straight into whatever it was she was going to say. Of course, he had to interrupt her and say 'Name and District?' It brought the house down because it was his own wife.

Frances Wilkinson mentioned the importance of regulations:

> They were really steeped in Oddfellowship, you had the rules and you had to stick to the rules. They would discuss heavily things at a point that they thought was right, that you shouldn't be doing it this way, it should be done that way. I can remember quite a lot of heated discussions over how things should be done.

After the war gradually the number of occasions when ordinary members could participate in investment decisions was reduced as power became more concentrated in fewer hands. Tony Crouch was one of three men from his lodge who wanted to become take the CAMU course at the same time:

> We used to have to go up to Stepney every week and Jim Morgan would instruct us. We learnt all about the rules of the organisation. It's a great thick book and they are very interesting to read. I did the course but by that time things were changing in political circles. You had to have a certified auditor not a CAMU person. You have to have your books audited by a bloke who sets up and says, 'I'm an accountant and I can audit'.

There were other skills which could be acquired. Eric Ogden claimed to be

> one of the very few bank managers who for 49 years held a double-decker bus driving licence. It was in that capacity that I used to organise the coach trips for the Oddfellows, not the Juveniles but the Oddfellows in general. We had an annual coach trip and I drove the bus to keep the cost down.

Ron Trenchard mentioned another skill people acquired through membership of the Society:

A lodge of the Order, the Loyal Laurel and Crown opened in Parwich in 1836, and there is a record of members carrying a banner in 1847. Parwich maintained its marching traditions until recent times. Like the Parwich golden axe, the staves displayed of Banbury in 1966 (*right*) were for ceremonial use. However, it is said that Oddfellows ceremonial swords were used in the 1839 Newport Rising.

ODDFELLOWS COLLECTION

BANBURY ANNIVERSARY CHURCH PARADE

(By Courtesy of the " Banbury Guardian"
Banbury District Officers with visiting members from other Districts in the Shennington Amicable Lodge's 125th Anniversary Church Parade.

'You get a person who comes and joins the society. They are timid but before you know where you are they are standing up and speaking. It gives people the incentive to speak at a meeting or speak at anything.' Derek Winbush joined the Leamington Lodge when he was 16 and suggested that it was through social rituals that he felt drawn into Oddfellowship. He gave the example of whist drives: 'I was dishing the cards out and things like that, nothing too exceptional but making a start, you build up a bit of a team together.'

Being an active member of the Society sometimes enhanced the social status as James Beard noted:

> We've got friends in Denmark and I was going down this street with one of these people and I saw a building with Oddfellows all over it and I said to Jan, 'Have you got Oddfellows here?' He said, 'Oh yes, it's something that if you're a member of Oddfellows, you're way up in the world.' 'Why,' I said, 'I'm a member of the Oddfellows in England,' and he looked at me and he said, 'You are high up in the world.'

Eric Ogden said that he was given time off to attend Board meetings which was perhaps a reflection of the high esteem in which the Society was held by his employer, a bank. Jean Facer, who worked in a school, received special dispensation to attend AMCs.

The work of an officer within the Oddfellows could be very time consuming. The formal recognition of the hours spent in ensuring the success of the Oddfellows was recognised in the regalia and Ritual. The engagement with Ritual was closely linked to gaining office and although those members who held office often look back on it as life-enhancing, some also remembered it being hard work for them and those around them. This has long been the case, as the example of Thomas Armitt indicates. Born in 1774 he went to work on a farm at the age of nine after his father died. He later moved to Salford and became Grand Master in 1824–1825, by which time he was describing himself as an earthenware dealer. A Grand Master spends a year in office In the year that he was the Immediate Past Grand Master, 1825–1826 he spent 18 days travelling to lodges with a new lecture known as the Patriarchal Degree. After he had visited Chester, Newcastle-under-Lyne, Wolverhampton, Birmingham, Worcester, Cheltenham, London, Brighton and elsewhere he returned home. He then set off for another 12-day trip later during that year and also attended Board and committee meetings. The route and the means of transport that a Grand Master takes has changed, but there is still considerable travel and effort for post holders.

Betty Mostyn acknowledged the effort involved when talking about her late husband, Len. He joined in 1949 and became Provincial Grand Master in 1966, Provincial Corresponding Secretary of the Mersey District and, in 1970, a member of the national Board of Directors. He became Grand Master in 1977. He was a Trustee for 15 years, was the National Conference of Friendly Societies President 1985/86 and he acted as full-time Secretary of the Order between August 1992 and May 1993. This took its toll on him as at one time he used to travel every day from Liverpool where he lived, to Manchester, where the Oddfellows was based, while also working in Carlisle. Betty explained:

> He'd go to Carlisle in the morning, come back, go to a Committee of Management and then go back to Carlisle. That's the dedication. It was a way of life. When Len was Secretary of the District our home was the office.

Many people recalled how they went 'through the chairs'. Bill Needham explained the system in his lodge, the Loyal Adventurers of the Peak in Taddington, Derbyshire, which he joined in 1919:

> It used to take you five years [to go through the chairs] – start from the Left or Right Supporter right up to Grand Master – and I went through three times. I had three thrashings of it because some of them, they weren't too keen on having it, because if you were Noble Grand you had a lot of talking to do … I was interested in that kind of work. I was young, fit and that's how it came about.

Bill Needham added: 'We'd got quite a lot of furniture. The seating was set out like a throne, with chairs on either side.' Albert Fox also referred to the materials: 'you've got your regalia, your boxes of stuff'.[19] Bill had little choice about taking up a post. *The Special Rules in Taddington* described how involvement within the Order was encouraged. Rule 16, Election of Officers, stated:

> On the annual election nights of the electing of officers there shall be seven brothers' names taken alphabetically from the book to serve inferior officers of the lodge; the secretary to choose his assistant; the NG to nominate his own supporters; the other one to act as Guardian … Any member entitled to benefits refusing to serve shall be fined two shillings.

Jean Facer described 'going through the chairs' in a later period:

> I went through the chairs of the lodge once and then I went through the district chairs twice. The first time was in 1977 which was our centenary year in the Watford district. I was a very lucky lady actually and then again in 1997. I had been involved with district affairs as well through Stan [her husband]. He went through district office twice and I supported him as his consort when he went on various district visits. To go through the lodge chairs you have to attend and hold various offices, minor offices as they are called, in the lodge before you can get through to the main lodge offices. You also have to take minor degrees which are lectures read out to you. You promise to do various things while you are holding this particular office. They have three chairs for you in the lodge, three stations, the first is the Vice Grand Chair. The main chair is the Noble Grand's Chair where you are the chairman of the lodge and you run the meetings together with the Secretary. Every Noble Grand always relies on the Secretaries. Then you are the Immediate Past, which is the last chair, so it's a three year office in effect. For each one you then have to take a Degree to be able to pass on to the next one which is again another lecture that is read to you and promises made.

Betty Mostyn said, 'I'd been through the chairs in the lodge before I was 21' and Derek Winbush went through the offices of the lodge at the earliest possible time 'just after 18 I suppose but I should have been 21 really'. Mike Trenchard pointed out one of the restrictions on holding office.

> I was initiated into the adult lodge on my 16th birthday and that was the youngest age you could join the adult lodge, but you were not allowed to be the Noble Grand until you were 21.

Syd Bolton was confident about the work. He remembered that within a year of joining the Oddfellows he was asked by the secretary, who was about to retire, to take over.

> He started working on me, 'You could do this job of mine, you could be secretary', and of course, I fell for it. Within a matter of six months I was an officer and within about eighteen months I was secretary … I had to give attention but I was fairly quick. I was 29 and I took to it like a duck to water.

However, he added, 'I had no time for anything else. It's a way of life and once you got involved in it and do it properly, attending meetings left right and centre, you've no time to start standing for local council or anything like that.' Mike Trenchard also found himself very busy.

> I was District Trustee for about 20 years. I was probably going to two or three meetings a week. The only paid officer is the Secretary because they are doing the work. There is no way they can pay the going rate so it is very much a kind of labour of love.

The possibility of work did not put off Jean Pye. She met Stan Facer at a holiday camp in East Anglia. On their return from holiday she noticed that the Oddfellows kept him busy

> During our early courting days he would turn round and say, 'I can't meeting you such-and-such a night because I've got a meeting,' and 'I can't meet you then I've got to go this or I've got to go to that.' I kept saying, 'Well what is it?' and he would tell me about the Oddfellows and that's how I came to be interested. At the time he was a member of the Loyal Phoenix Lodge in Watford. The year after we met we got engaged and I always remember he said to me, 'You're not stopping me going to the Odds are you?' Then he said, 'You're going to be a member when we are married?' I said, 'Yes, if I am going to be a member in two years I might as well be a member now.' That's when I joined the Oddfellows, when I got engaged to Stan. That was 1953.

Kath Vernon became a Provincial Secretary after a career as an Assistant Bank Manager. She found the work very varied: 'When you're used to saying, 'I get to work at nine o'clock in the morning and I start and I leave at five, and shut the door and finish, that's it, it isn't the case.' She indicated the nature of her involvement:

If you are Prov. Sec. it is not a nine-to-five job, it is not a Monday to Friday, it is twenty four hours a day, seven days a week. If you are not out somewhere, you are at the end of your phone. You are the first person that a lot of people get in contact with and in that respect you are very important because the impression that you give people when you answer the phone to them or when you answer their letters, is the impression that they keep and so it is onerous and not an easy job at all.

Others agreed that the work could take over their lives. James Beard became a Trustee and very active:

I went through all the chairs in the Meritorious Lodge, this was held in Stockport and became Noble Grand. I was really bogged down with Oddfellowship. One week I went out seven nights. I had to stop it, cut it down, my wife was getting a bit uptight about it.

This is a branch secretary, Pauline Pettigrove, giving an account of some of her recent activities:

[I do] everything from minute taking to being a good listener because members will phone up and sometimes you maybe the only person they have spoken to all day. No two days are ever the same. If I come in on a Monday morning with a list of 10 items to do, if I have ticked one off by the last week of the month I have had a cracking good month.

Edward Schofield, a third-generation Oddfellow, was appointed as District Secretary after the death of the previous secretary, who had been a family friend:

There is quite a lot of work with all the optical and dental benefits so although this job is an 18 hour per week job, it doesn't always work out like that. I enjoy the job. I love doing it and it's a way of life. For events which are now obviously to the fore in our fellowship, we usually have about 25. We are doing our best to try and revive the Oddfellowship as much as we can.

Michael Greatorex recalled the contribution of his father:

My father's work for the Oddfellows [Arnold Greatorex 1906–89, was a lodge secretary during the period 1959–77] was not always appreciated by my mother. He spent hours on end 'doing his Oddfellows books'. Large ledgers would be spread out in the front room while he made entries and did calculations. These would often litter the front room for days … Brothers calling at our house often did so unannounced and at all times of the day. Whatever my father was doing he would always deal with them, again to the consternation of my mother. I am convinced that my father would pay subscriptions for members he had not seen recently so that their subscriptions were kept up to date. He would then have the task of recovering the subscriptions from those in arrears.[20]

The recollections of these members indicate that the Society was structured so as to encourage people to take on posts and to progress, incrementally, towards greater authority and deeper involvement. Although Bill pointed out that not everybody wanted to become officers, for those who did there was some pleasure in their status. Jean for example called herself a 'lucky lady'.

The burdens, and pleasures, of being an active Oddfellow were sometimes shared. Betty Mostyn referred to 'our year' when her husband became Grand Master, Jean Facer mentioned how she was her husband's consort when he held office. Brenda Francis recognised the importance of her parents:

We lived for Oddfellows. Fortunately I had a mum and dad who lived next door to me when I had the children. They were very handy to babysit so I was fortunate on that score. We lived Oddfellowship. It was a way of life.

Recently another member, echoing Pat Morgan whose babysitter was later a Grand Master, mentioned the Oddfellow babysitting service provided for her son:

[My son] … refers to our current Grand Master Keith Adamson as 'Uncle Keith', and refers to his wife as 'Auntie Alison'. They spoil him rotten. I get to sit down and have a bit of a break and know full well that he is in safe hands.

The insistence that people frequently change posts was one of the ways in which Ritual helped structure life in the lodge and ensure that the same people were not overburdened without an opportunity to pass on their knowledge. This is the case at lodge, district and national level as Keith Adamson explained. He was elected to the Board of Directors and in due course became Deputy Grand Master and then Grand Master. At the time that he was interviewed he was the Immediate Past Grand Master charged with supporting the current Grand Master. He went on:

when this year is over I shall fall off the end of the Board never to go back unless I get elected as a Trustee. The system ensures that new ideas are being generated and the Board does not stagnate.

Ritual and ceremony were used to check on the authenticity and engagement of members and to ensure a flow of members through all the responsible posts. Through Ritual members of the Oddfellows have been able to act out and pass on ideas, structure their workload, to build their confidence and to enjoy themselves together. Confidential structures and information support and encourage trust between members, help to make the lodge a haven where members might meet other like-minded, discreet members and enable people to engage with ideas of solidarity and historical continuity. Through Ritual and actions members of the Oddfellows created social relationships and were guided towards institutionalised benevolence through a form of exchange which stressed the importance of loyalty and reciprocity.

III 'A peculiar and mysterious awe'[21]

The practical arguments for Ritual are only part of the explanation as to its functions and fascination over the years. The capacity of Ritual to cause fear and surprise has also been of value to the Oddfellows. It has helped bond together those who have been initiated and has kept them alert over the course of their membership. The early initiation appears to have been designed to frighten. Between 1810 and 1825 the first-degree initiation within the Oddfellows began with the blindfolding and binding of the candidate, the baring of his breast and his passage into the lodge between two Guardians who made challenges.[22] He heard the rattling of chains and was sometimes thrown into brushwood or had his head immersed in water. When his blindfold was removed there was a sword pointed at his heart. The man holding the weapon asked the members assembled, who were robed and masked, if he should be merciful. Once they had decided to be merciful the candidate was sworn in, unbound and shown a figure of Death and other symbols. There were four degrees, known by the colours White, Blue, Scarlet and Gold. The initiation for the fourth one included the following challenge and response:

Noble Grand: Whom do you represent?

Supplicant: The son of Onias, the High Priest, who repaired the House of God and fortified the Temple.

Noble Grand: In what light will you appear in the lodge?

Supplicant: As the morning star or the moon is full. I cheer and refresh the minds of my brethren like the Sun on the Temple of the Most High or the rainbow in the heavens.

This was a period when 'theatricality was a mode of public being, a representation of the self was not confined to dramas performed in the playhouses … was rooted in just about every imaginable sphere of contemporary life'.[23] Young urban working men attended penny theatres at some of which people could pay to perform. Worrall argued that 'no other single factor demonstrates the cultural reach of drama in this period'. In his recollections of the 1790s Henry Angelo described the speeches and singing at a number of clubs including the 'Good-Fellows' and the 'Free-and-easys'. He went on to mention a 'President who from a rostrum knocking with an ivory mallet hoarsely bawled', after which men stood and performed. Club life often included speeches, songs, drinking and smoking and theatre. Commercial companies saw a connection with drama. The Phoenix, Hand-in-Hand, Sun and Norwich insurance companies were all mentioned in the script of Dibdin's popular play, *Melodrame Mad*, 1819. Manchester had its own journal devoted to theatricals which reported in 1806 a spectacular entertainment based on a grand funeral while the 1773 production of Garrick's *A Christmas Tale* was called, by Worrall, a 'confident and visually innovative transmission of Masonic symbolism' and 'entirely typical of artisan spirtualities'. The composer of the piece, Dibdin, went on to write *Harlequin Freemason* in 1780 and his son, also a Freemason, later revived *A Christmas Tale*. There were a number of other dramatic 'embodiments of artisan fraternity'.[24] Drama and ritual were popular ways of expressing ideas and the discourses of politics and theatre were intertwined. Monod called the mid-eighteenth-century political movement, Jacobitism, 'a morality play' and an important root of later theatrical political culture.[25] Thompson connected drama and song with mutuality when he invited readers to remember

> the ballard-singer and the fair-ground which handed on the traditions to the nineteenth century (to the music-hall or Dickens' circus folk, or Hardy's pedlars and showmen); for in these ways the 'inarticulate' conserved certain values – a spontaneity and capacity for enjoyment and mutual loyalties.[26]

In October 1816 reformer Joseph Mitchell's 'melodramatic' *Address to the People* was distributed around the Manchester area, and in February 1817 there was the publication of Robert Southey's play *Wat Tyler* which had been written in 1794 and suppressed by the author. Selections were read at radical meetings and, in March when 25,000 people gathered in Manchester to launch a protest march on London, they 'adopted a melodramatic model of confrontation with authority'. A spy reported to the government that the contents of friendly society and sick club boxes were being used to fund protests in the belief that there was soon to be a larger-scale redistribution of wealth. Poole concluded that 'melodramatic postures, combining extravagant claims of legitimacy with dire threats of disaster, were part of the political currency of the age'.[27] The drama of politics may have informed, and been informed by, the Oddfellows.

Others have seen politics in terms of theatre. In 1809 and 1810, when theatre prices rose and the poor were excluded, there were protests during which people performed their own dramas in which they sang, danced and engaged in mock sword play. Over the next few years there were 'extraordinary changes in theatrical genres … gesture and expression now came to be perceived as indispensable parts of rhetoric'. Handclasps were codified and performances featuring skeletons, coffins and apparitions increased and were greeted with enthusiasm. Banners were used in on-stage processions and at least one play, about rioters, conflated the self-conscious theatricality of the free and easies and the conventions of the theatre. In 1822 the Coburg Theatre introduced a vast mirror which was lowered between the auditorium and the stage. Spectators could see reflections of themselves appearing on stage, they could become the subjects of their own spectacle and appear to cross the boundary between audience and players. The way that the world could be imagined was transformed by drama and attempts were made to capitalise on this. For example, one MP commissioned a theatre scenery designers and painters to produce flags and 'other showy paraphernalia' for his election campaign.

Oddfellows Ritual may also have been influenced by these developments. Many artisans were playgoers.[28] It is likely that during a period when popular drama addressed issues close to the heart of Oddfellowship there was some traffic of ideas between the lodge room and the stage. All around them working men could see the elements which contributed to Oddfellowship being portrayed. They could see drama, be it Christian, Masonic or secular, as a method of integration, control and tuition. There was a spectacular physicality to much working-class drama of the period. It kept men intellectually and spiritually involved and could be used to express core values and reinforce the way in which people looked at the world by providing a model, or a map, of the actual environment in which they operated. It was against this immediate backdrop of popular enthusiasm for spectacle and engagement in drama that the Ritual was developed.

Panto and pants

This account of initiation is from 1832. It makes it appear to be a daunting experience:

At the door of the Lodge I was blindfolded by the Outdoor Guardian, who had a drawn sword, and, with mysterious knocks and whispering, after giving the password I was admitted into the Lodge-room. All was intense silence. I felt a peculiar awe pass over me. I was told to step over imaginary steps and stoop under projecting beams, etc. All at once I was startled by the howling of members and rattling of ponderous chains; the noise subsided, and I was asked what I most wanted. My Conductor whispered me 'Say light'; I did so, and my interrogator asked me if I should know the person who proposed me. I said 'Yes'. The bandage was rudely torn from my forehead, and my conductor said, 'Is that him?' thrusting me close to a painted transparency representing a skeleton, or, as they called it, 'Old Mortality'. Two members dressed as priests stood beside the picture with drawn swords, who cautioned me to be very careful and discreet during my initiation, when a stentorian voice from behind the picture thus addressed me: 'Hold! approach me not, for know that in my presence monarchs tremble and princes kiss the dust; at my bidding the most potent armies disappear. My shadow is the pestilence, and my path the whirlwind. For thee, poor mortal, pass some few years of flowering spring, with pleasant, joyous summer and sober autumn fading into age. Then pale concluding winter comes at last and shuts the scene; then shalt thou be with me. But know, to the virtuous man my approach hath no terrors; to the guilty alone am I terrible.'

'So when the last, the closing, hour draws nigh,
And earth recedes before thy swimming eye;
Whilst trembling on the doubtful verge of fate,
Thou strain'st thy view to either state,
Then may'st thou quit this transitory scene
With decent triumph, and a look serene;
Then may'st thou fix thine ardent hopes on high,
And, having nobly lived, so nobly die.'

The last two lines were shouted out in chorus by all the members. I was now led to the father of the Lodge, the Warden. I was told he was very old and feeble, and he would further assist me in the ordeal of making. In my simplicity I tried to help him from his chair, being told to do so, when, to my surprise, he grasped me with Herculean strength and shook me violently, dragging me up and down the room. He ceased, and asked if the poker was ready, and asked me (as he said) in confidence if I had flannel drawers on. I had been told to say 'Yes,' and he announced to the Lodge that I had flannel drawers on, at which a tremendous yell of satisfaction was heard throughout the Lodge. Oh, it was fearful fun! They had a painted poker, similar to what clowns use in pantomimes. But the funniest appearance was their grotesque and ludicrous dresses, and all wore burlesque masks. I was led to the Vice-Grand, who administered the obligation; then taken to the Noble Grand, who was, I afterwards found, seated on a throne, with supporters similar to the Vice-Grand, splendidly attired in 'Regalia', as it was called. My Conductor told me the Noble Grand was not able to see me unless I particularly wished to see him; however, one of the supporters said he would prevail on him to see me. They accordingly drew aside the curtains which concealed him, when he appeared to be in a state of somnolency; and being asked should I like to have him waked, of course the simple candidate said 'Yes'. They aroused him, with which he appeared to be very indignant, but when told that a candidate stood before him for information he relaxed his anger, and addressing me said he would impart the secrets of Oddfellowship to me.

He [the Noble Grand] told me we admitted no one to become an Oddfellow under the age of 21, unless the son of a worthy brother; no bailiff or bailiff's follower, telling me to be cautious whom I introduced to become a member, and desired me to remove from my mind any impressions I might form from the evening's procedure, for in all ages past the best and wisest of men had been taken for Oddfellows. After admonishing me further he gave me the grip and password. There was a short lecture given me by the Grand Master, and the important ceremony was brought to a close.[29]

The reference to pantomime in Richardson's account (see *Panto and pants* below), need not be taken only as an insulting reference to children's entertainment. People flocked to pantomimes, which were not just performed at Christmas but right up until Easter Monday, to see examples of spectacle and tricks within a space seemingly outside conventional morality where 'performances seemed to represent a kind of emotional regeneration'. This was the period when the clown Joseph Grimaldi, 1779–1837, who was watched by thousands 'transformed pantomime into an entertainment at the cultural and financial heart of London theatrical life'.[30] Burn wrote of the blindfolded, 'poor affrighted novice, suspended, like Mahomet's coffin, mid-way between hope and fear' who was threatened with a sword, frightened by an image of a skeleton and surrounded by men in dresses which were 'in keeping with the rest of the mummery'. He dismissed the initiation as a 'harmless but nonsensical ordeal' and noted that 'we very properly discarded the mummery of the old school with its nonsensical forms and ceremonies'.[31] On the other hand he recognised that symbols were of importance across society. As Burn pointed out that a doctor's wig or silver-headed cane were 'emblems of deep learning and even supernatural power' while judges' wigs were 'of more importance than the ignorant or superficial have brains to comprehend'.[32] A similar point was made by historian Johan Huizinga who argued that the judge's wig 'is far more than a mere relic of antiquated professional dress. Functionally it has close connections with the dancing masks of savages. It transforms the wearer into another "being".'[33] The Oddfellows Ritual, which included the wearing of masks, was developed within and contributed to the living traditions of British society.

The account below, written in 1850s, describes initiation in more elevated terms than the above version which dates from 1832. The lack of any references to flannel drawers might reflect the enhanced sense of rectitude and care that the Society sought to promote:

> The candidate on being led into the lodge-room was carefully blinded, and after passing the Outside and Inside Guardians he felt a peculiar and mysterious awe steal over his senses, in consequence of the solemn and death-like silence that prevailed at the time. Anon, the perverted sense of hearing became fearfully awakened by the rattling of huge iron chains and the un-meaning sounds of men's voices. At this stage of the inauguration (that is provided he is not tossed and tumbled among the brushwood, or soused over the head in a large tub) the bandage is removed from his eyes and the first object that his visual organs discovered was the point of a naked sword close to the seat of his love. As soon as he could draw his attention from the worthy warden and his blade, ten to one but his eyes would rest upon a large transparency of the Old Mortality, whose ghastly grin would be sufficient to freeze the warm blood in his veins; while every part of the room was filled with symbols both of holy and profane things, the meaning of which few could explain ...[34]

Some of the elements of the Ritual were maintained. An elaborate account of initiation written in 1909 by an Oddfellow echoed these earlier accounts in it referred to how the initiation candidate 'found himself in utter darkness and surrounded by a solemn and deathlike silence. A sense of mysterious awe.'[35] By this time the ritual was seen as authentic compared to that of the Eisteddfod. A newspaper report 'from a Welsh correspondent' asked of the latter 'whether it is not time to bring to an end this silly parody of an Oddfellow's initiation'.[36]

Over the years many clearly felt a sense of foreboding when they joined as the account in the press in 1831 (see *Poking fun*) indicated. Bill Needham recalled his initiation in 1919 and subsequent initiations in Taddington, Derbyshire. There was a hot poker, rather than the painted poker mentioned in the account written 87 years earlier and a sense of nervousness that the men who had been initiated came to enjoy.

> If you were making new members, that was quite a performance. If somebody wished to become a member it was a – it put the breeze up me really, when I first come in 'cause with only being young. Of course after I'd been through the mill sort of thing I wasn't worried but anybody that were young they wondered what to expect! If there was a new member being made up one of the members would go outside with him, show him the procedure and show him how to get in. When they got him inside, we always used to have an open fire, some of the oldest members used to say 'Put the poker in the fire' and you used to wonder what the poker was going in the fire for. They put the poker in the fire and the chap that was behind the door, the Tyler, used to say 'Come on up to the fire', and he'd sort of put you to the fire and he'd draw this poker out of the fire and just put it across your bum, but not close to. It was supposed to be a sign of a brand and

that's what they used to be a bit scared of. And that is how you come to be a member. We had quite a lot of laughs about that. It was alright for us as knew, but it was them that didn't know, you see![37]

The use of fire may be an echo of an earlier initiation. The Patriotic Order of Oddfellows, from which the Oddfellows is said to have seceded, had five degrees: the Initiatory, the Covenant, the Royal Blue, Pink (or Merit) and Royal Arch of Titus (or Fidelity). The Initiatory degree involved the lodge room being in darkness except for a fire. Some loose rough planks made up a 'road'. The candidate, naked, blindfolded and tied with cords was prodded along the road, making three circuits of the lodge room. On the second circuit he was pushed off the road onto the 'rocks' (a pile of corks), on the third he was entangled in a 'forest' of brushwood and was then burned at a lit brazier before being drenched in the 'tempest' while the brethren shrieked and used metal sheets and a gong to make noises associated with a storm. While he was swearing his oath the props were removed and when the blindfold was removed he was faced with the members in masks, a real skull and cross bone and other emblems of mortality in the darkened room. He was threatened with death for 'trespassing', but was pardoned on the plea of his sponsor. He was then given a sermon on the skull and told to close his eyes while the death scene was removed, the masks removed and the lodge re-lit so that it 'resumed a placid appearance'. His nakedness was covered with a lambskin apron which symbolised the covering of lost innocence with aprons by Adam and Eve and the sacrifice of the Lamb of God (Jesus) to atone for the sins of humankind. He was told that his naked entry was symbolic of his birth and the two cords represented good and evil.

For many others the welcoming ceremony of initiation was a memorable occasion. Charles Willard was introduced to the Oddfellows at the age of six when he became a juvenile. Despite his familiarity with Ritual (his Juvenile Lodge, of which he was President, visited others to show how it was performed), and with the older members he still found joining the adults a little daunting. Writing in the 1970s he recalled:

> The night I was initiated into the Waterloo Lodge in 1930 is one I shall always remember. I approached the Lodge room with a load of butterflies in the pit of my stomach. As the Conductor spoke to the Guardian I very nearly gave it all up there and then, but some inner feeling urged me to go on with it and so we passed through the door. Anyone who remembers the Lodge Room at Queen's Road, [Beulah Lodge, Brighton] will know that the Officers were raised on a dais, with a square table four feet high in front of them. This has the knack of making the person standing in front of them feel very small, so one senses that you are really standing in the presence of the Gods.[38]

Charles Willard was not daunted because within two months he was a Supporter and by 1936 he was Noble Grand. Tom Nicholson was initiated aged 16 in 1935 in Preston and although his father was an Oddfellow they did not speak about initiation before the event.

> My father took me and I was interviewed by several men asking me different questions and then I was led into the Lodge Room … You were asked questions and if you gave a suitable answer you were allowed in. The questions were all related to loving God and the Queen, loving your fellow men, friendship, love and truth … I felt scared. I didn't know anything about it. I was led into the room, interviewed by these men and then taken into the Lodge Room as a suitable candidate.

In 1941, aged 16, Tony Crouch walked with his father to the Oddfellows Hall. His father went

LEFT

An early nineteenth-century Oddfellows mug. The three faces on the shield represent the masks used during initiations. Members could fill their homes with reminders of their membership.

The All-Seeing Eye gazes from a member's teacup and saucer: a reminder, perhaps, of the importance attached to sobriety during the transacting of Oddfellow business. One nineteenth-century Oddfellow handbook explained that the Eye symbolised charity, but it could be seen as representative of other ideas. Victorian men, who had few opportunities for display through their everyday clothing, might have been pleased to demonstrate their affiliation, to have imposed their Order, through decorated domestic items.
BY COURTESY OF THE LIBRARY AND MUSEUM OF FREEMASONRY

into the lodge room and Tony waited outside. Like Tom's father Tony's father had not told his son about the initiation. Tony admitted that he was a 'bit concerned a bit worried, didn't know what was going to happen to you'. He described the occasion:

> You had a man who came out who was what they call a Conductor. He instructed you on what to do. In this particular lodge, he knocked on the door and the Guardian opened the little slide to give the password. You went in and you paraded round in front of the Vice Grand. His name was Ted Day and the sash or the collar that the Vice Grand wore was pink with a blue edging and he had, his face was flushed, his face matched the collar and I can always remember that [laughter] it suited him. He was the Vice Chairman at the time. He said a little piece and he had two Supporters and then you moved to the Lecture Master who was Sid Lang. He did this lecture and I thought 'God, that's wonderful.' This man is not looking at any book, he did it all off pat. When I was Lecture Master I could never do that, I could remember bits of it but not all of it. He really was impressive when he delivered the lecture. He was very, very good ... '*Worthy and respected friend you have entered the society which is of far more importance than you may at first imagine it to be. It is based upon the great principles of philanthropy and self dependence, it admits nothing contrary to the allegiance we owe to the sovereign of the realm to ourselves and those dependent on us*' and that's as far as I will go. From him you go to the Noble Grand

and he does your initiation and shows you what to do. After you received a talking to from the Noble Grand, the Conductor has to demonstrate how you could get out of the lodge and how you could get into the lodge and so he gave a sign to the Noble Grand and turned round to the Vice Grand and gave the same sign there and then walked to the door and the Guardian opened the door and out he went. Then the Guardian, the Conductor came back, he knocked on the door twice and then the Guardian took his password and in he came, waited for the door to close and in the centre of the room he said 'Most Noble Grand' turned round and said 'Worthy Vice Grand' then he came back to us who were standing still in front of the Noble Grand and then we all had to go out and do exactly the same thing and come back in again in the same way and then we could take our seats and we were members. Our seats were just round the edge of the room. Everybody sat all round on the edge of the room, you weren't in like a cinema or anything like that with rows of seats.

Jeff Bartlett joined during the Second World War and mentioned his concerns:

When I went to be initiated it frightened me to death. There were all these old men, no young people there at all. Old men sat round tables with the Ritual books. The books contain the opening and closing of the lodge and al the things appertaining to that and the initiation ceremony … To a young person of 16 it was a bit frightening. I couldn't understand half the words. The age of the people who were doing it, to me they were all about eighty.

Betty Mostyn joined in 1946. She admitted to her fears, 'I was terrified. It took me years to relax.' She then described her memories of initiation:

The lodge had decided to go mixed [that is to admit women] and I joined the same night as the lodge secretary's daughter. It was a big room. There was a big leather chair on a plinth, on a box. Eventually I learnt after many, many months that was the Noble Grand's chair. The lodge was set out. You walked round the lodge and were initiated. There was Ritual. You don't take it in at all the first few times you see it done. Everybody used a book. You repeated what you were told to repeat. You were charged to keep the secrets of the society, to show you were going to be loyal and that sort of thing. I was shaking with not knowing what was happening. You didn't tell what went on in the lodge. I was a very nervous teenager. The gentlemen wore dark suits, collarettes and aprons and some of them had cuffs. Their aprons denoted whichever particular chair they were in.

Betty also found trips to other lodges nerve-wracking, 'I went to visit another lodge and they terrified me as well because their members could do it without the books. That was something that I knew I would never be able to do.' Brenda Francis was familiar with uniforms both because her father was a military tailor and because she sold school uniforms in her shop.

Furthermore, she had been told about some aspects of the initiation. She recalled that she both 'petrified' and in awe at her initiation:

> Sash, apron, collarettes … I thought it was very impressive. All different colours for different positions. I got to wear most of them as I got more involved. I thought it was great. They had the collar like a V shaped scarf with the insignia of your position on one side. If you were extra special on the other side as well and what I used to think of as a little satchel round their waist and cufflets. Big cuffs on their arms. Some of them had medals hanging on them as well if they had a high position.

These accounts reflect Oddfellowship's debt to mummery. Mummers' plays were folk performances which took place in the street or sometimes door-to-door or in pubs from the mid-eighteenth century. These non-professional peripatetic dramas were often built around seasonal visiting customs. They almost always involved a fight between a hero and a villain in which one is killed. Sometimes the vanquished was named for a national hero and the victor was a foreigner. The symbolic identity of the person slain or wounded was secondary to the need to supply someone on whom the comic Doctor could practise his miraculous cure of resurrection. He did this after much boasting of his abilities and his experience of travel. Sometimes the fighting and the treatment were repeated several times. It was usual for the play to end with singing and a collection of money from the audience.[39] Important Oddfellows' motifs, the interest in cures rather than combat, in Oddfellowship being a leaving of the old life and the start of a better one, of welcoming travellers and of raising money are contained in these popular dramas. An account of initiation, published in the *Oddfellows' Magazine* in 1832 foregrounded the link:

> Amid the mummery of that initiation there were gems of philanthropy and kind expressions towards our fellow-man interspersed, independent of the motto of the fraternity that Truth ought therefore to reign on the lips, Love in the affections, and Friendship in the heart of every Oddfellow.

In 1909 an account of the Ritual referred to 'gaudy tinsel and gilded trappings' and to how 'the dresses of the officers were in keeping with this mummery'.[40] The phrases echoed that of Burn who referred to 'gaudy trappings and idle formality' and also to 'useless toys', 'idle trappings', 'idle flummery and useless trappings' and the 'mania for regalia and other toys'.[41] Burn went on: 'The lectures or degrees were a crude digest of biblical cant and bombast. These were amended at the Kendal AMC in 1835. [However,] the degrees are still larded with much puritanical phraseology and superfluous nonsense.'[42] The concern to dismiss rituals and regalia perhaps indicates the powerful hold that they had over many members.

Many will not have realised that in their initiation they were re-enacting and re-interpreting very old ideas. The performance was for members, who took on roles perhaps more elevated than in their everyday lives. The ceremony may have inverted the social order in that the initiate, even if of high standing in the wider community, was in the lodge at the lowest level. The ceremony enabled the mundane to be transformed through the repetition of actions and the recitation of a script. This stylised performance reinforced the values of Oddfellowship and set members apart from others. While in the past initiation provided members with a variety of heightened emotions including fear ('the point of a naked sword close to the seat of his love') humiliation (if they got a soaking) and relief (at the conclusion), it continued to have the power to affect people.

Ann Harris was initiated in 1953, at the age of 16:

> I was petrified. Well I was going into strange surroundings I had only seen it from the kitchen before. I was going in and I was going to be the only one led round by two Conductors, which I had always seen my Dad and Fred Markham do but they couldn't do it because it was a ladies lodge.

In the same year Jean Facer found that

> It was quite a daunting experience walking into a room of fifty people to go through an initiation ceremony because Stan [her fiancé] wouldn't tell me anything. He just said 'You will have to do a couple of signs, and that is all. I thought 'Well, that's not too bad,' but it was a bit more than that. You have to say some words. The initiation ceremony is a little bit secretive. You are taken into a room where there are officers dotted about in regalia, you are asked to say certain words and make a certain promise and make a certain sign. Afterwards that's how you recognise other members of the Oddfellows who are outside, apart from the three links recognition badge that you are given.

Dulcie Pauley explained:

> We do have a little emblem that we should always wear is of the three links, little badge. It stands for Friendship, Love and Truth and it is three links joined together, the middle

From the 1890s women were permitted to join the Society in their own right. This image of Winifred Baulk, a Provincial Grand Master in Hertfordshire in the 1950s, might have been composed in order to indicate, through her conformity to the conventional dress codes of the Order, that women were not a threat to previously male-dominated lodges. However, the rise of women within the Order throws into relief some of the images on the apron that she is wearing.

BY COURTESY OF ANDY DURR

Noticeboards could serve as valuable reminders of the longevity of the lodge and the importance of recognising the service of office-holders. The noticeboard above is from Brighton and lists the Past Worthy Masters from 1874 until 1961. The Past Grands of the Blisworth Lodge are acknowledged on the noticeboard shown below, left. Several names occur more than once (e.g. Ayres, Goodridge, Holland, Leach) and the Whitlock and the Goode families were related by marriage.

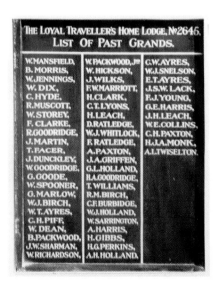

RIGHT

This picture of the gavel and the collar worn by a lodge chair (NG stands for Noble Grand) alongside the darts and teacup was created by Christine Payne in 2000. She explained that it represented the financial and social aspects of the Society: 'After the business – the friendship. Where we met there was always a cup of tea and a chat.'

one is Love which is uppermost and that one is slightly higher on the bar than the other two.

Frances Wilkinson, despite having been a junior, still found that initiation had some novel elements:

> There were things that happened that I hadn't expected. I was a bit in awe really I think. When you go into a strange place and everybody knows what they are doing and it's very formal, it was a bit awe inspiring. I think it helped when I taught my friend into joining as well and she came into it and went round the chairs after me.

After recalling his own initiation Tony Crouch explained how he had maintained the traditions of secrecy and dignity and how, through being given a relatively minor role, he was integrated into the life of the lodge.

> I became Conductor about twelve or eighteen months after I joined. They thought, 'Well, here's a youngster who is interested, let's give him something to do.' When I had candidates outside and I was Conductor, I didn't tell them what was going on but I told them they were going to be talked to by various people and I would have them in a particular order because you introduced them by name to the various people you took them round to and if I had them in order, then they knew who each candidate was, whereas if you just jumbled them up no one knew who was who and so I used to say to them, 'now when you come I want you to follow me and when I turn left I want you to turn left behind me, not alongside me but to come behind me like in a snake. When I stop I want you to left turn and you will be in one line.' You tried to get them central to whoever was going to talk to them and then when they'd finished I used to just touch the first one and they all right turned and followed me round to the next person who was going to say something to them. I think people appreciated it because I was Conductor for some time. They used to get me elected and re-elected.

Brian Merrell who was initiated aged 16 also recalled the role of the Conductor:

> Oddfellows was basically a secret society and you were only really told what to expect when you were standing outside the door ready to go in. You had the four officers of the lodge at the four points of the compass. The lodge Grand Master at one end and the Vice Grand or the Deputy at the other end. The Secretary and the Treasurer were at the other ones. You were sort of marched in with the person outside and he had to say a password to get in through the door.

If one of the reasons for the initiation to be secret and unusual was to make it memorable then in instances recalled by all these members it was a success.

Sometimes attempts to remain secret were foiled. One member recalled her childhood trips to the lodge with her father.

You're not allowed in until you are 16 but I used to peep through the keyhole [of the Oddfellows Hall] when I was allowed to go and sit in the kitchen to see my Dad doing his bit and all the regalia. We used to take the key out very quietly and our respective Dads, both tall, were always given the Conductors job because they looked very efficient and very regal with full regalia and the wands, which is a thing that you carry in one hand, it's got an open hand in it with a red heart in the middle.

The Ritual had served one of its purposes because, although the secret might have been revealed to the children, they remained in awe of the ceremonies and fearful of the consequences of revealing that which they had witnessed. Tony Crouch, a member in another lodge, knew the practical solution to the problem of prying eyes.

I did six or twelve months as Guardian. He stops people coming through the door if they didn't give the password. If you got there before the meeting started you just went into the lodge room and sat down. Once the lodge had been called to order then the door locked, the Guardian made sure it was closed. You had big heavy curtains across the door inside so that anybody outside, even if they put their ear to the door, couldn't hear what was going on.

Tony was doing the duty of a Guardian as described in the Universal Ritual Opening Ceremony, issued in 1935. The Noble Grand asks 'Guardian (*Guardian rises*), what is your duty?' The Guardian replies:

To receive the password or permission of the Noble Grand, previous to admitting members or visitors and guard the Lodge against intrusion; to refuse admission of anyone during initiation or ballot; to prevent any person other than a member listening to acquiring a knowledge of what is going on in the Lodge and to act in conjunction with the Officers of the Lodge in the execution of your commands.

Despite the use of the word universal there has clearly been some flexibility and variation on central themes. By the twenty-first century members no longer had to maintain the living traditions which have connected members of the Oddfellows for at least 200 years. However, many chose to help ensure the survival of these ceremonies and customs.

Ornate furnishings have long been a feature of lodges as has specific configurations of the furniture. The Lodge is traditionally set out in the way described by Bill Needham with officers at four corners of a diamond or square formation so that a person entering the lodge sees the Noble Grand at the far end of the room with supporters on each side. Part of the initiation ceremony can involve the candidate linking little fingers with officers and the singing of an Ode which starts with the lines 'Enter boldly, do not fear. None but brothers true are here.' Even if fear is not induced in the candidate, awe might be. When some members gave accounts of their initiation they framed it in terms of the material culture. Edward Schofield, the grandson of a Past Provincial Grand Master of the lodge and the son of a lodge member, joined in 1964, aged 16, did not indicate that he was frightened. However, the material culture did impress him: 'the lodge chairs with the symbols and with writing on the back, *Love, Friendship and Truth*, and long tables'. Karen Stuart did not know what to expect when she was initiated on Hallowe'en, 31 October 1995. She was not frightened and, like Edward, found the items on display of interest. I don't think I knew what I was walking into. Although I'd got some friends there who were keen, 'Oh, yes, you'll enjoy this.' I walked into a room with a lot of very elderly people and at the time, I would have been in my late twenties. I've always been used to being around older people so their age was not intimidating. It wasn't set up as a formal lodge in any way. You'd got a top table with the officers but then everybody else was just sat around almost in the form of a lecture, allegedly paying attention to the business of the meeting. The Provincial Grand Master was wearing his collar as were the Corresponding Secretary and the Deputy Provincial Grand Master, other members no. The Provincial Grand Master's collar is silver and it was, the night I had gone, it was a bright night and that was catching the light. I can remember feeling that it looked quite impressive.

Many of those who did not present their experience of Ritual as awe-inspiring focused on how it helped them to make friends. Daphne Harmer was relatively unworried when she was initiated in 1953. 'I didn't find it too bad because I knew a lot of people at the meeting that I had met before and I didn't find it very daunting at all.' Mary Wheeler was impressed by her initiation. It was in 1967 and it was not the furniture or the possibility of being blindfolded which awed her, but the warmth of the greeting:

> At the initiation I had no idea what to expect. They didn't tell me beforehand. It was lovely. They were extremely friendly. I was welcomed with open arms being the youngest in the lodge. The lady who ran the lodge was Alice Schofield who was the wife of Walter Schofield who was Grand Master later on. It was a very, very dingy little room. Two rooms. The front room was on the side of the road and very small little office type room and the backroom had a fireplace in and he used to put the kettle on and make us a cup of tea. Walter used to be there in the backroom while we had our meeting. It was the Oddfellows' office. What it lacked in décor it made up for in atmosphere. They were a lovely bunch.

Sue Doulton Smith was initiated in 1969 and she recalled friendship, not fear:

> All I can remember from the actual initiation was the heat from the room and the fact that they gave you a rule book when you were initiated. I don't remember being worried about it. They were all very friendly in our lodge and all very encouraging and pleased when there were young people going in.

For two hundred years initiates have had to be able to master their fears, follow directions and remain loyal to the society. Although in the twenty-first century there was no rattling of ghostly chains to bring to mind the punishments that might be carried out if the member behaved in anything except a fraternal fashion, the Ritual remained powerful. Here is Pauline Pettigrew describing both the fear and the friendliness:

> In January 2003 I was initiated. I sat downstairs trembling to death. It was a nerve racking experience because nobody told you what to expect. Brother Roy Bass came downstairs, sat with me and he said 'Right this is what is going to happen, you don't need to worry about it. I will hold you hand every step of the way through it.' He was absolutely fantastic.

Pauline's memories, like those of Bill Needham earlier, suggest that the common experience of initiation aided bonding between Oddfellows:

> Members sit down and afterwards they talk about when they did their experience and tell the newly initiated person or the next person who has done a Degree their experiences of it. It welcomes you to step into the family fold.

While a number of accounts of initiation evoked memories of trepidation, these were often overlaid with evaluations which reflected that which others felt at the time, pleasure and a sense that Oddfellowship had a meaning beyond insurance. It is because the Ritual evoked such strong emotions that it was successful in aiding fellowship.

IV   Debates about ceremony

For much of the nineteenth century there was an association between spectacle, prudent finances and sound governance. Martin Daunton argued that in 'the hands of Gladstone the annual budget became a matter of high theatricality, or perhaps more accurately of religious ceremony'.[43] The Oddfellows had at that time sought to promote trust in its finances and fiscal probity through performance, and may have drawn on the drama they witnessed. Booth concluded that 'melodrama and pantomime at Christmas was the Victorian working-class theatre'.[44] Ritual looked to the deceits, escape from daily routine and legends of these popular dramatic forms. In pantomime ritual social hierarchies could be disrupted. Similarly, an Oddfellows initiate could be of high rank outside the lodge, but low within it. He was reborn and could develop new relationships not based on hierarchical precedence. This inversion of values could be reinforced by the uses of masks. Bakhtin, writing about the topsy-turvy world of carnivals, described the mask as 'related to transition, metamorphosis, the violation of natural boundaries'.[45] Ritual, like pantomime, created a world of fantasy and engagement. Just as those on the stage could express their awareness of the audience's presence, could break the 'fourth wall' and make the audience take part in the action, so members engaged in the Ritual together. At the same time the late nineteenth century was a period of 'unprecedented honorific inventiveness … with costume, ceremony, heraldry, religion'. The British saw themselves as 'belonging to an unequal society characterised by a seamless web of layered gradations, which were hallowed by time and precedent, which were sanctioned by tradition and religion.'[46]

However, these ties began to loosen. When he opened the Oddfellows' Hall in Melbourne Australia in 1863 the Governor of the Colony, His Excellency Sir Henry Barkly, noted that 'many considered the walking in procession in a gay costume headed by painted banners was the only result obtained by the association', and felt the need to stress that he was 'convinced that the Order had a deeper significance'.[47] Perhaps there was a sense of embarrassment. Spry suggested that the abandonment of the oath was for both political reasons and because it was 'considered derogatory to the growing intelligence of the times and the increasing respectability of the Members'. He also argued, of members of a breakaway, that 'splendid banners and decorations cast a glare over their eyes'.[48] Moffrey was at pains to point out that it was only in 1888 that the Grand Master was provided with a distinctive badge.[49] An influential study argued that within oral cultures (and many working men in Manchester in the early nineteenth century would have had little formal education), learning was often dominated:

> by listening, by repeating what they hear, by mastering proverbs and ways of combining and recombining them by assimilating other formulatory material, by participation in a kind of corporate retrospection.[50]

By the late nineteenth century, after the time when children's schooling had been made compulsory, possibly Oddfellows did not wish to be associated with what may have been deemed as primitive pedagogic techniques.

In the twentieth century there were further challenges and amendments to Ritual. The National Health Insurance legislation of 1911 led the Secretary of the Charity Organisation Society, Charles Loch, to claim in 1913:

> The old and familiar usages of initiation into Forestry or Oddfellowship can hardly survive in their reality. With the old responsibility must disappear the old interests and the old customs. A sense of responsibility created them – and with the loss of it they must pass away.[51]

Within the Unity there was concern about the role of Ritual. In 1913, initiation, it was argued in the *Magazine*, had the effect of 'creating a feeling of nervousness'. In the same year the Grand Master told the AMC that in some lodges 'Ritual has fallen into utter disuse'.[52] There was a renewed interest with the reintroduction of older ceremonies in 1919 after the transformative First World War. A new manual of instruction for minor degrees was issued in 1922 in order 'to standardise the conferring of various degrees … add dignity to the ceremonial and increase enthusiasm amongst its adherents.' There was also an appeal to members to promote uniformity in the matter of grips and signs 'and so preserve the integral forms which embody

In 1939 members of the Pride of Clapham Lodge lined up behind Brother H Clare in their regalia and with a variety of symbolic items. Following the war there was a dramatic fall in membership and an interest in the revival of ritual.
GETTY IMAGES

the principles of Oddfellowship and sustain its constitution'.[53] Universal Ritual was introduced in 1935. In 1939 the AMC discussed Ritual once more. One Trustee pointed out that while National Health members could choose whether to be initiated, others had no choice and that 'it is against the principles of freedom of Odd Fellowship to enforce Ritual'.[54]

By the mid-twentieth century the lack of interest in spectacle was noted by playwrights. Although neither an Oddfellow nor writing exclusively about performance in the UK, the vision of French playwright Antonin Artaud (1896–1948) indicated the gap which had arisen. In 1938 he called for a rejuvenation of the theatre with a much greater emphasis on spectacle and action rather than text and a coherent plot. He focused on elements which would have been familiar to those who had practised Oddfellow Ritual:

> every show will contain physical, objective elements perceptible to all. Shouts, groans, apparitions, surprise, dramatic moments of all kinds, the magic beauty of all costumes modelled on certain ritualistic patterns.[55]

That the promoters of the theatre of the absurd sought to restore the importance of myth and ritual to remind people of the ultimate realities and to instill a sense of cosmic wonder and primeval anguish indicates the distance from the mystical Artaud and others felt that theatre had come. They wanted to draw on the traditions of dream and nightmare literature which goes back to Greek and Roman times, the allegorical and symbolic drama of the medieval guilds' morality plays, the rituals where religion and drama were one. Writing in the 1950s Jean Genet regarded his plays as attempts to recapture the ritual elements of the Mass, that is an archetypal event brought to life through a series of symbolic actions. As with ancient Greek theatre or the Mass, the audience is offered the possibility of transformation as a result of participation in a sacred drama. Oddfellows' Ritual was not part of the Theatre of the Absurd. What they shared was an approach to drama which was at odds with the realistic conventions of much of the theatre, and cinema, around them by the mid-twentieth century. *The Cambridge illustrated history of British theatre* refers to the mainstream 'class-ridden contemporary British drama' of the inter-war years, which it contrasts to the chanting, the tableaux and pageantry of the Workers' Theatre Movement.[56] Whereas in the nineteenth century many aspects of Ritual would have been familiar to members of the Oddfellows from popular performances, and there was an association between fiscal rectitude and drama, by the mid-twentieth century there was a considerable distance between Ritual and much conventional theatre. The unfamiliarity of Ritual, and perhaps its association with the vulgarity of music hall, may have accounted for its unpopularity.

Renewed interest after the Second World War led to demonstrations of Ritual being given in the latter part of 1945. *The Odd Fellow* reported: 'to stimulate interest in Ritual the Central Group (Propaganda) Committee of the South London District arranged a demonstration of Ordinary Lodge, Initiation and Installation of Lodge Officers'. The event provided an opportunity 'of seeing the beautiful Ritual of the Order rendered with becoming dignity'.[57] There were other ideas about the future of Ritual when, because the 'approved' work of the Oddfellows was about to be 'torn away' there was a concern that this might lead to the 'ultimate extinction of friendly societies'. One proposal was for 'the reorganisation of the fellowship side of the Society' with more frequent meetings at which Ritual was carried out in a

> dignified and proper way and where thereafter the Social atmosphere could be encouraged by the provision of meals and/or entertainment. This to some extent follows the idea of Masonry, where the Ritual and Social side takes precedence over the charitable or Insurance side. Instead of the entertainment as above, perhaps the Society might consider the desirability of having a Speaker at each Lodge meeting as is customary in Rotary.[58]

It appears that Ritual's ability to provide support during periods of change and uncertainty was retained. It was also the case that concern about secrecy within the Oddfellows has continued. In 1947 a survey of friendly societies concluded

> that the 'secret society' atmosphere which still characterizes the activities of some friendly

societies may be less acceptable to younger people nowadays and may in some degree be militating against the need for increased publicity.[59]

Arthur Jackson recalled opposition to Ritual after the war. His lodge met at *The Swan*, Kettleshulme until 1948 when 'the landlord decided he didn't want us any more, all the regalia'.

John Winkley joined in 1938 but was only became actively engaged after the war. By then some aspects of Ritual had died out in his lodge:

> We didn't have an initiation, it was a rather liberal lot and they didn't stand on the Ritual a lot. The Ritual was always held as being something apart and really when you came to understand it, it was only for the order of the meetings so that all things were done in a proper manner and people knew really what they were doing but for quite a long while I didn't enter into any of the Ritual at all, nor did the lodge. The Degrees were not practised. I know in my father's time they were because they did them religiously, I think from what he said, 'You know, if you come you will have to take degrees,' and he never really explained what a degree was. The regalia was in a big box but it never came out … when we went to district meeting there was an opening ode and closing ode to a popular hymn tune.

However, he did recall using regalia to attract interest in the Society:

Initially aprons were home-made and hand-painted. By the early nineteenth century, however, ready-printed and relatively inexpensive regalia began to be available. Some lodges required brethren to attend funerals not only wearing black armbands and hatbands but also additional regalia such as this mourning apron of white silk trimmed with black. Eighteenth-century workmen's aprons were fastened around the waist and tied in front. They had a bib attached to a waistcoat button. The bib, once unfastened, would flap downwards. This apron follows that tradition. However, the flap has been stylised into a decorative feature with two faces and a skull representing aspects of the initiation ritual. The three figures represent Faith (with a Cross) Charity (with the horn of plenty, cornucopia, representing abundance and Hope (with an anchor). Below them are the ten commandments (symbol of moral laws) and a coffin (a reminder of why many people joined the Society). Above are stars representing the Pleiades or the seven Liberal Arts.

BY COURTESY OF THE LIBRARY AND MUSEUM OF FREEMASONRY

My wife then didn't come up to meetings but she came up with an idea. 'You have got a hall up here and it does look pretty dingy. Let's brighten it up.' So we repainted the whole inside and at Christmas time we decorated it and then came out the old regalia and hung those round the walls and it looked quite nice with fairy lights and we had refreshments and things and started up a Christmas Party. When other members who didn't normally attend we got quite a few people to come and so we had quite a nice evening.

A report in *The Times* noted that by 1954 one in 11 of the UK population were members of friendly societies, a loss of a third since 1938 and most of those since 1947. In 1954 alone the Oddfellows lost 23,700 members and only gained 3,600. Similar losses occurred within the other main friendly societies. Between 1938 and 1954 wages rose by 190 per cent while the friendly society funds rose by 42 per cent. It concluded that 'fewer men now value fellowship in the particular forms they seek to perpetuate'.[60] Concerns about the decrease in membership framed the continuing debate about Ritual. It was argued that the Buffaloes and Freemasons were not losing members because of Ritual, that when approved the Society's focus had shifted to quantity not quality which had led to a reduction of interest in Ritual and that there was a 'current "couldn't care less" attitude'.[61] The Secretary of the Order suggested that the falling membership could be combated by personal contacts and the Grand Master stressed the necessity of Ritual, 'especially if the members translate its tenets into their everyday lives'.[62] Others invested Ritual artifacts with even more cultural weight by association with particular individuals. At the dedication of the new regalia in Cardiff in 1956 the Noble Grand's new chain was a memorial to a late brother and inscribed with his name. He had been a Treasurer for fifty years and never missed a lodge night throughout the war. As the item was placed on the shoulders of the Noble Grand there was a two minute silence in tribute.[63] In 1963 a PPGM argued that 'the spirit of benevolence seems to have gone out of our dealings because we are not practising the Ritual.'[64]

The Deputy Grand Master suggested that without Ritual 'with its Christian ethics' the Society would be 'become a collecting society', while H. F. Watson described Oddfellowship as 'a two-legged animal – one leg was the practical help they gave by the benefits of the Order and the second was the Ritual of the Order. The Ritual was the motive for the practical.'[65] In 1964 the Grand Master J. A. McBryde emphasised that the benevolent work of the Order was a practical expression of the Ritual. He mentioned the relief provided to victims of a recent hurricane and the Orphan Gift Fund and concluded: 'these benevolences are inspired and encouraged and practised through the Ritual which we practise and whilst we remain constituted as we are today and have been for many years, the future of the Order is secure.'[66] In the summer of 1966 Len Mostyn, at that time the Provincial Grand Master of the Mersey District, said while he personally 'questioned the Ritual in its broader aspects and its place and impact in the contemporary world, within his district it was 'an integral and essential part of the Order's activities'. He added that almost all the lodges in his district performed the ceremonies and that there was a demonstration team.

There was further debate in the 1980s when there were changes to both the status of Ritual and what it entailed. In 1983, when there were over 200,000 Oddfellows, it was still the case that to be a member 'he or she has to be initiated in accordance with the relative ceremony'.[67] In 1985 the Minor Degrees Ritual was revised and a new Ritual Book was produced in 1986. There was also a review and modernisation of the Biblical references in the Purple Degree.[68] Eric Ogden was a student at the St Cuthbert's Church Sunday School, Southport where he later taught. He recalled: 'I once saw a Ritual book where somebody had very carefully in pencil, annotated all the paragraphs and their origin from the Bible.' Grand Master Christine Feek mentioned that 'growing interest is apparent in the performance of our Ritual … This adds to the evening and helps to ensure that the historical heart and principles of Odd Fellowship continue.'[69] The changes to the Ritual were sometimes difficult. Roy Morris recalled that on one occasion he started a ceremony and found that when he paused nobody spoke:

> I investigated and found that I was reading from an older book than everybody else's. They gave me another book and I started again and the same thing happened again! I am very careful now because it's easy to make a mistake. If people don't know what's happening it can make a ceremonial activity turn into a shambles.

By the 1990s Derek Winbush reconciled the requirement that on the one hand on Lodge night lodges were required to be opened and closed and conducted throughout with Ritual, with, on the other hand, the need not to alienate new members:

> The word 'Ritual' frightens some people to death. A welcoming is a very much more pleasant sort of association with the Society so you will hear us talk … these days about a welcoming ceremony – just the same, not a scrap of difference … if we don't retain the ceremonial part of the society then realistically we could be anything. We could be a fishing club.
>
> [At the Heart of England we started an Afternoon Lodge] We decided that we'd start the Lodge off a little bit differently, a bit low key, collars only. No aprons at all at that Lodge. It might have been a bit off-putting to some people. We explained that there were aprons and showed then what one was. But we said 'Just try it. Let's see how we go.' It was fairly informal but they all said at the end of it how much they'd enjoyed it … Somebody said 'Can we sing one of these [Odes]?' and we sang the last one, the last ode and somebody said, 'I'm going to make sure that I come to another lodge when they do all of it.'[70]

Dorothy Deacon also suggested that 'the word ritual ought to be changed to ceremony'. Keith Adamson described the flexibility that had been introduced in his District:

> The society has taken a step towards compartmentalising the Ritual of the society. If members don't want to take part in the Ritual then they don't have to. They can still come to the meetings, they can still discuss the business of the society. If we want somebody

to go through the chairs or we want degrees doing then they are done at a different time, so that those people that want to do it can come along at that time as opposed to within the branch business meeting. There are some branches that still open their lodges with the ceremony of the society and there are others that don't.

Other members have said that people are now permitted to engage in social activities without reference to the Ritual because, as one put it, 'we don't want to scare them off with Ritual'. Once they indicate their interest in learning more they are given further information.

In 2000 there was an attempt to drop the need to have a Purple Degree in order to attend the AMC or be a Director. This issue had also been considered in 1858 when there was an attempt to change the name of the Society and many of the titles of officers.[71] In 2001 Peter Needham, a former Grand Master, spoke of the importance of the degrees and the need not to 'devalue our Rituals'. Dorothy Deacon stressed the need not to 'dilute the quality of the Ritual' but to open up the Oddfellows by allowing more members to take the Purple Degree and thus speed their route to higher posts. The concerns about ritual echoed the debate of 1858 on which Spry commented:

Destroy the distinctive character – reduce it to the level of an ordinary well-constituted provident institution and the charm is at once destroyed: and those incentives that have obtained so much free labour from the Members to build it up being once removed, in their place will spring up mercenary motives that must be paid to do the drudgery that is required to carry on the duties of the club … What the ribbon is to the peer, what titles are to the clergy and members of the bar what the sash and meal is to the military and naval professions, so is the emblematical sash and title of PG or PProvGM to the hard-working Oddfellow.[72]

In 2000 one Deputy pointed out that a person who joined aged 65 and wished to be further involved would be told 'Great, lad, you can do it when you are 72'. The reforms were rejected on that occasion but in 2008 it was decided that a person could attend the AMC without a Purple Degree as long as they had been a member for five years and served three years on a Committee of Management. Douglas Potter ruminated on some of the recent changes to Ritual:

The Ritual has been changed and rewritten and unfortunately it doesn't have the impact upon members that it did. We've got to the situation now whereby if a member is worried about their initiation and they don't want to go through with a lot of strangers, they have what is classified as a 'Welcoming Ceremony', which is almost, 'We are pleased to see you come in thank you very much and we hope you enjoy your stay with us.' Whereas the previous one, when you heard it, it meant something. The wording was very good and although it was 'oldie worldie' English that made it the interesting part … it was very sternly given and it meant something.

Despite the changes Roger Burley suggested that for those who joined without prior knowledge of Oddfellowship the initiation could be alienating.

> I can understand that if it's somebody comes in from the cold and it's a lodge that is very, very strict, 'You couldn't do this and you couldn't do that', it would be very frightening. If they'd got the ceremony you've got to do everything exactly according to the book, so, for instance, if you turned left instead of turning right there would be a load of mumbling. You felt a bit of a fool if you did something wrong … I mean I didn't experience too much of this in my lodge but I do know people that experienced it, when they came in their lodges and it drove a lot of people away. The juvenile lodge had a sort of simple ceremony so you knew what to expect.

Ritual required, he went on, periodic review and amendment.

> Every time that is changed there is always a hue and a cry. The original reason that the American Oddfellows split with us was over arguments over the ceremony and the Ritual. What we've got to do is that you keep enough of it, like the Trooping the Colour. You keep the traditional side alive but you send your soldiers into battle with the most modern machine guns. They only wear the bearskin hats and carry the swords on certain occasions.

Some Oddfellows have pointed to lack of interest in Ritual among those around them. It has ceased to be, in Joan Henry words, 'a cornerstone'. Brenda Francis enrolled all her children, grandchildren and great grandchildren in the Society but only Lesley Bull, her daughter, was active. She quoted another one of her offspring as saying. 'What do you want to dress up like that for?'

Elsewhere, too, interest in Ritual was fading. Syd Bolton remembered how in Cheadle there was some informality.

> Some of these lodges in those days weren't that formal. They didn't work to the book exactly, they worked to suit themselves … At the top end the Board of Directors practice the Ritual each year in the Grand Lodge which is held at the AMC. Down at the bottom end the Ritual is practised when it suits them.

Mike Trenchard said that while Ritual was important until the late 1990s, 'these days people think that Ritual is a bit quaint … an anachronism, out of its time'. Daphne Harmer pointed out that some lodges had insufficient people to do the Ritual properly and Jean Facer thought it was only 'a core of membership that sticks to the old-time Rituals'.

The Oddfellows had plenty of reasons and models which justified maintaining its fraternal secrets. Its interest in maintaining some privacy has continued, as Joan Henry recalled:

The Oddfellow were very secretive in those days. I wasn't too frightened but the Ritual
was a bit daunting at the beginning. In those days was taken a little bit more seriously.
Now it's not such a cornerstone of the Oddfellows. You could not be a member unless
you subscribed to the Rituals. At every lodge meeting there was a certain amount of
Ritual. I don't think I would want to describe it because it's still really for Oddfellows,
not for all and sundry. To a certain extent the Oddfellows is a secret society.

Syd Bolton enjoyed the sense of tradition when he performed Ritual, Brenda Francis entered
competitions for the best Ritual and Mike Trenchard felt that it 'gives you a standing in life,
a way to conduct yourself and behave yourself'. Lesley Bull, remembered growing up in a
household where Ritual was taken seriously in the 1960s:

My parents took part in the Ritual competition. It was nerve-wracking for them. My
mum would play the piano. It would be the initiation ceremony done to perfection run
by the District. My parents would be in the lodge team most years.

Andrew Porter recalled helping to organise a 'Ritual rally' for younger Oddfellows in
Yorkshire subsidised by the Head Office. In the morning the teams would practise, and in the
afternoon there was a competition: 'invariably Hull won it because they'd got a very strong
juvenile lodge'.

This was part of a longer tradition of such demonstrations.[73] Daphne Harmer mentioned
how, in 2008, in the Reading district 'we now belong to runs a Ritual team which enters a
team in the southern group area, a Ritual competition'. Speaking in 2008, Pauline Pettigrove
mentioned the continuing appeal of Ritual, especially to those who were formerly in the
Armed Forces.

We have become more Ritual-based or ceremonial-based because members have requested
it. We have bowed to pressure from the new members who want to see Ritual take place.
It's part of the reason why they joined. It's a regimental formula and if they've come from
a MoD [Ministry of Defence] background they need that formal structure.

A new branch was opened in Doncaster in 2003. Some of the new members chose to take
part in Ritual and 'have brought about a dramatic improvement in the ability of the District
Lodge to provide a full range of Ritual activities'.[74] Kath Vernon pointed out that it was still
possible to attend lodges where Ritual was performed and that this focused people's attention.
Ritual, she said,

changes an ordinary meeting into something that little bit more special, something more
significant. In Birmingham we always open the annual summer meeting and the half
yearly summer meeting with Ritual. I believe that sets into people's minds that today
we are doing something different.

The Grand Master's Degree Lodge, 1964. This lodge is open only to those who have attained the appropriate rank. This photograph appeared on the front cover of *The Odd Fellow* magazine, February 1964.

ODDFELLOWS COLLECTION

She described the Lodge of Past Grands, which is open to those who have been Noble Grands, as 'very Ritualistic'.

> They open with a strict Ritual and Ritual is observed all through the meeting. Apart from that it is no different to any other lodge but the Lodge of Past Grands doesn't tend to have a social programme in as much as all the members already belong to other lodges.

The current view of the Society in regard to Ritual is to present it as a voluntary element of Oddfellowship, as available but not as central as the social and care elements. For some it remains integral to their understanding of Oddfellowship. Pauline Pettigrove drew attention to the spectacle associated with degree ceremonies and to how her appreciation had developed:

> I've always sat there fascinated when other people have done their minor degrees. I always find it a very special occasion. I feel extremely honoured when I sit there and I watch other people go through their degrees because mine was done in such a rush, it didn't all sink in. Now I get to see it from the other side. Members get a lot from it. It's a beautiful thing.[75]

Derek Elmer made a similar point about how his understanding of Oddfellowship has matured over time.

We were just waiting outside the room when this elderly gentleman in all the regalia came out to us and said 'Give us your little finger,' and they led us two in and there was all the initiation ceremony and actually it meant nothing, like all Oddfellowship, you have to listen to it and witness it to understand more.

Karen Stuart agreed that Ritual's complexity made Oddfellowship continually interesting

Everybody will tell you that they don't learn very much when it is you having the degree conferred upon you, you learn far more the next time you sit and watch somebody else having a degree conferred because the nerves aren't there and you are quite happy to sit there and learn from somebody else.

Eric Ogden also felt that his appreciation of initiation developed:

I remember my initiation. It was in a fairly small room. I remember being led, somewhat confusingly, from one chair to the next to receive instruction and having it all explained to me. It's one of those things, where you don't really understand it until you see it being done to somebody else, but none the less it was relaxed. Everybody was friendly but businesslike.

Daphne Stephenson also explained what Ritual meant to her and how the significance grew with the passage of time:

Many people are finding that the interest in ceremonial is starting to wane. I think it's something that can bind people together. I think it's interesting from a historical point of view, I'm just not sure how new members now see this. A lot of them, because they've joined for the social aspect and the care aspect of the society, they see it as perhaps something alien, but of course, they don't have to come and it's not a good idea to invite them to come to the ceremonial lodge until perhaps they've been a member for quite a while. All our new members they are all welcome to come but I think perhaps they need to make friends within the branch first of all and to feel secure in that, to feel happy coming to the social occasions before you invite them to come to the ceremonial lodge. It reminds you how to appreciate other people and how to treat them. It reinforces the ethos of the society and tries to teach you to support one another and to be fair.

Lillian Leese, a member of a Past Grands lodge, said

I enjoy Ritual, I love the Ritual side of it and I hope they never lose the Ritual side. I think it makes you a better person. It's to do with the way it makes you feel but also if you look at some of the words of the Ritual there it is what you do in life. It's teaching you good things and how you should really see life and other people, you shouldn't turn around and say he is not the same as me or anything like that.

Debates about regalia and ritual continue. In 2008 outward garments were still being discussed in New South Wales. Brother Phil Keevers (a Past Grand Master in NSW) proposed and Sister Ronda Bramblen (the first female Grand Master) seconded a proposal to Grand Lodge meeting that members wear the Grand Lodge collaret to Society Dinners and other such functions.[76]

V   Conclusion

Ritual has enhanced the lives of numerous members. In the early years men could attend the lodge and, through the drama, both marginalise contemporary issues and express their nurturing and paternal emotion. The Ritual was a means by which members could construct a version of familial relationships and fellowship. They could reflect upon and reinforce values and ideas which were central to the Society. Since that period the Ritual has retained the power to evoke a variety of emotions in people, notably fear and respect. In addition, it has guided members through their careers within the Oddfellows without being inflexible. Some have progressed swiftly. Pauline Pettigrove, when a Provincial Corresponding Secretary, advanced from initiation through four minor degrees and the Purple Degree within four months. Others have taken their time. Some reached the point where they felt comfortable and stopped. Betty Mostyn had become a Noble Grand by the age of 21, took the Purple Degree, which enabled her to attend the AMC, and become a District officer, but explained, 'I never wanted to go higher than the lodge'. Whatever its future, and it remains popular, Ritual has supported Oddfellowship in many ways. The myths, symbolic practices, public performances, ornate certificates and jewels (badges) helped to constitute, and give meaning to Oddfellowship. They have indicated the internal hierarchies, ideas about roots and about the routes to higher social status. They were also useful advertisements. Ritual has attracted people to Oddfellowship, has evoked trepidation, encouraged friendship, framed consideration of ethical issues and reminded Oddfellows of the Unity's longevity and ethos. While some may have been alienated by Ritual, or antagonistic or indifferent towards it, for many active members it has strengthened their sense of distinctiveness, their understanding of the traditions and principles, their Oddfellowship. It has aided the survival of the Society into the twenty-first century for without the activists the Oddfellows would have disappeared long ago.

CHAPTER SEVEN

Families, fellowship and finance

A FTER the Second World War the Oddfellows was forced to drop one of its important roles, that of administrating, as an approved society, national insurance. In 1948 William Beveridge, who had proposed much of the welfare system which replaced approved societies, noted:

> The friendly societies have a difficult time ahead of them … The degree to which the friendly societies triumph over their difficulties will depend on the life and spirit of service in them, on their being ready to meet new needs by new methods in the old spirit of social advance by brotherly co-operation.[1]

Although the Unity continued to offer social activities, health and financial products including mortgages, Oddfellow membership fell. Members received different benefits, depending on which lodge they joined and for their investment strategy they were reliant on the financial acumen of fellow members, guided by advice from Manchester. They were restrained by regulations which increasingly meant more financial decisions were taken centrally and that the Oddfellows became more like the insurance companies with which some legislation categorised it. New financial options were made available to members but many were either unpopular or expensive to run. The Chief Registrar of Friendly Societies reported in 1952 that:

> It would be wrong to attribute the declining membership of friendly societies solely to the impact of National Insurance, or to assume that decline is inevitable. There is evidence in this report that an active and enterprising Society can recruit new members of all ages. It is clear that far more activity is needed than at any time in the past.

Gaining members through being 'active and enterprising' was a difficult task. The first section is about how the Oddfellows sought to encourage membership to grow by encouraging inter-generational activity. In the second section the importance of people being able to socialise with others their own age is considered. The third section is about the investment strategies adopted in the 40 years immediately after the conclusion of the Second World War. To counter decline the Oddfellows needed to show that it produced sound financial products. It was felt that the best way to do this was to rely on the enthusiastic engagement of the membership. This was the tactic that had been employed with such success in the past. The narratives of the members can be used to construct an explanation as to how, while other friendly societies failed, the Oddfellows reached the twenty-first century.

I   Families

A novel published in 1910 could realistically have a character whose 'whole life seemed to be nothing but a vista of Friday evenings on which he went to the society's office, between seven and nine, to "pay the club"'.[2] In 1932 an account of the decoration within 'the working-class home' suggested that the 'younger generation' were sweeping away the 'decadence' of their parents which was described:

On either side of the pleated satin-fronted piano would be the enlarged photographs

A prospective candidate completes his application to the Pride of Clapham Lodge in 1939. This shot was posed for *Picture Post* and the seriousness of the undertaking was emphasised by the presence of three others, almost certainly the proposer, seconder and the Secretary. Such scenes became less frequent after the war.
GETTY IMAGES

A FAMILY OF BRISTOL ODDFELLOWS.

Top Row (left to right):—F. E. BROCK, A. O. BROCK, A. E. BROCK, G. E. BROCK, and W. J. BROCK, jun.
Bottom Row—F. W. BROCK, J. BROCK (died April 1st, 1910), W. J. BROCK. H. G. BROOK.
All members of the Loyal Sincerity Lodge, Bristol District.

LEFT

These nine Brock family members, in 1910, were all members of the same lodge. Following the publication of their picture the *Oddfellows' Magazine* reported in October 1914 that Edward Davies, of Prince of Powis, Welshpool was the son of a founder of the lodge and had ten children and four grandchildren in it.

BELOW

Arthur Jackson, photographed aged 96, was one of a number of his family who have been in the same Lodge for generations.

FELLOW

...er of Odd Fellows Manchester Unity Friendly Society

1965

Three Generations In One Lodge In The Colchester And Maldon District.

APRIL   VOL. XCVI   No. 1068

Registered at the G.P.O. for transmission to Canada and Newfoundland

ABOVE

In 1965 three generations of Applebys attended the initiation of Roger Appleby into the Victoria Lodge in the Colchester and Maldon district. Roger's father, J. S. Appleby PG and his grandfather G. A. Appleby PPGM were active in the lodge. Roger and his father also had a common interest in the history of local Oddfellows. One published an account of their development in 1947; the other published one in 2002.

of the heads of the household and if the male head was a Buffalo or an Oddfellow there would also be one of those amazing coloured 'emblems' packed with as much hieroglyphic symbolism as a totem pole.[3]

A novel published in 1959 but set slightly earlier, featured a son, who, on hearing the coded conversation between of the friendly society members prior to their lodge meeting in the pub and learning that his father is to join them, is 'filled with an accumulation of nausea'.[4] While the latter is clearly exaggeration for comic effect, there was little interest among the young. The decline in adult membership was called a 'catastrophe' by the GM at the 1952 AMC who said that young people seemed to lack the understanding possessed by their parents and could not readily appreciate the desirability of making provision through additional safeguards.[5] Some districts admitted no juniors in 1953 and the overall number fell from 52,667 in 1951 to 50,648 while 20,000 adults also left the Unity. In 1955 half of the 3,000 lodges did not accepted a single new member. The number of branches of the larger affiliated orders, the Oddfellows, the Rechabites, the Foresters, Shepherds, Free Gardeners and Sons of Temperance, fell from around 16,000 in 1945 to 11,000 in 1955 (3,000 of these being Oddfellow lodges) and adult membership from 2,150,000 to 1,350,000 (about 500,000 of them being Oddfellows) during the same period.[6] Some 61,216 had left these societies during the previous year. There was concern that employing canvassers would undermine the incentive to attend on club night to pay contributions and would further undermine the initiation Ritual. However, in 1956 it was agreed to employ canvassers. By 1959 friendly society membership had fallen to 6.1 million and it was the affiliated orders which were most badly affected. There were about 570,000 in the Oddfellows. Many of the affiliated orders closed. There were 66 in 1945 and only 20 in 1990.

In the nineteenth century Oddfellowship was presented as a means by which men could maintain their dependants without necessarily socialising with them, a method by which men could form the heterogeneous ties necessary for broader mobilisation, rather than strengthen the more homogenous ties of blood or marriage kinship.[7] By contrast, the post-war focus on nuclear families was in line with the tenor of much social policy of the 1940s and 1950s. In 1945 the Grand Master argued that 'a small village lodge is a centre of Odd Fellowship and with a bit more energy on the spot might well increase in membership. Let every lodge be a family lodge, with men, women and junior members … keep the lodge in the village or town. [Take it away and] you lose the local contacts.' In addition, he proposed that contributions should be equalised and recruitment and attendance promoted.[8] He called for a revival of social activities, for more lodges to open and said that it was 'necessary to encourage the family membership of a lodge – father, mother and children – so that in future new lodges must make provision to that effect and admit females and junior members.'[9] Woolwich formed the first family lodge and there was an increased interest in ensuring that women could contribute to the Unity in a variety of ways including being elected to the AMC. A report on friendly societies in 1947 concluded:

A potential reinforcement of community feeling is provided by the 'family' atmosphere surrounding the societies. The fact is that many people belong to friendly societies either because their parents have enrolled them or because parents and friends are already members. Extension of membership, at first in a small way through people already knowing each other, may possibly prove a more useful approach to the future than any attempt to plan the larger group activities which invite comparison with commercial entertainment.[10]

The Stranger's Refuge is said to be the first Oddfellows lodge in Australia. Founded in 1840 the son of its first Noble Grand (C. M. Crighton) became a member of the Oddfellows. The founder's granddaughter became a Past Grand and his great-grandchildren also joined the Society.[11] There is also a case in a Grand Master in Australia, Robert Hanington, 1960, following his father, J. H. Hanington, who was a Grand Master in 1951.[12] Many people mentioned that others in their family were members of the Oddfellows. Arthur Jackson's great grandfather was one of the founder members of the lodge which Arthur joined and many other members of his family had held posts in that lodge. As he noted, 'the secretary was carried by the Jackson family right until we closed up'. Oddfellowship, while it may have started as being male-orientated, had always supported widows and children and had long encouraged the involvement of family members. Dorothy Deacon spoke about her membership as 'a family thing; we all belonged to the Odd Fellows.' Her father retired but then 'he found the lodge in Haslemere was in need of a Noble Grand so he decided to step in. They needed a secretary, so I took on the role. One of the highlights for many families was the trip to the AMC. Pat, perhaps ruefully, explained that Oddfellowship brought her family together

> We never had holidays because Board meetings were about four or five times a year which meant that we couldn't have a holiday because he [her father] had to keep all his leave for board meetings. So we had no family life as such. We went to conference because it meant we could spend some time together … We just grew up in an Oddfellows family, you just accepted the fact that, that's what, as far as we were concerned, that's what parents did …

Brian Merrell also remembered 'going to AMCs. We used to go with Pat [Morgan] and her sister. Everybody used to sit on the beach, there would be six to eight of us kids. The children played and the parents went off to the AMC.' Frances Wilkinson also went to the beach:

> Some years the family holiday would be Dad doing his AMC bit and us going along to Scarborough and the Isle of Man. We went as a family, Dad had his delegate job and he used to do that during the day and we'd go the beach with Mum and then we would meet up at night and there were a lot of other families that did the same, so we had quite a lot of friends. We weren't entirely used to going in hotels because usually our holidays were caravan holidays but when we went into a hotel it was really special, I remember

going into one and being totally fascinated by the lift. I think we were told in the end that the lift was for the oldies.

In 1951 Joan Henry's husband Reg, attended as a visitor while she stayed at home with their young children:

Reg went to Torquay and came back so full of enthusiasm that the next year they were going to Guernsey. That was my first one and Guernsey was fascinating and the whole thing was a wonderful, wonderful experience. Conferences were very much family

---

Recognise Social Ills   *Need to Change*   *Modernise Our*
of Our Times   *Structure*   *Principles*

GRAND MASTER'S SEVENFOLD CHALLENGE

The whole membership of the Order was challenged to put itself under the microscope, to examine itself and make the changes necessary to bring the Order into a state to meet the challenges of the 21st century.

The gauntlet was thrown down by the Grand Master of the Order, Bro Len Mostyn in an inspiring and challenging 7,000 word presidential address—believed to be the longest on record—at the opening of AMC.

I BID YOU all welcome to Margate, to this the 154th Annual Moveable Conference of our Society. I extend a particular welcome to those members who are attending their first A.M.C., and hope that you will find it interesting, informative and inspirational. If you are a deputy and have anything to contribute to the discussions I invite you to take part; those who are more experienced will I feel sure give you encouragement and a fair hearing.

Margate, though far from my home town, has a particular significance for me; it was here that I attended my first A.M.C. as a deputy in 1965. The facilities for a conference are excellent, the air is bracing and the Canterbury District through its A.M.C. Committee and the local authority have laid on some fine arrangements for our comfort and entertainment. I thank them for what they have done.

Our Annual Conference is the ruling body of the Society and whilst the purpose of our presence is to hear of the stewardship of the Board of Directors over the past twelve months and to debate and decide upon the policies of the Society for future years, it is my wish that the occasion be a happy one and that you will renew old acquaintances and make new friends. It is a unique opportunity when so many people of a like mind are thrown together, to exchange views on the many aspects of our Order and to practise the spirit of fraternity.

missed by myself and by all members of the Order. The deaths of Brother Fred Hammond and Brother Norman Thornton will also leave a void in the Manchester Unity we can ill-afford. For these friends and colleagues we grieve at their decease yet we are happy for their memory and give thanks for the service they rendered to us.

Retirements

At the close of this A.M.C. two close colleagues of mine will retire from service as Directors. I take this opportunity of remarking personally on this event. To Brother George Wyver I extend my thanks not just for the service he has given to the Unity as an Officer and Director but also for the kindness and friendship he has extended to me over the past eight years. To Brother John Poynton my thanks also for the services rendered the

Order in the years he has been a Director and again for the friendly comradeship we have shared together and the many acts of kindness he has done me. To you both and to your respective wives I express the wish that your retirement from service will be marked by a happy and well-earned rest.

Acknowledgements

I have been extremely fortunate during my term as Grand Master to have had so many people around me who have contributed so much to make the year successful and happy. I therefore desire to express my thanks to them at an early stage in my address. I begin at home, to my wife Betty who during the past twelve months has been constantly at my side, giving so much not only to me but also to the Order generally. No words of

In a more relaxed mood, Grand Master, Bro Len Mostyn with Sister Betty join "Auntie Jo" and 108 junior members at their party held in the Queen's Hall on Sunday afternoon.

"CHANGE OUR STRUCTURE"

mine can adequately convey the debt I owe to her for the dedicated and loving manner in which she has performed the duties placed on the consort of the Grand Master. From the bottom of my heart I thank you my love.

To my Lodge, The Loyal Good Intent Lodge of the Mersey District of which I am so proud, I extend thanks to the Officers and Members for their constant encouragement and support. If ever a Lodge typified the true spirit of Odd Fellowship it is the Good Intent. To the Officers and Members of the Mersey District, whom I have the privilege of serving as Provincial Corresponding Secretary, I extend my heartfelt thanks for sustaining me during this year; their unfailing readiness to assist me and to lend support can be without equal, and I shall be eternally grateful to them for the opportunity they have given me to serve the Unity. To my fellow Lancastrians in the County Palatine, my thanks for the support and inspiration they always give to me. Our Group Conferences serve the Manchester Unity in many ways, not-the-least of which is as a training ground, and the Lancashire and Adjacent Districts' Group Conference is an excellent example.

To you Sisters and Brothers in your Lodges and Districts: In our travels throughout the country we have been met with nothing but friendliness, kindness and great consideration. Your warm reception of us at your social

gatherings and meetings has been a revelation. Although our programme has been full and, at times, hectic, we have never failed to be inspired and excited by the degree of hospitality accorded to us. To you all I express my grateful thanks.

To my close colleagues—my Deputy Grand Master and immediate predecessor—I desire to place on record my thanks for all the assistance they have rendered to me. To my fellow Directors, who have worked so hard during this year, I am grateful for your efforts and I thank you for your friendship and comradeship. I reserve a particular thank you for the Secretary of the Order; you Sir, devote your life to the cause of this Society, perhaps it is only the Grand Master who realises the full extent of the energy and effort you expend in your duties. On behalf of the Society I extend all of our thanks but for myself a thank you for the ready manner and the spirit of co-operation and great courtesy you have accorded to me in my office.

To the Deputy Secretary and all the staff at Unity Office who work so devotedly for the membership of the Unity, thank you for your efforts. To all the other people who work for our Society, the Editor of the Magazine—Brother Frank Billinge—who manages each month against the most difficult of circumstances to produce a journal of unparalleled excellence and interest. To our many professional advisers, Accountants, Actuaries, Solicitors, Public Relations experts, my thanks.

My year of office has been marked by a number of events that have been a source of encouragement to me. In particular the celebration of the Queen's Silver Jubilee has shown that this country, despite a social revolution, still retains an appreciation of the old values of moderation and this is best-portrayed in the aims and objects and activities of our own Society. There is a crying need though for us to keep abreast of developments that have taken place and to provide for the needs of the present day. Such changes need not be accompanied by the jettisoning of our age-old principles and ideals but nevertheless changes are overdue and present us with a challenge.

I challenge this Society to change. I challenge the membership of the Manchester Unity to recognise the need for, and to accept, changes. I challenge you Sisters and Brothers to seek out and distinguish the changes that are necessary in the many facets of our Order. I challenge you to identify—as our forbears did—the social ills of the times in which we live and to seek means of alleviating them. I challenge you to examine our aims and objects and to consider whether they can be extended or changed in any way. I challenge you to change our structure so that some of the ponderous procedures we have

(continued on page 2)

Obituary

Since we last met many of our members have passed to higher service; we mourn their passing but remember them with joy, and give thanks for the service they rendered to Odd Fellowship. In particular I mention three of their number and whilst the opportunity will be taken later this morning of paying due tribute, I claim the privilege of a few words of my own. We have suffered the loss of two Past Grand Masters and one Past Director, all well-known to these assemblies and throughout the Order.

Shortly after the Blackpool A.M.C. the Unity and my own District in particular lost a man of considerable qualities and talents in the person of Brother John C. Kent; his presence will certainly be

Grand Master, Bro Len Mostyn, rings the bell to bring deputies to order at the start of AMC.

BRO
MOSTYN

Joan Henry (Auntie Jo), pictured above, recalled that 'At conference they had a newspaper in conjunction with the local newspaper. It carried photographs of the people installed and told people what had gone on. It was a general way of publicising the Order and we used to have a procession through the streets in those days.' Her picture appeared in this edition. There is also a picture of Len Mostyn.

affairs, they were a week long always at the seaside and in those days a different seaside each year. The whole family went. The children played on the beach with mother and father was usually in the conference. There was evening entertainment and Sunday afternoons.

A few years later Joan fostered further enthusiasm among younger Oddfellows when she took over from Auntie Nellie. Since at least 1939, when far-sighted Auntie Jeff's column looked forward to the introduction of decimal currency 32 years before the UK adopted the system, there had been a section of the Oddfellows literature aimed at children.[13] In February 1945 Uncle Tom was writing for 'Young Odd Fellows', and later that year Auntie Nellie starting writing in the magazine. During the 1960s she was joined by Uncle Leslie and Cousin Stan. It was from this trio that 'Aunty Jo' Henry took over. Between 1964 and 1986 she expanded two pages to *The Mini Link* magazine with a print run of up to 7,000, some going overseas. It was as she said, 'a new magazine for junior members, something a bit more modern'. Joan Henry invented the title but was not allowed to claim the prize for the person who named the publication.

> I said, 'Oh, I'll have my £5,' and my husband [Reg Henry] said 'No. Good gracious, you can't have it, otherwise they'll think it was a fiddle,' so I never got my £5. It was a purely voluntary job, the Oddfellows paid for the stamps, the birthday cards and the Christmas cards.

She and arranged for 7,000 cards to be posted to junior members all over the world adding

> I still had people come up to me at this last AMC who said, 'I was in your birthday club.'
> I now have mothers who say, 'I was in your birthday club'. Maybe one day some one will come up and say, 'I'm a grandmother, and I was in your birthday club.'

Her contribution was acknowledged by the Grand Master who in her 1985 address to the AMC referred to the 'good work' for junior members of Sister Joan Henry's Birthday Club.[14] In addition the Directors Report of that year mentioned that '*The Mini-Link* continues to have great success with the old and young. The Directors would like to thank "Aunty Jo" on behalf of the young members for her efforts in making *The Mini-Link* so successful.'[15]

Pat Morgan was active as both a junior and an adult member. She joined a juvenile lodge aged eight where she could socialise with people her own age with the support of their families:

> The lodge was already going when I joined. We had an adult committee that ran it and we had an overall Secretary. They supervised everybody and in some cases made sure that the juveniles got to the meetings because a lot of them hadn't got parents who would take them or they'd got long journeys. You were well looked after.

Pat's family was also involved at home:

> If there were any dinners in the area we always had some of the Board of Directors
> staying with us. You'd come back from wherever and there was always coffee and, my
> Mum or I, always done sandwiches before they went out. That's how you got to know
> them … Just ask me what social life we had, because we didn't.

A few days after she became 16 in 1956, Pat Morgan joined an adult women's lodge, of which
her mother was a member, and later a Trustee. It was that year that her father first joined the
Board of Directors, at the Scarborough AMC. Pat went on to hold a number of offices. In
March 1964 when she was the chair of the Jenny Warren lodge dinner, the guest of honour was
her father, the Grand Master and beside him sat the Provincial Grand Master of the Stepney
district, his wife Ruth. Pat's father ran a pension fund and her mother ran a pension fund ladies
committee, 'the ones that did all the jumble sales and the bazaars and coffee mornings and
things like that'. *The Odd Fellow* reported that this was 'believed to be unique in the history
of the Order', and that Pat was 'the youngest and most charming chairman we have ever had
at this dinner'. Frances Wilkinson was also a junior who went on to become a full member.
She compared her own time as a junior to that of her sons:

Promoting the Society at the Southampton AMC
in 1910 (*below*) and in Hull in 1965 (*right*).
ODDFELLOWS COLLECTION

Ellen Berner, Auntie Nellie, here surrounded by children at a post-war party. Ellen Berner, known to thousands as Auntie Nellie, wrote a column for children in the Society's magazine for almost 20 years after the war. She is pictured here pouring tea for Brighton Juveniles and in the centre of the group photograph, also taken in Brighton.

BY COURTESY OF CHRISTINE PAYNE

This Feast

ANOTHER CUP OF TEA is poured for Mr. President (Derek Betson, aged 13) during the Juvenile Odd Fellows' feast at the Belmont-street School, Brighton, the food for which was provided by 16 children of the U.S.

Little Americans Stand Young Brighton a 'Beano'

FOOD worth hundreds of points was used at a party given last night at the Belmont-street School, Brighton, for 38 members of the Brighton Juvenile Lodge of the Odd Fellows.

No points were, however, necessary for the whole spread was sent over to this country by sixteen members of the "Primrose" Juvenile Lodge of the Odd Fellows, New Bedford, U.S.A.

HUSBAND WINS APPEAL TO HIGH COURT

THE way in which a husband and wife lived their separate lives in the same house after the wife had secured a Magistrates' order for separation and maintenance was described to the Kings Bench Divisional Court yesterday.

The husband, Ioan Evans, of Ham-road, Worthing, appealed against a decision of the local Justices that he was obliged to pay his wife the £2 weekly and 10s. weekly in respect of each of their two children, ordered by the court on the wife's application for a separation order.

He maintained that after securing the separation order his wife had continued to reside with him and so made her order unenforceable.

Lord Goddard, the Lord Chief Justice, giving judgment, said Mr. Evans was the tenant of a house in Ham-road, Worthing, comprising a front room, kitchen and scullery on the ground floor and three bedrooms on the first floor. The husband slept upstairs and the wife downstairs.

Two large parcels of food, containing sweets, tins of pineapple, peaches and spam, and milk jellies and blanc-mange cakes and tea, arrived at Mrs. N. E. Berner's house at Victoria-road, Portslade, from the young Americans with a request that she would organise a party for one British Juvenile Lodge of the Society.

Mrs. Berner—"Auntie Nellie"—to thousands of children in the Odd Fellows throughout the world—decided for the children of the Brighton branch in which she has particularly interested herself most for a number of years.

PICTURES FROM U.S.

Derek Betson, 13-years-old President, with his red and gold band of office hanging from his neck, led the children to the tables supported by his Vice-President, 13-years-old Mary Bience, wearing a pink and blue band, the Past President June Hadland (13), and Junior Secretary Reginald Hora (11) and the youngest member of the party Michael Willard, aged two.

After their feast Mr. H. Newman used his endoscope to show them photographs of three of their young American hostesses, Harriet and Irene, and Nancy Noblett and Lynne Green will now settle down and write a long letter of thanks. Reginald, the Junior Secretary...

When I was junior member that they were absolutely hundreds of kids about. There used to an annual trip and the whole train would be Oddfellows children and families and there'd be endless coaches all going to Southport or Morecambe or Scarborough. When ours were little they didn't do the trips to the coast, but they went to the Bradford pantomime.

Those who joined when they were older often mentioned the importance of family in terms of sociability. George Kilford said that his wife joined the Oddfellows after he had, because 'it was a way for us to socialise together'. Joan Henry was also initially attracted by the idea of social activities. She and her husband had lived in a number of locations but by 1952 they settled in London with their two sons. A neighbour encouraged Reg Henry to attend a lodge in Cricklewood. Joan Henry decided to join because she

had lost touch with a lot of people during the war and it was to get me out of the house. I wasn't an active member as I had young children but my husband was knee deep in it and I felt, 'If you can't beat them join them.'

Daphne Stephenson attended some Oddfellow social events with her fiancé prior to her marriage.

Everybody made me ever so welcome and came to talk to me and were interested in what I did etc., but I didn't actually become an Oddfellow until after I had got married [in 1967. Her husband] seemed to spend an awful lot of time there and I used to say, 'What an earth do you do at that place?' Of course, he couldn't tell me very much about the business because you're not supposed to divulge the business to other people. He said, 'You could come if you want to,' so I went. I didn't quite know what to expect but everybody welcomed me.

Keith Adamson became aware of the Oddfellows through his wife. Despite her knowledge of Oddfellowship, and in common with others, she failed to provide accurate account of what to expect at initiation. He was initiated at his first meeting in 1993, when he was 39. He explained that his wife, a lifelong Oddfellow, 'said to me I'd got to raise my left trouser leg and do all sorts of weird and wonderful things and it was nothing like that. She is a terrible tease.'

Frances Wilkinson saw the Oddfellows as part of her family:

I remember lots of honorary aunts and uncles that I had through Oddfellowship. Aunts and uncles, all the brothers and sisters, they watch you growing up don't they? I can remember when we got married, people sent us towels and little gifts and they'd all be friends of Mum and Dad that were Oddfellows. It was like an extended family. Like a little community. Churches are the same you get that community spirit going. I think some religions have it as well but very much so in Oddfellowship. People cared about you they were interested and they did lots of things to encourage you.

Jean Facer described how the involvement of her parents-in-law, her late husband and herself provided a structure which linked them together:

Stan's Dad was very active. He was the District Chairman in 1940 and he served on the Management Committee of his lodge and the District Management Committee for many years. His Mum was a grassroots member, she loved going to the meetings. Stan joined as a baby in 1929 went through district office twice, in 1959 and again in 1994. He was secretary of two lodges and served 49 years as secretary. He used to have to do all the books for both lodges for sickness benefits with the different tables and pay out various benefits to various members. He was District Trustee for 28 years and served on the District Management Committee … I was an only child and Stan was an only child and my son's an only child, so I have no kin, near kin to be able to either rely on talk to or get a bit of support from. If you haven't got a sister you need friends. It helped the whole family business.

Others mentioned the role of fathers-in-law. Betty Mostyn recalled the effects of her father's words on her fiancé, later a Grand Master: 'My father said to Len in 1949, 'If you are getting married you might as well join the Oddfellows.' In the 1970s Andrew Porter, an apprentice engineer and also later a Grand Master, was recruited by his father-in-law, a lifelong Oddfellow who was one of a family of prominent local Oddfellows. Andrew's fiancée was also an Oddfellow.

Just before we got married, her father said to me, 'You're going to join the Oddfellows'. I went to this meeting that I knew nothing about or what I was going to do and I was initiated and had to sign the register. I paid my money and I was a member.

Keith Adamson explained about how, even though his sons were not active within the Oddfellows, they were supportive. After the dinner and speeches as his Grand Master's reception one of them said, '"Do you know something?" he said, "I'm proud of you". That meant the world, seriously, it really meant the world.' Members of the Unity wanted their relations to understand it, encouraged them to join and were pleased when those relations came to appreciate the nature of Oddfellowship.

Members recalled a variety of activities designed to aid recruitment and the retention of members by appealing to a wide age range. These included whist drives and plays, bowling, snooker, darts, football, cricket, quizzes, trips to the dogs and the theatre, wine and cheese quiz nights and dinner dances, garden fetes and river cruises. Ray Gibbens ran quizzes at his lodge between 1967 until 1990. His focus was social:

Children were encouraged to be active within the Society through most of the twentieth century. This is a Juvenile Section in Brighton, many of them wearing Unity collars.
BY COURTESY OF CHRISTINE PAYNE

In Skipton in 2005 there were echoes of the memories of Lesley Bull.

> We had a brass plaque on the front of our house that used to wait until it was virtually illegible and then one of us would go and clean it until a beautiful shine and wonder why we hadn't done it before. It said that our house was a registered office of the IOOFMU Lodge Number 6840, Loyal Imperial Lodge.

Children's parties may well have attracted families to the Society. The Mersey District's summer Field Day in 1936 (*below*) promised a fancy dress competition, while one lifelong Oddfellow recalled that when she was growing up in the late 1970s and early 1980s, 'It [was] really the parties that stick to mind because they were so well attended. They were absolutely packed with children.'

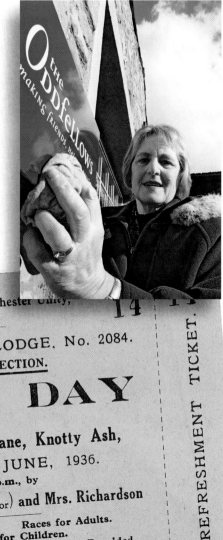

Independent Order of Odd Fellows, Manchester Unity, Mersey District.

LOYAL LORD STANLEY LODGE, No. 2084.
JUNIOR MEMBERS' SECTION.

A FIELD DAY

will be held at

Lower Finch Farm, Finch Lane, Knotty Ash,
On SATURDAY, 27th JUNE, 1936.

To be opened at 3-0 p.m., by

Bro. Ald. F. T. Richardson (Deputy Lord Mayor) and Mrs. Richardson

Races for Children (various ages).   Races for Adults.
Fancy Dress Competition for Children.
Novelties.   Orchestra will be in attendance.   Teas Provided.

TICKETS : Adults 1/- each *(including Refreshments).*

REFRESHMENT TICKET.

I was only interested in the social side … I wasn't impressed with Ritual. I joined purely for the social activities. Other people did as well. It paid dividends. The fact that I was able to write their plays for them … I played the piano. I accompanied them. I made the songs up. They were all musical plays. All the things I did were successful. I gave a lot of pleasure to people … I entertain the Oddfellows still. Aged 82 I gave them a musical afternoon last September. Half an hour with my guitar.

He recalled that in 1967 he wrote a song in a folk style, called 'Friendship, love and truth' later published in *The Oddfellows Magazine*, the first verse of which ran:

> It doesn't matter about the colour of your skin,
> It doesn't matter if you lose or if you win,
> It doesn't matter if you are rich or if you're poor
> But if there is friendship and love,
> You'll make the world go round.

Ron Trenchard mentioned the floats made for the Warwick and Kenilworth Carnivals, the annual lodge garden party and trips to the panto.

Brian Merrell recalled the Stepney District Sports Day at which he won medals. 'It was all very competitive against different lodges.' Dorothy Deacon also attended the Stepney District Sports Day at Snakes Lane. Ann Harris said, 'I am from an Oddfellow family, and I was made a member in February 1938. We were a very social district and attended many dinners and dances locally … My Mum used to play the piano, we had a knees up and we used to do quizzes, play darts, dress up have a big social event.' She particularly enjoyed one Children's Annual Christmas Party at which were served

> jam sandwiches and blancmange, just after the war when we were still on rationing. Mrs Crudge used to make lovely sponge fingers and decorate them like dominoes and there was a free fight for them and one of our lovely ladies was holding a rabbit mould and she got distracted and it fell over.

Douglas Potter recalled parties for the young after the war:

> I had the pleasure of arranging a lot of outings for the children. We used to have a lot of concerts in our lodge room, and on one occasion we took the children with their parents to Chessington Zoo and we had a slap-up tea party there. It was in Coronation year and we gave them all a Coronation Crown.

Mary Wheeler's father was frequently ill when she was growing up in the 1950s. The Oddfellows provided support and, as she recalled, 'My trips out with the Oddfellows meant a lot me, usually to the countryside. Children's trips, picnic days we used to call them and we would go out on a bus and play sports, egg and spoon races and sack races.' Lesley Bull recalled that

> The huge majority of my social events memories are to do with the Oddfellows. Christmas parties, darts matches, family walks with other Oddfellows. That is what I remember most about my childhood. We used to have the most enormous fun. Cricket matches, that was fun, all the ladies would make the teas. We had Christmas parties

in conjunction with Hale Lodge and dressing up parties. My mother was, and is, such a talented seamstress. She made some fabulous costumes. One that made us absolutely fall off chairs laughing was Bill and Ben and Little Weed [characters from *The Flowerpot Men*, a children's television puppet programme which was broadcast between 1952 and 1971] which was my Mum and Dad and a very good friend. There was one play called Fly-by-Night where my mum was a stewardess. I sat in the audience with my Gran and cried because my Mum said 'I'm leaving on the next plane,' and I was absolutely heartbroken that my Mum was going. They took part in a lot of amateur dramatics at the Oddfellows. Whenever we had social gatherings at the Oddfellows Hall, Ray Gibbens used to be the guitarist. He wrote a song called *Friendship, Love and Truth*. My Mum used to sing with two other people.

Lesley's mother Brenda Francis mentioned some of the same events.

It was a friendship society. We had a float in a carnival. Christmas parties every year. We used to have about 250 people in coaches, taking them all to the seaside. We had lots of fun.

Frances Wilkinson also enjoyed the social events:

Brenda Francis recalled that in 1961, 'in a play "Fly-by-night", George was dressed as an air steward and I was an air stewardess. Being in the trade I was I made the costumes.'

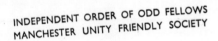

INDEPENDENT ORDER OF ODD FELLOWS
MANCHESTER UNITY FRIENDLY SOCIETY

NORTH AND SOUTH LONDON DISTRICTS'
125th JOINT ANNIVERSARY FESTIVAL 1963

ROYAL ALBERT HALL
KENSINGTON, LONDON S.W. 7.

SATURDAY, OCTOBER 26th 1963

The 125th anniversary was marked with a festival. Roger Burley recalled: 'One of the big highlights has got to be the 125th Anniversary of North and South London, 1963 in the Albert Hall. A big dance and cabaret and what have you. It certainly encouraged me.'
BY COURTESY OF DOUGLAS POTTER

When I met Paul and we became involved in Oddfellowship we used to go to the annual dinner dances, we got involved in suits and ties and the long frocks and we've been to many a dinner dance at Betty's Café in Bradford.

One interviewee recalled being a junior member in the early 1980s and the later involvement of her own child, Luke:

It is really the parties that stick to mind because they were so well attended. They were absolutely packed with children and whilst there was always the traditional party games, musical chairs, pass the parcel, there were also little games that my grandfather would make up. He put up a sheet of paper with anagrams of animals or flags of different countries. He put a poster up on the wall with different countries and we had to identify the flags and riddles … Luke was taken to the pantomime with all the rest of our junior members last year. That was lovely, I recall him smiling as he stood up on stage at the pantomime singing, 'There's a worm at the bottom of the garden.' I really hope that we can do a little bit more for children because I have got happy memories of the parties. Luke is having the time of his life at the moment with the social events.

These accounts suggest that, while finance and health were still of importance, in the post-war period the focus of Oddfellowship shifted as members of the Oddfellows made a concerted effort to include members of their families. This was through the publications, through activities arranged at the AMC, through sports days and trips and through encouraging family members to attend meetings.

II   Siblings and peers

Although in many accounts there are references to the influence of family in their decision to join, a lot of members pointed to the importance of mixing with their peers and their engagement with others of their own age, not with their parents. Recruitment of sons was

I.O.O.F.   M.U.F.S.

JUBILEE DINNER

GOOD INTENT LODGE 6264

ODDFELLOWS' HALL
ST. ALBANS ROAD
WATFORD
SATURDAY, FEB. 4TH, 1928

CHAIRMAN:
BRO. W. H. MEADOWS, I.P.P.G.M.

INDEPENDENT ORDER
OF ODD FELLOWS
Manchester Unity
Friendly Society

Countess of Warwick Lodge
1901 - 2001
Centenary Luncheon
at Moor Hall Hotel
Sutton Coldfield
on Sunday 3rd June 2001

Dining played an important role in binding members together. Grand Masters would tour the country meeting members at meals, and many who were interviewed had kept menus from special occasions, some signed by those present. Ann Harris is toasting the camera (*top*), while Mike and Ron Trenchard can be seen with their wives at a dinner (*bottom left*). Specially prepared menus, such as these from 1928 and 2001, often had information about the history and officers of the lodge. A number of members kept signed menus as mementos.

DINNER IMAGE COURTESY OF MIKE TRENCHARD; 2001 MENU COURTESY OF ROY MORRIS; 1928 MENU AND PICTURE OF HERSELF COURTESY OF ANNE HARRIS

Post-war Australia

At the conclusion of hostilities in 1945 the Oddfellows provided housing loans for much of Sydney through terminating building societies. In 1947 Australia's first credit union, the Small Loans and Savings Society, was established in New South Wales by the Oddfellows and in 1949 in Victoria it established the Co-operative Savings and Loans Society. In 1955 an Endowment Fund was created to provide cash benefits for members who reached the age of 65. Legislation limited trading with the public by friendly societies and between 1955 and 1982 the way that taxation was structured adversely affected the friendly societies far more than the private pharmacists. Nevertheless, the Oddfellows continued to provide health services. It opened a convalescent home in Woodend, near Melbourne in 1941 for members and staff of the Unity. Others followed in 1947 (a property near Mittagong about 67 miles south of Sydney and in 1949–50 (at North Parramatta). Aged Members Homelets were opened in 1953 and an 'Aged Members Section' building and hospital in 1957. It branched out into holiday homes in Cronulla in 1957 and in Port Macquarie in 1961. The Society also acquired property at Bream Beach on Saint George's basin when the National Independent Order of Oddfellows joined the Society in 1961. It purchased its home and hospital for older people in 1962. It sold Bream beach in 1976 and purchased Hawkes Nest and opened the Walmsley Retirement Village, Kilsyth, in 1980. In the 1990s the 24 self-contained holiday accommodation units at Hawkes Nest were refurbished and, because it was making a loss, sold. A new retirement village was built to replace the Aged Members' one. The new village had 230 residents living in a nursing home and a variety of other accommodation units. There were recreation and meeting areas, a library and a Credit Union banking facilities. In 2001 it acquired the Nursing Home at North Parramatta and in 2004 the Heritage of Hunters Hill Retirement Village. By June 2005 the Society provided 238 apartments and 183 places in high- and low-care beds.

In 1991 the Society was divided with Grand Lodge, operating as Manchester Unity in NSW, managing fraternal activities, opening lodges and controlling their budgets and a limited company, Manchester Unity Australia Limited, running the commercial operations and voting sums to its sibling. In 1999 Manchester Unity Australia Ltd becomes a public company limited by shares and guarantee. In 2008 Manchester Unity in NSW established itself as separate entity to prevent fraternal assets being seized in the event of a hostile takeover of Manchester Unity Australia Limited. Manchester Unity was by then a mutual company with about 90,000 members. The company provided care and services to more than 400 residents in retirement and aged care facilities, and provided financial products to more than 15,000 members. Following a ballot it then merged with a larger mutual company, Hospital Contributions Funds Limited, and became a wholly owned subsidiary of it. HCF was founded in 1932 as the Metropolitan Hospitals Contribution Fund which itself was created following negotiations between the charitable Hospital Saturday Fund and the Hospital Commission of New South Wales. It became one of Australia's largest not-for-profit health funds and the third largest private health insurer in the country. There were over 545,000 policyholders within the newly combined body. Members of Manchester Unity Australia received cash payments as part of the merger. However, the press reported that HCF 'intends to phase out the Manchester Unity brand over the next 12 to 18 months' and that Manchester Unity Australia employees would only have their jobs protected for a year.[16]

commonplace within friendly societies right up until the 1930s. As Whiteside noted, 'there is little evidence that new entrants shopped around for the society best suited to their needs. Most joined the society neighbours, friends or parents knew'.[17] A manager at the Liverpool Victoria Friendly Society explained:

> Liverpool Victoria traditionally gained new business through referrals. Our members were typically very loyal and their children would grow up with the agent coming every four weeks to their home, and when they grew old enough to need their own insurance they automatically came to Liverpool Victoria, as did their children. [By the 1990s] our customer base was ageing and oversold.[18]

However, after the war there was less desire among young men, or women, to follow their fathers into the same pastimes and workplaces. Eric Hobsbawm argued that while what he termed the 'invention of tradition' could legitimate an organisation, as the Ritual did in the nineteenth century, it could also prevent that organisation changing.[19] A number of those interviewed mentioned that they joined different lodges to those of their parents, preferring the company of their peers in Intermediate or Juvenile lodges. For much of the post-war period teenagers have been interested in socialising with their peers, not their families and have had the time and money to do this. In 2008 one lifelong member suggested that there might been some complacency within the Society:

> I did my Purple Degree last year. They said it has been eight to 10 years since they last had someone take their Purple Degree in the district because there has just been no recruitment drive at all; people had always assumed that people would join because their families were members, and that is just not the case any more. Even if they joined they joined because of the family connection and loyalty to the family rather to the society, so they pay, but they don't turn up to anything.

Julie Hill, writing about the Liverpool Victoria, argued that the members 'do not have a tendency to shop around or switch. But this is a very passive form of loyalty – the worst kind for us as the likelihood of the member acting as advocate is much lower.'[20]

When he joined the lodge Jeff Bartlett thought that it was full of older men. It was only at the conclusion of his military service, when the lodge was full of young people, that Jeff Bartlett became an enthusiastic Oddfellow and, as he explained,

> I've not missed a meeting since. They were anxious to get a sports and social club going. We had a cricket team, a bowls team and a tennis team. We used to play in the local league. We had a good time.

Others mentioned that they sought the company of those their own age rather than people who were the contemporaries of their parents. One person mentioned that he had been joined by his father at birth and attended trips to the seaside and the pantomime as a child. He showed no interest after the age of 16 until, on the death of his father, who paid a subscription for him, he was contacted and attended a meeting. He became involved and rose to be a Provincial Corresponding Secretary in the Leeds and Dewsbury District and in 1964, the President of the Yorkshire Group conference.[21] When Roy Morris, aged 14, joined during the war in Birmingham there was an explanation of Oddfellowship at the meetings, but his focus was on 'the fun and friendship'. He met up with children from other lodges and they went on trips to the local botanical gardens and for walks on the outskirts of the city. 'Discussion of the aims and ideals didn't occur very often, only once or twice a year.' Having been a juvenile member, Roy Morris joined an adult lodge aged 16 in 1946, probably influenced by his father: 'My father had given me a reasonable grounding in what went on. Personally I was much keener on Scouting than I was on Oddfellowship in those days.' Roger Burley found it difficult not to be disrespectful at his initiation, carried out by older Oddfellows. He remembered that 'the chairman couldn't pronounce "Return", and there was two of us being initiated and we couldn't help laughing and some of the older ones thought that was not really the done thing.'

Interest in an organisation which catered to their own age group was an attraction for several other members of the Society. In 1949 the 16-year-old Brenda Francis was not attracted by the prospect of sickness benefits or maintaining familial connections:

> I had a boy that I was sweet with and I went round to his house. We were planning a game of tennis. His brother was there. Jeff Bartlett. He said 'What you doing?' I said, 'We're just going out to play tennis.' He said, 'Do you want to play for the Oddfellows?' That was the first I'd heard of them. I said, 'Tell me more.' I was absolutely sports mad and within a week or two I was an Oddfellow and playing tennis for the Oddfellows.

Brenda went on to marry a member of the Oddfellows. In 1967 her husband said, 'I admit I only started because I was chasing Brenda, who is now my wife. She was an enthusiastic member, and that was good enough for me.' He became secretary of the sports club, Noble Grand and Provincial Grand Master of a District of 15 Lodges. Brenda became Lodge Secretary.[22]

Although Mike Trenchard is a fifth-generation Oddfellow, he stressed the companionship of his peers rather than his parents:

> The reason why people joined is for the friendship and the paternal side of the order. I've got friends that I have known since I was in my late teens in the society and I still know them and still visit them.

James Beard was another member whose father had been involved but whose own interest was related to social events. His father was an Oddfellow who went through all the chairs and was a lodge secretary for many years. James joined aged 16 with his cousin but showed little interest until the lodge was galvanised by a new secretary. 'We used to have very good lodge meetings, there was 30 to 40 people. In the 60s we were having trips out, dinners out.' Derek Winbush joined with his parents in 1950 and soon gained responsibilities

We all joined at more or less the same time. They followed me into the society fairly soon afterwards. I joined the Junior Section which was started after the war. There was some outings and one thing and another. At one stage it built up to a small ceremonial section for the juniors, but mainly we were there to enjoy ourselves. I was president of the Junior Section. I was the first Junior President.

During the 1960s there was a concerted attempt to recruit young people through arranging social events. According to Uncle Stan's column in 1964, Reading Juvenile Lodge members were entertained by 'a wonderful rendering of the Odd Fellows' idea of the Beatles', while in April that year Immediate Past Grand Master J. Gordon Barnes told those attending a annual dinner in Woking that 'those who belonged to lodges need never feel lonely'. He was Edmonscote and Stratford-on-Avon district secretary, 1951–65, and he appealed to 'the younger people to carry on this great work'. It was partly because those below the age of majority were not allowed to take substantial roles that, in the 1960s, the Oddfellows formed a new type of lodge for 16–25-year-olds called Intermediate Lodges. Mike Trenchard explained:

It was a kind of another youth club, but perhaps a more formal one. We had very similar Ritual to the adult lodge. Our regalia was similar to the adult regalia, except it was a different colour. In the same way as adult lodges have jewels, the juvenile lodges and intermediate lodges had something similar. We also had funds and could organise social events and dances to raise money for lodge activities. We used it to buy things like record players and records. The Intermediate Lodges were largely social. Around the

INTERMEDIATE LODGE MEMBERS

Edmondscote and Stratford-on-Avon Intermediate Lodge, 1964.

ODDFELLOWS COLLECTION

Bro. J. GORDON BARNES, I.P.G.M., with members of the Intermediate lodge in the Edmondscote and Stratford-on-Avon district.

country there were several of those Intermediate lodges. We held an annual conference of Intermediate Lodges and a representative of the board of directors came along. When I was 18 I organised the Intermediate Lodge Conference of that year. They had quite a tremendous effect on the society because I can name you half a dozen directors of the society who were leading members of Intermediate Lodges. They had quite a spectacular effect ultimately.

Roger Burley, who joined as a youth, recalled the success of providing social events:

We had such a big age gap in the Oddfellows, they started what they called Intermediate Lodges. The idea was that if the people coming at that age instead of being subjected to these people who wanted to turn the clock back all the time, they would be mixing with people of their own age. My people in the Flower of Kent lodge said, 'You'll have to go along, none of us are in that age group. Go along and find out what it's all about.' I got involved with Oddfellows from all over the country because I was involved in the Intermediate movement. Previously it would have been people that had been elected to district office, probably would be in their 30s. or 40s. I am doing it as a teenager. I found I had trouble with some of the older people. They kept saying 'You can't do that, the rules say this,' so I determined to find out what the rules did actually say. I took the auditors exam for the Oddfellows and passed. Well of course, that gave me a big status amongst the other youngsters.[23]

Brian Merrell recalled the conventions of the early 1960s:

Although I lived in Ilford and Barking, I used to go to Stepney because my father was in that one. You went with the father, you tended to follow your family. I was initiated

into the Gladstone lodge when I was 16 and I used to go to the lodge with my father. He was the secretary of the lodge … there was a lot of old people there, very old people, dressed in formal suits. My lodge was really dying on its feet. We met in a room at the top of a pub in Stepney, Six, seven just sufficient to open the lodge and close it again. I thought 'What am I doing? What's a 16-year-old doing with all these granddads?'

His mother, Dolly, who had many years experience of Oddfellowship, tried to engage with younger people:

Frances Wilkinson was one of those crowned Miss Intermediate.
BY COURTESY OF FRANCES WILKINSON

(By courtesy of D. I. Spencer Photo Agency)

During the conference of Intermediate lodges held at Warwick, the younger members of the Order who constitute these important lodges elected a " Miss Intermediate Lodge 1965 " and the winner, Sister N. Merrell of the Stepney Intermediate lodge, is seen here receiving congratulations from the then D.G.M., Bro. H. L. Hosking, and Sister Hosking.

Nicky Merrell of Stepney Intermediate Lodge was crowned Miss Intermediate Lodge 1965 at a ceremony in Warwick.

ODDFELLOWS COLLECTION

My mother started in the Stepney District what was called an Intermediate Lodge. It was a lodge that catered for the 16 to 21s. It had a Master and a Vice Master and a Secretary and a Treasurer. It adopted all the same principles but it was geared to the younger generation and we started it. We must have had eighteen people. Half the meetings ended up in a mini disco, records and dancing. The Intermediate Lodge did get double figures quite often at their meetings. It ended up as a youth club more than anything.

Frances Wilkinson also recalled a lodge for own age group:

In 1966 that we started the Intermediate Lodge in Bradford and I was instrumental in setting it up along with a lot of other people. We ran a football team [for which her future husband played] and there was a table tennis team that started from the Intermediate Lodge and in fact, I'm told that the tennis teams still runs but not as part of Oddfellowship unfortunately. We organised lots of different things for the district with dances, football and table tennis. We did night hikes and all sorts of different adventurous things. We had a night hike that ended in Baildon Woods and we had a little camp fire and cooked some sausages and we did sponsored things to raise money for charities … It was amazing when we were running the Intermediate Lodge, the support that we had from brothers and sisters of the other lodges, they were keenly interested in the young people.

She went on to recall a triumph at the 1968 Intermediate AMC:

> They had the Miss Intermediate competition that I was lucky enough to win. It was a beauty and personality competition. It was something that was awarded annually from this conference and I don't know how I came to find myself entering it but a few of us found ourselves in it. Not swimsuits but we did wear evening wear and then we had to be interviewed in front of the whole of the evening gathering, I think it was at a dance

Initiation of a new member at the Pride of Clapham Lodge, London, 1939. The tradition was that men would extend their right arms on the word friendship, move their hand to their hearts for the word love and clap once for truth. A similar scene was photographed about sixty years later, also in London.
GETTY IMAGES

An initiation ceremony in the 1990s.
BY COURTESY OF DOUGLAS POTTER

it was at. I can always remember being asked what sort of man I would like to marry and I said I quite fancied a man with a beard, so I think this guy who was interviewing me had a beard and he said 'Will I do?' and I said, 'No, my boyfriend had promised to grow one for me.' I am now married to that man. Yes it was quite a big thing when I came back into the lodge that I was Miss Intermediate and of course, my Dad, being lodge secretary I got a fuss made of and then that year I found myself going to the Annual Conference with my boyfriend Paul and we went on a scooter and I had to lead the dancing with the Grand Master of the Order, it was quite a trauma really.

Roger Burley pointed out that while the adult lodge offered a variety of sporting and social activities there were other attractions to the Intermediate Lodge:

The Intermediate Lodge would go for more, more younger things like discos. We used to go on camping trips and boating trips. I became friends with Oddfellows in different parts of the country. My Flower of Kent lodge at the time was lucky if it got ten people to a meeting.[24]

Members from eight Intermediate Lodges held a meeting, chaired by Chris Merrell about lodge finance, Ritual, initiation ceremonies and recruitment. The May 1964 edition of *The Odd Fellow* tried to report on the activities in an appropriate style:

A swinging time? A get-together? A discussion? A beanfeast? A time for youth? Yes, it was all this and more ... The Stepney Intermediate Lodge were hosts on this occasion and were 'irresponsible' for all the arrangements made ... A wooden spoon was presented to the member who had done the most 'stirring' throughout the debates ... Dancing was to Bro. Bert Cain's Trio ... After this, Stepney meeting intermediate members now say, watch out Leamington in 1965!

In February 1964 a hundred people gathered at the second annual dinner of the Stepney Intermediate Lodge including visitors from 14 lodges. According to 'our own correspondent' the tables were cleared by 8 p.m.', games and dancing continued until 11.30 p.m. 'Drinking stopped at 11 p.m.; hangovers continued for 48 hours'. In March that year 250 people attended a dance organised by the South London District Intermediate Lodge being entertained by the Aces Dance Band and, claimed *The Odd Fellow* 'the star attraction "the Deputies"'. Later that year 170 people went to a 'beat dance' and a second Intermediate Lodge was opened in south London. In the Edmonscote and Stratford-on-Avon District there was a 'Moonlight Twang' (200 people dancing to 'The Rangers') organised by the Intermediate Lodge which raised £20 for the social fund. Mike Trenchard, who was a member of that lodge, went on to organise the Intermediate Lodges conference in 1965 which was attended by members from a number of locations in England. The event included debates, chaired by Derek Winbush who at the time was the Past Provincial Grand Master, coach trips to places of interest in Warwick and

Stratford, and dancing to the Lew Roberts Four and 'the beat of the local Police checking all too regularly on the Bar licence'. In addition, there was a 'personality context for "Miss Intermediate Odd Fellow" of 1965', judged by among others, the local mayor. After parading and being interviewed Nicky Merrell won. Christine Burley was runner-up.[25] Pat Morgan became Vice Grand of the Stepney Intermediate Lodge when it opened, with Nicky and Brian Merrell in junior offices. She then became Noble Grand of her mother lodge.

Pat Morgan was not the only one in her family who enjoyed dancing as she mentioned when she recalled her father:

> There was a dinner in one particular place they went to, Billy Cotton had just become very famous and *I've got a Lovely Bunch of Coconuts* was famous [It was released in 1949]. There were these two district officers in company of people who were a bit snotty nosed; 'One had to respect the chain.' Their chains off, their coats off, [this was her father] they rolled up their sleeves and went on the dance floor with the band and sung *I've got a Lovely Bunch of Coconuts*. This apparently brought the house down but didn't go down too well with the older brethren.

It was perhaps because of the attraction of Oddfellowship to an older generation that it was less attractive to their children. A number of active Oddfellows commented on the difficulty they found in recruiting their own families. Jean Facer wanted her family to be Oddfellows. Her son was made an Oddfellow at the age of three months and remains one. However, she conceded that as his father was secretary of two lodges and his mother also active, 'it has become a little bit rammed down his throat, poor fellow!' James Beard said that his wife was 'a member and my two children are members but they won't put the grandchildren in. So I have talked to them but they won't have it,' and only one of Brenda Francis' daughters, Lesley Bull, became an active Oddfellow, though a number of her grandchildren have been enrolled.

It was not only young people who sought companions in the Oddfellows. Ricky Cubitt joined in 1991 but only became more involved when he met a fellow Oddfellow in Cape Town.

> This gentleman mentioned to my sister about going to the club. He said, 'Oh, you can come along too,' so I said, 'What club is it?' and he said, 'It's an organisation called the Oddfellows.' 'Snap,' I said. He said, 'Well, you would be welcome,' and while I was there I had very pleasant times in their company.

He explained that Oddfellowship was about being a link in a chain of friends, 'it goes further than friendship, its fellowship. You've got to think of other people.' Dorothy Deacon also mentioned South Africa when she spoke about the friendship she found within the Society:

> an Oddfellow could go to a lodge in any area and just say they are a member and they will be welcomed. It's marvellous really because you can do it abroad as well. You go out

to South Africa, if they know you are coming they will be ready for you, just because you are an Oddfellow.

Iris Capel had a similar view. During the war she attended a lodge with her father, which is where she met her husband. After they married and had a child they moved from London and Iris found it more difficult to attend meetings. However, she retained affection for the Oddfellows because it gave her 'the sense that you belong to something, part of a group of people with the same feeling. It's fellowship.' Daphne Harmer said that she felt that you had to put something in before you could take something out, to contribute before you can reap the benefits. Joan Henry felt that for her Oddfellowship was about 'friendship, and interest in other people. It was a very good way to meet people and socialize. Everybody had the same ideas for friendship with love and truth. You could trust people, you could have them in your home and you could go to their homes, there was never any question of any security or anything like that because they were your friends.' She suggested that fellowship meant taking responsibility about those who might join.

> You should not recommend anyone for Oddfellowship unless you personally felt that they were a person who would bring friendship, who was honest and straightforward and you knew them to be a good person. There was no advertisement for people, there is no 'Come and Join us'. It was rather more 'Would you like to join? We think you would probably enjoy it but it's up to you. I would like to recommend you if you would like to come.'

Daphne Harmer reflected on the companionship offered, particularly during two periods of her life.

> The main thing is the friends that I have made because when I moved to Farnborough, I didn't know any one at all, I had one young child and I made so many friends through it which I found was great support after my husband died.

For Jean Facer Oddfellowship offered 'a standard of living and a standard of how to live a life. If somebody you knew wanted a hand, you would be there. That's what going through the various offices in the lodge did for me.' She was delighted to also be a recipient of fellowship.

> When my son was born every time a nurse came into the ward there were cards for me. All from Oddfellows and I think practically every lady in that lodge knitted a matinee coat. I had so many present and matinee coats and flowers it was unbelievable.

For Daphne Stephenson Oddfellowship has:

meant a great deal of friendship and it's meant a great deal of support because we saw that when John had his accident at work and how much support there was from people. A fork lift truck reversed into him and there were so many messages of sympathy and support, we were quite overwhelmed.

A number of Oddfellows mentioned the sense of camaraderie. For Denis Rose Oddfellowship was the family. It is:

a realisation that there has always been somebody or organisation that I could look to if things went very crusty for me. If I needed help or companionship or guidance I know that I could look to the Oddfellows for advice if not help … It is carrying on quietly and doing all the good that they do to the people who are interested in them, they become a family, it's a family a brethren, a brotherhood of Oddfellows.

Oddfellowship was also a family for his father who had had to give up his secretarial and auditing work at the Oddfellows when he lost his sight in 1925.

After that he received a pound a fortnight less his two and sixpence a fortnight contribution. A Sick Visitor used to come to him every fortnight with seventeen and sixpence. They came round with the money and for a chat with my Dad. I don't know whether they enjoyed it but my dad was very glad to have a quarter of an hour's chat with them. He looked forward to them coming, not only to collect the money but to have chat with the old friends.

Sue Doulton Smith made a similar connection when she said that 'being an Oddfellow means you're never alone as a member of a world-wide family'.[26]

Ron Trenchard said, 'You get the friendship of people. If you are ill somebody will ring you up and ask how you are or they will come round and see or they will bring you a plant or a bunch of flowers.' Brenda Francis also mentioned the importance of companionship.

Because I opened my own shop I never met other people. I never had associates to go out with of an evening. Joining the Oddfellows was my way of life. It joined me together with my husband. It was the way to meet people.

George Kilford spoke of the opportunities and the fellowship:

the camaraderie of what was an all male lodge at the time, the discussions and debates, the opportunity to progress through the various positions in the lodge become a chairman and learn that sense of being able to make judgments following discussions. These were all things that interested me because I had always enjoyed getting on my feet or organising things.

Dorothy Deacon mentioned the companionship:

I was involved in a lot of the lodges, we could spend five nights out a week if we wanted to, my friend and I were both very much involved and it was just so very good, to me it was a way of life, In 1987/1988 I was going through a divorce and it was the Oddfellows that kept me going, you are always aware that if there is anything like that, that the friendship of the Oddfellows will always help you get through situations like that.

In this century Phil Norman's interest was also in camaraderie. In his account he made a connection to his father, who was not an Oddfellow but a member of the Royal Ancient Order of Buffaloes which Phil joined. He later learnt that the Oddfellows 'readily accepted women'. His wife and he joined 'because it was something we could do together'. Keith Adamson said he had a sense of security and affection because he was welcomed in all the branches. 'The ethos and the support and the friendship is exactly the same wherever you go. That's the good thing about it. If I go on holiday and I want something or I've got a problem, I know that I can turn to somebody and say "Help" and they'll be there.' These narratives are not representative of current members or of anybody who subsequently ceased to be a member. What the stories demonstrate is that many within the Society see it as welcoming. These are the people who recruit new members and they present the culture of the Society as warm and friendly.

There are numerous stories of Oddfellows who recruited many members and AMCs used to have ceremonies at which medals for such conduct were awarded. These illustrate the importance to the spread and success of Oddfellowship of individuals talking to their peers. For example, in 1831 an Oddfellow in Glamorgan, John Davies, produced a journal, *Yr Odydd Cymreig* and although it soon folded it appears to have influenced the 'Philanthropic Order of True Ivorites, St David's Unity, Friendly Society' which was established in Wrexham in 1836 with the motto: 'Cyfeillgarwch, Cariad a Gwirionedd' (Friendship, Love and Truth). He, along with John Renie of Monmouth 'carried the Order into South Wales where it has since increased and multiplied exceedingly'.[27] In the 1860s the population of Chipping Norton, Oxfordshire grew by around 16 per cent as new people arrived. James Pontifract from Saddleworth, a former Grand Master of the Saddleworth District Oddfellows, came in about 1867 to work at the mill owned by the largest employer in the town and established a new lodge of which he became the first Noble Grand in 1871. The secretary was also an Oddfellow from Saddleworth. The lodge thrived.[28] The reliance on members making members was recognised by Moffrey, who argued that the growth in membership was a magnificent achievement because it was 'not by compulsion, not by advertisements on street hoardings but by sheer force of its own merits which the love of brethren bear for the Order and its work'.[29] Both Syd Bolton and Mary Wheeler, who were nurses, joined following conversations at work, though both had previously heard of the Oddfellows. While in a church hall in 1950 Syd Bolton noticed on the wall

this very faded certificate 'In memory of the Oddfellows who had died in the 1914–18 war'. That's the first I had ever heard of them. It was quite fascinating. It's got a very nice engraved coat of arms. The next time I heard of Oddfellows I was working as a staff nurse at a mental hospital in Stockport and the chappie I was working with, he stood on one side of the bed and I was on the other side. 'By the way.' he said, 'I've got this, *The Oddfellows Year Book* you might be interested in joining.' I took the book and I read it all up … I said to this chap, 'Get us an application form.' I went to where they were meeting and gave the secretary the form and he said 'Very good. Nice to meet you.'

In 1967 Mary Wheeler, whose father had been an Oddfellow, was working in Huddersfield:

While I was on the ward I saw a 'Get Well' Card from the Oddfellows. I spoke the lady in question and she told me about the local lodge and invited me to go down. I went to the all-female lodge which is the Queen Mary, Huddersfield.

Terry Moore encouraged family, neighbours and those with whom he worked to join and when following illness he received convalescence care provided by the Oddfellows he recruited three new Oddfellows while at the Convalescence Centre. As he said: 'I'm an avid recruiter. When I see someone who will benefit I talk to them.' The Unity found it difficult to compete with the insurance companies in terms of advertising. 'They spent large sums on advertising, whereas we ploughed profits back into the funds of the Order,' noted the Grand Master, Brother J. W. Morgan in 1964.[30] Encouraging members to make members was cheaper and more effective. H. A. Andrews argued that while 'national advertising might be good for some commodities the personal touch was far more ideal for recruitment to the Order'.[31] Dorothy Deacon explained:

It was by word of mouth that you joined, if you knew someone you would say, 'How about coming and joining the Oddfellows?' You had to be welcomed into the society you didn't just join it … You had to recommend a friend to become a member, part of the Ritual says that if you recommend that person to become a member you have got to be sure that they would suit the society.

One problem with this approach was that it was slow work. The issue has long been pertinent within working-class associational culture. A question in *Labour Prophet*, 1895 made that clear:

I would ask the Socialist accountant to work out the following proportion sum: if it takes five years to make ten typical English boys into good citizens, how many Socialists will have to undertake the task to make England a Socialist state in 100 years?'

G. B. Shaw made a similar point in a lecture on 'The Ideal of Citizenship', 1909:

War memorials – this one is from Brighton – honoured dead
brethren. Such memorials could also promote the Society to the
living as Syd Bolton mentioned when he recalled how he came
to learn about the Unity.

Their programme was 'We will explain our good
intentions and our sound economic basis to the
whole world: the whole world will then join us at a
subscription of a penny a week; then, the whole of
society will belong to our society and we shall become
society, and we shall proceed to take the government
of the country into our hands and we shall inaugurate
the millennium'.[32]

Douglas Potter recalled a song with a similar message:
'May every good fellow become an Oddfellow and every
Oddfellow a good fellow be. If all the good fellows
would join the Oddfellows, what jolly good fellows
would Oddfellows be.'
    Despite the problems associated with the recruitment
of people one by one, recent recruitment campaigns have confirmed that those members
introduced by other members tend to stay for longer. George Kilford mentioned the difficulties
of other strategies.

We've had a policy in recent years of cold mail shots and lots of people have been
allocated to various districts and lodges. That's not the easiest of starts. A lot of these
people expected to be looked after and taken to meetings.

Although as early as 1916 the case had been made for centralised rates and benefits, which
would have made national advertising easier, it was only in the 1990s that such a scheme was
introduced.[33] This was, George Kilford argued, due to the energy of Derek Winbush and it
did not significantly increase membership. At the same time there was a mail shot to over
25,000 people which also failed to increase membership.
    The creation of the NHS and other state welfare measures reduced people's perceived need
for mutual insurance. Fewer people joined or remained within the Society. The lower numbers
put a larger burden on those who remained and reduced the social network of membership.
There were fewer lodges and this led to more people allowing their membership to lapse.
Encouraging families to become engaged may have led to false expectations, for example that
attending the AMC was a family holiday and not framed by the need for one or more parents

to act as Deputies. Moreover, while trips to the pantomime were part of the appeal of the Society, they were not the core business of the Society and arranging them may have been a distraction for hard-pressed officers. Recruitment of sons by fathers had been common in the past. Since the war sons, and daughters, have had more options and less inclination to follow their parents. Recruitment was also difficult because it relied on individual effort. Although Syd Bolton's earliest memory of the Oddfellows was seeing its symbol displayed, which harks back to those who must have seen the banners on parades a century earlier, it continued to be largely held within the Society that the most effective form of recruitment was by members who continued to recruit others like them. Brenda Francis wanted to play tennis with other young people while Kath Vernon was both recently bereaved and retired and was asked to join by another widow. Even when structural changes were made which made national recruitment easier, there was no rush to join. The message of Oddfellowship appeared diffuse not distinctive and, while there were attempts to connect it to, for example, The Beatles, other organisations were able to make such connections with greater effect.

III   Investment strategies

As membership fell, lodges began to merge, sometimes to form mixed sex rather than single sex lodges, and to close. This led to the breaking of local ties and greater difficulties for many who wished to attend meetings as they had to travel further. This led to further declines in membership. The number of Oddfellow lodges fell from 2,453 registered lodges in 1972 to 1,565 a decade later and 171 by 1992. Pat Morgan spoke of a 'cull'. 'Every time we close a lodge we close a shop window,' said the Grand Master, J. W. Morgan in 1964. Roy Morris described how in Birmingham after the sale of the lodge building in the city centre the lodge moved to Aston 'which was about a mile and half out of the city centre and that was more difficult to get to, so that the attendance seem to fade'. The lodge then moved two more times and although this meant it was centrally located members no longer lived in the area. Roy Morris mentioned one couple who travelled 30 miles each way and another with a round trip of 40 miles.

Syd Bolton, when talking about Stockport, suggested that sometimes rationalisation was not done on strictly rational grounds:

> When we started amalgamation of lodges we said we would amalgamate them all but we are not going to lose the oldest lodge in the Unity. Although that wasn't actually the most powerful or popular, we deliberately transferred all the members and funds into that one lodge so that we could keep the honour of being the oldest lodge in the world kind of thing.

He also pointed out that when fourteen lodges in his district amalgamated there was a reduction in the variety of activities. The unpopularity of mergers was also noted by Ann Harris:

> I was much more interested when we were a business lodge, when we became more social

I became less and less interested. We were taken over by another district and they do a lot of their social events in Harlow. Watford to Harlow in the winter, it's cross country.

Pat Morgan also expressed her worries:

In the late 70s membership was going down and Manchester decided that any lodge that had got less than 500 members had to amalgamate with another lodge. We started to do the cull, which was very sad. We had to do another cull in the 90s and we finished up with three lodges, then it came to it that we had to do it again.

The story of Old Elm Lodge, Chipping Norton can be used to stand for the fate of many lodges. In 1924 it had over 900 'state members' and 819 voluntary members who wished to supplement their National Insurance benefits. Voluntary membership fell to 765 by 1930 and 707 by 1940 while the average age grew from 35 in 1906 to 43 by 1931. In 1947 the district chair appealed to members to 'double their efforts to maintain the voluntary side of the Order'. The Old Elm did not fare as badly as other lodges in that it still had 587 members in 1950, but only 383 a decade later. In 1970 there were 340 and 214 by 1982, a year when only one person joined the Lodge. Posts were unfilled and there were few young people. By the mid-1980s 40 per cent of the members were aged 65 or over, and the Society launched a booklet about bereavement, *Dealing with death*. The business affairs were transferred to a financial lodge in Cheltenham and although the lodge continued to exist for a little longer, its meetings ceased to occur.[34]

The problems which arose when lodges closed were recognised. However, keeping them open was difficult. For example in the 1920s the 40 lodges of the Worcester area opened their own District Hall with a bar and a dance hall which was the base for a Dance School.[35] However, numbers dwindled and the hall was sold in 2000. Despite the concern about the adverse effects of merging lodges, many closed. Roger Burley explained:

The writing was one the wall for us after the war. We needed larger units. There just wasn't the rationalisation that there should have been at that particular time which meant it had to be much more draconian in 1988. The amalgamations then were pretty scary. A lot of people voted with their feet, we never saw them again because their branch had gone. Some of them left without even benefits.

As an investment strategy the maintenance of a network of lodges appeared to be of less value in the late twentieth century than it had in the early nineteenth century.

The Oddfellows also faced lack of concern within Westminster. In 1948 Beveridge expressed enthusiasm not for state intervention but for the Oddfellows. He argued that the government had only accepted parts of his report, *Social Insurance and Allied Services* and that he had not intended to undermine the friendly societies. He employed a metaphor of the family that echoed many of the Oddfellow references to brotherly love:

They have rejected my proposal to use the friendly societies as responsible agents for administrating State benefit … The marriage of 1911 between the State … and the voluntary agencies … has been followed by complete divorce. The State, like a Roman father, has sent the friendly societies back to live in their own house. The State is now engaged in constructing a complete and exclusive administrative machine of its own … The Act commits the State to setting up a centralised bureaucratic machine. Whether any such machine can grapple with the fundamental problem of sickness benefit, of reconciling a sound finance with sympathy and intimate local handling is uncertain.

Beveridge had been elected as a Liberal MP in 1944, wrote *Why I am a Liberal*, in 1945 and went on to become leader of the Liberals in the House of Lords. The Liberal Party was proud of the connection. Its 1945 manifesto stated that

mankind is a prey to Fear – fear of poverty and want through unemployment, sickness, accident and old age. With the Beveridge schemes for Social Security and Full Employment, the Liberal Party leads a frontal attack on this Fear.[36]

Beveridge concluded his *Voluntary Action. A report on methods of social advance*, by expressing his desire for the restoration of the conditions in which the Victorian pioneers of social advance had done their work. This was

so that at last human society may become a friendly society – an Affiliated Order of branches, some large and many small, each with its own life in freedom, each linked to all the rest by a common purpose and by bonds to serve that purpose. So the night's insane dream of power over other men, without limit and without mercy shall fade. So mankind in brotherhood shall bring back the day.[37]

In his response to Beveridge's *Voluntary Action* the Labour Minister, Baron Pakenham the Chancellor of Duchy of Lancaster, stressed that voluntary associations 'must be encouraged to continue to render great and indispensable services to the community', while the Prime Minister, Clement Attlee, who had, like Beveridge, been involved in voluntary social action in east London, emphasised the importance of 'the valuable lessons to be learnt from a study of the devices adopted by the great industrial democratic bodies' and the need for partnerships between paid officials and volunteers.[38] However, Beveridge's party was not in government, Attlee wrote those words in 1920 and there was little practical support for the Oddfellows during the years of the dramatic decline in the number of members.[39]

Whichever direction the Society wished to take its investment plans, it was limited by the strategies of earlier generations of Oddfellows and by the restraints placed on friendly societies by government. Throughout its existence there have been a number of reasons why the Oddfellows wanted to open its own halls. Halls provided an image of the Society. Commercial insurance companies were among the first to develop offices which made statements about the importance, rectitude and prudence of the owners. The Royal Exchange Assurance Corporation put an image of its office in the City of London on its publicity material. It was near to the Bank of England as were the offices of many other insurance companies. The Amicable's office, built in 1793 in Fleet Street, resembled the Treasury building in Whitehall and many offices sought to appear distinctive and significant.[40] Similarly, many Oddfellow Halls reflected the values of the Society. The association between drinking and Oddfellowship was deplored by many and some within the Society wished to appear respectable by staying away from pubs. Even Samuel Smiles, a supporter of friendly societies, only rather grudgingly recognised the need to meet in pubs. He said

> To some it may seem vulgar to associate beer, tobacco or feasting with the pure and simple duty of effecting an insurance against disablement by sickness; but the world we live in is vulgar and we must take it as we find it, and try to make the best of it.[41]

Although one publican, in advertising the sale of his property, the Chetham Arms, announced that 'a numerous lodge of Oddfellows' met there, others did not see such activity in a positive light.[42] In 1900 the Minority Report of the Royal Commission on the Liquor Licensing Laws concluded, 'it is extremely undesirable that Benefit Societies should hold their meetings in public-houses'. The Oddfellows' Parliamentary Agent noted that it was difficult to book pubs as members were so abstemious.[43]

The Unity celebrated when it gained control over its own space. In 1839 P. S. Tyson wrote a song to mark the laying of the foundation stone of the Oddfellows' Hall in Scarborough. It refers to the intention 'to ease each Brother's woes [and] to dry the tears from Widows' eyes and guide the orphan youth' when the members 'can freely meet in our Odd Fellows' Hall!'[44] In the same year an Oddfellows Hall was opened in Addingham, near Leeds, the occasion being marked by a band and a procession of Sunday School scholars and Lodge members. Members of the Foresters also attended. The hall had no bar but instead a library and reading room and provision for holding classes.[45] It was also in that year that the 64 lodges of Leeds decided to build their own hall. It was agreed that if shares of £1 were sold, and no member was permitted to won more than five, then £12,000 could be raised.[46] To build its hall Sheffield decided to raise £9,000, in shares of £1 each, payable, after a deposit of 1s. at the rate of 6d. a fortnight.[47] The opening of Halifax Hall in 1840 was celebrated with a procession, a dinner for about 1,500 people.[48] In 1855 a Past Grand Master of St Thomas Lodge, London argued that owning a hall 'would remove the stigma of being a pot-house affair and I have no doubt it would induce many persons of respectability to join the order who now stand aloof'. John Harris of Marc Anthony Lodge added that a hall would attract 'those who are at present averse to entering taverns as place of meeting', while E. J. Filsell noted that sometimes meeting were curtailed when another group wanted to use the same room.[49] In 1881 when the Unity opened a club house in Coventry business was transacted there but there was also a snooker table, a skittle alley and sales of beer. There were complaints about the beer from one lodge. In addition, halls advertised the solidity and values of the Oddfellows and could be opened

Although expensive to build and to maintain, Oddfellow halls were a source of considerable pride to members, a place where they could set out the furniture in the way they wanted and create a haven of Oddfellowship. These photographs show the hall at Dover (*above*), a plaque on the early hall at Pontypridd and ornate sculpture and shield on the Oddfellows Hall at Forrest Road, Edinburgh.

BY COURTESY OF ZACH PARADIS (DOVER); STEVE ANDERSON (PONTYPRODD); EFRAFAN DAYS (EDINBURGH)

There was often considerable celebration when a hall was opened. This material was produced for the opening of a new Oddfellows' Hall in Watford in 1925.

BY COURTESY OF ANN HARRIS

"OUR HALL"

I.O.O.F.   M.U.F.S.

PROGRAMME

Opening Ceremony

OF THE
ODDFELLOWS' HALL
ST. ALBANS ROAD
◇ WATFORD ◇
SATURDAY, MAR. 28, 1925
BY THE
GRAND MASTER *of the* ORDER
(BRO. H. H. BRIMBLECOMBE)

ARCHITECT:
MR. W. GRACE, A.R.I.B.A.

BUILDERS:
Messrs. GEO. WIGGS & SONS

CHAIRMAN:
BRO. W. SWAIN, P.P.G.M.

C. H. PEACOCK, LTD.
PRINTERS, WATFORD

with elaborate, public ceremonies. In Grimsby the hall was opened with a public dinner and shortly afterwards visited by the Queen while in Lancaster the local economic and political elite attended the opening of a hall.[50] The Bromsgrove hall was opened by the Rev. F. C. Davies, the Grand Master of the Order.[51] In 1966 a new hall was opened in Reading with both a formal ceremony and an 'unofficial opening' by 'Miss Unity 1966' (who, reported *The Odd Fellow*) was 'Bro. R Porton dressed as a ravishing blonde'.

A hall could also be used by others, thus promoting the fraternal charity of which the Oddfellows were so proud. Tony Viney recalled how the hall in Brighton was used:

> I received instructions to attend a medical inspection in preparation to being called up for the Forces at seventeen. This took place in The Oddfellows' Hall in Queens Road.[52]

Ann Harris referred to the war effort of the Oddfellows in her town when her lodge turned itself into a branch of the Women's Voluntary Service:

> They went out to soldiers coming back into Watford Junction, injured, hungry, homeless because of the bombing. The Oddfellows Hall had a kitchen where food would be prepared there for evacuees and then transported in [her aunt] Min's car and a car provided by Watford Borough Council driven by Chris Winch who also became a member of the lodge. We managed that until we got a Mobile Canteen which could provide two hundred meals at a time. At one stage over 14,000 evacuees within a two or three week period were catered for. Pride of Watford at that time was the largest woman's lodge in the Unity and the members were doing war work, some ATS some ARP, canteen workers,

ambulance drivers and there was also a large knitting group. 22 hour day on the canteen was quite often usual especially during the evacuation of France.

In the 1960s the Oddfellows of south London allowed the Grand United Order of Oddfellows to use its hall. Roger Burley added:

> In south London we were particularly friendly with them for a long time because they used to use one of our Oddfellow halls for their meetings, so we got on extremely well. Coincidentally, the Grand Master of their Order came from south London at the same time as I was Grand Master of our Order, which increased our friendship.

There were difficulties for those lodges without their own hall. Andrew Porter remembered that when he joined the atmosphere might have put off some people:

> They didn't have a lodge room. It was a very poor lodge in a very poor district in a poor area. They tended to pay out the maximum benefits they could so they never had any or much spare money to go around but they made sure that the members got what they deserved and what they could afford to give them. It was typical old men in a smoky room.

Douglas Potter mentioned that some lodges shared accommodation. His lodge had owned its own property since 1929. The lodge room has panelled walls, an All-Seeing Eye and signs painted on the furniture 'so that everybody knew what it was about ... knew exactly where they were going to sit'. It was rented out to other lodges: 'it was agreed at the time there that any lodges in the district, they were welcome to hire the room. When I became Secretary I was called the Duchess for Duchess House because I used to send the rent notice to them.' However, it was difficult to hold meeting there and the building was sold with a room leased back to the lodge for 125 years. A change of landlord rendered the lodges of Kettleshulme and Taddington homeless. There was also the expense of room rental. Andrew Porter, who became secretary of the Will of Salvation lodge in 1981, said:

> We used to have an annual Christmas Party but eventually this petered out because of lack of support, the kids weren't turning up. We hired a school hall one evening near Christmas and it cost us a lot of money to hire. Only about a dozen kids turned up. That was when we decided that we wouldn't go any further.

There were, however, often problems with the investment in property. The hall which was supposed to be used for the AMC on the Isle of Man in 1841 still required further work even as the Deputies arrived. It had to be sold by the coroner in 1842. It was only the intervention of a railway company which stopped a financial collapse of the King Street Hall, Birmingham. It was removed when New Street Station was built. This did not deter members from the building of a new Oddfellows' Hall for 1,000 people in Upper Temple Street in 1849. Legislation in the 1850s allowed lodges to appropriate part of their funds to purchase buildings to hold meetings, but there were legal constraints and difficulties.[53] In Barnsley the hall foreclosed at a cost of £2,300. In Halifax in 1872 the hall paid no interest on the money invested which caused local lodges financial difficulties as, according to one local commentator, their funds were 'locked up in the building and cannot be converted into cash'.[54] In 1957 the Unity had over £17,000 invested in halls but a survey of the West Country carried out in the previous year found one hall with part of its name missing, its windows dirty and in need of repairs and another with a tiny notice 'no larger than a shop keeper's tobacco licence notice' which was in an even worse state of repair.[55] By the 1980s many Oddfellows had moved away from town and city centres, as Roger Burley recalled:

> We had to sell our property because our members didn't live nearby. They were finding it increasingly difficult to get to it because of where they lived and the ones that had lived locally were moving out or died.

The offices of the Oddfellows in Grosvenor Street, Manchester, were used by the Society for over a century. By decorating their buildings in a manner reminiscent of a medieval cathedral the Society was able to enlist the stones as teachers. The walls provided clues as to how the interior space was used and the values of the Society. External decorative stonework such as this informed passers-by and members that this was an edifice owned by an association with taste and wealth which also recognised the skills of working men. The building is now home to the Language Centre of the University of Manchester.
ODDFELLOWS COLLECTION

Inside the Grosvenor Street offices mosaics lent the Society a sense of solidity, while stained-glass windows associated the Society with Christian values. Members could gaze upon symbols that would have been familiar to many Victorians. The beehive represented collective activity leading to prosperity; the lamb with the flag with a cross inscribed upon it symbolised Jesus and more generally humility and innocence. The crossed keys were a sign of security and stored treasures, and the hourglass a reminder that death comes to us all. In the centre were pictures of the plants associated with different parts of the UK (rose, thistle, shamrock and leek), and enveloping the lower part of the design was the Latin for friendship, love and truth. Above was the terrestrial globe denoting the worldwide spirit of benevolent Oddfellowship. At the pinnacle was the heart in an open hand. It signified that a requirement of friendship, the hand, required affection, the heart. It made it clear that charity could not be cold, but should be given with love.

ODDFELLOWS COLLECTION

Although there were financial benefits to ownership, for much of the post-war period in financial terms the ownership of halls and the resultant illiquidity of assets may have been a time-consuming investment strategy which offered a low expectation of a reasonable return.

The Oddfellows had long owned property. In the late nineteenth century there are examples of lodges that held small amounts of local property and received low returns.[56] By the 1920s the Loyal Constitution Lodge, Great Easton, Lincolnshire, owned two brick-built houses in Church Bank, the houses in The Jetty and a field at Drayton. The rental income was low, and fell even more during the Depression, and as there was a need for upkeep and modernisation it is doubtful if the Lodge made much money on its investment.[57] In 1935 the Secretary of the Order, H A Andrew had to make it clear that the lodges of the Society did not invest in slum homes.[58] In 1936 £200,000 was invested in mortgages and in 1937 the investments made by the Society were largely in mortgages and ground and chief rents.[59] In 1938 the AMC heard how the mortgages and property ownership were 'growing fields' for the Society, particularly as the government's policy of 'cheap money' (a bank rate of 2 per cent) restricted the possible local and national investments by the Society.[60] After the Second World War the Oddfellows increased its investment in mortgages to members. These had been available long before the war. For example, in the 1880s the Loyal Princess Charlotte Lodge, Newton Heath, Manchester provided for members to borrow money to purchase their own houses by fortnightly payments of 5s. 8d. per £100. The house became the property of the member in about 19 years.[61] In 1890 the Victoria Lodge, Chester began to advance sums to members and by 1901 13 had repaid the money and owned their own houses with another 47 still making payments.[62]

While many of the terms of the post-war mortgages are very unfavourable to the Society by later standards, they were beneficial to the members to whom the mortgages have been granted. In 1940 the total invested funds, over £8.6 million, was largely held in municipal and government securities and mortgages on land and buildings.[63] In 1951 at the Torquay AMC the Grand Master spoke of the 'tendency for local District and Lodge investment to develop, particularly in the direction of mortgage investment on the basis of periodic repayment of principal, which is a good sign'.[64] In 1953 the main item of investment was mortgages, £2.4 million of the £5.3 million invested in that year. In 1957 the Unity had investments of £5.7 million, over half of that sum was invested in mortgages.[65] Just as in the UK the Oddfellows diversified into investment in property and mortgages, so the Society in Australia had earlier made loans to enable members to buy houses, and by 1923 the Oddfellows in New South Wales was the largest building society in Australia.

The emphasis in both the UK (and Australia) on mortgages might have ensured that fewer members left. In the UK in 1949 more than 44,000 left the Oddfellows, in 1952 the membership figure fell by about half that figure. Mike Trenchard said that 'Mortgages were a central part of the society in the early part of the twentieth century. It was a safe investment and because they were lending to members they used a very cheap interest rate.' Syd Bolton agreed, 'Stockport District, of which I was Trustee, had rented property, a couple rows of terraced houses and we also used to give mortgages. We had a lot of mortgage business and lent money to members.'

Brenda Francis mentioned that it was the Oddfellows who

> set me up in business. We had one or two mortgages when my shop expanded. We had the fortune of buying the house next door to where we lived so that when my parents retired we bought it for them with the help of the Oddfellows.

Roy Morris recalled that:

> my father had a mortgage from the Royal Victory Lodge for his business. If you had a mortgage from a lodge you couldn't hold a position in the lodge, which was why my father didn't hold a position in the Victory Lodge but he could be the District Secretary for the juvenile lodge and he held office in the various offices in the district as well.

Ken Harding served in the Forces, married and received help from the Oddfellows to get a mortgage on a bungalow 'which wanted gutting before we could move in'. A builder and Provincial Grand Master C. H. Martin:

> didn't only get the loan for us, but did some of the building work, he was a tower of strength as was his entire family. Kindness and thought for others was his very life! We felt very much in debt to the Oddfellows so we took on the running of the youth club.[66]

Tony Crouch, a Trustee for many years, recalled his own mortgages and those of others. He said that mortgages were seen as long term investment and that borrowers had to provide 10 per cent as a deposit. The Trustees would value the properties but not ask members about their earnings.

> Our Trustees did the first industrial mortgage. It was with Duffin Containers, Ted Duffin was a member. He had a factory and he needed to expand it and came to the Oddfellows for a mortgage.

In regard to his own mortgages Tony explained that his wife and he wanted accommodation in 1951:

> You couldn't get on the council housing list so we bought a big house and let the top half and that was £1,800. I put up £180 deposit and I borrowed £1,620 for the Widows and Orphans Fund at 4.5 per cent. I think I was earning at that time £275 a year in the Health Service. I had a mortgage which I paid off when I was going to move to another house in 1958. I knew that Grays Thurrock [Lodge] had got money so I borrowed about £3,000 from them and that's when I gave up being a Trustee because you can't lend to yourself.

Jean Facer recalled that while she and her husband Stan did not have a mortgage from the Oddfellows, they were helped with their accommodation:

When Stan was secretary of the Lodge in Pinner, they had two little cottages there. After we were married four years the tenant in one of the cottages had to move away. The cottage became vacant and Stan asked the Lodge Committee of Management if he could take on the tenancy. We were lucky and we lived in one of the cottages of the Lodge for nearly 30 years.

Pat Morgan felt that her father's enthusiasm to promote mortgages and insurance did not stretch as far as it could have done.

In those days you had the lodges or the district help people with their mortgages. My Dad, he'd got a mortgage. He was a great one for arranging mortgages for other people and making sure that they had insurance to cover in case anything happened to any of them but he never did it himself. So when he died we had to manage … I had to take on the mortgage so I was working all hours going to keep up with the mortgage.

These narratives give a clue as to how the Oddfellows survived the last half of the twentieth century when so many friendly societies failed. These were financial decisions, but also personal ones. For Brenda Francis it meant that babysitter could move in next door and allow her to attend lodge nights. Ken Harding felt an obligation to organise 'sausage sizzles'. It was because Stan and Jean Facer were deemed acceptable risks by fellow Oddfellows that they got the cottage they wanted. The sense that recipients needed to reciprocate, to give back more than money to the Society, is a thread running through these accounts. Although Pat Morgan remembered her father's involvement in securing mortgages in a different light she spoke of her sense of mutual aid, of her father helping those within the Society and of her own sense of obligation.

There was a decline in interest in mortgages, particularly after the 1970s house price inflation. Roger Burley remembered this period:

A lot of lodges had War Stock. It was obvious even by the end of the war that it was a lousy investment and that you were stuck with what you had bought. People had to change their investment pattern and some branches went one way, some went another. South London [where he was a member] went into ground rents. When I came onto the District Committee of Management that would have been 1970, we were selling off ground rents. It was obvious that we had to get what we could for them and change our policy rather quickly. When I became District Secretary in 1980 I sold off two big lots and cleared the last ground rents out. It took over ten years to readjust our investment portfolio.

The Oddfellows Hall at Stamford, Lincolnshire. One Stamford resident recalls a song from the Oddfellow meetings of her youth: 'Sunshine corner, oh its jolly fine,/It's for children under 99/All are welcome, seats are given free,/Stamford Sunshine Corner is the Place for me!' (Stamford Memories Gateway)

These investments, like the halls, had social benefits but were insufficiently flexible to make the best financial returns. Winifred Felgate mentioned that her local lodge meeting place, which was owned by the lodge, was 'a bit dilapidated' and had to be sold in 1964. There was another property which failed to make the expected returns. 'We had a tenant who had a mortgage with the lodge because we did lend a lot of money out on mortgages. He failed to keep this mortgage up, so we had to foreclose on him.' It was experiences such as these one which encouraged the Oddfellows to seek a new balance between finance and fraternity, community and commerce.

There have long been calls for the Oddfellows to invest in a range of products.[67] Initially during the post-war period decisions about investment were made at lodge level. Mike Trenchard, explained that 'each lodge had its own investments and any surplus could be transferred to other funds within the lodge maybe to provide additional unpaid benefits, maybe to provide some money for marketing or even for some of the subsidising some of the social events.' Roy Morris recalled the process:

> We used to look after the Lodge's money which my father and his compatriots had gathered together over the pre-war years and early post war years. It was very carefully invested. We used to put it into a variety of [municipal] bonds having them running for various periods of time so that we always had a bond maturing in every calendar year. We were careful in looking after the money. A friend of my father actually took some money out of the lodge. The Investigation Committee, whose members would be selected from lodges all over the country, came in to sort out problems of that nature.

John Winkley recalled the constraints and freedoms of lodge finance:

> All lodges controlled their own finances but they had to do an annual report to the board of directors at Manchester on a set form AR2 and all the things had to be all tied up and equalled and balanced. You could move the interest each year that you earned into certain funds but only in certain percentages so you tried to put what you were allowed in to the funds that you could. There were two funds which I always thought was important, the benevolent fund and the additional benefits. The benevolent fund was an amount you could pay out according to the rules of the order, the additional benefits fund could be used to pay certain amounts to optical and dental and that sort of thing but up to a certain amount. There were some lodges that did avail themselves of that and only paid the smallest amount that they could with the additional benefits. We always tried to pay the maximum and therefore when we allocated the interest each year we put all we could do into those funds which you will see a bit later on did cause a bit of a problem.

Karen Stuart pointed out that few people 'can fully understand a set of accounts when they join', and Andrew Porter reflected that some of the decisions turned out to be riskier than people assumed. He mentioned the Company which was formed when the Mersey Docks and Harbour Board was reconstituted in 1972:

> We have made some poor investments. The Mersey Docks and Harbour Company that the Will of Salvation [the Lodge of which he was secretary] had money in went bust and issued unsubordinated, unsecured stock. We carried all these on our books at ten pence and when the Will of Salvation merged in with the Victory lodge we decided to sell it. We went to the broker and said 'Is it worth anything?' and he said, 'Well they've re-invented themselves and it's worth just as much as it was when you had it before.' So we sold it and made a fortune. We were extremely lucky.

These comments reflect a long term dilemma that the Oddfellows faced. In 1882 a curate and a station-master, neither of them local and both with better formal education than many lodge members, who were agricultural labourers, carried out an audit of the Loyal Constitution Lodge, Great Easton Lincolnshire. They noted the unpaid and illegal loans and the £33

Much of the work of an Oddfellow concerned keeping the books.

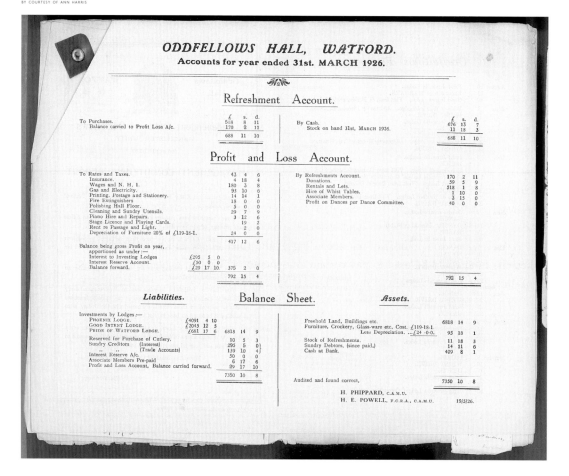

itemised in the expenditure of the sick fund as 'loss thro' mismanagement of former secretary (deceased) and late Treasurer'.[68] This example of mismanagement was not an isolated case. There are many examples of lodges making fraternal loans or miscalculations which crossed the boundaries of legality or involved amassing debt which could not be paid. In Nottingham in 1880 a report to the district's annual meeting indicated both the charity of the Oddfellows and its limitations. Members of the late Rock of Horeb lodge had not saved sufficient funds when younger and they were in need of support. The Oddfellows had guaranteed benefits to the last 70 members of the lodge who, during the last quarter, had paid in under £20 and received over £73. Watson, a Past Grand Master and Corresponding Secretary said that he thought that 'there was no other society in the world or district in the Manchester Unity where so good an act had been performed'. He then cited the example of six members who the society had been compelled to accept from a seceding lodge. They had cost the society over £68 and who had contributed under £7 and the district 'never had nor ever could receive any compensation whatever'.[69] When the *Oddfellows' Magazine* argued that those over the age of 50 had a right to payment, even 'if they should live to the age of Methuselah'. The Reverend J. Frome Wilkinson concluded that, 'The cause of humanity triumphs, but the outraged science of vital statistics avenges itself upon the society as a whole.' John Macnicol summarised the position: 'Mostly societies were generous to their older member – foolishly so, in the opinion of their actuaries.'[70]

The lack of book-keeping skills and understanding of the implications were continuing problems. Eric Ogden provided an example of the post-war version of the dilemma when he explained about Unity book-keeping.

The Unity system was always a bit of a problem for auditors because they couldn't quite understand it. It had to be designed for working-class people who had little training in the finer arts of accountancy and book keeping. The book keeping system was designed for a complete and utter amateur to be able to cope with it. In that sense, it coped remarkably well, it is quite inspired in my view. Anybody could have understood it. It didn't have all the cross linking that you'd do automatically on a computerised book keeping system. It had to be done manually, so you would post a total for the contributions and then you manually had to apportion them in a register for all the member's individual contributions. It was a time consuming job but none the less if you followed the rules it was impossible to go wrong. The people that did go wrong, which was quite often, were the people who didn't follow the rules, trying to cut corners.

Calculations often took a long time to complete as Ian Jones recalled. He started work for the Oddfellows in Grosvenor Street, Manchester, in 1966. His job included calculating the interest payments on the Unity United Investment Fund.

Alan [Powell] and I were destined to spend many hours locked away in the library doing these calculations and then preparing them for typing and checking. The whole process took about six weeks. Computers were devices that only existed in companies that had rooms large enough to store them and it would be several years before the first punched card computing machine was introduced into Unity Office. The interest calculations became a job to be dreaded but now, thirty years later, the whole process takes about one hour to complete. Levies were another headache. Lodges seemed to be levied for everything! Penny per member levies for the Orphan Gift Fund. A two-penny levy (old money) for the Unity Management Fund. A valuation levy for the additional benefits fund and another levy to finance all the other benefit funds. All these had to be calculated manually, typed out, checked and then distributed to the thousands of lodges that existed at that time. There seemed to be so many levies, I often wondered why lodges didn't rise up and storm the building in protest![71]

During a period when the sums of money involved were small, the investment opportunities limited and the accountancy methods unsophisticated the Oddfellows strategies had (without denying the evidence of theft and errors) been successful. In the post war period as the options broadened amateur control became a less desirable option. In 1996 Len Mostyn made the point that the recent legislation gave the Board (or Committee of Management) significant responsibilities and that for elected members to be expected to understand the complexities of the legislation was unrealistic. 'A poor chap hasn't got a chance to learn about the job. It was bad enough in my day but now since the 1992 Act he's got to learn everything.' This was the legislation which enabled friendly societies to sell unit trusts, PEPs and general insurance.

Until 1961 the Oddfellows was not allowed to invest in ordinary shares, being restricted to trustee securities and property. The Trustee Investment Act 1961 gave societies the power to invest in equity investments for the first time. In addition, to investments permitted by societies special powers, broadly in public funds, land and secured loans, including mortgages, societies could make authorised trustee investments. These were divided into 'narrower-range' investments such as government stocks and secured deposits and 'wider range' investments such as fully, paid UK stocks and shares of UK companies that had paid dividends on their shares in each of the previous five years, unit trusts and equities. No more than half the

With this postcard the Oddfellows connected its 1980 AMC to Liverpool, Manchester, Southport, Stephenson's 'Rocket' and the world's first inter-city passenger railway. Possibly a more forward-looking image would have aided recruitment and retention.

Listed in a 1936 directory as living at 6 Council Houses, Blisworth, Northamptonshire, Cyril Paxton poses for the camera here in collar, tie and ribbon, or sash (which denoted his rank). He became a Noble Grand of the Loyal Travellers Home Lodge, No. 2645 Blisworth, during the 1950s.

BY COURTESY OF THE PAXTON FAMILY

money invested could be in either one of the two categories. The aim was protect the value of charitable trust funds. One of the effects of being managed by committees and permanent staff who were not particularly well informed in investment matters was a tendency to invest in the more narrow market known to the individual investor, local authority annuities or War Loan for example. It was Oddfellows' money which went towards rebuilding war-damaged Britain but even so the Society had to adopt a rather complex accounting system and to seek additional advice about investments. Usually the split was made so that the wider range contained those investments which could more readily be sold or would mature earlier in order to facilitate reinvestment in ordinary shares. Each year, the money available for investment has to be divided equally between the narrower and wider ranges and if it is decided to put the whole of the new money into ordinary shares (or an amount greater than 50 per cent), then a transfer of other investments has to be made from the wider range to the narrower range to maintain the appropriate balance. The proportions were changed to 25 per cent narrower and 75 per cent wider range and the two funds were then allowed to managed separately. Over the period since 1961, wider range funds have generally outperformed narrower range funds.

The 1966 Finance Act enabled the Oddfellows to underwrite sums assured in excess of £500, subject to certain restrictions and to establish taxable assurance funds taxed in the same way as mutual insurance companies. The Unity could also underwrite sums assured of up to £200 per member, £3,000 in the case of mortgage protection business. The limits on taxable sums assured were increased over the subsequent years and then abolished 18 years later. The effect was to give lodges more choice and greater opportunities but not greater knowledge or skills. John Winkley mentioned how the Oddfellows had helped to fund the local government's post-war redevelopment:

> I was very lucky actually because I came into it when there were quite high interest rates. We used the Nottingham Council quite a lot, they paid quite good rates and you could put money in for a certain time to mature. I used a five year period so that we had money maturing every five years and then as one matured you would then re-invest it at the best rate you could get. One of the trustees in the lodge he happened to invest in these himself and as I worked as an accountant with a local firm I did most of the banking work, I had a little bit of background into that sort of thing so it came easy.

In 1968 the Friendly & Industrial & Provident Societies Act amended the law regarding audits and actuarial valuations of friendly societies and gave them powers to reinsure their risks. Roger Burley explained that the Oddfellows became constrained and isolated:

> Through the fifties and even the sixties the Oddfellows, all friendly societies, had a rough time from the government. The limits that they could insure for stayed the same until 1975 which was ridiculous because inflation was going wild through that period and it was very difficult for any friendly society to keep pace. A lot of them adapted to it by centralising and not being branch societies any more. They became like mutual insurance companies. The Oddfellows didn't go down that road. It tried to keep its branches for social and welfare side as well as the insurance. A lot of the old traditions that some of the other societies lost, we were able to retain.

The Friendly Societies Act, 1974 consolidated existing legislation while the Finance Act 1975 increased the limit for tax-exempt funds.[72] In 1975 there were 540 members of the National Conference of Friendly Societies. In 1995 it was only 350.[73] Under legislation in the 1980s individuals selling investment-related financial services had to be trained. Many agents were replaced by collectors and many people ceased to trust the new staff. Moreover the labour-intensive system was costly compared to sales made over the telephone. Legislation also restricted the ways in which members could be recruited and services sold. Further regulations restricted the roles that unpaid and unqualified staff could take and placed the Oddfellows in the same category as insurance companies.[74] Although one of the attractions of Oddfellowship was its fraternity and many members testified to the benefits they saw in local flexibility, the Society found itself manoeuvred towards behaving like the commercial sector.

In the 1970s a series of funds, called the Unity United funds, were created in Manchester. Soon most lodges were investing through the Fixed Interest Fund, the International Wider Range Fund and others. This was also a period when there was further debate, including a Special Conference in Blackpool, about the structure of the Society. In the late 1980s it was decided to to promote financial stability by encouraging the amalgamation of lodges. 'Financial Lodges', those with least 500 members and £150,000 worth of funds, were permitted to make investment decisions while 'Unregistered Lodges' (smaller ones) were not permitted to make decisions about investment. The change was also related to the amalgamation and closure of lodges. The number fell from about 1200 to 250 in a decade. As Syd Bolton pointed out, 'once they were all amalgamated the people at Head Office started to take charge of helping with the investment funds and that way we got some very good rates of interest'. Financial Lodges had only limited choices as to where to invest. Syd Bolton noted that the money had to go into 'government stocks, local government loans' and that it was only in the 1990s that the Unity was permitted to trade in shares. Mike Trenchard explained:

> You could only invest in safe securities. Until comparatively recently that meant gilt edged stock or [the now defunct] municipal securities. The board set up in dealing with property or equity investments on a broader scale, mainly blue chip companies administered by advisers directly from Manchester. The bulk of the money still went into safe investments. District Trustees, and I was one of them, had to have a balanced portfolio. It's all very well providing money for mortgages but you've only got a limited amount of money available and you don't want all your money in mortgages. The majority of the money was still in things like gilt edged stock and certainly in the last ten or fifteen years Head Office in Manchester has provided a number of safe investment funds.

Roger Burley said that he was 'a great champion of central investment funds', and that when the opportunity arose to invest more widely in

> companies, stocks and shares as opposed to what we could beforehand which was very restricted. I made it my business to try and extend that to fixed interest securities and then to property and to cash. We've now got a range of investment funds centrally that the branches can invest through. This makes the need for them to have investment skills much less. There's a range of them under the umbrella of the Friendly Societies Act which are tax-free because they are friendly society funds so an individual wouldn't not be able to participate in those. They would have to take a tax-free policy which we've now stopped selling.

These changes did not stop the fall in membership from 192,000 members in 1983 to 184,000 in 1984 and 175,500 in 1985. The Society had viable products, but was finding it difficult to find a market for them. Andrew Porter explained that The *Financial Times* found the 'Acorns and Oak Trees' policy to be 'the best product of its kind on the market but because we were a non-profit organisation, we weren't offering brokers any commission. They weren't pushing it forward so the best product on the market wasn't taken up by anybody because nobody knew about it.' The change in fortunes was recorded by John Winkley:

> Of course in this time now the interest you made had gone right down so quite a lot of the investments went to accounts which were held by Manchester. They would recommend but you didn't have to go along with them and of course we sold quite a lot of property as well which really made quite high funds for us. We kept the hall in Uppingham until it was decided that we would no longer go along as a non-registered lodge.

During the 1990s the trends towards greater central control were reinforced by further legislation. In 1992 the law stated that, in common with insurance companies, the Oddfellows had have an Appointed Actuary. This person's duties included the monitoring of the insurer's finances. In addition, the Oddfellows had to submit an annual actuarial valuation return. The law also made it impossible to create a new friendly society along the lines of the Oddfellows. The primary purpose of the Act was to enable existing friendly societies to re-register as incorporated friendly societies with limited liability. New societies could only follow this format. While it might have been designed 'to protect and foster the traditional values of which friendly societies were founded, whilst encouraging them to compete more effectively and secure the future of friendly societies for the foreseeable future', the Oddfellows decided not to be incorporated and thus become a limited company that was permitted to continue to provide financial services.[75] It was felt that incorporation could undermine the autonomy and the social activities of the lodges. Furthermore, there was a need to protect members. Friendly society trustees can sue and be sued on behalf of the society if it is not incorporated whereas an incorporated society would not have trustees but a corporate identity and people could sue the organisation itself. Roger Burley explained that the legislation provided

> insufficient protection for our branches. Branches' money could all be scooped into the centre which we didn't want. Within the framework of our main constitution our branches should be independent, providing they comply with the law of the land and with our main constitution.

John Winkley enjoyed being involved in finance:

> In 1990 there was a big shake up in the Odd Fellows. They had to have so many financial lodges in a district and the other lodges would be unregistered lodges which would only really be places in which people could go to have a meeting without any financial interest at all. There were some people who liked the social side and others who were interested from the running the lodge and seeing what they could do with it and I became involved then with the district.

At that time the Society found it difficult to market its financial products. Others offered better value insurance, insurance companies were merging in an effort to remain viable. Few people knew of the products that the Oddfellows offered and marketing was very expensive. The Sickness, Annuity and Death Fund, out of which small sums were paid, was closed to new members in 1978 and then transferred to the Unity Insurance and Reinsurance Fund which was soon also closed. In 1999 the Increasing Cash Benefit (ICB) Fund was closed to new entrants and as, this affected Junior membership, a new Junior membership package was developed. The Manchester Unity Healthcare fund was losing money and it was closed to new business in 2000. Sue Doulton Smith remembered the various packages:

We tried Manchester Unity Healthcare. It made you a member but there is never an obligation to turn up for meetings which is perhaps, part of the problem. We also did an over-fifties death benefit, insurance where people just paid in that for death benefits which lasted for quite some time. Then we had a link up with Northern Rock [which at the time was a limited company offering mortgages and was not in public ownership] in the 1980s for people who were taking out mortgages and associate membership with the Secretary which was slightly different. It wasn't an insurance product as such. We had the Unity Insurance Endowment Fund which sold insurance. They became members of the society but not quite the same in the branches. They could come to the branches but they didn't get the branch benefits and then we decided in more recent years that we would have to come out of insurance all together because we just weren't attracting enough people to make it competitive and worthwhile, so we finished doing insurance. We decided we wouldn't start any new products. Although we had one of the best products and it was rated as such by some of the national organisations, it just wasn't worthwhile.

The Annual Renewable Sickness fund and the Unity Insurance and Endowment and Retirement Annuity Fund were also closed. Sue went on:

We tried to sell larger amounts of insurance which didn't work awfully well because the bigger players in the insurance field did more in that way and people didn't know our name the same. People would go for the Liverpool Vics and the Norwich Unions of this world because they knew them as an established name, whereas they didn't think of Manchester Unity as a secure provider in that way. [Liverpool Victoria was the largest friendly society in the UK. It rebranded as LV= while Norwich Union became Aviva.] You didn't attract newer people in other than through personal contact, which is always the best way of making membership in any case. We did sell to small companies that had small amounts of people employed. They would do a sickness table through the Oddfellows.

These developments did not mean that the Oddfellows ceased to be a regulated society. A new Friendly Societies Commission was created which became part of the Financial Services

Authority (FSA) in 2001. The FSA registered and validated the rules of the Oddfellows. By 2005 the rationalisation of long term business, which had been under way since the Society closed to new insurance business in 2000, had led to pay-outs to those in the Branch Sick Annuity and Death Funds and the ICB. There were only four strands left. The Unity Insurance and Endowment and Retirement Annuity Fund and the Unity Insurance and Reinsurance Fund contained a variety of business both non-profit and with-profit. There were also 156 personal accounts (introduced in 1954 and 1970) of with-profit sickness and savings contracts and a pension service to the Society, the Meritorious Service Pensions, which later became the Unity Meritorious Service Award. In addition, many financial branches invested in the Unity United Investment Fund which closed to new business in 1998 and the Unity United (Fixed Interest) Investment Fund. There were also three equity funds and the Unity United (Property) Investment Fund. Roger Burley explained that the Oddfellows was still administering insurance products but it was 'extremely difficult'. He added that in the

> long term life business, everybody has to be qualified before you can sell it. Our thing was always word of mouth. An ordinary member would introduce another member. We are not allowed to do that now. We did try for a period of time, having full time representatives going out doing the selling but we found we couldn't compete with the High Street name like the Pru. That didn't work. It was bringing in insurance members but it wasn't bringing in people who would then attend a lodge which was part of what we wanted to keep going. It was keeping the society going but we were going down the route of the societies that had more or less closed all their branches and were really being run as like mutual insurance companies.

Even though the Oddfellows has remained committed to its branch structure, one outcome of the shift of power, dictated by regulatory authorities, towards the Committee of Management was that 2002 saw the first three day AMC since the early nineteenth century. This was partly because the areas which could be debated had been reduced. This was a matter which concerned some Deputies. George Kilford said, 'The floor of the conference thought they were being robbed', while Keith Adamson remarked that, 'It used to be five days and when the board wanted to reduce it from five days to three, ooh dear …'

The Oddfellows continued to have an interest in financial services. In 1992 it accepted a transfer of engagements from the Philanthropic Mutual Life Assurance Collecting Society which was based in Hyde, Cheshire and in 2006 the Oddfellows took over the insurance business of the Ideal Benefit Society. The 8,000 policy holders did not automatically become Oddfellows. They had to make independent decisions to join. It has also continued to maintain a credit union, a co-operative financial institution provided banking facilities, largely simple savings and loan products, to the financially excluded. In the UK membership of credit unions grew from 232,137 with assets of £124 million in 1991 to 658, 618 with £680 million in 2000. This was under 1 per cent of the population. In parallel, in Australia in 1985 the Manchester Unity (NSW) Credit Union was formed. By the end of the century it had evolved from an in-house savings and loans society to include banking and saving facilities, personal loans and credit cards. Under legislation passed in 1989 in Australia the Society was incorporated and, in 1990, it became 'The Manchester Unity Friendly Society in New South Wales'. The structure and governance of the society was dramatically altered, and then revised again following the 1997 Friendly Societies Act. A separate Grand Lodge was established to manage fraternal activities while the Directors concentrated on commercial operations. In the UK during the summer of 2000 the three locally based Manchester Unity Credit Unions held talks and decided to merge into a single Manchester Unity Credit Union, a financial, not-for-profit co-operative owned its members, all of whom were Oddfellows resident in the UK. This was approved by the 2001 AMC. These changes, while they did not arrest the decline in membership, attest to the vitality of the Society. It was trying a variety of strategies in order to comply with regulations and to retain and gain members.

IV   Conclusion

The period since the conclusion of the Second World War has been a difficult one for many organisations with semi-autonomous branches. The Labour Party centralised much of its activity and also lost members.[76] Some co-operative and mutual enterprises saw their activities taken over by the state. This is the case with those parts of the co-operative movement which were nationalised and those parts of the work of the Oddfellows which were taken over by Whitehall. In the period after the Society lost its approved status it struggled to find a new role. It offered the health care that the NHS could not, mortgages and a variety of social events that attracted families and young people. However, like others within the non-profit and voluntary sector, it struggled to compete with alternative leisure and financial products. The closure of lodges and other adaptations to new circumstances were not always popular, but appeared as the best option within a more subtly differentiated and specialist market where the same organisation was not deemed appropriate for such a wide variety of activities.

Neither the co-op nor the Oddfellows were organised like companies of the 1950s in which managers were relatively free to manage. In both there was democratic control by the membership which may have hindered the swift implementation of clear decisions. In the co-op only three per cent of the membership participated in elections or meetings and there was also a low participation rate within the Oddfellows.[77] This enabled sectional interests to gain control while the commercial sector provided cheaper and more effective services. Many within the mutual sector sought to bring about change in social and economic relations and to promote ideas which were seen as less relevant by the 1950s, such as the education of the membership and political and religious neutrality. Food safety legislation (the co-op had always prided itself on selling unadulterated food), anti-trust and monopolies legislation, state education and National Insurance and the National Health Service all removed the urgency of some of their original principles. In the 1950s the solution favoured for the co-op by the secretary to the first Co-operative Commission, Labour MP Tony Crosland, was a full-time executive management, appointed on merit at market rates, he also wanted to restrict the role of elected members to setting only broad policy. Crosland argued that the co-op was letting down the consumer by failing to compete. The Co-operative Insurance Society, with three million customers by the 1990s was still of importance but its membership had fallen. The retail co-operative movement had a similar formation to the Oddfellows with branches which connected members through shopping and also social activities. The Co-operative Wholesale Society was of significance but not be the biggest organisation in the food retail sector.

By the 1980s and 1990s there was extensive recognition of a widening welfare delivery gap. Costs rose while lower birth rates and greater life expectancy increased the number of people dependent on the welfare system. Governments emphasised that individuals should contribute to the cost of their personal welfare. Although private sector provision increased, there was wider recognition of the core competence and competitive advantages in this field of friendly societies. They handled the regular collection of small cash sums, engendered consumer trust and confidence and acted as vehicles for the development of social capital among financially and socially disadvantaged communities. On the left Labour MP Dr John Marek thought the mutuals could counter the government of Margaret Thatcher, the mutual society being 'a concept that ought to be cherished and developed. It rises above mere capitalism and profit making … it is noble and should be encouraged.' Donald Dewar, then Labour social security spokesman, said 'The friendly society movement has a very good pedigree. I believe there is a continuing place for it. We're certainly happy to talk with them about how they should be managed.' The left-wing Institute for Public Policy Research stated that self-help and specifically friendly societies must 'be at the heart of tomorrow's Welfare State'.[78] The think-tank Demos argued that mutuals could be could provide the heart to the idea of the Third Way proposed by Tony Blair and Gerhard Schroeder. Professor Nigel Waite, Executive Director, Financial Services Research Forum, agreed that friendly societies were potentially 'an important part of a Third-Way approach to solving the problems associated with the financing of future welfare'. Labour Minister Frank Field advocated proposed that 'stakeholder' welfare could be administered through friendly societies. A decade later another Labour Minister, Ed Balls, felt friendly societies could be vital in meeting the needs of consumers.[79] On the right John Major, when Chancellor of the Exchequer declared that 'the traditional values' of this venerable movement were 'worth protecting and fostering'.[80] The Institute of Economic Affairs perceived the friendly societies as beyond the state and vehicles for the advocacy of a smaller state sector and there was limited interest in mutual aid.[81] However, this interest in mutual enterprises was not reflected in supportive legislation.

In the 1990s leading building societies became shareholder-owned banks, some leading mutual insurers demutualised, co-operative retailers share of the market declined and trade union membership fell away. While the 70 remaining building societies had 2.8 million borrowers, 19 million investors and 37,309 employees at the end of 1997 and were still important, they accounted for only 17 per cent of retail deposits and 23 per cent of outstanding residential mortgages. Standard Life, the largest mutual life assurance company, had assets of £50 billion, and £60 billion under management for 4 million customers but this did not make it a market leader. The mutual insurers which included Equitable Life and Scottish accounted for about a quarter of the market. Similarly, the 80 largest friendly societies had £11.43 billion under management, 11.1 million policies and 4.76 million members. The Independent Order of Rechabites closed its branches (called tents) and consolidated its activities in a central office. In 1997 the Unity started the year with 99,047 adult members and 5, 291 juniors. It ended the year with fewer members in both categories as only 1,964 people joined and many more lapsed or died. In 1998 only 1,285 people were recruited and things got worse in 1999. Between 1976 and 1996 membership fell from over 200,000 to under 100,000. The versions of Oddfellowship which had been popular in the past looked increasingly inappropriate. Moreover, although many ideas had being mooted, there was no one mutually agreed, route forward for the Society. Reconstituting the Society with a focuson families, youth and new financial services may have aided its survival. However, none of these changes halted the overall decline in popularity of the Unity or the wider mutual sectors.

CHAPTER EIGHT

'A mutual, caring Society, but with an up-to-date twist'[1]

A SURVEY of friendly society members in 1947 suggested that they needed to recapture something of 'the group spirit and mutual aid feeling', and noted that the groups with 'the most active memberships were those which catered for special interests', giving the example of older people.[2] In 1948 Beveridge concurred about spirit and feeling in that he described the important elements of friendly societies as being charity, insurance, savings and also 'brotherly aid in misfortune'.[3] During the 1950s, according to some members' recollections meetings tended to focus on business and in 1966 there was concern that the insurance was being over emphasised. Brother Peet, the President of the Metropolitan District Officers Association, argued that the Board of Directors 'had a tendency to turn the Unity into a commercial organisation instead of a brotherhood', while Past Grand Master, Brother Hammerton argued that

> They should get back to the simple things in Odd Fellowship which were exactly the same as they were 150 years ago. We are drifting into commercialism ... Odd Fellowship is not something to sell – it is something to give for the benefit of the human race ... fraternity was of greater importance than finance.

Len Mostyn also took the view that

> they had to broaden their outlook. Some were committed to a policy of modernisation and realism in their administrative structure, others saw the answer in greater social activities and some favoured larger or more varied benefits. Perhaps they were all of equal importance.[4]

In 1985 the Grand Master, Christine Feek tried to reconcile the different elements within the Society, pointing out that they were connected: 'financial stability must receive our attention if our fraternal, benevolent and social activities are to continue'.

Apart from the debate about the best direction for the Society and the balance of elements within it, there was disagreement as to where power lay and who was in control. This was a matter of some concern to the regulators. The differences in outlook regarding the nature of the organisation and the extent of the shift in power away from lodges (later called branches) was exemplified in the analysis offered by Oddfellows. Roger Burley stressed the autonomy of the branches:

The Oddfellows is not like a company that is run from the top down. It's more like a franchise, each branch is an individual branch and they join together in the spirit of unity for support and mutual assistance. They've all got their own ideas and as long as they stick within the general rules, they are entitled to do things their way. Every branch is separately registered with its own Trustees that are responsible for holding in trust the property of that particular branch.

Others have mentioned the importance of the Deputies and pointed to the Oddfellows as a model for the civic culture. Keith Adamson pointed out: 'Oddfellows are passionate people. They are passionate about the Society. They voice their opinions quite openly and quite forcefully at times.' Joan Henry said:

We do not say delegates we say Deputy because a Deputy is able make his or her own mind up. If you find during the course of conference an argument which you have not thought of, you are free to cast your vote in whatever way you like and then report back to your District as to why.

Keith Adamson spoke about the role of the Deputies at the AMC:

Their word is law, if they say 'No,' it don't happen. It might cause us problems at Board level but that's what we are there for, to resolve those problems. If you look at the RLNI it's a major charity, they have their AGM and that normally lasts two hours and the rest of the day is taken up in presentations for bravery and whatever. You won't find that with Oddfellows, our AGM [i.e. the AMC] at the moment takes three days Monday through to Wednesday.

On the other hand George Kilford felt that power resided at the centre:

It's a pyramid. At the base are the social lodges and they report into various financial branches which are under district lodge control. At the top of the pyramid is the Board of Directors and AMC, the Annual Conference … Every four years there would be a valuation of what assets each individual lodge had and then it would be decided by the committee of that lodge how those benefits, how those surpluses would be distributed.

The metaphor of the pyramid and the simile of the franchise can be reconciled. Roger noted that branches 'join together', while George noted that lodge committees distribute surpluses and that Deputies at the AMC have authority. Nevertheless, the different perspectives are indicative of the range of views as to what the Oddfellows was and the way in which it should progress. Although branches, lodges, remained vital because the success of the Oddfellows continued to be built upon goodwill and trust, the delivery and commitment exercised at local level, the maintaining of lodge life, was difficult. Changing the investment policy by offering help with mortgages to members, by providing greater advice and guidance from Manchester and by merging lodges to create more financially viable units may have reduced the flow of people away from the Oddfellows. Gaining the support of politicians, often those far from power, ensuring that there was a range of social activities, many aimed at children and young adults, simplifying the Ritual, may also have helped the Society. However, membership continued to fall.

It was not until the 1980s and 1990s that the Society agreed on what it looked like and where it was going. This enabled it to implement a strategy which reversed the decline in membership. The first section outlines the implementation of a strategy designed to promote social and care networks based on semi-autonomous branches. It made clear that the Society was intended principally for those aged over 50. Around the time that the baby boomers born

The Society supported convalescent homes from 1889 and, following the donation of a philanthropist Passmore Edwards, it opened a home in Herne Bay in 1897. This was expanded several times until by 1930 it had 130 beds and extensive grounds. Speaking at the 1997 AMC one Deputy described his personal experiences of the support offered there: 'I don't think people realise what the convalescent home can do for you. The convalescent home, I would say, saved my life. A few years ago I had the big C and I was getting nowhere. I went to Herne Bay Convalescent Home and when I went there I couldn't carry my case. After a week I could walk down to town and when I came home from the convalescent home a fortnight later my whole outlook on life had completely changed. ... The convalescent home is one of the best assets that we've got in this Unity.' It was closed in 2009.

FULL TRANSCRIPT OF THE 1997 AMC, PAGE 73.

The Herne Bay Home Under Snow

when the 1947 report quoted above was published were starting to collect their pensions, the Oddfellows focused on them and membership began to climb. To return to Beveridge's description, the Oddfellows realised that it needed to readjust the balance between the elements he mentioned, to focus on being a channel for service and an aid in misfortune for, as Andrew Porter commented, 'we were never going to be a big player in the insurance world. I deal with the insurance business because I am a Director but to me, it's now a side issue.' For an individual who lived through the dramatic changes since the 1990s the shift remains distinctive. Andrew Porter went on: 'The thing that has stood out has been Pathfinder, changing to social care and welfare.' As a 200th birthday is also a time to reflect on the long term, the final section is an assessment of some of the most significant aspects of Oddfellowship over two centuries.

I Pathfinder

In the 1990s the Oddfellows had a strategic review. It included a comprehensive survey, which cost over £800,000 according to one account, involving interviews with all the Directors and Managers and with many existing and former members. The results indicated that although the Society offered sound financial benefits, fewer than 40 per cent of the members joined because of them.[5] Most of those who attended lodge meetings enjoyed the social events, while the ceremonial elements were less popular. Many did not attend as the lodge was too far away, they were too busy or 'they were not informed of meeting times'. Roger Burley told the 1999 AMC

> We commissioned a report as a result of listening to many members, many many members who said the Society does not seems to have a sense of direction, they do not seem to get the leadership they expect ... we commissioned outside advice. We listened to that advice. Unfortunately when we got the report it was rather an earth shaker, it was quite frightening.[6]

To ensure that the Oddfellows was the best branch friendly society in the UK a plan, based on the study, was launched. This aimed to reverse the decline in membership, increase branch activity, improve the services offered and assess the role of the Society within the financial services market. Pathfinder, as the new strategy was called, was to provide a clear purpose for the Society, recruit and retain members, and promote engagement by members without being either too expensive or losing the lodge structure. The strategy had also to 'be true to the Society's ideals and heritage' and ensure that it 'continue to promote the values of trustworthiness and integrity'. In 1996 the Society took the decision to move away from the provision of financial products, to concentrate on social and care provision for members and to focus activity in its branches across the country. It sought to encourage people to take a more active part in branch activities and to provide support and care for older and infirm members. The shift from attracting younger people to older one is indicated in Table 9.

Table 9   *Ages on joining the Oddfellows, 1938–2006*

	Percentage of initiations in age groups (to nearest whole percentage figure)					
	less than 19	*20–24*	*25–29*	*30–34*	*35–59*	*40–50*
1938	54	15	13	9	5	3
1939	58	13	12	8	6	3
1940	77	6	7	5	3	3
1941	77	6	6	5	4	3
1942	76	6	6	5	3	3
1943	79	6	4	4	3	3
1944	79	7	4	4	3	3
1945	77	6	4	5	4	4
1946	63	10	12	8	4	3
1947	63	12	12	7	4	3
1948	66	11	10	6	4	3
1949	63	12	11	6	4	4
1956	52	11	11	9	8	9
	16–18	*19–21*	*22–30*	*31–40*	*41–50*	*over 50*
1957	43	8	21	17	10	1
1958	44	9	20	16	9	1
1959	41	7	23	20	9	2
1960	40	8	23	17	10	2
1961	35	10	23	18	11	3
1967	30	12	22	16	13	7
1968	29	12	22	17	13	8
1969	25	15	24	17	12	8
1970	25	9	25	17	14	10
1971	26	9	22	17	14	11
1972	25	10	23	16	14	12
1973	24	8	22	16	14	16

	Age of new national members at time of recruitment, by year (percent)									
	18–49	*50–54*	*55–59*	*60–64*	*65–69*	*70–74*	*75–79*	*80–84*	*85–89*	*Average age*
2003	7	8	13	16	19	19	9	3	1	64
2004	7	8	14	22	26	11	5	3	1	63
2005	7	5	13	25	30	10	6	3	1	63
2006	10	5	12	21	21	15	9	5	2	64

Source: *Unity Report, 1945*, p. 246; *Unity Reports* 1950, p. 206; *Unity Reports*, 1962, p. 255; *Unity Reports*, 1973, p. 252 *Unity Reports*, 1974, p. 214.

To support companionable activities for the over-50s on such a scale was a market-leading proposition. Subsequently, others followed the lead. Age Concern established its Heyday membership organisation and the Royal British Legion expanded its number of clubs. However, the branch network and fraternal ethos, which has provided a firm basis for the Oddfellows to offer support and social opportunities to those facing bereavement, divorce and retirement, remained distinctive. A few years in later, in 2004, Frank Field told the Commons that at the next election 80 per cent of voters would either be pensioners, or within 'striking distance' of retirement. Certainly the majority of those who are likely to cast their votes at the next election were going to be pensioners. Those over the age of 50 were a group to which MPs needed to pay attention. Interest in social provision for older people increased. Kath Vernon said that in Birmingham 'I could go to a retired lunch from Monday to Friday with no problems'. There was also recognition of this age group from the government which, in 2008, appointed a 'Voice of Older People' within the House of Lords. Nonetheless, the strategy set the Oddfellows apart from other friendly societies.

The focus on older people was based on the recognition that there were to be about 19.6 million people aged over 50 in Britain in 2000 and that by the Oddfellows' bicentennial year of 2010 that figure was expected to be 21.9 million and 26.7 million by 2025.[7] At the same time the number of people in the UK aged between 16 and 50 was expected to fall.[8] It was also recognised that the over-45s in the UK were responsible for nearly 80 per cent of all financial wealth, and 30 per cent of all consumer spending.[9] A report in 2004 on the post-war 'baby boomers' indicated the trend which the Oddfellows had acted upon in the previous decade:

> Taken as a demographic group, they are the wealthiest cohort in contemporary society, healthier than any previous generation of middle-aged people and more than capable of looking after themselves … In order to challenge the prevailing gloom about ageing, we need urgently to invent a collective story about the value of growing older. Organisations that can assist in framing that story are likely to find a powerful and positive response.[10]

The Oddfellows was well placed to be able to realign its focus and 'assist in framing' that story, because the changes of the 1990s had been prefigured long before. In the post-war years there had been considerable interest in this element of Oddfellowship. An important aspect of the new strategy was to concentrate on revitalising the branches, something which the Grand Master had asserted in 1985 when she said that 'branch friendly societies are for the present and for the future'.[11] Continuity was emphasised in many of the reflections, made in 2008, by Oddfellows who presented the rebranding as organic growth. Sue Doulton Smith suggested that the Oddfellows has gone full circle – ensuring members join together to enjoy the social side of life, but also support each other in times of need. She said that Pathfinder took the Oddfellows 'back to our roots as a mutual, caring Society, but with an up-to-date twist.' Keith Adamson also saw the new route as one which led back to old roots:

The society took a decision to step back from insurance business, so we closed all our insurance to new business. We hold a closed insurance book. We looked at the Society and said 'Let's go back to our roots. Let's see what made the society what it is.' Basically it's looking after our membership and nurturing the up-and-coming membership. Back in the old days we used to have a thriving junior membership which then would extend into adult membership to sustain the society. We've gone back to doing what we do best and that's looking after our members, trying to make new members and enjoying ourselves in the process. It's almost like the comradeship that you get when you're in the Forces [he was in the Armed Forces for 12 years]. If I have a problem I know that there is somebody within this society that will help me to resolve it. There is always somebody there to watch your back and to catch you if you fall. That's the original ethos of the society.

In 1998 David Moss, Chief Executive and Secretary of the Order, agreed to terminate his joint appointments in order to support the creation of a new Board which could implement the Strategic Plan. His post was divided into two. The Chief Executive was to lead the Society in the development and execution of the strategy while the Secretary of the Order took responsibility for administration, the co-ordination of the AMC, compliance with the Friendly Societies Act 1992 and subsequent legislation. He also fulfilled ceremonial functions. Roger Burley explained the different roles, 'the Secretary needs to be pedantic. He needs to be right; he needs to be complying with legislation.' The Chief Executive on the other hand was to 'ginger up our strategy, he is supposed to formulate a business plan for us ... the leader of the team who is going to drive us forward. The aim was also to create a 'businesslike Board that is still accountable to the rest of us.'[12] Andrew Porter, later a Grand Master, remembered the atmosphere:

The pivotal moment for me was when we were all taken out of conference into a side room and given a presentation on Pathfinder. We were given this vision. The people who presented it on behalf of the Board were David Moss and the late Christine Feek. They presented their vision for the future. It was that we came out of providing insurance business and started concentrating on social and welfare and fun. In the early days it was different to what it actually came out to be, they were looking for ideas as well as putting a plan forward.

The new proposals led to a debate. Keith Adamson explained that, 'You get members who stand up at the annual conference and say, "Well, tell them [the Financial Services Authority, the regulatory body] where to go". We've been doing this for hundreds of years; tell them we are not doing it.' Andrew Porter presented the division in terms of age:

It caused a lot of excitement but consternation for quite a few people. A lot of the old guard wanted to cling onto what they had. We all decided that this was for us and we were the younger people. As long as I can remember I've always been the youngest in my Branch and the youngest in the District and youngest at Group Conference and when I got on the Board I was one of youngest Grand Masters.

Concerns were expressed about the use of professional expertise, greater centralisation, the lack of detail and the impact on the democratic structures of the Society. One former and one future Grand Master were supportive but hesitant about the rapidity of the change. Keith Adamson called the concept 'brilliant' but supported delay and George Kilford also favoured a new structure but sought greater clarification. Andrew Porter recalled the interest:

There were quite a lot of us who thought 'we can't carry on what we are doing which is nothing, last one out close the door. We have to have a future.' We saw the future perhaps not wrapped up in the package that they showed us originally but how it would develop as time goes on. We were crying out for some change, a purpose in life. We have, as Oddfellows, always had a purpose in life and that's to look after others, but we needed something that would be purposeful for the society to ensure its continuance. We were all concerned at the time that we were going nowhere, nothing to sell, nothing to do.

Roger Burley was blunt in his appraisal. He told the AMC that the decline in membership was a 'very severe problem', that Manchester Unity Assurance and Unity Health Care were 'two of our disasters', and that the Friendly Societies Commission was not satisfied with some of the responses it had received from the Unity. There was a need for change. The new arrangements for governance reflected the need for both executive and non-executive Board members and the need for accountability and acceptance of liabilities under the 1992 Act. The new Board was to be focused on strategy not administration and needed to recognise the benefits of support by those with experience outside the Oddfellows. After considerable, continuing debate about what Peter Needham, the Grand Master called 'the whys and wherefores of Pathfinder', the AMC decided to 'move ourselves away from insurance into caring and social activities' as Roger Burley put it at the 2001 AMC.

A Pathfinder team was established at the Unity office, overseen by Director Derek Winbush. Philip Howcroft was appointed to manage it on a day-to-day basis and a new Events and Public Relations Co-ordinator, Dawn Walters, was appointed. Although one Past Provincial Grand Master was worried that 'when professionals come in friendship, love and truth go out the door', a professional management team was deemed to be more efficient in terms of marketing and service development.[13] In the past the Society had recruited from within its own ranks. Andrew Porter pointed out that:

We are a truly democratic organisation in so far as a mediocre, educated person can come into the society and rise to the top having gained all the training and experience that they need.

However, the Friendly Societies Act demanded that operational control could not be in the hands of those without the qualifications it recognised. Four pilot areas were selected to implement Pathfinder in 1999 and a launch was soon held in Derek Wnbush's 'Heart of England' district. The project lay at the centre of Derek's concerns. As he said in 2000, 'being an Oddfellow means being willing to help others less fortunate than yourself, having a great time at various social events and being part of a team to maintain standards'.[14]

Roger Burley outlined developments:

In the 1990s we just hadn't been bringing in enough young people and those we had been bringing in we hadn't been retaining. The only ones that we were tending to keep were those that had come in for a long term insurance policy which was fine, but they didn't tend to attend meetings. We realised that we needed to get things going again but the gap was so great. We decided to target the over 50s, to try and bring in people that wouldn't feel so out of place … It started in '96 but it didn't really get going, the advertising and bringing numbers in, for a couple years after that. That was the beginning of the new look. We've paid up our old policies and we're purely concentrating on the social and welfare side. We know who can help you if you need advice, that's the line on the welfare side. The social side is trying to get the branches to do what they used to do, provide somewhere where people would like to go.

Oddfellows in the selected Pathfinder areas had priority access to advice from the Citizens Advice Bureau and could arrange free care assessments through Red Arc Assured (later these

The Grand Master lays the Foundation Stone

Laying of the foundation stone for the Red Rose Lodge, Blackpool, 1966.
ODDFELLOWS COLLECTION

were arranged through an Oddfellows Services Manager) while staff in the four areas were provided with appropriate additional training. By early 2000 the membership in the four areas was 23 per cent of the Unity's total membership. This rapid roll-out aided recruitment; 2,232 joined in 1999, and there was also an increase in members' activity. Thirteen districts gained more members than they lost, nine of them Pathfinder districts. Andrew Porter remembered the roll-out and felt that the implementation of the strategy was partly due to the energy of younger people:

> The younger element carried the change forward and moved it on and did everything they could to make it a success. I know that within my particular area, it was the younger end that pushed it forward and made it happen.

Things did not go entirely smoothly for, on the eve of the 2000 AMC, one of the directors who had been on the Board since 1996 and been influential in the implementation of Pathfinder, resigned.[15]

The number of adult members fell during the course of 1993 from over 93,000 to under 91,000 and the trend looked likely to continue. Even taking into account the investment costs, notably the research and provision of additional services, and the fact that the AMC agreed in 2000 that 'Pathfinder is making a positive impact on the Society'. Pathfinder lodges brought in 60 per cent of the new members and nine of the top ten districts in terms of recruitment had within them Pathfinder branches.[16] Whereas membership fell in non-Pathfinder lodges by 0.87 per cent it rose by 3.2 per cent in Pathfinder lodges. These lodges offered Care helplines, a Care Service and Care Lines. Prior to Pathfinder the selected lodges of Oddfellows offered 300 social events in a year. By 2000 it was 800. Indeed, so popular were the changes that the 2000 AMC made the extremely demanding decision that Pathfinder benefits be made available to all society members. Plans were brought forward in order to enable branches to adopt the Pathfinder approach. There was a reorganisation of the Society. Norman Heald held the joint role of Chief Executive Officer (CEO) and Secretary of the Order (SOO) and this became two roles with Philip Howcroft becoming CEO and Jane Nelson the first female SOO. In 2001, in an echo of Tony Blair, the person credited with coining the term New Labour and being responsible for the growth in Labour Party membership, the Grand Master, Eric Ogden, told the AMC: 'it is my ambition to see the word Pathfinder disappear as we accept that this is the New Oddfellows.'

Within a few years numerous branches had been reinvigorated as the Oddfellows tapped the growing market among those aged over 50. There were a wide range of social activities including quizzes, pig racing, pudding clubs and wine tasting. In 2000 Unity Brass (now Oddfellows Brass and another initiative associated with Derek Winbush) arranged a nationwide tour of the UK with the entertainer Pam Ayres. Both were contracted to help promote Pathfinder.

In 1964 Oddfellows aged between 20 and 40 met to discuss ways to encourage growth. *The Odd Fellow* reported that they wanted activities 'as well as the more conventional dinner dance', and also discussed social welfare work, an Oddfellows Week at a holiday camp or holidays abroad, concessionary price schemes and district Ritual teams. Some of those same youths might have gone on the holidays that Oddfellows ran about 40 years later. George Kilford, who was Deputy Grand Master 1989–90, explained:

> When I was Deputy Grand Master I chaired a committee dealing with membership and marketing. We entered into an arrangement with a public relations firm to sponsor the English Indoors Bowls Championship. We alerted all the lodges who had bowls clubs in their area of this and encouraged them to go along and make members. We provided score cards. The English Indoor Bowls Championships was quite big throughout the country and it had a big finals week up in Melton Mowbray. We were not only publicising the society but also of trying to recruit members from the bowls clubs, which we did in some parts, depending on the enthusiasm of the local members. A spin-off from that sponsorship was that the PR Company that we dealt with was also in contact with Warner Holidays, and we used to run a competition throughout the summer months at three of the Warner Holiday Camps in the south … From that a relationship was developed in providing an Oddfellows holiday.

The Housing Association, Red Rose Lodge, established in Blackpool for older Oddfellows in 1973, was maintained. However, in general there were to be no more mortgages or

In the new millennium there has been a renewed emphasis on helping members to get the most out of life. An important part of this has been the enthusiasm for social events. The wearing of regalia at the Cambridge District Dinner Dance 2009 was clearly no bar to exuberant dancing, which symbolises how the old traditions have been revitalised.
ODDFELLLOWS COLLECTION

In 1981, Rob Boulter was instrumental in founding a band called Unity Brass which has toured Europe and Barbados. It has its own base in Leicestershire and is now known as Oddfellows Brass. The band continues to blossom and tours extensively around the country performing at branch events and in competitions.
ODDFELLLOWS COLLECTION

insurance offered. Manchester offered advice on financial matters, and the focus at lodge level was on investing in people and social networks, not property. Districts continued to manage investments, a number own halls and one owned a swimming pool, but many followed the advice provided by Manchester which had a property department and IT support. It also had a Legal Aid Fund which dealt mostly with personal injury claims. It continued to be the case that few members claimed the dental and optical benefits and there was an assessment as to whether this was the most attractive option to offer those interested in joining. Members were more interested in the companionship, the sense of community and place, the opportunity to get involved and be active. Within a few years the Oddfellows had a firm sense of how to improve communication and activities at lodge level. In 2003 it was decided to create a new branch in a location where the Oddfellows had no presence. Doncaster, which had a high population in the target age range, was selected and a local Development Worker organised a series of events. Within two years there were 520 new members (excluding those who had left or died) and an average of 68 people attended each meeting.[17] Implementing the initiative appeared to involve a lot of effort but also some rewards and by 2008 members were claiming that they had 'the oldest and best club in South Yorkshire'.[18]

In 2005 *The Oddfellow* was merged with *Membership Matters* and was relaunched. Over 3,600 members responded to questions about their lives, likes and outlook. The 'Wonderful Life Report' concluded that the membership was lively, confident, fun, independent, busy and involved. Although the profile of the Oddfellows was raised through direct mailing, the website, press releases and advertisements and appearances on radio, it was the 'Member Get Member' scheme was the most cost-effective means of recruitment. This may have been because, compared to Saga and the University of the Third Age, relatively few people had heard of the Oddfellows or knew what it offered. Andrew Porter explained:

> Our biggest problem is having enough people to go out and shout from the roof tops what we are, who we are, what we're about, what we do, what benefits you can get. I am sure if you could get an advertisement in the middle of *Coronation Street* on television, telling everybody in a nutshell what benefits you could get for what they pay in, we would in inundated. We don't shout enough. People are put off by the name Oddfellows.[19]

An advertisement was not placed in one of the most expensive slots in broadcasting and, after the rises in membership in 2002, 2003 and 2004 the year 2005 saw only 6,471 new members, an overall decrease of 19.8 per cent on the previous year. Although the number of lapses was fewer the overall number of members fell and fell again in 2006, when only 3,000 people joined. However, it had not gone below the nadir of 2000. Turning around the fortunes of the Oddfellows was going to be a long and difficult task. Sue Doulton Smith reflected on the struggle to recruit as the economic changes occurred:

> At the time, the 1990s, everybody was going to be taking early retirement and we would all have so much time on our hands. That was what we expected and it's all turned the other way now because everybody is going to be working much longer. There would be people who would be looking for things to do who perhaps would like to get involved with a society which believed in mutual support, which looked after its members, which provided a social scene, which made sure that if there was something wrong, there was somebody who could visit you or that you could call upon. That was something which looked as if it was going to be missing and was going to be needed for people in their mid-fifties.

Some of the problems relating to recruitment and retention were noted in the 2007 *Annual Report*:

> the variety of ways to spend leisure time is growing … people have different expectations of life, demand better service, more choice, more control, more self-fulfilment. The values of duty and service to others are less prevalent. Without a family tradition of Oddfellowship or other long association with a Lodge there is no loyalty. It takes considerable effort on our part, therefore, to attract new members, particularly when

awareness of the Society is low. It takes even more effort to keep and nurture those members and over time, engender our values and traditions and develop loyalty.

By the bicentenary the Society had established a network of Care Coordinators managing a group of Welfare Officers. The Society offered benefits and services to members including help with travel and medical bills, advice from the Oddfellows Care Service and the Oddfellows Advice Service (which works in conjunction with the Citizens Advice Bureau) and opportunities to raise money for charity. Although, as Roger Burley said 'Anybody thinking in terms of expanding Oddfellowship into an organisation the size it once was is living in cloud cuckoo land', there is evidence that a vibrant culture has been developed and maintained.

The provision of social activities and care for members has always been central to the Society. These stories of the help provided by the Oddfellows can stand for many others. Keith Adamson provided an example of welfare work:

I've got a young family at the moment; the father died three or four years ago, two young girls and mum. Mum was doing her damnest to ensure that the girls lives were disrupted as little as possible, losing Dad is a major disruption in any young life. Mum was trying to ensure that, that disruption was kept to a minimum and we as a branch have done everything that we possibly can to help to ensure that that happens. If they've got a problem then they will talk to an Almoner who goes round and makes sure they are alright. If they've got any problems or any issues then we try and resolve them for them.

Deputies marched through the streets to mark the centenary of the Society. By 2010 such demonstrations were less commonly seen on the streets of the UK.

A Deputy told an AMC:

I had my house burnt down and I was away in Bradford at the time. All we had was our car and the clothes we stood up. Sister Woods came straight away and helped us out with an emergency grant … This is one of the things we can preach of Oddfellowship. We can talk about tables, we can talk about this and we can talk about that but it's the help we give to our people and other people when they are in desperate need.[20]

Derek Elmer also gave a personal example of Oddfellow welfare:

My parents joined in the late seventies and when my Dad sadly died in 1983 Mum found a lot of company and consolation. She's 92 now. She has gone into a residential home where there's Oddfellows round the corner and they pop in at least three times a week, take her out.

From 1810 Oddfellows have had to work, as Roger Burley put it, to 'keep the ethics and principles of the society alive. Everything in our history tells us that where you've got good

Members of the Active Travel Club on a trip to Bruges in 2009. The Club takes the Society in a new direction by offering members the chance to take part in a variety of holidays, both in the UK and abroad. Through the Society, members can also promote their own holiday homes to one another.
ODDFELLOWS COLLECTION

Marketing the Society has moved into the twenty-first century, in ways that include attendance at national exhibitions. This illustration shows an exhibition at the Retirement Show in London in 2008. It is the personal touch and the opportunity to talk to somebody who knows about the Oddfellows, which has consistently proved to be one of the most effective ways of increasing membership.

ODDFELLOWS COLLECTION

people you'll get good branches.' The ways in which the Oddfellows has ensured that the structures to support 'good people' are in place have changed. The need to welcome people with a skeleton may have diminished but the importance of conviviality and care remained. Pathfinder allowed the Society to focus on the reasons why people have joined and remained members in recent years. Their reasons have rarely been only financial as there have long been alternative ways of taking out insurance and saving money. Pathfinder enabled members to tell an agreed account of the Society. When Andrew Porter said 'We have, as Oddfellows always had a purpose in life and that's to look after others', and Roger Burley spoke of 'trying to get the branches to do what they used to do, provide somewhere where people would like to go' they were together providing a coherent narrative. A clear, plausible, uncontested explanation of the Society's roots and future provided a firm basis for them to build the membership.

II Two centuries of Oddfellowship

People have long struggled with the problems which occur in the event of illness or a death in the family. Recognising that reliable friends and neighbours could not be guaranteed, the Society provided resources. It built on the traditions and models provided by the guilds, box clubs, charities, Freemasons, trade unions, the savings banks, insurance companies and the

Fellowship, community and friendship: a group of Oddfellows pose for the camera at Hardy Green the year before the outbreak of the Second World War. Arthur Jackson can be seen on the left at the back.
BY COURTESY OF J.M. HEATHCOTE

Church. It also found ideas from within the conventions associated with drama, neighbourliness and the legal framework. The Unity looked backwards and forwards in time as well as to the sibling organisations and rivals at its sides. The result of connecting modernity and tradition, psychic and economic survival, commercial decisions and community-making was a distinctive reconceptualisation of structured reciprocity for members which helped, argued Frank Field, to promote social advance, to transform people's lives and to propel Britain 'to the top of the economic table'.[21]

The Unity has been more than an important node in the multi-directional network of British society. It has balanced democracy and patronage. It has liberated and relied upon members who have spread the skills and confidence required for self-improvement, collective self-help and democratic advance. It has systematised and commodified informal exchanges and also encouraged personal, social contacts. It has built and regulated trust and reciprocity, created rules and also supported flexibility. Through balancing 'friendship' and 'love' and 'truth' it has, as historian Tristram Hunt wrote, been 'fundamental to British identity'.[22] This remark, made in 2002, echoed that of Stanley Baldwin in 1934. The former and future Prime Minister spoke of 'the richness of our common heritage, of which Oddfellowship is one of the choiciest fruits'. He argued that much of the work which had benefited the nation originated with 'the people themselves' through their trade unions and friendly societies. He then asked 'Without vaunting ourselves, may we not look on this as our special contribution to a democratic civilisation?'[23]

In the twentieth century, while the need for the kindness of strangers remained, the needs of the Society, and those of the wider society, shifted. Many of the connections that it made in the nineteenth century were links which were of less value to it in the twentieth and twenty-first centuries as social, political and economic networks took on different formations. By the early twentieth century a greater engagement in civil life could be achieved through the political parties. Conservative MP Stanley Baldwin argued that the lodges provided 'the perfect training to fit men throughout the country for all the responsibilities that have been laid upon them in the past half-century in local government and national government'.[24] G. H. Roberts, one of the first Labour MPs, explained that he had 'graduated in the university of the friendly societies'.[25] In Australia three members of the Society became Prime Ministers of the Commonwealth, and two of those became High Commissioners. Many were members of legislative assemblies in Australia at local, state and national level.[26] However, other training grounds became available, leading to other routes to political power. The distancing from party politics as parties developed had some disadvantages as Roger Burley pointed out:

Oddfellowship always had this problem because we don't discuss politics or religion in the lodge room but of course, politics has a very great big effect on us. Conservative governments always tend to look on us as something like a trade union and therefore not be liked because we also had a connection with the Tolpuddle Martyrs. The Labour Party tended to look upon us as a private insurance which they didn't approve of.

In the early years of the Society the rituals, with their associations with magic, myth and drama were a means to check on the credentials of members, to reinforce the ideals of the Society and to transport members to a congenial and exclusive haven where the righteous were rewarded. Members, associated the language of Ritual with 'dignity' argued Eric Ogden and with 'the teachings of the Bible' suggested Terence Pauley. However, by the mid-twentieth century interest in both dignity and Christianity had declined. George Kilford noted that his lodge opened in the same year as the local church hall, and that both closed in 2008. He went on:

The values that the Society started off with still remain. It's a shame that basic teachings that we had, which were based on Christian principles, can't be shared by more people. There are people out there that could benefit from the wider education of democratic meetings, the comradeship.[27]

To be connected to Cottonopolis in the nineteenth century, when Sir Robert Peel, the son of a wealthy textile manufacturer, said, 'What Manchester thinks today, the world does tomorrow', may have benefited the Society. By the late twentieth century the link may have been of less value. Whereas Disraeli and Baldwin had addressed the Society, a later leader of the Conservative Party, when on a trip to near the Unity's home in 2009, indicated his greater interest in visiting the Salford Lads Club.[28] There was less need for the Society to

In contrast to the serious ranks of Deputies pictured at the 1910 AMC (see page 138), these revellers attending the Masquerade Ball at the 2003 AMC in Bournemouth are enjoying the more social side of Oddfellowship.
ODDFELLOWS COLLECTION

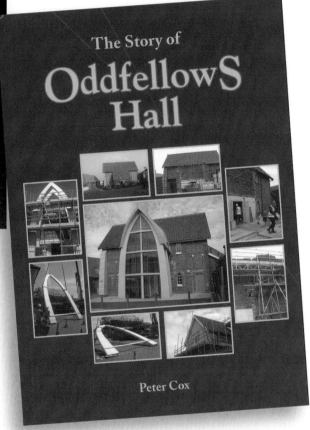

The Story of
OddfellowS
Hall

Peter Cox

RIGHT

This multi-award winning and distinctive venue in the heart of Sheringham, Norfolk, started life in 1867 as a lifeboat station. The upstairs was for many years used for its meetings by the Loyal Fishermen's Lodge of the Unity, and in 1931 the Society purchased the building, although it was sold after the war. When it was rebuilt in 2007, with a glass and steel entrance in the shape of the prow of a lifeboat, it was named Oddfellows Hall to reflect the long and continuing relationship between Sheringham and the Oddfellows, and in particular the support for the local lifeboat which the Society has provided for over a century.
ODDFELLOWS COLLECTION

position itself as respectable and independent, without being deferential, or to challenge the association of charity exclusively with middle-class women or the association of working men with short-sighted overindulgence. The franchise was won, the Poor Law abolished, the National Health Service created and the number of tramping artisans reduced. Societal and the legal pressures have always shaped, as well as being shaped by, the Unity. In the post-war period those external forces played significant roles in the fall in membership, the closure of lodges and the greater centralisation of financial decision-making.

There were always rivals to the Society and many of these grew in significance over the

ABOVE

In order to introduce people to the Society, a 'Wonderful Life' fair was held in 2008. This photograph shows exhibitors in Sheffield, where the Society also sponsored a local competition. Its Active and Ageless Awards celebrated all those who are creative, daring, intelligent, generous – and at least 50 years old. The fair exhibited 'Active and Ageless' photographs commissioned by the Oddfellows. This featured pictures of gliders and pilots, actors and musicians, mentors, dancers, marathon runners, marmalade makers and a fund-raising Santa.

ODDFELLOWS COLLECTION

RIGHT

Support for the Sheringham lifeboats has been important to the Society for many years. In 1994 the Manchester Unity of Oddfellows lifeboat, a gift from the Society, was launched there. She became Sheringham's longest serving offshore motor lifeboat. During her 29 years on station she was launched on service 127 times and saved 134 lives. This rigid inflatable boat is named 'The Oddfellows' because she too was paid for by the Oddfellows.

ODDFELLOWS COLLECTION

The more active Oddfellows, typified by these members from Suffolk, have enjoyed what the Society has become since 2000. Social events have encouraged recruitment and the 'recommend a friend' scheme has brought in friends as active members. Their District has seen over 800 new members join over ten years. This has been achieved mainly because their Branches have offered varied, enjoyable and value-for-money events.

ODDFELLOWS COLLECTION

period since 1810. They have sought to emulate its promotion of reciprocal obligation in a variety of ways. In 1874 there were at least 35 other societies with the word Oddfellows in the title and others with the words Odd Sisters and Odd Females in their names. Societies such as the Marple Bridge Independent Odd Fellows Provident Juvenile Burial Society and the Tilgate Forest Independent Odd Fellows existed for many years.[29] Others organisations specialised in particular elements of Oddfellowship. By the time the Society was officially a hundred years old members could buy insurance from commercial companies, open accounts with saving banks, commercial banks or building societies, gasp in awe at commercial magic shows, gain political power through the Labour Party or find warmth and reassurance within families which were often perceived as havens rather than simply economic units.

Important among the survival strategies for working men was the Prudential. The Prudential initially provided loans, secured by life assurance, to professionals. It soon started to sell penny premiums collected by agents to the people who might have otherwise joined the Oddfellows. At first it sought to copy the success of the Oddfellows and to present itself as treating people as if they had a moral dimension to their character as well as a material one. It tried to embody: 'England's rich charity' [which] promptly relived/The pitiful wants of hundreds bereaved'.[30] However, the ideas went in both directions. Under the 1896 Friendly Societies Act the

Oddfellows established the Manchester Unity Life Insurance Collecting Society. This offered policies similar to those of the Prudential and it was not necessary to be an Oddfellows to purchase them. It was not popular with many Oddfellows. At one AMC a delegate mentioned her preference for the Prudential and in 1922 Herbert White explained that 'in company with his colleagues of the South London district he had had a prejudice against this society for years.' This was because agents of the collecting society 'instead of doing the work for which the society was instituted were simply in the lodge room to clinch the business that belonged to the Manchester Unity'.[31] The Prudential had connected to modern networks in ways that the Oddfellows had not.

Friendly societies which did not offer club nights or social events grew in popularity. The Hearts of Oak conducted its business by post, providing postal orders for superannuation, sickness, funeral, lying-in and fire benefits. By 1874 it had almost 33,000 members all earning at least £1 2s. a week. Those who worked at many trades were excluded and men could only join if they were under the age of 36. There was an entrance fee and relatively high fees and policy holders had no direct control over the society. In 1905 the Royal Liver, the Liverpool Victoria Legal and the Royal London all had a membership of about two million each. When district membership In Bishops Auckland fell from 2,126 in 1900 to 1,230 in 1910 the local Oddfellows blamed the 'unfair competition of the Durham Miners' Permanent

It is not only members who are philanthropic. Staff from the central office in Manchester also support fundraising within the Society, demonstrated by their participation in the BUPA 10-kilometre run in aid of the Genesis Appeal.
ODDFELLOWS COLLECTION

There is a long history of Oddfellows supporting charities, and recently members raised £180,000 to support the Genesis Appeal — Europe's first purpose-built breast cancer prevention centre, at Wythenshawe Hospital. Above, some members of the Board of Directors sit in the completed lecture room which has been named after the Oddfellows. From left to right are John Hughes (Genesis Appeal), Philip Howcroft, George Lickess, Dorothy Deacon (Grand Master 2009/10), Karen Stuart, Charles Vaughan, Lester Barr (Chairman Genesis Appeal) and Alan Cole.

BELOW

Members of the Board of Directors promoting the Genesis Appeal. From left to right are Jane Nelson, athlete Diane Modahl, Margaret Lickess (Grand Master 2006/07) and Daphne Stephenson.

ODDFELLOWS COLLECTION

Relief Fund which pays … benefits from the common Trade Union Fund'.[32] Other aspects of Oddfellowship also became less popular in the face of specialist competition. Having thrived by being open to all trades it now looked like it was master of none.

Moffrey claimed that 'the victory over ignorance and financial superstition was not finally won until the year 1866 [when] the victorious majority [was] determined to walk in the paths of truth and honesty'. He added that 'the fundamental principle that every man entering the Unity should pay an equivalent value for the benefits he expected to receive was finally established at the Plymouth AMC in 1867'.[33] However, his dualist presentation, of familial modernity casting out 'superstition', marginalised the extent to which the Oddfellows can be conceived as serving both the old order and the new world. Its uneven reciprocity existed alongside the market because those worlds existed together, overlapping and in tension. In contrast to Moffrey, Pierre Bourdieu suggested that the gift could exist within a capitalist economy because gifting was manipulation, an ostensibly generous act which masked the infliction of self interest. The gift was a disguise that enabled capital to be misrecognised, a 'veil of enchanted relations' to cover up violence.[34] While avoiding Moffrey's teleology such an account also failed to recognise how far reciprocity was more than an economic survival strategy. It could also be an aid to the creation of communities based on obligation. This was different to self-interested neoclassical economic individualism in that even if everybody gave back as much as they had received there would still be the feelings and relations, the tying or tearing of which were involved in the process. To reduce gifting to simply masking relations of authority and domination marginalises the extent to which 'gifts at once express freedom and create binding obligations, and may be motivated by generosity or calculation or both'.[35] Both Whiggist interpretations and economic determinism offer incomplete images which marginalise the uneconomic and the archaic. It is because gift giving can be motivated and selfish without being alienating and impersonal, because the act of giving can turn into an act of revenge and respect into rivalry that the Oddfellows needed its Ritual. The Society's restructuring of reciprocity and respectability was not assured. Even after members had merged divergent discursive practices and created a novel form of flexible, formalised fraternity, they still had to struggle with the tensions between licensed exchange and unlicensed conviviality. Containing many contradictory elements including commercial insurance, Christian charity, heath care and the culture of tramping artisans, Oddfellowship, at the end of the nineteenth century was aided by the reiteration of the parable of the Good Samaritan.

Despite the outward triumph of the centenary, by the Edwardian period the Oddfellows had been weakened by changes in the distribution of wealth and shifts in ideas about health care. The banners at its centenary AMC 'Harmony, Peace and Concord' and 'Prosperity to our branches' may have reminded deputies more of the divisions and structures of the past than pointing the way forwards. The decision to apply to become a body which was approved by the government to administer national health insurance after 1912 took the Society in a new direction. Adjustment was difficult and the Society remained committed to Oddfellowship, not administration of the government's scheme. The Grand Master made this point to the 1914 AMC. Having spoken at length about National Insurance Walter Wright went on:

Speaking as an Oddfellow to Oddfellows I would beg to remind you that it is the least important part of our work. The Manchester Unity is a great, glorious, free, and independent brotherhood established for the purpose of spreading the principles of benevolence and charity. Our work is to relieve sickness by mutual voluntary insurance, not on mere commercial lines but by blending equity with brotherliness and real concern for each other's welfare. To relieve the widow, to succour the orphan, to help the traveller, to educate the young in the principles of thrift and at all times to stretch out our hands to brothers in distress.[36]

He concluded that the Unity would shrink in size but become nobler because of its values of self-reliance, self-education and independence. By refusing to conform to what he called the 'spirit of the age' the Grand Master was in danger of turning the Society from a survival strategy into a sect. The effects of approval were to increase the amount of time which had to be spent on administration, which drove up costs and reduced both the time available for other activities and the number of lodges. It also led to greater tensions with the medical profession and between members and Manchester. The Society's claims that 'the Insurance Act carries us backward to the servile Middle Ages', and that members became 'actuarial friendly society men rather than actual friendly society men' focused attention on the legislation rather than any other causes of problems that the Unity faced.[37] Members ceased to look for other reasons as to why so many joined the Prudential scheme and so few the Oddfellows one. Some of the secretaries probably ceased to look up very much at all, given the amount of paper work with which they had to deal. The scale of changes made adaptation difficult. The Society knew about localised economic downturns. Membership falls were often associated with recession. However, the inter-war period was a time when far larger parts of the country were in economic distress for far longer than in previous periods. Helping individual brethren was manageable; dealing with a crisis, especially when tied to the government's system of insurance, was more complicated. The position of the Society was weakened further by its association, in the eyes of the Labour Party, with the Sir George May's Pru and by the difficulties presented by the influx of women members.

The demise of approved status after the Second World War brought the exit of many of those who had run the Society for many years. These included the Grand Master of 1945 and many who had served in the Forces and broken their links to Oddfellowship. There was also a reduction of interest in joining by those who saw little need as the state arranged many benefits. The Society searched for new roles, seeking to attract younger people, the market it had sought particularly since the late nineteenth century and also women and their families. Those who joined in this period gave a variety of reasons. Most were invited to join by somebody they trusted, a family member, a friend, a work colleague. Once they had joined they remained for social reasons. For some the Oddfellows became their family, their sisters and brothers to use the Oddfellows' own terms. Lillian Leese said, 'I have got to know quite a lot of people so I can talk to them, and if they have got any problems then we can sort it out. It's like one big family.' However, fewer were joining than in the past. One reason was that centralisation, which saved money and reduced inefficiency, was unappealing to those who enjoyed local autonomy. Lodges control over money was reduced as regulations determined where money could be invested. Eventually 'unregistered' lodges were barred from accessing funds, while the national membership scheme determined what benefits could be paid. Another reason was that other forms of leisure appeared to be more accessible or more interesting. A third was that other routes to civic and civil authority were more rewarding. There was greater competition for people's time due to widened access to formal education, the lowering of social barriers and the increase in the types of organisations, such as trade unions, political parties or charitable bodies which offered opportunities that previously had not existed. Although there have been some political support for mutual aid, the regulatory framework encouraged a shift from management by activists towards governance for members and there was little interest in friendly society Orders with semi-autonomous branches. The decline of attention being paid to Oddfellowship reflected a wider decline of engagement with mutuality and member-run organisations. Moreover, families were changing. Assumptions about the pervasiveness of the male breadwinner model were no longer valid. The *2007 Annual Report* noted that, 'Without a family tradition of Oddfellowship or other long association with a Lodge there is no loyalty', and that tradition was not being maintained.

The construction of a new consensus culminated in the 1990s when the Society shifted focus. It became the mission of the Oddfellows 'to improve the quality of life of our members by meeting their social and welfare needs through a mutual, national branch network'. Although some aspects of the alterations had been considered over many years, Andrew Porter saw the shift as transformative:

> The change was from insurance to social care and welfare. That's the biggest change that the society has gone through since it took on the insurance business. That was a momentous occasion.

Margaret Lickess, the Grand Master in 2006, was close to the decision at the time. She presented it in terms of continuity, telling AMC that 'Our noble Order has the core value of helping our members and from this develops a respect of each other and also of ourselves'. Whether the developments were a change or a revival, the emphasis was to be on fellowship over finance and on sociability and care overall. Implementation could only occur with the consent of the membership. There had to be a shared understanding of the past and the present for the Society was to go forwards. In reviewing their experiences members of the Oddfellows often mentioned their sense of the past and of their role in the world. Andrew Porter mentioned that 'the Oddfellows has always had a purpose in life and that's to look after others'. He indicated where he saw 'the main focus':

> to make sure it's there for future generations. I'm grateful for my forefathers for having something that I could come into and take on and take over and run along with and I've got something that I can hand over.

Strength could be drawn from a sense of continuity with the past. As one member put it succinctly, 'we are not some sort of society which is going to be here today, gone tomorrow. That is not the case. We have got a very positive future.'

The narratives of the members help to explain the Society's trajectory during the post-war period. Their contributions, including their omissions, suppressions and interpretations, indicate how they relate the past to the present. To succeed the Society needed to be able to call on its members to be selfless, to devote many hours to ensuring that the Society was run in a correct fashion. Members spoke of their own efforts, of the input of members of their families and that they were moved by the devotion to the implementation of Oddfellowship of others. Some members spoke at length about the contribution of those who are now dead and unable to speak for themselves. Douglas Potter modestly referred to the 60 years that he had devoted to the Society as involving 'a lot of administration work to do as a secretary', and noted that was 'not always convenient for my wife and family'. Oddfellowship was presented as being about more than instrumental collective self-help in the face of concerns about mobility, urbanisation, anomie and the insecurity of waged labour. It was about social cohesion, the recreation of community and sense of mutual obligation. As such it required the engagement of the membership. As a Past Provincial Grand Master of West London pointed out in 1922, 'Men must feel a personal interest in the government of the Unity if it is not to become a mere benefit society, unworthy of its traditions as a great brotherhood'.[38] For members to be able to be effective in their recruitment and retention strategies they had to have some control over events. They had to have rights as well as responsibilities. A significant part of the stories that people related of their own experiences of Oddfellowship indicated how far the Society empowered its members.

Another thread running through the narratives is that members felt a pride in ownership of their own organisation. Douglas Potter went on, 'I still believe in it because it encourages people today to administer some semblance of thrift in their lives.' These members were able to be effective recruiters because they believed that they were giving people an exciting opportunity for self-improvement. Contributors' unique accounts of the Oddfellows offer insights into how they make sense of the past, how they have interpreted and developed Oddfellowship. Many structured their ideas within the discourses of Oddfellowship, using, for example, a discussion about Ritual as a vehicle for a contribution to a debate about the modernisation strategy. Some of those interviewed noted that the ineffectual had been allowed to make decisions beyond their competence, that there had been a lack of coherent criteria on which to base decisions and that the cushioning against change, due to the stocks of fixed and social capital that the Unity had accumulated, had allowed the Society to defer important decisions. It is because these members' accounts were framed by the culture, customs and history of the Society and presented through the prism of recent events, notably the changes inaugurated in the 1990s, that they enable others to understand how members saw the route from the post-war welfare reforms to the present day. The recollections of a few members, while not representative of the whole membership, indicate that the Society was able to survive because of its stalwarts. Although the Unity found it difficult to make the changes necessary for survival because of some of those very same people, in the end, it was members of the Oddfellows who drew upon the storehouse of Oddfellowship's resources and made the decisions to help themselves.

It is appropriate that an assessment of an organisation long run by its members should leave the last word to those members. The principles of the Society have been interpreted and reiterated on numerous occasions. James Burn simply stated that 'Friendship, Love and Truth' contains the whole duty of man'.[39] *Oddfellowship*, a popular poem first published in 1886, refers to the need to 'let love's golden tether, Embrace and bind us altogether' and the importance of the 'kindly, loving helping hand'.[40] It bolstered the idea of reciprocity, the virtuous circles that the Society engendered. In the same year a poem by Tom Coales of Stony Stratford answered the question as to who is 'Thy Neighbour' by stating that a neighbour was any 'human form less favoured than thine own'. The poem concluded in terms which reiterated the parable of the Good Samaritan:

> Oh pass not, pass not heedless by,
> Perhaps thou canst redeem,
> The breaking heart from misery
> Go share thy lot with him.[41]

Over a hundred years later Eric Ogden closed the 2000 AMC with the Ritual speech which echoed words that had been used over the last 200 years. He became an Oddfellow in the 1950s. He did not agree with all the changes which have occurred since that time but he remained within the Society. His account of the last half of the last century, during which he rose through the hierarchy, bridges the divide some perceive between the old and new approaches. In looking forwards he also looked backwards and reminded listeners that, since at least 1810, members have looked after each other, and thereby looked after themselves:

As our last thought, let us remember that Unity demands service from all its members and service. It can best be given by ever endeavouring to extend the principles of the Order, by sympathy with the sick and the afflicted, by giving comfort to those who mourn and by brightening the lives of those who toil. In the name of friendship, love and truth, I declare this Conference closed.[42]

Oddfellow membership, 1832–2009

Date	Number of members	Date	Number of members	Date	Number of members
1832	31,000	1874	496,529	1937	909,195
1834	70,000	1875	508,013	1939	908,175
1838	90,000	1876	518,802	1940	898,841
1842	220,000	1877	526,802	1941	891,978
1845	248,000	1878	531,559	1942	887,476
1846	259,374	1879	532,520	1943	881,208
1848	249,261	1880	543,485	1944	868,348
1849	234,490	1881	537,909	1945	871,033
1850	224,878	1882	565,358	1947	844,959
1851	229,040	1883	579,366	1950	718,868
1852	225,194	1884	593,520	1953	639,008
1853	225,001	1885	605,922	1955	595,170
1854	231,228	1890	673,073	1960	551,254
1855	239,783	1895	751,167	1965	539,886
1856	251,008	1900	837,040	1969	517,569
1857	262,883	1905	874,262	1970	533,907
1858	276,254	1909	882,668	1972	501,643
1859	287,575	1910	890,538	1975	264,928*
1860	305,241	1912	1,028,155	1980	215,098*
1861	316,215	1913	1,008,402	1985	175,500*
1862	335,145	1914	986,870	1990	129,970*
1863	342,953	1915	965,390	1997	101,770
1864	358,556	1916	947,676	1998	98,224
1865	373,509	1917	935,814	1999	95,783
1866	387,990	1918	919,967	2000	93,876
1867	405,255	1919	932,063	2001	102,345
1868	417422	1921	928,003	2002	102,696
1869	425,095	1922	925,399†	2003	103,192
1870	434,100	1924	908,218	2004	104,011
1871	442,575	1926	912,437	2005	102,351
1872	458,159	1930	908,280‡	2006	95,324
1873	481,630	1935	894,305	2007	95,462
				2008	97,569
				2009	119,995

Unless stated otherwise the figures exclude juveniles, junior members of adult lodges, honorary members and widows of members who subscribed for the funeral benefits. Overseas members are included. For example the 1909 figure could be read as 1,035,627 persons attached to the Order.

Notes:

   *   These figures include juveniles and other younger members.

   †   If juveniles and widows are included the figure is 1,080,058.

   ‡   *The Times*, 4 January 1944, reported the peak of two million members occurred before 1922 but that there were two million again by 1932 and 1942. Other sources suggest that between 1919 and 1933 the overall number of Oddfellows fell by over 36,000. However, the number overseas rose by 3,000. If the overseas members are excluded and only the UK membership is considered then there was a fall of over 65,700. The disparity continued. In 1949 there were 570,416 members in the UK, and 752,163 if the overseas members were included.

This information is derived from the annual lists which were published in the Unity Reports. It includes all members, that is those in Scotland, Ireland and abroad as well as England and Wales. In 1875 there were 426,663 Oddfellows in England and Wales. At that time the Ancient Order of Foresters had 388,872 members. Approximately two thirds of all the members of affiliated orders belonged to these two orders. Despite the attempts to gather statistics there continued to be lodges which did not make accurate or sometimes any returns. In some cases this may have been due an inability to complete the appropriate forms but there was at least one case of a dishonest Corresponding Secretary who was dismissed and refused to hand over any of the records he held. These events mean that the figures for membership should be treated as estimates. There is no direct correlation between the number of members and the number of lodges. In 1845 the average lodge in Lancashire had 87 members. In Devon, the figure was 34. Some of the sources contradict some of the other sources. If women and juniors are included then the Unity still had over a million members, 1,078,141, in 1944.

Some of the figures are derived from material presented to AMCs. However, the figures presented to each AMC are based on the Branch Numerical Return, i.e. statistics provided by the Branches themselves. Prior to 2006, the membership figures were held on a stand-alone DOS application called UBACS, and could not be corroborated by the central office in Manchester.

Part of the increase in membership on 2001 was due to the significant rise in marketing activity.

Through 2006 and 2007, the Society went through a data reconciliation exercise as Branches migrated to a common Access-based platform (Dynamics), and many anomalies came to light. This explains some of the decrease in 2006.

With the acquisition of Nottingham Friendly Society, the membership at the end of 2009 was approximately 120,000.

Sources:

Gosden, *The friendly societies*, pp. 30–5; C. Hardwick, *The history, present position and social importance of friendly societies*, 3rd edn, London, 1893 pp. 24–5; D. Neave, 'Friendly societies in GB', in M. van der Linden, pp. 49, 51, 64; Moffrey, *A century of Oddfellowship*, p. 185; *Quarterly Report*, October 1919; *Unity Reports*, 1949, 1950; AMC Agenda Books.

Glossary of some Oddfellows terms

Annual Moveable Conference (AMC)   The governing body of the Society which meets once a
year at a different venue. This is an opportunity for democratic discussion and voting by elected
Deputies on the business and management of the Society. It is also an important social event. It
was known as the Annual Moveable Committee between 1822 and 1904.

Annual Summoned Meeting   This is the Branch's AGM which every member is welcome to attend
and at which every member will have an equal vote. Historically attendance was compulsory
and each member was individually 'summoned' to attend. Members are still officially notified but
attendance is now optional. This meeting may contain ceremony.

Branch   The name now used for a lodge. Committees of Management run branches. Most consist of
a Chair, a Secretary, Trustees, a Social Co-ordinator and other members.

Brother   Term of address to a fellow member. The Oddfellows is a fraternal organisation.
Membership is likened to belonging to a family. In the manner of trade unions and other fraternal
bodies some members of the Society refer to men within it as Brother.

Certified Auditor of the Manchester Unity (CAMU)   Widely recognised auditing qualification
now disused. The acronym was also used for the later Certificate of Accounting Manchester
Unity, now also disused.

Committee of Management   The term used in the 1992 legislation for the body with significant
financial responsibilities. Within the Society this equates to the Board of Directors. There are
also Branch Management Committees that were in existence prior to 1992.

Conductor   *Q*: What are the duties of Conductors?

   A: To receive Candidates and care for them during the Ceremony of Initiation.
   (*Universal Ritual*, 1935)

Degree   Internal qualification

   Minor Degrees   After being initiated a member is entitled to take the minor degrees. There
   are four of these, listed below.

   White Degree   First of the Minor Degrees

   Blue Degree   Second of the Minor Degrees

   Scarlet Degree   Third of the Minor Degrees

   Gold Degree   Fourth of the Minor Degrees.

   Past Lodge Officers Degrees   A series of short Lectures, with accompanying signs and passwords, administered to members who have held the principal Offices in the Lodge (see below).

Purple Degree   This can only be taken by those who have served in each of the principal Offices of the Lodge (Elective Secretary, Vice Grand, Noble Grand and Immediate Past Noble Grand) and taken the Minor and Past Lodge Officers' Degrees. It qualifies a member to stand for higher office in the District or Society.

Past Elected Secretary's Degree   The first of the Past Officers' Degrees

Past Vice Grand's Degree   The second of the Past Officers' Degrees

Past Noble Grand's Degree   The third and final of the Past Officers' Degrees

Degree Master (or Lecture Master) (DM/LM)   A member who has taken the Purple Degree is qualified to act as a Degree Master to administer the Minor Degrees to other members. This member, charged with regulating degree ceremonies, informs those taking the degree of the obligations it entails by giving a lecture. The Lecture Master also examines a member on their previous degree. For example a member taking the 4th degree, the Gold, must demonstrate knowledge of the Scarlet, Blue and White Degrees.

Deputy   Members elected by a District to represent it at an AMC, or by a Lodge to represent it at a District Meeting. To attend AMC a Deputy has to hold the Purple Degree or have served on a Branch Committee of Management for three years and have been a member for five years.

Director   Member of the Board, elected by the AMC. Directors almost always remain on the Board until they become candidate for the post of Grand Master. Once they have served as Immediate Past Grand Master, they leave the Board unless they are elected as a Trustee of the Order. This provides both for continuity and innovation.

District   A regional grouping of lodges.

District Officer   Members who hold the Purple Degree are eligible to stand for regional offices, as District Officers. There are four officers at District level. These are the Provincial Grand Master (Prov GM), the Provincial Deputy Grand Master (Prov DGM), the Immediate Past Provincial Grand Master (IPPGM) and the Provincial Corresponding Secretary (Prov CS).

District Officers' Visit   District Officers have a duty to visit each local Branch in their District at least once a year. Historically this visit was effectively an audit but now it is more a social event. It may include a ceremonial element.

Elective Secretary (ES)   Person responsible for keeping the minutes and other administrative tasks.

Financial Lodge   During the 1980s Lodges were divided into those with over 500 members and £150,000 worth of assets (Financial Lodges) and other Lodges (Unregistered Lodges) that held no funds of their own.

Financial Secretary (or 'Permanent Secretary') (FS/PS)   This person has responsibility for organisational and financial activities. The Ritual description makes the commitment to clarity clear: 'To keep a fair and impartial account between every member and the Lodge; to explain and balance such whenever required by you or a majority of the Lodge and as far as in my power lies to keep the accounts clear and intelligible.'

Grand Master of the Order (GM)   Elected President of the Society. This post can only be held for one year. After the year of office is concluded the DGM (Deputy Grand Master) can then be returned as GM while the Grand Master becomes the IPGM (Immediate Past Grand Master) and subsequently one of the PGMs (Past Grand Master of the Order).

Guardian   Q: Guardian (*Guardian rises*), what is your duty?

A: To receive the password or permission of the Noble Grand, previous to admitting members or visitors and guard the Lodge against intrusion; to refuse admission of anyone during initiation or ballot; to prevent any person other than a member listening to or acquiring a knowledge of what is going on in the Lodge and to act in conjunction with the Officers of the Lodge in the execution of your [the Noble Grand's] commands. (*Universal Ritual*, 1935)

Herald   The term for the four officers who are placed at the North, South, West and East of the Lodge and have specific duties to perform during the ceremony which formally dedicates a new Lodge room.

Immediate Past Grand Master (IPGM)   Post held by a person who has just spent a year as Grand Master. Responsible for providing advice to the current Grand Master.

Immediate Past Noble Grand (IPNG)   Post held by a person who has just spent a year as Noble Grand. Responsible for providing advice to the current Noble Grand.

Immediate Past Provincial Grand Master (IPPGM)   Immediate Past District Chair. This post is held for a year.

Installing Officer (IO)   A director of the ceremony to create an officer of a lodge.

Initiation or Making   Welcoming ceremony. This is an optional ceremony for members who are interested in holding an office within the Society or taking part in the traditional ceremonies. Members who participate will make a promise to obey the rules and support their fellow members of the Society.

Intermediate Lodge   Branches for those aged 16–21, established in the 1960s.

Jewels   Medals or badges indicating either a rank or special status (such as attendance at an AMC).

Junior Section   This section is for those aged under 16. Now called Young Oddfellows.

Juvenile Section   A term no longer used for younger Oddfellows.

Left Supporter to the Noble Grand (LSNG)   Advisor to the NG. This person acts in conjunction with the Right Supporter of the Noble Grand and officiates if the Right Supporter is absent.

Lodge   A quasi-autonomous branch of the Oddfellows. A lodge can also refer to the meeting room of a branch.

Lodge of Past Grands   A group for members who have held office as chair ('Noble Grand') of a Lodge.

Minor Degree Lodge   This is a Branch which is set up purely to deliver the minor degree lectures which cover ethical teachings. Each degree lecture corresponds to a particular colour and those who have attained all four degrees are eligible to stand for office in their Branch. They are open to anyone wishing to learn more about the teachings and traditions of the Oddfellows.

Noble Grand (NG)   Lodge Chair. The equivalent of the Masonic 'Worshipful Master'. Once a member had held two assistant offices (Guardian, Warden and Conductor) served as Elective Secretary and completed two minor degrees (see under degrees) he (or she) could stand for the post of Vice-Grand. If (s)he then took the other two minor degrees (s)he could stand for the position of chair, Noble Grand. The post could be held for one year only. This provided frequent opportunities to stand for office and develop organisational and social skills.

To 'open' and 'close' a lodge.   Brief ceremonies which remind members of the principles of Oddfellowship. During the period that the lodge is 'open', that is in session addressing propositions about ill members, the welfare of the lodge or potential recruits, nobody may leave or enter without giving a signal, known only to members, of their membership.

Past Grand   Former chair of the Lodge who has taken the Purple Degree.

Past Noble Grand (PNG)   Former chair of the lodge. This post was held for a year and followed Immediate Past Noble Grand. Holders of these posts (PNG and IPNG) were ineligible to stand again until a year had passed. PNGs were eligible to sit for the Purple Degree and hold offices at District and national level.

Provincial Corresponding Secretary (Prov CS)   District Secretary.

Provincial Lodge of Past Grands   A group for Past Grands (PGs) interested in the history and meaning of ceremony, and who attend qualifying Degree Lectures.

Past Provincial Grand Master (PPGM)   Former District Chair.

Provincial Grand Master (Prov GM)   District Chair. The post is held for one year. After this period the Prov GM becomes the IPPGM, Immediate Past Provincial Grand Master.

Prov GM's Appeal   An important part of Oddfellowship is raising money for charity. Each year a Provincial Grand Master may nominate a charity which will benefit. The launch often involves a presentation by a representative of the chosen charity as well as refreshments. It is unlikely to contain any ceremony.

Regalia   Special clothing worn for Ritual purposes including sashes, aprons, gauntlets and collarettes. These items denote rank and can be supplemented by Jewels. There is also lodge regalia such as cloths and symbols.

Right Supporter to the Noble Grand (RSNG)   In the traditional lodge each NG had two advisors one was the experienced Right Supporter. The Ritual indicates the nature of the job. The response to the NG's question as to his or her duty is: 'To support you in keeping good order; to execute your commands; to see that all signs and tokens are given correctly and to open and close the Lodge in due form.'

Senior Past Grand Master   As being Grand Master of the Order is a post held only for a year there are often a number of former Grand Masters. This person is the one who was Grand Master earlier than any other one.

Sick Visitor   A lodge member who had the responsibility of ensuring that an ill member received the benefits due to them and checking on their well-being (now more frequently referred to as Welfare Officers (see below) or Visitors.

Sister   Term of address to a fellow member. The Oddfellows is a fraternal organisation. Membership is likened to belonging to a family and some members refer to female members as Sister.

Trustee   A member of senior rank with financial responsibilities.

Tyler   A Tyler is an old English word for the doorkeeper of an inn and within the Society it still refers to the Doorkeeper. The instruction 'Tyle the doors' means that nobody is allowed to enter or leave the room until the instruction to 'Untyle the doors' is issued. The title 'Guardian' (see above) is normally applied to the officer responsible. The title has long been used within Freemasonry where a Tyler is charged with examining the Masonic credentials of anyone wishing to enter the Lodge. It might have originally referred to a person who lays roof or floor tiles and is thus not as skilled as the higher status masons inside the lodge. It might also be a corruption of the word 'tether', to tie the door closed.

Unregistered Lodge   During the 1980s lodges were divided into those with over 500 members and £150,000 worth of assets (Financial Lodges) and other lodges (Unregistered Lodges). These are Lodges with no funds of their own.

Vice Grand (VG)   Vice chair of the lodge. The Ritual describes the post:

> *Q:* Worthy Vice Grand (*VG rises*), what is your duty in the Lodge?
>
> *A:* To act in conjunction with you Most Noble Grand, in restraining and suppressing disorder, to check anything improper and to keep a guard on the conduct of members during Lodge hours. (*Universal Ritual*, 1935)

Warden

> *Q:* Warden (*Warden rises*), what is your duty?
>
> *A:* To examine with care every person present before the lodge is opened; place and replace the regalia in a careful manner and report to the Lodge any damage or loss that may occur. (*Universal Ritual*, 1935)

Welfare Officer   An appointed member who ensures that older or infirm members receive benefits and care. See also Sick Visitor.

Biographical notes

These remarks about the lives of those who contributed their memories to this book are brief sketches. For reasons of space, much has been omitted. As the *Annual Report 1999* noted at the retirement of one of the contributors, Derek Winbush, 'the full list of his service to the Unity, even at local level, would fill this Agenda book'.

Keith Adamson was born in 1954. Shortly after his wife, lifelong Oddfellow Alison, became a Provincial Deputy Grand Master in 1993 Keith thought, 'I'll join and spend time with her.' The same year he had a heart attack and the Unity became a 'lifeline because it gave me something to get my teeth into'. Within a decade he was a Director. He became Grand Master in 2006. His two sons are Oddfellows and he obtained a mortgage through the Oddfellows.

Jeffrey Bartlett was born in Farnborough in 1926 and, on his uncle's recommendation, became an Oddfellow at the age of 16. He rose through the ranks to join the Godalming District Committee and become a District Trustee in the 1950s, Provincial Grand Master in 1960 and Senior Trustee until he retired in 1975. He has attended the annual AMC Past Provincial Grand Masters' lodge meetings.

James Beard was born in Hazelgrove, Derbyshire, in 1930. His father was an Oddfellow and had already been through all the chairs. During the war he became lodge secretary of Fox, Lilly of the Valley, 442 in Derbyshire, a post he held until his death in 1961. James was active in the 1960s and became a Trustee.

Syd Bolton was born in 1924 in Barrow in Furness. During the war he served in the Royal Navy and later trained to be a nurse at The Manchester Royal, Cheadle. On the recommendation of a colleague he became an Oddfellow and by 1984 had joined the Board of Directors, a post he held until 1992. He remained a director of the Red Rose Housing Association until 2004.

Lesley Bull was born to active members of the Oddfellows in 1955 and was enrolled as a baby. She was active for many years, has fond memories of growing up in a household of Oddfellowship and enrolled her own children soon after they were born.

Roger Burley was born in London in 1944 and was enrolled in the Unity as a child by his father, an Oddfellow and marine engineer on the Thames. Roger joined the John Evelyn Juvenile Lodge, was active in an Intermediate Lodge, was a District Secretary for 25 years and became Grand Master in 1996.

Iris Capel was born in 1927 to Oddfellow parents. She was a juvenile member in the 1930s in south west London and at the age of 18 joined Lorna Doone Lodge. In 1948 she married an Oddfellow.

She enjoyed life in the lodge, particularly the outings, picnics, Christmas parties and five-course lodge dinners.

Tony Crouch was born in Grays, Essex, in 1925. His father was a member of the Oddfellow and Tony joined when he was 16. He became a Conductor within a year and, aged 21, he became Vice Grand. He was a Noble Grand three times and was made a Trustee of the Lodge. He met his wife, a member of the Good Intent Ladies Lodge of which he was Secretary, on the Oddfellows' Hall ballroom. He arranged two of his mortgages through the Oddfellows.

Richard Cubitt was born in Durban, South Africa, in 1930 and about 60 years later joined the Oddfellows after careers in the British Merchant Navy and as a painter and decorator in London. The social aspects of Oddfellowship have been attractive, as has the fact that he can travel the world and meet other members of the Oddfellows.

Dorothy Deacon was born in Chelmsford in 1941. Her parents, cousin and aunt were members of the Oddfellows, and both her grandfathers were founder members of the Priory Lodge in Southend. Dorothy was joined when only a few hours old. Her father was a Noble Grand and a Sick Visitor, and he also helped run the lodge Loan Club. Dorothy has held many posts, including being a Director. She was a President and the first female Secretary of the Southern Group Conference.

Sue Doulton Smith was born in 1948 to Sister Dolly and Brother Jim. She joined in 1962, attended her first AMC in 1967, as a visitor with her mother, went through the chairs in Bedford and was active in the national Under 35s group. She has travelled to meet Canadian Oddfellows and Oddfellows in Europe and became the Grand Master in 1998. On the way she married Brother Steve and gave birth to Sister Natalie who attended a number of meetings in her carrycot. She is currently the Secretary of Bedford Lodge.

Derek Elmer was born in 1944 in St Neots. He used to sit in a pub and watch the Oddfellows go upstairs to the lodge. Curious, he joined in 1965, aged 21. He enjoyed the dinner dances and the ceremonial elements of the Oddfellows and served on the District Committee in the 1980s. He became a Trustee and has demonstrated British Ritual in Holland. He now acts as caretaker of Oddfellows' property in Camden.

Jean Facer was born in 1935 and grew up in Islington. It was her husband, Stan who introduced her to Oddfellowship. Her parents joined later. Jean has held many posts in the Oddfellows, including twice acting as District Chair.

Winifred Felgate was born in 1920 and when she was nine her father became an Oddfellow. Almost immediately he took on the task of being a Lodge Secretary, administering the National Health Insurance scheme. When Winifred was to be married he recruited her fiancé, Bill. On the death of her father in 1953 Bill was elected as Lodge Secretary. Winifred became Noble Grand for the first time in 1962, Provincial Grand Master in 1967 and President of the East Anglian Group Conference in 1975. She was delighted when her son-in-law, Keith Adamson, became Grand Master of the Order.

Brenda Francis was born in 1933 in Farnborough, the daughter of a tailor and a dressmaker and the grand daughter of an Oddfellow in the Royal Artillery Lodge, Woolwich. She joined her mother's business at the age of 15. By the age of 16 in 1949 she had established her own business, Brenda's, which she still runs, and joined the Oddfellows. Brenda held a number of posts, including being a Provincial Grand Master.

Ray Gibbens was born in Farnborough in 1926. His father was an Oddfellow but the reason Ray joined was because he was invited by his friends, Jeff and John Bartlett, to help encourage drama within the Lodge. Ray went on to write and produce three plays for the Lodge and to run quizzes for about 30 years. He was still singing and playing his guitar to Oddfellows in 2008.

Margaret Graham, born 1930 in Disley, is the daughter of and granddaughter of Oddfellows who were active at District level. Her mother continued to be an Oddfellow, even after she was widowed in 1952. Margaret's membership lapsed on marriage but was renewed in the 1990s.

Leonard ('Ken') Harding was born in 1929. His father, a builder and decorator, was a member of the Society. As a child Ken attended social events with his parents at the Phoenix Lodge Watford. After the war he received a 90 per cent mortgage from the Oddfellows and became involved in lodge social activities.

Daphne Harmer was born in Hamble, Hampshire in 1930. In 1946 she married a member of the Unity who she met at her place of work and they got a mortgage from the Oddfellows. He was a Lodge and District Secretary for many years and became a Grand Master. She joined in 1953, recalled Saturday night dances with affection and has pleasant memories of the Society's 150th anniversary celebrations in London.

Anne Harris was born in 1937 and lived in Watford. Both her parents were members of the Oddfellows, her aunt was chair of the Investigation Committee in 1933 and Matron of the Friendly Society's Convalescent Home at Herne Bay and her mother's uncle was a mother's uncle was Provincial Grand Master. Anne was joined to the Oddfellows aged three months in 1938 and held many posts, including being a District Trustee for many years.

Joan Henry was born in 1921, was married in 1941, and had two sons. Her husband was in the army and the family moved around a great deal. She knew nothing whatever about Oddfellowship until her husband Reginald joined, on the advice of a neighbour. He 'went through the chairs' within 18 months of joining and was Secretary to the Order 1972–85. She joined in the early 1950s and later became 'Auntie Jo' to thousands of members of the Society all over the world.

Arthur Jackson was born in 1912 in Derbyshire and like his father (who was the subject of a portrait in *The Odd Fellow Magazine*, January 1945) was a member of the Loyal Offspring of Truth Lodge Kettleshulme which was founded by his great grandfather in 1838. Arthur's grandfather was a secretary for 25 years and Arthur was Treasurer for 40 years, secretary for about 20, Noble Grand and Sick Visitor for 14.

George Kilford was born in Portsmouth in 1929. In 1946 he joined the civil service and in 1948 moved to Reading where he got married in 1954. In 1956 he was invited to join the Oddfellows by a friend. He held many posts and joined the Board of Directors 1981. He became Grand Master, representing the Order on trips to the USA, New Zealand and Australia, and was a Trustee 1990–95.

Lillian Leese was born on the Isle of Man in 1945 and joined the Oddfellows there after a recommendation from a work colleague. She was later active in Coventry becoming a Provincial Grand Master and also a member of a lodge for those who had been Grand Masters. She has attended a number of AMCs.

Brian Merrell was born in Becontree, Dagenham in 1943 to parents who were active Oddfellows. His grandfather was also an Oddfellow as was his great grandfather. His earliest memory is seeing his parents dressed in regalia to attend a lodge function. His father became a Provincial Grand Master and his mother, who was awarded the Meritorious Jewel in 1964, became the first female Grand

Master of the Order in 1978. Brian was active in an Intermediate Lodge in the 1960s.

Bertie Miles was born in 1923 in Norwich and has spent much of his life there. His maternal great uncle, Robert Farrow, was the subject of a portrait in the *Oddfellows' Magazine*, February 1901. When he left school Bertie was enrolled by his father, who worked for Colman's, a company run by a family which had long been supportive of Oddfellowship. Bertie worked in Birmingham and Wolverhampton where, during a bout of jaundice, he was supported by the Oddfellows.

Terry Moore was born in 1942. The eldest of six he grew up within a working-class family living south of Manchester. His father was a regular soldier until he was invalided out. Terry became a lay Minister, Buffalo and Freemason and joined the Oddfellows in his forties, influenced by learning about it through listening to a radio play.

Pat Morgan was born in Woodford Essex in 1940. In the early 30s her father, Jim Morgan, was secretary of a thrift club in Leytonstone. He was approached by two Trustees of a Stepney lodge, joined and became secretary until he died in 1966. He married an Oddfellow in 1938 and joined the Board in 1956. He was also secretary of the Metropolitan District Officers Association and a Trustee of Herne Bay Convalescent Home. He became Grand Master in 1963. Pat's mother, Ruth, was a lodge Trustee and her baby-sitter was the first female Grand Master, Dolly Merrell. Pat joined aged 16 in 1956, became a Vice Grand in the Intermediates and, after joining the adults, became Provincial Grand Master in 1974.

Roy Morris was born in the Moseley district of Birmingham in 1930. His father was an Oddfellow for 42 years, joining in 1920 and going through the district chairs several times. Roy's parents set up the Birmingham Juvenile Oddfellows district lodge in 1944 which Roy joined. Roy went to the Blackpool AMC aged 13. In the 1970s and 1980s Roy was a Noble Grand and Lodge Trustee.

Betty Mostyn was born in 1930. In 1937, after he was told about Oddfellowship by a fellowfootball referee, her father joined and took Betty to a meeting in 1946. She had 'gone through the chairs' by the age of 21 and she then married Len. Her father told Len 'If you are getting married you might as well join the Oddfellows'. Len went on to become Grand Master and President of the National Conference of Friendly Societies. He was awarded the OBE for his services to friendly societies.

Thomas ('Tom') Nicholson was born in 1919. His father was a member of Pleasant Retreat, Preston and his mother was a member of Preston Female Lodge. His grandfather Thomas was also an Oddfellow. Tom joined the Oddfellows in 1935 and after serving in the army, married. His wife became a Noble Grand and, following her death, he married Doris who he met at the 1964 AMC. Tom became a Grand Master in 1974–75 when he became the first Grand Master to address the Sovereign Grand Lodge in the USA in session. His daughter became a Noble Grand in Preston and his grandson is also a member there.

Phil Norman was born in Barnsley, south Yorkshire, in 1944. His father was a miner and Phil went underground as a mechanical craft apprentice before leaving to work in Copper Mines in Zambia between 1968 and 1973. On his return to England he became a member of the Society.

Eric Ogden was made a member of the Order on his birth in 1935 and initiated in 1954, prompted by a connection made in church. His great grandfather, his grandfather and his mother were all active within the Order. He attended his first AMC in 1958 and was Lodge Secretary from 1964 until 1975. In 1964 he also became Provincial Grand Master, the youngest ever in the district until his brother David became a Provincial Grand Master in the same district in 1978. Eric was appointed as Provincial Corresponding Secretary in 1969 and Grand Master in 2000.

Dulcie Pauley became a member after her marriage to Terence in 1963 and rose to become a Provincial Grand Master in the early 1990s. She took over as a Lodge Secretary from her husband Terence in 1974. She recalled that, 'we have had many a happy time with the society. We have made lots of friends.'

Terence Pauley was born in Plymouth in 1934 the son and grandson of Oddfellows. He was enrolled as a junior member at birth and admitted as an adult in 1950 when he was 16. After he became a Past Noble Grand he joined the Devonport Provincial Lodge of Past Grands. He remained active in his own lodge and from 1960 until 1974 when due to civil service regulations he had to give up all outside paid employment, he was a Lodge Secretary in another town as well. He passed the CAMU in 1970. He was a Trustee for 20 years and President of the Southern Group in 1988. In 1994 he was presented with a Meritorious Award.

Pauline Pettigrove was born in 1969 and has worked as a Branch Secretary for the Oddfellows in the Plymouth and Truro district Lodge since March 2004. She heard of the Oddfellows through the job advertisement she answered and on appointment became engrossed in Oddfellowship. Her husband has joined and at least one of her children helps out at social gatherings.

Andrew Porter was born in Huddersfield in 1952 and was encouraged to become an Oddfellow by his father-in-law, a Trustee. Andrew was active in Yorkshire for many years, particularly with the Yorkshire Juvenile Conference. He became a Provincial Grand Master and was then elected as Grand Master in 2004.

Douglas Potter was born in Acton, west London, in 1918 and he was introduced to Oddfellowship by his maternal grandfather, a Sick Visitor. Douglas joined in 1942, aged 24. One of his earliest activities was arrange a dance at Finsbury Town Hall in 1946. He and a Trustee were MCs for the evening. 'We charged a half a crown and we made a profit.' He became the Assistant Secretary for five years and Secretary 1952–2000, for 48 years. He has travelled to Europe to meet members of the Society on the continent.

Denis Rose was born in Chadwell Heath in 1920 above the family-run grocery and Post Office. His father, Henry, was a Lodge Secretary and auditor. He enrolled all three of his sons at birth. Denis retained his membership and got a mortgage through the Oddfellows. When Henry's eyesight failed the Oddfellows provided support until Henry's death in 1964.

Edward Schofield was born in 1948 in Glossop. He spent forty years working in local government. In the early twenty-first century he became District Secretary for the Pennine area with a brief to manage the refurbishment of the local Oddfellows Hall.

Daphne Stephenson was born in Hatfield, south Yorkshire in 1942, trained as a teacher, became a Youth Leader and married a Youth Leader who was an Oddfellow. She joined the Society and became a Provincial Grand Master and District Trustee, going on to join the Benevolence Committee and the Investigation Committee and to be elected to the Board of Directors. She was elected Grand Master in 2006 and has been secretary of the Yorkshire Group Conference for over thirty years.

Karen Stuart was born in 1965 and has lived most of her life in northwest Norfolk. Her great grandfather was an Oddfellow. In 1995 she was invited to join by a friend and by 1997 she had gone through the chairs and joined the District Management Committee. She got married during her first AMC and rose through the ranks to become Provincial Grand Master in 2001. In 2005 she became a Trustee and was elected to the Unity Special Arbitrators and to the Unity Benevolence Committee. In 2008 she was elected a Director.

Mike Trenchard was enrolled at birth in 1946 by his father Ronald (see below). He comes from a long line of Oddfellows. His great grandfather was a Past Grand and his great uncle, grandfather, father and mother were all Oddfellows. He was initiated aged 16 and became the Past President of a Junior Lodge the Noble Grand of an Intermediate Lodge, a Provincial Grand Master of the Watford District, a District Trustee and Secretary of the Minor Degree Lodge. His wife and daughter joined the Oddfellows.

Ron Trenchard was born in London in 1917. He joined the Society aged eight years old and attended meetings with his father who 'went through the chairs' and was awarded a merit jewel. Ron also went through the chairs at least twice and became a Provincial Grand Master, as did his wife. Their two children (one of whom is Mike Trenchard) and some of his grandchildren joined the Oddfellows.

Kath Vernon was born in 1934. She was introduced to Oddfellowship when she was in her fifties by a lifelong Oddfellow she met on holiday. She joined the Countess of Warwick lodge in Birmingham and subsequently became a Provincial Grand Master and Provincial Secretary. She has also been a Deputy to several AMCs.

Mary Wheeler was born in 1947 and made a member of the Cumbermere lodge, Stockport where her father, Philip, 1901–64 was a member. Her first formal meeting was when she was aged 20 and had married, moved to Huddersfield and was working as a nurse in the Royal Infirmary. She became a Noble Grand and then, she moved back to Stockport, went 'through the chairs' at her father's old lodge and became active at district level.

Frances Wilkinson was born in Bradford in 1948. Both her parents were active members of the Society. Her father became a Provincial Grand Master in 1956. As a Lodge Secretary he would 'quite often spend half the night looking for a halfpenny when they couldn't get the books to balance.' Her mother joined on marriage and also became a Provincial Grand Master among other posts. Frances was a junior, gained her Purple Degree and married an Oddfellow. They got a mortgage through the Society and both her sons joined the Oddfellows.

Derek Winbush was born 1934. He was a Provincial Grand Master by 1962 and organised trips, sea cruises and what became 'Oddfellows Brass'. He joined the Board of Directors in 1974 and went on to serve as a representative on the National Conference of Friendly Societies. He helped to launch the first Credit Union in the Oddfellows and in 2008 became the Senior Past Grand Master.

John Winkley was born in 1922 in Uppingham, Rutland. In 1938 he followed his father, a Provincial Grand Master and became an Oddfellow. After wartime military service John became involved in the Society as a Lodge Secretary, a Noble Grand, a Lodge Trustee and a member of the District Committee.

Conferences, Grand Masters and Secretaries of the Order

In addition to the main list, below, the following Grand Masters are recorded:

1814	James Christie
1815–1818	John Lloyd
1819–1820	James Mansell.

Year	Place where held and dates	Grand Master who presided
1822	Manchester, 30 May–1 June	William Armitt
1823	Hanley, 19–20 May	William Armitt
1824	Haslingden, 7–8 June	Thomas Armitt
1825	Huddersfield, 15–17 May	Thomas Armitt
1826	Manchester, 15–17 May	William Armitt
1827	Nottingham, 4–6 June	Thomas Derbyshire
1828	Dudley, 26–29 May	B. A. Redfern
1829	Sheffield, 8–11 June	Mark Wardle
1830	Leeds, 31 May–3 June	Joseph Bamett
1831	Liverpool, 23–27 May	John Ashurst
1832	Monmouth, 11–14 June	William Gray
1833	Bury, 27–31 May	Robert Naylor
1834	Hull, 19–22 May	John R. White
1835	Kendal, 8–12 June	John Ormond
1836	Derby, 23–28 May	James Mansfield
1837	London, 15–20 May	William Gray
1838	Rochdale, 4–9 June	James Gorbutt
1839	Birmingham, 20–25 May	John Peiser
1840	York, 8–13 June	James Davis
1841	Isle of Man, 31 May–5 June	David Carnegie
1842	Wigan, 17–21 May	E.K. Davis
1843	Bradford, 5–10 June	G. Richmond

Year	Place where held and dates	Grand Master who presided
1844	Newcastle, 27 May–1 June	James Mansfield
1845	Glasgow, 12–17 May	Henry Whaite
1846	Bristol, 1–6 June	John Dickinson
1847	Oxford, 24–29 May	R.R. Elliot
1848	Southampton, 12–17 June	W.B. Smith
1849	Blackburn, 28 May–3 June	John Richardson
1850	Halifax, 20–24 May	Thomas Luff
1851	Dublin, 9–14 June	John Bradley
1852	Carlisle, 31 May–4 June	S. Daynes
1853	Preston, 16–19 May	R. Glass
1854	London, 5–10 June	James Roe
1855	Durham, 28 May–1 June	Benjamin Street
1856	Lincoln, 12–16 May	John Schofield
1857	Norwich, 1–6 June	James C. Cox
1858	Swansea, 24–29 May	Charles Hardwick
1859	Leicester, 13–18 June	William Alexander
1860	Shrewsbury, 28 May–1 June	William Hickton
1861	Bolton, 20–24 May	Henry Buck
1862	Brighton, 9–14 June	John Gale
1863	Leamington, 25–30 May	Joseph Woodcock
1864	Birkenhead, 16–21 May	V. R. Burgess
1865	Worcester, 5–10 June	Fred Richmond
1866	Burton on Trent, 21–26 May	Thomas Price
1867	Plymouth, 10–14 June	James Curtis
1868	Cheltenham, 1–5 June	George Walker
1869	Sunderland, 17–21 May	Edwin Smith
1870	Chesterfield, 6–10 June	William Lovesey
1871	Bury St Edmunds, 29 May–2 June	George Ramsden
1872	Lancaster, 20–24 May	Reuben Ginn
1873	Weymouth, 2–6 June	James Gerrard
1874	Richmond (Surrey), 25–29 May	W.N. Westem
1875	Newport (Mons), 17–21 May	Reuben Watson
1876	Isle of Wight, 5–10 June	J.T. Cox
1877	Oldham, 21–25 May	John Geves
1878	Exeter, 10–15 June	J.J. Holmes
1879	Edinburgh, 2–7 June	J.A. Riley
1880	Lynn, 17–22 May	Henry Outram
1881	Cardiff, 6–11 June	Fred G. Pownall
1882	Southport, 29 May–3 June	Thomas Flanagan

Year	Place where held and dates	Grand Master who presided
1883	Nottingham, 14–18 May	Thomas Walton
1884	Reading, 2–6 June	John Bennett
1885	Aberystwyth, 25–30 May	Louis E. Wollstein
1886	Stafford, 14–19 June	William Grimes
1887	Dover, 30 May–3 June	J.J. Stockail
1888	Gloucester, 21–26 May	John Rust
1889	Dover, 10–14 June	Robert T. Eastwood
1890	Ipswich, 26–31 May	John Inglis
1891	Salisbury, 18–23 May	A. Sydney Campkin
1892	Derby, 6–11 May	John Bytheway
1893	Southampton, 22–27 May	Henry Flowers
1894	Northampton, 14–19 May	Sir C. Graham
1895	Swansea, 3–8 June	John Diprose
1896	Bristol, 25–30 May	Wm Orford White
1897	Isle of Man, 7–11 June	Samuel Turner
1898	Oxford, 30 May–4 June	Edward Lukey
1899	Middlesbrough, 22–26 May	Thomas Edmondson
1900	Portsmouth, 4–8 June	Tom Hughes
1901	Norwich, 27–31 May	Richard Rushton
1902	Newcastle, 19–23 May	R.J. Vallender
1903	Cheltenham, 1–5 June	R.W. Moffrey
1904	Manchester, 23–27 May	H.L. Woodesen
1905	Plymouth, 12–16 June	E.E. Hind
1906	Barrow In Furness, 4–8 June	Thomas Mills
1907	Folkestone, 20–24 May	J. Harford-Hawkins
1908	Cardiff, 8–12 June	A. Dempsey
1909	Bradford, 31 May–4 June	Ben Kilvington
1910	Southampton, 16–19 May	Edward Bourne
1911	Brighton, 5–9 June	Thomas Barnes
1912	London, 31 Jan–2 Feb	Alfred H. Warren
1912	Nottingham, 27–31 May	Alfred H. Warren
1913	Scarborough, 12–16 May	J.R. Barley
1914	Aberystwyth, 1–5 June	Walter P. Wright
1915	Manchester, 24–28 May	Rev F.C. Davies MA
1916	Bristol, 12–16 June	T.J.W. Siddal
1918	Cheltenham, 20–24 May	Wallace Smith
1919	Isle of Man, 9–13 June	W.H. Hayes
1920	Leamington, 24–28 May	Joseph Smith
1921	Glasgow, 16–21 May	Geo. L. Lingstrom

Year	Place where held and dates	Grand Master who presided
1922	Island of Guernsey, 5–9 June	Josiah Coulthurst
1923	Scarborough, 21–25 May	Thos G. Graham
1924	Folkestone, 9–13 June	George Wilkins
1925	Bournemouth, 1–5 June	H.H. Brimblecombe
1926	Torquay, 24–28 May	J. Fred Day
1927	Great Yarmouth, 6–10 June	Benjamin Ashdown
1928	Isle of Man, 28 May–June 1	Herbert White
1929	Portsmouth, 20–24 May	Edwin Heather
1930	Plymouth, 9–13 June	Amos Culpan
1931	Scarborough, 25–29 May	Robert Annis
1932	Island of Guernsey, 16–20 May	T.R. Morgan
1933	Brighton, 5–9 May	Samuel Barnes
1934	London, 21–25 May	John Holden
1935	Blackpool, 10–14 June	Edward Clark
1936	Isle of Man, 1–5 June	A.N. Wright
1937	Glasgow, 17–21 May	E.C. Baldock
1938	Margate, 6–10 June	E.H. Toogood
1939	Scarborough, 29 May–2 June	F. Cundall
1940	Southampton, 13–17 May	Thom. Duckworth
1942	London, 30 June–2 July	O.B. Meadmore
1943	Blackpool, 6–8 July	J.T. Little
1945	Leicester, 12–14 June	G.C. Seeviour
1945	London (sp), 22–24 October	M.V. Sweeney
1946	Scarborough, 24–28 June	M.V. Sweeney
1947	Douglas (I.O.M.), 16–20 June	H.E. Reiman MC
1948	Margate, 31 May–4 June	G.H. Barrow
1949	Morecambe, 20–24 June	J.A. Stephenson
1950	Great Yarmouth, 12–16 June	G.H. Harper
1951	Torquay, 4–8 June	E. Maxwell
1952	Island of Guernsey, 9–13 June	W.H. Simpson
1953	Folkestone, 15–19 June	H.P. Waller
1954	Southport, 21–25 June	W. Abbott
1955	Hastings, 6–10 June	A.B. Holland
1956	Scarborough, 28 May–1 June	H.E. Lacy
1957	Margate, 27–31 May	C.T. Flogdell
1958	Blackpool, 2–6 June	S.W. Roffey
1959	Scarborough, 25–29 May	F.R. Hammond
1960	Brighton, 30 May–3 June	H. Hammerton
1961	Douglas (I.O.M.), 29 May–2 June	W.A.S. Hiscox

Year	Place where held and dates	Grand Master who presided
1962	Island of Guernsey, 28 May–1 June	T.N. Kibble
1963	Torquay, 27–31 May	J.G. Barnes
1964	Morecambe, 25–29 May	J.W. Morgan
1965	Margate, 31 May–4 June	J.A. McBryde
1966	Isle of Man, 6–10 June	H.L. Hosking
1967	Bournemouth, 15–19 May	H.E. West
1968	Southport, 27–31 May	J.C. Kent
1969	Folkestone, 2–6 June	F.H. Sandom
1970	Scarborough, 18–22 May	G.P. Cooper
1971	Eastbourne, 24–28 May	R.H. Day
1972	Douglas (I.O.M.), 22–26 May	P.J. Martel
1973	Margate, 21–25 May	R.A. Perry
1973	Blackpool (Sp), 22–24 Nov	L. Blower
1974	Skegness, 20–24 May	L. Blower
1975	Eastbourne, 12–16 May	G.W. Wyver
1976	Scarborough, 17–21 May	W. Schofield
1977	Blackpool, 23–27 May	R.A. Bowler
1978	Margate, 22–26 May	L. Mostyn
1979	Douglas (I.O.M.), 21–25 May	Dorothy M. Merrell
1979	Installed Douglas (I.O.M.)	Elizabeth L.M. Lomax deceased July 1979
1980	Southport, 2–6 June	E. Fage
1981	Bournemouth, 11–15 May	E. Fage
1982	Scarborough, 10–14 May	D.W. Winbush
1983	Eastbourne, 9–13 May	L.D. Gaskin
1984	Torquay, 21–25 May	R. Johnson
1985	Blackpool, 27–31 May	T. Nicholson
1986	Bournemouth, 5–9 May	Christine H. Feek
1987	Scarborough, 11–15 May	J.A. Cowell
1988	Southport, 23–27 May	A. Tapp
1989	Scarborough, 29 May–2 June	R.F. Banham
1990	Eastbourne, 21–25 May	G.A.J. Kilford
1990	Installed Eastbourne	R.G. Harmer deceased January 1991
1991	Bournemouth, 6–10 May	S. Bolton
1992	Llandudno, 18–22 May	S. Bolton
1993	Blackpool, 3–7 May	E.N. Jaynes
1994	Plymouth, 23–27 May	H.F. Buckingham
1995	Eastbourne, 8–12 May	J.W. Goulding

Year	Place where held and dates	Grand Master who presided
1996	Scarborough, 10–14 May	K. Hughes
1997	Brighton, 26–30 May	Roger Burley
1998	Bournemouth, 12–15 May	Sue Doulton Smith
1999	Island of Jersey, 17–21 May	Ivan E. Ashborn
2000	Scarborough, 29 May–2 June	Peter Needham
2001	Eastbourne, 21–25 May	Eric A. Ogden
2002	Scarborough, 27–29 May	David G. Phillips
2003	Bournemouth, 24–27 May	David J Nelson
2004	Eastbourne, 24–26 May	Ron Munro
2005	Scarborough, 30 May–1 June	D.A. Porter
2006	Scarborough, 22–24 May	Margaret Lickess
2007	Eastbourne, 28–30 May	Daphne Stephenson
2008	Southport, 26–28 May	Keith Adamson
2009	Eastbourne, 28–30 May	Nicola O'Riordan Finley
2010	Manchester, 14–16 June	Dorothy Deacon

Secretaries of the Order

1815	W. Sandford
1816	Thos. Hignett
1820	Isaac Hardman
1824	Mark Wardle
1828	T. Armitt
1837–1847	W. Ratcliffe
1847–1877	H. Ratcliffe
1877–1878	John Schofield
1878–1906	Thos. Collins
1907–1926	Walter Collins
1926–1956	H.A. Andrews
1956–1972	H.F. Watson
1972–1985	R. Henry
1985–1992	J.G. Haughton
1992–1998	D. Moss
1998–2000	N. Heald
2000–	Jane Nelson

Notes and references

NB The full title of a text appears only at the first reference, and subsequently in a shortened form.

Introduction

1. The words Oddfellow, Oddfellows, Order, Unity and Society and the acronym IOOFMU refer to the Independent Order of Oddfellows, Manchester Unity, unless otherwise stated. There are other organisations with Oddfellows in the title. Over the years there has been inconsistency about whether members, and the Society, are Odd Fellows, Odd-Fellows or Oddfellows. The use of the term 'Manchester Unity' was first recorded in 1822. A previous name had been the 'Independent Order of Odd Fellows under the Manchester Compliance' and in a letter to the King in 1820 a Provincial Grand Master, James Mansell, called the Society 'the Loyal and Independent Order of Oddfellows for Lancashire'. There have also been those who refer to the Society with less accuracy, such as Erik Olssen who claimed that 'the organisation's full name was: Manchester United Independent Order of Oddfellowship'. See E. Olssen, 'Friendly societies in New Zealand, 1840–1990', in M. Van Der Linden (ed.), *Social Security Mutualism: The Comparative History of Mutual Benefit Societies*, Peter Lang, Berne, 1996, pp. 177–206. The spelling Oddfellow is used unless a direct quotation in which another spelling is employed is being cited.

2. J. D. Burn, *An historical sketch of the Independent Order of Oddfellows MU*, A. Heywood, Manchester 1845, p. 156. A decade later Burn recalled that he became a 'Grand Master of the district', that he lectured all over Scotland, sold one hundred copies of his book to the Society and in 1846 he was elected to the Oddfellows Board of Directors at the AMC. Despite his enthusiasm and commitment he left the Society within a year, describing how he felt cured of his infection with a 'species of insanity, in the shape of Odd-fellow-phobia'. See J. D. Burn, *The autobiography of a beggar boy*, 1855, edited with an introduction by D. Vincent, Europa,

London, 1978, pp. 157, 173.

3. T. B. Stead, *Foresters' Directory*, 1888, p. vi, cited in R. Logan, 'The role of friendly society orders in British society, 1793–1911, with particular reference to the Ancient Order of Foresters Friendly Society', Ph.D. thesis, Kingston, 2003, p. 1.

4. For two examples among many see *Western Mail*, 18 December 1900 which reported the case of Frank Ridings who was found guilty of claiming money on false pretences from both the Oddfellows and the Foresters. *The Guardian*, 21 April 1966 reported that a former Grand Master, John Barnes had been found guilty of embezzling almost £28,000 from the Society.

5. Some of the literature regarding personal behaviour and structures is discussed at greater length in J. Doris, *Lack of Character*, Cambridge University Press, Cambridge, 2002.

6. Burn, *An historical sketch*, pp. 40, 41.

7. A number of historians have linked friendly societies to trade unions. See, for examples, E. J. Hobsbawm, *Primitive Rebels*, Manchester: Manchester University Press, 1959, pp. 152–154; E. J. Hobsbawm, 'Artisan or labour aristocrat?', *Economic History Review* 37, 3, 1984, p. 361; S. Cordery, 'Friendly societies and the British labour movement before 1914', *Journal of the Association of Historians in North Carolina*, 3, 1995, p. 39; S. Cordery, *British friendly societies, 1750–1914*, Palgrave, Basingstoke, 2003, p. 135; P. H. J. H. Gosden, *The friendly societies in England, 1815–1875*, Manchester University Press, Manchester, 1961, pp. 55–6; M. Chase, *Early trade unionism, fraternity skill and the politics of labour*, Aldershot, Ashgate, 2000, pp. 2–3, 107; G. Finlayson, *Citizen, state, and social welfare in Britain 1830–1990*, Oxford: Clarendon, 1994, p. 6; Z. Bauman, *Between class and elite. The evolution of the British labour movement. A sociological study*. Translated by

S. Patterson, Manchester University Press, Manchester, 1972, p. 86.

8. E. P. Thompson, *The making of the English working class*, Penguin, Harmondsworth, 1963, revised edn 1968, pp. 461, 462, 464.

9. Burn, *An historical sketch*, p. 128.

10. S. Webb and B. Webb, *The history of trade unions*, Longmans, London 1893, revised 1920, p. 14. The Webbs noted how the leaders of two trade unions, the Amalgamated Society of Engineers and the Amalgamated Society of Carpenters and Joiners, sought to blur the distinctions between friendly societies and trade unions in evidence to a Royal Commission of 1867. The Webbs refer to the unions as 'primarily national friendly societies' and 'mainly occupied in the work of an insurance company' on pp. 265–6.

11. S. Webb and B. Webb, *Industrial Democracy*, Longmans Green, 2 vols, London, 1897, p. 89.

12. For a discussion of different theoretical frameworks within which friendly societies have been understood, see D. Weinbren, 'Imagined families: research on friendly societies', *Mitteilungsblatt des Instituts für die Geschichte der sozialen Bewegungen*, 27, 2002. See also D. Weinbren and B. James, 'Getting a grip – the roles of friendly societies in Australia and the UK reappraised', *Labour History*, 89, 2005. Brindley's 1909 story relating to Titus Caeser may be found at http://www.isle-of-man.com/manxnotebook/mquart/mq07598.htm, accessed 19 January 2010.

13. M. Gorsky, *Patterns of philanthropy. Charity and society in nineteenth-century Bristol*, Boydell, Woodbridge, 1999, p. 18; F. Prochaska, *Christianity and social service in modern Britain. The disinherited spirit*, Oxford University Press, Oxford, 2006, p. 11.

14. For a discussion see D. Weinbren, 'Freemasonry and friendly societies', in H. Bogdan and J. Snoek, *Handbook on contemporary freemasonry*, Brill, Leiden, 2010.

15. Burn, *An historical sketch*, p. 9.

16. *The Odd Fellow*, 16 February 1839.

17. *Aberdeen Weekly Journal*, 5 June 1900 report on the AMC.

18. Quoted in a booklet that the IOOFMU in Australia produced *100 years of achievement and friendly service*, IOOFMU, 1940, p. 20.

Chapter 1: Early years

1. *Odd Fellows Quarterly Magazine*, 9, 1847, p. 228.

2. *Unity Report*, 1986, p. 53. In line with Robert Moffrey, whose book helped to mark the centenary in 1910 for convenience a foundation date of 1810 is assumed throughout this book. See R. W. Moffrey, *A century of Oddfellowship. Being a brief record of the rise and progress of the Manchester Unity of the Independent Order of Oddfellows, from its formation to the present time*, Manchester, IOOFMU, 1910. Moffrey recognised the importance of predecessor bodies. Certainly parts of the Unity are older. For example the Loyal Independent Guernsey Lodge, which as an independent organisation dated back to the end of the seventeenth century, joined the Unity in 1845.

3. F. Prochaska, *The republic of Britain, 1760–2000*, Allen Lane, London, 2000, pp. 30–31.

4. For example, writing in 1819 Tom Paine devoted most of his essay on Freemasonry on its alleged origins in pre-Christian Druidism. See T. Paine, 'An essay on the origin of free-masonry'. This was written between 1803 and 1805. It first appeared in *The Complete Religious and Theological Works of Thomas Paine*, R. Carlile, London, 1819 and was republished by Bartlet Press, London, 2008.

5. Thompson, *The English working class*, p. 463.

6. Burn, *An historical sketch*, p. 146.

7. L. Colley, *Britons: the forging of a nation*, Yale University Press, New Haven and London, 1992, p. 88.

8. Colley's work is assessed in the Inaugural lecture by Andrew Prescott to mark the launch of the University of Sheffield's Centre for Research into Freemasonry, 5 March, 2001. http://www.freemasonry.dept.shef.ac.uk/index.php?lang=2&type=page&level0=243&level1=387&level2=391&op=264 accessed 15 September, 2009.

9. B. Anderson, *Imagined Communities: reflections on the origin and spread of nationalism*, 1983, revised edn, Verso, London 1991, pp. 6–7.

10. Burn, *An historical sketch*, p. 116.

11. *Northern Liberator*, 1 June 1839; *Northern Star*, 6 January 1838; 'Lines to the sacred memory of John Roach' appears in L. C. Hadley, 'Poetry and fiction from the friendly societies', Ph.D. thesis, De Montfort, 2006, p. 124.

12. J. Spry, *The history of Odd-Fellowship: its origin, tradition and objects with a general review of the results arising from its adoption by the branch known as the Manchester Unity*, Pitman, London, 1867, p. 55.

13. Spry, *The history of Odd-Fellowship*, p. 1.

14. George Brindley, Past Provincial Grand Master, Burslem Perseverance Lodge, Pottery and Newcastle District paper read to Mona Lodge of Oddfellows, Isle

of Man, August 1909. See http://www.isle-of-man.com/manxnotebook/mquart/mqo7598.htm accessed 3 December, 2008.

15. Moffrey, *A century of Oddfellowship*, p. 11, traced the Oddfellows back to 'a secret society existing among the captive Israelites in Babylon' but felt impelled to add that there was no historical collaboration for this story. The official Oddfellows website http://www.oddfellows.co.uk/history/introduction.htm when accessed 23 March 2005 said, 'The roots of the Oddfellows go back way beyond those of other organisations. Since the eighteenth century there has been a recorded legend of the Oddfellows which infers that the Oddfellows can trace its origins back to the exile of the Israelites from Babylon in 587 BC.'

16. *Oddfellows' Magazine*, July 1914, p. 278.

17. H. J. Hattersley, *The Odd Fellows Magazine*, February 1945, p. 39.

18. Moffrey, *A century of Oddfellowship*, pp. 12, 13.

19. Paul Eyre has suggested that the reference to the London meeting may be derived from John Thornley's 1914 *History of the Grand United Lodge of Oddfellows*. This refers to a meeting at the Bull and Mouth Inn, Sheffield, and a document dated 1452. This information may have become elided with the Grand Lodge of the Order in Sheffield which met at the Boulogne Mouth, in Waingate.

20. The song appears in Montgomery's *Verses written for the passing of the Loving Cup for the Threefold Toast at Lodge meetings*. It is reproduced in Moffrey, *A century of Oddfellowship*, p. 214. Montgomery was educated at the communitarian Moravian community at Fulneck, Pudsey. It was from within the Moravian Brotherhood that Methodist societies first arose and the Moravians popularised the language of brotherhood. See Thompson, *The English working class*, pp. 51–2.

21. G Brindley, 'The origin, rise and progress of Oddfellowship', *Manx Quarterly*, 7, 1909. This might be a confusion with the Société de Lintot which met in east London and existed between 1708 and the 1960s. See R. D. Gwynn, *Huguenot heritage: The history and contribution of the Huguenots in Britain*, Sussex Academic Press, Brighton, 2nd edn, 2001, p. 215.

22. Entry for Oddfellowship in J. M. Greer, *The New Encyclopedia of the Occult*, Llewellyn Worldwide, St Paul, Minnesota, USA, 2003.

23. Neave, *Mutual aid*, p. 100. Bob James noted that while the Minutes of a 'Loyal Aristarchus Lodge' of 'Odd Fellows' for 12 March 1748, and the 'Rules of Loyal Aristarchus Lodge, No 9 'Order of Oddfellows' have been cited, no copies are known to exist.

24. Report on speech of 7 November 1964 in *The Odd Fellow*, 1964, p. 669; *Annual Report*, 1997, p. 82.

25. Although Spry, *The history of Odd-Fellowship*, p. 3 distinguished between the 'myths' of the Unity's origins and the 'reality' of De Foe's claim, De Foe only described friendly societies. He did not mention the Oddfellows by name. Evidence for the claim made about the Order of Gregorians is unavailable.

26. *100 years*, p. 5.

27. R. Hutton, *The Triumph of the moon: A history of modern pagan witchcraft*, Oxford University Press, Oxford, 1999, p. 60.

28. *Odd Fellows Magazine*, Oct 1838, p. 171.

29. J. Brewer, *Party ideology and popular politics at the accession of George III*, Cambridge University Press, Cambridge, 1976, p. 194.

30. P. Clark, *British clubs and societies, 1580–1800. The origins of an associational world*, Clarendon, Oxford, 2000, p. 5. See also pp. 2–4, 383, 470–2.

31. Gosden, *The friendly societies*, pp. 13–16.

32. Clark, *British clubs*, p. 375.

33. J. Frome Wilkinson, *History of the friendly society movement*, Longmans Green, London, 1891, p. 116.

34. On the many possible reasons for societies to fail in this period see Clark, *British clubs*, pp. 365–8.

35. *General Evening Post*, 29 September 1789; *Public Advertiser*, 27 July 1790, *Morning Chronicle*, 20 July 1793; *Lloyd's Evening Post*, 17 February 1796; *Star*, 4 April 1796; *True Briton*, 4 December 1797; *True Briton* 31 October 1798; *Morning Post and Gazetteer*, 16 January 1798; *Whitehall Evening Post*, 7 April 1798.

36. There are lengthy reports of the case and Hadfield's claim in *Caledonian Mercury*, 30 June 1800, *Lloyd's Evening Post*, 25 June 1800 and the *Star* 19 May 1800.

37. This London lodge became the Grand Lodge of England, according to D. Smith and W. Roberts, *The Three Link Fraternity – Oddfellowship in California*, Linden 1993. It was later affiliated to London Unity in 1840 and the IOOFMU in 1883. The 'Union Order of Oddfellows was based on the 'Ancient and Honourable Loyal Order of Oddfellows'. *Oddfellows' Magazine*, July 1882, p. 506.

38. Gosden, *The friendly societies*, p. 69.

39. V. Solt Dennis, *Discovering friendly and fraternal societies: their badges and regalia*, Shire, Princes Risborough, 2005, p. 94.

40. Moffrey, *A century of Oddfellowship*, p. 15.

41. R. C. Lister, 'British friendly societies before 1834: an examination of their role, aims and activities', MA dissertation, Leeds, 1997, p. 86.

42. *Hampshire Telegraph and Sussex Chronicle etc.*, 18 May

1807; *The Aberdeen Journal*, 5 August 1807.

43. Entry for 18 December 1809. The diary is in a private collection and being prepared for publication by J. S. Appleby. Barnes' observations of a Masonic funeral two months later suggest that the Odd Fellows already had a distinctive appearance.

44. T. A. Ross, *Odd Fellowship: its history and manual*, M. W. Hazen, New York, 1888, pp. 9–11.

45. Neave, *Mutual aid*, pp. 101–2.

46. *Dictionary of the vulgar tongue*, 1811, quoted in Cordery, *British friendly societies*, p. 17.

47. *Odd Fellows Magazine*, October 1838, p. 171 suggested that the Oddfellows started in 1809. See also *The Odd Fellow*, 12 January 1839.

48. Lord Beveridge, *Voluntary action. A report on methods of social advance*, George Allen & Unwin, London, 1948, p. 59, suggested that the Oddfellows 'began by absorbing dissident Oddfellows from a Sheffield Lodge of Oddfellows'.

49. An image of the card is reproduced in B. James, *Secret handshakes & health care in Australia*, Grand United Order of Oddfellows, Williamstown, New South Wales, 1998, p. 26. This is available at http://www.takver.com/history/guoof1.htm, accessed 8 November, 2008. He also noted that in 1798 a sermon preached to the 'Original United Order of Oddfellows' in Sheffield was reviewed in the *Gentleman's Magazine*, September 1798, pp. 785–6. Paul Eyre has noted that the Sheffield City Library collection has a copy of a sermon preached to Sheffield 'Odd Fellows' on 7 December 1755. He has also noted that the claim is made by the Grand Lodge of the Grand United Order's *Elements of Odd-Fellowship*, 1812 of origins in either the seventeenth or eighteenth century.

50. *The Leeds Mercury*, 27 July 1811.

51. *Oddfellows (Manchester Unity) 175th Anniversary Souvenir Brochure*, 1985, IOOFMU, Manchester, p. 5.

52. Burn, *An historical sketch*, p. 15.

53. See http://www.uk.guoofs.com accessed 5 February, 2009.

54. James, *Secret handshakes*; *Oddfellows' Magazine*, December 1887, p. 356.

55. Neave, *Mutual aid*, pp. 100–1.

56. Burn, *An historical sketch*, pp. 26–7, called Bolton a marble cutter and the lodge the Victory which was opened in a pub called the British Volunteer, Marshall Street.

57. Clark, *British clubs*, p. 361.

58. R. W. Harris, *National Health Insurance in Great Britain 1911–1946*, George Pitman, London, 1946. For terms used within Oddfellowship see the Glossary, Table 9.

59. Moffrey, *A century of Oddfellowship*, p. 19.

60. Beveridge, *Voluntary action*, pp. 156–7.

61. Moffrey, *A century of Oddfellowship*, p. 19.

62. Beveridge, *Voluntary action*, p. 58 suggested that a 'benevolent society' started at the one address in 1808 but the first meeting of the Oddfellows was in 1810 at the other address.

63. *The Times*, 30 May 1978, when reporting the election of Dolly Merrell as Grand Master, collapsed the creation of the post and the creation of the first lodge when it claimed she was 'the first woman to hold this post in the 167 years since the Odd Fellows started'.

64. Burn, *An historical sketch*, p. 127.

65. Wilkinson, *History*, p. 11; E. W. Webbe, *The Oddfellows' Companion to Derby*, Bemrose & Sons, Derby, 1892, pp. 42, 46; Brindley, 'The origin ... of Oddfellowship'; *Leeds Mercury*, 27 December 1900.

66. Spry, *The history of Odd-Fellowship*, pp. 112, 39; Cordery, *British friendly societies*, p. 104.

67. *The Odd Fellow*, January 1964, p. 4.

68. Gosden, *The Friendly societies*, p. 27.

69. Ross, *Odd Fellowship*, p. 591.

70. Solt *Discovering friendly and fraternal societies*, p. 93.

71. M. Gorsky and B. Harris, The measurement of morbidity in inter-war Britain: evidence from the Hampshire Friendly Society' in I. Borowy and W. D. Gruner (eds), *Facing illness in troubled times. Health in Europe in the inter-war years*, Peter Lang, Oxford, 2005, p. 133 suggested 1814; J. R. Edwards and R. Chandler, 'Contextualising the process of accounting regulation: a study of nineteenth-century British friendly societies', *Abacus*, 37, 2, 2001, p. 196 plumped for 1816.

72. J. Goodchild, *The Freemasons and the Friendly Societies*, Prestonian Lecture 1996, p. 9 and also D. Neave, *Mutual aid in the Victorian countryside: friendly societies in the rural East Riding 1830–1914*, Hull University Press, Hull, 1991, p. 101, both opted for 1823. This last date was also that favoured by *Lloyd's Weekly London Newspaper*, 27 July 1845. For discussion about the formation of the Oddfellows see Bob James's website http://www.takver.com/history/benefit/ofshis.htm accessed 8 November, 2008.

73. A. Prescott, 'The Unlawful Societies Act of 1799' in M. D. J. Scanlon (ed.), *The Canonbury Papers, Volume 1. The social impact of freemasonry on the modern western world*, Canonbury Masonic Research Centre, London, 2002, pp. 120, 132.

74. Thompson, *The English working class*, p. 546.

75. *The Morning Chronicle*, 3 August 1819 reported both sides of this dispute and the matter was also covered in *Trewman's Exeter Flying Post or Plymouth and Cornish*

Advertiser, 5 August 1819.

76. D. Worrall, *Radical culture. Discourse, resistance and surveillance, 1790–1820*, Harvester Wheatsheaf, Hemel Hempstead, 1992, p. 7.

77. Burn, *An historical sketch*, pp. 12, 27.

78. Burn, *An historical sketch*, p. 46.

79. *Lloyd's Weekly London Newspaper*, 27 July 1845.

80. Spry, *The history of Odd-Fellowship*, pp. 55, 169.

81. R. D. Putnam, 'Let's play together', *Observer*, 25 March, 2001; M. J. Daunton, *State and market in Victorian Britain: war, welfare and capitalism*, Boydell and Brewer, Woodbridge, 2008, p. 114.

82. Burn, *An historical sketch*, pp. 18–23.

83. On the Chartist notions of family and marriage see R. G. Hall, 'Hearts and minds: the politics of everyday life and Chartism, 1832–1840', *Labour History Review*, 74, 1, 2009, pp. 33–7.

84. Spry, *The history of Odd-Fellowship*, pp. 50–1.

85. Moffrey, *A century of Oddfellowship*, p. 207.

86. Spry, *The history of Odd-Fellowship*, p. 47.

87. T. Porter, *Trust in numbers: the pursuit of objectivity in public life*, Princeton University Press, Princeton, New Jersey, 1996, I. Hacking, *The taming of chance*, Cambridge University Press, Cambridge; 1990.

88. G. F. Hardy, 'Friendly Societies', *Journal of the Institute of Actuaries*, 27 1888; A. Watson, 'The methods of analyzing and presenting the mortality, sickness and secession experience of friendly societies, with examples drawn from the experiences of the Manchester Unity of Oddfellows, *Journal of the Institute of Actuaries*, 25, 1900; Moffrey, *A century of Oddfellowship*.

89. Webbe, *The Oddfellows' Companion to Derby* reproduced the story of the foundation in 55 BCE and the recognition by Titus Caesar. The claim was also made that the Order came to Britain via North Wales, spread throughout the Roman Empire and returned to the UK from France.

90. H. L. Stillson, *The official history and literature of Odd fellowship. The three-link fraternity*, Fraternity Publishing Boston Mass, 1897, p. 50. See also *Odd Fellows Magazine*, October 1887, p. 231.

91. Stillson, *The official history*, pp. 50–1.

92. Stillson, *The official history*, pp. 49, 27.

93. Ross, *Oddfellowship*, p. 588.

94. D. Burton, D. Knights, A. Leyshon, C. Alferoff and P. Signoretta, 'Consumption denied?: The decline of industrial branch insurance', *Journal of Consumer Culture*, 5, 2, 2005, p. 200. See also B. Supple, *The Royal Exchange Assurance. A History of British Insurance 1720–1970*, Cambridge University Press, Cambridge, 1970, p. 310.

95. M. C. Carnes, *Secret ritual and manhood in Victorian America*, Yale University Press, New Haven, 1989, pp. 25–26.

96. Moffrey, *A century of Oddfellowship*, pp. 11, 16.

97. A. Briggs, *Victorian cities*, Odhams, London, 1963, p. 56 argued that 'Manchester was the Shock City of the 1840s'.

98. N. J. Smelser, *Social change in the industrial revolution: an application of theory to the Lancashire cotton industry, 1770–1840*, Routledge & Kegan, London, 1959, p. 182.

99. *Oddfellows' Magazine*, 1922, p. 229.

100. A. Ure, *Cotton Manufacture of Great Britain. Vol. l*, Charles Knight, London, 1836, pp. 191–192. Available at http://books.google.co.uk/books?hl=en&id=O8BFAAAIAAJ&dq= per cent22Cotton+Manufacture+of+Great+Britain per cent22&printsec=frontcover&source=web&ots=7N9-lrKsVF&sig=G9lOqTKX7rQzkDwNTyNGaoPaVYo&sa=X&oi=book_result&resnum=1&ct=result#PPR1,M1 accessed 12 December, 2008.

101. W. O. Henderson, *Industrial Britain under the Regency: The Diaries of Escher, Bodner, May and De Gallois 1814–18*, Frank Cass, London, p. 136.

102. An assessment of this literature is made in H. Barker, '"Smoke cities": northern industrial towns in late Georgian England', *Urban History*, 31, 2, 2004, pp. 175–6.

103. P. J. Corfield, 'From poison peddlers to civic worthies: the reputation of the apothecaries in Georgian England', *Social history of medicine*, 22, 1, 2009, p. 18.

104. Corfield, 'Poison peddlers to civic worthies', pp. 13, 15, 16–17.

105. Gosden, *The friendly societies*, pp. 4–5, 63; Clark, *British clubs*, pp. 350; 373; J. Foster, *Class struggle and the industrial revolution: early industrial capitalism in three English towns*, Routledge, London, 1977, p. 217; D'Cruze and Turnbull, 'Fellowship and family; J. H. Clapham, *A concise economic history of Britain from the earliest times to 1750*, Cambridge University Press, Cambridge, 1949, pp. 296–7; H. J. M. Maltby, *Early Manchester and Salford friendly societies*, Transactions of the Lancashire & Cheshire Antiquarian Society, 46, 1929. Registration did not guarantee financial soundness but it did meant that the rules were deemed acceptable by local JPs and that a society's officials could contest lawsuits and recover debts.

106. R. Wells, *Wretched faces: famine in wartime England, 1763–1803*, Alan Sutton, Gloucester, 1988, p. 326.

107. S. Gunn, *The public culture of the Victorian middle class. Ritual and authority and the English industrial city 1840–*

1914, Manchester University Press, Manchester, 2000, pp. 85–6.

108. R. Pearson, 'Thrift or dissipation? The business of life assurance in the early nineteenth century', *Economic History Review*, 43, 2, 1990, pp. 236–54; R. Person, 'Collective diversification: Manchester cotton merchants and the insurance business in the early nineteenth century', *Business History Review*, 65, 2, 1990, pp. 379–414.

109. D. Loftus, 'Capital and community: limited liability and attempts to democratize the market in mid-Nineteenth-Century England', *Victorian Studies*, 45, 1, 2002, pp. 107–8, noted that under the Limited Liability Act 1855 and the Joint Stock Companies Act, 1856 by signing a memorandum of association a group of seven or more people could pool their capital and enjoy limited liability for debts incurred.

110. L. S. Pressnell, *County banking in the industrial revolution*, Clarendon, Oxford, 1956, p. 443.

111. M. Poovey, *Genres of the credit economy. Mediating value in eighteenth- and nineteenth-century Britain*, University of Chicago Press, Chicago, 2008, pp. 31–2.

112. On the links between links ideas about the market, political economy and society see E. Janes Yeo, *The contest for social science: relations and representations if gender and class*, Rivers Oram, London, 1996.

113. Petitions of the manufacturers of Manchester and Bolton. Available at http://hansard.millbanksystems.com/commons/1811/may/30/petitions-of-the-manufacturers-of accessed 8 September, 2009.

114. For a discussion of Luddism see J. E. Archer, *Social unrest and popular protest in England, 1780–1840*, Cambridge University Press, Cambridge, 2000.

115. J. Tosh, 'Masculinities in an industrializing society: Britain, 1800–1914', *Journal of British Studies*, 44, 2005, pp. 331–2.

116. Barker, '"Smoke cities"', p. 189.

117. M. Huberman, *Escape from the market: negotiating work in Lancashire*, Cambridge University Press, Cambridge, 1996, chapter 5.

118. P. Joyce, *Visions of the people. Industrial England and the question of class 1848–1914*, Cambridge University Press, Cambridge, 1991, pp. 91, 100.

119. P. Joyce, *Work, politics and society. The culture of the factory in later Victorian England*, Methuen, London, 1982 edition, pp. 167–168.

120. Report in *Oddfellows' Magazine*, April 1858.

121. Joyce, *Work, politics*, pp. 167–8.

122. Quoted in J. K. Walton, *Lancashire: a social history 1558–1939*, Manchester University Press, Manchester, 1987, pp. 242–3.

123. *The Times*, 17 November 1862, printed a letter from Charles Hardwick about the Unity and the famine. His report in the Society's quarterly magazine was also reported in the press. See *The Times*, 10 October 1862.

124. Clapham, *A concise economic history*, pp. 296–7, 590.

125. Burn, *An historical sketch*, p. 29.

126. Burn, *An historical sketch*, p. 122.

127. Moffrey, *A century of Oddfellowship*, pp. 29–31, noted that the Patriarchial Order was established in 1825 and that the Grand Master, Thomas Armitt, travelled widely to inform members of it and try to quell rebellion against Manchester's authority.

128. Details of the London and Manchester methods of admitting strangers are set out in a letter dated 1820 from Isaac Hardman, who was probably one of the founders, see Moffrey, *A century of Oddfellowship*, pp. 25–6.

129. I am indebted to Paul Eyre for this information.

130. Burn, *An historical sketch*, p. 39, noted that the Nelson Lodge Hall, Kendall was erected in 1833 at a cost of £3,000.

131. Brindley, 'The origin … of Oddfellowship'.

132. E. L. Stanley, 'What legislation should follow on the Report of the Commission on Friendly Societies?', *Transactions of the Social Science Association*, 1874, p. 197 cited in Gosden, *The friendly societies*, p. 37.

133. *Parliamentary Papers, 1847–1848, Vol. 26*, p. 93, cited in Logan, 'Role of friendly society orders', p. 36.

134. Stillson, *The official*, pp. 50–57. On the growth in Yorkshire see Neave, *Mutual aid*, p. 36.

135. Williams, 'Friendly societies', pp. 281–3.

136. Spry, *The history of Odd-Fellowship*, p. 29.

137. For a comparison of the foundation dates of the Foresters and the Oddfellows between 1835 and 1860 see Logan, 'Role of friendly society orders', Table 5, p. 45.

138. Spry, *The history of Odd-Fellowship*, p. 165.

139. *Worcester News*, 16 April 2003.

140. *Coventry Herald*, 3 June 1842 cited in A. Prescott, '"We had fine banners": street processions in the Mitchell and Kenyon films', in V. Toulmin, P. Russell and S. Popple (eds), *The lost world of Mitchell and Kenyon: Edwardian Britain on film*, BFI Publications, London, 2004. Weller, 'Self help' also considered Coventry.

141. Burn, *An historical sketch*, p. 127.

142. Burn, *An historical sketch*, pp. 119, 154.

143. Burn, *An historical sketch*, p. 32.

144. Clapham, *A concise economic history*, pp. 590–1.

145. Spry, *The history of Odd-Fellowship*, p. 190.

146. For a discussion of the number of friendly society

members see B. Harris, *The Origins of the British Welfare State: Society, State and Social Welfare in England and Wales, 1800–1945*, Palgrave, Basingstoke, 2004, pp. 82, 194, and also E. P. Hennock, *The Origin of the Welfare State in England and Germany, 1850–1914: Social Policies Compared*, Cambridge University Press, Cambridge, 2007, pp. 166–81.

147. Burn, *An historical sketch*, p. 43. The Oddfellows of the USA seceded in 1843. Although the Oddfellows who founded lodges in America may have been Oddfellows in the UK prior to their migration it is not clear that they were necessarily members of the Independent Order of Oddfellows, Manchester Unity. However, they did affiliate to the IOOFMU.

148. Olssen, 'Friendly societies', p. 177, provided an account of the first friendly society in New Zealand being formed in November 1841 by emigrating members of the Unity on board the *Martha Ridgeway* between Liverpool and Nelson.

149. Spry, *The history of Odd-Fellowship*, p. 66.

150. Spry, *The history of Odd-Fellowship*, p. 119.

151. Spry, *The history of Odd-Fellowship*, p. 151.

152. Spry, *The history of Odd-Fellowship*, pp. 178, 183. On the growth in Australia and New Zealand also see Spry, *The history of Odd-Fellowship*, pp. 46–7.

153. Burn, *An historical sketch*, pp. 45–7.

154. Burn, *An historical sketch*, p. 106.

155. Spry, *The history of Odd-Fellowship*, p. 139.

156. Moffrey, *A century of Oddfellowship*, p. 100.

157. Moffrey, *A century of Oddfellowship*, p. 116.

158. Moffrey, *A century of Oddfellowship*, pp. 152, 155.

159. Burn, *An historical sketch*, p. 36.

160. Burn, *An historical sketch*, pp. 32–4.

161. *The Odd Fellow*, 2 March 1839.

162. The idea that members were the *omnium gatherum* outside of Freemasonry has been taken up by others, including W. Brabrook, *Provident societies and industrial welfare*, 1898, pp. 58–9 and Cordery, *British friendly societies*, p. 17.

163. *Freemasons' Monthly Magazine*, January 1855, p. 10; July 1858, pp. 103, 104.

164. Burn, *An historical sketch*, p. 13.

165. *North Wales Chronicle*, 7 June 1883.

166. Interview in *Worcester News*, 16 April 2003.

167. Spry, *The history of Odd-Fellowship*, pp. 186–8.

168. *The Manchester Guardian*, 21 May 1934.

169. The story appears in many publications. See, for example, *The Odd Fellow*, 16 February 1839.

170. Burn, *An historical sketch*, p. 14.

171. Burn, *An historical sketch*, p. 13.

172. Moffrey, *A century of Oddfellowship*, p. 17.

Chapter 2:   The setting

1. Anon., *The complete manual of Oddfellowship*, 1879, p. 94.

2. For a discussion of this idea see D. Valenze, *The social life of money in the English past*, Cambridge University Press, Cambridge, 2006, pp. 27, 59, 260, 263.

3. For a discussion of such items, see, S. Chapman, 'A unique friendly society plaque' *Journal of Antique Metalware Society*, 9, 2001 pp. 4–5 and S. Chapman, 'Friendly society antiques', *Journal of Antique Metalware Society* 8, 2000, pp. 35–40.

4. The lack of enthusiasm for bank notes may have been related to the widespread use of bills of exchange. These facilitated long-distance commerce by allowing a seller to receive a payment as soon as the product was dispatched.

5. *HC Debate*, 21 December 1819, vol. 41, cc1391–2.

6. *The Times*, 16 August 1842.

7. M. *Mauss, Theory of Magic, theory of magic*, translated by R. Bain, Routledge, & Kegan Paul, London, 1972 edn, 1st edn, 1950, p. 108.

8. *Mauss, Theory of Magic*, pp. 60, 43–4.

9. *Mauss, Theory of Magic*, pp. 47, 144.

10. On the fraternity of astrologers see O. Davies, *Witchcraft, magic and culture, 1736–1951*, Manchester University Press, Manchester, 1999, pp. 238–241.

11. H. A. L. Cockerell and E. Green, *The British insurance business 1547–1970. An introduction and guide to historical records in the United Kingdom*, Heinemann, London, 1976, pp. 16–18.

12. G. Clark, 'Life insurance in the society and culture of London, 1700–75', *Urban History*, 24, 1, 1997, p. 18; Supple, *The Royal Exchange*, pp. 10–11.

13. The association continued. It was through its subsidiary, Family Friendly Society that the British Industry Life Assurance issued the first industrial life policies in the 1850s thus addressing the recommendations of the Select Committee on Friendly Societies, 1852 which favoured the spread of life assurance 'among the humbler classes'. See Cockerell and Green, *British insurance business*, pp. 36–40.

14. G. Clark, *Betting on lives: the culture of life insurance in England, 1695–1775*, Manchester University Press, Manchester and New York, 1999, p. 73.

15. L. McFall, 'The disinterested self. The idealized subject

16. This was a different body to the London Union Odd Fellows Society mentioned in the previous chapter.

17. Other early examples include the Falkirk Sea Box Society, the Saint Andrews Sea Box Society, the Kirkcaldy Prime Gilt Society and the Anstruther Easter Sea Box Society.

18. It later amalgamated with the Landsmen's Society, the Friendly Society of Shipmasters, the Shipmasters' Society, and the New Friendly Society and became the United General Sea Box of Borrowstounness Friendly Society. Similarly, in 1804, the Sea Box Society in St Monans became a friendly society.

19. A minute book of the Free Gardeners of East Lothian exists from 1676 and there was a Society of Dyers of Linlithgow, formed 1679; De Foe, *An essay upon projects*, London, 1697, p. 142. Available online at http://www.gutenberg.org/etext/4087 and at http://www.online-literature.com/defoe/upon-projects, *accessed 9 September, 2009*, p. 19; Chase, *Early trade*, pp. 27, 28, 40, 42.

20. J. M. Baernreither, *English Associations of Working Men*, Swan Sonnenschein & Co., London, 1889, p. 160.

21. D.C. Barnett, 'Ideas on social welfare, 1780–1834, with special reference to friendly societies and allotment schemes', MA dissertation, Nottingham, 1961, p. 30.

22. Beveridge, *Voluntary action*, p. 24.

23. M. E Ogborn, *Equitable Assurances: the story of life assurance in the experience of the Equitable Life Assurance Company 1762–1962*, Allen and Unwin, London, 1962, pp. 166–92.

24. M. J. Cullen, *The statistical movement in early Victorian Britain*, Harvester, London 1975, p. 7.

25. J. Horton and R. Macve, 'The development of life assurance accounting and regulation in the UK: reflections of recent proposals for accounting change', *Accounting, business and financial history*, 4, 2, 1994, p. 298.

26. R. Pearson, *Insuring the industrial revolution: fire insurance in Great Britain, 1700–1850*, Ashgate, Aldershot, 2004, p. 157.

27. T. Alborn, 'The first fund managers: life insurance bonuses in Victorian Britain, *Victorian Studies*, 45, 1, Autumn 2002, pp. 65–92.

28. R. Blake, *Esto Perpetua. The Norwich Union Life Insurance Society: an account of one hundred and fifty years of progress and development in the service of the community*, Newman Neame, London, 1958, p. 19. The Norwich grew in parallel to the Oddfellows. By 1822 it had 550 agents across the country. It opened its first overseas agency in 1824.

29. R. Spear, 'The co-operative advantage', *Annals of Public and Cooperative Economics*, 71, 4, 2000, p. 508.

30. Minute to the 1841–44 Select Committee quoted by Horton and Macve, 'The development', p. 305. On the pervasiveness of advertising, 'puffs', in this period see L. McFall, 'The Language of the Walls: Putting Promotional Saturation in Historical Context', *Consumption Markets & Culture*, 7, 2, 2004, pp. 107–28.

31. Supple, *The Royal Exchange*, p. 141.

32. Supple, *The Royal Exchange*, pp. 111–12.

33. C. Hardwick, *The history, present position and social importance of friendly societies including Oddfellowship and other affiliated provident institutions of the working classes*, 2nd edn, John Heywood, Manchester, 1869, p. 143.

34. For the crest see Blake, *Esto Perpetua*, p. 54. The term 'community brokerage' is used in S. D'Cruze, 'The middling sort in eighteenth-century Colchester: independence, social relations and community broker', in J. Barry and C. Brooks (eds), *The middling sort of people: culture, society and politics in England, 1550–1800*, Saint Martin's Press, New York, 1994.

35. Clark, 'Life insurance', pp. 18, 22, 23.

36. De Foe, *An essay*, p. 142.

37. Clark, *Betting on lives*, p. 88.

38. Clark, *Betting on lives*, p. 200.

39. Babbage was also author of *A comparative view of the various institutions for the assurance of lives*, Mawman, London, 1826. Although he calculated a law of mortality in the form of an equation which would have been ideal for tabulation on his famous Difference Engine, he did not ever make this calculation. See M. Campbell-Kelly, 'Charles Babbage and the Assurance of Lives', *IEEE Annals of the History of Computing*, 16, 3, 1994.

40. H. J. G. Bab, 'The evolution of the British building society', *Economic History Review*, 9, 1938–39, pp. 56, 60, suggested that the earliest record of a building society is 1781 and that the building societies were 'founded as friendly societies'.

41. *Oddfellows' Magazine*, March 1901, pp. 69–71.

42. Z. Lawson, 'Save the pennies! Savings banks and the working class in mid-nineteenth-century Lancashire, *The Local Historian*, 35, 3, 2005, pp. 168–84.

43. H. O. Horne, *A history of savings banks*, Oxford University Press, Oxford, 1947, p. 128. The collapse of the Rochdale Savings Bank following a fraud by its actuary, a local mill-owner, is described in P. H. J. H. Gosden, *Self-help: voluntary associations in the nineteenth century*, Batsford, London, 1973, p. 224.

44. *The Times*, 3 December 1849.

45. A. Durr, 'William King of Brighton: Co-operation's

prophet', in S. Yeo (ed.), *New views of co-operation*, Routledge, London and New York, 1988, p. 17.

46. Clapham, *A concise economic history*, pp. 295–8.

47. R. A. Leeson, *Travelling brothers: the six centuries' road from craft fellowship to trade unionism*, George Allen & Unwin, London, p. 25.

48. Most guilds were only for men, though some let in members' widows and daughters and some admitted other women.

49. M. Chase, *Early trade*, p. 24.

50. D. T. Beito, '"This enormous army": the mutual aid tradition of American Fraternal Societies before the twentieth century', *Social Philosophy and Policy*, 14, 2, 1997, pp. 22–3.

51. For a broader discussion see M. J. Walker, 'The extent of guild control of trades in England, *c*.1660–1820', Cambridge University, Ph.D. thesis, 1986. In *Earthly necessities: economic lives in early modern Britain*, Yale University Press, New Haven, 2000 Keith Wrightson has indicated how the friendly societies developed some of the ideas of the guilds while Peter Clark's account of the rise of British associations in the early modern era (*British clubs*) also illuminates these origins. For the wider fraternal context, see D. Weinbren, 'Gender, fraternity order: seven hundred years of extending families', in M. Gross (ed.), *Lodges, chapters and orders: fraternal organisations and the structuring of gender roles, 1300–2000*, Palgrave, 2010.

52. S. D. Smith, 'Women's admission to guilds in early-modern England: the case of the York Merchant Tailors' Company, 1693–1776', *Gender and History*, 17, 1, 2005, pp. 99–126.

53. D. M. Owen (ed.), *The Making of King's Lynn: A Documentary Survey*, British Academy, Records of Social and Economic History, new series, IX, London, 1984, pp. 61–3, 295–317.

54. B. McRee, 'Charity and Gild Solidarity in Late Medieval England', *Journal of British Studies*, 32, 1993, p. 32; S. Epstein, 'Craft Guilds in the Pre-Modern Economy: a discussion' *Economic History Review*, 61, 1, p. 688; P. Richards, *King's Lynn*, Phillimore, Chichester, 1990, p. 103; L. F. Newman, '*Notes on some rural and trade initiation ceremonies in the Eastern Counties,*' *Folk-Lore*, 51, 1940, pp. 33–5; C. Muldrew, *The Economy of Obligation: The Culture of Credit and Social. Relations in Early Modern England*, Macmillan, Basingstoke, 1998, p. 109.

55. Thompson, *The English working class*, p. 457.

56. M. C. Jacob, 'Money, equality, fraternity: freemasonry and the social order in eighteenth-century Europe', in T. L. Haskell and R. F. Teichgraeber III, *The culture of the market. Historical essays*, Cambridge University Press, Cambridge, 1993, pp. 129–30.

57. M. Chase, 'A sort of Corporation (tho' without a charter): the guild tradition and the emergence of British trade unionism' in I. A. Gadd and P. Wallis (eds), *Guilds and association in Europe, 900–1900*, Centre for Metropolitan History, London, 2006, pp. 189–90, 192, 193.

58. Clark, *British clubs*, p. 353; Stillson, *The official history*, pp. 36–7.

59. J. Rose, *The intellectual life of the British working classes*, Yale Nota Bene, Yale University Press, New Haven and London, 2002, p. 58.

60. Rose, *Intellectual life*, pp. 16, 18, 59–63.

61. Prospectus of the Rochdale Oddfellows' Literary Institute, Oddfellows' Chronicle, April 1848, quoted in Gosden, *The friendly societies*, p. 235.

62. R. Colls, *The pitmen of the northern coalfield. Work culture and protest 1790–1850*, Manchester University Press, Manchester, 1987, pp. 70, 87, 246–248.

63. Home Office papers cited by Chase, *Early trade*, p. 55.

64. Thompson, *The English working class*, pp. 461, 459.

65. Chase, *Early trade*, p. 59.

66. H. Swanson, 'Crafts, fraternities and guilds in late medieval York' in R. B. Dobson and D. M. Smith (eds), *The Merchant Taylors of York. A history of the craft and company from the fourteenth to 20th centuries*, University of York, 2006.

67. *Joseph Warburton Lodge: centenary, 1835–1935*, 1935, p. 30, in J. J. Turner, 'Friendly societies in south Durham and north Yorkshire c1790–1914: studies in development, membership characteristics and behaviour', Ph.D. thesis, Teesside, 1992, p. 325.

68. P. T. Weller, 'Self help and provident friendly societies in Coventry in the nineteenth century', M.Phil. dissertation, Warwick, 1990, p. 127.

69. Weller, 'Self help', pp. 130, 132.

70. J. Goodchild, *The freemasons and the friendly societies. An historical study*, Prestonian Lecture 1996, privately printed.

71. Quoted in The Oddfellows, *The Oddfellows millennium book. A celebration of members and their meeting places*, Pemberton Wood, Manchester, 2000.

72. D. Knoop and G. P. Jones, *The genesis of Freemasonry: an account of the rise and development of Freemasonry in its operative, accepted and early speculative phases*, Manchester 1947 pp. 294–300; P. Elliot and S. Daniels, 'The "school of true, useful and universal science"? Freemasonry, natural philosophy and scientific culture in eighteenth-century England', *The British Journal for the History of Science*, 2006, 39, p. 207.

73. Clark, *British clubs*, pp 308, 313–22.

74. A. Durr, 'The origin of the craft', *Ars Quatuor Coronatorum, Transactions of Quatuor Coronati Lodge No. 2076*, 96, 1983, p. 181.

75. A. Prescott, 'Godfrey Higgins and his Anacalypsis', *Library and Museum News for the Friends of the Library and Museum of Freemasonry*, 12, April 2005, pp. 2–6.

76. D. Harrison, The Liverpool rebels', *Masonic Quarterly*, 13, April 2005, pp. 34–6.

77. R. Moffrey, *The Rise & Progress of the Manchester Unity*, 1904, IOOFMU, Manchester uses this term in the opening paragraph. Copy available at http://www.isle-of-man.com/manxnotebook/history/socs/odf_mdly.htm accessed 9 September, 2009.

78. H. Perkin, *The origins of modern English society, 1780–1880*, Routledge, London, 1969, p. 362.

79. *The Times*, 15 May 1851.

80. J. Money, 'The masonic moment: or, Ritual, replica, and credit: John Wilkes, the Macaroni Parson, and the making of the middle class mind', *Journal of British Studies*, 32, 1993, p. 384.

81. This is from the Lecture of the First Degree (Emulation Working). Freemasonry is communicated through Ritual dramas called 'Degrees' which are conferred in a lodge, the basic unit of Masonic organisation. Each lodge is responsible to the national governing body, 'Grand Lodge'.

82. *Lectures etc. used by the Manchester District* 1823, MS East Sussex County Record Office, p. 39 cited in A. Durr, 'Ritual of association and the organisations of the common people, *Ars Quatuor Coronatorum, Transactions of Quatuor Coronati Lodge No. 2076*, 100, 1987, p. 97.

83. Clark, *British clubs*, p. 385.

84. Preface to Ross, *Odd Fellowship*, p. 2. Moffrey and White might differed in their views partly because of the success of Freemasonry in the UK, where the heir to the throne was 'on the square', compared to widespread concerns about the society within the US during the nineteenth century.

85. Bristol Record Library, 7952 of Jeffries collection, cited in M. Gorsky, 'Charity, mutuality and philanthropy: voluntary provision in Bristol 1800–70', Ph.D. thesis, Bristol, 1995, p. 151.

86. A. Durr, 'Chicken and Egg – the emblem book and freemasonry: the visual and material culture of associated life', *Paper to Quatuor Coronati Lodge No. 2076 and Correspondence Circle*, 17 February, 2005, pp. 8–10. My thanks to Andy Durr for providing a copy of this paper.

87. Durr, 'Ritual of association', pp. 88–108. *Burn, An historical sketch*, p. 12 referred to the 'ennobling principle of fraternal charity and brotherly love'. The term 'affiliated societies' appears to have originated in the Report of the Registrar of Friendly Societies, 1858.

88. Minutes cited in Gosden, *The friendly societies*, p. 128, and *The Manchester Guardian*, 15 November 1815, quoted in *Oddfellows' Magazine*, January 1916, p. 18.

89. *Oddfellows' Magazine*, 1, 1829, p. 68.

90. D. G. Wickham, 'Beyond the wall. Ballarat Female Regue. A case study in moral authority', M.Phil. dissertation, Australian Catholic University, 2003.

91. *Oddfellows' Magazine*, April 1880, pp. 402–03; *Oddfellows' Magazine*, July 1882, pp. 449–451. There is also an account in *The Times*, 18 May 1880.

92. Moffrey, *A century of Oddfellowship*, p. 100.

93. *Oddfellows' Magazine*, January 1901 p. 11 noted the death, on 6 July 1900, of John Rust. Thanks to Karen Stuart I was able to locate his gravestone in Old Hunstanton, which indicates that he died in 1901.

94. Ives went on to become Provincial Assistant Grand Director of Ceremonies, Provincial Grand Senior Warden and Lodge treasurer.

95. Similarly, at the end of the nineteenth century there was a considerable overlap of membership between the Oddfellows and the Freemasons on the Isle of Man. Another active Forester and Oddfellow of this period was a printer John Fisher who was both a Provincial Grand Master and a Chief Ranger in South London during the latter half of the nineteenth century.

96. *Derby Mercury*, 14 November 1900.

97. *Oddfellows' Magazine*, January 1901, pp. 1–4.

98. *Full Transcript of the 2001 AMC*, Eastbourne, p. 38.

99. J. M. Gardiner, *History of the Leeds Benevolent or Strangers Friend Society, 1789–1889*, Leeds, 1890, cited in R. J. Morris, 'Voluntary societies and British urban élites, 1780–1850: an analysis', *Historical Journal*, 26, 1, 1983, p. 107.

100. On the role of friendly societies as an element within familial financial strategies see D. Weinbren, 'Relative value: the financing of families', *Family and Community History*, 2, 1, 1999.

101. Harris, *The Origins*, pp. 72, 77.

102. This is discussed further in D. Weinbren, 'Supporting self-help: charity, mutuality and reciprocity in nineteenth-century Britain' in B. Harris and P. Bridgen (eds), *Charity and mutual aid in Europe and North America since 1800*, Routledge, London and New York, 2007.

103. S. M. Pinches, 'Objects of charity: fads and fashions in founding charities over 400 years in Warwickshire',

104. T. W. Laqueur, *Religion and respectability. Sunday Schools and working class culture, 1780–1850*, Yale University Press, New Haven and London, 1976, p. xi.

105. A. P. Wadsworth, 'The first Manchester Sunday Schools', in M. W. Flinn and T. C. Smout (eds), *Essays in social history*, Oxford, 1974, pp. 101, 117, 119.

106. Gosden, *The friendly societies*, pp. 20–1.

107. K. D. M. Snell, 'The Sunday School movement in England and Wales: child labour, denominational control and working-class culture', *Past and Present*, 164, 1999, pp. 130–1.

108. *Hints for the institution of Sunday Schools and parish clubs*, York 1789, cited in Clark, *British clubs*, p. 371.

109. Kent Archive Office, P145/25/52, P145/25/54 cited in S. B. Black, 'Local government, law and order in a pre-reform Kentish parish: Farningham 1790–1834' Ph.D. thesis, Kent, 1991, pp. 45, 46, 55.

110. Laqueur, *Religion and respectability*, pp. 172–4.

111. E. A. Wrigley, *Population and History*, Weidenfeld and Nicolson, London, 1969, fig. 5.3.

112. Laqueur, *Religion and respectability*, pp. 163–4.

113. *Oddfellows' Magazine*, April 1859.

114. Quoted in T. R. Tholfsen, *Working class radicalism in mid-Victorian England*, Croom Helm, London, 1976, p. 292.

115. M. D. Fuller, *West Country friendly societies: An account of village benefit clubs and their brass pole heads*, Oakwood Press, Reading, 1964, p. 100.

116. On this role for charity see E. Isin and E. Üstündag, 'Wills, deeds, acts: women's civic gift-giving in Ottoman Istanbul', *Gender, place and culture*, 15, 5 2008, pp. 519–32; F. K. Prochaska, Women *and philanthropy in nineteenth-century England*, Oxford University Press, Oxford, 1980.

117. The Whitbread family went on to sponsor several friendly societies and to patronise the Biggleswade Loyal Dreadnought Lodge of the Oddfellows which met in the town near the family seat. See D. Weinbren, 'The social capital of female friendly societies' in Cross, *Lodges, chapters and orders*.

118. E. Higgs, 'Disease, febrile poisons and statistics: the census as a medical survey, 1841–1911', *Social History of Medicine*, 4, 3, 1991, pp. 465–78; C. Hamlin. *Public Health and Social Justice in the Age of Chadwick: Britain, 1800–1854*. Cambridge University Press, Cambridge, 1998, pp. 84–120.

119. E. Higgs, 'Colloquium on *The information state in England: the central collection of information in citizens, 1500–2000*, Palgrave, London, 2004', *Journal of Historical Sociology*, 18 1/2, 2005, p. 140.

120. Burn, *An historical sketch*, pp. 161, 159.

121. K. Waddington, *Charity and the London Hospitals 1850–1898*, Boydell, Woodbridge, 2000, p. 32.

122. P. L. Garside, 'The impact of philanthropy: housing provision and the Sutton Model Dwellings Trust, 1900–1939', *Economic History Review*, 53, 4, 2000, p. 750.

123. *Northern Star*, 13 June 1840.

124. D. G. Green and L. G. Cromwell, *Mutual aid or welfare state: Australia's friendly societies*, George Allen & Unwin, Sydney, 1984, p. 63.

125. Moffrey, *A century of Oddfellowship*, p. 60.

126. Spry, *The history of Odd-Fellowship*, pp. 146, 166.

127. Moffrey, *A century of Oddfellowship*, p. 73.

128. Weller, 'Self help', pp. 112–13.

129. AMC report, *Oddfellows' Magazine*, 1922, p. 337.

130. *Oddfellows' Magazine*, January 1884, p. 32.

131. Moffrey, *A century of Oddfellowship*, p. 81.

132. *Oddfellows' Magazine*, February 1886, p. 38.

133. Green and Cromwell, *Mutual aid*, pp. 61–2.

134. Moffrey, *A century of Oddfellowship*, p. 179.

135. *Master and artisan in Victorian England. The diary of William Andrews and the autobiography of Joseph Gutteridge* edited and with an introduction by V. E. Chancellor. 1969, pp. 103, 132, 135; V. E. Chancellor, 'Gutteridge, Joseph (1816–1899)', *Oxford Dictionary of National Biography*, Oxford University Press, 2004 http://www.oxforddnb.com/view/article/54368, accessed 25 Sept 2008.

136. Burn, *The autobiography*, p. 155. For the material about typhus see p. 147. He also related the same tale of being in arrears at the lodge, his family of seven getting typhus and the 'noble generousity' of the Oddfellows in Burn, *An historical sketch*, p. 153.

137. *Preston Chronicle*, 23 July 1886 quoted in S. D'Cruze and J. Turnbull, 'Fellowship and family: Oddfellows' lodges in Preston and Lancaster c.1830–c.1890', *Urban History*, 22, 1, 1995, pp. 27–28.

138. Weller, 'Self help', pp. 136–138.

139. Thompson, *The English working class*, pp. 47, 55.

140. L. J. Daston, 'The domestication of risk: mathematical probability and insurance 1650–1830' in L. Krüger, L. J. Daston and M. Heidelberger, *The probabilistic revolution. Volume 1. ideas in history*, MIT Press, Cambridge, Mass, 1987, p. 248.

141. There is an account of this in Spry, *The history of Odd-Fellowship*, p. 37.

142. *The Times*, 1 February 1842.

143. Hutton, *The triumph*, p. 61.

144. *The Northern Star and Leeds General Advertiser*, 16 June 1838.

145. *Leeds Mercury*, 16 November 1839.

146. Gosden, *The friendly societies*, pp. 168–9; Moffrey, *A century of Oddfellowship*, pp. 43–4.

147. In 1846 George Jacob Holyoake, a leading Chartist, Humanist and member of the co-operative movement, won fifty pounds in a competition on the themes and degrees of the Oddfellows, namely Charity, Truth, Knowledge, Science and the Golden Rule. The Oddfellows published his new Lectures for the White, Blue, Scarlet and Gold Degrees. These were inspired by the works of Burns, Coleridge, Dickens, Elliott, Scott, Shakespeare and others. G. J. Holyoake, *Sixty years of an agitator's life*, T. Fisher Unwin, London, 1906, pp. 205–207. Moffrey, *A century of Oddfellowship*, p. 60, reported that over fifty years later the older catechetical system was still in use in some areas.

148. M. E. Hotz, 'Down among the dead: Edwin Chadwick's burial reform discourse in mid-nineteenth-century England', *Victorian Literature and Culture*, 29, 2001, pp. 21–38.

149. *Northern Times and Newcastle Telegraph* in Green and Cromwell, *Mutual aid*, p. 28.

150. S. Cordery, 'Friendly Societies and the Discourse of Respectability in Britain, 1825–1875', *Journal of British Studies*, 34, 1, 1995, p. 49.

151. *Preston Guardian*, 4 May 1850.

152. B. Beach, P.Prov C.S., 'An Oddfellow's New Year wishes', *Oddfellows Magazine*, February 1901, p. 47; Moffrey, *A century of Oddfellowship*, pp. 44–5. Beach also called God 'our greatest Grand Master and Friend' in a poem published in *Oddfellows Magazine*, June 1901, p. 171.

153. *Oddfellows Magazine*, September 1914, p. 654.

154. This comparison draws on A. D. Buckley. '"Rise up dead man, and fight again". Mumming, the Mass and the Masonic Third Degree', in A. D. Buckley, C. Mac Cárthaigh, S. Ócathain and S. Mac Mathúna (eds), *Border Crossing: mumming in cross-border and cross-community context*, Dundalgan Press, Dundalk, 2007, pp. 19–38.

155. Burn, *An historical sketch*, p. 117.

156. *Warwick Advertiser*, 8 June 1845, quoted in M. A. Cluley, 'Mutuality, discipline and respectability: with special reference to nineteenth-century friendly societies in mid-Warwickshire', MA dissertation, Warwick, 1997, p. 22.

157. D. Neave, 'Anglican clergy and the Affiliated Order friendly societies' in E. Royle (ed.), *Regional studies in the history of religion in Britain since the later middle ages*, Humberside College of Higher Education, Hull, 1984, pp. 184–9.

158. Neave, *East Riding*, p. 23.

159. A. Jackson, *The Whaley Bridge Parish Magazine*, October 2007, pp. 12–13.

160. Horus, the ancient Egyptian lord of the skies who ensured good health, was represented by an eye. See also C. Ginzberg, 'Your country needs you': a case study in political iconography', *History Workshop Journal*, 52, 2001, pp. 8–11. Marcia Pointon, 'Quakerism and visual culture, 1650–1800', *Art History*, 20, 3, 1997, p. 407, notes that a single eye was a commonplace of Quaker discourse. Robert Greethead's sketch of a trade procession in Bristol in 1831 depicts brass-founders carrying a cast-iron model fire grate bearing images which included the All-Seeing Eye. See E. Cooper, *People's Art. Working-class art from 1750 to the present day*, Mainstream, Edinburgh, 1994, p. 84.

161. A. Briggs, *Victorian things*, Penguin, Harmondsworth, 1990, pp. 116–20.

162. R. A. Leeson, *United we stand: an illustrated account of trade union emblems*, Adams & Dart, Bath, 1971, p. 13, suggested that the 'All-Seeing Eye is that of the central executive'.

163. I. Loudon, *Medical care and the general practitioner 1750–1850*, Clarendon, Oxford, 1986, p. 254. *The Manchester Guardian*, 17 August 1844, reported that some doctors were not as enthusiastic about the Unity. They held a meeting in Glasgow at which they resolved to protect their dignity and the interests of the profession from the encroachment of Oddfellows' and other friendly societies.

164. Stedman Jones, *Outcast London*, p. 166.

165. J. E. Adams, *Dandies and desert saints: styles of Victorian manhood*, Ithaca, Cornell University Press, New York, 1995, p. 65.

166. These examples are drawn from Turner, 'Friendly societies', p. 337.

167. H. Southall and E. Garrett, 'Morbidity and mortality among early nineteenth-century engineering workers', *Social History of Medicine*, 4, 2, 1991, p. 240.

168. D. J. Salmon (ed.), *Malton in the early nineteenth century*, 1981, cited by Turner, 'Friendly societies', pp. 106–7.

169. *The Times*, 7 June 1895.

170. This may not have helped the AOF locally as by 1901 there were still no courts in a centre with a population of 685,000 while there were a number of major collecting friendly societies, notably the Royal Liver and the Liverpool Victoria.

171. Foresters' *Executive Committee Quarterly Report*, January 1894, p. 4, cited in Logan, 'Role of friendly society orders', p. 106.

172. *The Times*, 7 November 1844.

173. *The Times*, 10 February 1852.

174. H. T. Dickinson, *The politics of the people in eighteenth-century Britain*, 1994, p. 98.

175. D. Featherstone, *Resistance, space and political identities: the making of counter-global networks*, Blackwell, Oxford, 2008, p. 74.

176. Turner, 'Friendly societies', p. 98.

177. R. C. Lister, 'British friendly societies', p. 86.

178. *General Evening Post*, 7 March 1799. The tavern was the headquarters of a musical society where the Grand Lodge of English Freemasons first met in 1717. The Freemasons there revived the 'Antient Drama' commemorating the slaying of Hiram Abif which was later adapted to create the third degree.

179. Burn, *An historical sketch*, p. 146.

180. Gosden, *The friendly societies*, pp. 26, 29.

181. N. E. Key, 'The political culture and political rhetoric of county feasts and feast sermons, 1654–1714', *Journal of British Studies*, 33, 1994, pp. 226–47.

182. M. Gorsky, 'The growth and distribution of English friendly societies in the early nineteenth century', *Economic History Review*, 51, 3, 1998, p. 503. In his work on British clubs Peter Clark too has stressed the importance of both internal and international migration to the development of associational culture.

183. There are a number of examples cited in I. Krausman Ben-Amos, 'Gifts and favours: informal support in early modern England', *Journal of Modern History*, 72, 7, 2000, p. 318.

184. Tramping played an important role in the development of travellers cheques. On setting out a tramp would be given a book of cheques. These could be exchanged at a lodge for hospitality, thereby guarding against abuse of the system. When in 1865 John Mason Cook introduced coupons which could be used at participating hotels he may have been copying a system of which his father, Thomas must have been aware. Thomas Cook, before he set up as a travel agent, was an artisan in the printing trade.

185. This emblem is reproduced inLeeson, *United we stand*, p. 10. By the eighteenth century Quakers were using their registers as evidence for individuals' qualification for support from Quaker funds.

186. E. J. Hobsbawm, 'The tramping artisan', in E. J. Hobsbawm, *Labouring men: studies in the history of labour*, London, 1964, p. 34.

187. *Oddfellows (Manchester Unity) 175th Anniversary*, p. 5.

188. *Oddfellows' Reports* 1849–51; W Ranger, Report to the General Board of Health on Stockton, 1851, p. 57; Minute Book of the Rose of England Lodge, U/oD/1463, CCA all cited in Turner, 'Friendly societies', pp. 104–5.

189. Figures collated by Turner, 'Friendly societies', p. 376.

190. Hobsbawm, 'The tramping', p. 47.

191. Quoted in K. Y. Heselton, *The Oddfellows of Great Easton*, Bringhurst Press, 1986, p. 44. I am grateful to Ena Meechan for her hospitality and allowing me to see a copy of this text. An almost identical phrase appeared in the 'Arrangements for Travelling and for Clearances in the Manchester Unity of Oddfellows' set out in Gosden, *The friendly societies*, p. 221.

192. G. Stedman Jones, Outcast London: a study in the relationship between classes in Victorian society, Cambridge University Press, Cambridge, 1970; J. H. Treble, 'The seasonal demand for adult labour in Glasgow, 1890–1914', *Social History*, 3, 1, 1978, pp. 43–60.

193. Quoted in Moffrey, *A century of Oddfellowship*, p. 210.

194. Chase, *Early trade*, p. 62.

195. Information on tramping can be found in R. Leeson, Travelling Brothers: *The Six Centuries' Road from Craft Fellowship to Trade Unionism*, George Allen & Unwin, London 1979, pp. 125, 151, 172, 174–80, 193, 210, 213, 214, 215.

196. Neave, *Mutual aid*, pp. 81–2; Logan, 'Role of friendly society orders', p. 157.

197. D. Hunter, 'Vagrancy in the East and West Ridings of Yorkshire during the late Victorian period', *Local Historian*, 36, 3, 2006, p. 186 cited a Yorkshire Inspector's comment.

198. Spry, *A history*, pp. 111, 120, 122–4.

199. F.G.P. Neison's data cited by Gosden, *The friendly societies*, p. 79.

200. Spry, *The history of Odd-Fellowship*, pp. 176, 180.

201. K. D Kingston, 'Not gilden, but golden', *Oddfellows Magazine* May 1884, p. 12. For a discussion of this tale see L. C. Hadley, 'Poetry and fiction from the friendly societies', Ph.D. thesis, De Montfort, 2006, pp. 54–68.

202. *A Kidderminster Victorian Journal – based on the diaries Annie Tomkinson of Franche Hall kept from 1884–1920*. Transcribed by Michael Tomlinson of Jersey, http://www.scribd.com/doc/9672643/Annie accessed 17 September 2009.

203. B. Stibbins, '"A highly beneficial influence". Friendly societies in Norfolk in the nineteenth century, with particular reference to north Norfolk', MA dissertation, East Anglia, 2001, p. 41.

204. Spry, *The history of Odd-Fellowship*, pp. 180–1; Green and Cromwell, *Mutual aid*, p. 44.

205. Moffrey, *A century of Oddfellowship*, pp. 50–1.

Chapter 3:   Respect and reciprocity

1. M. Mauss, *The gift. Forms and functions of exchange in archaic societies* 1954. Translated by I. Cunnison, first published 1925, p. 76.

2. A. Ben-Amos, *Funerals, politics and memory in modern France, 1796–1996*, Oxford University Press, Oxford, 2000, p. 262.

3. J. Lynch, *Samuel Johnson's Dictionary: selections from the 1755 work that defined the English language*, Levenger Press, Delray Beach, 2002, s.v. 'gift'

4. I. K. Ben-Amos, *The culture of giving: informal support and gift-exchange in early modern England*, Cambridge University Press, Cambridge, 2008, p. 332.

5. These terms are derived from the work of Ferdinand Tönnies, in particular his *Gemeinschaft und Gesellschaft*, which was first published in 1887.

6. Mauss, *The gift*, p. 76.

7. Muldrew, *The economy*, pp. 306; 303–12.

8. R. Taylor, *The possibility of co-operation: studies in rationality and social change*, Cambridge, University Press, Cambridge, 1984, pp. 163–75.

9. K. Polanyo, *The great transformation: the political and economic origins of our time*, 1st edn 1944, Beacon Press, Boston, 1957, chapters 4–5; Valenze, *The social life*, p. 258; J. R. Gillis, *A world of their own making: myth, ritual, and the quest for family values*, Basic Books, New York, 1996, p. 79.

10. G. Stedman Jones, *Outcast London: a study in the relationship between classes in Victorian society*, Oxford University Press, Oxford, 1984, pp. 256, 257, 259.

11. H. Newby, *The deferential worker. A study of farm labourers in East Anglia*, Allan Lane, London, 1977, pp. 60, 21, 234, 42.

12. This view is promoted in P. Bourdieu, *Outline of a theory of practice*, trans. R. Nice, Cambridge University Press, Cambridge, 1977.

13. M. C. Finn, *The character of credit: personal debt in English culture, 1740–1914*, Cambridge University Press, Cambridge, 2003.

14. C. M. Arensberg, *The Irish countryman. An anthropological study*, Gloucester: Peter Smith, 1937; A. O'Dowd, *Meitheal: A Study of Co-Operative Labour in Rural Ireland (Aspects of Ireland)*, Comhairle Bhealoideas Eireann, Dublin, 1981.

15. Daunton, *State and market*, p. 127.

16. T. Owen, *Welsh folk customs*, National Museum of Wales, Cardiff, 1978, pp. 161–2.

17. J. A. Jaffe, *Striking a bargain. Work and industrial relations in England, 1815–1865*, Manchester University Press, Manchester, 2000, pp. 67, 136–7.

18. J. Benson, 'Coalminers, coalowners and collaboration: the miners' permanent relief fund movement in England, 1860–1895', *Labour History Review*, 68, 2, 2003, pp. 184, 191.

19. M. Finn, 'Working-class women and the contest for consumer control in Victorian county courts', *Past and Present*, 161, 1998, pp. 119–20.

20. J. Burchardt, *The allotment movement in England, 1793–1873*, Boydell, Woodbridge, p. 181.

21. J. E. Archer, 'The nineteenth-century allotment: half an acre and a row', *Economic History Review*, 50, 1, 1997, pp. 25, 27, 35.

22. A. Cameron, *Bare feet and tackety boots. A boyhood on Rhum*, Luath Press, Barr, 1988, p. 3.

23. G. J. West, 'Charity labour gatherings in rural Perthshire, 1850–1950', *Scottish Studies*, 33, 1999, p. 134.

24. J. Raven, *Judging new wealth: popular publishing and responses to commerce in England, 1750–1800*, Clarendon, Oxford, 1992, p. 198.

25. F. Engels, *The condition of the working class in England*, Oxford University Press, Oxford, 1958 edition, pp. 100, 102, 140.

26. *Porcupine*, 29 May 1880, p. 138.

27. Quoted in A. Davin, *Growing up poor. Home, school and street in London, 1870–1914*, Rivers Oram, London, 1996, p. 59.

28. L. H. Lees, *Exiles of Erin: Irish immigrants in Victorian London*, Manchester University Press, Manchester, 1979, p. 83.

29. E. Ross, 'Survival networks: women's neighbourhood sharing in London before World War I', *History Workshop Journal*, 15, 1983, p. 11.

30. J. White, *The worst street in north London. Campbell Bunk, Islington, between the wars*, Routledge & Kegan Paul, London, 1986, pp. 73–74, 274.

31. M. Anderson, *Family structure in nineteenth-century Lancashire*, Cambridge University Press, Cambridge, 1971, p. 137; M. Dupree, *Family structure in the Staffordshire potteries, 1840–1880*, Oxford University Press, Oxford, 1995, p. 350.

32. M. Tebbutt, *Women's talk. A social history of 'gossip' in working-class neighbourhoods, 1880–1960*, Scolar, Aldershot, 1995.

33. Cordery, *British friendly societies*, p. 181.

34. G. Stedman Jones, 'Rethinking Chartism' in G. Stedman Jones, *Languages of class: studies in English working class history 1832–1982*, Cambridge University Press, Cambridge, 1983, pp. 112–44.

35. J. Brewer,   'Commercialisation   and   politics'   in

N. McKendrick, J. Brewer and J. H. Plumb (eds), *The birth of the consumer society: the commercialisation of eighteenth-century England*, London, 1982, pp. 205, 197, 222, 220; Muldrew, *The economy*, pp. 58, 271; see also Craig Muldrew, 'Credit and the courts: debt litigation in a seventeenth-century urban community', *Economic History Review* 46, 1, 1993, pp. 25, 27, 30–1, 34–6; Y. Kawana, Trade, sociability and governance in an English incorporated borough: 'formal and 'informal' worlds in Leicester, c.1570–1640', *Urban History*, 33, 3, 2006, p. 325.

36. Even in the nineteenth century, when bankruptcy laws made negotiations over money less risky, the extension of credit remained of importance. Payment in kind and credit are part of the explanation for the continuation of low wages. For examples from Oxfordshire and Sussex see T. Vigne and A. Howkins, 'The small shopkeeper in industrial and market towns' in Geoffrey Crossick (ed.), *The lower middle class in Britain, 1870–1914*, Croom Helm, London, 1977, p. 201 and M. Reed, 'The peasantry of nineteenth-century England: a neglected class', *History Workshop Journal*, 18, 1984, pp. 61–3. In the case of the Oddfellows the lack of legal protection made claims about those who stole the funds difficult to pursue.

37. *Merthyr Guardian*, 5 January 1833, 9 August 1834, 17 December 1836 in G. A. Williams, 'Friendly societies in Glamorgan 1793–1832', *The Bulletin of the Board of Celtic Studies*, 18, 3, 1959, p. 276.

38. Burn, *An historical sketch*, pp. 127–36.

39. On this aspect of masculinity see Brewer, 'Commercialisation and politics', p. 215; J. Smail, 'Credit, risk, and honor in eighteenth-century commerce', *Journal of British Studies*, 44, 3, 2005, p. 454.

40. The term 'present' was used if there was no expectation of return. *Rose of England Lodge, Manchester Unity, Minute Book, 1842–1872*, March and October 1848 cited by Turner, 'Friendly societies', pp. 329, 360.

41. Moffrey, *A century of Oddfellowship*, pp. 188, 40.

42. Moffrey, *A century of Oddfellowship*, pp. 65, 74.

43. Spry, *The history of Odd-Fellowship*, pp. 59, 175, 176.

44. *Rose of England Lodge, Manchester Unity, Minute Book, 1842–1872*, January 1844, cited by Turner, 'Friendly societies', p. 329.

45. Rule 17, Yarm Tradesman's Society, 1772 cited in cited by Turner, 'Friendly societies', p. 328.

46. *Joseph Warburton Lodge centenary, 1835–1935*, p. 30 cited in Turner, 'Friendly societies', p. 330.

47. Lodge Minute Book cited by Turner, 'Friendly societies', p. 360.

48. V. A. Burrowes, 'On friendly societies since the advent of National Health Insurance', *Journal of the Institute of Actuaries*, 63, 3, 1933, pp. 307–82.

49. This phrase is taken from the 1935 initiation ceremony. The candidate was told to make a 'solemn Obligation regarding your duties and stated the following: 'I [Candidate states name] do most solemnly and sincerely promise that I never will on any occasion whatever tell, show or give by any means known any matters appertaining to the Order which its Rules or customs declare shall be kept secret.'

50. Thompson, *The English working class*, p. 485.

51. *Hansard's Parliamentary Debates*, 3rd series, T. C. Hansard, London, 1830–91, 23 137 quoted in A. D. Pionke, 'I do swear': oath-taking among the elite public in Victorian England, *Victorian Studies*, 49, 4, 2007, p. 613.

52. 'John Tester and the Trades' Union', *The Leeds Mercury*, 5 July 1834. There was also a union of flannel weavers in Rochdale, the emblem of which included a handclasp. See J. Cole, *Conflict and co-operation. Rochdale and the pioneering spirit, 1790–1844*, George Kelsall, Littleborough, 1994, p. 19.

53. My thanks to Paul Eyre for this story.

54. Burn, *An historical sketch*, p. 85.

55. Spry, *The history of Odd-Fellowship*, p. 39.

56. Moffrey, *A century of Oddfellowship*, p. 46.

57. Spry, *The history of Odd-Fellowship*, p. 39.

58. Moffrey, *A century of Oddfellowship*, p. 119.

59. Cordery, *British friendly societies*, pp. 105–7.

60. J. M. Roberts, *The mythology of secret societies*, Secker & Warburg, London, 1972, pp. 1–2.

61. W. Bagehot, *The English constitution*, edited with an introduction and notes by Miles Taylor, Oxford University Press, Oxford, 2001, p. 13.

62. Burn, *An historical sketch*, pp. 50–1.

63. *The sociology of Georg Simmel. Translated, edited and with an introduction by Kurt. H Wolff*, Free Press, New York, 1950, pp. 330, 332.

64. Quoted in Solt *Discovering friendly and fraternal societies*, p. 95. Hardwick was interested in ritual and wrote *Traditions, superstitions and folk-lore: chiefly Lancashire and the north of England, their affinity to others in widely distributed localities, their eastern origin and mythical significance*, A. Ireland, Manchester, 1872.

65. Cordery, *British friendly societies*, p. 145.

66. J. K. Walton, *The English seaside resort: a social history 1750–1914*, Leicester University Press, Leicester, 1983, p. 28.

67. D. Reid, 'The "iron roads" and "the happiness of the working classes": the early development of the railway

67. excursion', *Journal of Transport History*, 17, 1, 1996, pp. 57–73.

68. Spry, *The history of Odd-Fellowship*, p. 131.

69. Coventry City Library, JN 334.3 Oddfellows *Second Quarterly Report 1877*, in Weller, 'Self help', p. 118.

70. *Hull Advertiser*, 31 August 1838, in Neave, *Feasts*, p. 17.

71. J. C. Loudon, *A Catalogue of trees and shrubs and their upkeep*, 1840, held by Derby Local Studies Library. (Address to Town Council, drawings and account of the grand opening), pp. 92–5, available at http://www.derbyarboretum.co.uk/, accessed 8 September 2009.

72. A picture of the parade is in N. Mansfield, *Radical rhymes and Union Jacks: a search for evidence of ideologies in the symbolism of nineteenth-century banners*, University of Manchester Working Papers in Economic and Social History, No. 45, Manchester, 2000, illustration 23.

73. Quoted in V. Smith, *The town book of Lewes, 1702–1901 volume 1*, Lewes, 1973, pp. 270–3.

74. A report on the coronation of 1830 is quoted in Moffrey, *A century of Oddfellowship*, p. 43.

75. Report on the anniversary celebrations of the Temple of Peace Lodge, Newport in *The Odd Fellow*, 1 August 1840,

76. Discussion of the paper of F. G. P. Neison, 'Some statistics of the affiliated orders of friendly societies (Oddfellows and Foresters)', *Journal of the Statistical Society of London*, 40, 1, March 1877, pp. 87–9.

77. *Berrow's Journal*, 10 June 1865.

78. *Crewe Guardian*, 28 July 1909, quoted in F. Edwards, 'The treatment of poverty in Nantwich and Crewe, 1730–1914', MA dissertation, Keele, 1990, p. 523.

79. *Jackson's Oxford Journal*, 28 July 1900.

80. *North Wales Chronicle*, 7 June 1883.

81. S. Green, *The working classes of Great Britain: their present condition, and the means of their improvement and elevation*, J. Snow, London, 1850.

82. *Oddfellows' Magazine*, 1829, p. 68 quoted in Gosden, *The friendly societies*, pp. 125–7.

83. Clapham, *A concise economic history*, p. 591.

84. D. C. Richter, *Riotous Victorians*, Ohio University Press, Ohio, 1981, p. 87.

85. D. Cannadine, 'The transformation of civic ritual in modern Britain: the Colchester oyster feast', *Past and Present*, 94, 1982, pp. 128–9. By the early years of the twentieth century it was recognised that Edwardian men were more likely to join 'processions dominated by advertising for private companies and state agencies'; see J. M. MacKenzie, *Propaganda and empire: the manipulation of British public opinion, 1880–1960*, Manchester University Press, Manchester, 1984.

86. Cordery, *British friendly societies*, pp. 39, 50, 81; http://www.rward.clara.net/present.htm, accessed 8 March 2008.

87. My thanks to the People's History Museum for allowing me to access an image of this banner.

88. Letter of 3 May 1890, PRO MEPOL/2/248 cited in Richter, *Riotous Victorians*, p. 159.

89. *Warwick Advertiser*, 8 June 1894, in Cluley 'Mutuality', p. 22.

90. *Leicester Daily Mercury*, 6 June 1906.

91. Ten days before the AMC the King died and the celebrations were cancelled, leaving only the business proceedings intact.

92. Quoted in Winster Village History Group, *A Peak District village remembers*, Landmark, 2000, p. 54.

93. *Cecil Sharp's Folk Dance Notes* http://www.tradcap.com/folknotes.html, accessed 8 September 2009.

94. The difficulty of obtaining time off work on a Tuesday and the loss of the Club Room between 1931 and 1933, when the landlord would not permit the Unity to meet, contributed to the decline of the lodge. The last Club Day parade was held in the early 1930s, and the banner was sold to a dealer in 1975. See D. Bathe, 'Oddfellows and Morris Dancing in a Peak District village', *Certificate in English Cultural Tradition*, Sheffield University, 1984, pp. 46–7, 102–3.

95. Hardwick, *History ... of friendly societies*, p. 152.

96. T. R. Nevett, *Advertising in Britain: A history*, Heinemann, London, 1982, pp 53, 59.

97. *Oddfellows' Quarterly Report*, July 1847; *The Stokeley News and Cleveland Reporter*, 1 August 1843, 1 March 1844; lodge rulebook all cited in Turner, 'Friendly societies', p. 107.

98. *The Odd Fellow*, 2 March 1839.

99. R. Hird, *Annals of Bedale, Volume 3*, L. Lewis (ed.), North Yorkshire County Record Office, Publication No. 2, 1975, pp. 347–50, quoted in Turner, 'Friendly societies', p. 380.

100. J. R. Rogerson, 'The festival of charity', in *The Manchester Times and Gazette*, 15 January 1842.

101. Burn, *An historical sketch*, p. 89.

102. Shirrefs published a number of other newspapers but was bankrupt by 1849 when the privileges extended to Isle publishers were curtailed. See John Belchem, 'The neglected 'unstamped': the Manx pauper press of the 1840s', *Albion*, 24, 4, 1992, p. 607.

103. An account of the speech introducing it was published in the *Journal* and reproduced in Burn, *An historical sketch*, p. 97.

104. Moffrey, *A century of Oddfellowship*, p. 22.

105. *Blackburn Times*, 28 January 1893, available at http://

www.cottontown.org/page.cfm?pageid=3098&langua
ge=eng, accessed 7 December, 2008. Princess Charlotte
Augusta of Wales, 1796–1817, was the daughter of the
Prince of Wales, later George IV.

106. Wells, *Wretched faces*, p. 326.

107. For further analysis see R. Richardson, *Death, dissection
and the destitute*, Penguin, London, 1989.

108. *The Lancet*, I, 1844, p. 195.

109. *Northern Star*, 27 October 1838.

110. On the challenge from the private sector, see M. Smith,
'The Church of Scotland and the funeral industry in
nineteenth-century Edinburgh', *Scottish History Review*,
88, 1, pp. 108–33.

111. Moffrey, *A century of Oddfellowship*, pp. 85, 149–50.

112. D. Thomson, 'The decline of social welfare: falling
state support for the elderly since early Victorian
times', *Ageing and Society*, 4, 1984, pp. 451–82;
D. Thomson, 'The welfare of the elderly in the past: a
family or community responsibility?', in M. Pelling and
R. M. Smith (eds), *Life, death and the elderly: historical
perspectives*, Routledge, London, 1991, p. 204.

113. *Manx Liberal*, 6 June 1840. This is account is drawn
from the work of Frances Coakley.

114. *The Hull Advertiser*, 11 December 1840 in D. Neave,
*Feasts, fellowship and financial aid. South Holderness
friendly societies*, Hedon and District Local History
Society, Beverley, 1986, pp. 13–14.

115. For the rituals relating to funerals and the ways in which
Masonic cemeteries were designed as moral lessons,
see J. S. Curl, *The art and architecture of Freemasonry,
an introductory study*, 2nd edition, Batsford, London,
2002.

116. *Pioneer*, 7 June 1834, quoted in C. Behagg, 'Secrecy,
ritual and folk violence: the opacity of the workplace in
the first half of the nineteenth century', in R. D. Storch,
Popular culture and custom in nineteenth-century England,
Croom Helm, London and Canberra, 1982, p. 161.

117. Thompson, *The English working class*, p. 466, notes, by
contrast, that the Thames Shipwrights Provident Union
wore sprigs of oak on parades, perhaps in recognition
of the material with which they worked.

118. *Derbyshire Courier*, 13 July 1839, in Bathe, 'Oddfellows
and Morris Dancing', p. 42.

119. *Oddfellows' Magazine*, September 1901, p. 375;
Oddfellows' Magazine, November 1901, p. 440.

120. Quoted in Bathe, 'Oddfellows and Morris Dancing',
p. 42.

121. Coventry City Library, JN334.3 Annual Report 1867
quoted in Weller, 'Self help', p. 107.

122. G. Sturt [Bourne], *Memoirs of a Surrey Labourer: a
Record of the Last Years of Frederick Bettesworth*, London,

Duckworth and Co. 1st edition 1907, Caliban, Fifle,
1978, pp. 162, 218, 276 317.

123. *Manchester Unity in NSW Fraternity. The Lodge Branch
Journal*, March 2006, p. 16.

124. Stretford Burial Board regulations, cited in J. Strange,
'Tho' lost to sight, to memory dear': pragmatism,
sentimentality and working-class attitudes towards the
grave, c.1875–1914', *Mortality*, 8, 2, 2003, p. 153.

125. J. M. Clarke, *London's necropolis: a guide to Brookwood
Cemetery*, Sutton, Stroud, 2004.

126. *Odd Fellows Quarterly Magazine*, 1860, p. 246.

127. G. Best, *Mid-Victorian Britain, 1815–75*, Weidenfeld &
Nicolson, London, 1971, pp. 256–63; B. H. Harrison,
*Drink and the Victorians. The temperance question in
England, 1815–1872*, Faber & Faber, London, 1971,
pp. 23–6.

128. P. Bailey, 'Will the real Bill Banks stand up? A role
analysis of mid-Victorian working-class respectability',
Journal of Social History, 12, 3, 1979, pp. 338, 347.

129. B. B. Gilbert, *The evolution of National Insurance in
Great Britain. The origins of the Welfare State*. Michael
Joseph, London, 1966. pp. 166–7. Although the Order's
subscription rates were almost always higher than the
rates offered by local or patron-dominated societies,
members of the Oddfellows worked within a wide
variety of occupations. See, for examples, Gosden, *The
friendly societies*, p. 74; N. Kirk, *The growth of working
class reformism in mid-Victorian England*, Croom Helm,
London, 1985, pp. 198–9; M. Savage, *The dynamics of
working-class politics: the Labour movement in Preston,
1880–1940*, Cambridge University Press, Cambridge,
1987, p. 126; Neave, *East Riding*, p. 24.

130. D. Neave, 'Friendly societies in the rural East Riding,
1830–1912', Ph.D. thesis, University of Hull, 1986,
p. 198, Table 38.

131. Gosden, *The friendly societies*, pp. 88–93, 224–8.

132. Neave, 'Friendly societies in the … East Riding',
p. 241.

133. Henry Ratcliffe was born in 1808 in Tyldesley,
Lancashire, joined the Order aged 25 and died in the
Society's office aged 69. He rose to become Provincial
Grand Master within three years of initiation and
Corresponding Secretary of the Order by 1848. His
*Observations on the rate of mortality and sickness existing
among the friendly societies*, 1850, included the monetary
tables, known as Ratcliffe tables, which became the
basis of the actuarial soundness on which the Unity
relied. In 1852 and 1862 he issued supplements and
amendments and recommended quinquennial valuation
of the assets and liabilities of all friendly societies. This
was accepted and passed into legislation in 1870 and he

was nominated as a public valuer under the act. In 1871 he published a special valuation of the Order.

134. Cluley, 'Mutuality', discusses the backgrounds of the membership.

135. Kirk, *Growth of working class reformism*, pp. 198–9.

136. N. Mansfield. *English farmworkers and local patriotism, 1900–1930*, Ashgate, Aldershot, 2001, p. 182.

137. E. Edwards, 'The friendly societies and the ethic of respectability. Nineteenth-century Cambridge' Ph.D. thesis, Cambridge College of Art and Technology, 1987, p. 499.

138. D'Cruze and Turnbull, 'Fellowship and family', pp. 25–47.

139. *Northern Star*, 5 February 1842.

140. Turner, 'Friendly societies', p. 220.

141. P. Johnson, *Saving and spending. The working-class economy in Britain, 1870–1939*, Clarendon, Oxford, 1985, p. 62.

142. Turner, 'Friendly societies', pp. 229–39.

143. I am indebted to Karen Stuart for help with the collation of some of this information.

144. Turner, 'Friendly societies', pp. 229–32.

145. Gosden, *The friendly societies*, pp. 80–2. The Wigginton Lodge, Banbury District, was founded in 1899, and

14 of the 23 founders were labourers, 12 specifically farm labourers. Correspondence from Robert Schiff, 27 February 2006.

146. R. E. Moreau, *The departed village. Berrick Salome at the turn of the century*, Oxford University Press, London 1968, this edition, Country Book Club, Devon, 1971, p. 115. On the rival society see M. Bee, 'A friendly society case study: the Compton Pilgrims Benefit Society', *Southern History*, no. 11, 1989.

147. M. Bee, 'Within the shelter of the Old Elm Tree: Odd Fellowship and community in north Oxfordshire, 1871–2002', *Family and Community History*, 6, 2, 2003, pp. 85–97.

148. Cordery, *British friendly societies*, p. 149.

149. Spry, *The history of Odd-Fellowship*, p. 154. An extensive report of the trial of William Ratcliffe appeared in the *Manchester Times and Gazette*, 25 March 1848.

150. Turner, 'Friendly societies'. Increasingly miners formed their own friendly societies. See J. Benson, 'English coal-miners' trade union accident funds, 1850–1900', *Economic History Review*, 28, 3, 1975, pp. 401–12.

151. *The Manchester Guardian*, 12 June 1930.

152. Polonius in W. Shakespeare, *Hamlet*, Act 1, Scene 3.

Chapter 4:   Citizenship and security

1. *The Times*, 3 September 1907.

2. Moffrey, *A century of Oddfellowship*, p. 177. The italics are not in the original text.

3. Cordery, 'Friendly societies and the discourse', p. 40. See also Kirk, *Growth of working-class reformism*, pp. 189, 220–1, 222.

4. Cordery, 'Friendly societies and the discourse', p. 58.

5. Quoted in L. McFall, 'The disinterested self. The idealized subject of life assurance', *Cultural Studies*, 21, 4, 2007, p. 594.

6. J. H. Treble, 'The performance of the standard life assurance company in the ordinary market for life insurance 1825–50', *Scottish Social and Economic History*, 5, 1985, pp. 57–8.

7. On Curwen see Barnett, 'Ideas'.

8. J. Haslam, 'On the prescribing of accounting and accounting publicity by the state in early to mid-nineteenth-century Britain: accounting history as critique' Ph.D. thesis, University of Essex, 1991, pp. 141–2.

9. For examples of the granting of such rate payments see M. Barker-Read, 'The treatment of the aged poor in five selected West Kent parishes from settlement to Speenhamland (1662–1797)', Ph.D. thesis, Open

University, 1988, 60; Black, 'Local government' p. 60. On the payment of arrears up to and after 1834 see R. P. Hastings, *Essays in North Riding history, 1780–1850*, North Yorkshire County Council, Northallerton, 1981, pp. 117–18. On friendly societies as means of reducing the rates see J. N. Baernreither, *English associations of working men*, Sonnerschein, London, 1893, p. 371.

10. Barrister and civil servant John Tidd Pratt (1797–1870) exerted considerable influence upon friendly societies for much of his career. He was called to the bar in 1824 and four years later was given the job of certifying the rules of savings bank and, from 1829, friendly societies. He also received their mortality and sickness returns. He acquired some 30,000 sets of rules and amendments as his responsibilities increased, and he certified the rules of loan societies, building societies and co-operative societies. From 1855 he had to submit an annual report to Parliament, and within these he offered both statistics and managerial advice. He also wrote many legal manuals. He campaigned against 'wet rent', that is lodges having to buy a certain quantity of beer in order to be able to use a function room in a pub, and he insisted that each lodge of the Order be

treated as a separate organisation and register as such. He became, in the words of the 1874 Royal Commission which had to decide how to supervise friendly societies after his death, the 'Minister of Self-Help to the whole of the industrious classes'. That the Commission heard evidence from his son, a vicar, and that the legislation which followed his death extended rather than countered his achievements, indicates the influence of the man. On his death in 1870 his post was abolished for several years before a new post of Chief Registrar was created in 1875. Another barrister, J. M. Ludlow, was Chief Registrar until his retirement in 1891, aged 70, when the post was filled by E. W. Brabrook.

11. Williams, 'Friendly societies', p. 283.

12. Gosden, *The friendly societies*, p. 17; H. M. Coombs and J. R. Edwards, 'The evolution of The District Audit', *Financial Accountability and Management*, 1990. S. Cordery, 'John Tidd Pratt', *Friendly Societies Research Group Newsletter* 10, May 2003.

13. Edwards and Chandler, 'Contextualising … accounting regulation', p. 195.

14. *Northern Star*, 26 January 1839.

15. S. Fowler and W. Spencer, *Army records for family historians*, PRO Publications, London, 1998; N. A. M. Rodger, *Naval records for genealogists*, PRO Publications, London, 1988. See also S. Fowler, *Tracing army ancestry*, Pen and Sword, Barnsley, 2006.

16. *Oddfellows' Magazine*, August 1843, January 1844 and April 1844 quoted in N. Doran, 'Risky business: codifying embodied experience in the Manchester Unity of Oddfellows, *Journal of historical sociology*, 7, 2, 1994, p. 143.

17. Spry, *The history of Odd-Fellowship*, pp. 58–61.

18. The new society had just over 34,000 members in 1872, of whom 33,000 lived in Yorkshire and Lancashire. It was wound up in 2008 when there were only 145 members left.

19. This was the explanation provided by C. Hardwick, *A manual for patrons and members of friendly societies*, IOOFMU, Manchester, 1859, p. 40. See Gosden, *The friendly societies*, p. 28.

20. Moffrey, *A century of Oddfellowship*, pp. 54, 56, 57.

21. Gosden, *The friendly societies*, p. 103; Wilkinson, *History*, p. 35.

22. Burn, *An historical sketch*, p. 99.

23. Spry, *The history of Odd-Fellowship*, p. 182.

24. Perhaps wishing to avoid such struggles, the Foresters only began to expel Courts which did not adopt graduated tables in the 1880s.

25. *Oddfellows' Magazine*, 1922, pp. 226–9.

26. Poovey, *Genres of the credit economy*, p. 9.

27. Poovey, *Genres of the credit economy*, p. 9; Rose, *Intellectual life*, p. 95.

28. Cordery, 'Friendly societies and the discourse', p. 50.

29. Moffrey, *A century of Oddfellowship*, p. 64.

30. Gosden, *Self-Help*, p. 42.

31. The pattern of rapid expansion and rapid failure can be seen within the Ancient Order of Foresters, the main rival Affiliated Order as well. By 1840 the Foresters had 329 courts (the equivalent of lodges) in Lancashire, but over 26 per cent of them had closed by 1850. The percentage of closures in Yorkshire was higher, and in Derbyshire, Nottinghamshire and Northamptonshire, Durham and North Wales it was over 50 per cent. In Northumberland 21 of the 23 courts (that is over 91 per cent) had closed within a decade.

32. E. Hopkins, *Working-class self-help in nineteenth-century England. Responses to industrialisation*, UCL Press, London, 1995, pp. 55–6.

33. Gosden, *The friendly societies*, p. 106.

34. Logan, 'Role of friendly society orders', p. 143.

35. W. Watkins, *Statistical notes on the rate of mortality and sickness existing among the members of the Ancient Order of Foresters*, AoF, King's Lynn, 1855, cited in Logan, 'Role of friendly society orders', p. 148.

36. Hardwick, *History … of friendly societies*, p. 104.

37. Moffrey, *A century of Oddfellowship*, p. 56.

38. The Foresters only adopted them in 1871 but did not effectively enforce them until 1885.

39. Cordery, 'Friendly societies and the discourse', p. 56.

40. Hardwick, *History … of friendly societies*, p. 73.

41. W. G. Fretton, *A history of the Coventry Manchester Unity Order of Oddfellows, 1842–89*, held at Coventry Record Office, Accession 1231, as quoted in Weller, 'Self help', pp. 41, 61. For an account of Fretton (1829–1900) see *Coventry Evening Telegraph*, 5 March 1959. He was a head teacher in Coventry, joined the Oddfellows in 1861, became Grand Master of the Order and was the subject of a portrait in the *Oddfellows' Magazine* in 1874.

42. Quoted in R. Woods, 'Physician, heal thyself: the health and mortality of Victorian doctors', *Social History of Medicine*, 9, 1, 1996, p. 23.

43. Poovey, *Genres of the credit economy*, p. 9.

44. B. B. Gilbert, 'The decay of nineteenth-century provident institutions and the coming of old age pensions in GB', *Economic History Review*, 17, 1964–65, p. 555.

45. Poovey, *Genres of the credit economy*, p. 376.

46. Gilbert, *Evolution of National Insurance*, p. 169.

47. This was part of a broader move towards intervention. The Regulation of Railways Act, 1868, the Life

Assurance Companies Act, 1870 and legislation in the 1870s and 1880s covering gas water and electricity required disclosure of profit and loss accounts. See S. Jones and M. Aiken, 'The significance of the profit and loss account in nineteenth-century Britain: a reassessment', *Abacus* 30, 2, 1994, p. 198–199.

48. Gilbert, 'Decay of … provident institutions', p. 553.

49. Gosden, *Self-help*, p. 261; Gilbert, 'Decay of … provident institutions', p. 554.

50. *Oddfellows' Magazine*, April 1895, p. 102.

51. PRO FS/3/320 in A. Fisk, *Mutual self-help in Southern England, 1850–1912*, Foresters Heritage Trust, Southampton, 2006, p. 55; Society Minute Books and balance sheets cited in Turner, 'Friendly societies', pp. 126, 130.

52. J. Macnicol, *The politics of retirement in Britain, 1878–1948*, Cambridge University Press, Cambridge, 1998, p. 131; J. Riley, *Sickness, recovery and death: a history of ill health*, 1989, pp. 171–6.

53. Edwards, 'Treatment of poverty', p. 449.

54. Young is quoted in Gorsky, 'Charity, mutuality', p. 171.

55. A. W. Watson, *An account of an investigation of the sickness and mortality experience of the IOOF Manchester Unity during the five years 1893–1897*, IOOOF, Manchester, 1903 is based on a 1893–97 survey. This data was used to make the actuarial calculations which formed a central element of National Insurance after 1911.

56. Watson, *An account*, pp. 16–20; Gilbert, 'Decay of … provident institutions', p. 554.

57. Moffrey, *A century of Oddfellowship*, p. 56.

58. Turner, 'Friendly societies', pp. 127–30.

59. The issue is addressed in Weller, 'Self help', and in Baernreither, *English Associations*, pp. 224, 237, 273, 373, 434–7.

60. *Crewe Chronicle*, 20 November 1875, 4 December 1875, 11 December 1875 quoted in Edwards, 'Treatment of poverty', pp. 518–19.

61. Young is quoted in Gorsky, 'Charity, mutuality', p. 169.

62. Watson, *An account*, p. 11. Evidence by the actuary to the IOOFMU, Reuben Watson, *Royal Commission on the Aged Poor, Vol III* p. 622; Macnicol, *The politics of retirement*, p. 116.

63. Moffrey, *A century of Oddfellowship*, p. 176; Cordery, *British friendly societies*, p. 133.

64. For the case that many within the poorer sectors of society were wary of state activity and that compulsory education, housing schemes, health visitors and the Poor Law were seen as, at best, unwanted intrusions see H. Pelling, 'The working class and the origins of the welfare state' in H. Pelling, *Popular politics and society in late Victorian Britain*, Macmillan, London, 1968.

65. *Cambridge Express*, 28 January 1882 and 12 March 1893, quoted in Edwards, 'The friendly societies and the ethic', p. 425.

66. J. Redding Ware, 'How poverty and misery came to be always on Earth: a fairy tale', *Oddfellows Magazine*, June 1885, p. 241.

67. *Oddfellows Magazine*, October 1885.

68. *Oddfellows' Magazine*, July 1895.

69. William Brabrook, 1839–1930, was an accountant who engaged in research on friendly societies, savings banks and life insurance and joined the Institute of Actuaries in 1864. In 1869 he became assistant registrar to John Tidd Pratt and following Pratt's death in 1870, became assistant to J. M. Ludlow. In 1892 he succeeded Ludlow and held the post until 1904, when he retired. He wrote extensively about co-operative societies, trade unions, savings banks and building societies and was knighted in 1905 for his services to friendly societies. In common with the Oddfellows he had an interest in traditional Ritual and philanthropy. He was also a member of the council of the Charity Organisation Society and in 1901 became president of the Folk-Lore Society.

70. Moffrey, *A century of Oddfellowship*, pp. 124–5.

71. *Oddfellows' Magazine*, May 1895, p. 153. See also *Oddfellows' Magazine*, May 1900, p. 115 and *Oddfellows' Magazine*, July 1907, p. 291.

72. Cited in Gilbert, 'Decay of … provident institutions', p. 562. See also D. Goodman, *No thanks to Lloyd George: how the pension was won: the forgotten story*, Third Age Press, London, 1987, pp. 26–7.

73. J. Harris, *William Beveridge: a biography*, 2nd edn, Oxford University Press, Oxford, 1997, p. 168.

74. P. M. Thane, *Old age in English history. Past experiences, present issues*, Oxford University Press, Oxford and New York, 2000, pp. 221–2.

75. *Oddfellows' Magazine*, January 1901, p. 8. A report also appeared in *Leeds Mercury*, 2 June 1900.

76. *Aberdeen Weekly Journal*, 5 June 1900: report on the AMC.

77. *Oddfellows' Magazine*, January 1901, p. 6.

78. Moffrey, *A century of Oddfellowship*, p. 133.

79. Moffrey, *A century of Oddfellowship*, p. 67.

80. Moffrey, *A century of Oddfellowship*, pp. 149, 170, 183.

81. For a discussion of these reasons why legislation was welcomed, see G. R. Boyer and T. P. Schmidle, 'Poverty among the elderly in late Victorian England', *Economic History Review*, 62, 2, 2009, pp. 249–78.

82. Gilbert, 'Decay of … provident institutions', pp. 559–63; Cordery, *British friendly societies*, pp. 159–64.

83. M. Pugh, Working-class experience and state social welfare, 1908–1914: old age pensions reconsidered, *Historical Journal*, 45, 4 2002, p. 775.

84. Gilbert, 'Decay of … provident institutions', p. 551.

85. Moffrey, *A century of Oddfellowship*, p. 181.

86. *The Times*, 31 May 1848, reported that one Charter was presented on the same day that members of the Unity petitioned for the provisions of the Benefit Societies Act be extended to them.

87. Burn, *An historical sketch*, p. 88.

88. For a lengthy account see *Burn, An historical sketch*, pp. 106–7 and *passim*.

89. BL 8242.k.12, House of Commons, *Report from the Secret Committee on the Post office: together with the Appendix*, L, 5 August 1844.

90. *Bradford Observer*, 9 May 1839, *Northern Star*, 1 June 1839, cited in Theodore Koditschek, *Class formation and urban-industrial society: Bradford, 1750–1850*, Cambridge University Press, Cambridge 1990, p. 464.

91. *Northern Star*, 8 September 1838.

92. Burn, *An historical sketch*, pp. 170, 137.

93. Burn, *An historical sketch*, pp. 4, 49, 122, 149, 151.

94. E. J. Hobsbawm, *The age of revolution: Europe, 1789–1848*, Abacus, 1962, p. 261.

95. *The Odd Fellow*, 5 January 1839.

96. Such concerns were of interest to other societies. For example in Nottinghamshire the Hyson Green Friendly Society took part in a Chartist procession in 1838. See *Nottingham Review*, 9 November 1838 in J. A. O'Neill, 'The spirit of independence: friendly societies in Nottinghamshire 1724–1913', Ph.D. thesis, Nottingham Polytechnic, 1992, p. 77.

97. The Earl of Bessborough (ed.), *The diaries of Lady Charlotte Guest*, London, 1950, cited in Williams, 'Friendly societies', p. 280.

98. *The Times*, 29 November 1839.

99. On the Oddfellows' financial support see D. V. Jones, *The last rising: the Newport insurrection of 1839*, 1985, pp 31, 108.

100. *Northern Star*, 21 March 1840, 1 August 1840. List of Friendly Societies enrolled, Durham City, Q/D/S/56, Durham Record Office, cited by Turner, 'Friendly societies' p. 250.

101. M. Chase, *Chartism. A new history*, Manchester University Press, Manchester and New York, 2007, pp. 62, 142, 145, 229.

102. Burn, *The autobiography*. For his role as a marshall at mass meeting in Glasgow in 1832 see p. 142. For his comment that he 'identified myself with the Chartist movement', see p. 150.

103. http://www.chartists.net/Ashton-chartists.htm, accessed 6 December 2008.

104. *The Times*, 28 September 1841.

105. *Northern Star*, 3 July 1841.

106. http://www.chartists.net/Todmorden-Chartists.htm accessed 6 December 2008.

107. http://chartists.blogware.com/blog/_archives/2008/6/8/3733988.html, accessed 6 December 2008.

108. Some of this information comes from Tweddle's own accounts. See Turner, 'Friendly societies', pp. 251–3.

109. Turner, 'Friendly societies', pp. 255, 263.

110. *The Northern Liberator*, 30 March 1833, listed contributions to the fund for the defence of the radical Reverend Joseph Rayner Stephens.

111. *Northern Star*, 23 February 1839 and *Northern Star*, 2 March 1839.

112. Thompson, *The English working class*, pp. 462–3.

113. D. Thompson, *The Chartists: popular politics in the industrial revolution*, Ashgate, Aldershot, 1986 edition, p. 159. According to an Oddfellows booklet, *Centenary of the Halifax District 1833–1933*, p. 5, in that period Oddfellowship was 'something of an adventure and it had elements of secrecy about which we do not understand … meetings were often in different places because of the suspicion which rested upon those who supposed to be engaged in unlawful practices'.

114. *Northern Star*, 28 December 1839.

115. There is a description of the hall in the *Northern Star*, 3 February 1838. This was part of a report of a meeting there held to protest about the Poor Laws.

116. S. C. Robinson, 'Of "Haymakers" and "City Artisans": The Chartist poetics of Eliza Cook's songs of labour', *Victorian Poetry*, 39, 2, 2001, pp. 229–53.

117. Moffrey, *A century of Oddfellowship*, pp. 208–9.

118. Cordery, 'Friendly societies and the discourse', p. 48.

119. On Aitken see R. G. Hall, *Voices of the people: democracy and Chartist political identity, 1830–1870*, Merlin, Monmouth, 2007.

120. W. J. Linton, *Memories*, Lawrence and Bullen, London, 1895.

121. Samuel Fielden's autobiography is available at http://dwardmac.pitzer.edu/ANARCHIST_ARCHIVES/haymarket/Fielden.html, accessed 7 December 2008.

122. Benjamin Wilson, *The struggles of an old Chartist*, Halifax, 1887, pp. 22–3; in J. F. C. Harrison (ed.), *Society and politics in England, 1780–1960*, Harper & Row, New York, 1965, pp. 167–70. The Chartist Robert Gammage, to whom Wilson refers, was a sometime insurance agent.

123. *Blackburn Times*, 28 January 1893, available at http://www.cottontown.org/page.cfm?pageid=3098&language=eng, accessed 7 December 2008. The Chartists

aimed to sell shares in a company, buy land and distribute it among members.

124. Cordery, 'Friendly societies and the discourse', p. 48, notes that some friendly society members were enrolled as special constables to help suppress disturbances.

125. *The Times*, 18 July 1843.

126. E. D. Jones, 'A file of "Rebecca" Papers', *The Carmarthen Antiquary: The Transactions of the Carmarthen Antiquarian Society and Field Club*, I (3 & 4), 1943 and 1944, pp. 40–1, http://www.gtj.org.uk/en/small/item/GTJ25331//page/1/, accessed 11 May 2009.

127. *Laws for the Government of the Independent Order of Odd Fellows, of the Manchester Unity*, Richmond & Froggett, Manchester, 1841 quoted in Cordery, 'Friendly societies and the discourse', p. 49.

128. A. Clark, 'The rhetoric of Chartist domesticity: gender, language and class in the 1830s and 1840s', *Journal of British Studies*, 31, 1, 1992, pp. 62–88.

129. D Neave, *East Riding friendly societies*, East Yorkshire Local History Society, Series 41, Hull, 1988, p. 23.

130. *The Manchester Guardian*, 10 March 1841.

131. *Abingdon Herald*, 9 August 1873; 3 July 1875.

132. *Hampshire Telegraph and Sussex Chronicle*, 22 September 1875.

133. *Derby Mercury*, 9 September 1891.

134. *Derby Mercury*, 1 June 1892.

135. *Crewe Guardian*, 9 October 1909, in Edwards, 'Treatment of poverty', p. 524.

136. *Oddfellows' Magazine*, January 1913, p. 7; February 1913 pp. 48, 52, 55, 60.

137. On friendly societies and the correlation between associational density and political participation see M. Gorsky, 'Mutual aid and civil society: friendly societies in nineteenth-century Bristol', *Urban History*, 25, 3 1998, p. 316; D. Green, *Working-class patients and the medical establishment: self-help in Britain from the mid-nineteenth century to 1948*, Gower/Maurice Temple Smith, Aldershot, 1985; J. Garrard, *Democratisation in Britain: élites, civil society and reform since 1800*, Palgrave, Basingstoke, 2001, pp. 6, 184.

138. *Foresters' Miscellany*, March 1850.

139. Wilkinson, *History*, p. 67.

140. Hall, *Voices*, p. 55.

141. Mauss, *The gift*, p. 16.

142. *Bolton Chronicle*, 26 May 1877, quoted in Bailey, 'Will the real Bill' p. 342.

143. On the wider uses of the parable see D. Weinbren, 'The Good Samaritan, friendly societies and the gift economy', *Social History*, 31, 3, 2006.

144. *The Odd Fellow*, 26 September 1840.

145. *Jackson's Oxford Journal*, 28 July 1900.

146. *The Odd Fellow*, January 1964, p. 4. The parable is to be found in Luke, 10: 25–37. The term Golden Rule probably refers here to the words of the Oddfellows initiation, but may also refer to that which some Christians refer to as the 'Golden Rule' which is derived from Leviticus, 19:18, 'love your neighbour as yourself', and 19: 34, 'But the stranger that dwelleth with you shall be unto you as one born among you, and thou shalt love him as thyself'. Information about the banner is to be found in Coventry City Library JN334.3 *Annual Report* 1875 quoted in Weller, 'Self help', p. 107. On the Emblem see Moffrey *A century*, p. 203.

147. For examples of such complaints see Cordery, 'Friendly societies and the discourse', p. 51.

148. K. Waddington, *Charity and the London hospitals, 1850–1898*, Boydell, Woodbridge, 2000, p. 33.

149. A. Berry, 'Patronage, funding and the hospital patient c.1750–1815: three English regional case studies', Ph.D. thesis, Oxford, 1995, pp. 109–10; H. Marland, *Medicine and society in Wakefield and Huddersfield, 1780–1870*, Cambridge University Press, Cambridge, 1987, pp. 186, 196.

150. J. C. Riley, *Sick not dead: the health of British workingmen during the mortality decline*, Johns Hopkins University Press, Baltimore and London, 1997, pp. 99–104.

151. *The Odd Fellow*, 1966, p. 98.

152. Krausman Ben-Amos, 'Gifts', pp. 321–2.

153. *Oddfellows' Magazine*, January 1901, p. 36.

154. Account of a lodge anniversary, *Manchester Times and Gazette*, 12 February 1842.

155. Moffrey, *A century of Oddfellowship*, p. 202.

156. D'Cruze and Turnbull, 'Fellowship and family', p. 40.

157. Burn, *An historical sketch*, p. 116.

158. Report of a presentation at the Loyal Fountain of Friendship Lodge, Bollington, near Macclesfield, *Manchester Times and Gazette*, 13 May 1837.

159. *Derby Mercury*, 5 April 1837.

160. J. Spry, *The manual of Odd Fellowship, for the use of the initiated: being an attempt to explain the origin, degrees and emblems of the Independent Order of Odd Fellows, Manchester Unity*, IOOFMU, Manchester, 1862, p. 10.

161. The term 'Manchester man', meaning a virtuous public figure, is discussed in M. Rose, 'Culture, philanthropy and the Manchester middle classes', in A. J. Kidd and K. Roberts (eds), *City, class and culture*, Manchester University Press, Manchester, 1985, pp. 103–17. See also P. Shapely, 'Charity, status and leadership: charitable image and the Manchester man', *Journal of Social History*, 32, 1, 1998, pp. 157–77.

162. Doran, 'Risky business'. p. 134.

163. J. Larkin, *Leisure moments: a collection of miscellaneous*

poems, Woolwich, 1849, p. 85, cited in G. Crossick, *An artisan élite in Victorian society. Kentish London, 1840–1880*, Croom Helm, London, 1978, p. 196.

164. Oddfellows, *Preface to the Rules*, 1855.

165. Cited in Moffrey, *A century of Oddfellowship*, pp. 176–7.

166. G. A. Williams, 'Introduction', in J. Gorman, *Banner Bright. An illustrated history of the banners of the British trade union movement*, Allen Lane, London, 1973, p. 13.

167. All Saints Church, Nocton, Lincolnshire, has one example hanging on the wall. It has the words 'Loyal Ripon Lodge IOOF' and an instruction 'Thou shall love they neighbour as thyself'. There is also a depiction of the Good Samaritan. See http://www.allsaintsnocton.org.uk/nave.htm, accessed on 14 November, 2008. The Samaritan was also on the banner of the Loyal Adventurers of the Peak Lodge, Taddington, Derbyshire: see Bathe, 'Oddfellows and Morris Dancing'.

168. Friendly society banners are assessed in D. Weinbren, 'Beneath the all-seeing eye. Fraternal order and friendly societies' banners', *Journal of Social and Cultural History*, 3, 2, 2006.

169. There is a reproduction of an advertisement for Sunday School banners in J. Harvey, *The art of piety. The visual culture of Welsh nonconformity*, Cardiff, 1995, p. 22; R. Samuel, 'Editorial Introduction', *History Workshop Journal*, 6, 1978, pp. 104–5. On the company, George Tutill, see Gorman, *Banner*, pp. 49–55.

170. The buttons on the beadle's official coat have pictures of 'the Good Samaritan healing the sick and bruised man' and a replica of 'the parochial seal'. The beadle recalled, seemingly oblivious to the irony, that the first time he wore the coat was to attend an inquest on somebody who had died in a doorway from exposure and want. His colleague's responded to the tale with his own views on reciprocity: 'I pay a good deal towards the poor rates … I was thinking that if I pay so much towards 'em, I've a right to get as much out of 'em as I can.'

171. Cited in Moffrey, *A century of Oddfellowship*, pp. 176.

172. S. Yeo, 'Making membership meaningful: the case of older co-operative and mutual enterprises in Britain', in N. Deakin (ed.), *Membership and mutuality. Proceedings of a seminar series organised at the LSE Centre for Civil Society, Report No.3*, 2002, pp. 8–9.

Chapter 5:   Administering National Health Insurance, 1912–1948

1. Moffrey, *A century of Oddfellowship*, p. 185.

2. Moffrey, *A century of Oddfellowship*, p. 187.

3. *Oddfellows' Magazine*, January 1913, p. 13.

4. *Oddfellows' Magazine*, February 1913, p. 72.

5. *Charity Organisation Review*, 33, 328, June 1913. For his initiation as an honorary member see *Oddfellows' Magazine*, February 1901, p. 61.

6. G. D. H. Cole, 'Review of Lord Beveridge, Voluntary action: a report on methods of social advance', *The Economic Journal*, 59, 235, 1949, p. 400.

7. D. Green, 'The friendly societies and Adam Smith Liberalism', in D. Green (ed.), *Before Beveridge: welfare before the welfare state*, IEA Health and Welfare Unit, London, 1999, pp. 24–5.

8. Johnson, *Saving and spending*, p. 68.

9. Lloyd George described the National Insurance scheme as '9*d.* for 4*d.*' because workers paid 4*d.*, their employer 3*d.* and the state, 2*d.*

10. Cordery, *British friendly societies*, pp. 153–9.

11. Lee's initiation was reported in the *Hampshire Telegraph and Naval Chronicle*, 17 November 1900.

12. H. N. Bunbury (ed.), *Lloyd George's ambulance wagon: being the memoirs of William J Braithwaite, 1911–1912*, Methuen, London, 1957, p. 212.

13. *The Times*, 20 May 1910.

14. To gain approval societies had to apply to the National Health Insurance Commissions (there were four, one for each part of the UK), adhere to the scales of benefit set by the government, submit to periodical valuation (and impose a levy on members if there was a shortfall). They could propose schemes of additional benefits for approval by the Commission. The Commission adjudicated in the case of appeals and could withdraw approval.

15. Daunton, *State and market*, p. 82 cited figures of 21.9 per cent and 47.9 per cent.

16. Daunton, *State and market*, pp. 80, 114, 174.

17. This was in addition to the provision of hospitals through the Poor Law.

18. *Banbury Advertiser*, 17 June 1886.

19. Gilbert, *Evolution of National Insurance*, p. 168. Harry Lauder, 1870–1950, was a Scottish entertainer who was the first British performer to sell more than a million records.

20. *Oddfellows' Magazine*, January 1913, pp. 135–7.

21. *Oddfellows' Magazine*, January 1913, p. 31.

22. R. Roberts, *The classic slum*, Penguin, Harmondsworth, 1990, p 228.

23. Daunton, *State and market*, pp. 268–9.

24. Others who were paid less than £160 *per annum* but who did not qualify for compulsory insurance, the self-employed for example, could insure voluntarily. By 1936 there were 640,000 voluntary contributors.

25. B. B. Gilbert, *British social policy, 1914–1939*, Batsford, London, 1970, p. 53.

26. By the height of unemployment, 1931–34, the approved societies were bearing the cost of six million members who were in arrears. See N. Whiteside, 'Private agencies for public purposes: some new perspectives on policy making in health insurance between the wars' *Journal of Social Policy*, 12, 2, 1983, p. 183.

27. On the operation of the scheme, see N. Whiteside, 'Regulating markets: the real costs of poly-centric administration under the National Health Insurance scheme (1912–46)', *Public Administration*, 1997, pp. 467–85; G. Carpenter, 'National health insurance: a case study in the use of private, non-profit making organisations in the provision of welfare benefits', *Public Administration*, 62, 1, 1984 pp. 71–89.

28. Interview in *Worcester News*, 16 April 2003.

29. Interview in Women's Institute, *Never bored*. Derek Turner's obituary of Ralph Dawes appeared in *Parish News, covering Shillington, Pegsdon and Higham Gobion*, 74, February 2008.

30. J. A. O'Neill, 'The spirit of independence: friendly societies in Nottinghamshire 1724–1913', Ph.D. thesis, Nottingham Polytechnic, 1992, p. 49.

31. A. Fisk, *Mutual self-help in southern England, 1850–1912*, Foresters Heritage Trust, Southampton, 2006, p. 53.

32. Whiteside, 'Regulating markets', p 476; Whiteside, 'Private agencies for public purposes', p. 170.

33. These 'panels' were local committees representing doctors who took patients on their 'panel'. The 1911 National Insurance Act required the Local Insurance Committee to consult, through the Local Panel Committees, all panel doctors on a wide range of issues. In 1913 the Local Panel Committee became known as the Local Medical Committee.

34. *Oddfellows' Magazine*, January 1913, pp. 4–5.

35. *Oddfellows' Magazine*, July 1914, pp. 282–93.

36. Local Government Board 1914a, p. 86, quoted in Whiteside 'Regulating markets', p. 477.

37. *Oddfellows' Magazine*, February 1913, p. 477.

38. *Oddfellows' Magazine*, June 1914, p. 247.

39. *Oddfellows' Magazine*, January 1913, p. 25.

40. Bathe, 'Oddfellows and Morris Dancing'.

41. Quoted in N. Whiteside, 'Regulating markets', p. 476.

42. *Oddfellows' Magazine*, 46, 1915, pp. 639–40.

43. *Oddfellows' Magazine*, January 1913, p. 4.

44. *Oddfellows' Magazine*, October 1914, pp. 669–71.

45. *Oddfellows' Magazine*, June 1916, pp. 208–9.

46. *Oddfellows' Magazine*, January 1901, pp. 6–8; *Oddfellows' Magazine*, February 1901, p. 51.

47. The author was W. T. Hibberd, *Oddfellows' Magazine*, November 1914, p. 721.

48. Letter in *Oddfellows' Magazine*, October 1914, p. 686.

49. Correspondence in *Oddfellows' Magazine*, January 1915, pp. 28–30.

50. Whiteside, 'Private agencies for public purposes', pp. 31, 33.

51. B. B. Gilbert, *British social policy*, pp. 264–5; Finlayson, *Citizen*, pp. 207–8; Johnson, *Saving and spending*, pp. 205–7.

52. Beveridge, *Voluntary action*, pp. 30, 88.

53. Bunbury, *Lloyd George's*, p. 212.

54. Appendix to the Report … on Sickness benefit Claims under the National Insurance Act, London 1914 in T.L. Alborn, 'Senses of Belonging: The Politics of Working-Class Insurance in Britain, 1880–1914' *The Journal of Modern History*, 73, 2001, p. 601.

55. *Oddfellows' Magazine*, January 1913, pp. 23–4.

56. There is some evidence that most people still do not see National Insurance as a tax. R. Davies, M. Hill and T. Williams, *Attitudes to the welfare state and the response to reform*, Research Report, No. 88, Department of Social Security, Analytical Services Division, 1999, cited in F. Field, *Welfare titans: how Lloyd George and Gordon Brown compare*, Civitas, London, 2002, p. 51.

57. Field, *Welfare titans*, p. 37.

58. *The Manchester Guardian*, 17 May 1932.

59. The Society's rules changed. In 1871 Rule 1 of the General Rules stated that the society existed to provide 'proper medicine and medical attention for members'.

60. Edwards, 'The friendly societies and the ethic', pp. 262–4.

61. This latter rule was amended. According to rules 61 and 64, the cost of medical attendance was charged to the management funds of individual lodges and medical attendance was to be allowed to members of other lodges who lived beyond the limits of the surgeon of their own lodge.

62. Quoted in E. M. Roberts, *A woman's place. An oral history of working-class women, 1890–1940*, Blackwell, Oxford, 1984, p. 164.

63. Quoted in *Oddfellows' Magazine*, March 1901, p. 81.

64. Those covered by the 1911 scheme had no right to hospital care or medicine.

65. A. Digby, *The Evolution of British General Practice, 1850–1948*, Oxford University Press, Oxford, 1999,

pp. 318–22.

66. N Whiteside, 'Private provision and public welfare: health insurance between the wars', in D. Green (ed.), *Before Beveridge: welfare before the welfare state*, IEA Health and Welfare Unit, London, 1999, pp. 26–42.

67. Digby and Bosanquet, 'Doctors and patients', pp. 78, 91.

68. *Oddfellows' Magazine*, June 1909 and September 1911.

69. *Oddfellows' Magazine*, 43 1912 p. 376; Appendix to the Report … on Sickness benefit Claims under the National Insurance Act, London, 1914, cited in Alborn, 'Senses', p. 595.

70. Other lodges adopted the same standardised rules. For example the Loyal Constitution Lodge Great Easton, Lincolnshire, adopted these rules in 1916.

71. A. Cox, 'Seven years of National Health Insurance in England: A retrospect', *Journal of the American Medical Association*, 76, 1921, quoted in Digby and Bosanquet, 'Doctors and patients', p. 87.

72. *Oddfellows' Magazine*, July 1914, p. 489.

73. N. Whiteside, 'Counting the cost: sickness and disability among working people in an era of industrial recession, 1920–39', *Economic History Review*, 40, 2, 1987, pp. 228–46.

74. A Digby and N Bosanquet, 'Doctors and patients in an era of national health insurance and private practice, 1913–1938', *Economic History Review*, 41, 1, 1988, p. 80.

75. *Oddfellows' Magazine*, January 1913, p. 14.

76. *Oddfellows' Magazine*, January 1913, p. 7.

77. *Oddfellows' Magazine*, February 1913, p. 45.

78. J. Tosh, 'What should historians do with masculinity?', *History Workshop Journal*, 38, 1994, pp. 186–7.

79. Report from the Select Committee on the Aged Deserving Poor 1899, p. 95 cited in Macnicol, *The politics of retirement*, p. 31.

80. *Aberdeen Weekly Journal*, 5 June 1900, report on the AMC.

81. *Leeds Mercury*, 7 June 1900.

82. *Oddfellows' Magazine*, February 1901, p. 59.

83. Statement by R. Waite, *Report of the Old Age Pensions Conference held in the Memorial Hall, 14 and 15 January 1902*, 1902, p. 16 cited by Macnicol, *The politics of retirement*, p. 116.

84. *Report from the Select Committee of the House of Lords on Betting 1902*, p. 147 quoted in R. McKibbin, 'Working-class gambling in Britain, 1880–1939', *Past and Present*, 82, 1979, p. 170.

85. Quoted in S. Yeo, *Religion and voluntary organisations in crisis*, Croom Helm, London, 1976, p. 278.

86. Cordery, 'Friendly societies and the discourse', p. 55.

87. *National Insurance Gazette*, 2 1913, p. 634 cited in Alborn, 'Senses', p. 600.

88. Brindley, 'The origin … of Oddfellowship'.

89. D. Levine, *Reproducing families: the political economy of English population history*, Cambridge University Press, Cambridge, 1987, pp. 179–80.

90. S. Pedersen, *Family, dependence and the origins of the welfare state. Britain and France, 1914–1945*, Cambridge University Press, Cambridge, 1993, p. 48.

91. K. McClelland, 'Time to work, time to live: some aspects of work and the reformation of class in Britain, 1850–1880', in P. Joyce (ed.), *The historical meanings of work*, Cambridge University Press, Cambridge, 1987, p. 206.

92. L. T. Hobhouse, *Liberalism*, Williams and Norgate, London, 1911, p. 83.

93. Pedersen, *Family*, pp. 49, 51, 55.

94. *Oddfellows' Magazine*, January 1913, p. 6.

95. This paragraph is drawn from S. Alexander, *Becoming a woman and other essays in 19th- and 20th-Century Feminist History*, Virago Press, London, 1994, p. 219 and S. Alexander, 'Men's fears and women's work: responses to unemployment in London between the wars', *Gender and History*, 12, 2, 2000, p. 401.

96. J. Bourke, *Working-class cultures in Britain, 1890–1960. Gender, class and ethnicity*, Routledge, London, 1994, p. 108.

97. *Oddfellows' Magazine*, 1913, pp. 6–7, 244–56.

98. Gilbert, *Evolution of National Insurance*, p. 428.

99. Johnson, *Saving and spending*, pp. 231–2.

100. *The Times*, 18 May 1934.

101. *The Times*, 6 June 1936.

102. *The Times*, 17 May 1937.

103. Eighteen men were fined for not attending one funeral. The information about the lodge is held in the North Yorkshire County Record Office, and cited in Turner, 'Friendly societies', p. 323.

104. J. Frome Wilkinson, 'Lodges as educators', *Druids Quarterly Journal*, January 1880, pp. 79–80.

105. D. Bathe, 'Oddfellows and Morris Dancing in a Peak District village', *Folk Music Journal*, 5, 1, 1985, p. 7.

106. AMC report, *Oddfellows' Magazine*, 1922, p. 247.

107. *Oddfellows' Magazine*, April 1913, p. 144.

108. *Oddfellows' Magazine*, January 1913, p. 28.

109. K. Y. Stenberg, 'Gender, class and London labour politics, 1870–1914' Ph.D. thesis. Minnesota, 1993, p. ii.

110. P. Thane, 'Women in the British Labour Party and the construction of state welfare, 1906–39' in S. Koven and S. Michel (eds), *Mothers of a new world: maternalist politics and the origins of welfare states*, Routledge,

London, 1993, p. 345.

111. M. Francis, 'Labour and gender', in D. Tanner, P. Thane and N. Tiratsoo (eds), *Labour's first century*, Cambridge University Press, Cambridge, 2000, pp. 203–4.

112. P. M. Graves, *Labour women. Women in British working-class politics, 1918–1939*, Cambridge University Press, Cambridge, 1994, pp. 126, 163, 165, 167.

113. Diary entry of 25 August 1928, M. I. Cole (ed.), *Beatrice Webb's diaries, 1913–1924*, Longmans, London, 1952, p. 176.

114. On the roles offered to women in the Labour Party see D. Weinbren, 'Building communities, constructing identities. The rise of the Labour Party in London', *London Journal*, 23, 1, 1998.

115. Gilbert, *Evolution of National Insurance*, pp. 323, 320, 327–8.

116. *Oddfellows' Magazine*, January 1913, p. 5.

117. *Oddfellows' Magazine*, January 1916, p. 27; *Oddfellows' Magazine*, November 1916, p. 631.

118. *The Times*, 6 January 1937.

119. Quoted in M. Heller, 'The National Insurance Acts, 1911–1947, the Approved Societies and the Prudential Assurance Company', *Twentieth-Century British History*, 19, 8, 2008, p. 25.

120. Burton, Knights, Leyshon, Alferoff and Signoretta, 'Consumption denied?', p. 185.

121. Letter sent to various MPs quoted in B. B. Gilbert, 'The British National Insurance Act of 1911 and the Commercial insurance lobby', *Journal of British Studies*, 4, 2, May 1965, pp. 127–48, 143.

122. Burton, Knights, Leyshon, Alferoff and Signoretta, 'Consumption denied?', pp. 192, 191, 193.

123. *Oddfellows' Magazine*, January 1913, pp. 35–36.

124. On Labour's inter-war policy see, A. Marwick, 'The Labour Party and the welfare state in Britain, 1900–1948', *The American Historical Review*, 73, 2, 1967, pp. 380–403.

125. G. Sutherland, 'Social policy in the inter-war years', *Historical Journal*, 16, 2, 1973, pp. 425–6. Finlayson also took the view that Labour was critical of the way in which mutual aid appeared to be dominated by commercial companies and that charity was being substituted for social justice; see G. Finlayson, 'A moving frontier: voluntarism and the state in British social welfare 1911–1949', *Twentieth-Century British History*, 1, 2, 1990, pp. 187–8.

126. H. J. Laski, *The spirit of Cooperation*, Cooperative Wholesale Society, Manchester, 1936, pp. 7, 18; B. Lancaster and P. Maguire, 'The co-operative movement in historical perspective', in B. Lancaster and P. Maguire (eds), *Towards the Co-operative Commonwealth: 150 years of Co-operation. essays in the history of Co-operation*, Co-operative College, Loughborough, 1998, p. 12; H. Mercer, *Constructing a competitive order: the hidden history of British antitrust policies*, Cambridge University Press, Cambridge, 1995, p. 155. See also K. Manton, 'The Labour Party and the Co-op, 1918–58', *Historical Research*, 82, 218, 2008, online at http://dx.doi.org/10.1111/j.1468–2281.2008.00461.x, accessed on 27 December 2008.

127. On Labour's policies see D. Tanner, 'The politics of the labour movement, 1900–39', in C. Wrigley, *A companion to early twentieth-century Britain*, Oxford University Press, Oxford, 2003, pp. 44, 47, 52. On Labour's success at local level see M. Worley, *Labour inside the gate – a history of the British Labour Party between the wars*, I. B. Tauris, London, 2005. On Labour's popularity in London see D. Weinbren, 'Sociable capital' in M. Worley (ed.), *Labour's grass roots: essays on the activities of local Labour parties and members, 1918–1945*, Ashgate, Aldershot, 2005.

128. I. M. Rubinow, 'Standards of sickness insurance: I', *Journal of Political Economy*, 23, 1915, pp. 221–51.

129. M. J. Daunton, 'Payment and participation: welfare and state-formation in Britain 1900–1951', *Past and Present*, 150, 1996, pp. 169–216.

130. 'The development of the health services', 6 April 1938, MH 79/409 quoted in N. Whiteside, 'Regulating markets', pp. 467–85.

131. J. S. Clarke, 'National health insurance', in W. A. Robson (ed.), *Social security*, 2nd edn, Fabian Society, London, 1945, p. 121.

132. *East London Advertiser*, 12 April 1930.

133. Sir Alan Powell and E. C. Blight, 'Poor Law relief', *New Survey of London Life and Labour, 1929–1931*, edited by H. Llewellyn Smith, vol. I, P. S. King, 1930–1935, London, pp. 377, 387.

134. P. M. Graves, 'A blessing or a curse? Working-class attitudes to state welfare programmes in Britain 1919–1939, *Labour History Review*, 74, 2, 2009, pp. 181–182.

135. This section is largely derived from Green and Cromwell, *Mutual aid*, pp. xvi, 4, 9–12, 19–25, 28–30, 42, 56, 57, 62, 70, 71, 97, 131, 143, 145, Chapter 9; Mark Lyons, *Third sector: the contribution of nonprofit and cooperative enterprise in Australia*, Allen & Unwin, Sydney, 2001, p. 83; see also J. A. Gillespie, *The price of health: Australian governments and medical politics, 1910–1960*, Cambridge University Press, Cambridge, 2002, pp. 8–10.

136. Friendly societies arrived in Australia with some of the first white settlers. In 1826 a Female Friendly Society was in existence, and in 1829 the *Sydney Gazette*

announced a plan to establish 'a lodge of Odd Fellows'. Interest in friendly societies may have been aided when, in 1834 six men guilty of swearing illegal oaths as part of the creation of the Friendly Society of Agricultural Labourers, were transported to Australia. In 1836 the American Independent Order of Oddfellows (which had broken from the IOOFMU in 1826) established an Australian Grand Lodge in Sydney.

137. Bob James has cast doubt as to whether the men who were later claimed as members of the IOOFMU were in fact members of it in 1840. For an analysis as to why these early lodges may have been affiliated to other bodies see B. James, *They call each other brother. Secret societies, fraternalism and the strange slow death of mateship in Australia* (forthcoming). My thanks to the author for providing me with the information.

138. *The Times*, 30 November 1889.

139. *100 years*, pp. 1, 6, 10, 14, 18, 22.

140. The title of Part 3 of Beveridge, *Voluntary action*.

141. *The Times*, 4, January 1944.

142. *The Manchester Guardian*, 19 September 1942.

143. *Unity Report*, 1941, p. 23; *The Times*, 6 July 1943; *Odd Fellows Magazine*, June 1945, p. 121; December 1945, p. 248.

144. *The Times*, 2 July 1942.

145. *The Times*, 6 July 1943.

146. *The Times*, 12 May 1944. Andrews was honoured when, in 1971, a charitable fund was named after him. The fund is used for a variety of fundraising and sponsorship purposes.

147. *Odd Fellows Magazine*, January 1945, p. 5.

148. *Odd Fellows Magazine*, December 1945, pp. 248–9.

149. Davenport Hall, Catford, 1945, recalled in A. Brownjohn, 'Like 1945', in N. Ackowska (ed.), *Voices: from Arts for Labour*, Pluto, London and Sydney, 1985, p. 66.

150. *Odd Fellows Magazine*, December 1945, pp. 244–6.

151. *The Times*, 23 January 1946.

152. The NHI figure was compiled on 1 January 1946 and was a total of 1,033,964. The Unity total on 31 December 1945 was 1,070,795. *Unity Reports*, 1946, p. 233.

153. *Odd Fellows Magazine*, December 1945, p. 253; Sweeney was initiated in 1913, became Prov. GM and a Prov. CS before he joined the Board of Directors.

154. *The Manchester Guardian*, 1 June 1939.

155. *The Manchester Guardian*, 13 June 1950.

156. *Odd Fellows Magazine*, February 1945, p. 40.

157. *Odd Fellows Magazine*, February 1945, p. 42.

158. Green and Cromwell, *Mutual aid*, p. 55.

159. Charles Willard's autobiographical account was kindly provided by his daughter, Christine Payne.

160. *Oddfellows' Magazine*, August 1914, p. 605.

161. *Odd Fellows Magazine*, November 1945, pp. 208, 209.

162. Grand Master J. A. Stephenson at AMC 1949, *Unity Reports, 1949*, pp. 56–63.

163. Mass-Observation, *A report on the friendly societies*, Mass-Observation, 1947, p. 7.

164. Mass-Observation, *A report*, p. 30.

165. Mass-Observation, *A report*, pp. 22–3.

166. Beveridge, *Voluntary action*, pp. 78–9; W. Beveridge and A. F. Wells, *The evidence for voluntary action, being memoranda by organisations and individuals and other material relevant to voluntary action*, George Allen & Unwin, London, 1949, p. 20.

167. J. A. Lincoln, 'Problems of friendly societies' in Beveridge and Wells, *The evidence*, p. 270.

168. Cole, 'Review', p. 400.

169. *The Manchester Guardian*, 3 December 1958.

170. *The Manchester Guardian*, 3 December 1958.

171. Green, 'The friendly societies', pp. 24–5.

172. Cordery, *British friendly societies*, p. 174.

173. Daunton, *State and market*, pp. 288–9, 265.

174. R. Spear, 'The co-operative advantage', *Annals of Public and Cooperative Economics*, 71 4 2000, pp. 507, 521–2, 515.

175. A. Ware, 'On scale and scope and the history of the non-profit sector in the United Kingdom', *Voluntas* 7, 1 1996; M. Lyons, 'The history of non-profit organisations in Australia as a test of some recent non-profit theory', *Voluntas*, 4, 3 1993, p. 323; Spear, 'The co-operative advantage', p. 509.

176. G. Yarrow, 'The friendly societies', *Economic Affairs*, 14, 5, 1994, p. 34.

177. Foresters' *Executive Committee Quarterly Report*, October 1907, p. 65, cited in Logan, 'Role of friendly society orders', p. 88.

178. *The Times*, 24 May 1934. Baldwin was addressing an Oddfellows' conference held in the Albert Hall.

Chapter 6: Inside the lodge

1. This matter is considered more fully in A. D. Pionke, *Plots of opportunity. Representing conspiracy in Victorian England*, Ohio State University Press, Columbus, 2004.

2. For a discussion of these aspects of ritual see V. Turner, *Process, performance and pilgrimage*, Concept, New Delhi, 1979, p. 129.

3. D. Weinben, *Generating socialism. Recollections of life in the Labour Party*, Sutton, Stroud, 1997, p. 77.

4. According to the 1935 Universal Ritual, when the Conductor enters the lodge with the candidates for initiation and takes them from officer to officer this ode may be sung.

5. *Supplement to the lecture book of the Independent Order of Odd-Fellows, Manchester Unity Friendly Society*, 1875, Broadbent, Huddersfield, p. 41. My thanks to George Kilford for the loan of this book.

6. Burn, *An historical sketch*, p. 117 refers to the ritual wearing of 'white cotton gloves', and there are references in the accounts of funeral processions in Chapter 3.

7. There are differences in the spelling of this item. Here collaret is used for the singular, collarettes for the plural.

8. Clapham, *A concise economic history*, pp. 295–8.

9. E. J. Hobsbawm 'Inventing traditions', in E. J. Hobsbawm and T. Ranger (eds), *The invention of tradition*, Cambridge University Press, Cambridge, 1983, p. 8.

10. 'Lecture on the moral, social and friendly character of Odd-Fellowship of the Manchester Unity', Glasgow, 1840, p. 8 quoted in Burn, *The autobiography*, p. 23.

11. *Oddfellow Preface to the Rules*, Manchester, 1855.

12. Bathe, 'Oddfellows and Morris Dancing'.

13. *The Manchester Guardian*, 10 June 1930.

14. *Oddfellows' Magazine*, April 1880, p. 405.

15. Quoted in Women's Institute, *Never bored: Shillington village life, 1920–39*. Transcripts held at Bedfordshire and Luton Archives and Records Service, CR OH1/5.

16. *The Odd Fellow*. This broadsheet was loaned by Tom Nicholson. My thanks to him. It has no date but is late 1984.

17. *Oddfellows' Magazine*, November 1901, p. 428.

18. B. Foden, 'Keep the banner flying boys. A short history of the Parwich Oddfellows', *Parwich & District Local History Society Newsletter*, 4 January 2001 http://www.parwichhistory.com/Issue per cent204.htm. accessed 28 December 2008.

19. Bathe, 'Oddfellows and Morris Dancing', pp. 40–1, 133.

20. M. Greatorex, 'Winster Oddfellows', *Winster Local History Group Newsletter*, 31, March 2005.

21. Description of initiation from S.T. Davies, *Odd Fellowship: its history, constitution, principles and finances*, Richard Sutton Cheek, Witham, 1858.

22. There is an account in Spry, *The history of Odd-Fellowship*, p. 3.

23. Moody, *Illegitimate theatre*, pp. 166–7.

24. H. Angelo, *Reminiscences and friends*, 1828, pp. 284–7, quoted in D. Worrall, *Theatric revolution: drama, censorship and romantic period subcultures 1773–1832*, Oxford University Press, Oxford, 2006, p. 249. This paragraph is also drawn from pp. 2, 15, 134, 135, 138, 167, 218, 261, 265, 272.

25. P. Monod, 'Pierre's white hat: theatre, Jacobitism and popular protest in London, 1689–1760' in E. Cruickshanks (ed.), *By force or default? The revolution of 1688–1689*, John Donald, Edinburgh, 1989, pp. 174–5, 180–1. See also R. McWilliam, 'The mysteries of G. W. M. Reynolds: radicalism and melodrama in Victorian Britain', in M. Chase and I. Dyck (eds), *Living and learning: essays in honour of J. F. C. Harrison*, Scolar, Aldershot, 1996).

26. Thompson, *The English working class*, pp 63–4.

27. R. Poole, 'French revolution or Peasants' revolt? Petitioners and rebels in England from the Blanketeers to the Chartists', *Labour History Review*, 74, 1, 2009, pp. 8, 9, 12, 14, 18.

28. Moody, *Illegitimate theatre*, pp. 69, 83, 103, 123, 151.

29. R. Campbell, *A record of the origin, rise, and progress of the Independent Order of Rechabites, Salford Unity, from its institution on August 25th, 1835, to the present time*, Independent Order of Rechabites, Manchester, 1911.

30. J. Moody, *Illegitimate theatre in London, 1770–1840*, Cambridge University Press, Cambridge, 2000, pp, 226, 225.

31. Burn, *An historical sketch*, pp. 18–19, 46.

32. Burn, *An historical sketch*, pp. 28–9.

33. J. Huizinga, *Homo Ludens. A study of the play element in culture*, Paladin, London, 1970, 1st edn, 1949, p. 98.

34. Davies, *Odd Fellowship*, describing the initiation ceremony from earlier in the century.

35. Brindley, 'The origin … of Oddfellowship'.

36. *Liverpool Mercury*, 20 September 1900.

37. Bathe, 'Oddfellows and Morris Dancing' pp. 40, 133.

38. Charles Willard's autobiographical account was kindly provided by his daughter, Christine Payne.

39. For descriptions of a number of mummers plays see E. T. Kirby, 'The Origin of the Mummers' Play', *The Journal of American Folklore*, 84, 333, July–Sept. 1971, pp. 275–88.

40. Brindley, 'The origin … of Oddfellowship'.

41. Burn, *An historical sketch*, pp. 18–19, 141, 166.

42. Burn, *An historical sketch*, pp. 85–6.

43. Daunton, *State and market*, p. 73.

44. R. Booth ' Melodrama and the working-class' in C. H. MacKay (ed.), *Dramatic Dickens*, Macmillan, Basingstoke, 1989, p. 100.

45. M. Bakhtin, *Rabelais and his world*, translated by Helene Iswolsky, The MIT Press, Cambridge, 1968, p. 40.

46. D. Cannadine, *Ornamentalism. How the British saw their empire*, Penguin, London, 2001, pp. 4, 85, 99, 105.

47. Moffrey, *A century of Oddfellowship*, p, 76; Spry, *The history of Odd-Fellowship*, p. 164.

48. Spry, *The history of Odd-Fellowship*, pp. 50, 65.

49. Moffrey, *A century of Oddfellowship*, pp. 99, 112.

50. W. J. Ong, *Orality and literacy; the technologizing of the word*, Routledge, London, 1982, p. 9.

51. *Charity Organisation Review*, 33, 328, June 1913.

52. This is part of his speech to the AMC, see *Oddfellows' Magazine*, July 1914, pp. 282–93.

53. *Oddfellows' Magazine*, 1922, p. 89.

54. *Odd Fellows Magazine*, September 1939, p. 606.

55. A. Artaud, 'The Theatre of Cruelty (First Manifesto)', in *The theatre and its double*, translated by V. Conti, John Calder, London, 1977, p. 72.

56. S. Trussler, *The Cambridge illustrated history of British theatre*, Cambridge University Press, Cambridge 2000, p. 297.

57. *Odd Fellows Magazine*, December 1945, pp. 248, 249.

58. *Odd Fellows Magazine*, January 1945, p. 4.

59. Mass-Observation, *A report*, p. 28.

60. *The Times*, 30 April 1957.

61. *Odd Fellows Magazine*, March 1956, p. 90.

62. *Odd Fellows Magazine*, April 1956, p. 134; *Odd Fellows Magazine*, July–August 1956, pp. 268–9.

63. *The Odd Fellows Magazine*, April 1956, p. 135.

64. *Odd Fellow*, January 1964, p. 5.

65. Report of a meeting on 5 December 1963 in *The Odd Fellow*, 1964, p. 38.

66. *The Odd Fellow*, 1964, report of a speech made on 24 October in Chester.

67. IOOFMU, *An explanation of the object and meaning of the Order's emblem and certain lodge procedures*, Manchester, 1960, p. 1; National Conference of Friendly Societies, Report on Annual Meeting, 1984, p. 101.

68. *Unity Report*, 1986, p. 102.

69. *Unity Report*, 1986, p. 54.

70. *Full Transcript of the 2000 AMC*, pp. 76–7.

71. Spry, *The history of Odd-Fellowship*, p. 137.

72. Spry, *The history of Odd-Fellowship*, pp. 137–8.

73. *The Odd Fellow*, 95, 1964, reported that a unique feature of the opening of the annual meeting of the Yorkshire Conference of Juvenile Societies was the demonstration of juvenile ritual by the Goole Juvenile Ritual Lodge.

74. *Annual Report*, 2005, p. 90.

75. The minor degrees to which Pauline referred are White, Blue, Scarlet and Gold. Once a person has become a Past Noble Grand they are eligible for the Purple Degree. There are further degrees for Past Provincial Grand Masters and Past Grand Masters of the Order. Originally each involved a lecture from the Noble Grand, a secret grip and a password. An important element of each degree is still the lecture on a central aspect of the Order, e.g. White is Charity. The intention is that candidates can gradually accumulate knowledge and insights and that they are not overwhelmed at the Initiation.

76. *Manchester Unity in NSW Fraternity. The Lodge Branch Journal*, July 2008, p. 3.

Chapter 7:   Families, fellowship and finance

1. Beveridge, *Voluntary action*, p. 83.

2. A. Bennett, *Clayhanger*, Methuen, London, 1910, 1970 reprint, p. 242.

3. *The Manchester Guardian*, 12 April 1932.

4. K. Waterhouse, *Billy Liar*, Penguin, Harmondsworth, 1959, pp. 115–17.

5. *The Manchester Guardian*, 16 June 1953.

6. *The Manchester Guardian*, 3 December 1958.

7. On definitions of independent men see Keith McClelland, 'Time to work, time to live: some aspects of work and the reformation of class in Britain, 1850–1880', in P. Joyce (ed.), *The historical meanings of work*, Cambridge University Press, Cambridge 1987, p. 206. On fictive brotherhoods see Hobsbawm, *Primitive rebels*, p. 154; R. J. Morris, 'Clubs, societies and associations' in F. M. L. Thompson (ed.), *The Cambridge social history of Britain, 1750–1950*, iii, Cambridge University Press, Cambridge, 1990, pp. 395–443. On different forms of social ties and networks see Perri, *The power to bind and lose: tackling network poverty*, London, 1997 p. 6; S. Tarrow, *Power in movement: social movements, collective action and politics*, Cambridge University

Press, Cambridge, 1994, p. 60.

8. Inaugural address, Margate AMC, 1948, *Unity Reports*, 1948, pp. 67–70.

9. *Odd Fellows Magazine*, December 1945, p. 250.

10. Mass-Observation, *A report*, pp. 24–8.

11. *100 years*, p. 22.

12. *Manchester Unity in NSW. Fraternity. The lodge branch journal*, Special History issue, 2007, p. 27.

13. *Odd Fellows Magazine*, September 1939 p. 619.

14. *Unity Report*, 1986, p. 52.

15. *Unity Report*, 1986, p. 107.

16. *Sydney Morning Herald*, 16 December, 2008; *The Age*, 29 August 2008.

17. Whiteside, 'Private provision and public welfare', p. 37.

18. J. Hill, 'Keeping customers loyal at Liverpool Victoria Friendly Society', *Managing Quality Service*, 6, 4, 1996, p. 28.

19. E. J. Hobsbawm, 'Introduction', in E. J. Hobsbawm and T. Ranger (eds), *The invention of tradition*, Cambridge University Press, Cambridge, 1985, pp. 1–14.

20. J. Hill, 'Keeping', p. 29.

21. Mr L. Auty was interviewed by Sherridan Steel (née Brown) in 1976. See S. J. Brown, 'The development of the friendly society', MA dissertation, Leeds, 1976. On Mr Auty see also *The Odd Fellow*, 1964, p. 37.

22. *Surrey and Hants News*, 4 November 1967.

23. *The Odd Fellow*, 1965, p. 9, reported that four South London district Intermediate lodge members studied for the CAMU examination under Provincial Corresponding Secretary, Wally Cutts. Roger Burley remembered him as a good teacher, a lifelong Oddfellow who knew the work thoroughly: 'he knew the ins and outs of it, he cared'.

24. In 1966 the Provincial Corresponding Secretary noted that The Flower of Kent was known for its enthusiasm. See W. Lovelock, *The Saint Mary Cray and Dartford District No. 1081. A century of Odd Fellowship, 1866–1966*, Smith, Sidcup, 1966, p. 7. I am grateful to George Kilford for the loan of this book.

25. *The Odd Fellow*, 1965 p. 241.

26. Quoted in The Oddfellows, *The Oddfellows millennium book*.

27. Moffrey, *A century of Oddfellowship*, p. 39.

28. Bee, 'Within the shelter'.

29. Moffrey, *A century of Oddfellowship*, p. 185.

30. *The Odd Fellow*, March 1964, p. 77.

31. *The Odd Fellow*, March 1964, p. 39.

32. *Labour Prophet*, May 1895, pp. 65–7; W. S. Smith, The religious speeches of George Bernard Shaw, New York, London 1965, pp. 20–8, both cited in S. Yeo, 'A new life:

the religion of socialism in Britain, 1883–1896', *History Workshop*, 4, 1977, pp. 45–6.

33. Amos Culpan in *Oddfellows' Magazine*, January 1916, p. 13.

34. Bee, 'Within the shelter'. On the booklet see *The Guardian*, 18 August 1980.

35. *Worcester News*, 16 April 2003.

36. http://www.psr.keele.ac.uk/area/uk/man/lib45.htm, accessed on 13 December 2008.

37. Beveridge, *Voluntary action*, pp. 80–2, 62, 323–4.

38. Lord Pakinham, quoted in N. Deakin, 'The perils of partnership', in J. Davis Smith *et al.*, *An introduction to the voluntary sector*, Routledge, London, 1994, p. 46; C. R. Attlee, *The social worker*, G. Bell & Son, London, 1920, pp. 252, 87.

39. For further discussion see D. Weinbren, '"Organisations for brotherly aid in misfortune": Beveridge and the friendly societies', in M. Oppenheimer and N Deakin (eds), *Beveridge and Voluntary Action: a transnational perspective*, Manchester University Press, Manchester, 2010.

40. L. McFall and F. Dodsworth, 'Fabricating the market: the promotion of life assurance in the long nineteenth century', *Journal of Historical Sociology*, 22, 1, 2009, pp. 39–40.

41. S. Smiles, *Thrift*, 1875, p. 118. Available from http://www.gutenberg.org/etext/14418, accessed 12 December 2008.

42. *The Manchester Guardian*, 26 December 1855.

43. *Leeds Mercury*, 7 June 1900.

44. Reproduced in *The Odd Fellows Magazine*, September 1939, p. 605.

45. *Northern Star*, 6 April 1839.

46. *Northern Star*, 26 January 1839.

47. *Northern Star*, 20 April 1839.

48. *Leeds Mercury*, 13 June 1840 and *Northern Star*, 13 June 1840.

49. Cordery, *British friendly societies*, p. 62.

50. T. H. Storey, 'The Oddfellows Hall, Grimsby and its place in the social history of the town', *Lincolnshire History and archaeology*, 12, 1977; D'Cruze and Turnbull, 'Fellowship and family'.

51. *Oddfellows' Magazine*, July 1914, p. 584.

52. See My Brighton and Hove living history website: http://images.google.co.uk/imgres?imgurl=http://www.mybrightonandhove.org.uk/images/uploaded/scaled/Tony_Viney_s.jpg&imgrefurl=http://www.mybrightonandhove.org.uk/page_id__6961.aspx&usg=__E5X38wfod0DzfDMq65JTxstm9m4=&h=430&w=300&sz=45&hl=en&start=18&um=1&tbnid=TPEM4IMYNWn3YM:&tbnh=126&tb

nw=88&prev=/images per cent3Fq per cent3Dwartime per cent2Boddfellows per cent2BUk per cent26um per cent3D1 per cent26hl per cent3Den per cent26client per cent3Dfirefox-a per cent26rls per cent3Dorg.mozilla: en-GB:official per cent26sa per cent3DG, accessed 24 February 2009.

53. Spry, *The history of Odd-Fellowship*, p. 142.

54. Cordery *British*, pp. 115–18, 147. Spry, *The history of Odd-Fellowship*, p 56, noted that the Halifax Hall had already been had to appeal to the wider membership for funds at the 1843 AMC.

55. *Unity Reports*, 1958, p. 145; *The Odd Fellows Magazine*, September 1956, p. 449.

56. For examples from Cambridge see Edwards, 'The friendly societies and the ethic'.

57. Heselton, *The Oddfellows*, p. 64.

58. *The Manchester Guardian*, 15 June 1935.

59. *The Times*, 17 May 1937.

60. *The Times*, 9 June 1938.

61. Reported as part of the biographical account of William Pass, *Oddfellows Magazine*, January 1913, pp. 2–3.

62. *Oddfellows Magazine*, April 1901, p. 116.

63. *Unity Reports*, 1941, pp. 128–55.

64. *Unity Reports*, 1951, p. 54.

65. *Unity Reports*, 1958, p. 145.

66. *The Odd Fellows Magazine*, March 1956, p. 101.

67. For example in 1843 the Owenite *New Moral World* argued that the Oddfellows should invest in co-operative workshops and not put funds 'in the hands of monopolists' who in turn invested the funds and employed them as a whip wherewith to flog their own backs'. However, although lodges have remained relatively financially autonomous, there have been restrictions of expenditure on alcohol, regalia and halls. Cordery, *British friendly societies*, p. 62.

68. Heselton, *The Oddfellows*, p. 50.

69. *The Oddfellows' Magazine*, April 1880, p. 406.

70. J. Macnicol, *The politics of retirement*, pp. 118–19.

71. Reminiscences in personal correspondence with the author.

72. L. Eagles, 'Friendly societies' in D. Renn (ed.), *Life, death and money, actuaries and the creation of financial security. Making financial sense of the future*, Blackwell,

Oxford, 1988.

73. *The Observer*, 26 February 1995.

74. The Life Assurance and Unit Trust Regulatory Organisation reduced the roles of members, while the European Community Insurance Directives (implemented by the Friendly Societies (Long Term Insurance Business) Regulations 1987 and the Financial Services Act 1986 enforced the new taxonomy.

75. A. Wilson, *Friendly societies; a guide to the new law*, Lexis Law Publishing, London, 1993, p. 10.

76. Labour Party membership was at its most popular in the 1950s. It declined and then rose briefly to 407,000 members in 1997. In the decade which followed membership fell to 117,000.

77. A. Crosland, *Co-operative first principles*, p. 6, cited in Manton, 'The Labour Party'.

78. *The Observer*, 26 February 1995.

79. Frank Field was Minister of Social Security, May 1997 to July 1998. Ed Balls was Secretary of State for Children, Schools and Families who, in an address to the Association of Friendly Societies, argued that mutuals are playing a 'vital role in meeting the needs of modern consumers' and cited the role of friendly societies in the success of Child Trust Funds. C. Leadbetter and I. Christie, *To our mutual advantage*, Demos, London, 1999; F. Field, *The state of dependency. Welfare under Labour*, Social Market Foundation, London, 2000; F. Field, *The future of welfare reform*, Politeia, London, 1998; F. Field, *How to pay for the future: building a stakeholder's welfare*, Institute of Community Studies, London, 1996; N. Waite, *Welfare and the consumer society. New opportunities for the Third Way*, The Canford Centre for Consumer Development on behalf of the Association of Friendly Societies, London, 2001, p. 95.

80. *The Observer*, 20 January 1991.

81. R. Whelan, *Involuntary action. How voluntary is the 'voluntary' sector?*, Institute of Economic Affairs, London, 1999, p. 11; The speeches and copies of the reports by the Conservatives regarding social cohesion and communities can be found at www.conservatives. com and *From here to fraternity: perspectives on social responsibility* can be found at www.jessenorman.com

Chapter 8: 'A mutual, caring Society, but with an up-to-date twist'

1. Sue Doulton Smith's description of the Pathfinder strategy.

2. Mass-Observation, *A report*, pp. 24–8.

3. William Beveridge said 'friendly societies have been and are organisations for brotherly aid in misfortune

and channels for the spirit of voluntary service as well as being agencies for mutual insurance and personal saving'. See Beveridge, *Voluntary action*, p. 62.

4. *The Odd Fellow*, 1966, p. 99.

5. Estimate of costs by Brother Troilett, of Lakeland. *Full*

transcript of the 1999 AMC, p. 75.

6. *Full transcript of the 1999 AMC*, p. 71.

7. Figures from the Datamonitor report 'Senior Consumers', 30 April 2002. See www.datamonitor.com/~ba010c0666424ac58d8b4a4b917f2b28~/consumer/reports/product_summary.asp?pid=DMCM0088, accessed 3 December 2008.

8. Employers Forum on Age, *Ageism: too costly to ignore*, 2001 available from: http://74.125.77.132/search?q=cache:LWEMnT8FTPMJ:www.efa.org.uk/publications/default.asp+Ageism:+too+costly+to+ignore+(Employers+Forum+on+Age&hl=en&ct=clnk&cd=1&gl=uk accessed 3 December 2008.

9. M. Carrigan and I. Szmigin, 'Advertising in an ageing society', *Ageing and Society*, 20, 2, 2000, pp. 217–33. According to the Office of National Statistics, the median age rose from 34.1 years in 1971 to 38.4 in 2003, and was projected to rise to 43.3 in 2031. In 1971, 25 per cent of the population were aged under 16. This fell to 20 per cent in 2003 and is projected to fall further to 17 per cent in 2031. The percentage of older people (aged 65 and over) increased from 13 per cent in 1971 to 16 per cent in 2003 and is projected to rise to 23 per cent in 2031. In 1971 there were 52 people aged 65 and over for every 100 children under 16. In 2003 there were 81 and in 2031 it is expected that there will be 136.

10. J. Harkin and J. Huber, *Eternal youth. How the baby boomers are having their time again*, Demos, 2004, pp. 104–5, available at http://www.demos.co.uk/files/EternalYouths.pdf, accessed 3 December 2008.

11. *Unity Reports*, 1986, p. 44.

12. *Full transcript of the 1999 AMC*, pp. 72–4.

13. Christine Feek, *Unity Reports*, 1986, p. 44; Brother J. A. Toilett. Debate reported in the *Full transcript of the 2001 AMC*.

14. Quoted in The Oddfellows, *The Oddfellows millennium book*.

15. He then attended the AMC in 2001 as a deputy and exercised his right to speak.

16. Peter Needham told the AMC that 21 per cent of the lodges were making 58.8 per cent of the new members.

17. *Annual Report*, 2005, p. 90.

18. http://www.activityexchange.com/Doncaster Oddfellows/default.asp, accessed 30 December 2008.

19. *Coronation Street*, a television series that started in 1960, is set near to the original home of the Oddfellows.

20. *Full transcript of the 1997 AMC*, p. 73.

21. F. Field, *Welfare titans: how Lloyd George and Gordon Brown compared*, Civitas, London, 2002, pp. 35–6.

22. T. Hunt, 'Who made us what we are?' *Observer*, 2 June 2002.

23. Speech in the Albert Hall quoted in *100 years*, p. 20.

24. Speech in the Albert Hall quoted in *100 years*, p. 20.

25. *Oddfellows' Magazine*, November 1914, p. 701.

26. Baldwin's speech in the Albert Hall quoted in *100 years*, p. 20; list of members who attained high office, p. 21.

27. For a discussion of the shifts since the mid-nineteenth century, when over half the British population frequently went to church and Christianity was central to much charitable activity and associational culture see F. Prochaska, *Christianity and social service in modern Britain. The disinherited spirit*. Oxford University Press, Oxford, 2006.

28. For an account of Cameron's trip see *The Times*, 23 March 2008.

29. These two examples from *The Times*, 27 December 1958 and *The Times*, 28 February 1961.

30. C. Burchell, *Songs and poems on life assurance*, London n.d., quoted in Alborn, 'Senses', p. 596.

31. *Odd Fellows Magazine*, September 1939, p. 607; AMC report in the *Oddfellows' Magazine*, 1922, p. 321.

32. Turner, 'Friendly societies', p. 147.

33. Moffrey, *A century of Oddfellowship*, p. 80.

34. P. Bourdieu, *The logic of practice*, translated by Richard Nice, Polity, Cambridge, 1990, p. 127.

35. M. Osteen, 'Introduction: questions of the gift', in M. Osteen (ed.), *The question of the gift: essays across disciplines*, Routledge, London, 2002, p. 14.

36. *Oddfellows' Magazine*, July 1914, p. 293.

37. These quotations are referenced earlier.

38. *Oddfellows' Magazine*, 1922, p. 229.

39. Burn, *An historical sketch*, p. 169.

40. S. Newman, 'Oddfellowship', *Oddfellows Magazine*, April 1886, p 155.

41. T. Coales, 'Thy Neighbour', *Oddfellows Magazine*, October 1886, p. 346.

42. *Full transcript of the 2000 AMC*.

List of subscribers

A G Smith
A G Whittaker
A L Khajeh
A Newing, North London District
Aaron S T Mountford
Adrian Lines
Aidrie Felix
Aileen Petts
Alan & Frances Bonner
Alan A Hillier
Alan Bula
Alan Cole
Alan Gellatly
Albert & Lucy Rogers
Albert Allan Rice
Albert Eaglen
Albert Stocker
Albert Trevor Swain
Albion Lodge, Guyana District
Alex Edwards
Alexander Bean
Alfred De Souza, Beds & Bucks District
Alice Mary & Stuart Edwards
Alison Adamson
Allan Rogers, Border Counties District Lodge
Alma Gear
Amy Smith
Andrew Gell
Angela Harmsworth
Angela Hooker, North London District
Ann Kight
Ann Sheila Baker
Anne Breeze
Anne Harris
Anne MacKinnon
Annie W Fulton
Anthony Crouch
Anthony Danton
Anthony T Wignall

Arthur & Maureen Cawood, Leeds District
Arthur Cotterill
Arthur Vivian Garratt
Audrey E Kirkwood
Averil Joan Perks
B Bedford
B Jackson
B M Earl
Barbara Lupton, Derbyshire Peak District Lodge
Barbara Pinder
Barrie S George, Lily of the Valley Branch
Barry A Dye
Barry Kennington
Barry Wheaton-Mars, Great Berkhampstead District
Barry William Cawkwell
Ben Clough
Bernard G Harrington
Bertie G Miles
Beryl & John Harman
Beryl & William Baxter, Poole Bridport & Yeovil
    District
Beryl Toogood
Beryl Wikes
Betty Powici
Betty Whitaker, Todmorden District
Bill Millitt
Bob Parris
Bob Reeves
Bonita Hesketh
Bradford District Lodge
Brenda Williams
Brian & Ann Boyle, Beds & Bucks District
Brian & Jana Evans
Brian & Mary Walker
Brian & Renee Gross
Brian A Read
Brian Harper
Brian J Print
Brian Jennings

Brian Johnson, Great Western Branch
Brian McGlenn
Brian Sparks
Brian W Smith
Brian Woodward
Brighouse Branch
Britons Pride Lodge
Bryan E Dawson
Bryn R B Marshall, Todmorden District
Burton on Trent District Lodge
C M Clark
Carol Bullock
Carole Rosemary Kallend
Centre Vale Lodge, Todmorden District
Charles A H Barton
Charles Edward Smith
Chris Sargeant
Christina Wakefield
Christine & Derek Smith
Christine Howman
Christine Kemp
Christine Payne
Christopher W Moss & Eva A Moss, Castle Lodge
City of Canterbury Lodge
Cleveland & Durham District
Cliff Wright
Clifford Gray
Clive Elcock, Severn & Trent District Lodge
Clive Tayler
Colin Mills
Colin T Sankey
Combermere Lodge, Stockport District
Connie Hilton
Constance & Albert Santus
Corrie Rhianon Thompson
Cumbria District Lodge
Cynthia Tucker
Cyril Collins
Cyril Vincent Murgatroyd
Cyril Wright
D Bean
D Dewgarde
D E Hammond, North Gloucestershire District
    Lodge
D Ford
D H Mashford
D J Ray
D Randall, Erewash Valley District Lodge
Daisy Jones
Daphne Chilvers
Daphne Harmer

Dave Simmons
David & Anita Rose
David Arthur Norrell
David Bramwell-Kemp
David Edward Cox
David Gage
David H H Norris
David J D Groves
David John Browne
David R Ogden
David Stanage
David Struthers
David William Lewis
David William Stephens
Dawn & Alfred Taylor, Mitcham District Lodge
Deeside Lodge Office
Derek E Pollecutt
Derek Elmer
Derek Green
Derek R W Cleveland, Richmond (Surrey) District
    Lodge
Derek Warrington
Diana Bryan
Diana M Mercer
Diana Randall
Diane & David Nelson PGM
Diane Richards
Donald Hamilton
Doreen Foster
Dorian Palmer-Minnis, Mitcham District
Doris Lily Baker & B Grounsell
Dorothy Deacon, Grand Master 2009–2010
Dorothy Varley
Douglas John Stephens
Duchess of Devonshire Lodge, Stockport District
Duchess of Kent Lodge
Duke of Cambridge Hurlingham Lodge
E G Wedderburn MBE
Edgar Welff
Edmund Hudson, Bradford District Lodge
Edna Florence Ralph
Edward Hoar
Edwin David Halliwell
Edwin Roy Harris
Elaine & Tony Barker, Heart of England District
    Lodge
Elaine Brown
Elsie Joy & Maurice Bobbitt, Norwich District
Eric & Elizabeth Karklins
Eric Foston, North Gloucestershire District
Eric Middleton

Eric Ward
Esta Wilkinson
Evans Aberepikima
Evelyn Betty Westlake
Exley Payne, North London District
Faye LeBon & Family
Fely Doloroso
Fiona McKay-rae, Cambridge District Lodge
Flo & Charlie Willard
Flower of Kent Lodge
Frank & Betty Garrod, Bradford District Lodge
Frank & Valerie Jones
Frank Burton
Frank Walter Watson, Norwich District
Fred & Susan Potts
Fred Phillips
G A Hague, Derbyshire Peak District Lodge
G Baxter
Gareth Williams
Geoff Whitaker
Geoffrey Hoar
Geoffrey Latham
Geoffrey W Bracewell
Geoffrey W Clarke
George A J Kilford PGM
George Edward & Doris Amy Fuller
George Knox
Gerald Houghton
Geraldine Neil
Gillian Buck
Gillian Hamblin
Gladstone Walker, Temple of Peace Lodge
Gloria J James
Glyn & Sylvia Thomas
Gordon & Rita Sinclair
Gordon Womersley PPGM
Grace Holmes
Graeme Ward
Graham Elliot
Grand Lodge of Alberta
Great Berkhampstead District
Guernsey District Lodge
Gustaaf Vijnck
Gwynneth, Peter & Lee Robertson
Hal T Schoonover
Handel & Jenny Morgan
Handforth & Altrincham District Lodge
Harald Thoen, Grand Sire
Harold F Buckingham PGM, South London District
Harry & Jean Mary Rose
Harry & Pauline Fisher

Harry Thorp
Haydn & Barbara Illingworth, Great Berkhampstead
    District
Hazel Deacon
Hazel Puttick
Heather Alexandra
Heather J Stopps & Donald John Ware
Helen Evans
Helen Watson
Henry Leonard George Clow
Hilda M Matson
Howard Gerald Malin
Hugh & Janet Jolly
I D Field
Ian G Malcolm
In memory of Charles Joseph Pidcock
In memory of Eric Fowler
In memory of Jack Wilkinson
In memory of Joyce & John Hudspith, Beds &
    Bucks District
In memory of Leslie H Granger
In memory of S Roffey PGM, Stockport District
In memory of Thomas Edmondson PGM, Skipton
    District Lodge
Ipswich District Oddfellows
Irene & Harold Clark
Irene Pope
Irene Ryan
Iris Barrell, Ipswich District Lodge
Isabel Sherlock, Border Counties District Lodge
Ishmael Williams
Ivan Ashborn PGM
Ivy F Penighetti
J E Hustwick
J H Elphick
Jack Elvin Whitt
Jack Thomas Jenkinson, Skipton District Lodge
Jack Wakefield
Jacqui & Colin Worley
James & Annie Prizeman
James (Jim) H. Earl
James Alan Troilett
James Henry Hayward
James Kemp
James Stanage
Jamie McAndrew, North London District
Jan & Nora Leenders
Jan Swain
Jane Barlow
Jane F Nicole
Janet Allum

Janet Hannah Blinkhorn
Janet Sylvia Saveall
Janis L Souza
Janis Reynold & Family
Jean Baldwin
Jean Diamond
Jean Facer
Jean Mason
Jean Whitehead, Kings Lynn and West Norfolk
    District Lodge
Jeff Bartlett
Jenny Winder, Cinque Ports Warden District Lodge
Jim & June Middleton
Jimmy Cowell PGM, Cambridge District Lodge
Jo Baxter
Joan Bailey
Joan Haresign
Joe Whelan
Joe Winstanley
John & Bernice Newman
John & Bloss Dunn
John & Daphne Stephenson
John & Pam Leah
John (Joe) Hayes
John A Leach
John Arthur Austin Adams
John Batchelor & Family
John Bird
John Bodman
John Bradley
John Burgin, South Yorkshire & North Derbyshire
    District Lodge
John Burridge
John C Moore
John Cooper
John Corner
John D Wright
John Edgar Jones, Brighton & Sussex District Lodge
John Edward Rust-Andrews
John Edward Scillitoe
John Ellis
John Gwilym Price, South Yorkshire & North
    Derbyshire District Lodge
John H Collins
John Haynes
John Houghton
John King
John Lavender
John Livesey
John Twitchett, Exeter District Lodge
John W Tuck

John Wellington
John William Balaam
John Wills
Jonathan H Roberts
Jordan Spauls
Josephine Orman
Joy Old
Joyce Baigent
Joyce Hall
Joyce Lewis
Judith A Bramwell, Heart of England District
    Lodge
Judith Laine
Julia Watts
Julie Winup
June E Linkins
June Geer
June Holt
K E Earth
K Jackett, Beds & Bucks District
K M Butcher
K Vernon
Kai Hughes
Karen Pye-Smith
Karen Stuart & Nick Beckwith
Kathleen Nixon
Kathleen Stansfield
Keith Graham Blood
Keith Hewitt, Humber Wolds District
Keith James Andrews, Phoenix Branch
Ken Holt
Ken Martin
Ken Mills
Kenneth & Yvonne Roberts
Kenneth George Linstead
Kenneth W D Turner
Kenneth William Richards
Kesley Petty, Southampton District
Kevin Hosking
L A & B A Crawford
Lance English
Laurence Manning
Lawrence Inniss, Birmingham District Lodge
Leeds District
Les Viles
Lesley Bull
Leslie & Joyce Jenks
Leslie & Mary Herbert
Leslie Blunden
Leslie Chennells
Leslie Hayes

Leslie Needham
Leslie Smith
Leslie Torry
Liam Hayden
Lilian & Eric Ogden PGM
Lillian Leece
Lily & Lewis Lambert
Lionel W H Woods
Louise Keys
Louise Smith
Loyal Cambridge District Lodge
Loyal Good Samaritan Lodge
Lucille Verle Hopps Cameron
Luqman Raymond Whittinger, Mitcham District
    Lodge
Lynette Heywood
Lynn E Bradbury
M D Potter
M Tyrrell, Lord Nelson Lodge
Maggi & David Winter
Malcolm Day
Malcolm H Brett
Margaret & Bill Henchliff
Margaret & Chris McGarraghy
Margaret H Morgan
Margaret Lindsay, Beds & Bucks District
Marie J Shelton
Marion & Brian Hayhoe
Marion Bird
Marion Sawyer
Marjorie & Brian Elliott
Marjorie Arbury
Marjorie Lucas
Marjorie Morgan
Martyn Ripley OBE, Nantwich & Crewe District
    Lodge
Mary Ethel Lilly
Matthew John Young
Maureen Best, North London District
Maurice Fairall
Meirion & Tracey Edwards
Melvin Edwards
Melvyn Clynes
Mervyn Hall
Mervyn J Eaton
Michael & Jane Hill
Michael & Lana Bright
Michael & Wendy Debenham
Michael A Lloyd-Jones
Michael C Nolan, Ormskirk & Southport District
    Lodge

Michael E Phelan
Michael J V Bevis & Marie J Bevis
Michael Ledgard
Michael Stokes
Michael Trenchard
Michel Philistin
Michelle Benedit
Mick Mitchell
Mike & Barbara Malloy, Preston District
Miss Teresa Collins
Moira & Bernard Dye
Molly & Len Bastock
Molly & Mac McFayden
Monica Margerrison
Mr & Mrs F G Whatley
Mr & Mrs R Bowker
Mr & Mrs T A J Pawley
Mrs & Mrs Wilkinson
Mrs Brenda Bartholomew
Mrs Doreen E Burnett
Murray A Lethbridge, Grand Lodge of Alberta
Neil Thompson, Todmorden District
Nelson Family, Stockport District
Nicholas McKenna
Nicholas Norman
Nigel Martin
Noel Neville
Noreen M Lewis, Bedford Lodge
Norry Tetzlaff & Chris Tucker
North Gloucestershire District Lodge
North London District
Norton Western Lodge
Norwich District
Olna Manyan
Olwen Bellis
Oswald Branch, Southampton District
Oswestry District Lodge
Owen Brewster, North London District
P F Brook
P J Jackson
P Proctor, United Lodge
P Statham
Pam & Iuan Piggott
Pam English
Pamela Hazel Moule
Pamela Henry
Pamela M Boseley
Pamela Rose Osborne
Pat-Tricia Whitcher
Pat and Mike Park
Pat Flynn

Patricia Knight & Robert H Gibson, South East
    Lancashire District Lodge
Patricia L Murray
Paul & Denise Turner
Paul & Patricia Sidorczuk
Paul Ferraro
Paul Thomas Odgers
Pauline & Nigel Pettigrove
Pauline J Coltman
Peggy D White
Penny Doyle
Peter & Barbara Needham
Peter & Janet Holmes
Peter & Pam Maxwell
Peter A Burbridge
Peter Clarke
Peter Hartley
Peter Ilsley, Reading District
Peter John Adams
Peter John White
Peter Kearnes
Peter L Buckingham
Peter L Smith
Peter Matthews
Peter Michael Holmes
Peter Nicholas Robertson
Peter R Lewin
Peter Webb
Philip A Maria
Philip Frederick George Wicks
Philip H Slade
Philip Howcroft
Phillip A Kinson & Megan A Harvey
Phillip Francis
Phyllis May Tayler
Pride of Bermondsey Lodge
Pride of Islington Lodge
Pride of Leicestershire District Lodge
Princess Royal Branch
Prue Osborne
R J Turner, Offa's Dyke Lodge
R North, Gloucestershire District
R W Bowdery
Ray Hentze
Ray Shelford
Raymond Barrett
Raymond Jeffery William Perry
Raymond John Howard
Raymond Williams
Reg Hook, Brighton & Sussex District Lodge
Ricardo Gonzalez

Richard Cawte
Richard George Hackwell
Richard Talbutt
Richmond (Surrey) District Lodge
Robert & Patricia Eyre
Robert A Smith, North London District
Robert Alston
Robert C Warnock, St Marnock Lodge
Robert Gordon Higgins
Robert Laing
Robert Michael Lloyd
Robert Monk
Robert Penfold
Robert R Callcut
Robert Reeves
Robert Robinson
Roland Vincent Walton, Pride of Leicestershire
    District Lodge
Romeo & Ann Tambini
Ron Bannister, Leeds District
Ron Munro PGM
Ronald Richmond
Ronald W Perkins
Rose Cugley
Rose, Gary & Howard Pemberton
Rosemary Pacey
Roy & Patricia Kelsey
Roy Bottomley, Huddersfield District
Roy Emmington
Roy Morris
Russell & Fiona Vince
Ruth & Harry Bennett
Ruth H Nicholson
Ruth Hutin
S A O Hutt, North London District
S Bolton PGM, Stockport District
S C Lindsey
Sally Markham
Sandra Leighton, United Lodge
Sarah J Fox, Ipswich District Lodge
Sarah Nevill
Shaun Michael Turner
Sheila Evison
Shirley Hill
SI Metric Matters
Sidney Robert & June Maureen Rider, Leeds
    District
South London District
St Edmundsbury Branch
St Mary Cray & Dartford District
Stan Fenton

Stephen D G Parr
Stephen Lewis
Stephen Mitchell
Stockport District
Stuart & Sybil Williams
Stuart Littlejohn, Maidstone Fernlea District Lodge
Sue C Maltby
Sue Weston
Susan & Paul Burton
Susan Ruth Eaglen
Sybil Lamb (née Day)
Sylvia Dunn
Sylvia Hardy, Erewash Valley District Lodge
T R & J Naylor
Ted Veal
Terence David Moore
Teresa & Denis Daly
Terry & Linda Harding
Terry A Hirst
Terry Butcher
Terry E Elks
The Grand Lodge of Norway
The La Touche Family
The Wheeler Family
Theresa Haynes, Portsmouth District Lodge
Theresa Samples
Thomas Badger
Thomas Henry 'Harry' Cloke
Thomas James PPGM
Three Counties Lodge
Tom Asquith

Tom Nicholson PGM
Tony & Christine Luckett
Tony & Lynda Bantock
Tony G Barnard, Ipswich District Lodge
Tony Lewis
Tunbridge Wells District Lodge
United Lodge
V & E Colby
Valerie & David Phillips PGM
Vecta Lodge, Southampton District
Vera James
Vera May Pepperell
Victor R Partridge
Vincent Griffiths
Vo - Huu Hoang
W H Ridd
W J (John) Powell, Boston & Lincoln District
    Lodge
W P Fowles
Walter & Vera Payne
Waveney Lodge
Wendy & John Swinburn
Wendy Kitchener
West London District
Willi O Riha
William E Whitfield, Laurel and Crown Lodge
William King
Winifred M Felgate
Winnie Jameson
Zandra Tomes
Zena M Morgan